A HISTORY OF THE SOUTH

VOLUMES IN THE SERIES

I THE SOUTHERN COLONIES IN THE SEVENTEENTH CENTURY, 1607–1689
by Wesley Frank Craven

II THE SOUTHERN COLONIES IN THE EIGHTEENTH CENTURY, 1689–1763
by Clarence Ver Steeg

III THE SOUTH IN THE REVOLUTION, 1763–1789
by John R. Alden

IV THE SOUTH IN THE NEW NATION, 1789–1819
by Thomas P. Abernethy

V THE DEVELOPMENT OF SOUTHERN SECTIONALISM, 1819–1848
by Charles S. Sydnor

VI THE GROWTH OF SOUTHERN NATIONALISM, 1848–1861
by Avery O. Craven

VII THE CONFEDERATE STATES OF AMERICA, 1861–1865
by E. Merton Coulter

VIII THE SOUTH DURING RECONSTRUCTION, 1865–1877
by E. Merton Coulter

IX ORIGINS OF THE NEW SOUTH, 1877–1913
by C. Vann Woodward

X THE EMERGENCE OF THE NEW SOUTH, 1913–1946
by George B. Tindall

Volume IX

ORIGINS OF THE NEW SOUTH

1877–1913

A HISTORY OF THE SOUTH

Volume IX

EDITORS

WENDELL HOLMES STEPHENSON

E. MERTON COULTER

Origins of the New South 1877-1913

BY C. VANN WOODWARD

LOUISIANA STATE UNIVERSITY PRESS
THE LITTLEFIELD FUND FOR SOUTHERN HISTORY OF THE UNIVERSITY OF TEXAS

Designed by Robert Josephy

SECOND PRINTING, 1956
THIRD PRINTING, 1959
FOURTH PRINTING, 1962
FIFTH PRINTING, 1964
FIRST PAPERBACK EDITION, 1966
SECOND PAPERBACK PRINTING, 1967

AUTHOR'S PREFACE TO THE PAPERBACK EDITION

IN the fifteen years since the original edition of this book appeared the shadow of an anachronism has already overtaken part of the title. It was with some reluctance, the reasons for which I explained, that I used the phrase "New South" in the first place. But those misgivings had to do mainly with connotations the phrase had acquired in the past, the slogan-like usage and the optimistic faith it implied. Whether one shared that faith and cherished the social order that sustained it or not, however, there could be little doubt that that order was still a going concern. In the 1940's one could study the 1870's and the decades that followed with confidence that he was dealing with the origins of living institutions. Those institutions were subject to constant criticism, to be sure, but they had survived and resisted all but minimal change. In matters racial, economic, political, and social, lines of continuity still linked the South of the present with the South of the past.

By the mid-1960's, however, the links of continuity appeared more often than not to be broken. The breaks were probably as sharp as those that divided any two previous periods in Southern history. For the changes the South has experienced in the last two decades have come with a concentration, abruptness, and force equaling those of any comparable period of the past—including the period following Appomattox and the one following Reconstruction. The most conspicuous changes were those in racial relations, but hardly less profound have been those of an economic and political character.

What could still be called, a mere decade and a half ago, the "New South" had in the meantime become one of the several Old

Souths. The period admittedly shares characteristics with the order replacing it. But it is as distinctive as the "Old South" that ended in 1865, or the "Old South" that preceded the Cotton Kingdom. It spanned three score years and ten, relatively long as the lives of Southern regimes go, longer in fact that the life span of the Old South of the Cotton Kingdom. In reprinting this book without change in title or text, I shall expect the reader to profit from advantages of perspective that time and change have added and that the author himself did not share.

C. V. W.

AUTHOR'S PREFACE

AMERICAN historians, generally speaking, have taken the New South at its word and accepted its professions of nationalism to justify a neglect of regional history. After a more-or-less detailed treatment of the South during Reconstruction, the general histories of the United States have been governed by the tacit assumption that the South is adequately covered by the various phases of national history, and the perverse section is disposed of with cursory reference to progress, poor whites, and the race problem. The historians cannot be blamed for this neglect, as Southern scholars themselves have connived in it and sometimes justified it.

Part of the difficulty lies in the phrase "New South." It is not a place name, as is "New England," nor does it precisely designate a period, as does "the Confederacy." From the beginning it had the color of a slogan, a rallying cry. It vaguely set apart those whose faith lay in the future from those whose heart was with the past. It suggested moods ranging from forthright recantation to an affable and uncritical optimism. It was invariably ladened with a hopeful nationalism suggesting that the lately disaffected South was at last one in faith with the country—or would be as soon as a few more bonds were sold, another appropriation was passed, the depression was ended, or the new railroad was completed. Those who have undertaken to write of the New South have not always been careful to dissociate themselves from the implication of the phrase as a popular slogan. Unconsciously, perhaps, they have emphasized those aspects of the region's history that are most congenial to the New-South mentality.

If it were possible to dispense with a phrase of such wide currency, I would not use the name "New South" except to designate an ill-defined group of Southerners. Unfortunately, the vocabulary of the subject and period is cluttered with a remarkable number of clichés that give the historian trouble and lead to popular misapprehension. In addition to "New South" there are, for example, "Bourbon," "poor white," "Solid South," "Redemption." Some of them are productive of so much mischief that I have consciously avoided them. Others, equally mischievous, seem unavoidable. The historian may deplore the injustice of the term "carpetbagger" when it falls alike upon the just and the unjust, but he is no more able to dispense with it than was the carpetbagger himself.

Disinfected as much as possible, the term "New South" will be used in the following pages without its slogan-like connotations. By the South I mean the eleven former Confederate states plus Kentucky and, after it became a state, Oklahoma. The newness of the New South will be subject to considerable qualification. That it was new enough to have outgrown those peculiarities that in earlier periods had set the region apart and necessitated separate consideration by historians is frankly questioned. In some ways it was more distinctive as a region than it had been earlier. Politically the South achieved, on the surface at least, a unity that it had never possessed in ante-bellum times. Economically it was set apart from the rest of the nation by differentials in per capita wealth, income, and living standards that made it unique among the regions. War and Reconstruction, while removing some of the South's peculiarities, merely aggravated others and gave rise to new ones.

It would be impossible to acknowledge adequately all the assistance I have received in this book from scholars, librarians, and editors. I am especially obligated to Rupert B. Vance of the University of North Carolina, who read the entire manuscript and illuminated the margins with colored pencils. Charles A. Barker of the Johns Hopkins University, Howard K. Beale of the University of Wisconsin, Francis B. Simkins of Louisiana State University, and William G. Carleton of the University of Florida have read parts of the manuscript and contributed valuable suggestions. My indebtedness to the editors of this series for their painstaking work is very great. The paragraph on the page preceding this Preface is taken from Arnold J. Toynbee, *The Prospects of Western Civilization* (New York, 1949), and is quoted with the permission of the author and the Columbia University Press. I was assisted in completing research for this book by fellowships from the Rosenwald and the Guggenheim foundations.

C. V. W.

PUBLISHERS' PREFACE

A HISTORY OF THE SOUTH is sponsored by Louisiana State University and the Trustees of the Littlefield Fund for Southern History at The University of Texas. More remotely, it is the outgrowth of the vision of Major George W. Littlefield, C.S.A., who established a fund at The University of Texas in 1914 for the collection of materials on Southern history and the publication of a "full and impartial study of the South and its part in American history." Trustees of the Littlefield Fund began preparations in 1937 for the writing of the history that Major Littlefield contemplated. Meanwhile, a plan had been conceived at Louisiana State University for a history of the South as a part of that institution's comprehensive program to promote interest, research, and writing in the field of Southern history.

As the two undertakings harmonized in essentials, the planning groups united to become joint sponsors of *A History of the South.* Wendell Holmes Stephenson, then professor of American history at Louisiana State University, and the late Charles W. Ramsdell, professor of American history at The University of Texas, were chosen to edit the series. They had been primarily interested in initiating the plans, and it was appropriate that they should be selected to edit the work. Upon the death of Professor Ramsdell in 1943, E. Merton Coulter, professor of history at the University of Georgia, was named his successor.

Volumes of the series are being published as the manuscripts are received. This is the fifth published volume; it follows Volume VII. When completed, the ten-volume set will represent about twelve years of historical planning and research.

I remember watching the Diamond Jubilee procession myself as a small boy. I remember the atmosphere. It was: Well, here we are on the top of the world, and we have arrived at this peak to stay there—forever! There is, of course, a thing called history, but history is something unpleasant that happens to other people. We are comfortably outside all that. I am sure, if I had been a small boy in New York in 1897 I should have felt the same. Of course, if I had been a small boy in 1897 in the Southern part of the United States, I should not have felt the same; I should then have known from my parents that history had happened to my people in my part of the world.

ARNOLD J. TOYNBEE

CONTENTS

CHAPTER I

THE REDEEMERS

ANY honest genealogy of the ruling family of Southern Democrats would reveal a strain of mixed blood. The mixture sprang from a forced union with the house that had been Democracy's bitter rival for the throne. A Mississippian once whimsically acknowledged this union. "A few years after the war," he wrote, "all lovers of good government in the South concluded to celebrate a marriage. The high contracting parties were Whiggism and Democracy and the ceremony took place in 1875, though the betrothal may antedate that time. . . . As is usual in such cases the parties have now one and the same name, but the Whig party is no more dead than is one of our fair damsels, because she has concluded to cast her lot with the man of her choice for weal or for woe." [1]

The fact was that instead of assuming the submissive role suggested by a change of name, Whiggery often took the dominant position—along with the bulk of desirable offices. A North Carolina editor who described himself as one of the "unterrified Democracy" boasted that "the Democratic nominees for Governor since the war had been Worth, a Whig; Ashe, a Whig; Merrimon, a Whig; Vance, a Whig; and Jarvis, who was too young before the war to have had much political leaning one way or another." The Democrats of the First North Carolina District had in that period nominated five men for Congress, "every one of them former Whigs," and the state supreme court was "composed of three sterling Democrats, all former Whigs." By 1884 it appeared that "the Democrats of today admire Henry Clay just as much as the men of

[1] Jackson *Clarion*, September 19, 1883.

Whig traditions."[2] On the other hand, so repugnant had the marriage with their old enemies been to the Whigs that it was not until eight years after the war that the very name "Democratic" was avowed by the Conservative party of North Carolina.

The Whiggish tendency was widespread. "It is almost impossible to find a disciple of Benton among Southern Democrats," wrote an observer in 1882. The older generation had "apparently determined to adopt the views of the old Whigs," while the younger leaders were uninterested in Jacksonian dogma.[3]

Henry Watterson, thoroughly in accord with all but details of the New Order, took occasion to attack Colonel Arthur S. Colyar, commander of the dominant wing of the Tennessee Democrats. Colyar, he charged, was "in sympathy with the iron, coal, and manufacturing interests of Tennessee exclusively, and, being an old high-tariff Whig, has not emancipated himself from the crude opinions which prevailed among the shortsighted and narrow minded political economists among whom he grew to manhood." The reply came promptly from the Nashville *Daily American:* "Better be careful, Mr. Watterson, the Democratic party of Tennessee is made up, at least in part, of old Whigs, and, being now all of the same family, it might hurt the party to establish that the old Whigs were 'short sighted' and 'narrow-minded!' " If the Kentuckian were uninformed, he might make inquiry in his own state concerning the master of all those "narrow minded political economists." "His name was Clay, and no doubt some of the old men will remember him."[4]

All in all the union was a *mésalliance.* With every crossroad hustings and county courthouse the memorial of some battle between the old parties, any semblance of domestic harmony was likely to be forced and artificial. "I despise the very name of Democrat," declared a Democrat of Whig background from the Lower South. "There is not a principle or a tradition belonging to the organization which I approve." Another unwilling adherent described himself as "in principle an Old Line Whig, but, under ex-

[2] Raleigh *News and Observer,* February 23, 1884.

[3] Henry L. Nelson, "The Political Situation in the South," in *International Review* (New York), XII (1882), 415.

[4] Nashville *Daily American,* January 19, 1883.

isting circumstances, in practice and from necessity, a Southern Democrat." [5] Even the name Democrat fell into general disuse in the South during the seventies and eighties. The substitute, "Conservative," though originating in the battle against "Radical" Republicans, proved too appropriate a name to abandon for many years. In some states it was adopted as the official name of the party, sometimes in combination, "Conservative and Democratic Party." "Conservative" was not dropped from the official title of the Democratic party of Alabama for forty years after the war.

The shape and character of salvation promised the South by "Redemption" are in some measure revealed by the extrapolitical concerns of the "Redeemers." The first ex-Confederate state to be restored to Democratic rule, Tennessee had as her first Democratic governor, General John C. Brown, a former Whig and brother of the ante-bellum Whig governor Neill S. Brown. Governor John Brown took prominent part in the ambitious schemes of Thomas A. Scott for a southern transcontinental railroad and served as vice-president of Scott's Texas and Pacific Company. Later he became president of the Bon Air Coal Company, and at the time of his death he was president of the expanding Tennessee Coal, Iron, and Railroad Company. His successor, also a former Whig elected by the Democrats, was James D. Porter, a Confederate veteran. After two terms in office, Governor Porter was elected president of the Nashville, Chattanooga and St. Louis Railroad. He was also a director of the Tennessee Coal, Iron, and Railroad Company, along with several other financial enterprises of Nashville.[6]

The dynamic leader of this Whig-industrialist wing of Tennessee Democrats was Colonel Colyar. There were, according to Watterson, six prominent newspapers in the South that supported every Republican and opposed every Democratic policy. Three of these were published in Tennessee, and the "king" of this whole school of journalists was Colonel Colyar, who controlled the Nashville *American*. Watterson described him as a brilliant captain of industry, "backed by abundant capital of protected industries" issuing

[5] Letter to editor, dated Washington, February 27, 1877, in New York *Tribune*, March 3, 1877; and "an ex-Confederate officer," quoted *ibid.*, June 20, 1881.

[6] William S. Speer, *Sketches of Prominent Tennesseans* (Nashville, 1888), 37–40.

orders to his lieutenants throughout the Lower South.[7] His paper fought the free traders and the railroad commissions and defended the policies of the Tennessee Coal, Iron, and Railroad Company, of which Colyar was a director and general counsel. The company leased the convicts of the state penitentiary for an annual rental of $101,000. "One of the chief reasons which first induced the company to take up the system," explained Colonel Colyar, "was the great chance which it seemed to present for overcoming strikes." [8] Governor Albert S. Marks, who succeeded Governor Porter, was a kinsman and former law partner of Colonel Colyar.[9]

Redemption came early in Virginia and was accomplished under peculiar auspices—a combination of Confederate Democrats, conservative Republicans, old-line Whigs, and Negroes. This mongrel group left "Democrat" out of the party name entirely, and for thirteen years was known simply as the Conservative party. "This combination," according to one historian, "was effected by city capitalistic leaders, and to it (and them) was entrusted the inauguration of the new regime." The city man's rule of a countryman's state had as the first Conservative governor a Carpetbagger-Republican and banker from Norfolk, Gilbert C. Walker. The nine men who acted as an executive committee for the state central committee of the Conservatives were all residents of Richmond, and for years all state conventions of the Conservatives were held in that city.[10]

The General Assembly that laid the foundation of the New Order passed two bills of great consequence in quick succession. One of these provided for the sale, at a sacrifice, of the state's valuable holdings in the stock of its own railroads, a sale which proceeded at "immense loss" until virtually all the state roads had fallen into private hands, usually those of expanding Northern railroad systems. The railroads retained the special privileges and exemptions enjoyed under state ownership, but were relieved of state control

[7] Quoted in Daniel M. Robison, *Bob Taylor and the Agrarian Revolt in Tennessee* (Chapel Hill, 1935), 19. This book has the best account of the Tennessee Redeemers.

[8] Knoxville *Daily Chronicle*, July 7, 1883; Nashville *Daily American*, August 23, 1892.

[9] Speer, *Sketches of Prominent Tennesseans*, 74–75.

[10] Charles C. Pearson, *The Readjuster Movement in Virginia* (New Haven, 1917), 22–23. See also, Allen W. Moger, *The Rebuilding of the Old Dominion* (Ann Arbor, 1940), 4–5.

or regulation—an arrangement which made virtually inevitable "railroad control over the legislature." [11]

The second measure, passed within two days of the railroad bill, was the Funding Act of 1871. The act fastened upon an impoverished, war-broken state an annual interest upon the funded debt almost equal to the entire revenue of the state. The funding and railroad acts were obtained by corrupt pressure methods of a combination of bankers, bondholders, and railroads. To a recent student it is clear that "if ever Virginia bowed to money interests and pressure against the will of her people and contrary to the exigencies of the situation, it was on this occasion." [12] Launched in this manner, the Hamiltonian financial policy of the Conservatives soon occupied such a conspicuous place in the new system that the party members came to be known as the "Funders."

Railroads continued to share honors with bondholders in the degree of influence they exerted over the Conservative party. Whether the Funders or their rivals were in power the railroads were prominently represented. General William Mahone's extensive railroad interests led him to seek power in the Conservative party and to take perhaps the largest individual part in bringing the Conservatives to power.[13] Out-of-state railroads, gaining predominant influence with the Conservatives, then assisted in overthrowing Mahone's schemes and driving him into a political revolt that removed the Conservatives temporarily from office. Even after defeat, subsequent reorganization, and return to power under the name "Democratic," the party remained thoroughly identified with railroad interests. This is clearly indicated by the composition of the state committee of the party in the seventies, eighties, and nineties, during which period nearly every state chairman was a railroad president or director.[14]

11 Pearson, *Readjuster Movement,* 28–31; Nelson M. Blake, *William Mahone of Virginia, Soldier and Political Insurgent* (Richmond, 1935), 120, 136.

12 Moger, *Rebuilding of the Old Dominion,* 7. See also, Pearson, *Readjuster Movement,* 30, 32; and Blake, *William Mahone,* 136, 160.

13 Blake, *William Mahone,* 108–109, 135. Governor Gilbert C. Walker acknowledged his obligation to Mahone handsomely.

14 George M. McFarland, "The Extension of Democracy in Virginia, 1850–1895" (Ph.D. dissertation, Princeton University, 1934), 154–55. See also, Ralph C. McDanel, *The Virginia Constitutional Convention of 1901–1902,* in Johns Hopkins University *Studies in Historical and Political Science,* XLVI (Baltimore, 1928), 304–305.

Despite Kentucky's failure to secede and join the Confederacy, no state below the Ohio River presented a more solidly Confederate-Democratic front in the decade after Appomattox. For a short time after the fear of Radical and Negro votes was quieted, a rift in the ranks opened between a weak "Bourbon" wing led by J. Stoddard Johnson's Frankfort *Kentucky Yeoman,* and a powerful "New South" or businessman's wing, whose spokesman was Henry Watterson's Louisville *Courier-Journal.* The struggle was uneven and short-lived.[15]

Watterson's policy called for "an intelligent appeal to the business interests and conservative elements of Northern society" and a firm alliance of those elements against radicals of all sorts. He demanded a program of subsidies, tax exemptions, and privileged franchises in order to accommodate Eastern capital and encourage its flow into the state. The constant theme of New-South editors and orators was cheap resources, business opportunities, railroad developments, and commercial enterprise.[16] "Even though they might look like Southern colonels," writes one student of the new leaders of Kentucky, "with goatee and moustaches, and speak like Southern orators, retaining these outer trappings of the olden days, the program of the 'New Departure' was a program of surrender." [17] The "Bourbon" opposition soon faded into the past. By September 7, 1880, Watterson could write in the *Courier-Journal* of the old secession leaders that "not one of them remains upon the stage of active political life."

A multitude of interests, both in and out of the state, were served by the New Order in Kentucky, and joined in loyal support of its leaders. The railroads, the great wholesale merchants, the liquor and tobacco interests—none should be overlooked. It would be a mistake to identify the new structure with any one of its pillars and buttresses. However, the Louisville and Nashville Railroad should be singled out for special notice, not only because of its unique importance in Kentucky, but because of its remarkable influence in the affairs of other states to the southward into which

[15] Thomas D. Clark, *A History of Kentucky* (New York, 1937), 585–86.

[16] Henry Watterson, *"Marse Henry", An Autobiography* (New York, 1919), I, 183. See also, Louisville *Courier-Journal,* May 9, 1880; August 6, 1881; October 5, 1882.

[17] Edward F. Prichard, Jr., "Popular Political Movements in Kentucky, 1875–1900" (Senior thesis, Princeton University, 1935), 16–17.

it penetrated. By process of aggression, colonization, city building, and acquisition, the "L and N" gained predominance in Kentucky, and established connections with Memphis, New Orleans, Mobile, Atlanta, and Savannah. "Having here in Louisville a Railway Emperor and a Railway Bismarck," Watterson wrote, celebrating the latest *"coup de chemin de fer"* of the L and N, it was not to be wondered at that they were "making a 'United Germany' of the Southern railways which were lying about loose . . . instead of leading to Louisville as they should." [18]

It was characteristic of the times that in its battles to achieve monopoly, which differed in no essential from similar struggles the nation over, the L and N managed to identify its cause with that of the downtrodden South. This is the more curious in view of the road's service to the Union army during the war, the passage of control and ownership to Northern and European capital, and the appearance in the lists of its directors of the names Jay Gould, Thomas Fortune Ryan, Jacob Schiff, and August Belmont.[19] As chief lobbyist and leading light of its legal staff, however, "General Basil W. Duke, C.S.A.," as he described himself in the title of his *Reminiscences,* served the L and N for twenty years. Not only in his Confederate military record, but in his family connections, his striking appearance (including the standard mustache and goatee), his literary service to the Confederate memories, and his chivalrous and attractive personality, General Duke was all that the age expected in the Kentucky colonel of the old school.[20]

"The only inducement for railroad companies to enter politics—become parties to the dirty work—is to protect their property," remarked Milton H. Smith, president of the L and N. He was the first to admit that this inducement alone was considerable. It was found necessary to retain "legislative agents" in various states, lawyers in all county seats through which the road ran, and in strategic places friendly judges, legislators, and officeholders of all

18 Louisville *Courier-Journal,* January 19, 1880.

19 John L. Kerr, *The Story of a Southern Carrier . . . The Louisville and Nashville* (New York, 1933), 45, 49–51; George R. Leighton, "Louisville, Kentucky: An American Museum Piece," in *Harper's Magazine* (New York), CLXXV (1937), 409–10.

20 See Thomas M. Spaulding, "Basil Wilson Duke," in Allen Johnson, Dumas Malone, and Harris E. Starr (eds.), *Dictionary of American Biography* (New York, 1928–1944), V, 495–96; *Reminiscences of General Basil W. Duke, C.S.A.* (Garden City, 1911), *passim.*

sorts with passes in their pockets or relatives on the L and N pay roll.[21]

Revealing light is shed upon the nature of Redemption and of the Redeemers of Alabama by following the course of the Louisville and Nashville empire builders in that state. Albert Fink, one of the ablest railroad superintendents of his time, foreseeing the immense potentialities of the undeveloped mineral resources of northern Alabama, began soon after the war to make large investments in that region for the L and N, subsidizing numerous developments and encouraging the building of new towns. In this manner there were affiliated with the fortunes of the L and N many of the new industries, along with a rising class of industrialists. In the front ranks of these men was James W. Sloss, said by the Birmingham *Iron Age* to be "identified with the development of the industrial interests of Alabama to a greater extent than any other man in the State." [22] Sloss was closely associated, in business as well as in politics, with the most prominent leaders of the Democratic party in Alabama. Although the Panic of 1873 resulted in the transfer of ownership to Northern and European capital, the L and N continued as in the past to work in close co-operation with the state Democratic organization.[23]

Behind the fury of partisan conflict during Reconstruction there proceeded a struggle between the L and N and a rival system for access to the riches of the mineral region of northern Alabama. The opposing system, the Alabama and Chattanooga Railroad, seeking to divert ore shipments from Louisville to Chattanooga for smelting, was linked in its fortunes with the Republican party through the investments of such men as Henry Clews, Russell Sage, and William D. ("Pig-Iron") Kelley. During Reconstruction both railroads were beneficiaries of extravagant state-government aid that virtually bankrupted the state. Liabilities assumed for these two

[21] Interstate Commerce Commission, *Hearings Relative to the Financial Relations, Rates, and Practices of the Louisville & Nashville Railroad Co., The Nashville, Chattanooga & St. Louis Railway, and other Carriers* (Washington, 1916), *Senate Documents*, 64 Cong., 1 Sess., No. 461, pp. 407–10, 430–31, 439, 447–48.

[22] Birmingham *Iron Age*, December 24, 1879. See also, Albert B. Moore, "Railroad Building in Alabama during the Reconstruction Period," in *Journal of Southern History* (Baton Rouge), I (1935), 421–41.

[23] Ethel M. Armes, *The Story of Coal and Iron in Alabama* (Birmingham, 1910), 245, 249.

railroad systems alone, in the form of loans and endorsements of bonds, accounted for $17,000,000 of the total estimated $25,000,000 "debt" incurred after the war. That the system of state aid was inaugurated by the provisional Democratic government and manipulated to the advantage of a number of prominent party leaders did not deter the Democrats from playing up the state debt as the most sensational charge against the Carpetbag government.[24]

The election of 1874 had more than a racial or political significance, for it would determine not only the fate of the Republican party and Reconstruction in Alabama but also which of the financial interests involved would be able to make the best possible settlement with a state government they had both brought to the point of bankruptcy. Walter L. Fleming wrote that "the campaign fund was the largest in the history of the state," and mentioned especially the contributions of "northern Democrats and northern capitalists who had invested in the South or who owned part of the legal bonds of the state." [25] It should be remembered, however, that it was just this question of the "legality" of bonds that would be determined by the outcome of the campaign to which the Northern capitalists contributed. The Conservatives won by a large majority. The L and N was by this time firmly identified with the downtrodden South and the victory of White Supremacy in Alabama.

George S. Houston, Redeemer governor of Alabama, described in campaign literature as "the Bald Eagle of the Mountains," won his office with the usual slogans of "White Supremacy" and "home rule." A northern Alabama lawyer with industrial interests, he was a leader of the Unionists of the state. "How much will the young men . . . be enthused by H[ouston]'s nomination?" demanded one Alabama Democrat. "Can it be expected that they will vigorously exert themselves for a man selected because he is supposed to be strong with that element which in all this region is known in common parlance as Tories?" [26] Houston was a close associate of

[24] Horace M. Bond, *Negro Education in Alabama; A Study in Cotton and Steel* (Washington, 1939), 42–50; Walter L. Fleming, *Civil War and Reconstruction in Alabama* (New York, 1905), 589–604.

[25] Fleming, *Civil War and Reconstruction in Alabama*, 792.

[26] Rufus K. Boyd to Robert McKee, April 29, 1874, in Robert McKee Papers (Alabama Department of Archives and History, Montgomery).

Sloss and the L and N, for one of whose affiliated lines he was a director.[27]

Houston hastened to bring about a settlement with the state's bondholders and the railroads. His friend Rufus W. Cobb, who framed the plan later adopted with modifications, was a local attorney of the L and N and president of the Central Iron Works at Helena, which was subsidized by that railroad.[28] Governor Houston served as ex-officio chairman of the debt commission. Levi W. Lawler, one of the commissioners and director of a railroad competing with the Alabama and Chattanooga, confessed privately that in view of his party's complicity in the railroad-bond legislation, "we, the commissioners, and the party, are environed with embarrassments of no ordinary magnitude." [29] The settlement agreed upon was satisfactory to some bondholders and highly advantageous to those railroad systems favored by the Redeemers, particularly L and N affiliates with which Sloss and Houston were in one way or another associated. Since the debt was always a potential debt, and would have become an actual debt only by the state's becoming the owner of the railroads endorsed, the "debt settlement" took the form of relieving the state of its potential debt and relieving the railroads of the threat of foreclosure on mortgages held by the state. The "settlement of 1876 left the residual obligations of the State Government . . . at approximately $12,000,000." [30]

After serving two terms Governor Houston was elected to the United States Senate. He was succeeded in the governor's chair by Cobb, whose connections with Houston and his interests have been described. On Houston's death Governor Cobb appointed to the

[27] Armes, *Story of Coal and Iron in Alabama,* 245; Bond, *Negro Education in Alabama,* 55.

[28] Rufus W. Cobb to McKee, September 8, 1874, in McKee Papers; Bond, *Negro Education in Alabama,* 54–55.

[29] Levi W. Lawler to McKee, June 12, 1875, in McKee Papers. A most revealing letter on Democratic responsibility for policies ordinarily attributed to Negroes and Carpetbaggers. Lawler wrote from New York City, where he was in touch with bondholders.

[30] Bond, *Negro Education in Alabama,* 55–62; Fleming, *Civil War and Reconstruction in Alabama,* 583–86; also memorandum on stationery of "Executive Office, State of Alabama," dated May 15, 1883, presumably by McKee, private secretary to Governor, in McKee Papers.

Senate as his successor Luke Pryor, Houston's law partner and also a business associate of Sloss and the Louisville and Nashville interests.[81]

Redemption was sometimes accomplished by means that did much toward determining the character of the new administrations. Tactics, habits, and vices that established the plane of public morals during Reconstruction were not abandoned overnight, and sometimes persisted for a decade or even longer. Impoverished state committees of the Conservative party were at times driven into alliance with the very forces against which the Redeemers' crusade was launched. In such cases the privileged interest was likely to continue in the enjoyment of its privileges and take as powerful a hand in the Redeemers' regime as it had in the Radicals'.

According to one of its enemies the Louisiana State Lottery Company was "conceived in the miscegenation of reconstruction and born in inquity." It was, as a matter of fact, chartered in 1868 by an act of the Louisiana legislature which gave it a monopoly of the lottery business in the state for a period of twenty-five years. The profits of the company were enormous, and its political power in the state was said to be "stronger than the Tweed ring in New York." Its money went not only to the legislature but to the Radical campaign fund in every election: "There has never been a Radical judge or recorder in New Orleans who has not been the subservient tool of the Lottery managers."[82] However close the ties between Lottery and Radicals, the connections between the Lottery and the Redeemer regime became quite as intimate.

In the tense days of April, 1877, Louisiana had two governors, each claiming to have been rightfully elected, and two rival legislatures, each lacking a quorum. When other persuasions failed, money was used to induce enough of the Republican legislators to desert the government led by Stephen B. Packard and move over to the Democratic legislature to give it the desired quorum. There is considerable evidence, including statements of Lottery spokes-

[81] Montgomery *Advertiser and Mail,* January 7, 1880; Armes, *Story of Coal and Iron in Alabama,* 245.

[82] New Orleans *Democrat,* January 17, 1879; Richard H. Wiggins, "The Louisiana Press and the Lottery" (M.A. thesis, Louisiana State University, 1936), 58; Berthold C. Alwes, "The History of the Louisiana State Lottery Company" (M.A. thesis, Louisiana State University, 1929), 19.

men, that much of the money used to attain this end was supplied by the Lottery Company. One account, purporting to give the "inside history," places the cost to the company at "nearly or quite $250,000." [33] Though this seems an excessive amount, even considering the flourishing market for Louisiana legislators that particular season, other estimates indicate a considerable investment on the part of the Lottery.[34] The editor of a paper that was an outspoken defender of Lottery interests went so far as to assert that Francis T. Nicholls, Redeemer governor, "could never have been Governor of the State of Louisiana but for the Lottery Company," which "upon earnest solicitations, came forward and put up the money which was absolutely necessary to win over the negro Senators." [35]

In 1879 the legislature, in the mood for wiping out another Carpetbag landmark, passed an act rescinding the Lottery Company's charter. The act was signed by Governor Nicholls, and the monopoly was faced with a death blow. Quick response from the Federal circuit court in the form of a temporary restraining order, and later an injunction, averted this threat, but a decision of the Supreme Court promised danger from another quarter. The Lottery lobbyists next stormed the doors of the state constitutional convention, sitting in 1879 to replace the Radical constitution with a home-rule product. The Lottery this time demanded nothing less than the writing of its charter into the fundamental law of the land, where it would be beyond the reach of fickle legislatures and ungrateful governors. The Lottery had its way. On the floor of the convention "the Caesarean operation which evolved the Nicholls government was fully explained," and one member pointed out how unreasonable it was to ask the New Order "to wipe out the institution to which it owed its existence." [36]

[33] *Colonel Alexander K. McClure's Recollections of Half a Century* (Salem, Mass., 1902), 104, 178.

[34] Alwes, "History of the Louisiana State Lottery Company," 56–57; C. C. Buel, "The Degradation of a State," in *Century* (New York), XLIII (1891–1892), 625; Wiggins, "Louisiana Press and the Lottery," 58–59; Garnie W. McGinty, *Louisiana Redeemed: The Overthrow of Carpetbag Rule, 1876–1880* (New Orleans, 1941), 185–92; Ella Lonn, *Reconstruction in Louisiana after 1868* (New York, 1918), 523; Thomas E. Dabney, *One Hundred Great Years; The Story of the Times-Picayune From Its Founding to 1940* (Baton Rouge, 1944), 342–43.

[35] New Orleans *Times-Democrat,* August 6, 1890.

[36] Report on proceedings of the convention, in New Orleans *Times,* July 10, 1879.

Not only was the company's charter placed beyond the threat of legislative repeal, but the Nicholls government, which had antagonized the Lottery, was removed from power by a constitutional provision calling for the election of a new governor and legislature, to assume office in January, 1880, thus shortening Nicholls' term of office by more than a year. Furthermore, by a provision reorganizing the supreme court, the judges who had sustained the government's policy were removed and replaced by a new court.[87] In the midst of these changes the New Orleans *Democrat*, party organ of the Redeemers, found itself bankrupted by a Federal court decision rendering worthless the state warrants it held for a year's printing for the government, and by the Governor's withdrawing the state printing from the newspaper. The *Democrat*, which had been the most outspoken opponent of the Lottery, promptly fell under control of Major E. A. Burke, Charles T. Howard, and the Lottery Company, and suffered a sudden reversal of editorial policy. The Federal court then reversed its decision on the state warrants after a rehearing, thereby giving the new proprietor of the *Democrat* the full value of the state warrants.[88]

The next ten years were the most prosperous in the history of the Lottery. Collecting $28,000,000 a year through the sale of tickets for its monthly and semiannual drawings, the company distributed in prizes less than $15,000,000, and kept about 46 per cent of collections—a shockingly bold take compared with that of foreign lotteries. Exempt from other taxes, the company paid a flat fee of $40,000 annually to the state. Newspapers over the nation were offered double and sometimes quadruple prices for Lottery advertisements. Banks, business houses, and manufactures were brought under Lottery domination. The number of regular pensioners on the company's fund, some of them in public life, was said to be "enormous"; the list of employees was extensive. The support of the masses was courted by spectacular charities.[89] "With

[87] Diedrich Ramke, "Edward Douglas White, Statesman and Jurist" (Ph.D. dissertation, Louisiana State University, 1940), 146–48.

[88] Wiggins, "Louisiana Press and the Lottery," 36, 45, 98–100; Alwes, "History of the Louisiana State Lottery Company," 62–63.

[89] *The Cornucopia of Old, The Lottery Wheel of the New. The Generous and Tender Hand-Maiden of All the Virtues,* By a Louisianian (New Orleans, 1877), a pamphlet in Howard-Tilton Library, Tulane University; Frank McGloin, "Shall the Lottery's Charter be Renewed?" in *Forum* (New York), XII (1891–1892), 560–61;

its gigantic 'slush' fund it debauched legislators, muzzled the press, made and unmade public officials," declared a Louisiana historian. He believed that the Lottery "subtly exercised a power greater than that of the State government itself." [40]

Important institutions in the South of that day sought to identify themselves with the romantic cult of the Confederacy. It was a poor subsidiary of an Eastern railroad that could not find some impoverished brigadier general to lend his name to a letterhead. General Robert E. Lee's austere example in this regard was much admired but rarely followed. Some surprising naturalizations of Yankee capital into Confederate citizenship were effected. The Louisiana Lottery, with its well-known Carpetbag origins and Yankee owners, took rather more pains than usual. A few weeks after the Carpetbag government collapsed in 1877, there appeared on the platform, to act as personal supervisors of the "Extraordinary Drawing" from the great glass wheels of the Lottery, two distinguished personages—General P. G. T. Beauregard and General Jubal A. Early. It would have been hard to find surviving figures of greater prestige in Confederate legend. Both gentlemen had seen lean days before they accepted the Lottery's offer of handsome salaries. Their signatures in facsimile were soon familiar to newspaper readers the country over, appearing year after year in Lottery advertisements endorsing the honesty of the drawings the men supervised. Another tie binding Lottery and Confederacy was the Confederate Memorial Building in New Orleans, built by descendants of the Lottery owner, Charles T. Howard, a Carpetbagger who was said to have "loved the dignifying memories of the war." [41]

It is one of the rarer ironies of the period that the Redeemers of so coy and inconstant a widow of the Confederacy as Georgia should have come to be known as "Bourbons." No group of Southern rulers less deserved that much-abused epithet, with its implications of obstinate adherence to the old loyalties and abhorrence of the new, than did Georgia's so-called "Bourbon Triumvirate." Con-

---

John C. Wickliffe, "The Louisiana Lottery: A History of the Company," *ibid.*, 575–76; *Proceedings of the Anti-Lottery Democratic Convention of 1890* (New Orleans, 1890), 28–30; Buel, "Degradation of a State," *loc. cit.*, 627–28.

[40] Henry E. Chambers, *A History of Louisiana* (Chicago, 1925), I, 707.

[41] Alwes, "History of the Louisiana State Lottery Company," 27, 97.

cerning the justice of the term "Triumvirate," however, there was little question. During the eighteen years following the overthrow of the Carpetbaggers, either General John B. Gordon or Joseph E. Brown occupied one of the state's places in the United States Senate, and after 1883, Alfred H. Colquitt, the third member of the Triumvirate, held the other. For the major part of the same period General Colquitt or General Gordon served as governor. Here was a concentration of authority that, if rightly understood, would reveal much of the nature of Georgia's new order.

"Henceforth let it not be said that Georgia is not reconstructed," commented a Mississippi editor upon the news of former Governor Brown's election to the United States Senate by a Democratic legislature.[42] Governor Brown's career in war and peace is, in fact, another striking illustration of the continuity between Reconstruction and Redemption. "First in secession, first in reconstruction, and very nearly first in the restoration of Democratic home rule," Brown, as one historian observes, "came up on top at every revolution of the wheel of destiny." [43] Supplanted as war governor in 1865, he wrote that "The Statesman like the business man should take a practical view of questions as they arise." He urged upon the South a policy of acquiescence in Radical Reconstruction, became a Republican himself, and was appointed chief justice of the state supreme court by Rufus B. Bullock, Radical governor. Though not personally involved in the corrupt bond issues that disgraced the Republican administration, Brown was closely associated with many beneficiaries of them. Just before Governor Bullock fled the state in fear of indictment, the legislature leased the Western and Atlantic, a state-owned railroad, to a company of which Brown was president. Later investigation pronounced the lease and the formation of the company fraudulent, but no action was brought. The following decade saw the rise of Brown to a rank among the leading industrialists of the South. Not only was he president of Western and Atlantic, but also of the Southern Railway and Steamship Company, the Walker Coal and Iron Company, and the Dade Coal Company. In his coal mines Brown used convict labor leased from the state at about seven cents a day. These and other industrial inter-

[42] Jackson *Weekly Clarion*, November 25, 1880.

[43] C. Mildred Thompson, *Reconstruction in Georgia* (New York, 1915), 223.

ests made him a wealthy man in a short time, while his large philanthropic gifts and endowments tended to soften the hostility aroused by his political apostasy.[44]

One enthusiastic supporter of Brown in the political contest of 1880 was former Governor Bullock. His case illustrates from another angle the indulgent spirit of the times as well as the lack of sharp distinction between Reconstruction and Redemption. Bullock returned to Georgia in 1876 and stood trial on an indictment for embezzlement of public funds. Neither his acquittal for lack of evidence nor his published defense of himself has convinced historians that his administration was other than a "carnival of public spoliation!" [45] Yet, remaining in Atlanta after his trial, Bullock soon became one of its most honored citizens: he was president of an Atlanta cotton mill, president of the Chamber of Commerce, and a director of the Piedmont Exposition. H. I. Kimball, a Carpetbagger from Maine, second only to Bullock among Georgia Radicals and second to none of them in his reputation for public plunder, was also president of an Atlanta textile mill and served as "director general" of the Atlanta Cotton Exposition of 1881. His popularity was attested by his near victory in a race for the mayoralty of Atlanta in 1880, which he lost by fifty-four votes. Alexander K. McClure attended a dinner at the home of Henry W. Grady in honor of Governor Colquitt and found as fellow guests Kimball and Bullock, whose "political filthiness" had once been the subject of Grady editorials. "Their general agreement as to State policy was somewhat a surprise to me," said McClure. He "did not meet any Atlanta prominent business Republicans who desired Republican control in the State. . . . All had absolute confidence in Grady." [46] "Ex-Governor Brown is in a marked degree a representative of this New South," wrote Bullock. "He fully understands her

[44] *Ibid.*, Chap. IX, 251–54; Herbert Fielder, *A Sketch of the Life and Times and Speeches of Joseph E. Brown* (Springfield, Mass., 1883), 465–80, 488–90, 568–87; Isaac W. Avery, *History of Georgia, 1850–1881* (New York, 1881), 48–49, 167–70, 339–40, 606; Haywood J. Pearce, Jr., *Benjamin H. Hill, Secession and Reconstruction* (Chicago, 1928), 218–30.

[45] Ulrich B. Phillips, *The Life of Robert Toombs* (New York, 1913), 262; Robert P. Brooks, "Rufus Brown Bullock," in *Dictionary of American Biography*, III, 258–59.

[46] *Colonel Alexander McClure's Recollections of Half a Century*, 401–402. For Henry W. Grady on Bullock and H. I. Kimball, see Raymond B. Nixon, *Henry W. Grady: Spokesman of the New South* (New York, 1943), 72–73.

practical needs and will foster her commercial advantage." [47]

Confusion regarding General Gordon, second of the Triumvirate, is more understandable. The General's distinguished military record, his popular title "Hero of Appomattox," his chivalrous bearing and courtly appearance, and above all his office of commander in chief of the United Confederate Veterans from the time of its organization until his death, combined to make him a popular idol in the South and the incarnation of the Lost Cause in the North. More revealing about the significance of the General as a Redeemer than his romantic *Reminiscences* were his business connections. These included the Central Pacific and later the Louisville and Nashville, which he served as counsel at a salary of $14,000. Gordon became an adventurous speculator in Southern industry and business. A mere listing of his schemes, mainly railroad ventures but also including insurance, publishing, mining, manufactures, and real estate, would require more space than is available here.[48]

Colquitt, third member of the Triumvirate, at first appeared out of place in the New Order. A gentleman of distinguished family, coming from the Black Belt, and one of the largest planters in the state, he seemed to belong to the old aristocratic planter-statesmen. His interests were not exclusively agricultural, however, nor his association with the Triumvirate exclusively political. At the height of its political teamwork, Governor Colquitt was reported by a friendly source to be co-operating with General Gordon and his brothers in large-scale speculations in two Southern railroads, a New England textile mill, and a Tennessee fertilizer factory, and in coal mining. These gentlemen were understood to have cleared $1,000,000 by their transactions in less than a year.[49]

Colquitt's case is only one illustration of the growing attachment between representatives of the New Order and the few survivors of the old planter class who entered its service. Senator L. Q. C.

[47] Letter from Bullock, in New York *Tribune,* October 25, 1880.

[48] General John B. Gordon, *Reminiscences of the Civil War* (New York, 1903), *passim;* Lucian L. Knight, *Reminiscences of Famous Georgians* (Atlanta, 1907), II, 872–73; Rebecca L. Felton, *Memoirs of Georgia Politics* (Atlanta, 1911), 484–85, 494–95, 538–40; Augusta *Chronicle,* September 29, 1890; Montgomery *Advertiser,* January 16, 1881.

[49] Atlanta *Constitution,* quoted in Jackson *Weekly Clarion,* July 19, 1882.

Lamar of Mississippi was also associated with Senator Gordon in sundry speculations.[50] Mississippi, in fact, had almost as much of a triumvirate as Georgia. Its members were Lamar, Edward C. Walthall, and James Z. George, all United States Senators. Among them they occupied both of their state's seats in the Senate throughout the eighties. They were the three men most influential in state politics, yet neither they nor their lieutenants had exercised important influence in ante-bellum Mississippi. All three Senators were corporation lawyers. Lamar and his intimate friend General Walthall, a man of considerable wealth and aristocratic connections, were avowed friends of the railroads and corporations and hostile to any attack from agrarians. Although Senator George had the largest corporate practice in his state and had built a fortune for himself, he came up from the ranks, took pride in the name "Commoner," and gained the confidence of the small-farmer element. After George's election to the Senate in 1881, Lamar's supporters said that he was "of the same political school" as Lamar and that the two "saw eye to eye on many matters." George, however, was never on intimate terms with his two colleagues.[51]

During the two decades following Redemption in Mississippi the governorship was exercised by only two men—John M. Stone and Robert Lowry. Conservative railroad lawyers, both men resisted regulatory legislation and conformed to the Lamar-Walthall approach toward Northern capital and corporate interests in the seventies and eighties. Stone, like Senator George, was to prove more adaptable to the ground swell of agrarian sentiment. Governor Lowry, a former Whig, proved a consistent friend of factories, railroads, and textile mills in quest of tax exemptions and freedom from regulation. Among the seventeen Democratic Congressmen elected by Mississippi between 1876 and 1890, a careful investigator was able to find only seven who "sympathized with, worked for, and were approved by the farmers." [52]

50 "I made another little turn for you in a speculation & enclose you the result." John B. Gordon to L. Q. C. Lamar, October 1, 1881, in L. Q. C. Lamar–Edward Mayes Papers (Mississippi State Department of Archives and History, Jackson).

51 Albert D. Kirwan, "A History of Mississippi Politics, 1876–1925" (Ph.D. dissertation, Duke University, 1947), 81–85; Willie D. Halsell, "The Bourbon Period in Mississippi Politics, 1875–1890," in *Journal of Southern History,* XI (1945), 519–27.

52 Halsell, "Bourbon Period in Mississippi Politics," *loc. cit.,* 529–30.

Redemption, like Civil War and Reconstruction, meant only one more postponement of the eventual reckoning between the "two South Carolinas, the one of the masses, the other of the classes," between which there had long existed "a fatal lack of touch." [53] In the crisis of 1876–1877, as in the presence of external dangers in earlier times, the upcountry democracy once more subordinated its ancient grievances to the common cause and submitted to the leadership of the low country and the men with the old names. Senators Wade Hampton and Matthew C. Butler, whose family connections, manners, and patrician outlook identified them with the Old Order, gave superficial color to the picture of Redemption as a "restoration." But like the Redeemers of sister states, those of South Carolina definitely allied themselves with the business interests—with the factory owners, railroad men, and merchants of Charleston, Columbia, and other cities. If their manners and names were of authentic planter origin, their votes and deeds were of the middle class, and to that class the Redeemers lent all the prestige of aristocratic lineage and glorious war record. One heated contest after another arose to divide the white man's party. In each conflict—whether with the bondholders over the state debt, with the bankers over a usury law, with the merchants over protection of fertilizer consumers, or with railroads over rates—the popular side of the issue was opposed by the Redeemers with striking consistency.[54]

Florida was ushered into the ranks of redeemed states in 1877 upon the arm of Governor George F. Drew, a native of New Hampshire, who moved to Georgia in the fifties and settled in Florida in 1865. Like many of the leaders of Redemption, Governor Drew was an old-line Whig. He was a Union man in sympathies and took no part in the war. Locally he was known as "Millionaire Drew" because of his "vast and successful enterprises," chiefly in the lumber industry, but including also "the largest mercantile house in

[53] David D. Wallace, *The History of South Carolina* (New York, 1934), III, 108–109, 343–44.

[54] Charleston *News and Courier*, May 1, 7, 1877; July 23, December 6, 1878; January 5, 1880; Francis B. Simkins, *Pitchfork Ben Tillman, South Carolinian* (Baton Rouge, 1944), 80; William W. Ball, *The State that Forgot; South Carolina's Surrender to Democracy* (Indianapolis, 1932), 175; Wallace, *History of South Carolina*, III, 326–28.

the State." In partnership with a New York capitalist, he bought great tracts of timber land during Reconstruction. "The firm now owns the largest saw-mills in the State, and ships immense quantities of yellow pine to New York," it was reported in 1877.[55]

Harriet Beecher Stowe, a resident of Florida since the year after the war, was glad to reassure Northern friends that "although Gov. Drew is a Democrat, the Republican papers cordially support his administration," a sign that "the lion and the lamb . . . may yet lie down together." Prospects for Uncle Tom's children seemed to her "all they ought to desire," and since "about all the money circulating in the State comes from Northern immigrants and visitors," Yankees were thrice welcome.[56] Governor William D. Bloxham, Drew's successor, improved handsomely upon the policy of hospitality by granting to visiting capitalists considerably more land than the state owned. The path for Henry B. Plant and Henry M. Flagler, the Rhodeses of the American tropics, lay open before them. Men of this type found it easy to co-operate with Drew, Bloxham, and their two successors in the governor's office.

So far in this account of the Redeemers the emphasis has been upon the dominant element and its leadership. In the main they were of middle-class, industrial, capitalistic outlook, with little but a nominal connection with the old planter regime. This is not to suggest that all Redeemers and all elements of their party were so aligned. Other elements that took part in the struggle for Redemption were more strongly associated by their point of view and leadership with the ante-bellum order. They sometimes resisted capitalistic encroachments, but they usually constituted a minority within the Conservative party and were dominated by the New-South Redeemers. In three states these factions were led by figures important in Confederate history.

General Robert Toombs, former member of the Confederate cabinet, joined hands with Joseph E. Brown to overthrow Bullock's Radical administration in Georgia, but quickly broke with his ally. His personal prestige enabled him to dominate the Constitutional

[55] Tallahassee *Weekly Floridian*, June 5, 1877; William W. Davis, *The Civil War and Reconstruction in Florida* (New York, 1913), 692; *Biographical Souvenir of the States of Georgia and Florida* (Chicago, 1889), 872–73.

[56] Letter in New York *Tribune*, February 17, 1877.

Convention of 1877 and, in spite of Brown's stiff opposition, to write into the new constitution prohibitions against irrevocable franchises, railroad monopolies, and state subsidies to railroads. Disfranchised and deprived of citizenship, Toombs had no coherent following and soon ceased to wield important power. His old friend Alexander H. Stephens bitterly disappointed him by making peace with Grady and the Bourgeois Triumvirate.

In Tennessee Senator Isham G. Harris, secessionist and war leader, commanded a strong wing of the Conservative party based mainly on a cotton-planter constituency in western Tennessee. Adhering to the old state-rights line of John C. Calhoun, the Harris-planter wing wrestled annually with the more powerful Colyar-Whig-industrialist wing for control of the party. Gaining temporary ascendancy in 1882, the Harris-planter wing infuriated the industrialist faction by repudiating some of the state's fraudulent bonds and by establishing a commission to regulate railroads. The policy nearly split the party.[57]

There was comparable discord among Redeemers of other states. In Texas, for example, Congressman (later Senator) John H. Reagan, former Postmaster General of the Confederacy, and his agrarian lieutenants, who fought for state and Federal railroad regulation, offer some contrast to the dominant element of Texas Redeemers. As a rule, however, the planter and industrialist Redeemers were able to compose their differences amicably and rule by coalition. As later analysis will reveal, the planters who remained found ways of merging with the new middle class through the avenue of the supply merchant. And finally, in some states, when the major offices were held by industrialists, the disproportionate voting strength of the Black Belt gave big landed interests a significant veto power. Until the end of the eighties any insurgency of the lower-class whites usually enabled the dominant industrial Redeemers to whip the landed interests into line.

If the Redeemers themselves are an indication of the character of their regimes, it would seem a mistake to assume that Redemption was in any real sense a restoration. Even though a few of the old names were prominent among the new leaders, Redemption was not a return of an old system nor the restoration of an old ruling

[57] Robison, *Bob Taylor*, 20–21.

class. It was rather a new phase of the revolutionary process begun in 1865. Only in a limited sense can it be properly called a "counter-revolution."

It is quite possible that the Carpetbagger and the Scalawag have been allotted by the historians a share of attention out of all proportion to their true importance in the revolutionary process. In no Southern state did Radical rule last so long as a decade. Apart from South Carolina, Louisiana, and Florida, where the Radicals did manage to prolong a troubled and contested authority for nearly that long, the Radical regime in the average state—from the time it was recognized by Congress till it was overthrown—lasted less than three and a half years. The amount of good or evil the Radicals could accomplish was limited by this fact if by no other. In the long range of more than three centuries of the white and the black man's history in the South the Radical's role was brief. Radical Reconstruction, like the Confederacy, was an ephemeral experiment. By comparison the work of the Redemption was more enduring. For it was not the Radicals nor the Confederates but the Redeemers who laid the lasting foundations in matters of race, politics, economics, and law for the modern South.

CHAPTER II

THE FORKED ROAD TO REUNION

DECISIONS of great moment confronted the South in the winter that brought the end of Reconstruction.[1] They were decisions that affected the welfare and future course not merely of the South alone but of the nation as a whole. The occasion for these decisions, the thing that gave the South, for the first time in years, a measure of freedom to choose her course, was the disputed Presidential election of 1876.

A great deal more was at stake in the winter of 1876–1877 than the question of which of two citizens, Samuel J. Tilden or Rutherford B. Hayes, would occupy the White House. To many Northerners it seemed that all the hard-won fruits of the Civil War and Reconstruction were in jeopardy. On one plane there were the North's more idealistic war aims, those centered about the freeing and protecting of the Negro and reflected in the new amendments of the Constitution. On a different plane there were the less idealistic, less publicized war aims, those centered around the protection of the peculiar interests and privileges of a sectional economy. They were reflected in new statutes regarding money, banks, tariffs, land, railroads, subsidies—all placed on the lawbooks while the South was out of the Union. People who thought of themselves as realists were already talking of saving the fruits of Northern victory on one plane by sacrificing those on the other.

It was a depression year, the worst year of a bad depression. In the East radical labor elements and unemployed were working themselves into a violent temper that foreshadowed the insurrec-

1 This chapter is based on the author's *Reunion and Reaction: The Compromise of 1877 and the End of Reconstruction* (Boston, 1951), in which the story is much more fully elaborated and documented. Permission was kindly granted by Little, Brown and Company.

tionary riots of the summer. In the West a tide of agrarian radicalism was rising in the shape of Granger, Greenback, and silverite doctrines. From both East and West came threats against the elaborate structure of protective tariffs, railroad subsidies, banking privileges, and monetary arrangements upon which the new economic order was founded.

And now the South, kept at bay for sixteen years, presented a third threat to the New Order. Traditionally hostile to the new capitalistic legislation, believed to be nursing bitter grievances, and suspected of all manner of mischief, the South was at last returning in full force, united as never before, to upset the sectional balance of power. Which way would the South throw her weight in the impending struggle over national issues? Would she make common cause with other rebellious elements? Would she join hands with restless labor in the East as she once had? Or would she rush into the arms of her ante-bellum ally, the agrarian West, break up the East-West alliance that won the war, and leave the East once more an isolated minority section? Or could the South be induced to combine with Northern conservatives and become a bulwark instead of a danger to the new capitalistic order? If the South were given a share in some of the more tangible fruits of the New Order, might she not prove more friendly toward it? And if so, what inducements would be found necessary?

These questions loomed large in the deliberations of those who sought a practical solution to the Presidential election crisis and had an important influence upon the Compromise of 1877.

The circumstances of the national electoral crisis will be readily recalled. A closely contested election gave Tilden and the Democratic ticket more than a quarter of a million more popular votes than Hayes received and 184 uncontested electoral votes, or just one short of the number required to elect. Hayes trailed with only 166 undisputed electoral votes, but Republican managers immediately laid claim to the 19 doubtful votes of South Carolina, Florida, and Louisiana. Democratic managers laid a counterclaim to one Oregon vote on the ground that the elector was a Federal officeholder and therefore disqualified. There seems to be no positive way of determining what the results of a perfectly fair election in the three Southern states would have been. The consensus of recent historians is that Tilden deserved the 4 electoral votes of Florida and was therefore elected.[2] Republican returning boards in each of the three states "canvassed" the returns, however, and under pressure of visiting Republican delegations certified all electoral votes for Hayes. Rival Democratic state authorities at the same time certified another set of returns for Tilden. Congress was therefore presented with conflicting returns for 20 electoral votes, including the one from Oregon. Hayes would have to be awarded every one of these votes to win, while Tilden required only one to complete a majority.

The question was, who was to count the votes? Neither the Constitution, nor the law and rules, nor precedent and custom offered an acceptable solution. The strongly Democratic House of Representatives and a stanchly Republican Senate were completely at odds on methods proposed. A deadlock ensued, and as the weeks slipped by without prospect of agreement, tension mounted in Washington and gripped the nation. It had been only sixteen years since a Presidential election had precipitated a civil war, and each quadrennial election since then had turned, in the last analysis, on the employment of military force or the threat of it. It remained to be seen whether the country could regain the ability to choose a President without resort to force. To Abram S. Hewitt, national Democratic chairman, a peaceful solution seemed extremely doubtful in 1876. He knew of fifteen states in which Democratic war veterans were organizing for military resistance to the election "fraud," and to him "it seemed as if the terrors of civil war were again to be renewed."[3] One historian concluded that more people expected a bloody outbreak in the crisis of 1876–1877 than had anticipated such an outcome in the crisis of 1860–1861.[4]

In the meantime, as soon as Congress convened in December,

2 Among historians holding that Tilden carried Florida are Allan Nevins, *Abram S. Hewitt, With Some Account of Peter Cooper* (New York, 1935), 373; H. J. Eckenrode, *Rutherford B. Hayes, Statesman of Reunion* (New York, 1930), 227; Alexander C. Flick, *Samuel J. Tilden, A Study in Political Sagacity* (New York, 1939), 415–16; Leon B. Richardson, *William E. Chandler, Republican* (New York, 1940), 193. The older historians, James Schouler, William A. Dunning, and James Ford Rhodes, also put Louisiana in Tilden's column.

3 Allan Nevins (ed.), *Selected Writings of Abram S. Hewitt* (New York, 1937), 177–78.

4 Paul L. Haworth, *The Hayes-Tilden Disputed Presidential Election of 1876* (Cleveland, 1906), 168.

friends of Governor Hayes discerned a difference between the attitudes of Northern and Southern Democrats on the subject of the electoral crisis. The Southerners, "especially those who were old Whigs," observed James A. Garfield, counseled peace and moderation, deplored the violent talk of Northern Tildenites, and seemed less zealous for Tilden's cause. Garfield urged that "in some discreet way" overtures be made to the Southerners immediately.[5] Murat Halstead had already attempted unsuccessfully to get L. Q. C. Lamar to visit Hayes, and in lieu of that he arranged a long interview between Hayes and Lamar's friend W. H. Roberts, editor of the New Orleans *Times*. The talk was gratifying but inconclusive.[6]

What was needed was negotiators who were on easier personal terms than were Northern Republican and Southern Democratic politicians at that particular time. Just such men were the officials of the Western Associated Press, a nonpartisan organization of which the leading newspapers of the Mississippi Valley, North and South, were members. Halstead of the Cincinnati *Commercial* was president, and William Henry Smith of Chicago, Hayes's closest personal friend and political adviser, was general agent. On the board of directors sat Joseph Medill of the Chicago *Tribune*, Colonel Andrew J. Kellar of the Memphis *Avalanche*, Richard Smith of the Cincinnati *Gazette*, and W. N. Haldeman, publisher of Watterson's Louisville *Courier-Journal*. William Henry Smith and Colonel Kellar called a meeting of several of these men in Cincinnati on December 14. Smith reported to Hayes that they had "arranged a programme" for splitting the Southern Democrats from their party and that Kellar was leaving at once for Washington to "enter zealously on the great work." [7]

Smith believed that Kellar was "an admirable man" for the job,

[5] James A. Garfield to Rutherford B. Hayes, December 12, 1876, in Rutherford B. Hayes Papers (Hayes Memorial Library, Fremont, Ohio).

[6] Murat Halstead to Hayes, November 30, 1876, *ibid.;* Cincinnati *Enquirer*, December 2, 1876; New York *Herald*, December 4, 1876.

[7] William Henry Smith to Hayes, December 14, 1876, in Hayes Papers. On the origins of the plan, see Andrew J. Kellar to William Henry Smith, November 14, December 10, 1876, in William Henry Smith Papers (William Henry Smith Memorial Library, Indiana State Historical Society, Indianapolis; copies in Hayes Memorial Library).

that he was "discreet and wise and fully sympathizes with us." [8] A Douglas Democrat and a Union man, Kellar nevertheless fought for the Confederacy. After the war he entered newspaper work in Memphis and identified himself with the Whig-industrialist wing of the Tennessee Democrats led by Colonel Colyar of Nashville. Kellar was to collaborate with General Henry Van Ness Boynton, Washington representative of the Cincinnati *Gazette* and one of the Capital's most distinguished newspapermen. Of New England abolitionist background, the General had won his rank on the opposite side of the firing line from Colonel Kellar. Union general and Confederate colonel admired each other enthusiastically from the start and worked in complete harmony. Boynton wrote Smith that the Colonel was "able to do that part of the work which was most difficult for us, namely sounding certain Southern men. He has their confidence & he easily got near them." [9]

Under the guidance of Kellar and Boynton the Republican strategists conducted the most searching analysis ever made of the mind of the Redeemers, and the correspondence and journals that record their findings constitute the richest available source of information on the nature of the New Order in the South. Garfield's diary records his first interview with Kellar, in which the Colonel demonstrated that the so-called "Solid South" was weakest along the seams where the old Whigs and Unionists had been forcibly joined with Democrats and Secessionists. If Hayes could break the South along those seams by detaching the old Whig element he could not only gain support in the current crisis from the South but "build up a sound Republican party there" in the future.[10]

The forgotten history of Southern Whiggery became a subject of absorbing interest to practical politicians. State by state they canvassed the South to tabulate the ante-bellum voting power of Whig and Unionist elements that now voted Democratic.[11] They derived great comfort from the fact that these elements had cast a

8 Smith to Hayes, December 14, 1876, in Hayes Papers.

9 Henry V. Boynton to Smith, December 18, 1876, in Smith Papers.

10 Garfield Diary, December 17, 18, 1876, in James A. Garfield Papers (Division of Manuscripts, Library of Congress).

11 New York *Times*, January 11, 1877; Chicago *Tribune*, January 3, 1877; Cincinnati *Daily Gazette*, December 19, 1876.

majority of Southern votes in 1860. Hayes's friends were enormously gratified to note the remarkable proportion of old Whigs and Unionists among the new Southern Senators, Congressmen, governors, and Democratic leaders. Approaches were made to many Southern leaders—to Governor Augustus H. Garland of Arkansas, Senator David M. Key and two other Congressmen of Tennessee, Hampton of South Carolina, Benjamin H. Hill and Gordon of Georgia, Lamar of Mississippi, and several Congressmen from Louisiana and Texas. One of Hayes's advisers counted twenty-six Southern members of Congress "who before Secession were Whigs" and who were pledged "to resist all extreme measures, and who are at least desirous that you may be inaugurated." [12] One thing the Republicans learned about these Redeemers was that whether they were old Whigs or not, they were not the old ante-bellum planter type of conservative. They spoke for much the same type of railroad and industrial interests as did the Republicans and took a "practical" view of things. The various business alliances and lobbies with which Southern Congressmen were identified were carefully noted by Boynton and Kellar for future reference.

Republicans began to see the Southern problem and the Redeemers with new eyes, and the more they saw the more anachronistic seemed the Southern policy of the Republican party. It dated back to the revolutionary days of Thaddeus Stevens and Charles Sumner. The party of abolitionist radicalism had now become the party of vested interests and big business; the old Whig element was on top, its program had been enacted, and its leader was Rutherford B. Hayes, an ex-Whig and a stanch conservative. Yet in the South the party still appealed for the votes of a propertyless electorate of manumitted slaves with a platform of radical equalitarianism. The contradiction was obvious. And while the Northern Whigs were taking over leadership of the Republican party from Free-Soilers and Radicals, Southern Whigs and conservative Democrats had to a considerable extent replaced Jacksonians as leaders of the Democracy of their region. In the old days Federalists and Whigs had combined naturally, without regard to sectional barriers, but now that the Northern conservatives were sorely pressed by radical farmers and laborers in West and East, they found them-

12 A. H. Markland to Hayes, January 5, 1877, in Hayes Papers.

selves estranged from their normal allies in the South. This was the more regrettable in view of the demonstrable futility of leaning on black labor votes. "We have tried for eight years to uphold Negro rule in the South officered by carpet baggers," lamented Medill, "but without exception it has resulted in failure." [13] Medill and large numbers of Hayes's advisers in North and South urged him to abandon the Carpetbaggers, place the Negro under political fealty to his former master, and appeal to the latter along the lines of the old Whig conservatism. The revolution in Republican policy was debated publicly and privately and was eventually adopted. "The whole subject is a constant theme of earnest talk in Washington," reported the New York *Times*.[14]

Hayes was advised by realists, however, who knew that practical politics is not based merely on appeals to tradition. "Just what sort of assurances the South wants is not quite so clear," Garfield wrote Hayes, "for they are a little vague in their expressions." [15] Kellar and Boynton set out to clear up that vagueness. It was obvious that the Southerners wanted to get rid of the last Carpetbaggers, but Tilden could do that. Hayes would have to go further. A little discreet inquiry indicated the lay of the land.

The South's extreme poverty and her hunger for capital were the basic considerations. They were no mere sociological abstractions but powerfully felt needs of a dominant class and of many of the plain people. No ruling class of our history ever found itself so completely stripped of its economic foundations as did that of the South in this period. Involved in the downfall of the old planter class were the leading financial, commercial, and industrial families of the region. The hard struggle of these people to get back on their feet and recoup their losses took on a measure of desperation. Early in 1877 the more desperate of them were said by one of their number to be "willing for almost anything to turn up which gives promise or possibility of change." [16] Numerous leaders of old families attached themselves to Yankee capitalists, economic Carpetbaggers who came South for profits. These adventurers often pros-

13 Joseph Medill to Richard Smith, February 17, 1877, *ibid.*

14 New York *Times*, January 11, 1877.

15 Garfield to Hayes, December 12, 1876, in Hayes Papers.

16 J. L. M. Curry, "The South, Her Condition and Needs," in *Galaxy* (New York), XXIII (1877), 544, 548.

pered with the aid of extravagant subsidies from Carpetbag state governments. But the Panic of 1873 forced the economic Carpetbaggers to retreat on their home bases, and the political Carpetbaggers left the states that they turned over to the Redeemers impoverished or bankrupt.

As a last resort the South turned to the Federal treasury, and as the depression deepened to its gloomiest year that seemed the only hope left. The Southerners could make a respectable case for government aid. They pointed to the flood of subsidies, grants, bonds, and appropriations bestowed upon Northern enterprise during the South's absence and asked why, since they were taxed to pay for them, they could not ask for a share of these blessings. Surely the clearing of the fine harbors of Savannah, Mobile, and New Orleans, still choked with wartime obstructions or mud, meant improvements of national interest. And there were millions of acres of the richest lands in four states annually subject to floods for lack of an adequate system of levees and flood control along the Mississippi. The South's uncompleted railway system, one of the victims of war and invasion, was surely as worthy of Federal subsidies as were the new railroads that wandered among the buffalo over the uninhabited plains of the West. Deteriorating public buildings, fallen bridges, choked canals, unbuilt waterways, and obstructed river channels all waited their turn for an appropriation. For the construction of such projects a corporation had usually been organized and stock floated, and usually operations had been suspended in the Panic of 1873 to await news of the earnestly petitioned bill for a Federal subsidy. Popular support for many of the bills was not wanting, for they often promised to fulfill real needs. Around each of these bills—and there were hundreds of them—gathered a group of capitalists, politicians, and civic leaders—a lobby. And on the progress of that lobby sometimes hung the hopes of rebuilding the fortunes of once-mighty families.

No sooner had the Southerners returned to Washington and presented their internal-improvement bills, however, than they were informed that the Great Barbecue was over and they were too late. It was now time for reform. Northern leaders of their own party adopted the slogan "Retrenchment and Reform" and greeted their returning friends from the South with lectures on economy. One

Northern Democratic reformer introduced a resolution forbidding all future subsidies and grants to private enterprises. Introduced on the eve of an election, the bill passed by 223 to 33. All but seven of the opposition votes came from the South.[17] Colonel Kellar's Memphis paper called the bill "an insult to the South," and noted that "When a practical question like paying a Southern claim, or assisting an internal improvement such as the Texas and Pacific Railroad or the Mississippi levees came up," Yankee Democrats "could be relied on to take the extreme Northern ground of opposition." [18] The New Orleans *Times* marveled that "an excessive fit of economy should have seized the country when the North was gorged and the hungry South was begging a modicum of the same fostering generosity." And the worst offenders were the perfidious Northern Democrats.[19] By comparison the Republicans showed a sympathetic understanding. Garfield wrote Hayes that numerous Southerners had told him that "in the matter of internal improvements they had been better treated by the Republicans than they were likely to be by Democrats." [20] He thought this point worth developing in the current crisis.

General Boynton and Colonel Kellar quickly fixed upon the South's hunger for Federal money as one of the means of solving the national political crisis. This hunger took as many forms as there were Southern bills for internal improvements in Congress. None of the lobbies behind these bills, however, was so well organized, shrewdly directed, liberally financed, and widely supported in the South as that demanding a Federal subsidy for the Texas and Pacific Railway Company. The president of the Texas and Pacific was Colonel Thomas A. Scott of Philadelphia, who was also president of the Pennsylvania Railroad, the biggest freight carrier in the world and probably the most powerful corporation in America at that time. Seeking to round out a nationwide system and to challenge the transcontinental monopoly of the Union Pacific and Central Pacific, Scott entered Texas in 1872 to build a southern route to the Pacific coast. His resources included claims

[17] *Congressional Record,* 44 Cong., 1 Sess., 227.

[18] Memphis *Daily Avalanche,* January 11, 1877.

[19] New Orleans *Times,* February 25, 1877.

[20] Garfield to Hayes, December 12, 1876, in Hayes Papers.

to some 16,000,000 acres of public lands in New Mexico, Arizona, and California, the last great land grant made to a railroad by the Federal government. Scott also had a large grant of land in Texas made by that state to two companies acquired by the Texas and Pacific, plus a grant of $6,000,000 in bonds by the Reconstruction legislature of Texas, passed over the Republican governor's veto.[21]

Construction was placed in charge of General Grenville M. Dodge, already famous as chief engineer of the Union Pacific and known as one of the ablest railroad lobbyists in the country. The Panic of 1873 brought construction to a sudden halt, prevented Scott from floating bonds in Europe, and confronted both the Texas and Pacific and Scott with financial disaster. In this plight Scott turned to the Federal treasury as the means of repairing his fortunes and sought the advice of General Dodge with regard to securing a subsidy.[22] Dodge pointed out that the Crédit Mobilier scandal had discredited railroad subsidies, that both major parties had forsworn the policy, and that the West, where he had once mobilized great support, was under Granger influence. The South, he thought, was the only hope. "Every convention in the Northwest is putting resolutions in their platforms against that class of legislation," Dodge wrote Scott, "so that our fight has got to be made by the combined South and what votes we can get from the middle and eastern states." [23] The General, with this program in mind, plunged into the task of mobilizing the South for the Texas and Pacific bill.

A formidable part of the army Dodge and Scott enlisted were the four projected eastern branches of the Texas and Pacific, all of which were incorporated in Scott's bill, and all likewise asking subsidies. One of the three southernmost branches was to connect the eastern termini of the Texas and Pacific in east Texas with

[21] Charles S. Potts, *Railroad Transportation in Texas,* University of Texas *Bulletin,* No. 119 (Austin, 1909), 95; Charles W. Ramsdell, *Reconstruction in Texas* (New York, 1910), 307–308.

[22] Jacob R. Perkins, *Trails, Rails and Wars; The Life of General G. M. Dodge* (Indianapolis, 1929), 257.

[23] Grenville M. Dodge to Thomas A. Scott, June 16, 1874, letter-book in Box No. 346, in Grenville M. Dodge Papers (Iowa Historical and Memorial Building, Des Moines).

New Orleans, one with Vicksburg, and one with Memphis. Each of the companies incorporated to build these branches claimed a land grant but boasted few other assets save large stock issues of dubious worth that would be greatly enhanced by the passage of the Scott bill. Two rival companies, one affiliated with the Carpetbaggers and one with the Redeemers, were ready to build the New Orleans branch. A fourth branch was projected to leave the Texas and Pacific in west Texas and wander for 436 miles through uninhabited plains, much of it in Indian Territory that was closed to settlement, to Vinita, where it was to connect with a line to St. Louis.[24] In all, the branch lines amounted to more mileage than the Texas and Pacific trunk line. Around each branch was grouped a collection of interests—holders of the relatively worthless paper of the corporations who hoped to build the line, landlocked towns awaiting the "great day," and numerous politicians, some of them personally interested. Eight states and three territories were directly touched, and eastward from the terminal cities of the branches stretched railroads through other states seeking outlet to the west. The Vinita branch alone, Dodge estimated, controlled twenty-five votes in Congress.[25] One Arkansas Senator was president of the Memphis branch and the other a director. "Each branch," observed the *Nation*, "represents so many Congressional Districts and so many votes, and it represents so many thousands of tons of iron which are to be manufactured in so many other districts which have so many more votes." [26] If the branches were incomprehensible from the viewpoint of railway economics, they were thoroughly understandable from the viewpoint of railway politics.

General Dodge did not rely upon the branches alone for Southern support. "There was no success here," he wrote in 1875, "until I changed my whole policy, by reaching men from their homes not in Washington." [27] To do this he used the press of the South. Early

[24] *Railroad Gazette* (New York, Chicago), IX (January 19, 1877), 29–30; New York *Times*, January 22, 1877; House of Representatives, *Reports of Committees*, 44 Cong., 2 Sess., No. 139, Pt. II, 4.

[25] Dodge to Scott, January 12, 1875, letter-book in Box No. 346, in Dodge Papers.

[26] *Nation* (New York), XXIV (1877), 24.

[27] Dodge to Frank S. Bond, vice-president of the Texas and Pacific, March 1, 1875, letter-book in Box No. 346, in Dodge Papers.

in his campaign he was able to list forty-two Southern newspapers from Virginia to Texas, among them the most influential journals of the region, that were lending him strong support.[28] "The people behind the press at home is what has done this work," declared Dodge, explaining his success.[29] But not altogether. For Dodge also undertook to secure formal endorsement of the Texas and Pacific bill by all of the state legislatures of the South, and was successful in all states save Virginia and Louisiana.[30] State action usually took the form of a resolution instructing Senators and requesting Representatives to vote for Scott's bill. Chambers of commerce in Atlanta, Augusta, Louisville, Macon, Memphis, Nashville, New Orleans, Richmond, Vicksburg, and other cities of the South petitioned Congress for passage of the Scott bill. Of all his achievements, Dodge was proudest of securing the endorsement of the National Grange itself, a stronghold of opposition, at its convention in Charleston.[31] The prestige of old Confederate chieftains was too strong in the era of Redemption to be neglected, and Dodge was able to secure the active support of Jefferson Davis, Stephens, General Beauregard, and R. M. T. Hunter. Two former governors, James W. Throckmorton of Texas and John C. Brown of Tennessee, both old Whigs turned Democrats, were elected officials of the Texas and Pacific.

In November, 1875, a national railroad convention met in St. Louis to organize pressure in support of the Texas and Pacific bill. It was attended by 869 delegates from thirty-one states and territories, the largest number from the South.[32] President of the convention was Stanley Matthews, kinsman of Governor Hayes, counsel to Tom Scott, and later Senator from Ohio. Older members

[28] *The Press and the People on the Importance of a Southern Line Railway to the Pacific and in Favor of Government Aid to the Texas and Pacific Railway Co.* (Philadelphia, 1875), 25–47.

[29] Dodge to Bond, March 1, 1875, letter-book in Box No. 346, in Dodge Papers.

[30] *Resolutions of the Legislatures, Boards of Trade, State Granges, Etc., Favoring Government Aid to the Texas & Pacific Railway* (Philadelphia, 1874), 35–38; *Press and People on the Importance of a Southern Line Railway*, 6–10.

[31] *House Miscellaneous Documents*, 43 Cong., 2 Sess., No. 89, *passim*.

[32] *Proceedings of the National Railroad Convention at St. Louis, Mo., November 23 and 24, 1875, in Regard to the Construction of the* TEXAS & PACIFIC RAILWAY *as a Southern Trans-Continental Railway Line from the Mississippi Valley to the Pacific Ocean on the Thirty-Second Parallel of Latitude* (St. Louis, 1875), vii–viii, 45–57.

recalled the St. Louis convention of 1849, also held to urge a Federal subsidy for a Pacific railroad. Jefferson Davis, chairman of the Mississippi delegation, was present in 1875 to defend his report of 1855 on the route that Scott later adopted. The road to the Pacific had been one of the favorite panaceas for the South's ills in the fifties. The movement stirred historical memories of earlier sectional disputes and compromises.[33] Scott's plan revived the Cotton Kingdom's ante-bellum impulse to expand the Southern system westward and make colonies of the territories between Texas and California. It promised realization of the old planter-statesmen's dreams of a Southern route to the Pacific. It offered "justice to the South" in the form of subsidies that other regions had enjoyed, and it accommodated itself perfectly to the ground swell of reviving Whiggery in the region.

Despairing of aid from Northern Democrats, the Southern Congressmen returned to Washington in December, 1876, determined "not to wait any longer for outside help, but help themselves in the matter of internal improvements." They were said to be "a unit upon two questions": Mississippi levees and the Texas and Pacific. On "the very best authority," a Washington correspondent reported, "They mean to have these things." [34] The New Orleans *Times* saw in the "presidential complication" the South's opportunity, because the crisis had "made a 'new departure' of some sort necessary to both parties of the North, in order to secure the favor of the South." [35]

"What we want for *practical* success," General Boynton wrote William Henry Smith on December 20, a week after Kellar had arrived in Washington, "is thirty or thirty-six votes. West Tennessee, Arkansas, a large Kentucky element, Louisiana, Texas, Mississippi *and Tom Scott* want help for the Texas & Pacific Road." He proceeded to outline "strong arguments" in favor of Scott's bill. "If such arguments & views commend themselves to Gov. Hayes," he continued, "& Tom Scott, & the prominent representatives of the States I have named could *know* this, Scott with his

[33] Robert R. Russel, *Improvement of Communication with the Pacific Coast as an Issue in American Politics, 1783–1864* (Cedar Rapids, 1948), 25–26, and *passim.*

[34] St. Louis *Post-Dispatch,* January 15, 1877.

[35] New Orleans *Times,* February 24, 1877.

whole force would come here, & get those votes in spite of all human power, & all the howlings which blusterers North & South could put up. . . . If Gov. H. feels disposed toward this enterprise as many of the best & most honest men of the republican party do—there would certainly be no impropriety for some recognized friend of his giving *Scott* to understand it." [36]

Smith showed Boynton's proposal to Medill, who pronounced it "of grave importance" and asked Smith to tell Hayes that he did "not think the price too high for the end proposed to be accomplished." Smith thought the Boynton letter "of great interest" and forwarded it to Hayes with Medill's opinion.[37] Hayes's reaction was guarded but encouraging. "I do not wish to be committed to details," he wrote. "It is so desirable to restore peace and prosperity to the South that I have given a good deal of thought to it. The two things I would be exceptionally liberal about are education and internal improvements of a national character." He continued with the reflection that the South needed to put business above politics, and asked Smith to meet him in Xenia, Ohio.[38] A few days after the conference Hayes wrote Smith that he doubted "the trustworthyness [*sic*] of the forces you hope to rally." [39] Smith replied that he was puzzled by the statement, but would pursue the Southern policy on his "own responsibility." [40] Boynton was satisfied with Hayes's statement that he would be "exceptionally liberal" about internal improvements, and continued his work. Hayes was kept fully informed.

In the meantime, three simultaneous developments were increasing pressure for a drastic departure in the strategy of the Hayes men. The first was a serious threat of defection from Hayes's cause among Republican Congressmen that alarmed Hayes's most trusted advisers.[41] The second was an intensification of the threat of violent or revolutionary tactics on the part of Democrats. This

[36] Boynton to Smith, December 20, 1876, in Smith Papers.

[37] Smith to Hayes, December 22, 1876, in Hayes Papers.

[38] Hayes to Smith, December 24, 1876 (presumably a copy), *ibid.*

[39] Hayes to Smith, January 3, 1877 (presumably a copy), *ibid.*

[40] Smith to Hayes, January 5, 1877, *ibid.*

[41] John Sherman to Hayes, January 3, 1877, in Charles R. Williams, *The Life of Rutherford Birchard Hayes, Nineteenth President of the United States* (Boston, 1914), I, 521; Garfield Diary, January 5, 1877, in Garfield Papers; James M. Comly to Hayes, January 8, 1877 (copy), in Hayes Papers.

came mainly from the North, but a few Southerners participated. Watterson called for 100,000 Democrats to march on Washington and ensure Tilden's inauguration.[42] The third development lay in railroad politics. For four years the most effective opposition to Scott's bill had come from the powerful lobby of Collis P. Huntington, who sought to block Scott's challenge of the transcontinental monopoly and get government consent to build the southern route himself. Using the same methods as Scott, Huntington complained that the Forty-fourth Congress was "composed of the hungriest set of men that ever got together," and that "It costs money to fix things so that I would know his [Scott's] bill would not pass." [43] The two men fought each other to a deadlock, but on December 24, 1876, they met in Philadelphia and agreed upon a compromise of mutual advantage.[44] Then during the first week in January the House Committee on Pacific Railroads, of which Lamar was chairman and Garfield a member, agreed to report a subsidy bill in which both Scott and Huntington would share benefits.[45] Thenceforth the two great antagonistic lobbies would join forces, and their combined power would be formidable indeed. General Dodge, director and lobbyist for the Union Pacific as well as for the Texas and Pacific, saw to it that the lobbies of Jay Gould and Sidney Dillon, which were seeking passage of Senator John B. Gordon's sinking-fund bill, were co-ordinated politically with the lobbies of Huntington and Scott.[46]

General Boynton had been seeking for some time "a perfectly *safe* way" to approach Scott. Finally, on January 14 Dodge brought Scott to Boynton's home and the three had a long talk. "Col Scott feels sure," Boynton reported to William Henry Smith, "that the

[42] Louisville *Courier-Journal*, January 8, 1877; New York *Times*, January 7, 8, 9, 1877; Washington *National Republican*, January 9, 1877.

[43] Collis P. Huntington to David D. Colton, November 20, 1874, and January 17, 1876, in Chicago *Tribune*, December 27, 1883.

[44] Huntington to Colton, December 25, 1876, *ibid.* On Scott's side the compromise was foreseen in Dodge to James A. Evans, November 6, 1876, letter-book in Box No. 384, in Dodge Papers.

[45] Garfield Diary, January 11, 1877, in Garfield Papers; New York *Times*, January 5, 13, 1877.

[46] Dodge to Bond, March 1, 1876, letter-book in Box No. 346; Dodge to Sidney Dillon, December 14, 1876, letter-book in Box No. 382; Dodge to Jay Gould, February 12, 1877, letter-book in Box No. 384, in Dodge Papers.

attitude of Gov H towards the South, & his willingness to help them in their material interests can be so used here among prominent Southern democrats as to effectively kill all measures looking toward revolution. He will go to work in the matter *personally,* & with the skill & *directness* for which he is justly celebrated. The talk we had was a long one, covering all the ground, & I am sure you would have been much pleased & encouraged by it. From today there will be no lack of help, for Scott's whole powerful machinery will be set in motion at once, & I am sure you will be able to detect the influence of it in *votes* within ten days. . . . This is a short letter, but it weighs a *ton.*"[47] According to Boynton, Scott had "the *very greatest confidence*" in his ability to bring the Southerners into line. A few days later, reporting on Scott's progress, Boynton wrote Smith: "You would not guess in some time who was the first man to surrender without hesitation to Scott after the talk I wrote you about. You will hardly believe it but it *was* Watterson."[48] Whether for this reason or not, Watterson's Louisville *Courier-Journal* suddenly changed from the most bellicose to one of the most moderate papers in the South. Medill's *Tribune* congratulated Watterson on the alteration.[49]

On January 24 Lamar arose in the House in the midst of debate on the Electoral Commission and reported, with cordial endorsement for passage, the Texas and Pacific bill. It was a remarkable proposal. The government was asked to guarantee for fifty years the annual payment of 5 per cent interest on bonds of 1,187 miles of trunk line at $40,000 a mile and a possible 1,378 miles of branches at $30,000 to $35,000 a mile. The annual interest came to $4,473,500 and the aggregate for fifty years to $223,675,000. The security offered left much to be desired, while the profits all went to the railroads.[50] Realizing that he was speaking in "the midst of serious political perplexity and threatened danger," Lamar offered the

[47] Boynton to Smith, January 14, 1877, in Smith Papers. As usual, Boynton wrote two letters to Smith on the same date, covering the same ground. Why this was his practice the writer cannot imagine.

[48] Boynton to Smith, January 26, 1877, *ibid.*

[49] Chicago *Tribune,* February 13, 1877. Compare the tone of the Louisville *Courier-Journal,* January 24, 1877, with issues in the weeks following.

[50] House of Representatives, *Reports of Committees,* 44 Cong., 2 Sess., No. 139, Pt. II, 4.

Texas and Pacific bill as "one of the simplest and yet surest means of reconciling the interests and harmonizing the sentiment of this whole country." It would promote not only "reconciliation" of the sections but "material reconstruction" of the South, and "mutual respect and affection" at a time they were desperately needed.[51]

William S. Holman of Indiana, Democratic chairman of the House Committee on Appropriations, was immediately on his feet with objections to Lamar's request for unanimous consent to give the bill priority. This was no surprise, for Holman had introduced the resolution against subsidies and a later one calling for an investigation of alleged shady practices used to put the original charter of the Texas and Pacific through Congress.[52] The latter resolution was a slap in the face of Southern Democrats and a notice that the Democracy was the party of reform and not of Whiggery and revived Grantism. Other Northern Democratic Congressmen joined Holman in denouncing subsidies, railroad jobbery, and the Texas and Pacific bill.[53] Scott's Southern friends got no comfort for their "reconciliation" scheme from Northern members of their own party.

The Northern Democratic press took up the outcry against the Texas and Pacific "job" and heaped merciless criticism upon its Southern Democratic supporters. The New York *Sun,* popularly believed to be the mouthpiece of Tilden, pronounced Lamar's bill "the most nefarious railroad jobbery yet attempted in this country," a revival of Crédit Mobilier tactics.[54] The *Nation,* voice of liberal Republicans and reformers, had hoped to find "in Southern politicians like Mr. Lamar himself and Senator Gordon of Georgia, powerful assistance in ridding the Government of the corrupt and jobbing practices," and declared it "almost incredible that they should be seen rising up in company with Mr. Tom Scott and his kind." The editor was particularly concerned about Lamar, "representative, *par excellence,* of the South in the new order of things," and warned him "that suspicion of bribery will just as naturally rest on the supporters of a Texas and Pacific as of a Union Pacific

[51] *Ibid.,* Pt. I, 8; *Congressional Record,* 44 Cong., 2 Sess., 924.

[52] *Congressional Record,* 44 Cong., 1 Sess., 598.

[53] *Ibid.,* 2 Sess., 922–24.

[54] New York *Sun,* January 9, February 6, 13, 16, 1877.

job."[55] More galling to Southern Congressmen than anything else were the bitter attacks of the Democratic Washington *Union* and its editor Montgomery Blair. As Tilden's counsel and editorial voice in the Capital, Blair was extremely well informed and merciless in his attacks on "*Southern* Democrats—Tom Scott's Democrats." To Blair it seemed that Scott's subsidy was playing the role that Biddle's bank had played in Jackson's time and was being used to revive Southern Whiggery in the guise of Democracy.[56] He wrote Tilden of connivance "between the Radicals & the men of the Lamar order," and warned, "you will be defeated by the lobbies."[57]

The Texas and Pacific subsidy was only one of numerous issues that illustrate the cleavage between Northern and Southern Democrats. The Southerners got more aid from the Republicans than from Northerners of their own party in their drive for money to free the mouth of the Mississippi from mud bars.[58] And again, almost twice as many Republicans as Northern Democrats voted with the South in favor of an appropriation for repairing Mississippi levees and reclaiming flooded lands.[59] Time and again the South would gain Republican support in the Senate or on the floor of the House for an appropriation—for the Galveston harbor, for a Southern steamship line, or for some other local bill—only to have it killed by the Democratic Committee on Appropriations.[60] The Washington *National Republican* openly urged Republican Congressmen to vote with the South in order to compel a roll call on the Texas and Pacific bill and fix responsibility for its defeat on "the Tilden wing" of Democrats.[61] Friends of the bill, however, were unable to force a roll call. The lobbies of Scott, Gould, and

[55] *Nation*, XXIV (1877), 65–66, 82–83.

[56] Washington *Union*, February 19, 20, 1877.

[57] Montgomery Blair to Samuel J. Tilden, February 8, 1877, in Samuel J. Tilden Papers (New York Public Library).

[58] *Congressional Record*, 44 Cong., 2 Sess., 1066–73, 1086, 1347; *Letter from James B. Eads to Hon. W. S. Holman, January 29, 1877* (Washington, 1877), a pamphlet.

[59] *Congressional Record*, 44 Cong., 2 Sess., 2232.

[60] James M. Comly to Hayes, January 8, 1877 (copy), in Hayes Papers. Referring to the defeat of a ship subsidy, the New Orleans *Times* warned: "These repeated rejections of similar bills for Southern aid or relief on the part of a strongly Democratic House may prove at last too much for patient endurance." Quoted in Memphis *Avalanche*, March 1, 1877.

[61] Washington *National Republican*, January 29, 1877.

Huntington brazenly invaded the House, creating such confusion at times as to stop proceedings on the electoral crisis.[62]

Meanwhile, it began to seem that a peaceful solution had been found for the dispute over the counting of the electoral votes in the Electoral Commission, which had been created with bipartisan support the last week in January. But as soon as the Commission cast its first vote on February 8 it became clear that the decision was going against the Democrats by a vote of eight to seven. Then the Democrats heard that Justice Joseph P. Bradley, who cast the deciding vote on the Commission, had suddenly changed his opinion the night before he cast his first vote. When it was charged that he had been influenced by Scott and other Pacific railroad lobbyists, they raised the cry of "conspiracy" and refused to abide by the Commission's decision.[63] Northern Democrats at once opened a filibuster in the House that was designed to prevent completion of the count of electoral votes. It could prevent Hayes's election, and it could lead to violence, even revolution. Its success would depend upon the support of the Southern Democrats.

Boynton, Kellar, and Dodge all expressed confidence that the Southerners could be dissuaded from joining the filibuster. "I shall expect to see hard & effective work there," wrote Boynton, referring to the "Scott help." For the Southerners the problem had been "much simplified" since "they have only to say that good faith, honor, & respect for law all bind them not to impede the execution of the new law for the counting." [64] As tension mounted in Washington over the threat of the filibuster, however, some of Hayes's advisers, including Boynton, urged him to give the South additional assurances. Hayes wrote John Sherman that the Senator could assure Southerners that he would live up to his promises and that Sherman could "not express that too strongly." [65] But by this time the South was asking for something more. Shortly after the filibuster opened, a group of Southern Congressmen met in

[62] Chicago *Tribune*, January 31, 1877.

[63] On Joseph P. Bradley's change of opinion, see Nevins (ed.), *Selected Writings of Abram S. Hewitt*, 173; Charles Bradley (ed.), *Miscellaneous Writings of the Late Hon. Joseph P. Bradley* (Newark, 1902), 220–22; on the influence of Scott and the railroads, see New York *Sun*, February 20, 1877.

[64] Boynton to Smith, February 11, 1877, in Smith Papers; Dodge to Gould, February 12, 1877, letter-book in Box No. 384, in Dodge Papers.

[65] Hayes to John Sherman, February 15, 1877, in Hayes Papers.

Washington and dispatched a messenger to Chicago to present Medill and William Henry Smith with the request that Hayes appoint Kellar's friend Senator Key of Tennessee postmaster general. The portfolio of the traditional cabinet dispenser of patronage was a high price for Democrats to demand of Republicans—an unprecedented price. But the Southern bargainers had it in their power to deliver in exchange two prizes denied the Republicans by a majority of the electorate in 1876: the Presidency and control of the House. The election had narrowed the Democratic majority in the new House to about eight votes. The messenger of the Southern Democratic caucus told Smith that nine of their number were "pledged to aid in giving the Republicans the organization of the new House by electing Garfield, Speaker." These elaborations of the Compromise were enthusiastically endorsed by Medill, Halstead, Boynton, William Henry Smith, and Richard Smith, who urged them upon Hayes. Henceforth the additions were referred to as part of "the purely political plan," as distinguished from "the Scott plan." [66]

At a Democratic caucus on February 17 the Northern filibusters sought to get the official endorsement of the party for their movement to stop "the inauguration of the usurper." Their support in a stormy session came "almost entirely from the North and West," while "the South was almost a unit" against the filibuster. Southern leaders succeeded in passing a motion by a vote of sixty-eight to forty-nine in favor of completing the count.[67] At a second caucus two days later the filibuster met another defeat in spite of a fire-eating speech by Speaker Samuel J. Randall, in which he accused the Southerners of disloyalty and warned them that Hayes would revive bayonet rule in the South and "overwhelm any southern man in ruin who aided in carrying out their agreement in good faith." [68] Though visibly shaken, the Southern ranks held firm. The caucus did agree to put a clause in the army appropriation bill forbidding

[66] William Henry Smith to Hayes, February 17, 1877; Joseph Medill to Richard Smith, February 17, 1877; Boynton to William Henry Smith, February 27, 1877, *ibid.*

[67] Cincinnati *Enquirer,* February 19, 1877. New York *Times,* February 19, 1877, reports fifty-six negative votes.

[68] Charles Foster to Hayes, February 21, 1877, in Hayes Papers; Albert V. House, Jr., "The Political Career of Samuel J. Randall" (Ph.D. dissertation, University of Wisconsin, 1934), 98–99.

the President to intervene in the South with troops. When the Senate refused to agree, the House eventually adjourned without passing the bill, thus leaving Hayes without pay for the army. That action put "teeth" and "sanctions" in the Compromise.[69]

When Boynton learned that the Southerners had stood their ground in the caucus he was overjoyed. "It is difficult," he wrote William Henry Smith, "to distinguish between the comparative effect produced by the two elements—the purely political, & the Scott forces." He doubted that either could have held the South in line alone. "I am sure," he added, "the Scott force has performed enough of the work to entitle it to claims the execution of which appeared in the letters I received." [70] General Dodge, from a less disinterested point of view, wrote Tom Scott attributing the stand of the Southerners entirely to the fact that he had "come to a very clear understanding with those people." Dodge thought he and Scott should see Hayes, who had "a clear understanding" that he was to give them aid in his inaugural, as soon as the President-elect reached Washington. It was even more important for "our Southern friends" to see the President, since "Lamar and a few of that class of men would have great weight with him." [71]

As soon as the South's defection became known, all the leading Republican papers, including those that had for years, and as recently as the summer campaign, pictured the South as treasonous, brutal, and disloyal, broke into effusions of praise for the "decency," "statesmanship," "honor," and "immovable good faith and loyalty of the South." [72] The *National Republican* called the South's vote against the filibuster on February 20 "the bravest and wisest act that has been recorded in the annals of political history for half a century." To the editor it appeared but natural and proper that the "governing classes" in the South should combine with like elements in the North against the Northern Democratic "riff-raff" and assume leadership over "the native menial classes" of the South, especially since the latter had proved "incapable of the in-

[69] New York *Times,* February 20, 1877; *Congressional Record,* 44 Cong., 2 Sess., 2248–52.

[70] Boynton to William Henry Smith, February 18, 22, 1877, in Smith Papers.

[71] Dodge to Scott, February 20, 1877, letter-book in Box No. 384, in Dodge Papers.

[72] New York *Times,* February 19, 1877; Chicago *Tribune,* February 19, 1877; New York *Herald,* February 19, 1877.

telligent exercise of the privileges of citizenship."[73] To Northern Democrats the South's course seemed more like apostasy, if not something worse. "Thus jobbery can effect reconstruction and '*conciliation*' when the military failed," brooded Montgomery Blair, "and we are enabled to see that it was not Wells, Packard, Kellogg, Stearns & Co. [Carpetbaggers] who gave Southern votes to Hayes, but *Southern* Democrats—Tom Scott's Democrats!"[74]

Then on February 22, when all seemed to be settled, the Columbus *Ohio State Journal,* edited by a close friend of Hayes, came forth with a typical bloody-shirt editorial attacking Louisiana Democrats in contemptuous terms. The editorial was quickly disavowed, but the excitement over the incident created a temporary diversion. Seizing upon this opportunity, three Louisiana Congressmen with Major E. A. Burke, the personal representative of the Democratic claimant for the Louisiana governorship, succeeded in arranging what became famous as the "Wormley House Bargain." Using the threat of a renewed filibuster, Burke and his friends managed to frighten Sherman, Charles Foster, Matthews, and Garfield into repeating such pledges of Hayes's good intentions toward the South as had already been given, and in pinning down somewhat more definitely the understanding about withdrawing troops from Louisiana and South Carolina. John Young Brown of Kentucky and Senator Gordon independently wrung written and signed versions of these pledges from Matthews and Foster.[75] Since these pledges were well publicized they may have helped in weakening Republican resistance to Hayes's policy.

The importance of the Wormley Bargain, however, has been greatly exaggerated. Major Burke later admitted under oath that he was playing a "bluff game," that he could not have held his temporary recruits from the South in the filibuster, that his "bargain" had no appreciable effect on the outcome of the electoral crisis, that the South would have helped complete the electoral count anyway, and that Hayes was already committed to the policy he pursued "before these negotiations were entered into."[76] But as an explana-

[73] Washington *National Republican,* February 19, 20, 21, 1877.

[74] Washington *Union,* February 20, 1877.

[75] "Presidential Election Investigation," in *House Miscellaneous Documents,* 45 Cong., 3 Sess., No. 31, I, 974–81; III, 619–29.

[76] *Ibid.,* I, 990, 1015.

tion to offer angry and puzzled constituents for the apostasy of Southern representatives the Bargain had its uses. Pictured as a knightly deed, the rescue of distressed sister states from the heel of the Carpetbagger, it was much easier to explain than complicated arrangements regarding patronage, postmasters general, speakerships, control of the House, railroad subsidies, branch roads, and internal improvements. The story also served to enhance the reputation of certain politicians as "Redeemers," though Lamar, Watterson, Hill, Brown, John Hancock, and other leaders who shared the enhanced reputation, never once broke rank and joined the filibuster with other Southerners to assist Major Burke's maneuver.[77] When that maneuver was completed the filibuster suddenly ceased, the count was completed, and Hayes was peacefully inaugurated.[78]

Then began a period of eight months during which "reconciliation" flourished, and Hayes, with the co-operation of Southern conservatives, launched his policy to win support in the South. The inaugural address contained a boost for Southern internal improvements. The President told Garfield and Matthews that he favored Scott's bill "if that will bring Southern support to the Administration to make it worth while." [79] To the press he "expressed himself in very decided terms in favor of a system of internal improvements calculated to benefit and develop the South, and especially of such Government aid as may be appropriate to secure the completion of the Texas and Pacific Railway." [80] Hayes promptly sent in the nomination of Senator Key for postmaster general, and when Republican Senators resisted this and other appointments, Hayes was glad to note that "the resolute support of the Southern Senators like Gordon, Lamar, and Hill" overcame the opposition.[81] After a brief delay and some awkwardness the President removed the troops from the statehouses of Louisiana and South Carolina, and the last Carpetbag regimes immediately collapsed.

[77] *Congressional Record,* 44 Cong., 2 Sess., 2007-2009, 2025, 2030, 2048–49.

[78] Meantime, Samuel J. Randall turned against the filibuster. Hewitt and other New York Democrats also joined in opposing it.

[79] Garfield Diary, April 3, 1877, in Garfield Papers.

[80] Louisville *Courier-Journal,* April 26, 1877.

[81] Hayes Diary, March 14, 1877, in Charles R. Williams (ed.), *Diary and Letters of Rutherford Birchard Hayes* (Columbus, 1922–1926), III, 427. L. Q. C. Lamar and Benjamin H. Hill entered the Senate in March, 1877.

In spite of the need for an army appropriation, Hayes postponed the calling of an extra session of Congress until fall in order to give the South time to respond to his new policy. Postmaster General Key, with Hayes's blessing, began rapidly filling post offices and higher posts with ex-Confederates, old-line Whigs, Douglas Democrats, and plain Democrats. According to a Southern paper friendly to Hayes, one third of his Southern appointments of the first five months were Democrats.[82] So encouraging were the letters Hayes received from Southern conservatives, businessmen, and politicians in praise of his policy that in May he wrote: "I am confident it will secure North Carolina, with a fair chance in Maryland, Virginia, Tennessee, and Arkansas, and am not without hopes of Louisiana, South Carolina, and Florida." [83] With members of his family and cabinet, accompanied by Wade Hampton, the President made a triumphant speaking tour through the Southeast in September. In Atlanta he told Negroes that their "rights and interests would be safer" in the hands of the Southern white man than in the care of the Federal government. Southern exponents of the Compromise of 1877, Gordon, Lamar, Hill, Hampton, and Stephens, made speeches in the North that assisted in the rituals of reconciliation and gratified conservative opinion in the Northeast. "If this is Southern Democracy," exclaimed the ex-Radical *Harper's Weekly*, "it is wonderfully like the best Northern Republicanism." [84] So long as this mood prevailed the rejuvenation of Whiggery proceeded apace, and the South was drawn closer into alliance with the conservative Northeast.

The first serious breach in the Compromise of 1877 occurred on October 15, 1877, when the Southern Congressmen failed to deliver the votes necessary to elect Garfield speaker and organize the House for the Republicans.[85] Hayes's policy of conciliation began to deteriorate from that point, for a large wing of his own party

[82] Louisville *Commercial* (Republican paper), August 21, 1877.

[83] Hayes to W. D. Bickam, May 3, 1877, in Williams (ed.), *Diary and Letters of Rutherford Birchard Hayes*, III, 432.

[84] *Harper's Weekly*, XXI (1877), 343. For a full discussion of the mood of reconciliation, see Paul H. Buck, *The Road to Reunion, 1865–1900* (Boston, 1937), 100–106.

[85] Garfield had been skeptical of the plan from the start. See Garfield Diary, April 6, 1877, in Garfield Papers.

came forth in open revolt against it. Opponents of the policy found one vulnerable point of attack in the enormous number of internal-improvement bills pressed by Southern Congressmen. "We must conciliate the Solid South, undoubtedly," remarked the New York *Tribune*. "But what will it cost?" [86] The cost added up to national bankruptcy, in the editor's opinion. The second breach of the Compromise came at the hands of the President himself in December when he publicly expressed "grave doubt" regarding the Texas and Pacific bill and declared against "any more Credit Mobilier operations." [87] Scott continued to pile up political victories with the aid of Southern Democrats, but in the meantime Huntington, once more at war with Scott, was laying rails eastward over the same route—without subsidy and with Hayes's blessing.[88] The South got her road to the Pacific, but not in the way she had planned.

The Whiggish alliance between Republicans and Southern conservatives might have survived these breaches of the Compromise had it not been for a sudden wave of agrarian radicalism in 1878 that swept the South out of control of conservative leaders and into temporary alliance with the West. Southern farmers of the Jacksonian tradition who had submitted to the leadership of the Whig-Democrats only in the emergency of Redemption now grew restive and unhappy. The millennium of subsidies promised by the Redeemers failed to materialize, and the depression deepened. Desperate for relief, the agrarian debtors embraced the Greenbacker, silverite, and antimonopoly doctrines of the West and called for the regulation instead of the subsidization of railroads. Yielding to this sentiment in spite of all that Lamar, Hill, Stephens, and other conservatives could do to prevent it, the Southern delegation in the House voted solidly with the West against Eastern opposition to pass Richard P. Bland's free coinage bill and the Bland-Allison

[86] New York *Tribune*, December 19, 1877.

[87] General Boynton, who reported this story in the Cincinnati *Daily Gazette*, December 22, 1877, was "both surprised & disgusted" at Hayes's change of position. He thought of publishing his correspondence regarding the Texas and Pacific deal, but never did. Boynton to Benjamin H. Bristow, December 24, 1877, in Benjamin H. Bristow Papers (Division of Manuscripts, Library of Congress).

[88] Huntington to Colton, October 10, 1877, in Chicago *Tribune*, December 28, 1883.

silver purchase bill, to repass the latter over Hayes's indignant veto, and to repeal the law for the resumption of specie payments.[89] In the South powerful movements got underway in a majority of states to repudiate state bonds worth millions of dollars, held largely by Northeastern capitalists.

Agrarian leaders of the South revived the ante-bellum sectional diplomacy of a Western alliance. They dusted off the old arguments for unity between the agrarian sections—the geographic and ethnic ties, the "natural" system of river, versus the "artificial" system of railroad, transportation, the common cause of farming economies against an industrial economy. Senator John T. Morgan of Alabama declared that a community of interest would "draw the South and West together . . . beyond the power of resistance or of future disseverance." [90] "United politically, they are invincible," contended a Mississippian. "They can defy the world, the flesh, and the devil." [91] Toombs of Georgia swore that the West always had been the South's "most valuable ally." [92] Facing West, the Southern Democrats wrote state platforms for the campaign of 1878 that flamed forth defiance of Eastern capitalism, its banks, monetary system, railroads, and monopolies. The election resulted in the first "Solid South." Not one of the states that Hayes had courted did he win.

As soon as the West-South combination became apparent and the South began voting for agrarian money and antimonopoly bills and repudiating state bonds, the spirit of conciliation vanished among Republican circles. The *National Republican,* which had praised the South as the home of honor and loyalty in 1877, discovered in 1878 that "the spirit of rebellion still lives and is liable at any moment to be again entrenched in arms." [93] The Southern ideas regarding money, debts, banks, and state bonds

[89] *Congressional Record,* 45 Cong., 1 Sess., 241; *ibid.,* 2 Sess., 1112, 1410–11, 1420; *ibid.,* 1 Sess., 632–33.

[90] John T. Morgan, "The Political Alliance of the South with the West," in *North American Review* (New York), CXXVI (1878), 318.

[91] Editorial, Jackson *Weekly Clarion-Ledger,* February 6, 1878.

[92] Robert Toombs to Alexander H. Stephens, March 25, 1880, in Ulrich B. Phillips (ed.), *The Correspondence of Robert Toombs, Alexander H. Stephens, and Howell Cobb,* in American Historical Association, *Annual Report,* 1911, II (Washington, 1913), 740.

[93] Washington *National Republican,* June 13, 1878.

proved to the New York *Tribune* that "the South is not yet ready for the new civilization," that it "still stands in need of reconstruction," and that between it and the North there was "a radical, irrepressible conflict." [94] Wendell Phillips thought that since "the South and West are naturally allies" on the "material question" and the East and West on "moral issues," the Republicans blundered in dropping issues of the latter type in 1877. "The Southern question . . . properly treated, might have delayed this material question for some years," he believed.[95] William Lloyd Garrison declared that the lesson of the 1878 campaign was plain: " 'The bloody shirt!' *In hoc signo vinces!*" [96] By that time the party had rejected Hayes's policy and returned to the bloody shirt.

A general debate over sectional diplomacy took place in the South after the election of 1878. Because the West had proved more responsive to the bloody-shirt issue than to appeals for agrarian unity, the Southern advocates of a Western alliance were discredited and on the defensive. Lamar and the conservatives, "who persistently resisted this movement," maintained stoutly that they had been "justified by events" and that "a further Western alliance is now out of the question." It was plain that the road to reunion was a forked road, that the right fork led to the East and the left fork to the West. Between the right-forkers and the left-forkers the debate raged for months.[97] It was to break out intermittently again and again over the years, but in the immediate issue the counsel of the right-fork conservatives—the architects of the Compromise of 1877—was to prevail. There is no better statement of their position than one found in the Charleston *News and Courier:*

"We see no hope that a platform will be framed that is acceptable to both East and West. . . . With one section or the other the South must go, and our fixed opinion is that the *permanent interests of the South lie with the East rather than with the West.* The aim of the South being to . . . avoid whatever is revolutionary in politics, sociology or finance, the South must go with the East, de-

[94] New York *Tribune,* January 4, February 4, March 27, 1879.

[95] Wendell Phillips, "The Outlook," in *North American Review,* CXXVII (1878), 102.

[96] Quoted in New York *Tribune,* January 4, 1879.

[97] For an illuminating discussion of the debate, see Charles Nordhoff in New York *Herald,* November 19, 1878.

spite its aggregating self-assertion, rather than join hands with the West, which is learning the A, B, C, of statesmanship." [98]

The partners of the South's Eastern alliance were Democrats instead of the Republicans Hayes had hoped they would be, but they were quite as conservative. Meekly the South lined up in 1880 behind a national Democratic platform reported by Henry Watterson that contained the phrase "strict maintenance of the public faith" twice in one sentence. And in the successive Cleveland campaigns the South submitted tamely to doctrine dictated by the sectional interests of the Northeastern economy. The reconstructed South came to be regarded in the eighties as a bulwark of, instead of a menace to, the new economic order. "For actual sectional issues," observed the New York *Journal of Commerce,* "we must look north of Mason and Dixon's line. Future storms will come not from the South, but from the West." [99] The Southern states, agreed the *Industrial South,* were the "breakwater for all fanaticism. They are the bulwark against all the storms of political passion. They send forth conservative influences." [100]

It took a lot of hallooing and heading off by the conservative leaders to keep the mass of Southerners herded up the right fork. Agrarian mavericks were eternally taking off up the left fork followed by great droves that they had stampeded. With the aid of the New-South propagandists, however, and by frequent resort to repressive or demagogic devices, the right-forkers contrived to keep the South fairly faithful to the Eastern alignment—until the advent of the Populists.

[98] Charleston *News and Courier,* December 13, 1878. A similar treatment of the question is in the Richmond *Dispatch,* October 22, 1878.

[99] Quoted in Galveston *Daily News,* January 4, 1885.

[100] *Industrial South* (Richmond), VI (June 3, 1886), 247.

CHAPTER III

THE LEGACY OF RECONSTRUCTION

THE loyalty and discipline that prevailed in the white man's party were inspired by the revolution that established it in power. After the two objects of that revolution were achieved—the crushing of Negro power and the ousting of foreign control—party discipline was still dependent upon keeping vividly alive the memories of these menaces. They were the only reliable bases for white solidarity. Almost any other issue ran the risk of dividing the whites and was hushed whenever possible. The Redeemers tried by invoking the past to avert the future. The politics of Redemption belonged therefore to the romantic school, emphasizing race and tradition and deprecating issues of economics and self-interest.

"The fact is that the present Democratic party in Virginia was formed . . . without any reference to economic questions," asserted the leading spokesman of that party.[1] "In other States it may be different," wrote the editor of Mississippi's most powerful paper. "In this State for some time to come there is but one issue. All know what it is."[2] Another Democratic paper of Mississippi announced that its columns were closed to any "discussion of the merits or claims of gentlemen for the Democratic nomination for Congress."[3] An Alabamian declared that "we care not the snap of our finger who the next Governor shall be, provided that he is a sound Conservative-Democrat." This sentiment was praised by the Montgomery *Advertiser* as "the spirit of genuine patriotism. It is the spirit that should prevail in all elections."[4] Edward Mayes,

1 Richmond *Dispatch*, May 6, 1888.

2 Jackson *Weekly Clarion*, August 23, 1882.

3 Raymond *Gazette*, quoted in Jackson *Weekly Clarion*, August 2, 1882.

4 Montgomery *Advertiser*, July 6, 1881.

chancellor of the University of Mississippi and a historian of some distinction, proudly announced in public that "In all my life I have never voted any other ticket, I have never failed to vote, I have never scratched a ticket, and I would not, no matter whom the party might nominate for its candidate." [5] It would be difficult to match this blind devotion to the "party line" even among devotees of modern revolutionary organizations.

Had the white man's party of conservatism been democratically organized, had the "party line" been determined and criticized democratically, the one-party system might not have been stultifying. But the organization and control of the party was anything but democratic. Issues, candidates, platforms—everything was the private business of a few politicians known by the discontented as the "ring" or the "courthouse clique." The extent of their domination and the nature of their machinery of control varied among the state rings, but the ring was always present. An examination of the workings of one machine will reveal typical methods.

The key man in the Democratic organization of Virginia was the county chairman, who received his orders from the state chairman. The county official picked out an electoral board whose names were approved by the state legislature. The electoral board appointed election judges and clerks designated by the county chairman. Through these "election officials and the use of money and local pressure," the county chairman "was able to see that only his men were chosen as treasurer, sheriff, clerk of court, commissioner of revenue, member of the legislature, and supervisors." Since the General Assembly by custom appointed the county judge recommended by the member from the county, it could be accurately said "that the county chairman and his immediate assistants determined who would be chosen to every office in the county." This tiny group was the "courthouse clique," and "In them lay the real power of the only organization which could control Virginia." [6] The political aspirant or hopeful lawyer who did not reach an understanding with this ring was condemned to almost certain failure.

[5] Jackson *Clarion-Ledger,* September 18, 1890.

[6] Allen W. Moger, "The Origin of the Democratic Machine in Virginia," in *Journal of Southern History,* VIII (1942), 206–208.

The political soil on which this growth of rings flourished had long produced crops of incorrigible individualists, as independent as any who could be found in the land. Political conflict was a deep-rooted tradition in the South. Now that peace was restored and the invader removed, an unquestioning obedience was exacted that had previously been refused Southern rulers even in time of war.

The tide of democratic faith was at low ebb on all American shores after the Grant administration, and it would be a mistake to fix upon a reactionary temper in the South as a sectional peculiarity.[7] Still there was an obvious explanation for the extremes to which reaction was carried in that section. Never in our history was there a more radical application of the democratic dogma than that which suddenly enfranchised the liberated Negro slave. Once reaction set in, it could hardly be expected to be mild.

The Richmond *Dispatch,* which spoke for the Redeemers and Funders in Virginia, thought that "Every step towards pure democracy in the States has increased the depravity in the political arena. . . . Any backward step that may re-establish conservative checks upon the corruptions of demagogism will protract the duration of republicanism." [8] It was the opinion of the Richmond *State* that "The true teaching is that both 'caste' and 'class' must exist in all organized society, and their abolition, admitting such a thing possible, could result in nothing else but a return to primitive barbarism, for they are the outcome of civilization." The preachment of leveling doctrine was especially futile in Virginia, "wherein equality by birth as a general principle has been taught ever since Mr. Jefferson made so strong a presentation of it in the Declaration of Independence; yet where classes and race distinctions have constantly grown and become more marked each year." It remained true that the "best Government in the world" was the "rule of the best people." "All men may aspire to the highest ranks in their caste, and each class may continue to improve its condition," but there the matter ended.[9]

Over against such pronouncements could be set contrasting pro-

[7] See, for example, Francis Parkman, "The Failure of Universal Suffrage," in *North American Review,* CXXVII (1878), 1–20.

[8] Richmond *Dispatch,* August 2, 1877.

[9] Richmond *State,* October 7, 1882.

fessions of democratic principles. Josephus Daniels, growing up at this time in the adjoining state of North Carolina, believed that his was "a community free from caste or social chasms, as true a democracy as the world has known." [10] Theoretical and abstract statements, however, are less descriptive of the true nature of democratic processes in the redeemed South than an examination of the "conservative checks" themselves, the "backward steps" taken to protect and entrench the new regimes after the overthrow of Carpetbag governments. These devices were so numerous and varied that they can only be sampled.

In Daniel's own democratic North Carolina, almost the first step taken by the legislature after the downfall of Republican power was the passing of a county-government act that, according to one historian, "violated every principle of local self-government." [11] The law provided that the legislature should name the justices of the peace, who in turn were to elect the commissioners of their respective counties, thus making the principal county officers appointive. By this means the "black" counties of the east were assured white government, but by the same device western "white" counties lost control of their local affairs to a highly centralized party machine. Thirty members of the legislature of 1876 signed a "solemn protest" against the act upon its passage. Twenty years later they were echoed by a Populist outburst that pronounced the system "as mean a piece of political machinery as ever was devised," for it "put the financial affairs of every county into the hands of an irresponsible oligarchy." [12]

The corresponding device in Louisiana was even simpler. In the hands of the governor, instead of the legislature, was placed "an inordinate appointive power." He appointed the police jury of every parish, which levied local taxes and enacted local laws, as well as all rural school boards, all executive boards and boards of

[10] Josephus Daniels, *Tar Heel Editor* (Chapel Hill, 1939), 113.

[11] J. G. de Roulhac Hamilton, *North Carolina Since 1860* (Chicago and New York, 1919), 192–93.

[12] North Carolina *House Journal,* 1876–1877, pp. 875–76; Raleigh *Daily Caucasian,* February 10, 1895. See also, William A. Mabry, *The Negro in North Carolina Politics Since Reconstruction,* in Trinity College Historical Society, *Historical Papers,* Ser. XXIII (Durham, 1940), 18–19.

trustees of state institutions, numerous judges, and all registrars, who passed upon the eligibility of voters.[13]

The successors to Carpetbag rule in Florida discovered in the Republican Constitution of 1868 an instrument so well adapted to their purposes that they successfully resisted all attempts to change it for eight years after Redemption. The constitution placed in the hands of the governor the power to appoint (with confirmation by the senate) in each county the tax collector and assessor, treasurer, surveyor, superintendent of schools, county commissioners, sheriff, clerk of court, county judge, and justices of the peace—thus leaving to the uninhibited franchise of free Floridians the choice of constables. The original intent of these provisions, Republican supremacy in the white counties, was equally as suited to Conservative control of black counties as to machine domination of all counties. Clearly the restoration of "home rule" in Florida did not bring sovereignty very close home.[14]

The device of gerrymandering had a long history, but its refinements by the Redeemers were often a legacy of Radical rule. "I have nothing to conceal in the matters," said the chairman of the committee of the Tennessee senate that proposed a redistricting bill shortly after the overthrow of the Radicals in that state. "One main object was [so] to redistrict the State that for the next ten years not a Republican can be elected to the Legislature. . . . I believe in the law of revenge. The Radicals disfranchised us, and now we intend to disfranchise them." [15] With somewhat less candor other states put into practice the same method.

The legal devices for limiting Negro votes which were most favored in the Redemption period were intricate registration and election laws varying from state to state. Striking at weaknesses of the Negro, these laws could be employed against whites of the same economic or educational status. The requirements of regis-

13 Henry E. Chambers, "Modern Louisiana, 1876–1909," in Julian A. C. Chandler *et al.* (eds.), *The South in the Building of the Nation . . .* (Richmond, 1909–1913), III, 169–70.

14 Eldridge R. Collins, "The Florida Constitution of 1885" (M.A. thesis, University of Florida, 1939), 7, 89–92, 101.

15 Quoted in Philip M. Hamer (ed.), *Tennessee; A History, 1673–1932* (New York, 1933), II, 676.

tration several months before voting and possession of the certificate at the time of voting struck at a class not accustomed to preserving papers, as it did at a landless class of tenants constantly changing residence and having to obtain new vouchers. The fact that registration and election officials were usually Democrats should not be overlooked in estimating the effect of the registration requirements.[16] Virginia's law adding petty larceny to the list of disqualifications was imitated because of its effect on the Negro vote. Numerous forms of what was loosely called the "Australian" system provided for a ballot that did not identify candidates by party, either with emblem or name, and limited the voters to two and a half minutes in the polling booth. Those illiterates who were not too proud, or timid, or suspicious might ask the Democratic election judges for whatever degree of assistance the law permitted. South Carolina's eight-box law of 1882 confronted the voter with a Chinese puzzle, for he had to match ballot to box or invalidate his vote. Election managers were permitted to read box labels on request, but opportunity for confusion abounded.[17]

Elaborate extralegal devices of fraud and chicanery which had developed during Reconstruction became habits that lingered long after Redemption. The stuffing of ballot boxes, the use of boxes with false bottoms, the casting of tissue ballots, the doctoring of returns, the manipulation of counts, the repeating of votes, and the tampering with registration books were all highly developed arts. Methods of less subtlety were not rare: "I ask if there is a member on this floor who will pretend to deny that nine ballot-boxes were stolen from the clerk's office in . . . [Pulaski] county," demanded the speaker of the Arkansas house of representatives in 1889.[18]

[16] Mabry, *Negro in North Carolina Politics Since Reconstruction*, 22.

[17] Stephen B. Weeks, "The History of Negro Suffrage in the South," in *Political Science Quarterly* (New York), IX (1894), 690–703; Paul Lewinson, *Race, Class, & Party. A History of Negro Suffrage and White Politics in the South* (New York, 1932), 63–68; James O. Knauss, "The Growth of Florida's Election Laws," in *Florida Historical Society Quarterly* (Tallahassee), V (1926–1927), 10–11.

[18] A member from Pulaski promptly denied the charge. "Only six were stolen," he maintained.

"Very well, I stand corrected," replied the speaker of the house. "Only six ballot-boxes and poll books were stolen from . . . the county in which stands the capitol of the beloved Arkansas." Little Rock *Arkansas Gazette*, February 3, 1889.

Polling places were changed without general notification, or located at points remote from Negro communities. White men might vote in so leisurely a fashion that Negroes might find closing time had come before they had their turn. Bribery remained useful, but was rarely necessary except when the white men divided. The most casual consideration of the extent of the Negro's psychological and economic dependence upon the white man will indicate the narrowness of his margin of political freedom. It was scarcely necessary for the "Democratic Farmers and Employers of Labor" to be reminded, as those of one Georgia community were, to "bring to bear the power which your situation gives over tenants, laborers, and croppers"; [19] or for a South Carolina editor to suggest that "if every employer of colored people in Charleston will constitute himself a political missionary . . . the bulk of the colored votes will be cast for the Democratic candidates." [20]

Intimidation by outright violence and force did not disappear with the Ku Klux Klan and the Red Shirts, though its use became rarer and less necessary. The "southern outrage" story was a standard feature of the Republican press, and congressional investigations for partisan purposes often exaggerated the amount of violence in the South. In large areas of the region elections were as fairly and peacefully conducted as in any part of the country. On the other hand, the continual repetition of "riots" along a peculiar pattern, especially in the Lower South, was an undeniable part of the picture. The Louisiana elections of 1878 cost between thirty and forty lives and after the election of 1884 sixteen bodies were found along the Bayou Teche.[21]

It would be a mistake to assume that such methods were always cynically adopted or that the Southern conscience was callous toward the moral degradation they involved. It was with deep mortification that Judge J. J. Chrisman, in urging disfranchisement of the Negro, made the following confession in the Mississippi constitutional convention of 1890: "Sir, it is no secret that there has

19 "To the Democratic Farmers and Employers of Labor of Wilkes County," a handbill dated September 8, 1892, in Thomas E. Watson Papers (University of North Carolina Library, Chapel Hill).

20 Charleston *News and Courier,* December 4, 1879.

21 *Senate Reports,* 45 Cong., 3 Sess., IV, No. 855, pp. 28–37; Louisville *Courier-Journal,* November 3, 1884.

not been a full vote and a fair count in Mississippi since 1875—that we have been preserving the ascendency of the white people by revolutionary methods. In plain words, we have been stuffing ballot-boxes, committing perjury and here and there in the State carrying the elections by fraud and violence until the whole machinery for elections was about to rot down." No one would deliberately choose to perpetuate such methods, he declared, who was "not a moral idiot." [22] Describing the situation in the Upper South, William L. Royall stated that "the elections in Virginia became a farce. We got rid of negro government but we got in place of it a government resting upon fraud and chicanery, and it very soon became a serious question which was worse, a negro government or a white government resting upon stuffed ballot boxes." [23] Private letters of the period reveal again and again the writhings of the best consciences of the South under the lash of this problem.

"Retrenchment," a policy causing bitter complaint in the South when applied by the Federal government, became the watchword of the Redeemers in their state and local governments. The special significance of the word for that generation had two derivations: first, the extravagance of Carpetbag legislatures, and second, the Panic of 1873 and the long shadow of depression that followed it. The extravagance of the Radical governments has doubtless been exaggerated, but expenditures had raised tax rates in certain states to oppressive heights. "No other part of the union was half so poor as the South," writes one historian; "yet the South groaned under levies which were unapproached elsewhere. When computed according to wealth, it was a more oppressive taxation, in all probability, than has ever been borne before or since in the United States." [24]

Retrenchment meant many things, but the proposition laid down by Governor Drew of Florida as the principle of his administration provides a working definition: "spend nothing unless absolutely necessary." And in amplifying that principle he said to his legislature in 1877 "that government will be the most highly esteemed

[22] Jackson *Clarion-Ledger*, September 11, 1890.

[23] William L. Royall, *Some Reminiscences* (New York, 1909), 201–202.

[24] Allan Nevins, *Emergence of Modern America, 1865–1878* (New York, 1927), 355–56.

that gives the greatest protection to the tax payer." [25] Redemption governments, often describing themselves as the "rule of the taxpayer," frankly constituted themselves champions of the property owner against the propertyless and allegedly untaxed masses. "Intelligence and property must rule over imbecility and pauperism," proclaimed Henry Watterson, for this was the "law alike of nature and society." [26] Cheapness, even niggardliness, under this tutelage became widely accepted as the criterion of good government. Measured by that standard the achievements of the new dispensation were sometimes rather remarkable.

Salaries of state officials were slashed drastically, sometimes to absurdly low amounts.[27] Some states made salary reductions of as much as 50 per cent. In the middle eighties only two Southern states paid their governors as much as $5,000, and four paid only $3,000. Observing that "the Gov. of Tennessee boards at a hotel," Lamar suggested to Governor Stone that the executive mansion of Mississippi be "sold or applied to some Public Service." Stone thought it a good idea.[28] If the members of the Texas legislature prolonged their deliberations over sixty days, their pay fell from $5.00 a day to $2.00. Large numbers of offices were abolished, departments were cut to skeleton staffs, and occasionally public services were simply dropped. By means of these strict economies, and in some states by scrupulous administration, spectacular reductions were made in state expenses and in state taxes.

Achievements in retrenchment and low taxes later constituted a mainstay in the defense of the Redemption governments' record. Yet the figures used to support the argument are sometimes not all they seem on the surface. State services were often shifted back to the counties, with little change in total taxation.[29] Tax reductions, while not so large as they appeared, were, however, sufficient to make a deep impression on impoverished landowners. Millions of

[25] Quoted in Kathryn T. Abbey, *Florida, Land of Change* (Chapel Hill, 1941), 324.

[26] Richmond *Dispatch*, April 26, 1890.

[27] Montgomery *Advertiser*, December 9, 1884.

[28] Lamar to John M. Stone, March 31, 1876, in Governor John M. Stone Papers (Mississippi State Department of Archives and History); Stone to Lamar, April 1, 1876, in Lamar-Mayes Papers.

[29] James S. Ferguson, "The Granger Movement in Mississippi" (M.A. thesis, Louisiana State University, 1940), 149.

acres forfeited for nonpayment of taxes during Reconstruction were redeemed.

Apart from the amount of taxes, the systems of taxation resorted to were generally deplorable. The poll tax was regressive; general-property taxes placed an unequal burden on owners of realty, while personalty easily escaped taxation; assessment and valuation laws encouraged dishonesty. Among those interests specially favored by Redemption tax policies were railroads, utilities, and insurance companies. They were frequently granted valuable franchises that escaped taxation, and assessments of their property, especially that of railroads, were generally far below their true value.[30] Urged on by the dominant wing of Redeemers, several state legislatures and numerous municipalities adopted measures exempting from taxation new manufacturing capital entering the state or community. The South Carolina law was inherited from the Reconstruction legislature and continued by the Redeemers. The Mississippi law, adopted in 1882, declared the machinery and everything in and about a new factory, save railroad capital, "to be exempt from all taxation, State, county, and municipal, for a period of ten years from the time such factory is completed and in operation." [31] By 1886 Florida, Louisiana, and South Carolina had similar laws, and a tendency was established that was to become widely characteristic of the South.[32] This liberality with manufacturers and railroads went hand in hand with stern "retrenchment" in the matter of school funds. Governor Oran M. Roberts of Texas, who vetoed the state appropriation for public schools on the ground of economy in 1879, was soon urging the legislature to exempt manufacturing capital from all taxes for ten years.[33]

To be properly evaluated, the policy of retrenchment must be viewed in relation to the accompanying record of public services and social legislation. The extreme poverty of the South would

[30] J. H. Hollander (ed.), *Studies in State Taxation with Particular Reference to the Southern States,* in Johns Hopkins University *Studies in Historical and Political Science,* XVIII (Baltimore, 1900), 99–111, 202, 231–33, 237.

[31] "Published by Authority," in Jackson *Weekly Clarion,* March 29, 1882.

[32] New Orleans *Times-Democrat,* September 1, 1886; James W. Martin and Glenn D. Morrow, *Taxation of Manufacturing in the South* (University, Ala., 1948), 102–106.

[33] Galveston *Daily News,* February 18, 1882; Rupert N. Richardson, *Texas, The Lone Star State* (New York, 1943), 330.

have made a satisfactory program of public education and services impossible under any regime. Before passing judgment on the Redeemers one should always recall the handicaps under which they worked. But poverty can not explain away the shortcomings of Redemption. Measured in terms of ignorance and suffering the results of the Redeemers' neglect of social responsibilities were grave. Perhaps a more permanent injury was the set of values imposed upon the Southern mind by the rationalization of this negligence.

Public education, bearing in many minds the stigma of a Carpetbag measure, was first to suffer. This was even true in Virginia, though the school system was launched by native Conservatives of that state. By 1878 the unpaid sum due Virginia schools was over a million dollars. Despite the warning of the school commissioner that one half of the schools would fail to open in the fall, the state auditor ignored an act of the legislature requiring him to pay the schools their constitutional quota of state funds in cash, on the ground that the state's obligation to its bondholders came first. John W. Daniel thought that "It were better for the State to burn the schools" than to readjust the state debt; Governor F. W. M. Holliday considered public schools "a luxury . . . to be paid for like any other luxury, by the people who wish their benefits"; while William L. Royall, editor and one of the counsel of the bondholders, thought that free education beyond the barest rudiments was "imported here by a gang of carpetbaggers," and that taxation to support it was socialistic. It should be provided for pauper children only, as before the war.[34]

The attitude of the Virginia Funders was no doubt extreme, yet in each of the Southern states there was an element who shared the Funders' philosophy. In Texas, Tennessee, Mississippi, Alabama, Louisiana, Arkansas, and Florida reaction crippled the schools, and throughout the South public education suffered under the pinch of the Redeemers' policy of retrenchment as well as under the general poverty and depression. The average length of the common school term in the South fell off approximately 20 per

[34] John W. Daniel, quoted in Richmond *Whig*, December 3, 1880; William L. Royall, in Richmond *Commonwealth*, March 17, 1880. See also, McFarland, "Extension of Democracy in Virginia," 96, 110–15.

cent after Redemption, and the 100-day term, the highest average attained during Reconstruction, was not restored until after 1900. The amount of money expended per pupil enrolled in the common schools of the South Central census division of states fell off by 1880 to 59.5 per cent of the amount spent in 1871, then slowly increased to 81 per cent by 1890. Expenditures per pupil in the South Atlantic division [35] were $10.27 in 1871, $6.60 in 1880, and $7.63 in 1890. In the last year the national average expenditure per pupil was $17.22, state expenditures ranging from $3.38 in South Carolina to $43.43 in Colorado. Between 1871 and 1890, however, the percentage of the total population of the South enrolled in public schools almost doubled, and climbed to the national average. Over the same years, on the other hand, the national average remained almost stationary. The amount expended per capita of population declined in the South Central states from 81 cents in 1872 to 51 cents in 1877, and in the South Atlantic states from 80 cents in 1875 to 63 cents in 1879. By 1890, after the pressure of the farmers' movement had been felt, the per capita expenditure climbed to about 97 cents in the South, as compared with $2.24 in the country as a whole.[36]

In each of the states there was a heroic minority who battled against reaction and struggled tirelessly for the cause of the schools and social betterment. Assisted by small Northern endowments, such as the Peabody Fund and the Slater Fund, J. L. M. Curry of Alabama and Virginia recruited a small staff of crusaders in each Southern state and awakened some localities to a pitch of self-sacrificing zeal. The important victories of these crusaders, however, were not won until after the turn of the century. Reaction and retrenchment prevailed generally during the first decade of the New Order and well into the second. Thirteen years after Redemption a Louisiana newspaper complained that "there is an illiterate majority to-day, whereas there was none in 1880, that this illiteracy prevails not among the negroes alone, but among the whites as well." These were but the "natural effects of a poor public school system"; yet all appeals to the legislature had been met with

[35] Including Delaware, Maryland, District of Columbia, and West Virginia.

[36] *Report of the Commissioner of Education for the Year 1889–90* (Washington, 1893), I, 31, 36–37, and charts on pp. 38–40.

"the stereotyped reply that there is no money for the schools." [37] The year after the Tennessee Redeemers had all but destroyed the public-school system of their state it was realized "that while the white population had increased only 13 per cent during the preceding ten years, white illiteracy had increased 50 per cent." Yet little effective public action was taken to check the retrogression before the end of the century.[38] Retrenchment in Texas left the people with "scarcely a decent pretense" of an efficient public-school system. "The sons and daughters of the poorer classes, except here and there in favored localities, are thus condemned . . . to grow up in ignorance." [39]

Even if the Redeemers had abandoned retrenchment and championed the cause of the schools, they would not have been able to provide an adequate system of education. Neither Southern resources of that day, nor the small handouts of Northern philanthropists, nor the two combined would have been enough. The only answer, many Southerners were convinced, was Federal aid. Their argument was that emancipation and Negro enfranchisement were national, not Southern, policies, that the nation had evaded its responsibilities for the education of the freedmen and left the burden upon an already overburdened South. The South's opportunity for national aid came in the form of a bill of Senator Henry W. Blair of New Hampshire, introduced into the Senate on December 4, 1883, and reported favorably out of committee on January 31 following. The bill provided for ten annual appropriations, beginning at $15,000,000 and diminishing by $1,000,000 each year, to be distributed among the states in proportion to the amount of illiteracy in each. Segregation of the races was permitted, but no inequality in the benefits derived from the bill.[40] Because of the enormous amount of illiteracy in the region, the South would receive the lion's share of the appropriations—$11,000,000 out of the first $15,000,000, according to one estimate. This was

[37] Editorial, New Orleans *Times-Democrat,* August 3, 1890.

[38] Charles W. Dabney, *Universal Education in the South* (Chapel Hill, 1936), I, 302–305.

[39] Editorial, Galveston *Daily News,* December 9, 1880.

[40] Henry W. Blair, *National Aid in the Establishment and Temporary Support of Common Schools: The Education Bill* (Washington, 1887), 47; *Congressional Record,* 48 Cong., 1 Sess., 758.

more than the entire sum spent on the public schools of the South in 1880.[41]

The Blair bill was debated furiously in the press, legislatures, and schoolhouses of the South from 1883 to 1890. Perhaps no other Federal bill, unless it was Henry Cabot Lodge's "force bill," received half so much space in the Southern press. Opinion was sharply divided.[42] Unfortunately for its Southern defenders, the Blair bill, not unlike other humanitarian measures from the same general source, contained a dilemma that confused the issue. A Republican measure, the bill was designed to relieve that party of the embarrassment of a large surplus in the treasury which was due mainly to the high protective tariff. In order to receive the desirable education funds, therefore, the South had to give tacit assent to a tax that its party stamped as iniquitous and from which it derived no real benefit. It was not surprising that the industrialist wings of the Redeemer state parties were among the advocates of the Blair bill.[43] The bill never came to a poll in the House, but in the Senate in 1884 thirteen Southern Senators, or one more than half, voted "aye," five "nay," and six were recorded absent. In 1886 fifteen voted "aye," and in 1888 fourteen Southern Senators favored an altered version of the bill.[44] The Republicans dropped the bill after the election of 1888 ended the threat of tariff reform.

Constitutional objections predominated among the arguments of the Blair bill opponents from the South. The reflections of Curry, who labored hard for the bill despite his state-rights credo, are especially interesting. "I cannot, *inter nos,*" he wrote Robert C. Winthrop, "help from suspecting that race-prejudice at the South and a fear that the education of the negroes would make them less easily manipulated in elections had more influence in the adverse action than constitutional scruples." [45]

[41] *Report of the Commissioner of Education for the Year 1889–90,* I, 27.

[42] For varied press opinion, see New Orleans *Times-Democrat,* May 11, 1882; Jackson *Clarion,* April 9, 1884; Louisville *Courier-Journal,* November 9, 1885; Richmond *Dispatch,* January 3, 1888; Raleigh *News and Observer,* March 19, 1884; Birmingham *Daily Age–Herald,* July 2, 1890; Birmingham *Iron Age,* April 17, 1884.

[43] Nashville *Daily American,* July 31, 1886. Robison, *Bob Taylor,* Chap. IV, has an illuminating analysis of the Blair bill–tariff issue.

[44] For the roll call of 1884, see *Congressional Record,* 48 Cong., 1 Sess., 3024; for 1886, *ibid.,* 49 Cong., 1 Sess., 2095; for 1888, *ibid.,* 50 Cong., 1 Sess., 1223.

[45] Jabez L. M. Curry to Robert C. Winthrop, September 1, 1886, in Jabez L. M.

Provision for the care of state prisoners, the insane, the blind, and other dependents, as well as measures for safeguarding public health, were largely governed by the philosophy of retrenchment that guided the Redemption policy on public schools. Public facilities for these purposes continued in a primitive state, shockingly inadequate to meet increasing needs.[46] The Redeemers sought, in many instances, to revert to the ante-bellum system of local responsibility that relieved the state of these unwelcome burdens. The attempt did not work.

Reaction against Reconstruction took forms other than retrenchment. Under Radical control, state as well as Federal government exceeded all previous limits of interference with the property, habits, and life of the individual. Reaction against these Radical intrusions became reaction against governmental interference of any kind. The distrust and suspicion of legislative action and political power that accompanies any laissez-faire philosophy was more deep-seated in the South than elsewhere. *Laissez faire* became almost a test of Southern patriotism.

This reaction was only natural and would have yielded in due time to the pressing needs for government services, regulation, and action had it not happened that at the height of the reaction many states adopted new constitutions that froze a passing mood into fundamental law for decades. Written shortly after Redemption, new constitutions were adopted by Alabama in 1875, Arkansas in 1874, Georgia in 1877, Louisiana in 1879, North Carolina in 1876, Tennessee in 1870, Texas in 1876, and Virginia in 1870. Almost all of the new instruments show the fears and prejudices of the times, though they are embodied in different degrees and ways.[47] The most common characteristic was an overweening distrust of legislatures. Of the fifty-eight sections in the chapter of the Texas con-

Curry Papers (Division of Manuscripts, Library of Congress). Unless otherwise stated subsequent citations refer to this Curry collection, rather than the one in the Alabama Department of Archives and History.

[46] See below, pp. 212–15.

[47] For examples, cf. Alabama Constitution of 1875, Art. IV, Secs. 29, 30, 32, 33, 40, 41, 53, 54, in Francis N. Thorpe (comp.), *The Federal and State Constitutions, Colonial Charters, and Other Organic Laws* (Washington, 1909), I, 161–63; Arkansas Constitution of 1874, Art. V, Secs. 29–33, *ibid.*, 341; Georgia Constitution of 1877, Art. III, Sec. 12, Art. IV, Sec. 2, *ibid.*, II, 853, 854–55; Louisiana Constitution of 1879, Arts. XLIII, XLIV, XLVI, XLIX, *ibid.*, III, 1478–79.

stitution dealing with the legislature, over half of them place limitations on its authority. The Louisiana legislature was forbidden to pass local or special laws on twenty-one carefully enumerated subjects and was restrained from incurring any debt except for the purpose of suppressing insurrection or repelling invasion. Pledging the state's credit to corporations was forbidden by several constitutions. Limitations on power over taxation and appropriations were often rigidly set, and minute provisions for procedure laid down. Besides reducing legislative prerogatives to a minimum, the tendency was to emasculate discretionary authority of civil servants, and in general to tie all the knots in the skein of the famous "checks and balances."

Looking over the handiwork of the Texas convention a contemporary critic gave his opinion of the document in words that would have been appreciated in several Southern states. "The harness is so small," he wrote, "the straps drawn so tight, the check rein pulled up to the last buckle hole, and the load to draw so heavy, that the legislative horse will be galled from collar to crupper in the attempt to work, and the State wagon will go creaking along the highway of progress, in the rear of the procession." [48] The Texas constitution of 1876 was to remain the law of the land for many years to come.

A reputation for scrupulous honesty in public office—the virtue most notoriously lacking in the Carpetbag governments—was widely enjoyed by the Redeemers. It was a reputation that has been spared the test of searching scrutiny. Few American governments have enjoyed such immunity from criticism as those of Redemption. Public curiosity regarding corruption and graft in government had been jaded by the campaign of exposure against the Carpetbaggers. The Redeemers bore the banner of reform and were usually protected by Confederate war records, while the exclusiveness of ring politics spared officeholders the ordeal of defending their records and re-elected them term after term. Press criticism was rarely searching, and the absence of any effective party of opposition was an additional invitation to laxity.

[48] Houston *Daily Telegraph,* quoted in S. D. Myers, Jr., "Mysticism, Realism, and the Texas Constitution of 1876," in *Southwestern Political and Social Science Quarterly* (Austin), IX (1928–1929), 180.

Robert McKee of Alabama possessed an unusual insight into Southern affairs of his day. Secretary and mentor to two governors, and himself an influential editor, he watched events from the inside, brooded over their evils, and exchanged musings with his friend Senator John T. Morgan. By 1882 McKee was apprehensive. On the whole he believed his party's administration had been "honest and economical," had "reduced taxes and secured the public debt." Yet he hardly dared look below the surface. The whole administration, he said, writing from the governor's office, had been "conducted without order, system, plan, design, or purpose; without method, or checks, or safeguards other than the personal integrity of the several heads of departments and the clerks themselves. It is amazing there has been no dishonesty with so many opportunities for it. Looseness invites corruption. At any moment a scandal might overthrow the party." [49] Within a year McKee saw his prophecy materialize at very close quarters.

The first mutterings of a reawakened public conscience came in 1879 in Georgia, where an exceptionally strong independent party dared challenge the Bourgeois Triumvirate of Redeemers. A series of investigations of Governor Colquitt's administration resulted in the impeachment and resignation of the state treasurer, the impeachment and conviction of the comptroller general on eight counts, the resignation of the commissioner of agriculture, and the disclosure of disgraceful scandals in the convict-lease system involving highly placed Redeemers.[50] Ben Hill thundered against "official rogues" who "threaten our popular institutions with ignominious shame, rottenness and ruin." The following year, however, Governor Colquitt was re-elected in a campaign of "vindication," with the assistance of Gordon, Brown—and Ben Hill. The state treasurer, upon restoring misappropriated funds, was allowed to escape punishment.

A few years earlier, in 1873, the Conservative state treasurer of Virginia had been indicted for defalcation and embezzlement, but had escaped trial upon the plea of insanity. In 1877, however, large additional embezzlements came to light in the form of can-

[49] McKee to John T. Morgan, January 8, 1882, letter-book copy, in McKee Papers.

[50] Georgia *House Journal,* 1879, Pt. II, 1522–24; Georgia *Senate Journal,* 1879, pp. 685, 688, 703, 717–18; Georgia *Acts and Resolutions,* 1878–1879, pp. 431–32.

celed bonds illegally refunded and added to Virginia's staggering debt.[51] These revelations did not strengthen the Funders' case for sacrificing the public schools to the rights of the bondholders in the name of Virginia's unspotted honor.

After the various independent movements were crushed all over the South in the early eighties, there remained little danger of exposure for official miscreants except their own blundering.

Marshall T. Polk, Democratic state treasurer of Tennessee since 1877, had all that family name and social position could provide in prestige. Nephew and adopted son of former President James K. Polk, relative of Bishop (later General) Leonidas Polk, he had served on the latter's staff in the Confederate army. Great was the astonishment of the state when in January, 1883, Polk's disappearance and his defalcation to the amount of more than $400,000 was suddenly revealed. His bond was only $100,000. The office had not been investigated in years. A joint committee of the legislature reported after investigation that Polk had for years used state funds for large-scale private investments in Louisville and Nashville railroad stock, Alabama iron mines, Mexican silver mines, and Tennessee state bonds. Of special interest were the speculations in state bonds, since Polk was known as a leader of the "State Credit" faction of his party, which contended in the name of Tennessee's honor against any readjustment of the state debt. "There are readjusters and readjusters," remarked one observer. Polk was convicted of embezzlement, sentenced to twenty years imprisonment, and fined $366,540.10, the amount of the remaining deficit in the treasury.[52]

Three weeks after the Tennessee scandal came the news that Isaac H. Vincent, state treasurer of Alabama, had disappeared. His default amounted to $232,980.79. The law requiring the treasurer to file a bond of $250,000 had not been observed when Vincent's new term began in November. Like Polk, Vincent was a popular Confederate veteran. He had been private secretary to Houston, Redemption governor, from 1874 to 1878, was elected treasurer in

[51] New York *Tribune*, December 7, 1877.

[52] Nashville *Daily American*, January 19, July 14, 26, 27, 1883; Knoxville *Daily Chronicle*, January 6, 7, 9, 12, 14, February 27, March 1, 3, July 29, 1883; *Nation*, XXXVI (1883), 23, 29.

1878 and re-elected in 1880 and 1882. Speculation in cotton futures with public funds had been his undoing. Vincent escaped to Mexico and remained at large for four and a half years, during which state authorities were much criticized for neglecting the case "because of knowledge Vincent might have involving the good names of others." Eventually captured, he was tried and received a sentence of fifteen years.[53]

Less than a month after Vincent became a fugitive, an investigating committee of the Arkansas legislature reported its findings of a shortage of $294,876 in the accounts of the late treasurer, who was subsequently the governor, Thomas J. Churchill. Churchill was elected treasurer upon the Redemption of Arkansas in 1874, and served three terms in that office before his election as governor in 1880. The amount of default was fixed at $80,522 by the state supreme court. The defendant's plea that irregularities were due to faulty bookkeeping was generally accepted with the feeling that Churchill was exonerated. No proper investigation of the treasurer's books had been made since Carpetbag days.[54] Churchill was succeeded as treasurer in 1880 by Major William E. Woodruff, who occupied the office for ten years, at the end of which an investigation revealed a shortage of $138,789, and a sordid record of irregularities and incredible laxity from the beginning. The affair was pronounced by a Democratic paper "the worst thing of its kind that has happened in all the history of the State"—including Reconstruction.[55]

In the meanwhile, one state after another was treated to the same painful spectacle. Kentucky and Mississippi present no variation except in the length of terms of office served by their defaulting treasurers: twenty years in the one and fourteen in the other—in both cases, ever since Redemption. Treasurer James W. Tate of

[53] Governor Cobb to McKee, February 1, 1883; McKee to Governor E. A. O'Neal, February 17, 1883; Governor Thomas Seay to McKee, April 21, 1887, in McKee Papers; Huntsville *Gazette,* February 10, November 17, 1883; Birmingham *Iron Age,* March 17, 1887.

[54] Little Rock *Arkansas Gazette,* March 17, 20, 21, 1881; February 28, 1883; David Y. Thomas (ed.), *Arkansas and Its People, A History, 1541–1930* (New York, 1930), I, 182–85.

[55] Little Rock *Arkansas Gazette,* February 20, June 27, October 1, 1891; Thomas (ed.), *Arkansas and Its People,* I, 233–34.

Kentucky, affectionately known as "Uncle Dick," was said to have been "a man reverenced by the people." His popularity is attested by his election to the office ten consecutive times. Tate absconded in 1888, leaving a shortage of $229,009, and disappeared.[56] Treasurer William L. Hemingway of Mississippi, whose shortage was $315,612, remained to face trial for embezzlement and receive a sentence of five years.[57] One earlier scandal in Mississippi involved a Democratic treasurer shortly before the Radical Republican took control. Another Democratic treasurer was exposed as an embezzler in 1902. There were no treasury scandals and no dishonesty among any other officials of importance in Mississippi during Reconstruction.

Louisiana could usually be depended upon to bring a certain Latin exuberance to her part in such drama, but an Irish flavor lent zest to her performance in this case. The scene broadens to include Central America and London.

The pivotal figure in the Redemption of Louisiana and the regime it inaugurated was Major E. A. Burke. Burke's origins were veiled in much obscurity. His statement on oath that he was born in Kentucky has been questioned by several sources. He appeared first as an employee of the Erie Railroad in Pennsylvania, and in 1856 as a local agent of the Ohio and Mississippi in Xenia, Ohio. His field of operations shifted abruptly to Texas, where during the war he acquired the title of major. After the war his name was connected with a whisky revenue scandal in Galveston. Burke appeared first in New Orleans as a day laborer in a stonecutter's yard in 1870, the heyday of Carpetbag activities. Two years later he was an important official in the old Jackson Railroad and chairman of the Democratic campaign committee. His part in the White League revolt in New Orleans in 1874 consisted in sidetracking and delaying a train bearing Federal troops on his company's road.[58] Major

[56] Louisville *Courier-Journal,* March 21, 23, 26, April 24, 1888.

[57] Jackson *Clarion-Ledger,* February 27, March 20, July 3, December 4, 1890; John R. Lynch, *The Facts of Reconstruction* (New York, 1913), 165–68. The writer is indebted to Vernon L. Wharton for calling his attention to this and three other cases of state-treasurer scandals.

[58] W. M. Aikman, New Orleans, to William E. Chandler, January 30, 1878; J. R. G. Pitkin to Chandler, January 30, 1878; R. K. Smith, Austin, Texas, to [?] Moore, March 5, 1877, in William E. Chandler Papers (Division of Manuscripts, Library of

Burke's endeavors in Redemption next broadened to a national scope. His maneuvers in Washington during the electoral crisis of 1877, resulting in the so-called "Wormley House Bargain," have already been reviewed.[59] Whether he was playing for Presidential stakes amid rumors of civil war or smaller stakes in his numerous business speculations, the Major was always the same cool-headed and daring gambler.[60]

Returning to Louisiana with the laurels of Redeemer extraordinary, Burke was elected state treasurer, an office he held for ten years. The constitutional convention, under strong Lottery influence, made a clean sweep of state officials in 1879 but made special exception of Treasurer Burke. The day the constitutional convention convened, the New Orleans *Democrat,* bitterest enemy of the Lottery, passed into the control of Major Burke and Charles Howard, Lottery owner. In 1881 the New Orleans *Times* was acquired and the two papers were consolidated under Burke's ownership and editorship, giving him direction of his party's most powerful organ.[61] As became a Southern editor of his responsibilities, the Major fought his duel with a rival editor (pistols at twenty paces) and sustained honorific wounds. His popularity soared. At the great World Exposition at New Orleans in 1884, of which he was director general, he was toasted as "The Man of Iron." The next year he was mentioned in the press as an ideal choice for Grover Cleveland's cabinet, in fact "one of the foremost men in all the South." [62]

It was at the New Orleans Exposition that the Major met Louis Bogran, President of Honduras. In some way the visiting President became indebted to Burke for "enormous sums," and in turn

Congress); W. O. Hart, "The New Orleans Times and the New Orleans Democrat," in *Louisiana Historical Quarterly* (New Orleans), VIII (1925), 579–80; *South Illustrated* (New Orleans), II (November, 1887), 1; New Orleans *Daily Picayune,* November 24, 1889.

[59] See above, p. 44.

[60] For Burke's comments on his methods at Wormley House, see *House Miscellaneous Documents,* 45 Cong., 3 Sess., No. 31, Pt. I, 990, 1015.

[61] Hart, "New Orleans Times and the New Orleans Democrat," *loc. cit.,* 579–80; Alwes, "History of the Louisiana State Lottery Company," 62–63.

[62] Louisville *Courier-Journal,* January 3, 1885. See also, Herbert S. Fairall, *The World's Industrial and Cotton Centennial Exposition, New Orleans, 1884–85* (Iowa City, 1885), 153–54.

granted the Major territorial concessions that were said to have made him "the dictator, practically, of the mining as well as the fruit shipping interests of Honduras." [63] In January, 1889, Burke sailed for London to organize international syndicates to exploit his concessions. While he was so engaged, his successor in the state treasurer's office in Louisiana began to discover that great quantities of state bonds ordered destroyed had not been destroyed, that the coupons had been regularly paid, and that the bonds themselves were in the market. Grand jury investigation revealed that Burke had begun a systematic course of bond frauds in 1880, the second year of his office as treasurer, and that the state had been robbed altogether of $1,777,000, exclusive of interest. This amount was reduced to $793,600 by the deduction of bonds found in Burke's private bank box. *In absentia,* the Major was indicted for embezzlement and forgery. From London he promised an early return to face his accusers, but the return was continually postponed. Extradition procedure missed fire, and the Major transferred his field of operations back to the banana belt—farther south this time. In the face of talk of extradition he had floated his companies in London with a capital of £750,000. An interviewer the following year found Major Burke established at the remote capital city Tegucigalpa, and judged him "virtually the controlling force in Honduras," with "the government at his beck and call." "Whatever he is in the States," said the reporter, "he is here a bigger man than President Bogran." Thrilled with the potentialities of his new domain, the Major exclaimed that it was "as primitive as in the days of Cortez," its population "utterly ignorant of any trade or practical knowledge." From this backward condition he promised the republic a glorious "redemption." [64] The process of redemption was in progress for many years in Honduras, while its redeemer remained a fugitive from Louisiana courts.

The sums involved in these numerous embezzlements seem relatively small, yet their significance is better weighed in relation to the Redemption policy of retrenchment in the South. The total

[63] New York *Herald,* quoted in New Orleans *Daily Picayune,* November 12, 1889.

[64] New Orleans *Daily Picayune,* September 27, October 19, November 12, 24, 1889; New Orleans *Times-Democrat,* February 10, 1890.

expenditures of the state government of Mississippi during the first year of Redemption amounted to only $547,000, and were reduced in succeeding years. Explaining a reduction in the pitiful public-education fund of Alabama in 1883, Robert McKee, secretary to Governor E. A. O'Neal, wrote: "The embezzlements of the late treasurer have swept away nearly every dollar of the surplus funds of the state, the accumulations of eight years of almost niggardly economy in public expenditures." [65] The same month that the treasurer of Alabama absconded, the state superintendent of education reported defalcations among county superintendents of education over a period of three years amounting to over $40,000.[66]

The simple reflection that personal honesty came at a discount among Redemption circles does not suffice as an explanation. Several of the individuals involved seem to have been victims of circumstances beyond their control. "For let us confess it," wrote Watterson, when the Kentucky treasurer absconded after twenty years in office; "all of us are more or less to blame for this wretched business." He went on to point out that the treasurer's salary was only $2,400, or $2,000 less than the current rate charged by security companies for giving the bond required of the office. "This is no exceptional case," he added. "There is scarcely a salaried officer in this State adequately paid." [67]

To supplement Watterson's explanation, it is well to consider that many of the evils of Reconstruction, ordinarily held peculiar to Carpetbag government or to racial factors, were rather the result of economic and social conditions that continued long after Redemption. This is not to suggest that the evils of Redemption were so gross as those of Reconstruction. Nor is it suggested that this situation was peculiar to the South. Public morals were low generally. It is suggested, however, that some revision is due in the commonly accepted view, which was expressed by one historian as follows: "The incredible waste and robbery of the Reconstruction Era was followed as soon as that era ended by the most careful methods in the handling of the public funds. Nowhere has there been so little peculation and defalcation on the part of officials in charge of

[65] McKee to Captain W. P. Armstrong, May 24, 1883, in McKee Papers.

[66] Huntsville *Gazette,* February 17, 1883.

[67] Louisville *Courier-Journal,* March 23, 26, 1888.

the public treasuries."[68] Another declares that "No governments in American history have been conducted with more economy and more fidelity than the governments of the Southern States during the first years after the Reconstruction period."[69]

George W. Cable, the Louisiana writer who became an exile in Massachusetts, ventured an appraisal of Redemption in 1890. Suspect as an agitator, Cable nevertheless gave the Redeemers credit for "honest intentions" at the outset of their experiment. He knew better than "to mourn the extinction of the Reconstruction governments as one mourns the death of the righteous." For all their stress on "equal free government" the Radical administrations had lost "the nation's respect and good-will by an acute moral and financial defalcation." The Conservatives, using a one-party system and making small pretense of equality and freedom, then took control with the promise of "pure government first, free government afterward." This had proved a "twin fallacy," for "the governments that started out twelve years ago full of honest intentions to be or become pure, have grown confessedly corrupt." The experiment proved it a "delusion," thought Cable, "that a policy of pure government first, free government afterward, could produce either free or pure government."[70]

[68] Philip A. Bruce, *The Rise of the New South* (Philadelphia, 1905), 439–40.

[69] Holland Thompson, *The New South* (New Haven, 1921), 25.

[70] George W. Cable, *The Southern Struggle for Pure Government. An Address* (Boston, 1890), 10, 15–19; also printed in his *The Negro Question* (New York, 1898), 134–37, 146.

CHAPTER IV

PROCRUSTEAN BEDFELLOWS

THE expression "Solid South," like its companion and contemporary expression, "Bourbon," [1] is of questionable value to the historian. The solidarity of the region has long been exaggerated. Thus one New Yorker wrote in 1879: "Find what a Virginian or a Georgian is thinking on any question of National politics and you need not ask what a Louisianan or a Texan is thinking . . . . the mountaineer on the Blue Ridge and the 'Tarheel' of the Carolina turpentine forests will be of one mind with the sugar-planter on the Mississippi and the herdsman on the Texas plains." [2]

The classic lines of cleavage in Southern society were not erased magically by Reconstruction. The very geographical distinctions mentioned above were constants in the history of the region. Against the Appalachian peninsula that pushed deep into the heart of the South the waves of Lower-South opinion continued to beat with small effect, while the levees of the Delta region withstood free-trade doctrine at flood tide. The Black Belt, the very backbone formation of regional coherence, seemed to withstand every seismic disturbance that shook the land.

No love was lost between Black-Belt gentry and hillbilly commoners—then or now. The persistence of this particular feud is illustrated nowhere better than in the memoirs of a modern Delta

[1] It is time this expression was abandoned as a source of confusion. An anonymous writer in the eighties observed accurately that "In the Southern States the term Bourbon has no distinct significance. It is applied indiscriminately by all classes of politicians to anybody who differs from them. It is there a convenient though empty epithet or name of reproach." "Studies in the South, II," in *Atlantic Monthly* (Boston), XLIX (1882), 191.

[2] New York *Tribune*, March 8, 1879.

planter and poet, the legitimate heir to his attitudes. Into his otherwise urbane and genial pages there is obtruded this reference to his neighbors of the hill country: "the present breed is probably the most unprepossessing on the broad face of the ill-populated earth. . . . I can forgive them as the Lord God forgives, but admire them, trust them, love them—never. Intellectually and spiritually they are inferior to the Negro, whom they hate." [3] Men of the hill country, the "white" counties, answered in kind—then as now. In 1877, the year of Redemption, there came notice from the uplands of South Carolina, served by Martin Gary of Edgefield County, to "those elegant, smooth mannered, oily tongued bondholders, bond speculators, banks and members of financial boards," and all the lowland minions of "the Duke of Charleston" and "the Earl of Columbia" that the upcountry would bolt the party before it would permit the lowlands to monopolize the benefits of Redemption. Colonel E. B. C. Cash, who took up the Independent banner after General Gary's death, accused Wade Hampton of leading *"the thieves, tyrants and cowardly murderers* who are crushing out the life and liberty of our state." [4]

So intense were the repressed feuds between white factions that the disaffected partners could scarcely wait until Redemption was achieved to air their grievances and fall upon the leaders of the dominant element of Redeemers. Disaffection had been unnaturally bottled up for a generation—first by the threat of war, then by invasion, and finally by Reconstruction. The Redeemers' plan to prolong repression by threat of Negro domination and constrain all warring factions within their Procrustean one-party system met with trouble from the start. Independent movements renouncing allegiance to the Democratic party broke out in nearly all Southern states almost as soon as they were redeemed. Boasts of white solidarity that impressed outsiders were often loudest in the presence of division.[5]

[3] William A. Percy, *Lanterns on the Levee; Recollections of a Planter's Son* (New York, 1941), 20. The writer was well aware that no more insulting comparison was possible in his region. For an articulate spokesman of the hillbilly, see Herman C. Nixon, *Possum-Trot; Rural Community, South* (Norman, 1941), *passim.*

[4] Martin Gary, quoted in Wallace, *History of South Carolina,* III, 326–27; E. B. C. Cash, quoted in Charleston *News and Courier,* October 25, 1882.

[5] The state convention of the Democratic-Conservative party of Alabama resolved

The first state to be relieved of Radical Republican rule was Tennessee. There in 1872 former President Andrew Johnson led a movement from within the Democratic party against the "military ring." Nominated for Congressman at large by a "workingmen's mass meeting" after the Democratic convention had rejected him, Johnson lost his race, but wrested from the Conservative machine the control of the state legislature. Under Johnson's guidance that body repealed the poll-tax qualification for voting, reapportioned representation, passed an act providing for a state system of public schools, and in 1875 elected Johnson himself to the Senate.[6]

Andrew Johnson might be taken as the prototype of the Independent—the hillman of the white counties, traditional enemy of the lowland planter gentry, the man who could make his peace neither with the Republicans nor with the Democratic-Conservative party, who resented the uses both parties made of the Negro vote, and who was repelled by the social and economic doctrines of both camps. There was really no permanent political place of abode for these latter-day Jacksonians who lived on into a totally Whiggish world. Yet their restless and unhappy quest for some refuge continued to disturb the political equilibrium of the South for another generation.

The earliest manifestations of independence were usually local revolts against county rings in the interest of candidates for the legislature or county offices. The Macon *Telegraph* of the Black Belt complained as early as 1874 of "a rank crop of 'independent' candidates, so-called, for the legislature, growing on Georgia soil just now!"[7] The widespread appearance of such candidates was commented upon in 1877, but with the observation that they had "no general principle in common except the spirit of revolt against the dictates of the solid Democracy." At the same time it was ad-

in 1876 that the "white people, whether residing in the mountains and valleys of North Alabama, or in the prairies of Middle Alabama, or among the pine-hills of South Alabama, and whether rich or poor, learned or unlearned, is one great family." But the delegates were well aware that the fires of revolt were raging in the hill country at that moment. *Appletons' Annual Cyclopaedia . . . 1876* (New York, 1877), 18.

[6] Hamer (ed.), *Tennessee; A History*, II, 678–80.

[7] Quoted in Glenn W. Rainey, "The Negro and the Independent Movement in Georgia" (manuscript in possession of its author), Chap. IV.

mitted by Conservative leaders who "recognized the inevitable" that in all probability these local factions would "in a year or two coalesce into formidable opposition parties in many of the States." [8]

The tendency of local independents to coalesce was marked from the first. In 1874 northern-Georgia independents of a mountain district united to elect the parson-doctor-farmer William H. Felton to Congress over the powerful opposition of Joseph E. Brown. Four years later another hill district of Georgia returned the young independent Emory L. Speer to Congress. William M. Lowe, described as "one of the most picturesque figures ever to participate in Alabama politics," and "a man of commanding personality" was elected to Congress in 1878 from an Alabama district in the far-northern part of the state. Lowe ran, he wrote privately, "as an independent Greenbacker on financial matters, and as an administration [Hayes] man on sentimental politics"—a curious but not unique distinction.[9] The same year G. "Wash" Jones, running upon a Greenback-Labor ticket, was successful in his race for Congress in Texas. By this time the whole state of Virginia was under third-party control, and the alarm was sounded throughout the Democratic-Conservative South that a concerted drive to break white solidarity was under way.

Faced with a common danger, Redeemers of various states collaborated across state borders as they had recently combined against the Carpetbaggers. "We want you to come to Ga.," wrote Senator Gordon to Senator Lamar, "& help us kill Independentism, which is . . . threatening us with the loss of our state." [10] Hampton was also having his troubles in South Carolina; Colonel Colyar, in Tennessee; and Garland, in Arkansas.

Before carrying the account of the Independent revolt into its more advanced stages, it would be well to examine the issues over which the Independents deserted the party of Redemption. These issues were as deep lying as any over which American parties have ever clashed—more basic, in fact, than the issues that supposedly

[8] New York *Tribune*, October 27, 1877; Edward Mayes, *Lucius Q. C. Lamar, His Life, Times, and Speeches, 1825–1893* (Nashville, 1896), 319.

[9] William M. Lowe to Colonel R. M. Reynolds, November 22, 1878, in Hayes Papers; also in John P. Dyer, *"Fightin' Joe" Wheeler* (University, La., 1941), 251–55.

[10] Gordon to Lamar, October 7, 1878, in Lamar-Mayes Papers.

divided the national Democratic and Republican parties in that age.

The first of these clashes came over the one issue upon which it is generally assumed that all white men were of one mind—the Negro. Once Redemption was accomplished, the white rulers of the Black Belt found themselves in somewhat the position their predecessors, the Carpetbaggers, had enjoyed. They became heirs to the control of the more-or-less submissive or intimidated Negro voters, plus whatever constitutional devices had been erected (and were not forthwith destroyed) for the control of the white counties. In effect, the ante-bellum planter's prerogative of casting three fifths of a ballot for every slave, so much resented by the ante-bellum uplander, had been amplified to something approaching a five-fifths prerogative in some sectors of the Black Belt. Jealousy on the part of the uplanders was not diminished by this amplification of lowlander power. The apportionment of representation in the Democratic-Conservative party conventions of Alabama was determined by the vote cast for the party's candidate for governor in the previous election. Thus Dallas County in the Black Belt, with a population of only 9,285 whites but 45,372 Negroes, was apportioned thirty delegates to the convention of 1890, while Cherokee, with 18,080 whites and only 3,618 blacks, was granted a mere ten seats. This was due, of course, to the heavy polling of black votes for the white-supremacy party in Dallas.[11]

An implicit part of the Black-Belt policy toward the Negro as voter was the planter-patrician's paternalism. Hampton proudly boasted in the year of Redemption that he was "the first man in America—certainly the first in the South—who advocated the granting of the right to vote to the colored man. That is on record." [12] Addressing Negro voters in a campaign against the white Independents, Hampton said: "The best friends of the colored men are the old slaveholders. . . . They will defend your right to vote because it gives to the South infinitely more power than we ever had before." [13] The purpose of Hampton's party, declared the

[11] John B. Clark, *Populism in Alabama* (Auburn, 1927), 101–102.

[12] Quoted in New York *Tribune*, April 21, 1877.

[13] Charleston *News and Courier*, September 20, 1878.

Charleston *News and Courier,* would be "so to legislate, and so to administer public affairs, as to win over tens of thousands of colored voters." And the same paper proudly described "a long line of black faces peering out of red shirts" at the polls led by "two sturdy dusky sons of the soil [who] bore a banner . . . inscribed 'Waccomaw Democrats.' "[14]

General Martin Gary of upland Edgefield County found the spectacle of Negroes parading in the red shirt of white-supremacy night riders too confusing for his taste. "It was the Straightout [white-supremacy] aggressive policy which saved the State [in 1876] in spite of Grant's bayonets, as every one knows, not 17,000 Negro votes, as Hampton says," declared Gary. Yet once Redemption was effected, the upland plebeians found they had redeemed the state from the Carpetbaggers only to lose it to the lowland bosses. Hampton's coddling of Northern prejudices, his traipsing about with President Hayes "to reconcile the South to the greatest electoral fraud ever perpetrated," and his truckling to the Negro vote and Carpetbag judges of the state supreme court were more than Gary could stomach. Gary would "sooner have [his] . . . right arm cut off" than support the lowland policy of "fusion" with Negroes. While Hampton deplored "any resort to violence or wrong, or any adoption of the 'shot-gun policy,' " the forthright Gary called for a return to the "Mississippi plan."[15]

While not so important in some states as in others, this cleavage over racial politics cannot be overlooked in any state. In Georgia Benjamin H. Hill gladly marched "arm in arm" to the polls with a Negro, "glad to be voted by a colored Democrat."[16] Thomas M. Norwood, Independent candidate for governor of Georgia in 1880, charged that the machine had stolen the election from the Independents with Negro ballots. When the North Carolina General Assembly elected several "colored magistrates in and for certain counties," nine white Democratic members signed a protest against their election as "inconsistent with the principles and purposes of the party" as proclaimed "by its thousands of speakers" in the campaign of Redemption. Most notably flouted was the dogma that

[14] *Ibid.,* April 28, 1877; October 9, 1878.

[15] *Ibid.,* May 4, 1877; September 20, 1878; February 3, 1880.

[16] Jackson *Weekly Clarion,* November 22, 1876.

Negroes "were absolutely unfit for these public positions." "If Democrats do what they have persistently abused and condemned Republicans for doing," read the protest, "how can they hope to escape just censure?"[17] Likewise, disaffected white Democrats of Mississippi were infuriated by the "fusion" policy of Senators Lamar and George, by which Negroes were regularly given minor offices and smaller white politicians were deprived of them.

Closely related to the issue of racial politics was that of machine politics. Outcry against "king-caucus" and "ring-rule" was heard in all of the Southern states in this period. By 1876 Conservative leaders of Alabama were already warning the lowland bosses that "the people are tired and heartily sick of the caucus rule. They long for an opportunity to throw off the galling yoke."[18] The leaders of the strong Independent party in Georgia were to find their most popular issue in the widespread resentment against the dictatorial methods of the machine.[19]

Corruption of the ballot box and the forthright stealing of elections were also grievances of the Independents. Since the same tactics of fraud and violence were employed against the Independents that had been and continued to be used against the Republicans, the two minority parties, though usually standing at opposite poles on economic issues, were drawn into co-operation against a common foe by this common grievance. "I am a hard-money, national-bank man," wrote the chairman of the Republican Committee for the Eighth Congressional District of Alabama. "Why, then, did I and the mass of Republicans here support the Greenback-Labor candidate? Let me frankly tell you. There are questions of more vital importance in Southern politics than banking and currency. . . . They are issues such as fair elections, an honest count, free thought, free speech, free government itself. . . . The Republicans felt bound . . . to stand by the Greenbackers upon this issue. We had a common grievance, and we made a common cause against it."[20] The odd practice of endorsing a ticket and repudiating the platform on which the ticket ran was

17 North Carolina *House Journal*, 1876–1877, pp. 872–74.

18 H. R. Hood to McKee, July 29, 1876, in McKee Papers.

19 For evidence of the same feeling in other states, see William H. Skaggs, *The Southern Oligarchy* . . . (New York, 1924), 18, 64, 104.

20 A. W. McCullough to the editor, in *Harper's Weekly*, XXV (1881), 302–303.

a common phenomenon of Procrustean politics the South over.

Although nearly all the sharply defined economic issues that divided the militant Populists from the Democratic-Conservatives in the nineties were powerful causes of disaffection in the seventies and eighties, the Independents never developed the keen, interest-conscious realism that served the Populists as an agrarian critique of the New-South capitalism.

For one thing, the Independents lacked the background of economic and political education that the Farmers' Alliance of the eighties provided for the Populists. Although the Granger movement in the South has been examined for evidence of its influence upon the Independent and Greenback movements (with the analogy of the Farmers' Alliance in mind), the results have been surprisingly negative. Several possible explanations suggest themselves. For one, the Grange, entering the South about 1873, had reached its peak and even started its decline in some states before Redemption had been accomplished—and therefore before Independent revolt could be seriously contemplated. In Mississippi the decline of the Grange was evident by 1875; in Alabama, shortly after 1875; in Kentucky, by 1877; in South Carolina, before 1877; and in Texas, after 1878.[21] Again, the prominent "Masters" of the state granges in the South, men like Putnam Darden of Mississippi, later National Master of the Grange, or William W. Lang of Texas, while at odds with their party over many important issues, could always be depended upon to "go down the line" at election time. When the Mississippi Grangers failed in their effort to seize control of the white man's party by nominating Darden for governor, they solidly, if sullenly, voted for Governor Lowry, a man they knew to be thoroughly identified with the forces they feared. Nor were they attracted by the Greenbackers. "Some Grange counties gave fairly strong support to the Greenback candidates, but it was no stronger than the support of normal counties. Not a single strong Grange county gave [Greenbacker Benjamin] King a majority." [22]

[21] Ferguson, "Granger Movement in Mississippi," 59–64; Prichard, "Popular Political Movements in Kentucky," 41–42; statement of D. Wyatt Aiken, master of state grange, in Charleston *News and Courier,* March 2, 1877; Roscoe C. Martin, "The Grange as a Political Factor in Texas," in *Southwestern Political and Social Science Quarterly,* VI (1925–1926), 367–68.

[22] Ferguson, "Granger Movement in Mississippi," 134, 137, 139.

In Kentucky, "the Granges were practically all located in the Democratic sections of the State, and, as one observer stated 'they were Democrats first and Grangers afterward.'" This is not to say they had no political influence. From within the party the Grangers were able to elect one of their number speaker of the Kentucky house of representatives in 1876, and to defeat for the United States Senate the candidate said to be allied with the Louisville and Nashville Railroad.[23] Outside the old party, Granger ideas and demands were frequently on the tongue of Independent party leaders in various states and appeared in third-party platforms. For all this, it would appear that the Southern Grangers were too conservative, or too timid, to play the role for the Independents that the Alliance later played for the Populists.

The early phases of the national Greenback movement, from 1872 to 1877, coming as they did before Redemption was fully achieved, left the South pretty much unscathed. Then in 1878 the Democratic strategy of out-Greenbacking the Greenbackers proved fairly effective in forestalling revolt.[24] As the leading Democratic paper of Mississippi framed the appeal: "There is no reason for any . . . member of the Democratic Conservative party to abandon it and join the new fangled combination calling itself National or Greenback party, if his real motive is set forth in the platform of the latter—viz., to reform the financial policy." [25] A short while later, however, Senator Lamar was expostulating excitedly to his constituents on the "boundless, bottomless, and brainless schemes" of the Greenbackers, whose doctrines threatened "the direst calamities." [26] The situation changed with the dominance of the "right-fork" conservatives after 1878 and the writing of the "honest-money" and "public-faith" platform of the National Democratic party for the presidential year 1880. The strategy of guile was frankly abandoned, for the new platform was a slap in the face of the soft-money faction. The road south now lay open to missionaries of the Western Greenbackers, who had reorganized under the name National Greenback-Labor party.

Even in 1878 there were some defections. The election to Con-

23 Prichard, "Popular Political Movements in Kentucky," 41–42.

24 See above, pp. 47–48.

25 Jackson *Weekly Clarion,* April 23, 1879.

26 Mayes, *Lucius Q. C. Lamar,* 353, 410.

gress of the Independent William M. Lowe, a former Democrat "of means and influence," by the strong support of northern-Alabama Greenbackers was one case. The Texas Greenback-Labor party, claiming 482 Greenback clubs throughout the state, nominated General W. H. Hammond for governor and gave him 55,000 votes, or about one third the ballots polled by the Democrats. The Texas Greenbackers elected ten state legislators and one Congressman.[27] Organization was progressing in other states in 1878, and in Kentucky the Greenbackers gave the Democrats a scare in 1879.

It was not until the election of 1880, however, that the new party made any strong showing in the South. Contests of a more-or-less serious character were made in six states. In Alabama the Greenback-Labor party nominated a full state ticket calling itself the "People's Anti-Bourbon" party and wrote a platform that endorsed the candidates and reaffirmed the Chicago platform of the national Greenback-Labor party, denounced the new Democratic-Conservative party for its favoritism to railroads, banks, insurance companies, and other corporate interests, its inhumane convict labor system, its inefficient and unfair common-school system, and for its "ring-rule." The party's candidate for governor, the Reverend James M. Pickins, from the northern county of Lawrence, received 42,343 votes. The Republican party put forth no regular ticket and gave nominal support to the "Anti-Bourbon" nominees; but the contemporary explanation, that the insurgents owed their chief successes to the Negro vote, was belied by the election returns, which revealed that the party of white supremacy got almost twice the vote from Negroes of the Black Belt in 1880 that the Redeemer governor, Houston, commanded there in 1874. In 1880 the Democrats came into complete control of the Black Belt. Congressman Lowe was defeated by the Democratic-Conservative candidate, "Fightin' Joe" Wheeler, a prominent spokesman and director of the Memphis and Charleston Railroad. The Greenback strength was broken in Alabama by this election, but warning of the deep cleavage between white men that was to come in the Populist nineties had been served.[28]

[27] Roscoe C. Martin, "The Greenback Party in Texas," in *Southwestern Historical Quarterly* (Austin), XXX (1926–1927), 161–77.

[28] Clark, *Populism in Alabama*, 25–27; Montgomery *Advertiser*, July 2, 3, Septem-

Rufus K. Garland of Arkansas, brother of that state's Redeemer governor, was disillusioned by the reaction after 1878. He charged that "the Democrats had undermined the Greenback movement temporarily by promises which had not been fulfilled." W. P. ("Buck") Parks, Greenback nominee for governor, was said to have been, like Garland, "a sincere and capable man." Together they campaigned "with dead earnestness and stirred the emotions of the farmers and small businessmen." Parks received 31,284 votes to 84,088 cast for Churchill, the Democratic winner.[29] The Greenback-Laborites also made contests in Kentucky, Mississippi, and North Carolina in 1880, with insignificant results. After the strong showing of 1878, the Texas Greenbackers weakened in 1880, when they rejected a fusion with Republicans. In the next election, however, Greenbacker Congressman Wash Jones, running as an Independent, received "the largest popular vote ever polled by a losing candidate [for governor] in a Texas state election up to that time," a total of 102,500 votes against his opponent's 150,900 votes.[30]

The fact that these Greenback ballots were cast in the year of a presidential election, a particularly hard year for insurgents in the South, and that this was the first such election since Redemption, is not without significance. It should also be noted that several strong insurgent movements were under way contemporaneously in other Southern states, though not taking the Greenback label.

The economic issues that divided Southern whites in this period were predominantly local. Struggles over taxation, interest rates, and the lien law, over the disgraceful convict-lease system and the plight of the share cropper, over public schools, fence laws, fertilizer inspection, exorbitant grants of land to corporations, and railroad regulation raged on the hustings and in the legislatures of a dozen states. In general they were indexes of the country-versus-town character of the cleavage. The Redeemer governments were regularly aligned against the popular side of the struggle. Hampton and the Charleston Chamber of Commerce, which claimed

ber 14, 1880; *Nation,* XXXI (1880), 103; Dyer, *"Fightin' Joe" Wheeler,* 246; Fleming, *Civil War and Reconstruction in Alabama,* 798.

29 Thomas (ed.), *Arkansas and Its People,* I, 175–77.

30 Martin, "Greenback Party in Texas," *loc. cit.,* 171–77; Galveston *Daily News,* September 17, 1882.

that Charleston contained one third of the taxable property of the state, took up the cudgels against Gary's usury bill. This sought to re-enact a law repealed by Carpetbaggers that limited interest rates, which had climbed to 18 or 20 per cent. Hampton and his faction argued that it was "against the established principles of personal liberty for the State to touch individual rights of person and property, and that money is as much property as land"; but Gary's bill was passed.[31]

None of the numerous local issues, however, was to assume the political importance of Southern state debts and their "readjustment." This issue alone excited sufficient opposition to overthrow temporarily the Democratic-Conservative control of certain states. The complexities of the Southern state-debt question of the seventies and eighties make those of the interallied war debts of the twenties and thirties seem simple by comparison. For included in the Southern computation were not only numerous questions regarding the legality of the Reconstruction bonds but the niceties of distinction between fraudulent and honest issues, between actual debts and potential obligations, between direct and endorsed bonds, between the ante-bellum and post-bellum debts, and between "home-rule" and "Carpetbag" debts.[32]

To disinfect the account from partisanship it should be observed that the process of scaling down the inflated Reconstruction debts began in three states before Redemption was accomplished, and under the auspices of Carpetbag governments.[33] The wholesale readjustment, repudiation, and scaling process in the South, however, began after Redemption. The procedure differed from state to state. Usually, upon the overthrow of the Radicals, all issues of bonds were stopped and a committee was appointed to ascertain the extent of the debt or the "honest debt"—a term of remarkable flexibility, as it turned out. Then by statute, constitutional revision,

31 Charleston *News and Courier,* May 10, 1877; Wallace, *History of South Carolina,* III, 326–27.

32 Competent studies will be found in Benjamin U. Ratchford, *American State Debts* (Durham, 1941), especially pp. 162–245; Reginald C. McGrane, *Foreign Bondholders and American State Debts* (New York, 1935), especially pp. 282–389; William A. Scott, *The Repudiation of State Debts . . .* (New York, 1893), *passim;* and Pearson, *Readjuster Movement in Virginia, passim.*

33 These states were North Carolina, South Carolina, and Louisiana.

court decisions, or a combination of these methods, debts and various kinds of liabilities, potential as well as actual, were repudiated, scaled down, or "adjusted." With notable variations this process was repeated in Alabama, Arkansas, Florida, Georgia, Louisiana, North Carolina, South Carolina, Tennessee, and Virginia. The extent of reduction in "debts" by all methods ranged from an estimated $29,278,000 in North Carolina down to $4,000,000 in Florida. In all but three states estimated reductions ran over $13,000,000.[34] The amount of debt in Texas, while under much dispute, was small. Neither Mississippi nor Kentucky repudiated or scaled down debts in this period.

Professor B.U. Ratchford places the total of all state "debts" in 1874 at $274,578,000 or an increase of $101,232,000 over the total for 1868, at the beginning of the Carpetbag regime. To the latter sum he adds $12,000,000 reduced from the Tennessee debt. He concludes that by the whole process of scaling down and repudiation "the Southern states reduced their total and ultimate liabilities by not less than $150,000,000." Ratchford carefully warns that his figures are "open to question" in several instances, and is never dogmatic about his conclusions. It should be noted, however, that he adopts the same usage of the word "debt" as does Professor Fleming, in placing the Alabama "debt" at over $30,000,000, thus including much that was potential or contingent debt. Estimates and conclusions of other scholars differ widely.[35]

The Southern defense of repudiation was buttressed by arguments from the law and from history. The Reconstruction acts were measured against the Federal Constitution and found wanting. Flagrant instances of bribery in the passage of acts authorizing bonds and of fraud and criminal carelessness in the issue and sale of the bonds were enumerated. Appealing to ethics and justice, the argument maintained that the majority of citizens had not favored the bond issues, and had given ample warning that they would not be honored; that the absurdly low rates at which the bonds were

[34] Ratchford, *American State Debts,* 192. The figure for North Carolina includes accrued interest on scaled debt not paid.

[35] *Ibid.,* 176–96, especially Table 14, p. 183, and Table 15, p. 192. Cf. Scott, *Repudiation of State Debts,* 231; McGrane, *Foreign Bondholders and American State Debts,* Chap. XIV; Thompson, *New South,* 227–33.

sold should have put investors on guard; that the states got little if any benefit from the sale of the bonds, the proceeds of which were largely loot for bands of adventurers. Finally, contended the readjustors, it was impossible for the impoverished and ravaged states to carry the additional burden of Reconstruction debts, and it was only just that holders of the securities last issued should share the inevitable loss.

The New York *Times* was aghast at the "naked rascality" of the Georgia convention that wrote a repudiation clause into that state's constitution in 1877. A Raleigh editor denied that Georgia had "the honor of inventing that particular mode of repudiation," and reminded the *Times* that the Constitution of the United States contained a Fourteenth Amendment that anticipated Georgia in repudiating debts by a decade. "We take no stock in that honor," he continued, "that sees no harm in repudiating an obligation to one of our citizens and does see harm in repudiating one due to a Northern man, who helped to bring all our woes upon us." He made the same reply to the New York *Nation,* which solemnly declared that there was "no principle of public law and morals better settled" than that any government was responsible for the public debt of the government it succeeded in ousting.[36] "Wherever slavery existed," said the New York *Tribune,* "there the moral sense was so blunted and benumbed that the white people as a whole is to this day incapable of that sense of honor which prevails elsewhere." [37]

It was, after all, an old dispute. Farmer John E. Massey, of Albemarle County, who called himself "Father of the Readjuster movement" in Virginia, delighted in quoting the words of an Albemarle planter of another generation, Thomas Jefferson: " 'The earth belongs always to the living generation. . . . neither the representatives of a nation, nor the whole nation itself assembled, can validly engage debts beyond what they may pay in their own time.' " [38] To defend their fraudulently gotten gains the modern aristocracy of "paper and patronage exclaims, national faith! sacred charters! disorganization! and security of property!" observed John Taylor of

[36] Raleigh *Observer,* February 24, March 18, August 17, 1877.
[37] New York *Tribune,* August 30, 1879.
[38] John E. Massey, *Autobiography* (New York, 1909), 64.

Caroline County, with reference to Federalist dogmas.[39] " 'The inviolability of contracts,' 'the ability of the State,' 'our boundless resources,' 'our increasing revenues,' 'the retrenchment in expenses,' etc., etc.,—these are all the old familiar phrases," wrote the editor of the leading Readjuster paper of Virginia in 1881, with reference to the Funders of Richmond, heirs to John Marshall's Federalist doctrines.[40] The Readjusters could have interchanged pamphlets with the Jeffersonians.

The leading authority on the debts, while admitting that Arkansas, Florida, and North Carolina "acted drastically in repudiating all Reconstruction bonds without discrimination," and that "the action of the states which scaled down their pre-Reconstruction debt cannot be justified so easily," believes that "on the whole the repudiations can be defended." For all their repudiations the Southern states in 1890 carried a much larger burden of debt than other sections. The South Atlantic states in that year, for instance, had a per capita debt of $10.12 compared with $1.44 for the North Atlantic states, and this in the most impoverished section of the nation.[41]

Up to this point the debt controversy has been viewed only as an intersectional struggle. As an intrasectional struggle, however, the issue was of great importance. In virtually all the states involved there were factions of the dominant party of greater or lesser significance that opposed repudiation and readjustment. In Alabama, Georgia, Florida, North Carolina, and South Carolina the opposition was not very important, but in Arkansas, Louisiana, Tennessee, and Virginia the "Debt-Payer," or "State-Credit," or "Funder" faction was strong enough in some cases to control state policy and dominate the Readjusters for a time. Always identified with the most conservative wing of the Redeemers, this faction used the slogans "public faith" and "the state's honor" and stressed the importance of debt paying in inducing capital to move South. Some of the leading Funders were bondholders themselves or legal representatives for creditor organizations. Republican capital-

[39] John Taylor, *An Inquiry into the Principles and Policy of the Government of the United States* (Fredericksburg, Va., 1814), 31.

[40] Richmond *Weekly Whig*, September 30, 1881.

[41] Ratchford, *American State Debts*, 193–96.

ists were not the only beneficiaries of the lavish Carpetbag bond issues. Charles Nordhoff, whose testimony is anti-Reconstructionist, observed that "where conspicuous jobbery took place Democrats have, oftener than not, been parties in interest." [42]

"Few questions in the history of the State," writes an Arkansas historian, "ever agitated the public mind like the proposition to repudiate a part of the State debt." [43] In 1881 this issue had "rendered imminent a disruption of the Democratic party." [44] The fight began shortly after Redemption, when a Democratic investigating committee returned a report condemning certain railroad and levee bonds as fraudulent, and stating that "the bonds themselves were distributed among Democratic and Republican politicians in such a manner as would fortify the iniquity against a repudiation by the people." A Republican writer later maintained that "there were some *Democratic* politicians who were as deep in the mud of these transactions as certain Republicans were in the mire. The pot should not call the kettle black." [45] In spite of strong opposition from the Little Rock *Gazette* and the *Arkansas Democrat,* the repudiation faction won its fight by 1884, and the threatened party split was avoided, though not without difficulty.[46]

The country parishes of Louisiana were not content with the moderate scaling of the state debt, to sixty cents on the dollar, devised by the Carpetbaggers before Redemption. They determined to strike a blow at the "bloated bondholders" of New Orleans in the constitutional convention of 1879. "Will the gentlemen from the pine hills of North Louisiana mass together and descend by night upon New Orleans to level it with the dust?" asked the New Orleans *Times.* Conceding that much of the state debt was fraudulent in origin, city businessmen and Funders pointed out candidly that among the lobbyists who had urged those bond issues were Democrats as well as Republicans. "When you look closely into the matter," Donelson Caffery told the constitutional

[42] Charles Nordhoff, *The Cotton States in the Spring and Summer of 1875* (New York, 1876), 89.

[43] Thomas (ed.), *Arkansas and Its People,* I, 170.

[44] *Appletons' Annual Cyclopaedia . . . 1881,* p. 32.

[45] Pamphlet by Albert W. Bishop, *What is the Situation Now? A Review of Political Affairs in the Southern States* (Buffalo, 1894), 31–32.

[46] Little Rock *State Gazette,* March 17, April 16, 19, 22, 1881; March 26, 1882.

convention, "you will find that nearly one-half of the bonds had their origins in Democratic sources." [47] Even so, the hill people did not want to be taxed to pay fraudulent bonds or to finance the river people's levees and railroads. The *Times* was pleased that the election resulted in a city delegation "virtually solid for upholding the public faith and rebuking the communistic spirit" of the pine hills. The country-parish returns, however, showed that repudiation sentiment was "strong enough to threaten to split the Democratic party." [48]

While the Louisiana convention was sitting upon the debt question it was "a matter of common remark" in Wall Street "that 'Louisiana was for sale' "—again. The New York *Tribune* reported that "bondholders in this city were asked to subscribe money to a fund for securing from the convention a decision less unfavorable than absolute repudiation," and that it could be secured "only by the payment of sundry thousand dollars." [49] The New Orleans *Times* corroborated the report.[50] London bondholders joined the lobby by cable. Complete repudiation was headed off, but the pine-hill boys could point to the partial repudiation effected as something of a triumph. "Sugar coat it as they may," commented the *Times,* "it is a mere act of repudiation," with enough objectionable features to "damn the entire scheme in the eyes of the financial and commercial world." [51]

Governor John C. Brown of Tennessee, stanch champion of state credit, considered Andrew Johnson "the father of repudiation in Tennessee," since under his influence the legislature suspended payment of interest on the state debt after the Panic of 1873.[52] Had he lived, Johnson might have accepted the title without quarrel, for the ten-year struggle over the debt question was fought along lines of cleavage that he would have found familiar even in ante-bellum days. The "Low-Tax Democrats," whom their ene-

[47] New Orleans *Democrat,* June 13, 1879; New Orleans *Times,* January 13, 1879.

[48] New Orleans *Times,* March 20, 1879; McGinty, *Louisiana Redeemed,* 163.

[49] New York *Tribune,* July 3, 1879.

[50] New Orleans *Times,* July 9, 1879.

[51] *Ibid.,* July 23, 1879; New Orleans *Democrat,* June 13, 1879; *Official Journal of the Proceedings of the Constitutional Convention of the State of Louisiana . . . 1879* (New Orleans, 1879), Appendix, 23–25; Marguerite T. Leach, "The Aftermath of Reconstruction in Louisiana" (M.A. thesis, Louisiana State University, 1933), 57–58.

[52] John C. Brown, quoted in New York *Tribune,* February 16, 1882.

mies called the "repudiationists," charged the State-Credit faction with truckling to railroads, banks, and bondholders, and insisted that part of the tax burden be shifted from landowner to capitalist, and that the debt be scaled down drastically. In 1879 a referendum upon a proposed settlement seemed to indicate that a substantial majority in the state favored complete repudiation. The following year the Democrats split into two hostile parties, the bolting Low-Tax wing nominating their own ticket. As a result the Republicans returned to power in 1880.[53]

The Whig-industrialist or State-Credit wing of the Democrats was in complete agreement with Republicans upon the menace of agrarian bolters. "This contest is a struggle between ill-disguised communism and conservatism. The appeals of the repudiation party are all directed to . . . arousing that feeling against all accumulations," warned a Democratic paper of Nashville.[54] A Republican organ of Knoxville thought that "There is a growing disposition . . . to disregard property rights. In some places it takes the form of 'strikes;' in others it is called 'readjusterism,' and in others 'repudiation'. . . . We call on business men of all parties to take warning. Communism, socialism, agrarianism, nihilism and diabolism are on the increase in America." [55] Again in 1882 the Democrats were split, though a compromise modifying to some extent the demand for repudiation attracted enough support to the Democratic ticket to defeat the Republicans. The morale of the champions of Tennessee's honor was somewhat shaken when one of their own leaders, Marshall T. Polk, the state treasurer, defaulted to the tune of over $400,000 and fled the state.[56]

Nowhere else did the debt issue attain the importance it did in Virginia. In spite of the evil name attached to the origins of the Funding Act, the Conservative party, led by city lawyers and businessmen and members of the old aristocracy, planted itself rigidly against the rising tide of sentiment for readjustment. The answer to all protests regarding war-ravaged battlefields, the state's inability to pay, and the misery of bankrupt farmers, was "the unspotted

[53] Hamer (ed.), *Tennessee; A History*, II, 681–88.

[54] Nashville *Daily American*, September 21, 1880.

[55] Knoxville *Daily Chronicle*, January 2, 1883.

[56] Nashville *Daily American*, May 15, 29, 1882; Knoxville *Daily Chronicle*, January 2, 1883; *Nation*, XXXVI (1883), 23, 29.

honor of Virginia." The Funders plunged the state deeper and deeper into fiscal difficulties as the seventies drew to a close and depression intensified. To begin with, the interest on the principal funded in 1871 took all the state's revenue provided under the new tax, minus the small sum provided for public education by the constitution. Nothing at all was left for government expenses, which were estimated at a million dollars. Having contracted away the state's most valuable assets, the railroads, the Funders had to look elsewhere for revenues. The corporate interests, next to the bondholders the loudest defenders of state honor, employed old charter exemptions to escape taxation. Declining assessments of property, falling wages, and disappearing profits did not permit increase in taxation. Niggardliness in all expenditures, however severe, could not avail against an empty treasury, millions of accrued interest unpaid, and the increasing suspicion and antagonism of the people.[57]

Eventually the Funders diverted money belonging to the new public schools. The state auditor, disregarding both constitutional and statutory requirements, simply withheld sums due the schools, amounting by January, 1879, to one and one-half million dollars. State School Superintendent William H. Ruffner in his report of 1878 said that in the previous two years educational appropriations had declined from $483,000 to $195,000. He doubted "that more than one-half as many schools will be opened this year as last." [58] Governor Holliday, John W. Daniel, and other Funders declared themselves willing to scuttle the schools in order to fund the debt.[59] Even Curry, great exponent of philanthropic education, was a rigid Funder who denounced readjustment of the debt as "sheer demagoguism or communism." [60] The colleges and the religious press of the state, identified in interest with the bondholders, joined in placing the moral obligation to bondholders above the "luxury" of educating the masses.[61] The Funders cut school funds still lower

[57] Pearson, *Readjuster Movement in Virginia,* 31, 55–56, 58, 62, 90–93; Moger, *Rebuilding of the Old Dominion,* 7–8.

[58] Quoted by McFarland, "Extension of Democracy in Virginia," 96.

[59] *Ibid.,* 110–11; Richmond *Commonwealth,* March 17, 1880; Richmond *Whig,* December 3, 1880.

[60] Curry to Winthrop, December 9, 1881, in Curry Papers.

[61] Pearson, *Readjuster Movement in Virginia,* 62.

and proposed measures virtually stopping free schools. Under their guidance Virginia was in full retreat to the ante-bellum system of privilege.

The same social philosophy was reflected in Funder policy toward other state social services. Were penitentiary facilities appallingly antiquated? The Richmond *Dispatch* offered a solution: "The whipping-post would save the State in two ways: first by diminishing the number of criminals . . . ; second, by diminishing the amount of crime." [62] Was it proposed to make wealthy corporations shoulder their share of the tax burden? William L. Royall, counsel for English bondholders and editor of a Richmond paper that fought the proposed tax, believed that the "very rich corporation . . . has a right to make all the money it can make, and the more it makes the better it is for society." [63]

If Virginia Funders had discovered a satisfactory answer to Falstaff's queries regarding the emoluments of honor, Virginia Readjusters were still asking, "Can honor set a leg?" and declaring that "Honor won't buy a breakfast." Readjusters were convinced that Funders were stripping the people of their schools and their very livelihood. It was "cowardly," they held, "to cater to the opinion of those who 'having stripped us, think it rascally that we should not submit to be skinned.' " [64] Without separate party organization, opponents of the Funders had twice forced their bills for readjustment through the legislature, only to meet with the vetoes of Funder governors. Upon other measures they were thwarted by court decisions. Many were convinced by 1879 that no hope remained inside the Conservative party, and that revolt was essential.

The chaotic mixture of party lines made independence somewhat more respectable in Virginia than elsewhere. There had been some kind of independent movement in every campaign after 1869. Restiveness was increased by the entrance of the Grangers, who by 1876 claimed 685 granges with a membership of 18,783. The Grangers' demands for railroad regulation, fertilizer inspection, and a department of agriculture had met with uniform op-

[62] Richmond *Dispatch*, October 9, 1877.

[63] Richmond *Commonwealth*, January 30, 1880; Royall, *Reminiscences*, 171.

[64] Pearson, *Readjuster Movement in Virginia*, 122.

position from the Conservative party.[65] Readjusters were generally friendly to the ideas of the Greenbackers and silverites and hostile to those of bankers and capitalists.[66]

In February, 1879, the Readjusters met in convention and organized for a campaign that year. In "Parson" Massey of Jefferson's county in the Piedmont, Abram Fulkerson of the "Southwest," H. H. Riddleberger of the "Valley," and General William H. Mahone of the "Southside," the new party found strong leadership. The Richmond *Dispatch* declared that Massey, "head and front of their rebellion," was preaching "communism of the worst sort. If this is not a war upon society we know not what it is." [67] With the debt question as the chief issue, and with both sides appealing to the Negro vote, the Readjusters won a hard-fought contest. Returns indicated that they were especially strong among the mountain-locked whites of the Southwest and Valley, and among blacks and Republicans of the Tidewater and Southside. "The towns, even little villages, usually went Funder; the districts surrounding them, Readjuster." [68]

Although they won control of the legislature, the Readjusters were temporarily thwarted in carrying out their debt policy by the conservative Governor Holliday, who promptly vetoed their readjustment bill in 1880. The following year, in a still more bitter campaign, however, the Readjusters elected William E. Cameron governor, a young man of distinguished family who, like John S. Wise, had joined the insurgents. The next year he signed the Riddleberger Act, which wrote into law the principles of the Readjusters. Although the Funders denounced it as a "bill of abominations" that had dishonored the mother state, the act stood the test of the highest courts, and the Funders themselves accepted it the following year.

With the rush of undammed waters a flood of liberal measures burst upon Virginia, leaving conservatives gasping, their worst predictions confirmed. Swept away by the flood were the whipping post, the poll tax as a prerequisite for voting, and official connivance

65 *Ibid.*, 59; McFarland, "Extension of Democracy in Virginia," 88, 99–100.

66 E.g., Richmond *Whig and Advertiser*, February 22, September 27, October 11, 1878; Massey, *Autobiography*, 135–36.

67 Richmond *Dispatch*, August 19, 1879.

68 Pearson, *Readjuster Movement in Virginia*, 130.

at dueling. Mechanics' wages were made more secure, stricter bond was required of insurance companies, labor unions were chartered, and Granger measures were given sympathetic hearing. The farmers received relief by a lowering of their tax rates. The public schools were snatched from near ruin and restored to life. The funds diverted from education were restored; back salaries were paid; the public-school appropriation was increased about 50 per cent; and scores of new schools were opened. Education entered a period of growth it had never before enjoyed in Virginia.[69]

To offset consequent loss in revenue and pay additional expenses, the Readjusters turned to corporate wealth, which the Funders had allowed to escape with ridiculously low taxes. The new tax policy more than tripled the taxable value of railroads, made them liable to local taxes, tightened collections, and settled old claims. Funds flowed in abundantly. Virginia had reversed its retreat to antebellum reactionism and stepped forward to take a lead among Southern states.[70]

It was soon apparent that General Mahone was master of the victorious Readjusters. In the whole gallery of Southern figures of his generation, he stands out as one of the boldest and most enigmatical. A full-bearded, dapper little figure, fastidiously dressed, under five feet six in height and less than a hundred pounds in weight, Mahone was a self-made man, not to the manner born, yet possessed of "an imperiousness of will and manner," and an overweening confidence in his destiny. Chief engineer of a railroad at twenty-six and president of one at thirty-three, he proved as gifted and ambitious a railroad executive as he was a soldier. He had finished the war with the rank of major general and a name that was famous. Mahone plunged again into railroad organization after the war and pushed his schemes of consolidation against those of rival combinations (chiefly the Baltimore and Ohio) as though waging a military campaign.[71]

[69] *Ibid.*, 144–47; John S. Wise, in Richmond *Whig and Advertiser*, September 25, 1883.

[70] Moger, *Rebuilding of the Old Dominion*, 12–13; Richmond *State*, October 25, 1883; Richmond *Dispatch*, February 3, 1884; H. H. Riddleberger, "Bourbonism in Virginia," in *North American Review*, CXXXIV (1882), 427.

[71] Blake, *William Mahone*, 11, 35, 38, 87–89, 264–65, 271; Pearson, *Readjuster Movement in Virginia*, 68–71, 114–15.

Finding control of public opinion and political power essential to his large-scale railroad plans, Mahone bought control of the Richmond *Whig*, and took a leading part in organizing the Conservative party. Thereafter every successive change in administration found the railroad president on friendly terms with the new governor, whether Carpetbagger or aristocrat, Funder or Readjuster. In this adaptability, Mahone bore strong resemblance to one of his contemporaries, Senator Brown of Georgia. Mahone's powerful lobby obtained liberal franchises and charters for his roads. His railroad system, however, soon passed into the hands of receivers. Mahone believed his loss was the result of the more-or-less open co-operation of Richmond businessmen and Conservative politicians with "foreign" railroads of Pennsylvania and Baltimore, which owned or controlled rival newspapers, the *Enquirer* and the *Dispatch*. It was "with the hope of regaining ultimate control" of his lost railroad that, according to his biographer, "Mahone now turned his attention definitely to politics"—that is, to seeking office himself. Thwarted in an attempt to get the Conservative party nomination for governor in 1877, he was quickly converted to the Readjusters' faith, became leader of their campaign in 1879, and was seen "everywhere—planning, speaking, bargaining." [72]

A hint of the little General's conception of his political role is found in the columns of his own newspaper: "The fact is, Mahone is one of those men who only emerge at distant intervals, like Julius Caesar or Napoleon Bonaparte, to show what nature can do, and to serve some wise end of Providence." [73]

Immediately after the victory of 1879 Mahone declared with regard to officeholders that "not one of them shall go unexpelled—and that quickly." The General meant exactly what he said. Higher offices, such as those of state auditor, treasurer, secretary, and school superintendent, were filled with his followers. Then all controlling boards of state colleges and asylums were declared vacant, and some of the institutions were reorganized. School superintendents and local boards were replaced with men in "touch with the people," so that the whole school system came under the "influence of poli-

72 Blake, *William Mahone*, 88–89, 147; Pearson, *Readjuster Movement in Virginia*, 27–29, 114–15.

73 Richmond *Weekly Whig*, July 27, 1877.

tics unabashed." The supreme court judges and about three fourths of the county and corporation judges were removed as their terms expired, and replaced by Mahone men. Gerrymandering of Congressional districts and strict control of the Negro vote further strengthened the General's power. Candidates for the legislature were required to sign a written pledge to abide by caucus decisions. Conventions came together merely to learn the General's wishes. State employees in Richmond and, later, Federal employees were openly assessed a percentage of their salaries for campaign purposes. The Readjuster party had become a machine with Mahone as boss, and according to one scholar, "a very real and a very debasing tyranny." [74]

Entering the United States Senate in March, 1881, General Mahone found himself in a promising situation. With thirty-seven Republicans and thirty-seven Democratic Senators seated, and with one Independent who sided with the latter and a Vice-President, with the former, the Virginia Senator's vote would decide which of the national parties would control the organization of the Senate. He doubtless enjoyed being called " 'the most interesting personage in American politics.' " Mahone cast his lot with the Republicans and took over control of Federal patronage in Virginia.[75]

The General's decision marks also a change in the policy of the Republican party toward the whole South and therefore requires attention to developments beyond the boundaries of Virginia.

President Hayes had, for the most part, hewed to the line of the commitments of 1877 in his policy of *laissez faire* toward the Negro. Although he rewarded overthrown Carpetbaggers of Louisiana and Florida with lucrative offices, he turned a deaf ear to the pleas of Southern Republicans to revive the old Carpetbagger-Negro organizations. Some Southern Republicans, especially those secure in Federal office, were acquiescent. "Indeed, Sir," wrote former Governor William W. Holden of North Carolina to Hayes, "we

[74] Pearson, *Readjuster Movement in Virginia*, 147–59; also Massey, *Autobiography*, 219, 224–25.

[75] Blake, *William Mahone*, 206, 210.

occupy pretty much the same ground of Zaccheus and Matthew, tax-gatherers for the Romans among the Jews. But we do not complain." [76] Still others, admitting the hopelessness of a "straight-out" Republican revival, urged the President to encourage fusion or co-operation with Southern independent movements of one kind or another. Foster Blodgett was sure that in Georgia "the independent movement is the best to destroy the democracy and build up a good strong party," but warned that "it must be *at first under the name of independent democrat.*" [77] Although some patronage was put under control of Georgia Independents, the Republican leaders of the state were bitterly disappointed in Hayes, declaring later that he "was practically on the side of the Southern Bourbons" and that "in no way" did he "aid the party in the State." [78] Republican organizations in several other states co-operated at times with Greenbackers, Readjusters, and Independents, but such arrangements were usually local and temporary.

President Hayes abhorred the soft-money, repudiationist views of the Southern agrarian third parties as much as did the conservative Southern Redeemers. This was clear in his policy toward the Virginia Readjusters. The Republican party of that state was split over the debt issue and the question of co-operating with Mahone. The aristocratic tidewater element that had joined the party and had control over many Negro votes was strong for a combination with Mahone. There is an engaging picture of John Tyler, Jr., the President's son, denouncing the "crushing public debt" that should never "have been imposed upon us, and least of all upon those among us who were slaves [*sic!*] and not citizens." [79] Judge R. W. Hughes had co-operated with Mahone "so often in Railway mat-

[76] William W. Holden to Hayes, January 1, 1877, in Hayes Papers.

[77] Foster Blodgett to Hayes, May 25, 1877; J. E. Bryant to Hayes, August 28, 1877, *ibid.*

[78] *Sixth Annual Report of the Southern Advance Association* (Atlanta, 1883–1884), pamphlet in Hayes Memorial Library, 10–11.

[79] Richmond *Whig*, December 7, 1880. Privately John Tyler was writing Hayes that he considered the debt question a "subordinate and secondary consideration" of no real importance, and urged Hayes to join in backing Mahone "to the end of destroying Bourbonism, and breaking up the solidarity of the South." "Mahone," he wrote, "is nothing to me except as an instrument of national and Republican ends." John Tyler, Jr., to Hayes, December 8, 1880; January 31, 1881, in Hayes Papers.

ters, and always so pleasantly," that he urged "co-operation with him in politics." [80] On the other hand, William C. Wickham, chairman of the Republican committee of Virginia, adopted a policy that would "throughout the whole state combine the republican vote on the debt paying candidates," against Mahone and the Readjusters. Wickham, head of the Carpetbag element of the party, was second vice-president of the Chesapeake and Ohio Railroad, a bitter rival of Mahone's railroad schemes.[81] Hayes sided with this "straight-out" faction against Mahone, urging Republicans "to co-operate with the debt payers," who were Democrats in national elections. He thought that "Republicans who acted with the readjusters should cease to be considered good Republicans." [82]

Toward the end of Hayes's administration more and more Southern state Republican organizations gave up the fight, or refrained from making nominations and co-operated with Independents. This happened in South Carolina, Georgia, and Arkansas. Albion W. Tourgée declared, "The Republican party of North Carolina is dead—dead beyond hope of resuscitation or resurrection!" [83] William E. Chandler, severest critic of Hayes's policy, declared that it had "resulted in the enforced dissolution of the Republican party at the South," and the nullification of the Fifteenth Amendment.[84]

The succession of James A. Garfield brought to the control of the Republican party several of the most outspoken enemies of Hayes's Southern policy. Garfield, spokesman of creditor interests, was embarrassed by an open alliance with debt repudiators, and while reaping its benefits and helping Mahone substantially, sought to do so without "tainting our party with the flavour of repudiation." Simon Cameron, untroubled by such scruples, had in 1879 made a Southern tour "ostensibly for health," and established arrangements with Mahone that facilitated the Readjuster victory in that year. During the campaign of 1881, Senator J. Don Cameron,

[80] R. W. Hughes to Tyler, November 9, 1879, enclosed in Tyler to Hayes, November 11, 1879, in Hayes Papers.

[81] William C. Wickham to Hayes, October 6, 1879, *ibid.*

[82] Clipping, quoting Hayes, in R. M. Mayo to Hayes, November 28, 1879, *ibid.*

[83] *The "C" Letters as Published in "The North State"* (Greensboro, 1878), 21–25.

[84] *Letters of Mr. William E. Chandler Relative to the So-Called Southern Policy of President Hayes, Together with a Letter to Mr. Chandler of Mr. Wm. Lloyd Garrison* (Concord, N.H., 1878), 16.

following up his father's "schemes to aid the new combination by which the 'Solid South' was to be broken," was reported to be "daily engaged in New York City raising funds for Mahone," while "revenue officers throughout the United States were asked to contribute." [85]

After Garfield's death Chester A. Arthur elevated William E. Chandler to the cabinet as secretary of the navy. Chief of the "visiting statesmen" of 1876, and a specialist in the art of manipulation of Negro and Carpetbag legislatures, Chandler had become the leading opponent of Hayes's policy, and a defender of straight-out Republican organizations and of the intimidated Negro voters. By 1882, however, he had become convinced of the futility of the Negro-Carpetbagger combination, and abandoned the old method for an alliance with disaffected white independents of whatever economic persuasion in all states below the Potomac with the object of splitting the Solid South. Chandler became ex-officio minister for the Southern department. He promptly brushed aside the straight-out Republicans of Virginia and turned over to Mahone 200 offices in the Treasury, 1,700 in the Post Office, 70 in the Federal Courts, and many in the Norfolk Navy Yard. He proposed to employ similar devices in eight other Southern states, more if possible.[86]

Among those Republicans who were embarrassed to eat their many words regarding public faith and the downtrodden Negro was James G. Blaine. Chandler explained his policy carefully to the Senator: "If we lose the next House we can hardly hope to carry the presidential election . . . . we shall need more than 20 southern votes instead of the 10 we had to give us the organization of the House. . . . The real question can not be evaded by caviling about Mahone and the readjustment . . . nor about Chalmers and his Fort Pillow record. Those are only incidents. . . . Our straight Republican, carpet-bag, Negro governments, whether fairly or unfairly, have been destroyed and cannot be revived . . . ; do not be narrowminded, or hesitating but place yourself unmis-

[85] Thomas V. Cooper, *American Politics* (Boston, 1890), 263–64; Theodore C. Smith, *The Life and Letters of James Abram Garfield* (New Haven, 1925), II, 1117.

[86] Mahone to Chandler, May 5, 1882, in Chandler Papers; Massey, *Autobiography*, 201–203; Richardson, *William E. Chandler*, 344–47.

takably on the side of progress at the South." [87] Blaine took his stand for "progress." It is worth mentioning, perhaps, that the bonds of Virginia, unlike those of other states, were owned principally in England, not in the North.[88]

The coalitions resulting from Chandler's stratagem were a test for the social conscience of a Machiavelli. Beginning by making bedfellows of repudiationists in Virginia, the coalitionists next turned to the aid of the State-Credit party of Tennessee in the fight against repudiation. "In Alabama the Republican party has enthusiastically endorsed the Greenback and Independent fusion State ticket," announced Chandler's *National Republican* in 1882; and the same connection was formed with Greenbackers in Texas, South Carolina, and Mississippi. As if to outdo himself Chandler proclaimed for Arkansas "a coalition of all Liberal Democrats . . . who repudiate repudiation, [plus] the Greenbackers . . . with the Republicans." It was hoped that this coalition would result in a victory for the Greenback leader Rufus K. Garland, "which would crown him as the Mahone of Arkansas." [89] Republicans were further bewildered to find their President endorsing General James R. Chalmers, Independent leader in Mississippi, familiar to all bloody-shirt orators as the Confederate villain of the "Fort Pillow massacre." He was now a renegade Democrat. The bewilderments multiplied. "In South Carolina we have all been made to believe that one Col. [E. B. C.] Cash was guilty of murders so atrocious that they shocked a community accustomed to scenes of blood," exclaimed a New York Republican. But Cash quarreled with his party and came out as an independent Greenbacker. "Forthwith the Administration adopts him, and its patronage is given in aid of his election." [90] Chandler's paper dismissed all such talk as impractical quibbling and declared that "The cry should be 'anything to beat the Bourbons.' " [91]

It was too much for some Republicans. "There is no moral

[87] Chandler to James G. Blaine, October 2, 1882, in Chandler Papers. See also, Chandler to Whitelaw Reid, December 17, 1883, *ibid.*

[88] Royall, *Reminiscences,* 118.

[89] Washington *National Republican,* July 15, 1882; previous quotation, July 12, 1882.

[90] New York *Tribune,* October 26, 1882.

[91] Washington *National Republican,* August 5, 1882.

strength to such a movement," said the New York *Tribune*, "It is inherently and inevitably bad." [92] The *Nation* thought it no wonder "that the Federal Government and the Republican party should still seem to many honest Southerners the incarnation of political wickedness." [93]

The natural reply to Machiavellianism is more Machiavellianism. The Redeemers had been schooled in this principle during Reconstruction and the revolution that overthrew it. They did not forget the lesson, nor did they cease to act upon it.

There were certain important advantages accruing to the white-supremacy party of the Redeemers from the maintenance of Negroes or discredited Carpetbaggers in control of the Southern state Republican organizations. By aiding the Negro leaders in maintaining control over their party and the Federal patronage, they could thereby exclude capable native white leadership from control and thus minimize the danger of Republican victories. At the same time they could by these means identify the Republican party with the colored race, and more easily solidify their own party by the old cry of white supremacy. These tactics would also make it more difficult for any white third party or independents to co-operate with the Republicans. The strategy was well understood by white-supremacy leaders and was adopted in numerous instances. Understandings between white Democrats and Negro politicians were naturally not committed to writing. The correspondence of Secretary Chandler, however, is full of charges of this co-operation made by white Republicans or independent politicians who bitterly resented it.

In Mississippi, for example, George C. McKee, able leader of the white wing of the Republican party in his state, complained to Chandler that "Bruce & Lamar humbug the different [Republican] administrations and keep up negro rule in the Rep party in order that fear of negro rule in the State may keep white men in the Dem. party." [94] The Negro Republican wing, led by Senator Blanche K. Bruce, John R. Lynch, and James Hill, had enjoyed Federal pa-

[92] New York *Tribune*, October 26, 1882.

[93] *Nation*, XXXVII (1883), 301.

[94] George C. McKee to Chandler, July 6, 1882, quoted in Willie D. Halsell (ed.), "Republican Factionalism in Mississippi, 1882–1884," in *Journal of Southern History*, VII (1941), 93.

tronage since Reconstruction, dominated the white wing, and received support for Federal patronage from Redeemer Congressmen in Washington. Thus Senator Lamar had moved the unanimous confirmation of former Senator Bruce for register of the Treasury. The *quid pro quo* exacted of the Negro politicians, so white Republicans charged, was secret support for the Democratic candidates in state and local elections. In 1882 Democratic Congressman Chalmers, charging his defeat for re-election by Lynch to Lamar's connivance with the Negroes, left his party and announced his candidacy on the Independent ticket of the disaffected agrarians. The white Republicans then joined hands with Chalmers and the Independents and persuaded Secretary Chandler to attempt the experiment of making Chalmers the "Mahone" of Mississippi. With Chandler's aid the anti-Democratic combination elected Chalmers, carried two districts, including Lamar's home county and district, and polled 31,256 votes against 47,960 Democratic votes, "the strongest opposition to the Democrats since Reconstruction days." The attempt to "Mahoneize" Mississippi won no further successes. Negro politicians as well as Democratic leaders fought the White Republican–Independent combination from the start.[95]

Collaborations and understandings between the Conservative party and the Negroes, however, did not prevent Conservative leaders from lifting the cry of race treason against the Independents. Thus Senator Lamar denounced the leaders of the Greenbackers and Independents as "selfish and unscrupulous men who have publicly made a shameless partnership with the negroes of Mississippi." [96] A Virginia editor could one week declare that the slogan "This Way Freemen," as a Democratic appeal for Negro votes, was "worthy of a place in the story of our great State, side by side with her deathless legend, '*Sic Semper Tyrannis,*' " and a few weeks later assert of the fight that overthrew Mahoneism: "It is black against white; ignorance against intelligence; vice against virtue; barbarism against civilization." [97]

[95] *Ibid.,* 84–101; Willie D. Halsell, "James R. Chalmers and 'Mahoneism' in Mississippi," *ibid.,* X (1944), 57–59; Vernon L. Wharton, *The Negro in Mississippi, 1865–1890,* in the *James Sprunt Studies in History and Political Science,* XXVIII (Chapel Hill, 1947), 202–203.

[96] Quoted in Mayes, *Lucius Q. C. Lamar,* 435.

[97] Richmond *State,* July 26, October 30, 1883.

Once the color line was firmly drawn and the charge of the Independents' alliance with Republicans was fixed in the public mind, the third-party men had little chance. When this was not enough, there remained the resort to older tactics. A Mississippi scholar describes the methods used in that state: "Independent candidates were run out of their counties, beaten, or murdered. . . . Ballot boxes were stuffed, fraudulent returns were made, and thousands of opposition votes were thrown out on technicalities. With mock solemnity, newspapers reported that boxes containing anti-Democratic majorities had been eaten by mules or horses." [98] The reaction of the Independents is reflected in one of their papers: "Greenback men, you must learn to shoot. You must make up your minds to kill. Nothing will check this hellish spirit of intolerance but lead." [99] From South Carolina came reports of four political murders, a lynching, and intimidation of many kinds.[100] The Virginia campaign that overthrew Mahone and the Readjusters ended in the bloody Danville riot and several deaths.

"We have Virginia once more in our possession, and we will keep her this time, be sure of that," asserted a spokesman of the Conservatives—now reorganized officially as "Democrats." [101] Royall, a leading Funder, told with remarkable candor how this was to be done: "They thereupon determined that they would never run the risk of falling under negro domination again, and they accordingly amended the election laws so that the officers of election, if so inclined, could stuff the ballot boxes and cause them to make any returns that were desired." [102]

With the party of white supremacy in alliance with the Negro against lower-class white men; with the Republican party of hard money and Negro rights in alliance with Greenbackers and repudiationists against the Negro and debt payers; and with agrarian antimonopolists in alliance with the party of big business, what wonder is it that the average Southerner retreated into some form of political nihilism? This nihilism of the common man might be expressed in an excessive devotion to bird dog and shotgun, or in the

98 Wharton, *Negro in Mississippi,* 204.

99 Houston *Patriot,* quoted in Jackson *Weekly Clarion,* September 17, 1879.

100 "United States *vs.* A. Quay Dunovant," Report of William P. Snyder, assistant district attorney, to Chandler, February 21, 1883, in Chandler Papers.

101 Richmond *State,* November 7, 1883.

102 Royall, *Reminiscences,* 201–202.

towns and cities by a heedless absorption in money getting and progress. For several years after the collapse of the movements of the early eighties insurgency was almost unheard of in the South. The region lapsed into a period of political torpor more stultifying, perhaps, than any in its long history. Future Populist leaders began their political education in the Independent campaigns of the seventies, however, and it was then that the seeds of later revolt were planted.

CHAPTER V

THE INDUSTRIAL EVOLUTION

"FIFTEEN years have gone over the South," observed Whitelaw Reid, "and she still sits crushed, wretched, busy displaying and bemoaning her wounds." The reporters he sent to tour the South, as well as foreign travelers and commercial agents, came away with the same impression of the region in the late seventies. While they usually mentioned Atlanta, Nashville, and Richmond as exceptions, they were generally agreed that "tried by Northern standards, there are only a few cities between the Potomac and the Rio Grande that can be said to be growing and prospering." The exceptions were ordinarily attributed to "an infusion of Northern blood." [1]

By the fall of 1879 Charleston was still unable to rebuild the great district in the heart of the city which had been burned over during the war. Commerce in almost none of the seaports was increasing and in some it was falling off. New Orleans was handling more cotton and sugar than before, but she was neither erecting new buildings nor repairing many old ones. Her streets were to remain cesspools and open sewers for years.[2] Mobile looked "dilapidated and hopeless," Galveston's population had declined since 1873, Norfolk was "asleep by her magnificent harbor," while Savannah, Wilmington, and New Bern were "at a standstill." [3]

On the interior an English traveler found "wide gaps and ruins of crumbling stone and charred wood" along the streets of Columbia, "utter desolation that lies where once were lovely homes." [4]

[1] New York *Tribune*, October 3, 1879; August 16, 1880.

[2] Roger W. Shugg, *Origins of Class Struggle in Louisiana . . .* (University, La., 1939), 283, 289.

[3] New York *Tribune*, October 3, 1879.

[4] Lady Duffus Hardy, *Down South* (London, 1883), 273–74.

Montgomery was "showing no signs of growth" in 1879, and Vicksburg was "looking just as unattractive as ten years ago." Yellow jack added terror and death to economic blight in cities and towns of Louisiana, Mississippi, Tennessee, and Alabama. The fever killed 1,138 in and around Vicksburg, 3,977 in New Orleans, and 4,200 in Memphis in 1878.[5] So devastating was the effect on Memphis that one historian writes of "two cities . . . one which existed prior to the pestilence, and a second metropolis which sprang up like some fungus growth on the ruins of the first." [6]

Throughout the countryside and in the small towns travelers found the same grim poverty and dilapidation. Roads were in a "shocking condition," with "few bridges across the rivers, and almost none across the creeks." Railroads, "save for a few through lines operated by Northern capitalists," were "barely passable for trains running ten or fifteen miles an hour." In Alabama "the towns are lonesome and the stores empty of customers; hotels subsist on the patronage of drummers from Northern cities." Planters' homes were often abandoned and falling in ruins, and Negroes "live in the old cabins . . . or have built for themselves wretched huts." The picture was much the same in other states. "Everywhere the people show by their dress and manner of living that they are poor. Even the owners of large plantations wear coarse clothing, live on plainer fare than ordinary mechanics in the North, and are oppressed with debts." [7]

In the older South, "the people on the poor, thin lands of the Carolinas, Georgia, and Alabama," seemed to be breaking up and moving west. In Jackson, Mississippi, were seen "lines of emigrant wagons filled with hard-featured men and women bound for Texas and Arkansas." New Orleans witnessed in the middle seventies "the daily arrival of hundreds of refugees from the older Southern states, seeking homes on the Texan prairies." [8] Occasionally the younger son of a patrician Virginia family joined the trek of the plebeians. A nephew of Raleigh Travers Daniel wrote his uncle in

[5] *Appletons' Annual Cyclopaedia . . . 1878*, pp. 315–22.

[6] Gerald M. Capers, Jr., *The Biography of a River Town; Memphis: Its Heroic Age* (Chapel Hill, 1939), 204.

[7] New York *Tribune*, May 16, 1877; April 2, 1879; Montgomery *Advertiser*, August 12, 1881; Armes, *Story of Coal and Iron in Alabama*, 269–70.

[8] Edward King, *The Great South: A Record of Journeys* (Hartford, 1875), 99, 314.

1877 describing the revolutionizing effects of "the change from Richmond to Texas," and expressing amazement at the way "immigrants are pouring into this State." [9] The overwhelming majority, of course, were of the common stock, the stock that had peopled Alabama and Mississippi and Tennessee. Edward King described "lean fathers and lank and scrawny mothers entering the cars, followed by a brood of ten or more children of all sizes," the father toting the family rifle, the mother a basket of food. "The ignorance and timidity of these poor people, during their journey to new homes," remarked King, "was painful as well as ludicrous to witness." [10]

They were "the natives," a name by which, according to a New Yorker in Tennessee, "all Northerners call the people of this country." [11] Northern visitors could not readily reconcile the poverty of the South with the national faith in opportunity and boundless progress. Such wretchedness belonged to those "backward peoples" whom the leading imperial powers of Western Europe were in those days seeking to "develop," and to whom was applied by common international usage the curious term "natives." [12] The teeming millions of kerchiefed Negroes in the Black Belt, with their "happy-go-lucky disposition," and the quaint "highlanders" of the mountains, with their "Elizabethan flavor" (invariably noted), fitted conveniently into the imperialistic pattern of "backward natives." But the observant traveler from the Northeast found some difficulty in accounting for other millions of Southerners of approximately the same economic status who were not black, who bore English, Scotch, and Irish names, and about whom there was no appreciable Elizabethan flavor.

A term of remarkable elasticity was found useful in identifying this troublesome class and at the same time disposing of the problem of accounting for them. The term consisted of two adjectives,

[9] Mitchell Daniel, Paris, Tex., to Raleigh Travers Daniel, Richmond, January 29, 1877, in Robert A. Brock Collection (Huntington Library, San Marino, Calif.).

[10] King, *Great South*, 774–75.

[11] New York *Tribune*, February 18, 1881.

[12] According to *Webster's New International Dictionary* (1950), "native" as a noun in Sense 3 means: "One of a race inhabiting a region or country at the time it was discovered or became familiar to those using the expression;—chiefly used of non-Caucasian peoples of inferior civilization. . . ." For a discussion of the origins and implications of this usage, see Arnold J. Toynbee, *A Study of History* (London, 1935–1939), I, 151–53, 156, 160, 162, 212–13, 346, 465–66.

"poor" and "white," each of which was undoubtedly appropriate, yet which in combination came to possess for the Northerners a sinister, if somewhat elusive, connotation. At times the habitat of this class was identified as the Black Belt, at others, the pine barrens or the sand hills. The "local contempt for them" was said to be "reflected in the names by which they are best known," that is, such expressions as "hillbillies," "crackers," "Tarheels," terms the average Southerner was likely to apply indiscriminately to any down-at-the-heels countryman. Thus the residue of frontier riffraff, which still lingered in the South and to which the term "poor white" was originally applied, was multiplied faster than ever rogues in buckram. For Northern intellectuals the poor-white concept became the standard means of rationalizing the poverty of an exploited region. A Harvard professor called this "the most numerous element in the Southern population" and estimated that there were "five or six millions of Poor Whites scattered through the South." [13] In a moment of extreme provocation, a New York editor referred to them as "the vast majority" of the Southern people.[14] In 1879 a journalist wrote that these degenerates had "peopled the great States of Kentucky, Tennessee, Alabama, Mississippi, Arkansas, and Missouri, and they are now filling up Texas." They had "no progress in them, no love for adventure, no ambition . . . and the worst of it is that they all vote the Democratic ticket." [15] For some reason never fully explained the "poor whites" seem to have been more numerous in periods of economic depression than in other times!

The year 1877 marked the end of a period of social, economic, and political revolution in the South. This revolution had as one of its avowed aims the ending of the "house divided," and as the objective of a secondary phase of coercive reorganization the removal of such remaining differences as set Southern society apart. The end result, however, was actually to widen and deepen the disparity between the revolutionized society and the rest of the

13 Albert B. Hart, *The Southern South* (New York, 1910), 38, 41. Compare a modified version in Arthur M. Schlesinger, *The Rise of the City, 1878–1898* (New York, 1933), 4–6.

14 Editorial, New York *Tribune,* August 16, 1880.

15 Correspondent, *ibid.,* June 7, 1879. The myth persists. Thus, Vincent Sheean, in the New York *Herald Tribune Book Review,* October 23, 1949, writes that the poor whites "at all times formed the vast majority of the paleskins in those regions."

Union in several important respects, particularly those of wealth, living standard, and general welfare. The South's share of $47,-642,000,000, the estimated true valuation of property in the Union in 1880, was $5,725,000,000. This meant a per capita wealth of $376 in the South as compared with $1,086 per capita in the states outside of the South. The national average per capita was $870. The range in the South was from $286 in Mississippi to $533 in Kentucky, and outside the South, from $577 in Kansas to $1,567 in Massachusetts and $1,653 in California. Thus no Southern state came within $300 of the national average, nor within $550 of the average outside the South. In fact, Virginia, the richest ex-Confederate state in 1880, did not come within $100 of the per capita wealth possessed by Kansas, the poorest state outside the South.[16]

The marked contrast between the South's poverty and the North's wealth suggests more than a minor regional disparity in a national living standard. It is more readily comparable with the contrasts between European nations of that time. In 1880 the estimated per capita wealth of Russia was approximately 27 per cent of that of Germany.[17] In the same year per capita wealth in the South was almost exactly 27 per cent of that in the Northeastern states of New England, New York, New Jersey, and Pennsylvania. In the Northeast it was $1,353 as compared with $376 in the South.

It was little wonder that visitors from more privileged regions were struck with the discouragement they encountered in the South. "These faces, these faces," exclaimed King as he walked the streets of New Orleans. "One sees them everywhere; on the street, at the theatre, in the salon, in the cars; and pauses for a moment, struck with the expression of entire despair." [18] Surveying the situation in 1879 Reid wrote, "Manifestly something is wrong," and suggested helpfully that "Economic laws are violated in some way." [19]

Yet it was toward the end of this decade of despair that there oc-

[16] Fletcher W. Hewes and Henry Gannett, *Scribner's Statistical Atlas of the United States* (New York, 1883), lxix–lxx, and Plate 70; for a discussion of methods used in arriving at basic figures, see Henry Gannett, "The Wealth of the United States and the Rate of its Increase," in *International Review*, XII (1882), 497–504. Per capita wealth of the territories is not embraced in the comparison between sections.

[17] Hewes and Gannett, *Scribner's Statistical Atlas*, xliv, lxix.

[18] King, *Great South*, 34.

[19] New York *Tribune*, April 2, 1879.

curred that sudden quickening of life in commerce and investment in certain areas of the South that has sometimes been taken to mark the opening of a completely new era in the region's history. From New Orleans, in whose streets and noisome alleys King had seen nothing but black gloom a few years before, an exultant editor hailed the new day: "The stagnation of despair has, by some magic transformation, given place to the buoyance of hope, of courage, of resolve. The silence of inertia has turned into joyous and thrilling uproar of action. We are a new people. Our land has had a new birth." He pronounced it "a commercial evolution unparalleled in the annals of American progress," and he dated it from the beginning of 1879.[20]

Impressed by similar outbursts from orators and editors of other seaports and piedmont cities about the same time, particularly after the election of 1880, some scholars have fixed upon the latter year as the beginning of "the industrial revolution" in the South. One author declares that his "whole study really is a justification of the assertion that this date ushered in industrialism." [21] The chief reliance of this school in explaining the South's sudden "plunge" into industrialism on this date is "The shock of Hancock's defeat." [22] The South is said to have been guilty of "lashing itself to a false ambition" in relying upon Winfield S. Hancock's victory to "cure Southern sorrows." Once this false hope was disappointed Southerners were brought to their senses and resolved that "Out of our political defeat we must work . . . a glorious material and industrial triumph. We must have less politics and more work." [23] This might be called the "voluntaristic" explanation of Southern recovery and industrialization—a revolution worked by Southern will power. In fact "a fundamental distinction between the English Industrial Revolution and that in the South" is said to have been that "the latter was deliberately planned." [24]

Coupled with this theory is a moralistic explanation. Following

[20] New Orleans *Times-Democrat,* December 4, 1881.

[21] Broadus Mitchell, *The Rise of Cotton Mills in the South,* in Johns Hopkins University *Studies in Historical and Political Science,* XXXIX, No. 2 (Baltimore, 1921), 69.

[22] *Ibid.,* 88.

[23] Raleigh *News and Observer,* November 9, 1880, quoted *ibid.,* 89–90.

[24] *Ibid.,* 78–79.

the example of the abolitionists, who applied a moralistic interpretation to Southern political history, modern economists have applied a moralistic interpretation to Southern economic history. While the causes of the industrial revolution in England were "narrowly economic," it is said that "in the South they were moral as well." [25] "During Reconstruction the South, like a man thrown into prison, had time to reflect on past sins." Some sort of moral regeneration occurred in this prison, and "the South found itself." It experienced "a change of heart." A "veil was torn off," a "fever subsided," and "normal thinking brought frank avowal of the past distemper." In fact, the whole movement "was emphatically in response to a moral stimulus." [26]

Undoubtedly the will, ambition, and even the cupidity of a class of Southerners had much to do with the speeding-up of Southern industrialization. And no doubt moral forces played a part in this, as in all historical movements. But forces that were impersonal and quite amoral assumed a role that was not negligible. For one thing, a great depression came to an end in 1879 and released Northern and English capital that sought a Southern outlet for investments. If the political and economic revolutions that had swept away the Old Order were not determined primarily in the South, neither were industrialization and the character of the New Order left entirely for the South to decide.

By 1877 political exploitation of the South, at least by outright control, was discovered to be of dubious value, out of all proportion to cost. Nor was it any longer essential, if the assurances of the Redeemers could be trusted. The Redeemers pointed out the moral of the violent strikes and riots of 1877. "The peaceful, self-contained attitude of the Southern States presents too striking a contrast with that of the convulsed and panic-stricken, mob-ridden States of the North not to attract attention," read a typical comment. "Money invested here is as safe from the rude hand of mob violence as it is in the best United States bond." [27] The unstable Carpetbag governments were, moreover, considered positively

25 Broadus Mitchell and George S. Mitchell, *The Industrial Revolution in the South* (Baltimore, 1930), 93.

26 Mitchell, *Rise of Cotton Mills in the South,* 56–57, 81, 85.

27 Raleigh *Observer,* August 8, 1877.

harmful to important Northern interests. The Philadelphia *Times* declared that "Republican capitalists would today withdraw their investments if they apprehended a restoration of the only Republican authority that the South could furnish." [28] The missionary and political phase of the North's Southern policy that followed upon conquest was abandoned for a policy of economic exploitation.

In the sixties and early seventies the North had been interested in the "natives" of the South mainly as subjects for conversion or reform—outlets for missionary and political expansionism. By the late seventies they were pictured more and more as opportunities and outlets for economic expansionism. "The plantation negroes," observed the Philadelphia *Press* in 1879, "are beginning to see beyond bare floors, 'nigger's' shoes, and gaudy head 'kerchiefs.' Neat carpets, good Lynn shoes, and tasteful millinery begin to find a market in the South. Even the corset trade finds a developing outlet." [29] Profit motive and missionary motive have often gone hand-in-hand in the development of "backward people." The "natives," white as well as black, not only constituted an expanding market but a limitless source of cheap labor as well. As the Philadelphia *Telegraph* pointed out in 1877, in the South "land, labor, fuel, water power, and building facilities are cheap. The way to clear and large profits is open." [30]

Northern economic interest in the South did not, of course, originate in the seventies. So stable a citizen as Hamilton Fish is reputed to have remarked privately in the summer of 1860 that "the South was or would be splendid colonies to the North," [31] and a month after hostilities opened the New York *Times* observed that the North would "soon have the great portion of . . . [Virginia's] territory as a prize, which will a hundredfold compensate for the losses sustained by the great outbreak." [32] The Southern life of

28 Quoted in Birmingham *Iron Age,* October 23, 1884.

29 Quoted in Montgomery *Advertiser and Mail,* January 1, 1880.

30 Quoted in Richmond *Dispatch,* July 18, 1877.

31 Thomas H. Turner to Hamilton Fish, November 28, 1860, quoted in George W. Smith, "Some Northern Wartime Attitudes Toward the Post-Civil War South," in *Journal of Southern History,* X (1944), 255.

32 New York *Times,* May 13, 1861, quoted in George W. Smith, "Ante-bellum Attempts of Northern Business Interests to 'Redeem' the Upper South," *ibid.,* XI (1945), 213.

luxury pictured in abolitionist tracts seems to have inspired numerous ill-fated economic adventures immediately following the war. One Union veteran who turned Southern planter in 1866 described his dream of "the grand sweep of an eleven-hundred-acre plantation, with a roll of laborers running up in the hundreds; riding on a fine horse, with . . . a ringing spur, under a Southern sky." He attributed his failure and that of his fellow veterans to unregenerate, hostile Southerners. "The wrecks of that superb stream of immigration which flowed into the South at the close of the war," he wrote, "mostly drifted back to the North within the year." By the end of the seventies, however, the same writer discovered that hospitality toward Yankee capital was increasing and predicted a second stream of immigration.[33] Later publications indicated the same trend. A book entitled *How to Get Rich in the South. Telling What to Do, How to Do It, and the Profits to be Realized* reported that there was "no country that offers such tempting inducements to the capitalist for profitable investments." [34] A similar volume was entitled *Road to Wealth Leads Through the South*.[35] Chauncey M. Depew told Yale alumni that "The South is the Bonanza of the future. We have developed all the great and sudden opportunities for wealth—or most of them—in the Northwestern States and on the Pacific Slope," he said. Pointing to the "vast forests untouched, with enormous veins of coal and iron" that awaited pre-emption and exploitation below the Potomac, he emphasized the title of his address, "Go South, Young Man." [36]

The transition from the missionary and political to the economic and exploitative phase of Northern policy is nowhere better illustrated than by a comparison of the Federal land policy toward Southern states in the period from 1866 to 1876 with the policy from 1877 to 1888.[37] In 1861 some 47,700,000 acres in the five public-land states of the South (Alabama, Arkansas, Florida, Loui-

[33] [George C. Benham], *A Year of Wreck; A True Story, By a Victim* (New York, 1880), v, 14–17, 472.

[34] William H. Harrison, Jr., *How to Get Rich in the South . . .* (Chicago, 1888), 5–7, 192.

[35] Eugene C. Robertson, *Road to Wealth Leads Through the South . . .* (Cincinnati, 1894), 200.

[36] Quoted *ibid.*, 57.

[37] The following account is based on Paul W. Gates, "Federal Land Policy in the South, 1866–1888," in *Journal of Southern History*, VI (1940), 303–30.

siana, and Mississippi) or about one third of their area remained in Federal ownership. In 1866 the Indiana Congressman George W. Julian, a fiery abolitionist, took the lead in shaping Radical Reconstruction land policy toward the South. Julian, chairman of the House Committee on Public Lands, and his Radical followers proposed the drastic measure of ending all cash sales in the five Southern states, reserving public lands for homesteaders, limiting the size of grants to eighty acres, but excluding from the homesteading privilege all ex-Confederates. Thus at one blow the Radical leader intended to punish Southern whites, double the elusive forty acres for the landless freedman, open the way for impecunious Federal army veterans, and scotch the growth of monopoly and speculation. Although Julian's proposal that land grants to Southern railroads made in 1856 be forfeited was frowned down by railroad Congressmen like Blaine, the discriminatory bill applying to the South alone was passed by almost a strict party vote.[38]

By 1876 Depew's "sudden opportunities for wealth" in Northwestern lumber were showing signs of depletion, and the clamor for throwing open to unrestricted speculation the rich Southern empires of timber, coal, and iron was becoming irresistible. The voices of the Southern Redeemers, eager for progress, were added almost unanimously to the chorus. "Clearly by 1876," writes Professor Paul W. Gates, "the southern land question had ceased to be confused with reconstruction issues and had become a problem in land economics and business policy." [39] An act of that year repealed all limitations, and after some delay the lands were opened to unrestricted cash entry. The Illinois Central Railroad was obliged to run a series of special trains from Chicago to Mississippi and Louisiana to accommodate the speculators, such was the excitement among Northern capitalists. Huge domains were carved out of the rich timberlands and mineral regions of the Lower South. One Congressman of 1876 purchased 111,188 acres in Louisiana; a group of Chicago capitalists bought 195,804 acres; a Michigan firm acting as land brokers selected and located nearly 700,000 acres of pine land; one purchaser from Grand Rapids acquired 126,238 acres in Louisiana, to which his company later added well over half a million acres more in the same state. In Louisiana alone forty-

[38] *Ibid.*, 308.

[39] *Ibid.*, 311.

one groups of Northerners bought 1,370,332 acres and nine from the South, 261,932 acres. In Mississippi thirty-two Northern groups acquired 889,359 acres and eleven Southern groups bought 134,270 acres. Between 1877 and 1888, 5,692,259 acres of Federal lands were sold in the Southern states. When, in the latter year, under the spur of agrarian alarm and resentment, Southern representatives succeeded in reviving some of the restrictions of 1866, it was too late. "Northerners," writes Professor Gates, "controlled the best stands of yellow pine and cypress lands and were to reap the benefit by taking the cream of the profits from the rising lumber industry." [40]

Contemporaneous with the era of largess in Federal-land sales was a period of state-land sales that far outstripped it in prodigality. With both hands legislators dealt out their states' lands to speculators. Florida sold 4,000,000 acres at twenty-five cents an acre to a syndicate headed by Hamilton Disston of Philadelphia in 1881. The transaction, attended by illegal practices, uprooted many squatters and left behind it a trail of resentment discernible in a Populist campaign fifteen years later.[41] This sale was a mere priming of the legislative pump. As the Philadelphia *Times* merrily put it: "The Florida Legislature doesn't want to make anybody feel bad by saying no and so it says yes to everybody." A Floridian summed up the "land office" business by writing in 1884 that "the three last Legislatures have granted, or attempted to grant to projected railroads . . . out of a public domain which had never at any time exceeded 14,831,739.04 acres, the enormous quantity of 22,360,000 acres, or thereabouts." [42] The Carpetbaggers in all their glory could hardly match such deeds.

Texas awoke in 1885 to find its vast public domain virtually exhausted, including the half of the huge holdings dedicated in 1875 to the public-school fund, which had "not received by ten or twelve million acres the half of the public domain thus dedicated." It was revealed that under Democratic Redemption rule "frauds covering

40 *Ibid.*, 330, 314–29.

41 T. Frederick Davis, "The Disston Land Purchase," in *Florida Historical Quarterly*, XVII (1939), 200–10.

42 Letter to editor, Jacksonville *Florida Times-Union*, January 26, 1884, also quoting Philadelphia *Times*, as above. See also, Rowland H. Rerick, *Memoirs of Florida* (Atlanta, 1902), I, 360–61.

immense quantities of these lands have been committed . . . a Democratic commission's investigation showing fraudulent sale of 700,000 acres in two or three years." In all, Texas granted to twelve railroad companies a total of 32,400,000 acres, an area larger than the state of Indiana.[43]

Entering along the railroads and joining with them in the profitable business, Northern lumber syndicates sliced wide swaths through Southern forests, stripping them of timber. This happened, for example, in the "backbone grant" of the Texas and Pacific Company in Louisiana. Lumber production in Louisiana increased in value from $1,764,644 in 1880 to $17,408,513 in 1900. In the five Gulf states the increase in that period was from $13,068,353 to $73,077,050.[44] Early warnings against denuded forests and irreparable waste were brushed aside as "immeasurably stupid" by a Tennessean in 1886. "Such stuff, if taken seriously would leave all nature undisturbed," was the argument. "As for these investments of Northern capital, the South is glad to have it come. . . . We welcome the skilled lumberman with the noisy mill." [45] The work of the noisy mills was thorough. Twenty years after this welcome was extended, a government forestry expert pronounced the result in the South "probably the most rapid and reckless destruction of forests known to history." [46]

Of the splendid hopes of developed resources by which the Redeemers had justified their support of the Federal land law of 1876 little was heard in later years. The Redeemers soon found the South returned to a status comparable with that occupied prior to 1776, though the great majority of the new empire builders lived north of the Potomac rather than along the Thames.

A surprising number of them, however, did live along the Thames. So active were English investors in the region that for a time it seemed as if the mother country, after the lapse of a century,

[43] Dallas *Morning News,* October 1, 2, 3, 4, 1885; Reuben McKitrick, *The Public Land System of Texas, 1823–1910,* University of Wisconsin *Bulletin,* No. 905 (Madison, Wis., 1918), 70.

[44] *Twelfth Census, 1900,* IX, *Manufactures,* Pt. III, 807–809; Shugg, *Origins of Class Struggle in Louisiana,* 269; *Northwestern Lumberman,* quoted in *Manufacturers' Record* (Baltimore), IV (November 3, 1883), 340.

[45] *Tradesman* (Chattanooga), XIV (May 1, 1886), 16.

[46] J. F. Duggar, "Areas of Cultivation in the South," in *South in the Building of the Nation,* VI, 17.

were about to renew an old relationship with the South. One English syndicate bought 2,000,000 acres of the Disston purchase in Florida in 1881, and a Scotch company took up a half-million acres in the same state. Phillips, Marshall and Company of London purchased 1,300,000 acres located mainly in the Yazoo Delta from the State of Mississippi in 1881. General Gordon served as broker extraordinary in the transaction. It was reported from London that "nearly all classes are interested in the scheme—noblemen, members of Parliament, country squires, journalists, army and navy officers. Government officials favor the enterprises, as they will afford a good outlet for what they regard as pauper emigration." [47] The following year an English company purchased 4,500,000 acres in western and northwestern Texas, and a member of Parliament for Peterborough bought 311,000 acres for an English company in the Texas Panhandle.[48] "Foreign capital is pouring into the South at an unprecedented rate," observed a Philadelphia journal in 1883. "Not since the fiasco of the Emma Mine" in the seventies had there been anything like it.[49] The London *Standard* believed that "the time of the South has come again," and reported that in London "company after company is being organized for the exploration of the old Southern States." [50]

None of the English ventures equaled that of the North American Land and Timber Company, Limited, as a colonizer of the New South. It was organized in London in 1882 under the chairmanship of a member of Parliament. In combination with other English companies, it bought more than a million and a half acres of unsettled land on the Louisiana Gulf Coast between Vermilion Bay and the Texas border at 12½ to 75 cents an acre. In 1884 the syndicate employed Seaman A. Knapp of Iowa, one of the great pioneers of the New South and one destined to be of incalculable service to its farmers. Under Knapp's guidance rice-production methods were revolutionized by the use of wheat machinery in upland prairies, and the yield per man was increased ten- to twenty-

[47] Jackson *Clarion,* June 6, 1883; New York *Tribune,* December 27, 1881.

[48] *Manufacturers' Record,* II (November 23, 1882), 286; Jackson *Clarion,* June 6, 1883.

[49] Philadelphia *Iron,* quoted in *Manufacturers' Record,* II (February 8, 1883), 461.

[50] London *Standard,* quoted in New Orleans *Times-Democrat,* May 28, 1884.

fold. In five years Louisiana became the leading rice-producing state. The combined advertising efforts of the syndicate and the newly completed Southern Pacific Railroad, which tapped the colony, boomed land values dizzily, attracted many Midwestern settlers, and made the London colony in Louisiana a spectacular success.[51]

A more powerful magnet than Southern lands to attract Northern and foreign capital was Southern railroad development. For all the bond issues and shady railroad politics of the seventies, the Southern states east of the Mississippi [52] had but 13,259 miles of rails by 1880 as compared with 10,609 miles in 1870, an increase of 2,650 miles or only 24.9 per cent. In the decade that followed 14,396 miles were added, making a total of 27,655 miles, or a gain of 108.6 per cent. Even more rapid was expansion west of the Mississippi, in Texas, Arkansas, and Louisiana, where the increase in mileage during the eighties amounted to 211.4 per cent. In the South as a whole railroads increased from 16,605 miles in 1880 to 39,108 in 1890, or 135.5 per cent as compared with the national expansion of 86.5 per cent.[53]

The construction boom got under way in 1879, during which twice as many miles of rails were laid as in any year since 1873.[54] In the two years following July, 1879, more than $150,000,000 was invested by Northern and foreign capitalists in Southern railroads exclusive of the trans-Mississippi states, and the speculative boom had scarcely begun.[55] Between 1881 and 1890 some 180 new railroad companies, most of them small, opened operations in the South east of the Mississippi.[56] Railroad building inflamed the imagination and hopes of whole states and regions. For example, the old ante-bellum dream of a Southern route to the Pacific, revived by the Redeemers in the middle seventies, was finally realized in 1882 when the Southern Pacific linked New Orleans with San

[51] Joseph C. Bailey, *Seaman A. Knapp, Schoolmaster of American Agriculture* (New York, 1945), 109–32, 184–85.

[52] West Virginia is included because of the nature of the census data, and will be included hereinafter when the "states east of the Mississippi" are referred to in connection with railroad development.

[53] *Eleventh Census, 1890, Transportation by Land*, Pt. I, 4, 6.

[54] *Tenth Census, 1880*, IV, *Transportation*, 349.

[55] New York *Herald*, July 27, 1881; Montgomery *Advertiser*, August 11, 1881.

[56] *Eleventh Census, 1890, Transportation by Land*, Pt. I, 79–91.

Francisco. Many lesser dreams were pounded into realities by gangs of sweating blacks and whites who cut and graded and bridged their way across the Appalachians and the Piedmont, through steaming delta and swamp of the Gulf region, the arid Texas plains, and the scrub and hammock of Florida to link the subtropics with the temperate zone. Overexpansion, shoddy construction, and mismanagement attended the process, as it had in the North and West.

Simultaneous with the construction boom went a wave of consolidation in which scores of smaller companies were swallowed up by stronger ones. The Richmond and Danville Railroad, which opened its line between the two Virginia cities in 1856, combined by purchase and other methods twenty-six railroads. In 1890 this system had 3,123 miles and linked Washington, D.C., with the Mississippi River at Greenville.[57] In the meantime, the Richmond and Danville itself had been, in 1886, brought under the control of the Richmond and West Point Terminal Company, which had launched a movement of consolidation to eliminate competition and reorganize failing lines. The next large coup of the Terminal Company was the purchase in 1887 of voting control over the East Tennessee, Virginia and Georgia Railroad, itself the result of numerous consolidations which combined 1,745 miles of rails. The following year the Central Railroad and Banking Company of Georgia, with 2,361 miles, was added to the expanding system. Together with two steamship companies and some smaller railroads the Terminal system included 8,558 miles of rail and water lines. It was the largest system in the South—and the basis of the future Morgan railroad empire. Of the twenty directors elected in 1890, seventeen, including Gould, Hewitt, and Plant, were of New York City, though some—for example, John C. Calhoun, Patrick Calhoun, and John H. Inman—were transplanted Southerners operating in New York.[58]

Other consolidations effected by 1890 placed more than half the railroad mileage of the South in the hands of a dozen large companies and their affiliates. They were very largely directed from New York. There remained, however, some four hundred smaller companies to divide the rest of mileage among them in parcels

[57] Henry V. Poor, *Manual of the Railroads . . . 1891* (New York, 1891), 457–70.
[58] *Ibid.*, 471–75; Stuart Daggett, *Railroad Reorganization* (Boston, 1908), 146–64.

averaging not more than forty miles apiece.[59] It could still be said with much truth that Southern railroads constituted "a system of branches with trunks yet to be built." [60] The great era of consolidation under Morgan and the New York bankers was not to come until the depression of the nineties.[61] Until that time much was done toward the elimination of cutthroat competition and rate wars through the Southern Railway and Steamship Association, a gigantic freight pool organized during the depression of the seventies by Albert Fink of the Louisville and Nashville Railroad. It "was, in fact, with one exception, the first practical pooling arrangement in this country." [62] The pool practiced its system of basing points, freight differentials, and apportionment of traffic and earnings unimpeded until 1887, after which the prohibitions of the Interstate Commerce Act began to interfere with the power of the Association. For a brief period before the Morgan reorganization there ensued a revival of competition and rate-cutting in the South.[63]

When violence attended the wars and maneuvers of railroad consolidation it was likely to follow a pattern unique to the South. Trouble arose in 1889 between officials of the small, independent Chattanooga, Rome, and Columbus road and the giant Richmond Terminal system. J. D. Williamson of Rome, Georgia, president of the independent line, was said to have been fighting "to prevent the road's being swallowed up by monopoly." Patrick Calhoun, grandson of the great Carolinian, was general attorney and director of the Richmond Terminal and at that time in the early stages of his rise as one of the most powerful servants of national corporate interests. Instead of sending forth armed retainers to battle,

[59] *Eleventh Census, 1890, Transportation by Land,* Pt. I, 79–91.

[60] George B. Cowlam, *The Undeveloped South. Its Resources, and the Importance of Their Development as a Factor in Determining the Future Prosperity and Growth of Wealth in the United States* (Louisville, 1887), 17–19.

[61] Morgan's reorganization is treated in Chapter XI.

[62] Henry Hudson, "The Southern Railway & Steamship Association," in William Z. Ripley (ed.), *Railway Problems* (Boston, 1907), 100.

[63] "In re Tariffs and Classifications of the Atlanta and West Point Railroad Company and Other Companies," in *Interstate Commerce Commission Reports* (New York, 1890), III, 21–25. Origins and activities of the pool are described in E. Merton Coulter, *The South During Reconstruction, 1865–1877,* in *A History of the South,* VIII (Baton Rouge, 1947), 244–45.

as Northern and Western officials sometimes did, the two principals, Calhoun and Williamson, settled the altercation according to "the code." "Twelve paces were stepped off in a clearing in the woods right off the railroad," and a signal was given. Fortunately no one was hit.[64]

Southern railroad executives could rival some of the exploits of their Northern peers. The Tennessean John H. Inman, one of the founders of the Tennessee Coal, Iron, and Railroad Company and of the New York Cotton Exchange, earned the name of "a Southern carpetbagger in Wall Street." In 1888 Inman was elected president of the huge Richmond Terminal Company, and within the following year two brothers, Patrick and John C. Calhoun, who were directors of the Central of Georgia, were also made directors of the Richmond Terminal. In October, 1889, the three of them with two other directors induced the Terminal Company to purchase for $7,500,000 the worthless stock of the Central of Georgia, for which the five men had paid about half that sum. "Not only had the Terminal Company been swindled," concludes an investigator, "but the board of directors had not proceeded legally in approving the transactions." [65] This scandalous mismanagement and the deterioration of the road's physical condition contributed to the failure of the Richmond Terminal, a prelude to the great Panic of 1893.

Of the numerous disparities that set Southern apart from Northern society, one was entirely man-made: a difference of three inches between the predominant railroad gauges of the two sections. The resultant bottleneck at the Ohio and Potomac border was an awkward and expensive hindrance to traffic. Here, at least, was one impediment that an aroused South bent on progress could remove. As in other cases of difference, it was the Northern gauge that was regarded as "standard," and the Southern gauge that had to be "adjusted." After prolonged preparations the day set for changing some 13,000 miles of rails arrived, and traffic was suspended. At dawn on Sunday, May 30, 1886, the Louisville and Nashville, one of the biggest lines involved, had an army of 8,000 men poised

[64] Birmingham *Daily Age-Herald,* August 11, 1889.

[65] Edward G. Campbell, *The Reorganization of the American Railroad System, 1893–1900* . . . (New York, 1938), 100–104; Daggett, *Railroad Reorganization,* 164–66.

along its 2,000 miles of rails, armed with sledge hammer and crowbar and fired with zeal. By sundown their heroic labors had shifted the west rail three inches east along the whole 2,000 miles and adjusted the iron wheels of 300 locomotives and 10,000 pieces of rolling stock to conform to the "standard." [66]

The strain and sweat of that desecrated Sabbath in 1886 might symbolize the South's desperate determination to conform, to "adjust," to "standardize." For it should never be imagined that the changes here described were entirely imposed, unwanted, from outside. They were desperately sought, implored, cajoled. For the South had come to believe—with at least part of its divided mind—in Progress. No better evidence of this can be found than the great industrial expositions of the region in the eighties and nineties. Atlanta took the lead with her International Cotton Exposition of 1881. Louisville expanded the conception in 1883 with her Southern Exposition, which covered fifteen acres of floor space. New Orleans, with the aid of a Federal appropriation for her Cotton Centennial Exposition of 1885, outstripped all forerunners, including the Philadelphia Centennial of 1876, by placing thirty-three acres of exhibits under roof. Atlanta enlarged her pioneer effort by her Piedmont Exposition of 1887 and her still more ambitious Cotton States and International Exposition of 1895. Nashville capped the Chicago Exposition's splurge of classical architecture with a replica of the Parthenon for her Centennial Exposition of 1897. If Henry Adams found "matter of study to fill a hundred years" in the Chicago spectacle, a Southern historian may find food for reflection in these solemn circuses of Atlanta, Nashville, and New Orleans. The huge exposition structures of plaster and iron were temples erected to the alien gods of Mass and Speed. In their halls Southerners joined with millions of Yankee guests to invoke the spirit of Progress and worship the machine. Here they performed rituals of "reconciliation" and nationalism, and held reunions of Blue and Gray—without which none of these affairs were complete. More prosaically, the expositions were modern engines

[66] Kincaid A. Herr, *The Louisville & Nashville Railroad, 1850–1942* (Louisville, 1943), 45–49. To avoid profaning the Sabbath, some companies made the change shortly before or after May 30.

of propaganda, advertising, and salesmanship geared primarily to the aims of attracting capital and immigration and selling the goods.

One victim of progress was the steamboat of the region's magnificent system of rivers and inland waterways. The golden age of river traffic, chronicled by Mark Twain, passed in the mid-century. In the sixties and seventies steamboats staged a spirited comeback, only to slump rapidly into obsolescence after the eighties under the demands of a more hurried age and the competition of railroads. Flanked by trunk lines, the Lower Mississippi and its tributaries saw their freight decline rapidly from over 6,000,000 tons in 1889 to 2,500,000 in 1906. Traffic of the inland waterways of Virginia, the Carolinas, and Georgia fell off even more drastically. The river boats lost their business in cotton, grains, and passengers and took over the dirtier jobs of coal, ore, and petroleum. The stately white river queens of the Old Order, with their pillared crinolines and side-wheel bustles gave way to stubby black barges with sooty cargoes for the new masters. Like other paraphernalia afloat and ashore, the river boat became the handmaid of industrialism.[67]

Ocean shipping and seaport cities responded quite differently to the expanding railroads. Seaports and even river ports were special beneficiaries of the favoritism of the railroad basing-point rate system, and under its stimulus they sprang vigorously into new life. Another stimulus was the large appropriations made by the Federal government for river and harbor improvement in the South. Among them were over $8,000,000 for the Mississippi below New Orleans, $7,500,000 for Galveston harbor, $3,000,000 for Mobile harbor.[68] Between 1880 and 1901 exports from the Southern states increased 95.5 per cent in volume, while exports from the rest of the country grew only 64.9 per cent. Of the larger ports of the South, only Charleston and Norfolk suffered any appreciable decline. The greater gain was made by the Gulf ports, for while they increased the value of their exports 142.7 per cent in the

67 Bureau of the Census, *Transportation by Water, 1906* (Washington, 1908), 36–38, 43–44, 178–80; Bruce, *Rise of the New South*, 293–95.

68 These appropriations were expended between 1891 and 1906. *Transportation by Water, 1906*, pp. 83–84; also *Report of the Commissioners of Corporations on Transportation by Water in the United States* (Washington, 1909), Pt. I, 49–58.

twenty years after 1880, the ports of the South Atlantic gained only 56.8 per cent.[69] In the two decades after 1892 export values from the Gulf ports nearly quadrupled. New Orleans was second to New York and Galveston, for a time, a close third.[70] These gains were explained, in part, by the diversion of Western products from Atlantic ports along the trunklines southward over the quickest and shortest route to the seaboard. By 1901 the flour shipped from Southern ports was ten times what it had been in 1880, and their share of the traffic had mounted from one tenth to over one third. Another explanation was the enormous increase in the raw materials produced by the South itself in those years, during which the exports of cotton almost doubled, and corresponding or greater increases were made in lumber, tobacco, oil, coal, and pig iron.[71]

The business revival of 1879 opened the way for the Southern iron industry, until then largely a hopeful potentiality. "Then, and not until then, was there any sign of life in the city of Birmingham," observed John T. Milner, a pioneer of that iron center.[72] In 1879 an English syndicate with millions at its command opened its first furnace in Tennessee, and the same year Northern and English capitalists made large investments in the mines and furnaces of Virginia. Reporting the arrival of two parties of English capitalists, the Birmingham *Iron Age* declared that "scarcely a week passes but the city is visited by capitalists from a distance." [73] Expansion was rapid in several Southern states, but in none so fast as in Alabama. Her production of 1889 was over ten times her tonnage of 1880, more than twice the combined production of her nearest Southern rivals, Tennessee and Virginia, and more than all the other Southern states together.[74]

The great empire builder of the Alabama mineral region was the Louisville and Nashville Railroad. In 1876 the L and N, whose stock was owned largely by foreigners, had approximately half a

[69] Bruce, *Rise of the New South*, 251–52. Baltimore is included among the South Atlantic ports.

[70] New York *Tribune Almanac and Political Register, 1912* (New York, 1912), 235–37.

[71] Bruce, *Rise of the New South*, 252–55.

[72] Armes, *Story of Coal and Iron in Alabama*, 273–74.

[73] Birmingham *Iron Age*, April 5, 1883.

[74] *Statistical Abstract of the United States, 1892* (Washington, 1893), 210–11.

million acres of land in Central Alabama.[75] In the early eighties the company laced the mineral area with a mesh of rails connecting Birmingham with Ensley, Bessemer, Helena, Talladega, Anniston, and other iron and coal towns, running spurs to mines and furnaces. There were thirty-two furnaces on its lines by 1887.[76] With the powerful leverage of land and transportation in its hands, the L and N directed the investment of more than $30,000,000 in mines, furnaces, and rails in twenty years. It founded towns and scattered agents over the country and abroad to bring in immigrants.[77] In 1888 the road handled a tonnage of pig iron and minerals exceeding the average annual weight of the entire cotton crop of the country for the past fifteen years.[78] The mastermind of this empire was President Milton Hannibal Smith, intrepid executive of the L and N for half a century. "This man has been the strongest force in the industrial history of Alabama," writes Ethel Armes. She quotes the pioneer Milner as saying in 1889, "The Louisville and Nashville is now not only Birmingham, but Alabama." [79]

During the depression of 1884 and 1885 Southern iron made its first successful invasion of any extent into the Northeastern market. This precipitated a hard-fought struggle for sectional dominance in the iron industry that was almost as much discussed as that between Northern and Southern cotton mills. At first it seemed to ironmasters of the North that certain Southern advantages might prove decisive. A delegation that included Andrew Carnegie, Hewitt, and the banker Frederic Taylor, squired by John C. Calhoun and Inman, toured the coal and iron districts of the South in 1889—"to spy out the land." Carnegie declared that "the South is Pennsylvania's most formidable industrial enemy"; Taylor thought the South had "every possible advantage," and Hewitt was quite as positive.[80] By the late eighties the South was producing far more pig iron than the nation produced before the war; investment in blast furnaces was mounting faster than in any Northern state;

75 Herr, *Louisville & Nashville Railroad*, 39.

76 *Ibid.*, 37–44, 50–53. On the role of railroads in Virginia and Tennessee mineral districts, see *Manufacturers' Record*, IV (September 29, 1883), 195.

77 Armes, *Story of Coal and Iron in Alabama*, 281–82, 298.

78 Herr, *Louisville & Nashville Railroad*, 52.

79 Armes, *Story of Coal and Iron in Alabama*, 281–82, 298.

80 *Manufacturers' Record*, XV (April 6, 1889), 12–14.

and between 1876 and 1901 pig-iron production increased seventeen times in the South and only eight times in the country at large.[81] Later in the history of the sectional conflict in iron and steel it became apparent that the decisive factors were not unrivaled deposits of raw materials in unique proximity—ore, coal, and limestone within a stone's throw—but the long arm of the banker and control over transportation.

Quite early Northern capital became prominent in Southern mineral industries. For a time it seemed that "the Federal brigadier was almost as prominent in the iron world of the South as the Confederate brigadier was in the political world at Washington."[82] Truman H. Aldrich, a member of the eminent New England family, headed the list of the first big coal operators of Alabama, while his associate, Daniel Pratt, another New Englander, was high in that list himself. In the early period, however, Southerners also took a leading role. Among them was Henry Fairchild De Bardeleben, son-in-law and business associate of Pratt. He was called "the most picturesque and dramatic character in the coal and iron history of the South," and described as "savagely energetic, restless, and impatient." His part in the Pratt Coal and Coke Company was compared with that of Andrew Carnegie in the Carnegie Company. "Life," exclaimed the young ironmaster, "is one big game of poker." Unlike Carnegie, the Alabamian delighted in the games of finance capitalism. In 1889 he consolidated his holdings under the De Bardeleben Coal and Iron Company, capitalized at $10,000,000. " 'And every sheaf in the field rose up and bowed to my sheaf,' " exclaimed the whimsical millionaire. Indeed, his company controlled seven blast furnaces, and (with Biblical repetitiveness) seven coal mines, and seven ore mines, together with nine hundred coke ovens and several railroads and quarries. "I was the eagle," exulted De Bardeleben, "and I wanted to eat up all the craw-fish I could,—swallow up all the little fellows, and I did it."[83] But there followed lean years unforetold in his dreams, and De Bar-

[81] Victor S. Clark, *The History of Manufactures in the United States* (New York, 1929), II, 215, also 211–20; Bruce, *Rise of the New South*, 213. Southern iron was invading the East by 1883. See Boston *Economist*, quoted in *Manufacturers' Record*, III (May 10, 1883), 269.

[82] Clark, *History of Manufactures in the United States*, II, 214.

[83] Armes, *Story of Coal and Iron in Alabama*, 239–42, 268–78, 335, 339.

deleben was swallowed by Inman—who in turn was swallowed by Morgan, the biggest eagle of them all.

The manufacturing of tobacco, the South's oldest staple crop, was not new to the region, nor was its recovery delayed until the eighties. Four years after the war the Virginia–North Carolina district, which had produced 61 per cent of the country's smoking and chewing tobacco in 1859, manufactured 31 per cent, and in 1879 about 41 per cent, in spite of a 35 per cent national increase.[84] By 1880 Virginia, the foremost tobacco manufacturer of the South at that time, had doubled both the capital and the output of her ante-bellum factories.[85] Florida won an unanticipated boon from the tariffs, which drove Cuban cigar manufacturers to her shores to escape import duties.[86] Kentucky overtook and outstripped her ante-bellum production in the seventies.[87]

Until about 1885 tobacco was largely manufactured by ante-bellum methods in much the same areas as before the war. Then came a series of sweeping changes in the decade following 1885 that completely revolutionized the old industry. The making of cigarettes, smoking tobacco, and chewing tobacco was so thoroughly mechanized that by 1900 it could be said of what had been largely a handicraft industry that "Everything, from the stemming of the leaf to the payment of wages to the employees of the factory, is done by machinery." [88] In the same period there occurred a remarkable shift of consumers' taste to cigarettes and a corresponding shift of production in the same direction. Simultaneously there took place a wide expansion of bright-tobacco culture into the Carolinas, a change in leadership from Virginia to North Carolina in manufacturing, and a vast concentration in control and an increase in the size of factories.

[84] Nannie May Tilley, *The Bright-Tobacco Industry, 1860–1929* (Chapel Hill, 1948), 489.

[85] Benjamin W. Arnold, *History of the Tobacco Industry in Virginia from 1860 to 1894*, in Johns Hopkins University *Studies in Historical and Political Science*, XV, Nos. 1–2 (Baltimore, 1897), 64.

[86] Willis N. Baer, *The Economic Development of the Cigar Industry in the United States* (Lancaster, Pa., 1933), 106–107.

[87] Meyer Jacobstein, *The Tobacco Industry in the United States*, in Columbia University *Studies in History, Economics and Public Law*, XXVI, No. 3 (New York, 1907), 69.

[88] *Twelfth Census, 1900*, IX, *Manufactures*, Pt. III, 671.

The South took the lead in several phases of this revolution. The most important single mechanical innovation was the cigarette machine invented by James A. Bonsack, a young Virginian still in his teens, and patented in 1880. Southern inventors added numerous devices for packing, bagging, labeling, and processing tobacco.[89] The passing of leadership from Virginia to North Carolina was in part a reflection of the shift in the center of bright-tobacco culture and the demand for cigarettes, but it was also due to the superior aggressiveness and bold tactics of a group of young Southern entrepreneurs rising with the raw towns of Durham, Winston, and Reidsville. New men, uninhibited by the traditions and complacency of the Old Order, William T. Blackwell, James R. Day, Julian S. Carr, R. J. Reynolds, the Dukes, and their kind, were of the breed that had seized control of beef, petroleum, and steel in the North. With superior ruse and craft they broke the strangle hold upon their towns that Richmond had imposed by her control of the Richmond and Danville Railroad. They seized upon the "narrows" of commerce, cornered patents, smashed competitors. "Let buffalo gore buffalo, and the pasture go to the strongest," was the motto of the Bull Durham firm, a motto which President Carr interpreted as "simply the survival of the fittest." [90] By 1883 Bull Durham was producing five million pounds of smoking tobacco, and Carr, a pioneer wizard of American advertising, was spending $300,000 a year to spread posters of the famous Bull from the Golden Gate to the Pyramids.[91]

Carr's challenge of the bull pasture was taken up by the tall, rugged, redheaded son of Washington Duke, of Durham, James Buchanan Duke, called "Buck." "I had confidence in myself," he declared. "I said to myself, 'If John D. Rockefeller can do what he is doing for oil, why should not I do it in tobacco.' " [92] "Tobacco is the poor man's luxury," he observed, thereby announcing the foundation principle of several Southern fortunes and religious endowments based on the minor vices. Duke's role in American

[89] Of the several accounts of the tobacco revolution, none is so good as that in Tilley, *Bright-Tobacco Industry*, 568–92.

[90] Quoted *ibid.*, 550.

[91] *Manufacturers' Record*, IV (January 12, 1884), 619.

[92] John W. Jenkins, *James B. Duke, Master Builder* (New York, 1927), 84, also vii–xi, 52–53, 59, 70–72.

tobacco—as the eliminator of competition and the founder of monopoly—belongs with the account of the part that Morgan played in Southern railroads and Rockefeller in Southern oil and will be included with their story. But Buck Duke was no empire builder from the Northeast. He came right out of the colony.

The dramatic elements in the rise of the Southern cotton mill gave the movement something of the character of a "crusade." The successful competition with New England, the South's old political rival, the popular slogan, "bring the factories to the fields," and the organized publicity that attended every advance, have combined to enshrine the cotton mill in a somewhat exalted place in Southern history. Burdened with emotional significance, the mill has been made a symbol of the New South, its origins, and its promise of salvation. Facts that embarrass this interpretation of cotton-mill history have been somewhat neglected.

Rising in the Old Order, the cotton mills of the South showed a rather remarkable tenacity and even prosperity in the troubled decades that followed secession. Of the three leading cotton-manufacturing states of the South, North Carolina doubled the value of her output between 1860 and 1880, Georgia tripled her ante-bellum record, and South Carolina quadrupled hers.[93] These gains continued right through the supposedly blighting years of Reconstruction. The case of a large Augusta mill was by no means unique. Running some 30,000 spindles and 1,000 looms, this mill paid cash dividends averaging 14.5 per cent a year during the seventeen years following 1865 and laid aside a surplus of about $350,000.[94] These and other facts call into serious question the tradition of dating the beginning of the cotton-mill development of the South from 1880.[95]

93 *Eleventh Census, 1890, Manufacturing Industries,* Pt. III, 188–89. See also, Elizabeth H. Davidson, *Child Labor Legislation in the Southern Textile States* (Chapel Hill, 1939), 4–5.

94 This and similar examples will be found in *Manufacturers' Record,* IV (December 15, 1883), 503. Columbus, Georgia, had ten textile mills and a bagging factory in 1881. Columbus *Enquirer-Sun,* quoted in *American; a National Journal* (Philadelphia), II (1881), 166.

95 While Professor Mitchell, in his *Rise of Cotton Mills in the South,* 59, has "not meant to insist dogmatically upon this precise point of time," he nevertheless concludes, and repeats the view, that "There is every reason for selecting the year 1880 as the beginning of cotton manufacturing development in the South."

In the eighties the rate of cotton-mill expansion was simply accelerated, but it was accelerated to a speed never attained in earlier years, a pace vastly exceeding the rate of growth outside the South. In his report on the cotton-textile industry in the Census of 1890, Edward Stanwood wrote that "the extraordinary rate of growth in the south" during the eighties was "the most important" aspect of the period. In 1900 he was even more emphatic, saying that "The growth of the industry in the South is the one great fact in its history during the past ten years." [96] The number of mills in the South mounted from 161 in 1880 to 239 in 1890, and to 400 in 1900—an increase of 48.4 per cent in the eighties and 67.4 in the nineties. This, as compared with a national increase of 19.7 and 7.5 per cent in the two decades, and an apparent decrease in New England. A great number of the new mills, moreover, were equipped with more up-to-date machinery than the mills of the old textile regions. The first factory operated entirely by electricity was located in the South, and many improvements first found their way into the country through that region. The increase in the number of mills reveals only a fraction of the expansion. In the four leading states of North and South Carolina, Georgia, and Alabama—in which virtually all the increase took place—the average number of spindles per mill increased from 3,553 in 1880 to 10,651 in 1900. In total number of spindles the same states rose from 422,807 in 1880 to 1,195,256 in 1890, a gain of 182.7 per cent; and in the next decade the total mounted to 3,791,654 or an additional increase of 217 per cent in the nineties. Between 1880 and 1900 the total number of operatives in all Southern mills rose from 16,741 to 97,559; the number of bales consumed, from 182,349 to 1,479,006; the capital invested, from $17,375,897 to $124,596,874. Not untypical of the relative rate of expansion was the increase in capital

---

If the fact that South Carolina "was one of the last States to be freed from carpetbag rule" was a factor "Contributing to the lateness of the economic awakening" in the South, *ibid.*, 62, it is of interest to note that between 1860 and 1880 her mills grew more rapidly than those of any other Southern state, faster than those of Georgia and North Carolina, which were redeemed earlier. In that period South Carolina more than tripled her cotton-mill capital and more than quadrupled the value of her output. *Eleventh Census, 1890, Manufacturing Industries,* Pt. III, 188–89

[96] *Eleventh Census, 1890, Manufacturing Industries,* Pt. III, 172; *Twelfth Census, 1900,* IX, *Manufactures,* Pt. III, 28.

invested in cotton manufactures, which, between 1890 and 1900 amounted to 131.4 per cent in the South as compared with 12.1 per cent in New England.[97]

Both the historians and the promoters of the cotton-mill campaign have held that the movement was motivated by "moral incitement" and became "a form of civic piety" in the South. While the incentives common to most industrialization were admittedly present, "the moral considerations brought the matter to a focus." The cotton-mill executives were "thinking for the whole people." [98] The extent of this motivation should be carefully explored, but it is well to point out first that in the early years of the movement, according to the census report of 1900, "the return upon investment in Southern cotton mills has greatly exceeded that upon factories in the North." [99] In 1882 an average of 22 per cent profit was received on investments in Southern mills, under good and bad management—and there was much of the latter. There were failures as well as successes among the new mills. But profits of 30 to 75 per cent were not unheard of in those years.[100]

As important as these inducements undoubtedly were, they cannot account for the public zeal that, in the Carolinas, Georgia, and Alabama, converted an economic development into a civic crusade inspired with a vision of social salvation. Not only did this process occur in cities like Charleston, Atlanta, and Charlotte, with their efficient chambers of commerce, big newspapers, and Northern visitors and settlers, but even more typically in isolated Piedmont towns. Old market villages of a few hundred citizens that had drowsed from one Saturday to the next since the eighteenth century, were suddenly aflame with the mill fever and "a passion for rehabilitation." Stock was often subscribed in small holdings. Among the professions from which early mill executives were called, Broadus Mitchell lists lawyers, bankers, farmers, merchants, teachers, preachers, doctors, and public officials. City dailies and country weeklies devoted columns to the crusade and itinerant

[97] *Twelfth Census, 1900,* IX, *Manufactures,* Pt. III, 28–59.

[98] Mitchell, *Rise of Cotton Mills in the South,* 133, 135, 153.

[99] *Twelfth Census, 1900,* IX, *Manufactures,* Pt. III, 29.

[100] Mitchell, *Rise of Cotton Mills in the South,* 265; Daniel A. Tompkins, *Cotton Mill, Commercial Features . . .* (Charlotte, N.C., 1899), 51; Francis W. Dawson, in Charleston *News and Courier,* February 10, 1880.

evangelists added the theme to their repertoire. With a headlong zeal not uncharacteristic of the region in war as in peace, the Southeast embraced the cotton mill. "Even machinery was wrapped with idealism and devotion," according to one account.[101]

Much was made by mill promoters of the philanthropic motive of giving "employment to the necessitous masses of poor whites." Undoubtedly this motive was sincere in some cases. Its force, however, is somewhat diminished by evidence submitted by the promoters themselves. Francis W. Dawson of Charleston, one of the most forceful propagandists for cotton mills, wrote in 1880 that employment in the mills subjects the poor whites "to elevating social influences, encourages them to seek education, and improves them in every conceivable respect." In the same editorial he stated that in South Carolina there were at that time "2,296 operatives, upon whom 7,913 persons are dependent for support. The amount paid out in wages monthly is $38,034." The average worker and dependent thus enjoyed an income of a little over twelve cents a day. In the same article Dawson estimated that the profits of these factories "ranged from 18 to 25½ per cent a year . . . under the most unfavorable circumstances." [102] The profit motive did not necessarily preclude the philanthropic motive, but it does seem to have outweighed it in some instances.

The question of the relative proportion of Southern and Northern capital in the Southern cotton mills is hedged with difficulties. Acknowledging the importance of Northern investment in Georgia and in areas of other states, authorities are in substantial agreement that after the seventies and before the depression years of the nineties, when Northern capital moved southward in quantities, the initiative lay with the South, and the chief source of capital was local.[103] One writer finds "no evidence of any cotton mill estab-

101 Mitchell, *Rise of Cotton Mills in the South,* 160; William H. Gannon (comp.), . . . *The Land Owners of the South, and the Industrial Classes of the North* . . . (Boston, 1882), 8.

102 Charleston *News and Courier,* February 10, 1880.

103 Holland Thompson, *From the Cotton Field to the Cotton Mill* . . . (New York, 1906), 81; August Kohn, *The Cotton Mills of South Carolina* (Charleston, 1907), 32–33; George T. Winston, *A Builder of the New South; Being the Story of the Life Work of Daniel Augustus Tompkins* (Garden City, 1920), 103–104.

lished in North Carolina by Northern interests before 1895." [104] This could not be said of any other mill state. A widespread practice was to raise only part of the required capital locally and then issue a large percentage of the stock of a new mill to Northern textile machinery and commission firms. Dependence upon these absentee firms, which often charged exorbitant rates of interest and employed injurious marketing practices, resulted in milking off a sizable proportion of profits.[105]

Although the first cottonseed-oil mill in the United States was built at Natchez in 1834, the industry had no commercial importance until after the war. By 1880, however, 45 mills were producing nearly 7,000,000 gallons for export alone, an amount not exceeded until 1890. By that date there were 119 mills and by 1900 there were 357, all but four of which were in the Southern states.[106] Northern capitalists and large oil consumers became interested in the new Southern development, and the story of cottonseed oil soon took on the familiar pattern of consolidation and monopoly. About 1884 numerous associations consolidated to form the American Cotton Oil Trust. Modeled on the Standard Oil Company, it controlled some 88 per cent of production in the United States and dictated the policies of the industry.[107]

Under the plume of the smokestack and the shadow of the blast furnace grew the New South—the industrial towns of the Piedmont. William G. McAdoo remembered "a reddish look about the whole town" of the Chattanooga of his boyhood in 1882.[108] But the clay dust of Chattanooga and Atlanta and Knoxville soon yielded to soot and coal dust that modified the "reddish look" to a uniform griminess. The black mouths of the mines, like magnets, drew in the population—sallow whites from the hill country, black boys from the cotton belt, speculators from the ends of the earth.

104 Dan Lacy, "The Beginning of Industrialism in North Carolina, 1865–1900" (M. A. thesis, University of North Carolina, 1935), 74.

105 Mitchell, *Rise of Cotton Mills in the South,* 241–53.

106 *Twelfth Census, 1900,* IX, *Manufactures,* Pt. III, 589–94.

107 Clark, *History of Manufactures in the United States,* II, 519–23; Winston, *Builder of the New South . . . Daniel Augustus Tompkins,* 95–97, 101–13.

108 *Crowded Years, The Reminiscences of William G. McAdoo* (Boston, 1931), 32.

The mining towns were the newest of the New South, so new that many had had no previous existence. Birmingham: "a staring, bold, mean little town: 'marshes and mud roads everywhere and shallow pine shacks and a box car for a depot, and gamblers and traders from all over the globe.' "[109] Born in an old cornfield in 1871 of the union of a land company and a railroad, the speculators' town was throttled first by cholera and then by the alternate diseases that have beset it all its days—depression and boom. It wavered between exaltation and bankruptcy until 1879, when for the first time it seemed to strike its stride. By 1880 Birmingham counted 3,086 inhabitants; by 1900, 38,415. Anniston: conceived two years after Birmingham and laid off along the rows of an abandoned cotton farm, planned and built by Samuel Noble, an Englishman. The very type of paternalistic industrialism, Anniston was owned almost entirely by the members of two families, the Nobles and the Tylers, until 1883. When property was formally opened to public sale for the first time that year, Anniston already had a population of 4,000, three blast furnaces, a cotton mill, car-wheel works, rolling mills, and a freight-car factory, along with churches and schools.[110] Bessemer and Sheffield: brashly proclaiming their origins and aspirations with their names, sprouting out of piney gullies and promoters' imaginations in the eighties. Chattanooga: a railroad junction and a military post in 1865, a city of 30,000 by 1890. Big Lick: a "sleepy country village" of 400 in 1881, taking the statelier name of Roanoke, being Virginian, but quickly assuming the appearance of "a typical New England manufacturing town" under the direction of the Philadelphia capitalists who called it into being. By 1892 it boasted a population of nearly 20,000 with $8,000,000 invested in manufactures—though not by its inhabitants.[111]

The textile and tobacco towns of North Carolina usually, though not always, had some tiny nucleus of tradition and shade trees around which to grow. Winston could never be quite so crassly new for growing up under the shadow of old Salem, and Greensboro

[109] Armes, *Story of Coal and Iron in Alabama,* 234.

[110] *Ibid.,* 310–15, 321; *Virginias* (Staunton), V (1884), 134; *Harper's Weekly,* XXXI (1887), 767.

[111] Moger, *Rebuilding of the Old Dominion,* 35–36.

was Bill Porter's village of 497 souls in 1870 before it became an O. Henry city of 10,035 in 1900. Salisbury in the same period rose from 168 to 6,277; Winston, from 443 to 10,008; Charlotte, from 4,473 to 18,091; and Gastonia between 1880 and 1900, mounted from 236 to 4,610. Durham, entirely omitted from the census of 1870, had 6,679 by 1900, while High Point, also unlisted in 1870, had a population of 4,163 by the end of the century.

The old cities, the river and seaport towns, came in for a share of the newness of the New South. Reviewing scenes of his pilot days in 1883, Mark Twain had expected to see strange changes in the course of the Mississippi, "but," he added, "I was not expecting to live to see Natchez and these other river towns become manufacturing strongholds and railways centres." [112] The metamorphosis of Memphis was complete. "In the history of the city the year 1880 marks a distinct cultural break. . . . The old Memphis, with all its filth, was unique; the new city, with all its improvements, was typical and in time became a southern Middletown. . . . Once heterogeneous, it became homogeneous and progressive; formerly cosmopolitan, it became hopelessly provincial." [113] New Orleans, for all its concessions to Progress, managed to remain in 1889, according to Dudley Warner, "in its aspect, social tone, and character, *sui generis.*" [114] To Grace King of New Orleans, Paris in 1890 seemed "so natural, so what we are accustomed to," that it was like "letting out a French Opera matinée at every corner" of Royal Street of her home town.[115]

Beginning about 1887 and reaching a peak in 1890, a speculator's boom in town real estate swept the South, especially the mineral region. Scarcely a town in that section was too small to be without its Land Improvement Company, capitalized at preposterous figures, and making its heaviest investment in advertising. For Birmingham the boom was only one of several fevers that shook the town, but perhaps the most violent. "Why, men would come in at four o'clock in the morning and begin making trades before break-

112 Mark Twain, *Life on the Mississippi* (Boston, 1883), 411.

113 Capers, *Biography of a River Town*, 205–207.

114 Charles Dudley Warner, *Studies in the South and West, With Comments on Canada* (New York, 1889), 62.

115 Grace King, *Memories of a Southern Woman of Letters* (New York, 1932), 117.

fast," recalled an old citizen. "Property changed hands four and five times a day. . . . Men went crazy two hours after getting here. . . . A brand-new sensation was born every day." [116] Pig-Iron Kelley saw a swampy lot of 100 square feet on which was located a peanut stand sold for $100,000.[117] The wildest plunging went into brand new towns, or cities "yet to be established." The Chattanooga *Tradesman* declared in 1890 that at least a dozen such establishments had been launched within a seventy-five mile radius of that city in less than a year. "The great bulk of both capital for the projects and people who buy the lots, come from the East and North, some of the money from England," said the *Tradesman*.[118]

Middlesboro, Kentucky, unknown to maps in the middle of 1889, was seized upon by English capitalists who were said to have invested "fully $10,000,000" in the town and surrounding timber and mineral lands, and gathered a population of 3,000 by the end of the year.[119] About the same time New Englanders invaded the unknown village of Fort Payne, Alabama, and in less than a year "invested several million dollars there in building an industrial town." [120] Tactics of the boomers are illustrated by the projected town of Cardiff, Tennessee, for which an auction of lots was announced for April 22, 1890. An advertisement proclaimed it "the Richest and Most Inexhaustible Coal and Iron Region in the South," and announced that "Ten Solid Vestibuled Special Trains Will be Run from New England Alone, besides Specials from All Over the South and West." Cardiff's rise is unchronicled in the census reports, in which it never achieved the dignity of a listing.[121] When the inevitable collapse began the *Tradesman* rather peevishly declared that "Southern people are not responsible for the starting of a single new town in the coal and iron region. They were all without a single exception New England and old England projects." [122] Southerners did their bit, however. Even conservative Virginia was infected with the fever. Captain Robert E.

116 Quoted in Armes, *Story of Coal and Iron in Alabama*, 344–45.

117 William D. Kelley, *The Old South and the New* (New York, 1888), 8.

118 *Tradesman*, XXII (May 1, 1890), 111.

119 *Manufacturers' Record*, XVI (December 21, 1889), 7.

120 Richard H. Edmonds, *The South's Redemption. From Poverty to Prosperity* (Baltimore, 1890), 10–12.

121 *Tradesman*, XXII (April 15, 1890), 52–53.

122 *Ibid.*, XXII (July 1, 1890), 42.

Lee, son of the great general, headed a company to boom the tin mines around Cornwall. Money poured in and a large hotel was built. It was belatedly discovered that the tin was not of sufficient quantity for profitable exploitation. The hotel was never occupied.[123] General Fitzhugh Lee, the great general's nephew, former governor of Virginia, and president of a railroad, became president of the "Rockbridge Company" to boom Glasgow. It was not clear whether the projected metropolis was to be a health resort or an industrial center, but what was more important was General Lee's solemn announcement of the sale of "Lots number 35 and 37 in Block 153 on Rockbridge Road to Her Grace Lilly the Duchess of Marlborough," and two more "to George Charles Spencer Churchill, Duke of Marlborough." Large stock sales were made and a handsome hotel constructed. The crash unhappily halted the transplanting of English aristocracy, and the hotel was never opened. It stood for years, a decayed ruin.[124]

The fact of the matter was that, in spite of the spectacular rise of completely new cities in an old section of the country and the growth of many old ones in the last two decades of the century, the sum total of urbanization in the South was comparatively unimportant. According to census definitions and figures the percentage of urban population in the South Central division of states reached 10.3 by 1890, and rose to 11.1 in 1900. This, while the North Central states rose from 25.9 to 30.6 per cent. Urban population in the South Atlantic states climbed all of one per cent, from 16 per cent in 1890 to 17 per cent in 1900, while the percentage in the North Atlantic states mounted from 51.7 to 58.6. Omitting Maryland, Delaware, and the District of Columbia, the urban population of the South Atlantic states at the end of the booming eighties was 8.5. North Carolina, one of the states most affected by the industrial movement, had 3.9 per cent of its population classified as urban in 1890; Alabama, another, had 5.9 per cent. By 1900 there was not a single city in North Carolina with a population of 25,000 and only six with more than 10,000. The Southern people remained, throughout the rise of the "New South," overwhelmingly a country people, by far the most rural section of the Union.[125]

[123] Moger, *Rebuilding of the Old Dominion*, 40. [124] *Ibid.*, 40–41.

[125] *Twelfth Census, 1900*, II, *Population*, Pt. II, cxxxii.

It does not appear that the South as a whole advanced in manufactures faster than the nation as a whole. In 1860 the South had 17.2 per cent of the manufacturing establishments of the country and 11.5 per cent of the capital, and in 1904 these figures stood at 15.3 and 11 per cent respectively. Between those same dates the value of manufactures produced in the South rose from 10.3 per cent of the total value produced in the United States to 10.5 per cent. These figures by no means imply a static condition, of course, for in those years the product of American factories increased ninefold, and at the same time there took place a vast territorial expansion. For the South, with a comparatively fixed area, to have held its own in this march of giant strides, was no inconsiderable achievement. But it was one thing for enthusiasts to hail the arrival of industrial South Carolina, the cotton-mill state, in 1900; another to point out that 69 per cent of its people were still employed in agriculture and only 3.6 per cent in manufactures. The proportion of people in Southern states east of the Mississippi engaged in manufactures in 1900 was about the proportion in all the states east of the Mississippi in 1850. All these comparisons support Victor S. Clark's conclusions in 1909 that "the South was and continues to be mainly an agricultural region," and that it had "not in this respect, followed the example of Great Britain and New England." [126]

It is questionable that anything in the extent and character of industrialization in the South described above would justify the statement that there "arrived nearly overnight an Industrial Revolution as swift and vigorous as that in England." [127] Changes of a profound and subtle character in the Southern ethos—in outlook, institutions, and particularly in leadership—*did* take place in this period. They are even comparable with those changes in English society in the two generations between the establishment of the factories and the Reform Act of 1832, about which scholars have speculated in thinking of the South.[128] The "victory of the middle classes," and "the passing of power from the hands of landowners

[126] Victor S. Clark, "Modern Manufacturing Development in the South, 1880–1905," in *South in the Building of the Nation*, VI, 297–302; *Twelfth Census, 1900*, II, *Population*, Pt. II, cxxxv; *Manufactures*, Pt. II, 982–89.

[127] Mitchell and Mitchell, *Industrial Revolution in the South*, 294.

[128] *Ibid.*, 106–107.

to manufacturers and merchants," which required two generations in England, were substantially achieved in a much shorter period in the South, yet with nothing approaching the same amount of industrialization. The extent of the industrial revolution simply does not account for the changes. To understand them one must explore beyond the limits of economic history.

CHAPTER VI

THE DIVIDED MIND OF THE NEW SOUTH

CANVASSING the Southern problem in 1880, Edwin L. Godkin felt that he had hit upon the essence of the matter. "The conversion of the Southern whites to the ways and ideas of what is called the industrial stage in social progress, which is really what has to be done to make the South peaceful, is not a more formidable task than that which the anti-slavery men had before them fifty years ago," he wrote. He believed that the conversion could be effected "by the kind of speaking which persuades men and not that which exasperates them." Admittedly there were obstacles. "The South," he said, "in the structure of its society, in its manners and social traditions, differs nearly as much from the North as Ireland does, or Hungary, or Turkey." The common religion, language, and law were important, "but they are only a basis." [1]

Godkin was not the first to entertain such ideas. They seemed especially common, in fact, among critics of foreign or New England extraction. Alexis de Tocqueville had thought that the perverse South would be "assimilated" by "the civilization of the North." [2] Ralph Waldo Emerson, the New England sage, shared his views. Speaking at Washington in 1862 to an audience that included President Lincoln and members of his cabinet, Emerson asked, rhetorically: "Why cannot the best civilization be extended over the whole country, since the disorder of the less-civilized portion menaces the existence of the country?" [3] Once Lincoln's policy

1 *Nation,* XXXI (1880), 126.

2 Alexis de Tocqueville, *Democracy in America,* trans. by Henry Reeve (New York, 1904), II, 444.

3 Ralph Waldo Emerson, quoted in Charles and Mary Beard, *The American Spirit* (New York, 1942), 310.

of moderation was overthrown, the idea of revolutionizing Southern society in the image of the North became the avowed policy of the party in power. In the words of Thaddeus Stevens, "It is intended to revolutionize their principles and feelings . . . [to] work a radical reorganization in Southern institutions, habits, and manners." For Governor Horatio Seymour that revolution would not be complete "until their ideas of business, industry, money making, spindles and looms were in accord with those of Massachusetts." [4]

Inhabitants of "the less-civilized portion," from the days of Thomas Jefferson down to the period under consideration, had shown little hospitality toward these conceptions and some truculence in rejecting them. As late as 1880, only a week after Godkin's analysis of the situation appeared, Whitelaw Reid despaired of converting the refractory Southerners. "To us," he wrote, "the principles to which they cling are heresies not to be entertained after such bloody refutation as they have had. . . . [Yet] no facts, no statistics, no arguments, can make them comprehend that the Northern masses are their superiors, intellectually, physically, numerically, and financially." [5] Had Reid and Godkin scanned the Southern scene more carefully, however, they would have discovered much to inspire hope.

In comparing the difficulties of converting the South to "the industrial stage of social progress" with those encountered by the abolitionists, Godkin might have taken heart in reflecting that whereas the abolitionists had been met with resolute hostility, their tracts having been banned from the mails and their sympathizers summarily ejected, the new revolutionists were able to penetrate the South's borders with ease. Their tracts filled Southern journals, and their Southern converts stormed and took whole cities.

Among the spokesmen of Northern industry who caught the ear of the South was the Boston capitalist Edward Atkinson. Although one of the aims of Atkinson's mission, as spokesman of New England's cotton manufacturers, was to divert the South into primary industries and the preparation of raw materials, he was listened to eagerly and read widely. His biographer describes him as "a

[4] Quoted in Howard K. Beale, *The Critical Year* (New York, 1930), 149, 276.

[5] New York *Tribune*, August 30, 1880.

former Abolitionist who had his first Southern contact in helping to equip John Brown's raiders with Sharp's rifles."[6] But whereas Atkinson's armed emissary had been dealt with harshly, Atkinson himself was given an honorary degree by a leading Southern university, and was much sought after as a speaker. Speaking in Atlanta in 1880 he said: "When we, who are business men take a firm hold upon political questions, and try men and measures by their effect on industry and commerce, a great advance in the true science of politics will have been made." North and South would then be "one in faith, and one in hope." He was "warmly congratulated" upon his speech by Governor Colquitt, former Governor Bullock, Kimball, and the two Inman brothers—now presumably all "one in faith."[7]

William D. Kelley, often called "Pig-Iron" because of his advocacy of protection, performed the mission from the Pennsylvania ironmasters to the Southern mineral region that Atkinson performed for the New England manufacturers in the textile South. Back in 1867 the Radical Republican Kelley had appeared at Mobile to preach his doctrines to a mixed group of whites and blacks and precipitated a riot that threatened his life. Less than twenty years later, however, in an extended speaking tour in the same region Kelley professed himself touched by "The eager desire of these energetic, hopeful, and courteous people" to hear a man they once "regarded as the chief apostle of a system of oppressive sectional taxation, which had reduced the Southern people to the condition of hewers of wood and drawers of water."[8]

The South gave willing ear to other Northern evangelists, but far more influential than the Northerners were their Southern apostles. Some of them, not old enough to recall the Old Order, combined the zeal of the new convert with the impetuosity of youth. Richard H. Edmonds was only twenty-five when he founded the *Manufacturers' Record* of Baltimore in 1882, and William Wadley Yonge was twenty-three when he helped launch the *Tradesman* of

[6] Harold F. Williamson, *Edward Atkinson; The Biography of an American Liberal, 1827–1905* (Boston, 1934), 176.

[7] Quoted in Hannibal I. Kimball, *International Cotton Exposition, 1881 . . .* (New York, 1882), 12–14, 26.

[8] Kelley, *Old South and the New*, 138–39.

Chattanooga. Born in Augusta, Georgia, in 1856, Yonge, with the support of Adolph S. Ochs, started the *Tradesman* in 1879. Yonge died at the age of twenty-nine, but his journal continued to expand in influence. The young Virginian Edmonds gained greater influence, not only through the Baltimore journal, but through pamphlets, books, and speeches. Spread on the pages of the *Manufacturers' Record* were weekly reports on the triumphs of the Southern capitalism: investments, new establishments, letters, and speeches of Northern capitalists. The journal described itself as "a thoroughly Southern paper," "thoroughly identified with the New South." [9] Edmonds employed statistics for hortatory purposes, with something of the orator's license. A businessman himself, and eventually director in several large corporations, Edmonds scorned politics and politicians and, as he said, "labored persistently to impress upon the people of the South the importance of giving every possible encouragement to Northern and foreign capitalists to invest their money in the South." He inveighed against "demagogues and blatherskites," who provoked "the agrarian spirit against railroads," and he pressed the protests of Northern capitalists against "local taxation and other shortsighted but sugar-coated communism in many Southern states." [10] Inspired by the *Record*, many similar journals were founded in the South. One of them, the *Texas Trade Review*, declared that "Mr. Edmonds has set an example that may well and profitably be followed by others." [11]

In a day when newspapers were regarded as the voice of their editors, the editors of city dailies—Francis W. Dawson of the Charleston *News and Courier*, Henry Watterson of the Louisville *Courier-Journal*, Henry W. Grady of the Atlanta *Constitution*—were public figures of supreme importance. Their organs were regarded in the eighties as "metropolitan and unprejudiced," as distinct from small papers that reflected "local surroundings and interests" and were therefore "prejudiced" [12]—a distinction, incidentally, which sounds, more surely than volumes of statistics,

[9] *Manufacturers' Record*, VI (August 16, 1884), 7; IX (February 13, 1886), 7.

[10] *Ibid.*, VII (May 2, 1885), 359; VIII (December 5, 1885), 544.

[11] Quoted *ibid.*, XXXIV (December 16, 1898), 349.

[12] New Orleans *Times-Democrat*, quoted *ibid.*, VII (June 13, 1885), 556.

the depths of change in the New South. The country editors themselves, eager to keep up with the city oracles, "echoed them with tiny peals in the local weeklies." [13]

Dawson, the romantic Anglo-Southerner who had enlisted in the Confederate navy at Southampton in the opening year of the Civil War, began his persistent campaign for Southern capitalism and industry in the early seventies from the columns of the *News and Courier.* In Dawson's metropolitan and unprejudiced eyes there was nothing in old Charleston that could not be improved with an eye to Pittsburgh. "As for Charleston," he wrote, "the importation of about five hundred Yankees of the right stripe would put a new face on affairs, and make the whole place throb with life and vivid force." He preferred "a cross between the Bostonian and the Chicagoan." [14] Although Dawson and his compatriot Godkin, who preceded him to the New World by five years, chose opposing sides in the Civil War of their adopted land, they saw eye to eye on the deeper consequences of that unpleasantness. If Atkinson and Kelley were the emissaries of Boston and Philadelphia, Dawson and Godkin spoke with the voice of Manchester to the New South.

There was a magic in Henry Grady's name that still has potency. "What a radiant and charming and accomplished man he was!" exclaimed Josephus Daniels half a century after Grady's death.[15] To his own times Grady was "a genius born for an era—a marvel of inspiration to every faltering industry." [16] He came by his businessman's philosophy honestly, for he sprang not from planter stock but from ante-bellum tradesmen, promoters, and gold prospectors, and he married into a pioneer cotton-manufacturing family. Grady's business associates and friends included John H. Inman, Major Burke, and Victor Newcomb, young president of the Louisville and Nashville. Hard luck stalked his newspapers, three of which failed within five months. His luck turned in 1880, however, when Cyrus W. Field loaned him $20,000 to buy a quarter interest in the Atlanta *Constitution,* and Newcomb guided him in

[13] Thomas D. Clark, *The Southern Country Editor* (Indianapolis, 1948), 28–29.

[14] Charleston *News and Courier,* August 11, 1882.

[15] Daniels, *Tar Heel Editor,* 382.

[16] Walter G. Cooper, *The Piedmont Region . . .* (Atlanta, 1895), 97.

stock speculation to pay off the loan. By 1887 the weekly edition of his paper was claiming the largest subscription list in the South, and the following year it was acknowledged to have the largest circulation of any paper of its kind in the United States. But Grady became more famous and influential than his paper. As a practical politician with the wires of a powerful machine in his hands, he helped see to it that Georgia was governed by the new industrialists. As an orator of national fame he advertised opportunities for investment in his region, celebrated the self-made man, and preached "reconciliation" with the Northeast. Both Grady and Dawson died in 1889, still young men, yet men who had lived to see their message accepted as the creed of their people.[17]

Rarely were the new captains of industry sufficiently articulate to speak their message directly to their people. Yet not only was Daniel Augustus Tompkins a great industrialist, but he was also supremely articulate, and fired with a zeal to proselytize his unregenerate countrymen. Brought up in the county of Edgefield, South Carolina, Tompkins was educated at Rensselaer Polytechnic Institute in New York, served his apprenticeship as engineer at the Bethlehem Iron Works, and in 1882 moved to Charlotte, North Carolina, to open his own business. This included, according to his biographer, the work of "industrial missionary and apostle of the New South." His business prospered wonderfully. He became "chief owner and president of three large cotton mills, director of eight mills, and stockholder in many more," besides a manufacturer and distributor of cotton-mill machinery and machinery for other kinds of mills all over the South. Edmonds quickly discovered in young Tompkins a kindred spirit and invited him to write for the *Manufacturers' Record*. As owner of three newspapers and writer of innumerable pamphlets and articles, Tompkins became a publicist in his own right. In his papers he "made use of all possible material that could be used either to point the moral or adorn the tale of industrialism. . . . Anything, everything, and everybody—all the world—was grist in the voracious Tompkins mill of industrialism. He ground it out and gave it to Piedmont Carolina for its meal." Capable of some subtlety, the propagandist realized that "these changes had to be carefully expressed and

[17] Nixon, *Henry W. Grady*, 26–32, 45, 122, 167–69, 183, 238, 257–58, 262.

worked out to keep from offending the delicate sensibilities of a fine race of people." Like some modern Augustine, Tompkins elaborated a whole theory of the history of his people to justify his faith. "In the early days of the republic," ran the theory, "the South was the manufacturing end of the union." Then arose false prophets—"Mr. Jefferson," with his "mistaken theory," for example, not to mention Tompkins' distant relative Calhoun—and there followed years of wandering in the wilderness. The new gospel, then, was not recantation but asseveration. Like Carnegie a reader of Herbert Spencer, Tompkins believed that "the survival of the fittest is, has been, and will always be the law of progress." In his papers he fought child-labor legislation and sought to save "Democracy from Communistic Populism," and capitalist enterprise from governmental regulation of any sort.[18]

It is perhaps worth observing of Tompkins, as well as of all the apostles of his persuasion so far mentioned, that it is a mistake to view them merely as advocates of "industrialism"—of which there were several ante-bellum examples in the South. What is more important, they were preaching laissez-faire capitalism, freed of all traditional restraints, together with a new philosophy and way of life and a new scale of values.

Influences of other kinds brought to bear on the dominant minority in the South were changing the region's character more subtly and powerfully than it could be altered by frank propaganda. Recalling that in the old days "the Lowndeses, Randolphs, Rutherfords and so on married right and left into the Knickerbocker blood," a Richmond newspaper in the nineties was not surprised to observe that more recently "intermarriage has given New York's best society a distinctly southern blend." [19] Both Cornelius Vanderbilt and Collis P. Huntington, in their second marriages, chose young brides from Alabama. Henry M. Flagler at seventy-one married a young North Carolina belle and built her a $2,500,000 palace at Palm Beach. For these aging buccaneers the South was a belated romance upon which they lavished endowments, investments, and the devotion of dotage.

[18] Winston, *Builder of the New South . . . Daniel Augustus Tompkins,* 12–16, 75–78, 126, 234, 242–44, 253, 299.

[19] Richmond *Dispatch,* June 9, 1895.

Charles Dudley Warner remarked in 1889 that "society becomes yearly more and more alike North and South. It is becoming more and more difficult to tell in any summer assembly—at Newport, the White Sulphur, Saratoga, Bar Harbor—by physiognomy, dress or manner, a person's birthplace." [20] Irene Langhorne of Virginia established her claim to the title of the all-American "Gibson girl" by marrying Charles Dana Gibson in 1895. About Miss Langhorne there was said to be "no trace of languor." She was "in tune with the times," "capable and energetic." Even Southern belles could be brisk and businesslike. And over the gilded court of New York's exclusive Four Hundred, as arbiter of a thousand fine points ("One is taken, the other left"), presided the renegade Georgian, Ward McAllister. On his arm Irene Langhorne led the grand march at the New York Patriarch's Ball in 1893.

He does not reign in Russia cold,
Nor yet in far Cathay,
But o'er this town he's come to hold
All undisputed sway.[21]

New Southerners invaded not only Fifth Avenue but Wall Street, where there were "several Aladdins who came from the South." Some ancient names appeared in these alien courts: a Beverley Tucker, "for many years a successful counsel before congressional committees for large railroad corporations," [22] or a John C. Calhoun, railroad speculator. But most of the names were new: John H. Inman, from broker's clerk to Fifth Avenue mansion. "What an exemplar is here for our young men," exclaimed Henry Grady over Inman's rise. "What a brilliant promise to draw them away from the arid ways of politics . . . at thirty-six worth a million and a half." [23] Some were found useful as presidents of Southern firms controlled from Wall Street: Samuel Spencer, from section boss to president of Morgan's Southern Railway. "Being found exceedingly

[20] Warner, *Studies in the South and West*, 35–36.

[21] Ward McAllister, *Society as I Have Found It* (New York, 1890), 162, 232; Fairfax Downey, *Portrait of an Era as Drawn by C. D. Gibson* (New York, 1936), 215, 222.

[22] Richmond *Dispatch*, July 5, 1890.

[23] Quoted in Russell F. Terrell, *A Study of the Early Journalistic Writings of Henry W. Grady* (Nashville, 1927), 163.

faithful over a very few things," it was said of him, "he was soon given authority over many." [24]

One evidence of the South's acceptance of Northern ideas as the "national" standard was its pathetic eagerness for Northern approval: A little Mississippi weekly paper, quoting the Detroit *Free Press,* congratulating Mississippians on their "push"; a Baltimore journal basking in the approval of Henry Ward Beecher; the Galveston *News* snatching at a compliment from Jay Gould; Atlantans rejoicing in a donation to their Cotton Exposition from General William T. Sherman. "We wanted commendation at that time from our conquerors," remembered a New Orleans woman, "and we needed it." [25]

Northern families were sometimes important elements in the new dominant society. Especially in the mineral region were they prone to make of some towns not only economic but political outposts of empire. Writing to Secretary William E. Chandler, who had inquired about prospects for the Republican party in Alabama, a Northern immigrant replied: "Large manufacturing interests have sprung up at Birmingham just outside; and all in this District: Alabama Furnace; Anderson Furnace, controlled by Genl. Tyler of Pennsylvania, Tecumpsa [*sic*] Furnace controlled by Ohio people, Shelby *Iron* Furnace, the largest in the state—some millions of Capital, controlled by *Hartford Connecticut people*—The Stonewall Furnace, the Aetna Furnace, Cedar Creek Furnace, & other large manufacturing interest—*all controlled by Northern men* who will cooperate if the proper influences are brought to bear." [26]

Within the little islands of industrialism scattered through the region, including the old towns as well as the new, was rising a new middle-class society. It drew some recruits from the old planter class, but in spirit as well as in outer aspect it was essentially new, strikingly resembling the same class in Midwestern and North-

[24] Richmond *Dispatch,* June 9, 1895.

[25] King, *Memories of a Southern Woman of Letters,* 53.

[26] W. E. Horne, Talladega, Ala., to Chandler, September 15, 1882, in Chandler Papers. A similar instance was that of a Pennsylvanian who wrote Chandler: "While not wishing to be egotistical I think I can control the Electoral vote of Florida in the coming national contest." He explained: "I am the man who originated the Disston scheme which has put several millions of dollars in that state and put them on their feet." A. B. Linderman to Chandler, December 19, 1883, *ibid.*

eastern cities.[27] Richmond, former capital of the Confederacy, observed the social revolution within its walls with complacency: "We find a new race of rich people have been gradually springing up among us, who owe their wealth to successful trade and especially to manufactures. . . . [They] are taking the leading place not only in our political and financial affairs, but are pressing to the front for social recognition. . . . 'The almighty dollar' is fast becoming a power here, and he who commands the most money holds the strongest hand. We no longer contemn the filthy lucre. . . . They may be parvenuish, and want something of the polish which is the heritage of birth or only acquired by many generations of refining influences; but these are trifling matters. . . . Our provincial characteristics are fast disappearing, and we are not only advancing towards metropolitan development, but are losing our petty, narrow prejudices and becoming truly cosmopolitan. . . . We are not longer a village but a city." [28]

The *Industrial South* asked in the title of an editorial, "Shall We Dethrone Our Idols?" and answered with a thumping affirmative. It seems that "the founders of our American system . . . forgot to consider that the American public was to be peculiarly a community of business men, and that what it would most need was the practical wisdom of business men in the administration of its affairs. And so from the beginning the places of trust and honor were filled by warriors and orators." The inference was plain: "Beyond all question we have been on the wrong tack and should take a new departure." [29] With Virginia leading the way, this heedless iconoclasm swept the South. "If proselytism be the supreme joy of mankind," declared Henry Watterson in 1877, "New England must be pre-eminently happy, for the ambition of the South is to out-Yankee the Yankee." [30] There were even breaches in that irreducible citadel of Southernism—Mississippi. "We are in favor," announced a Vicksburg paper to a hushed Delta, "of the South, from the Potomac to the Rio Grande, being thoroughly and permanently Yankeeized." [31]

27 *Figaro* (New Orleans), I (1883–1884), 8.

28 Richmond *Whig and Advertiser*, April 4, 1876.

29 *Industrial South*, V (1885), No. 3, p. 2.

30 From a speech delivered in New York, quoted in New York *Tribune*, November 21, 1877.

31 Vicksburg *Herald*, quoted in *American*, II (1881), 166.

The facts of the record would not seem to warrant the contention that "whereas in England many from the middle class became captains of industry, here [in the South] the characteristic leadership proceeded from the aristocracy." According to this interpretation, the English industrialists were "small men who struck it lucky," whereas the Southern mill men were "gentlemen." [32] A study of the background of 254 industrialists in the South of this period reveals that "about eighty per cent came of nonslaveowning parentage." Out of a total of 300 studied only 13 per cent were of Northern birth.[33] Professor John Spencer Bassett, the historian, who took a peculiar delight in the rise of the new and the decline of the old ruling class, wrote that "The rise of the middle class has been the most notable thing connected with the white population of the South since the war. . . . Everywhere trade and manufacturing is almost entirely in the hands of men who are sprung from the non-planter class, and . . . the professions seem to be going the same way." As for the old planters, a decadent class, Bassett thought, "They have rarely held their own with others, and most frequently they have been in the upper ranks of those who serve rather than those who direct business. . . . But the captains of industry . . . are men who were never connected with the planter class." [34] A shrewd New England observer corroborated the Southerner's view when he wrote in 1890: "now, like a mighty apparition across the southern horizon, has arisen this hope or portent of the South,—the Third Estate,—to challenge the authority of the old ruling class." He advised his section against "exclusive observation of the old conflict of races" in the South. "For the coming decade, the place to watch the South is in this movement of the rising Third Estate. What it demands and what it can achieve in political, social, and industrial affairs . . . on these things will depend the fate of this important section of our country for years to come." [35]

[32] Mitchell and Mitchell, *Industrial Revolution in the South,* 32, 106.

[33] George W. Adams, unpublished paper quoted in Schlesinger, *Rise of the City,* 15 n. The industrialists studied were "random instances" from Virginia, North Carolina, South Carolina, Georgia, Alabama, and Tennessee.

[34] John S. Bassett, "The Industrial Decay of the Southern Planter," in *South Atlantic Quarterly* (Durham), II (1903), 112–13.

[35] A. D. Mayo, "The Third Estate of the South," in *New England Magazine* (Boston), N.S., III (1890–1891), 300.

Mark Twain on a Southern junket in the eighties was brought face to face with these men of the New South: "Brisk men, energetic of movement and speech; the dollar their god, how to get it their religion." [86] Somewhat awkwardly, but with great show of self-assurance, this new man adjusted to his shoulders the mantle of leadership that had descended from the planter. Some considerable alteration was found necessary: less pride and more "push," for example. Punctilio was sacrificed to the exigencies of "bustle," and arrogance was found to be impracticable in the pursuit of the main chance.

Up and down the ranks of society the professions began to cut their garments to the new pattern. "The way of the successful author is pointed out by the successful business man," affirmed Bassett of Trinity College, an institution already associated with the Duke fortune. Professor Bassett found it to be "in harmony with the general social development here" that "the future of authorship in the South will be in the hands of the new men," men unburdened by the incubus of "the blood of a dozen generations of slaveowners." The businessman was the Southern author's best model, because he had "no prejudices against work, no habits of extravagance, and no false loyalty to the worn out ideas of a forgotten system." [87] Even the college student, paragon of conservatism, was reported to be abandoning "the pleasant vices, the midnight brawl, the lawless pranks, the roystering vagabondism of the old days," and, at least in Nashville, to be "earnestly intent upon business, preparing to promote a new progress." [88] Edmonds could report with a degree of truth that "the easy-going days of the South have passed away, never to return. . . . The South has learned that 'time is money.' " [89]

For the ambitious if backward Southerner there were manuals of instruction in the new morals and manners. One, for example, entitled *The Law of Success,* appeared in 1885 under the imprint of the Southern Methodist Publishing House. The Southern author adduced his maxims empirically "from the crystallized experiences

86 Twain, *Life on the Mississippi,* 412.

87 John S. Bassett, "The Problems of the Author in the South," in *South Atlantic Quarterly,* I (1902), 207–208.

88 Nashville *Daily American,* September 19, 1880.

89 *Manufacturers' Record,* XIV (November 3, 1888), 11.

of twelve hundred successful men," for the most part Southerners who were "all self-made." His rules, "in harmony with all moral obligations," were primarily laid down for "success in private business." But they were also the assured "means by which to accomplish any purpose," including those of "artists, authors, bankers, dentists, editors." The reader was instructed in "selecting a wife with a view to making his life a success," and in "the commercial value of the Ten Commandments and a righteous life." The theory was advanced that "even social calls and visiting the club-room may prove paying investments of one's time." Allegedly an educator himself, the author evidently kept up with the "trend" and perhaps was a little in advance. "The educator of the future," he wrote, "will teach his pupils what will pay best. He will teach them the art of thinking, which, for the purpose at hand, I may define to be the art of turning one's brains into money. He will not teach dead languages, obsolete formulas, and bric-a-brac sciences . . . which are never used in the ordinary transactions of the forum, the office, the shop, or the farm." The proof, again, was empirical: "The richest man in Arkansas never had any schooling whatever." [40]

Well might Bishop Atticus G. Haygood ask, "Does History record an example in any race or age, where a people of strong character went so far in fifteen years as the Southern people—a race of Anglo-Saxon blood—have gone since 1865 in the modification of opinions, in the change of sentiments that had been, through generations, firmly fixed in all their thinking and feeling? The change in the opinions and sentiments of the Southern people since 1865 is one of the most wonderful facts of history." [41]

Perhaps the most curious aspect of the revolution in values, manners, and institutions that was daily leveling those distinctive traits that Godkin believed set the South as far apart from the North as Ireland was the romanticism that accompanied and partially obscured the process. For along with the glittering vision of a "metropolitan" and industrial South to come there developed a cult of archaism, a nostalgic vision of the past. One of the most significant

[40] William S. Speer, *The Law of Success* (Nashville, 1885), 5–8, 14, 19–20, 43, 84–85, 226.

[41] Atticus G. Haygood, *Our Brother in Black: His Freedom and His Future* (Nashville, 1881), 101.

inventions of the New South was the "Old South"—a new idea in the eighties, and a legend of incalculable potentialities.

The first step was the Lost Cause itself. In 1880, in the earlier and more abject stage of the Great Recantation, Watterson's paper could say blandly that "The 'bonny blue flag' is the symbol of nothing to the present generation of Southern men. . . . The Southern Confederacy went down forever fifteen years ago. Its issues and ensigns went down with it."[42] An exaggeration, to be sure, but such a statement, even a suggestion of it, ten years later would have been well-nigh unthinkable. By that time the official position on the progress of the Lost Cause was typified by the editor who declared simply, "It is not lost! On earth it may be lost forever. But might never did make right."[43] The deeper the involvements in commitments to the New Order, the louder the protests of loyalty to the Old.

Jefferson Davis, hardly the most popular Confederate official, was resurrected from his plantation exile in 1886 by Henry Grady (as one means of repairing the political fortunes of General Gordon) and borne in triumph up and down his old domain. Watterson's paper reported the progression "a continuous ovation." Standing on the spot in Montgomery where he had taken his oath as Confederate President twenty-five years before, Davis said, "Your demonstration now exceeds that which welcomed me then. This shows that the spirit of southern liberty is not dead."[44] An observer from Lowell, Massachusetts, declared the ovations were such "as no existing ruler in the world can obtain from his people, and such as probably were never before given to a public man, old, out of office, with no favors to dispense, and disfranchised!" He reported to Lowell that there must be "something great, and noble, and true in him and in the cause to evoke this homage."[45] Thus Yankeedom took to its heart the Lost Cause—a favorite theme in Northern theaters in the nineties, and one not unknown to later generations. The composer of "Carry Me Back to Old Virginny," which glorified the old slave regime, was a native of Long Island

[42] Louisville *Courier-Journal,* September 7, 1880.

[43] Richmond *Times,* May 29, 1890.

[44] Richmond *Dispatch,* April 29, 1886; Louisville *Courier-Journal,* May 3, 1886.

[45] Lowell *Weekly Sun,* quoted in *Industrial South,* VI (1886), 333.

and a descendant of slaves.[46] Southern romanticism was highly contagious.

Local reunions of Confederate brigades were known earlier, but it was not until 1889, in New Orleans, that the United Confederate Veterans was organized, with General Gordon "unanimously elected general commander." Lacking the lucrative incentive of Corporal James Tanner's billions extracted from the public treasury for the G.A.R., the commanders of the U.C.V. nevertheless mobilized hosts of ragged Confederates, who thronged to the annual reunions. At the reunion in Richmond in 1896 thousands, many without money, slept in "all the parks, on roofs, on doorsteps, in yards, and even in the streets." Upwards of 10,000 veterans attended, 444 from Texas, and spent the day cheering Mrs. Davis and her daughter ("the chivalric Gordon at the head of the procession") and listening to oratory. The "Adjutant General" reported to Gordon at this session that his office had "now become a vast bureau, with an enormous accumulation of books and papers," conducting an immense correspondence. To the reunion in the same city eleven years later were attracted 80,000 people.[47]

In 1895 the United Daughters of the Confederacy was organized in the capital of the New South, Atlanta. Only then, when the movement was taken into custody by Southern Womanhood, did the cult of the Lost Cause assume a religious character. Monuments were planted in courthouse squares—usually the figure of a soldier facing North, gun in hand. "Our Confederate Column" of the Richmond *Dispatch* had its manifold counterparts, filled with reminiscences, dying words, heroes of godlike mold, battles, skirmishes, and alarums, often giving the impression of news fresh from the front. A week before Bryan was nominated in Chicago, on the occasion of a veterans' reunion, the Richmond *Times* devoted nineteen of its twenty-four pages to the Confederacy and the Old South, and its rival, the *Dispatch,* not to be outdone, twenty of its twenty-four pages. It is a matter for speculation whether any lost cause in modern history, from that of Bonnie Prince Charlie to

[46] There was an ante-bellum song of the same name, but the familiar one was composed by James A. Bland in 1878.

[47] Richmond *Times,* July 2, 1896; Richmond *Dispatch,* June 30, 1896; Richmond *Times-Dispatch,* June 5, 1907.

that of Wilhelm's legions, has received the devotion lavished upon the Stars and Bars.

The romanticism and sentimentality of that generation of Southerners, however, was too copious to spend itself upon the Lost Cause. Genealogy became the avocation of thousands. Its more esoteric branches yielded their treasures to seekers after the heritage of grandeur. The fabled Southern aristocracy, long on its last legs, was refurbished, its fancied virtues and vices, airs and attitudes exhumed and admired. Homage even from the plain man, who for ages had been unimpressed by doings of the upper crust, was added in this period. Drippings from the plantation legend overflowed upon race and labor relations, public charities, and even the organization of factory villages. The Natchez Cotton Mills were adorned with "three spires or turrets of mansard style to give them grace and beauty," and the Female Institute of Columbia, Tennessee, boasted in an advertisement of "its resemblance to the old castles of song and story, with its towers, turreted walls, and ivy-mantled porches."

Mark Twain saw the paradox, but only through the glasses of his age and therefore darkly: "practical common-sense, progressive ideas, and progressive works, mixed up with the duel, the inflated speech, and the jejune romanticism of an absurd past that is dead." [48] Henry James came closer with a cast of one of his loose, netlike sentences. "The collapse of the old order," he speculated, "the humiliation of defeat, the bereavement and bankruptcy involved, represented, with its obscure miseries and tragedies, the social revolution the most unrecorded and undepicted, in proportion to its magnitude, that ever was; so that this reversion of the starved spirit to the things of the heroic age, the four epic years, is a definite soothing salve." [49]

In addition, the South suffered from a prevailing sense of inferiority and a constant need for justifying a position. But the really curious thing is that oftener than not this archaic romanticism, this idealizing of the past, proceeded from the mouths of the most active propagandists for the New Order. And this with no apparent sense of inconsistency, certainly none of duplicity. It is true, as al-

[48] Twain, *Life on the Mississippi*, 468.

[49] Henry James, *The American Scene* (New York, 1907), 371.

ready pointed out, that Tompkins (who penned romantic pictures of "Life in the Old South") elaborated a theory to prove that the New South was merely a revival of the "true" genius of the Old South, as it existed prior to certain heresies. Edmonds went so far as to scorn the very name "New South," insisting that it was "simply a revival of the South as it existed thirty-five years ago," that is, in 1860![50] But such strained rationalizations did not embarrass the oratory of Henry Grady, of the young Woodrow Wilson, or even of Walter Hines Page, all of whom paid reverent homage to ancestral shrines. Joel Chandler Harris worked for Grady in the Atlanta *Constitution*'s editorial hatchery with no consciousness of serving two masters. After all, if the United Confederate Veterans could follow John B. Gordon as the living embodiment of the legend, what need was there for awkward rationalizations!

The bitter mixture of recantation and heresy could never have been swallowed so readily had it not been dissolved in the syrup of romanticism. Political servants of the New Order used this formula to advantage. In 1894, when the tide of Populism was rising fearfully, Senator Matt W. Ransom's political fortunes were foundering in North Carolina. The mayor of Charlotte wrote him that "The country people, as it seems to us, are at present against you." Then he proposed a well-tested stratagem: "getting Genl Gordon to deliver his lecture on 'the last days of the Confederacy' inviting the country people, and getting him to make an allusion to you!"[51]

No paradox of the New South was more conspicuous than the contrast between the earnestly professed code of shopkeeper decorum and sobriety and the continued adherence to a tradition of violence. For violence was, if anything, more characteristic of the new society than of the old. In the place of the code duello, the traditional expression of violence in the Old South, gunplay, knifing, manslaughter, and murder were the bloody accompaniments of the march of Progress. The old state of South Carolina, with less than a quarter of the six New England states' population, reported nearly three times their number of homicides in 1890.

[50] Quoted indirectly in New Orleans *Times-Democrat,* November 10, 1895.

[51] R. J. Brevard to M. W. Ransom, July 3, 1894, in M. W. Ransom Papers (University of North Carolina Library, Chapel Hill).

For all its cities and slums and unassimilated immigrants, Massachusetts had only 16 homicides as compared with 65 in Virginia, 69 in North Carolina, 88 in Kentucky, 92 in Georgia, and 115 in Tennessee. Yet none of the Southern states mentioned came within a quarter of a million of the population of Massachusetts, and all were among those having the highest percentage of native, rural population. In the western tiers of states, Michigan had 31 homicides and Alabama 108, Wisconsin 20 and Mississippi 106, Minnesota 21 and Louisiana 98. Kansas and Nebraska were no further removed from frontier conditions than was Texas, but the Northern states reported respectively 34 and 23 homicides and Texas 184. Yet the census figures were admittedly unreliable, since they fell far short of the actual number of homicides, especially those of the rural, sparsely settled areas.[52] A Kentucky editor published figures in 1885 demonstrating that there had been an average of 223 murders a year for the past six years in Kentucky, though the census returned only 50 for 1880; and a Mississippi paper declared in 1879 that there was an average of a murder a day in that state, while the census of the following year reported only 57.[53] It is not improbable that the amount of homicide was two or three times that reported.[54] Italy, with what appeared to be the highest homicide rate in Europe, did not have in her prisons in 1890 as many convicts charged with murder as did the South Central states, which had less than a third of Italy's population.[55] The South seems to have been one of the most violent communities of comparable size in all Christendom.

The record of violence should not be hastily attributed to the Negro, for at least in South Carolina, Kentucky, and Texas white men killed much more often, in proportion to their numbers, than did Negroes. Race violence there was, undoubtedly, but it was only

52 On the unreliability of homicide data, see Bureau of the Census, *Special Reports, Mortality Statistics, 1900–1904* (Washington, 1906), cv–cvi; for the above figures, see *Eleventh Census, 1890, Vital and Social Statistics*, Pt. III, *Statistics of Deaths*, 27–425; to compare 1880, see *Tenth Census, 1880*, XII, *Mortality and Vital Statistics*, Pt. II, 388–427.

53 Hardinsburg (Ky.) *Breckinridge News*, in Clark, *Southern Country Editor*, 223; Vicksburg *Herald*, May 25, 1879.

54 Horace V. Redfield, *Homicide, North and South* (Philadelphia, 1880), 172.

55 Burr J. Ramage, "Homicide in the Southern States," in *Sewanee Review* (Sewanee, Tenn.), IV (1895–1896), 221.

a part of the general milieu of Southern violence and can be understood best against that background. Nor could lower-class whites bear disproportionate blame, for the newspapers of the day were crowded with homicidal frays between lawyers, planters, railroad presidents, doctors, even preachers, and particularly editors. Guns blazed in banks, courtrooms, and schoolhouses as well as in bars and ginhouses. Casualties were fewer in the spectacular mountain feuds than in bustling towns of the lowlands. And the immediate causes were often absurdly trivial. Of the quarrels resulting in the shooting of five men on one day in a Mississippi county, two arose over the opening of doors and two over petty debts. Dueling persisted, but in diminishing proportions. In one year there were 128 homicides and only 3 duels in South Carolina. In place of the relatively civilized duel there arose the barbarous custom of "shooting-on-sight." According to Southern editors dedicated to reform, the practice of toting a pistol was "almost universal" in some parts. The state auditor of Alabama in 1881 reported the valuation of tools and farming implements in his state to be $305,613; that of guns, pistols, and dirks, $354,247.[56] Turning the chronicles of Southern communities—Edgefield, Vicksburg, Memphis—one is reminded forcefully at times of Marlowe's London, or the Highlands of the wild Scots.

Another anachronism from the Old Order that contrasted queerly with the new society was a lingering grace and simplicity of life. Even its detractors could not quite deny the persistence of this heritage from the country life of ante-bellum Virginia, Carolina, and the Bluegrass. Of the two relics—the heritage of violence and that of grace—the former undoubtedly had more to feed upon in the new society and proved the hardier tradition. Grace and gallantry were more vulnerable to the new climate of push and progress and survived only in sheltered places. Specious varieties of the genuine article were, of course, cultivated for the tourist trade, adopted sedulously by the ancestor societies and the *nou-*

[56] *Nation*, XXXVI (1883), 14; also Redfield, *Homicide, North and South*, 90, 95–96, 101, 151–52, 159, 202; Ramage, "Homicide in the Southern States," *loc. cit.*, 215–19, 222–23; Clark, *Southern Country Editor*, 218–23; Nathaniel S. Shaler, "The Peculiarities of the South," in *North American Review*, CLI (1890), 487. In 1913 the homicide rate in Southern cities was 21.2 per 100,000 population and in Eastern cities 5.6. Frederick L. Hoffman, *The Homicide Problem* (Newark, 1925), 23.

veaux riches (of Northern as well as Southern origins), and associated in numerous ways known to the advertiser's art with brands of tobacco, liquor, stage beauties, and politicians. When the New South was personified by the cartoonist it was, significantly, in the garb of the ante-bellum planter.

Distressed at the poverty of Southern achievement in the arts and sciences during this period, Nathaniel Southgate Shaler speculated on the reasons for "the failure of the Kentucky people to make good their promise." He ascribed it to "a peculiar combination of circumstances, of which the Civil War was the most potent," especially the resulting sacrifice of life. "This sacrifice," he wrote, "was in peculiarly large measure from the intellectual, the state-shaping class," and it was made in the South "in far larger proportion than the Northern states." Before the war he had seen evidence that "men and women were seeking, through history, literature, the fine arts, and in some measure through science, for a share in the higher life. Four years of civil war . . . made an end of this and set the people on a moral and intellectual plane lower than they occupied when they were warring with the wilderness and the savages." [57]

As a matter of fact, Shaler's own career, filled with achievement and renown in geology, was partial refutation of his picture of intellectual barrenness. In his own bluegrass South there was an unusual burst of scientific activity in the eighties. A thriving group of geologists, among them Robert Peter and John R. Proctor, flourished in Kentucky. Lucien Carr, another Kentuckian, won high praise among ethnologists for his studies of the Mound Builders of the Mississippi Valley, and Ellen Churchill Semple of Louisville later became a pioneer in human geography. Edward E. Barnard of Tennessee achieved international fame as an astronomer, and J. Lawrence Smith of Louisville made significant contributions in chemistry. Alert surgeons of the region maintained productive medical schools and flourishing professional journals and estab-

[57] *The Autobiography of Nathaniel Southgate Shaler* (New York, 1909), 76–77. Mr. Justice Holmes wrote a concurring opinion: "the best part of the South was simply wiped out." Oliver Wendell Holmes to Sir Frederick Pollock, April 25, 1920, in Mark A. de Wolfe Howe (ed.), *Holmes-Pollock Letters* (Cambridge, 1941), II, 40–41.

lished the first state board of health in Tennessee in 1877 and in Kentucky in 1878.[58]

Apart from the sciences and the more practical arts the picture was darker. Even those creative spirits who survived the ordeal of war and clung to their purpose found the odds heavily against them. Sidney Lanier's nightmarish struggle against poverty and hemorrhages was only one of the tragedies of the period. Lanier, however, was more fortunate than some; he found a berth for the last three years of his life, first at the Peabody Institute and then (from 1879 to 1881) at the newly founded Johns Hopkins University. A mixture of the Old and the New Order, Baltimore was at one and the same time the last refuge of the Confederate spirit in exile and a lying-in hospital for the birth of the New Order. There William H. Browne's *Southern Magazine* expired in 1875 and Albert T. Bledsoe's *Southern Review*, in 1879; there also the first number of Edmond's *Manufacturers' Record* appeared in 1882; and there Basil L. Gildersleeve wrote his *Creed of the Old South*. To Baltimore came the young Southerners—Walter Hines Page, Woodrow Wilson, and scores of others—to hesitate between the Old and the New. Gildersleeve and about a third of the Hopkins faculty were Southerners.

Others found no refuge. Paul Hamilton Hayne lived in this period near Augusta, Georgia, in a shack furnished with goods boxes and papered by his wife with pictures cut from magazines, like the shacks of Negro croppers. Praise for his verse came from Tennyson and Swinburne, and he continued to write at the carpenter's bench that served him as a desk. Virtually his only associates were the illiterate crackers who worked at a nearby sawmill. He lived in the shack until his death in 1886.

Perhaps Shaler's gloomy analysis and Edward King's belief that "a generation has been doomed" were overstatements of the case. Yet multiple instances of frustration could be cited to support those views. "There's failure in the very air," declared one of Ellen Glasgow's young Virginians. And he echoed a hundred aspirations when he exclaimed, "No, I want to get away, not to spend my life as a missionary to the broomsedge." [59]

[58] F. Garvin Davenport, "Scientific Interests in Kentucky and Tennessee, 1870–1890," in *Journal of Southern History*, XIV (1948), 500–21.

[59] Ellen Glasgow, *Barren Ground* (New York, 1925), 112.

Flight was an all-too-common impulse. The swelling migration of Southern talent to the Northeast began quite early. Shaler himself was one instance. The leading American architect of the period, Henry Hobson Richardson, was born on a Louisiana plantation and educated in New Orleans, Harvard, and Paris. In the seventies and eighties his buildings sprinkled the entire country—with the exception of his native region. Likewise, John Wellborn Root of Georgia won his fame as an architect entirely in the North. Joseph Le Conte and his brother John, Georgians, gained high distinction as scientists in California but found no opportunity at home after 1865. The South of the eighties was a bleak place for the young scholar. "The studious man is pronounced impractical and is suspected as a visionary," wrote young Woodrow Wilson from Atlanta in 1883.[60] Wilson soon left for the Johns Hopkins to prepare for a teaching career, a career he pursued outside the South. Walter Hines Page took his departure for the golden cities about the same time, flinging back a farewell to the "mummies" of North Carolina. The South could have its own golden cities and skyscrapers, he prophesied, if it would only forget "constitutional questions which have been irrevocably settled." [61] Page left for New York "dead broke." In ten years he had put the *Forum* on its feet, become editor of the *Atlantic Monthly,* and, to keep a hand in the work of converting his unregenerate homeland, acquired part ownership of the *Manufacturers' Record.*[62] His headquarters, however, remained in Boston and New York.

Withdrawal of the artist or critic sometimes became a secession that was spiritual as well as physical, and resulted not only in the alienation of the writer from his people but in a schism within the spirit of the man himself. A recurrent tragedy in the intellectual history of the South, this phenomenon had its cruder prototype in Hinton Rowan Helper, and its clearest example from this period in George W. Cable, the novelist. Cable's story, complicated by psychological crosscurrents, by the heritage of a hapless Virginian

[60] Woodrow Wilson to Robert H. Dabney, May 11, 1883, in Ray S. Baker, *Woodrow Wilson; Life and Letters* (Garden City, 1927–1939), I, 169.

[61] Burton J. Hendrick, *The Training of an American; The Earlier Life and Letters of Walter H. Page, 1855–1913* (Boston, 1928), 146.

[62] In 1895 Page was the second largest stockholder, Edmonds the largest. "List of Stockholders, May 23, 1895," filed under the name of Richard H. Edmonds in Walter Hines Page Papers (Houghton Library, Harvard University, Cambridge).

father and a mother of New England stock against a Creole background of New Orleans, presents too many complexities to unravel here. The crisis of the conflict within him, however, is described in his own words. As he watched the "great Reconstruction agony from its first day to its last," Cable found his emotions deeply torn —"with his sympathies ranged upon the pro-Southern side of the issue, and his convictions drifting irresistibly to the other," he wrote. The pull of his convictions and of New England eventually asserted themselves. In 1885, the year Page left for New York, Cable published *The Silent South,* the most radical indictment of Southern racial policy written by a Southerner in that period, and in 1885 he moved his family to Northampton, Massachusetts. He had the right, as he said, to speak as "a native of Louisiana, an ex-Confederate soldier, and a lover of my home, my city, and my State." [63] Yet he never again lived in the South. Both Cable and his people were losers—the writer, of his art, which never fulfilled its rich promise; the South, of a fearless critic and a point of view that could thenceforth be more readily dismissed complacently as foreign. Later Cable would look homeward and melt with ruth: "I felt that I belonged still," he wrote, "peculiarly to the South." [64]

It was in the field of fiction that the postwar generation found fullest expression. The Southern literary revival of the eighties came with a concentration and suddenness that made it unique in the region's history. There were a few transitional figures—the poets Hayne and Lanier, the story-writer Richard M. Johnston—but all of the new major writers burst upon the national consciousness about the same time. Whatever lasting fame these writers were to earn was to depend, with striking similarity and quite regardless of the extent of later publication, upon one or two books, in each case their earliest. All of these books appeared between 1879 and 1887. Cable's *Old Creole Days* was published in 1879, *The Grandissimes* in 1880, and *Madame Delphine* in 1881. Irwin Russell of Mississippi, precursor of the dialect school, died in 1879 at the age of twenty-six. Joel Chandler Harris' *Uncle Remus* appeared in 1881 and his *Mingo* in 1884, Thomas Nelson Page's *In Ole Virginia*

[63] George W. Cable, *The Silent South* (New York, 1885), 25, 47.

[64] Lucy L. C. Biklé, *George W. Cable: His Life and Letters* (New York, 1928), 162; see also Arlin Turner, "George W. Cable, Novelist and Reformer," in *South Atlantic Quarterly,* XLVIII (1949), 539–45.

in 1887,[65] "Charles Egbert Craddock's" *In the Tennessee Mountains* and *Where the Battle Was Fought* in 1884. A dozen lesser luminaries, among them Grace King and Kate Chopin, took their first bows within the same years.

It was a propitious moment to gain the national eye. The decline of New England's long dominance, New York's neglect of Melville and Whitman, and the subsidence of the vogue enjoyed by the West in the seventies had cleared the stage for the New South. The ninth edition of the *Encyclopaedia Britannica,* 1886, in a badly outdated article on "American Literature," said that Southern letters, "mainly by their connection with the North," had been "saved from sinking to the level of Mexico or the Antilles." Yet the following year the New York *Critic* declared that "Southern literature is a sort of craze" and complained of the "excessive praises" lavished on it.[66] In 1888 Albion W. Tourgée, hardly a pro-Southern critic, observed in the *Forum* that "A foreigner studying our current literature, without knowledge of our history, and judging our civilization by our fiction would undoubtedly conclude that the South was the seat of intellectual empire in America, and the African the chief romantic element of our population." As evidence, he pointed out that a few months before "every one of our great popular monthlies presented a 'Southern story' as one of its most prominent features; and during the past year nearly two-thirds of the stories and sketches furnished to newspapers by various syndicates have been of this character." The Southern revival, then, was a national as well as a regional phenomenon, called forth, in part, by a freakishly romantic turn of Northern fancy. Indeed, according to Tourgée, "it cannot be denied that American fiction to-day, whatever its origin, is predominantly Southern in type and character"; not only that, but "distinctly Confederate in sympathy." [67]

If credit for the revival be assigned in the South, it would be a

65 "Marse Chan," the most famous story in the collection, was first published in 1884, after the publisher had held it four years.

66 Anonymous, "Literature in the South," in *Critic* (New York), VII (1887), 322–23.

67 Albion W. Tourgée, "The South as a Field for Fiction," in *Forum,* VI (1888–1889), 406–407. According to Shields McIlwaine, *The Southern Poor-White from Lubberland to Tobacco Road* (Norman, 1939), 100, "Between 1882 and 1887, the annual average of articles published on the South was about ten times that during the preceding eighty years."

mistake to overlook Joel Chandler Harris. "What strange habitations does genius choose among men," observed the sleekly groomed Walter Hines Page, noting the "red unkempt hair," "the freckled face and freckled hands" of "Joe Harris." [68] This shy, inveterate countryman, illegitimate son of an itinerant Irish laborer, could write unflattering truths of literary criticism. "The stuff we are in the habit of calling Southern literature," he wrote in 1879, "is not only a burlesque upon true literary art, but a humiliation and a disgrace to the people whose culture it is supposed to represent. . . . The truth might as well be told: we have no Southern literature worthy of the name." [69] Writing across a desk from where Henry Grady was exhorting the South to exploit her "mountains stored with exhaustless treasures," Harris was telling the Southerner with idle literary capital that "all around him, untouched, undeveloped, undisturbed, unique and original, as new as the world, as old as life" were literary materials of unparalleled richness. "But they must be mined. They must be run through the stamp mill," he added.[70]

With a zeal approaching that of the speculators who were combing the Piedmont for mining stakes, the literary prospectors began a veritable gold rush to the unexplored corners of the region—and much they unearthed that glittered. Scratch the surface, they believed, and one would find "local color," picturesqueness, quaintness. Provided with the divining rod of current literary fashion, they could not have wished for richer deposits of the material they sought. Where else could one unearth such a variety of "types": cove-locked mountaineers of the Smokies, ex-slaves who practiced voodoo and told African fables that were philological nuggets, picturesque poor whites, decadent aristocrats, homespun provincials, romantic Creoles, and Cajuns along every bayou? Harris' success with Negro dialect in *Uncle Remus* precipitated a national flood of dialect literature. Again Southern resources led the boom. Did not "our contemporary ancestors" still speak "Shakespeare's English"? Not to mention Sea-Island Gullah, Cajun patois, and poor-white English!

[68] Hendrick, *Earlier Life and Letters of Walter H. Page,* 149.

[69] Atlanta *Constitution,* quoted in *Harper's Weekly,* XXIV (1880), 19.

[70] Quoted in Cary McWilliams, "Localism in American Criticism," in *Southwest Review* (Dallas), XIX (1933–1934), 422–23.

It would be stretching a point to claim Lafcadio Hearn for the Southern revival, in spite of his ten years in New Orleans, from 1877 to 1887, several of them on Major Burke's *Times-Democrat.* In fact, both of these strange birds of passage took flight about the same time—Major Burke to seek the gold of Honduras, Lafcadio in quest of the golden women of Martinique. It was in his New Orleans years that Hearn achieved his first recognition, however, and *Chita* (1889) was not unrelated to the milieu of "Marse Chan" (1884). Nor did Hearn misrepresent the mood of his Southern contemporaries when he exclaimed, "I have pledged me to the worship of the Odd, the Queer, the Strange, the Exotic, the Monstrous" —with the possible exception of the last named of his idols.[71]

Not that the outpourings of the eighties were alien to the spirit of the New South. On the contrary they gave expression to many of its moods, especially its florid romanticism. "And the Southerner, be he never so progressive," wrote progressive Professor Edwin Mims of Thomas Nelson Page, "cannot but now and then sigh, amid some of the raw expressions of the new South, for the charm and leisure of the old." [72] And what delectable sighs! What bittersweet tears washed Nashville's grimy cheeks over Page's *In Ole Virginia!* "Dem wuz good ole times, marster—de bes Sam ever see! Dey wuz in fac'! Niggers didn' hed nothin' 'tall to do." Embarrassing race conflict dissolved in liquid dialect, angry Populist farmers became merely quaint in Billy Sanders' vernacular, depression rolled aside, and for a moment, "de ole times done come back again."

Boston and New York shared the illusion and cheered the dashing Confederates. Even the polemical literature of the South in ante-bellum years had not lavished such praise upon the plantation legend. Yankee imitators of the Dixie school sought to outdo it in sentimentality. Maud Howe, daughter of the composer of "The Battle Hymn of the Republic," declared in her novel *Atalanta in the South* (1886) that the Negro was happier in slavery than in freedom; Thomas Wentworth Higginson, onetime militant abolitionist and commander of a Negro regiment, dissolved in

[71] Lafcadio Hearn to W. D. O'Connor, June 29, 1884, in Elizabeth Bisland, *Life and Letters of Lafcadio Hearn,* 2 vols. (Boston, 1906), I, 328.

[72] Edwin Mims, "Thomas Nelson Page," in *Atlantic Monthly,* C (1907), 113.

tears over "Marse Chan." A favorite theme of the Southern school and its Northern imitators was "reconciliation," preached with little more subtlety than in Grady's orations or Edmonds' editorials. The conventional ending of their novels was a union between Confederate heroine and true-blue Federal hero. Bronson Howard outdid the novelists by uniting *five* such lovelorn pairs in his play *Shenandoah* (1889). By 1892 it seemed entirely appropriate for the Boston *Atlantic Monthly* to publish Gildersleeve's "Creed of the Old South," an uncompromising panegyric.[73]

The Southern school, like the rest of the country, was, of course, inundated by Victorian prudery—all except Hearn, who complained of "a Sunday-school atmosphere" about Cable. Harris assured his publisher that "In all my writings you will find nothing that cannot be read and explained to a young girl." *The White Rose of Memphis,* a novel by Colonel William Falkner [74] of Mississippi, was characterized by another Mississippian in 1882 as "hallowed with an atmosphere of purity and sweetness." It probably was.

For all their shortcomings and the comparative brevity of the revival (it reached its peak by 1887), the Southern writers undeniably possessed solid virtues. Among them, however, one will search in vain for a realistic portrayal of their own times. But for an occasional interest of Harris and Cable, the writers were too preoccupied with their quaint "types" of the hinterland to notice what was going on in their own parlors. The importation of shoddy standards from the North and the encroachment of rank indigenous evils, the preachment of an alien ethics, and the spreading helotry among the farmers went largely unchallenged in their pages. "Life, as a whole," philosophized the rising Kentucky novelist James Lane Allen in 1885, "presents a scene of happiness and success; shall the

[73] These and other illustrations of Yankee acquiescence are ably discussed in Buck, *Road to Reunion,* 220–35. See also, Francis P. Gaines, *The Southern Plantation: A Study in the Development and the Accuracy of a Tradition* (New York, 1924), 81–82.

[74] The grandfather of the novelist, William Faulkner, though he spelled his name differently. A veteran of General Nathan B. Forrest's raiders, Colonel Falkner, besides writing a novel, found time to build a local railroad, fight many duels, and kill his quota of opponents. He was finally shot dead in the main street of his home town by a former friend and business associate in a shoot-on-sight fray for which he refused to arm himself. *Mississippi, A Guide to the Magnolia State* (New York, 1938), 456–58.

novel of life present a spectacle of wretchedness and failure?"[75] Joel Harris knew better than that, but he clung tenaciously to the doctrine of neighborly love that among his Middle Georgia countrymen ("the most democratic people the world has ever seen," he thought) proved the talisman against all evil. Why not, then, among sections and races and classes, however estranged? On that theory, at least, he tried to believe that Atlanta was only an enlargement of Snap Bean Farm.[76]

As acknowledged shepherds of Southern folds, the Protestant clergy enjoyed a position that was unchallenged in this period. "There is no part of the world in which ministers of the Gospel are more respected than in the Southern States," declared a distinguished minister in 1885.[77] This was more fact than boast. Bishop Haygood was on equally safe ground when he observed that since the Civil War "The controlling sentiment of the Southern people in city and hamlet, in camp and field, among the white and the black, has been religious."[78]

Observers from outside the region were struck by Southern religiosity. "The South is by a long way the most simply and sincerely religious country that I was ever in," wrote an English traveler. "In other countries men are apt to make a private matter of their religion . . . ; but the Southerner wears his upon his sleeve."[79] Northerners were prone to account for the trait after the manner of Warner, who wrote that "Life in the South is still on simpler terms than in the North, and society is not so complex." He found the people "more frank and impulsive . . . it may be less calculating." A New York journalist wrote that "There is everywhere much of primitive-simplicity in their methods of life and in their manners and character." On all hands he heard talk of "things marvelous, supernatural and impossible generally . . . the same as that

[75] Quoted in Grant C. Knight, *James Lane Allen and the Genteel Tradition* (Chapel Hill, 1935), 53.

[76] John Donald Wade, "Profits and Losses in the Life of Joel Chandler Harris," in *American Review* (New York), I (1933), 17–35.

[77] Dr. O. P. Fitzgerald, quoted in Hunter D. Farish, *The Circuit Rider Dismounts; A Social History of Southern Methodism, 1865–1900* (Richmond, 1938), 105.

[78] Atticus G. Haygood, *The New South: Gratitude, Amendment, Hope . . .* (Oxford, Ga., 1880), 9–10.

[79] Sir William Archer, *Through Afro-America: An English Reading of the Race Problem* (London, 1910), 73–74.

which was heard a quarter of a century ago in the log cabins of . . . Indiana." [80]

Evangelical fervor, revivalism, camp meetings, mass conversions were no new phenomena in the South. But in this period, religious zeal was abnormally intensified. Membership in the Southern Methodist Church, lower in 1866 than in 1854, doubled in the fifteen years following the war. The greatest gains were made when revivalism was at highest pitch, and the eighties were "a time of extraordinary revivals." Net gain in members of the Methodist Church in 1885 was the highest in its history, and a rapid rate of growth was maintained throughout the century.[81] Scenes recalling the Wesleyan revivals of early industrial England were not unknown to the New South. It was the heyday of such masters of pulpit demagogy as Sam Jones. "When I get up to preach," said the Reverend Mr. Jones, "all I do is to KNOCK OUT THE BUNG and let nature cut her caper." Thousands thronged the special trains that ran to his performances to witness these wonders of nature. "His power is felt not only by the lower classes . . . but by the purely intellectual as well," it was reported.[82]

To a remarkable degree this religious ferment was the work of only two Protestant sects, the Methodists and the Baptists, which in the middle eighties were said to have "very nearly a monopoly of church membership" in eight Southern states. "In Alabama and Mississippi the members of these two sects . . . [made up] 95 per cent. of the total church membership; in Georgia, 94 per cent.; in Florida, 93; in South Carolina, 91; in North Carolina, 86; in Virginia, 81"—this, as compared with a little over 47 per cent accounted for by the two sects in church membership of the nation as a whole. Thus the Methodists and Baptists had about twice the relative strength in the South that they had in the whole country.[83]

Edwin A. Alderman, president of the University of Virginia, contended that "The fancied home of the cavalier is the home of the nearest approach to puritanism and to the most vital protestant evangelicalism in the world to-day." [84]

80 Warner, *Studies in the South and West,* 32; New York *Tribune,* March 11, 1881.

81 Farish, *Circuit Rider Dismounts,* 69, 74–76.

82 Nashville *Daily American,* June 6, 1887; Jackson *Clarion,* April 28, 1886.

83 *Nation,* XLI (1885), 211.

84 Edwin A. Alderman, *The Growing South* (New York, 1908), 20.

Further evidence of the strength of Southern puritanism—or perhaps, more accurately, the surrender to the middle class—was the increase of blue laws, and restrictions of various sorts aimed at the saloon, the prize fight, and what a leading Methodist journal called "one of the antechambers of hell," the theater. Even before the Civil War all the Southern states except Virginia and Tennessee had experimented with local prohibition of saloons through special state legislation, a method peculiar to the South. In 1874 Arkansas, Kentucky, and North Carolina, and in 1876, Texas, supplemented their special laws with general local-option laws for townships. The eighties saw a burst of prohibition activity. This took the form of general county local-option laws in Arkansas, Florida, Georgia, Louisiana, Mississippi, and North Carolina, and local option for townships in South Carolina and Virginia. "Blind tiger" and "scientific temperance education" laws were becoming popular.[85] An editor in sinful New Orleans might denounce "the Medieval bigotry and religious tyranny" of Sunday blue laws in adjacent states, but it is the conclusion of a scholar that Sabbath observance prevailed "to a greater extent in the South than in any other section." [86]

The rupture between North and South had come earliest in the great Protestant sects, and there it was slowest to heal. The Northern branches sought to imitate the state during Reconstruction in using force to effect union, sometimes seizing Southern churches and their funds by force. They were bitterly and effectively resisted by Southern churchmen. The Northern "connections" then established their own churches in the South and the struggle continued. "We claim the South," declared the New York *Christian Advocate* in 1879, "because the Republic which we have recently saved by Methodist conscience and Methodist bayonets, now demands at our hands another salvation by Methodist ideas and faith." Missionaries established Northern journals in the South, one of which in New Orleans based its right to leadership on the theory "that New England has developed a stronger arm, a more active

[85] Leonard S. Blakey, *The Sale of Liquor in the South,* in Columbia University *Studies in History, Economics and Public Law,* LI, Whole No. 127 (New York, 1912), 12, and Table I, 39.

[86] New Orleans *Times-Democrat,* November 8, 1895; Farish, *Circuit Rider Dismounts,* 340.

brain, a greater love of freedom, and a higher form of civilization." Another in Atlanta announced in 1881: "There is a struggle now going on as to the character of the Methodism of the future in this section. Shall it be under American or Southern ideas? This is the bone of contention between us and the Southern Church." [87]

As a result of the continuation of a temporal struggle on an ecclesiastical plane, and of the clerical championship of the Southern cause after the surrender and defection of its secular defenders, the Southern churches became for a time centers of resistance to the invasion of Northern culture. "All through the South," noted a Northern observer in 1881, "the ministers appear to view 'progress' with a degree of alarm, and certainly with decided reprobation. I should say that Southern ministers very generally appear to feel instinctively that it brings new dangers to religious institutions." [88] The attitude was expressed in the leading religious journals. "Let us have a rest on this sort of talk we have had about the New South," demanded one. "It begins to sound like cant. It seems to cast unjust reproaches upon the dead." And again, "When Mammonism thus possesses the people they soon become prepared to make almost any concession of moral principle to the demands of commercial expediency. . . . Cursed be the wealth which comes to us at such a price! Blessed be the poverty which gives us immunity from such temptations." [89] A churchman of Chapel Hill, warning the flock against "the perils in the New South," wrote, "Nothing is surer than that much of the lauded change in the South consists mainly in the *money-mania*. . . . The standard of character erected by the blatant portion of the New South—that portion that reviles the Old South—is the *brazen* standard of money making." [90]

For a time the churches showed a disposition to take up cudgels against "mammonism" in its secular entrenchments. "Nearly all the necessaries of life," affirmed the Nashville *Christian Advocate*, in 1888, "are now controlled by 'the trusts,' even to the medicine for the healing of the sick, the oil that feeds the light. . . . Noth-

[87] Quoted in Farish, *Circuit Rider Dismounts*, 108–109, 117–18. For evidence of a similar struggle in the Presbyterian Church, see Thomas Cary Johnson, *The Life and Letters of Benjamin Morgan Palmer* (Richmond, 1906), 440, 457, 472–74.

[88] New York *Tribune*, March 11, 1881.

[89] Nashville *Christian Advocate*, March 5, 26, 1887.

[90] A. W. Mangum, letter, *ibid.*, May 14, 1887.

ing escapes the extortion of these worst publicans the world ever saw." [91] Increasingly, however, as the churches, with their huge publishing houses, their large investments in colleges, universities, and schools, and their private endowments became vested interests, and as they became dependent upon the "publicans" North and South—the tobacco trust, for example, and various Northern philanthropic endowments—the earlier tendency faded. The "blessed poverty" that gives "immunity from temptations" seemed less important than a suitable endowment. Old-fashioned sins, like that of the bottle, came to absorb the attention of the churches with crusades for temperance and prohibition. Presidents of handsomely endowed church universities, and publications, such as the *Biblical Recorder* of the North Carolina Baptists, became defenders of the trusts. Publicans and sinners of the newer type had less to fear from ecclesiastical wrath in later years, and the New Order and its standards and values received little more criticism from the clergy than it had from the writers.

In the dustbins of the eighties—where the eighties hastily swept them—are the remains of an elaborately reasoned critique of the Brave New South. The critique was identified with the Lost Cause, since the men who proclaimed it, men like Robert L. Dabney of Virginia and Charles Colcock Jones of Georgia, wore the uniform of the Confederacy and spoke in its name and memory. The doctrines they pronounced, however, like the style in which they pronounced them, were closer to the eighteenth than to the nineteenth century, closer to Thomas Jefferson than to Jefferson Davis. They were more like the polemics of John Taylor of Caroline against the Federalists than those of Robert Barnwell Rhett against the Abolitionists. They linked "plutocracy" and "communism" in a way Taylor would have understood, and spat the word "privilege" with his special vehemence. They regarded huge cities not as "metropolitan and unprejudiced" but as "sores on the body politic." They were unimpressed by the splendors of the "new equality": "the regal luxury of a Vanderbilt, in his gaudy palace, beside the hireling laborer in his sordid tenement-lodging, who is his theoretical EQUAL!" Nor did they fancy the new "free enterprise": "Capital is collected in commanding masses, at whose bidding the free-holding citizen is sunk into the multitudinous hire-

[91] Quoted in Farish, *Circuit Rider Dismounts*, 334.

ling proletariat." Nor the "free press": "Its sheets come up, like the frogs of Egypt, into our houses, our bed chambers, our very kneading troughs . . . a deluge of perversions . . . the creatures of money." As for the great twin gods Mass and Speed, they were really demons in disguise, and would end by swallowing their foolish worshipers. These gentry were, in short, more old-fashioned than the Lost Cause itself: they were not only incorrigibly "unprogressive," they were "reactionary," and Walter Hines Page would have pronounced them "mummies" without a moment's hesitation.[92]

In his address "The New South," Robert L. Dabney, Stonewall Jackson's chief of staff and biographer, warned against the "special temptations to which a subjugated people are exposed while passing of necessity under a new and conquering system," particularly the temptation "to become like your conquerors." He said: "I hear our young men quote to each other the advice of the wily diplomat Gortstschacoff to the beaten French: 'Be strong.' They exclaim: Let us develope! develope! develope! Let us have like our conquerors, great cities, great capitalists, great factories and commerce and great populations; then we shall cope with them. . . . To exclaim as so many do of factories, and mines, and banks, and stock boards, and horse-powers of steam, and patent machines, 'These be thy gods, O Israel!' This would be a deadly mistake."

Never, of course, was there the remotest chance of Dabney's goose quill prevailing against the clattering presses of Grady and Dawson, Tompkins and Edmonds. Anyway, the New South had no ear for pessimism—not with Georgia boasting eleven millionaires in 1892, and Kentucky twenty-four, and New Orleans alone thirty-five![93] Not with Edmonds proclaiming that throughout "the real South"—the urbanized, capitalistic South—could be heard "a continuous and unbroken strain of what has been termed 'the music of progress—the whirr of the spindle, the buzz of the saw, the roar of the furnace and the throb of the locomotive.'" Not until the New South was confronted by the Populists did it meet with a challenge that set it back on its heels for a spell.

[92] Robert L. Dabney, *The New South. A Discourse* . . . (Raleigh, 1883), *passim;* Charles C. Jones, Jr., *The Old South. Addresses Delivered before the Confederate Survivors Association* (Augusta, Ga., 1887), *passim;* John Donald Wade, "Old Wine in a New Bottle," in *Virginia Quarterly Review* (University, Va.), XI (1935), 239–52.

[93] Shugg, *Origins of Class Struggle in Louisiana,* 291 and note.

CHAPTER VII

THE UNREDEEMED FARMER

SIDNEY LANIER consulted the census reports when, in 1880, he undertook to define "The New South." The result was a vision of beauty. "The New South means small farming," he announced, and quoted statistics to prove it. Had the returns of 1880 been available to the poet, he could have buttressed his thesis with even more startling evidence—of its kind. It would then appear that since 1860 the number of Southern "farms" had more than doubled, while the average "farm" had been cut to less than half its size in that year. To Lanier this "quiet rise of the small farmer" seemed to be "the notable circumstance of the period, in comparison with which noisier events signify nothing." For, he explained, "Small farming means, in short, meat and bread for which there are no notes in bank; pigs fed with home-made corn . . . yarn spun, stockings knit, butter made and sold (instead of bought); eggs, chickens . . . products of natural animal growth, and grass at nothing a ton." [1]

It was an inspired vision, and it represented everything that the Southern farmer was *not* and *had not*. But the vision was made of the tough stuff of myths and was destined to endure. The new myth fulfilled the old Jeffersonian dream of an independent yeomanry, self-sufficient lords of a few acres. Later elaborations pictured this yeomanry "breaking up the plantation system," or "wiping out the last vestige of the planting aristocracy," and vindicating the Civil War as the bringer of "economic democracy" to the South. "Emancipation freed the poor whites more than it did the Negro!" This cliché was heard so often that it came to be repeated even by re-

[1] Sidney Lanier, "The New South," in *Retrospects and Prospects* (New York, 1899), 104–105, 110–11.

spected Southern historians and is still a favorite generalization of modern textbooks, one of which goes so far as to compare the liberation of the poor white man by the Civil War with that of the peasants by the French Revolution. Out of this tissue of theory was spun that curious postulate "The Rise of the Poor Whites"—an expression that, as one writer has pointed out, "reduces to a paradox the problem it was coined to describe." [2]

From time to time the oracles of the New Order took turns at instructing their country cousins. The farmer's "provincialism," his "unprogressive outlook," and his "unscientific methods" were deplored. He was given lectures on what was once called the American System—the putative dependence of the farmer's prosperity on the rise of big cities. It was generally agreed that he was behind the times. A Vanderbilt professor advised him to "recognize that farming is a 'business' also, requiring 'business' talents," and a city Congressman exhorted him to strive for a "liberalized state of mind" freed from "narrow local concerns." A Louisiana farmer complained "that it has become fashionable for every quill driver in the land to inform us, 'that we are not abreast of the age, that we don't know how to farm.' " [3]

Poring over the proceedings of the agricultural societies of Louisiana, Alabama, and Virginia, one comes to the conclusion that while the farmer became increasingly vocal about his wretched plight, he did not, during the decade following Redemption, seriously question the philosophy of the New Order that was dinned into his ears from the cities. There were occasional rumblings. An upland farmer of South Carolina growled, " 'Northern brains and capital' as the phrase goes. They want to civilize us from without, not from within, and all must confess it has been thus far a most lamentable failure." [4] But the rule was submission, until the coming of the Farmers' Alliance.

Meanwhile the prophets of the New South were hard put to it

[2] Shugg, *Origins of Class Struggle in Louisiana*, 275–76. See also, *ibid.*, 235–37, on "Survival of the Plantation System."

[3] W. S. Frierson, in *Proceedings of the Fourth Annual Session of the* [Louisiana] *State Agricultural Society . . . 1890* (Baton Rouge, 1890), 6.

[4] Benjamin R. Tillman to the editor, Charleston *News and Courier*, December 7, 1885.

to explain where the farmers, the great mass of the population, fitted into the New Order, and why it was that as the cities rose the country seemed to decline. Even Pig-Iron Kelley admitted that "apart from the New South, by which I mean the country around the region of the rapidly developing iron industries . . . the same wretched poverty prevails among the Southern people now, twenty-two years after the close of the war." [5]

Evidence in abundance was at hand to substantiate Kelley's impressions. In Alabama a planter reported that "want and gaunt, haggard despair have prevailed everywhere in the Black Belt" of Alabama; in Louisiana a farmer pointed to "old fields abandoned in every direction" that he had seen cleared as a boy on the frontier as rich new land; in Mississippi, there was a poverty-driven exodus from the farm "so strong and wide as to threaten whole sections of our country with desolation"; in Virginia, Colonel Robert Beverley declared that "since the Red man left us tobacco-seed the farming interest has not been so depressed." [6] "You Richmond affluents," said Beverley later, "know but little more than the New York money kings, what is the trouble among the masses." [7]

Pig-Iron Kelley pronounced the farmer's plight "the result of fatally vicious economic and agricultural theories," such as free trade, or fell back on the theory that "the 'poor whites,' 'the low downs,' 'the clay eaters,' and 'the crackers' of the old South" still had to be civilized.[8] With greater patience and often with genuine concern, Southern spokesmen of the New Order explained the condition of the farmer by his failure to practice diversified or scientific agriculture. There were some explanations that did not contribute to the cause of reconciliation and were customarily passed over by the New-South school. One of them was the enduring effect of devastation and pillage by invading armies. The loss of every third horse or mule and almost half the agricultural machinery in the South meant reduction in productivity and in some

[5] Kelley, *Old South and the New*, 121.

[6] *Proceedings of the Fourth Annual Session of the Alabama State Agricultural Society* (1888), 35–36; *Proceedings of the Second Annual Session of the* [Louisiana] *State Agricultural Society . . . 1888* (Baton Rouge, 1888), 37; Jackson *Clarion*, December 10, 1884; Robert Beverley, in Richmond *Dispatch*, January 11, 1888.

[7] Quoted in Richmond *Virginia Sun*, May 18, 1892.

[8] Kelley, *Old South and the New*, 121.

states reduction in the acreage cultivated. Two mules and one plow could not do the work of three mules and two plows.[9]

As for the celebrated breakup of the old plantations into democratic small farms, which so captivated the fancy of Lanier and many others, the statistics did not mean all they seemed to mean. The census figures indicated that in the nine large cotton-planting states, Alabama, Arkansas, Georgia, Louisiana, Mississippi, North Carolina, South Carolina, Tennessee, and Texas, the size of the average "farm" declined from 347 acres in 1860 to 156 acres in 1880. In the same states during that period the number of farms increased from 449,936 to 1,110,294, a total increase of 660,358 farms, and more than 17,430,000 acres were added to the amount of land in farms. What is likely to be overlooked is the rapid rise of sharecropping. By 1880 sharecroppers cultivated 301,738 of the farms in the nine states.[10]

Henry Grady observed in 1881 that the planters were "still lords of acres, though not of slaves." [11] Although considerable redistribution of land ownership did take place, the parceling-out of plantation lands in small plots among croppers was more a reflection of the revolution in the labor system than it was a revolution in land tenure. Under the sharecropping system the plantations were worked by families instead of by gangs. Yet each "cut" of land assigned to a sharecropper constituted a "farm" within the definition under which the census marshals worked. The consequence was that the persistence of the plantation pattern, particularly in the Black Belt, tended to be obscured. In one Louisiana parish, for example, the census taker found 171 farms of less than 20 acres in 1890, although the local tax assessor could find only 19 taxpayers with holdings that small.[12] A study of the manuscript tax-assessment rolls in representative areas of Louisiana has indicated that the plantation in that state "not only survived but also expanded after the Civil War," that while the number of farms actually decreased between 1860 and 1880, "there was nearly a

[9] James L. Sellers, "The Economic Incidence of the Civil War in the South," in *Mississippi Valley Historical Review* (Cedar Rapids), XIV (1927–1928), 183–89.

[10] *Tenth Census, 1880,* III, *Statistics of Agriculture,* 25.

[11] Henry W. Grady, "Cotton and Its Kingdom," in *Harper's New Monthly Magazine* (New York), LXIII (1881), 722.

[12] Shugg, *Origins of Class Struggle in Louisiana,* 236.

threefold increase in the number of plantations" in the same period, and that whereas the state "had contained more farms than plantations in 1860, it was dominated by agrarian monopoly in 1900." [13] Finally recognizing the need for more realistic definitions for peculiar conditions in the South, census officials in 1910 authorized a special study of 325 Black-Belt counties in the eleven states of the old Confederacy. When that was completed it was revealed that more than one third of the landholdings in the area studied were organized in "tenant plantations," and the average size of these estates was 724 acres, or more than six times the average size of holdings reported in 1900 for all holdings.[14]

To say that plantations of a sort were preserved and enlarged is not to say that the ante-bellum planter was preserved also. The ante-bellum planter of Louisiana whose plantation remained in his family after 1880 was rather the exception than the rule. In the Sugar Bowl there was a veritable "revolution in land titles" resulting increasingly in "a new, capitalistic sugar aristocracy, organized in corporations and financed by banks"; and "At least half the planters after 1870 were either Northern men or were supported by Northern money." [15] F. C. Morehead, President of the National Cotton Planters' Association, estimated in 1881 that not one third of the cotton plantations of the Mississippi Valley were "owned by the men who held them at the end of the war," and that others were daily passing "into the hands of the commission merchants" at that time.[16]

Moreover, the survival and expansion of the plantation did not mean the preservation of the ante-bellum "plantation system." It was often the plantation without system, at least in cotton culture —the plantation minus such scant efficiency, planning, responsible supervision, and soil conservation as the old system provided. It was minus the ordinary minimum of economic virtues associated with proprietorship, for the plantation was usually minus even an owner

[13] *Ibid.*, 235–40.

[14] A "tenant plantation" was defined as "a continuous tract of land of considerable area under the general supervision or control of a single individual or firm," all or part of which was leased to at least five tenants. *Thirteenth Census, 1910*, V, *Agriculture*, 878.

[15] Shugg, *Origins of Class Struggle in Louisiana*, 248–49.

[16] Quoted in Grady, "Cotton and Its Kingdom," *loc. cit.*, 727.

who lived on its soil and spent the profits of another's labor on his own family. The evils of land monopoly, absentee ownership, soil mining, and the one-crop system, once associated with and blamed upon slavery, did not disappear with that institution but were, instead, aggravated, intensified, and multiplied.

The key to the New Order in agriculture was the lien system, said by an authority to have "been the main feature of southern agriculture since the war, as slavery was previous thereto." [17] In fact, it came to be more widespread than slavery had been, for it was no respecter of race or class; and if it be judged objectively, by its economic results alone, the new evil may have worked more permanent injury to the South than the ancient evil.

The lien system was one of those growths, like the convict lease and sharecropping, that sprang up out of ruins of the old regime, and spread like Jimson weed, a curse to the soil. It was not a plot but a makeshift. The Mississippi law of February 18, 1867, entitled with unconscious irony "Act for Encouraging Agriculture," authorized the pledging of crops to merchants for future supplies and provided summary means of enforcement. The farmer had to have credit or starve, and there was no other means of getting credit. The system did hold together with financial bailing wire the shattered machinery of Southern agriculture—liberated slave, bankrupt planter, and supply merchant—in sufficient co-ordination to support life, but it represented one of the strangest contractual relationships in the history of finance. The seeker of credit usually pledged an unplanted crop to pay for a loan of unstipulated amount at a rate of interest to be determined by the creditor. Credit was advanced in the form of supplies—pork, plowpoints, calico, hay—to the extent the merchant considered safely covered by the probable crop. The "interest rate" was greatly augmented by the price charged on the goods, and the universal practice was a two-price system, the cash price and the credit price. The latter price was always higher, "never less than thirty per cent., and frequently runs up to seventy per cent.," said Grady, though reports vary widely (as did the extent of usury).[18] Quoting a report to Parliament accus-

[17] Matthew B. Hammond, *The Cotton Industry; An Essay in American Economic History* (New York, 1897), 122.

[18] Grady, "Cotton and Its Kingdom," *loc. cit.,* 723; Birmingham *Weekly Iron Age,* December 4, 1884.

ing an English creditor of charging an Irish peasant of Connaught an interest rate of 43.5 per cent, a Federal judge asked the Arkansas State Bar Association in 1886, "What is 43½ per cent. compared to the profits charged by the holders of anaconda mortgages on tenants in Arkansas? They would scorn 43½ per cent." [19]

His critics asked why the farmer did not bargain for better terms with other merchants. But once a lien was executed to one merchant no competitor would sell the farmer so much as a side of fat back, except for cash, since the only acceptable security, his crop, had been forfeited. "The lien credit almost destroyed competition," according to one authority.[20] While the farmer was buying in the highest market, moreover, he was selling in the lowest market, for normally he did not control the marketing of his own crop or "hold" it for better prices. If that was done, it was done by the furnishing merchant, who paid the farmer "inside" prices when it was gathered. Under this arrangement it was not surprising when, at the end of the season, the farmer was told he had not "paid out." His contract then bound him to renew the lien on his next crop under the same merchant. "When one of these mortgages has been recorded against the southern farmer," wrote Matthew B. Hammond, "he has usually passed into a state of helpless peonage. . . . With the surrender of this evidence of indebtedness he has also surrendered his freedom of action and his industrial autonomy. From this time until he has paid the last dollar of his indebtedness, he is subject to the constant oversight and direction of the merchant. Every mouthful of food he purchases, every implement that he requires on the farm, his mules, cattle, the clothing for himself and family, the fertilizers for his land, must all be bought of the merchant who holds the crop lien, and in such amounts as the latter is willing to allow." [21]

19 Quoted in Cable, *Southern Struggle for Pure Government,* 16. See also, Thomas D. Clark, "The Furnishing and Supply System in Southern Agriculture since 1865," in *Journal of Southern History,* XII (1946), 27–31.

20 Thomas D. Clark, "Imperfect Competition in the Southern Retail Trade after 1865," in *Journal of Economic History* (New York), III (*Supplement,* December, 1943), 40.

21 Hammond, *Cotton Industry,* 149. See also, George K. Holmes, "The Peons of the South," in *Annals of the American Academy of Political and Social Science* (Philadelphia), IV (1893–1894), 265–74; Charles H. Otken, *The Ills of the South* (New York, 1894), 17–19, 68; Robert P. Brooks, *The Agrarian Revolution in Georgia, 1865–1912* (Madison, 1914), 32–36.

It was sometimes said that this economic nightmare in which the Southern farmer writhed could have been dispelled had he only waked up. If he did not, was it not another evidence of "Southern indolence," or perhaps of the degeneracy of the poor white? Why, for example, did he stupidly cling to the one-crop system?

It is true that the Southern farmer bought Indiana hay, Milwaukee flour, and Chicago bacon—all of which in Lanier's vision grew in his own back yard "at nothing a ton." South Carolina raised 15,000,000 bushels of corn in 1860 and only 11,700,000 in 1880, while in the same period her hay crop declined from 87,000 tons to 2,700, but her cotton crop increased from 353,000 bales to 522,000. "Let . . . the soil be worn out, let the people move to Texas . . . , let almost anything happen provided all possible cotton is produced each year." [22] Part of the trouble was traditionalism and the inertia of habit, as critics of the one-crop system charged, but the critics overlooked factors that were of equal importance. Some of these were lack of markets or of marketing and storage facilities, and of adequate roads and transportation that would have permitted or encouraged diversification of crops.[23] Critics also forgot that the farmer was rarely a free agent. "Cotton raising has grown to be a necessity more than a choice," an Alabama farmer told a Senate committee. The farmer was "forced to raise it to get credit." [24] Cotton was "the" cash crop and together with the other cash crops the only security upon which the furnishing merchant would advance credit. "The majority of cotton growers," wrote an economist in the nineties, "including the greater part of the tenant farmers and small land owners, as well as some of the large planters, are bound to cotton by a law as inexorable as any ever promulgated by the most despotic earthly governments." [25] Annual production of the cash crops eventually doubled or trebled ante-bellum records, and to the present day the swelling totals in bales and hogsheads are cited as proof of the superiority of the new system. They were proof instead of the greater enslavement of the one-crop system.

[22] Ulrich B. Phillips, "Conservation and Progress in the Cotton Belt," in *South Atlantic Quarterly*, III (1904), 5–6.

[23] Clark, "Furnishing and Supply System," *loc. cit.*, 34–39.

[24] *Report of the Committee on Agriculture and Forestry on Condition of Cotton Growers*, in *Senate Reports*, 53 Cong., 3 Sess., No. 986, Pt. I, 317.

[25] Hammond, *Cotton Industry*, 195.

If credit was the core of the problem, why could not the Southern farmer resort to a simple mortgage as did the Northern farmer, instead of using the crop lien? A Mississippi merchant answered that one: "Merchants can't furnish goods on property that would be an incumbrance to own," he said, referring to farm lands. "Unless they can get some guarantee of receiving crops for supplies, the supplies will remain in New Orleans." [26] This, and not the more optimistic inference sometimes suggested, was the reason for the somewhat lower number of Southern than Western farms under mortgage.

Then why not a businesslike arrangement with the banks? Unfortunately, the Southern farm vote was not as influential in Congress when the new bank policy was adopted in 1862 as it had been in the debates of 1832, and the National Banking Act was framed during the Civil War to fit the convenience of Northern and nonagricultural interests. In 1895, when there was in the whole country one bank to every 16,600 inhabitants, there was in the cotton states, excluding Texas, only one to every 58,130. One hundred and twenty-three counties in Georgia in 1894 were without an incorporated bank of any kind, state or national.[27]

In several states there were efforts to repeal or amend the lien laws, but that fight did not come to grips with the real issue. The struggle as it developed in Mississippi, Alabama, and South Carolina, for example, lay primarily between the merchants and the planters for control over the planters' own lands and tenants, with the tenants artificially aligned with the merchants against repeal. It was the planter's object, generally, to obtain some measure of control over the mortgaging of crops grown by tenants on his own land. The merchant opposition insisted on "freedom of contract" for the tenant. Thus one Mississippi planter, calling the lien law "extortion, genteel swindling, legitimate larceny," denounced it as a "plan of dealing which shut out the landowner as an insignificant factor. . . . The negro and poor white men of the country made nothing; the factors and the country merchant were the divinities presiding over the agricultural interests . . . ; the land-

26 A. H. F. to editor, Jackson *Clarion*, December 15, 1886.

27 Hammond, *Cotton Industry*, 160; George L. Anderson, "The South and Problems of Post-Civil War Finance," in *Journal of Southern History*, IX (1943), 181–95.

owners were out in the cold ignored even by their tenants; lands were being worn out." [28] The lien system had, in fact, divorced landownership from its age-old prerogatives. The tenant, for his part, powerless in any case, seemed to prefer the more remote and irresponsible control of the lien-merchant peonage to the immediate control of the planter. Thus a Negro paper of Alabama, speaking "in the interest of the poor tenants," asked of the planter: "Does he want to prohibit the tenant from a choice of supplying himself, and force a dependence on him alone? This is what will result from the repeal. The poor laborer will then be turned away by all merchants and must meekly depend for all advances on the landlord, who could then dictate what terms as he pleased." [29]

In the earlier years of the rise of the supply merchant, this class seems to have been of less indigenous origin than later.[30] A strong tendency early asserted itself, however, for merchant and planter to become one—that is, for the merchant to acquire the farms of the hapless landowner, and for the more fortunate planters to move to town and become supply merchants. In fact, the latter were almost driven to this if they remained planters. Thus the conflict between these two classes was resolved in their tendency to merge. Absentee ownership with its multiple evils was thus increased, and the lien system was more deeply entrenched than ever.[31]

It would be a mistake to make the supply merchant the villain in the piece. He has long been accused of sharp practices, and certainly the opportunity for them was not lacking. A historian who has checked numerous accounts in old books, however, reports "remarkably few errors," and those were "minor slips in bookkeeping rather than intentional manipulation." The prices and interest rates were exorbitant, but so were the risks the merchant took. Nor did he pocket the take of his till. He in turn paid outrageous rates of interest to factors, who paid their tributes to the ultimate lords of credit. The merchant was only a bucket on an endless chain by

[28] "N" in Jackson *Weekly Clarion,* April 30, 1879. For revealing insight on this problem, see letters from merchants, planters, and small farmers in the *Clarion,* October 17, November 14, 1883; October 7, 14, November 18, 1885; March 3, December 15, 1886; also editorial in Charleston *News and Courier,* June 18, 1890.

[29] Huntsville *Gazette,* December 16, 1882.

[30] New York *Tribune,* May 23, 1881.

[31] Alex M. Arnett, *The Populist Movement in Georgia,* in Columbia University *Studies in History, Economics and Public Law,* CIV, No. 1 (New York, 1922), 53.

which the agricultural well of a tributary region was drained of its flow.[32]

The Southern farmer was thus heir to a combination of special sectional disadvantages and deprivations. The threefold revolution in labor, land tenure, and credit, together with the heritage of military defeat and pillage, would have been enough to keep generations of Southern farmers in a slough of depression. But heaped on top of these exclusively regional shackles were virtually all those burdens that eventually drove the Western farmer to outright revolt in alliance with the South. If these additional grievances receive less attention here than the special regional ones, it is only because they are more familiar as a part of the national story.

The steady, year-by-year drop in crop prices was the farmer's most obvious and inescapable grievance. If the Western farmer found bankruptcy written in the decline of corn from an average market price of 40.9 cents a bushel between 1874 and 1877 to an average of 29.7 cents between 1894 and 1897, the Southern farmer read even worse disaster in the decline of cotton from 11.1 to 5.8 cents a pound over the same periods, for while the price of corn was declining 32.8 per cent, the price of cotton dropped 47.7 per cent.[33] Nor does the "market price," as of December 1, represent the price received by the farmer, who had to sell his crop much earlier, when the market was glutted and the price was much lower. Neither do the quoted prices take into account the frequent deductions for bales of inferior quality, for warehouse charges, and for dealers' commissions, nor the generally helpless bargaining position of the farmer in relation to the lien merchant who actually marketed his crops. The farmer got less for the 23,687,950 acres he planted in cotton in 1894 than for the 9,350,000 acres of 1873. The crop of 1894 broke all records, but the "farm price" was 4.6 cents a pound as compared with 14.1 cents in the panic year 1873.[34] In plain words, under the new system he had to work more than twice as long for the same pay. If the "general consensus of opinion" was correct "that cotton can not, except under the most favorable

[32] Clark, "Furnishing and Supply System," *loc. cit.*, 26, 43–44.

[33] Department of Agriculture statistics, in John D. Hicks, *The Populist Revolt; A History of the Farmers' Alliance and the People's Party* (Minneapolis, 1931), 56.

[34] Fred A. Shannon, *The Farmer's Last Frontier, Agriculture, 1860–1897* (New York, 1945), 114, 415.

circumstances, be raised profitably at less than 8 cents per pound, nor without loss under 7 cents," [35] then a majority of the cotton farmers in the late eighties and through most of the nineties were actually operating at a loss. In general, tobacco prices followed the same downward trend, and the Virginia and Carolina farmers found that "tobacco proved as vulnerable as any other product" to the world-wide agricultural depression.[36]

As a chronic debtor the farmer had more to suffer from the national contraction of currency than did any comparable interest. His embittered complaint was that as the price of his crops declined by half, the value of his debts in terms of bales and bushels sometimes doubled. In their attack upon the national banking system the agrarian economists were on solid ground in contending that private privilege was exercising a sovereign power, the power of regulating national currency, for private gain rather than for meeting the needs of the country.

The protective tariff, like national currency and banks, was not a new concern of agrarian politics in the South, but also, like those two problems, the tariff menace to the region's welfare had loomed vastly larger since the restraining combination of South and West had been broken during the Civil War, and tariff rates had mounted higher and higher. The immemorial pattern of colonialism—the dependence upon the sale of cheap raw materials on a world market and upon buying back manufactured goods from protected industrial and commercial areas—continued to hold sway in the South despite the much-vaunted "industrial revolution." Everywhere it was the pattern for poverty. As a producer and seller the farmer was subject to all the penalties of free trade, while as a consumer he was deprived of virtually all its benefits. It did not soften his resentment to reflect that out of his meager returns was extracted the tribute that built up the monopolies he hated.

If Southern agrarians were never able to convince the Western farmers of the seriousness of the tariff oppression, the sectional allies were of one mind on many other common oppressions—the trusts,

[35] *Report of the Committee on Agriculture and Forestry on Condition of Cotton Growers,* in *Senate Reports,* 53 Cong., 3 Sess., No. 986, Pt. I, iv.

[36] Tilley, *Bright-Tobacco Industry,* price table on pp. 353–56. See also, *ibid.,* 367–72, 405.

for example. While the Westerner complained most bitterly of such combinations as the beef trust, the Southerner was more acutely aware of the jute-bagging trust, the cottonseed-oil trust, the tobacco trust, the fertilizer trust. He believed that the prices he paid for many necessities were no more fixed by competition among domestic manufacturers than they were between domestic and foreign manufacturers. Instead, they were fixed by pools, monopolies, trusts, and combines, who levied tribute on his machinery and tools, his fuel, his food, his clothing. Southeastern railroads were members of a pool that fixed rates and discriminations against agricultural shippers quite as ruthlessly as did the pools and combinations against which the West took up arms, and with even less interference from state commissions and legislation. These same railroads, along with Northern lumber speculators, insurance companies, and English syndicates monopolized millions of acres of Southern land, while the sons of families that had owned their farms for generations sank into the ranks of tenants and sharecroppers.

When 606,674 acres of farm land were flooded by the Mississippi in 1882, relief was not forthcoming from the government. In 1886 and 1887 an "unprecedented drought" lasting twenty-one months in twenty-five or more counties of western Texas plunged 30,000 people into destitution and sent thousands of them reeling back from the frontier. Congress voted a paltry amount for seed loans as a gesture of relief, and Cleveland, their Democratic President, promptly vetoed the bill. Yet Federal generosity to railroads and land speculators was notorious, and Southern state legislatures advertised in the North their eagerness to hand out liberal franchises, subsidies, and exemptions to manufacturers and railroads. In the meantime, upon the backs of the farmers "fell the burden of taxation, out of all proportion to the value of their property or their ability to pay." [87]

It was little wonder that in 1886 Darden of Mississippi, National Master of the Grange, found that his followers did not "work with that spirit and animation that characterizes a hopeful people," [88] or that Benjamin R. Tillman the same year complained bitterly of a "fatal lethargy" among the farmers of his state in which "our

[87] Arnett, *Populist Movement in Georgia*, 72.

[88] Jackson *Clarion*, December 15, 1886.

minds become benumbed, deadened," [39] or that Thomas E. Watson spoke of a strange "apathy" among Georgia yeomen as they slipped deeper into peonage, "like victims of some horrid nightmare . . . powerless—oppressed—shackled." [40]

The annual defeat of the crop market and the tax collector, the weekly defeat of the town market and mounting debt, and the small, gnawing, daily defeats of crumbling barn and fence, encroaching sagebush and erosion, and one's children growing up in illiteracy —all added up to frustration. The experience bred a spirit of desperation and defiance in these people. "The basest fraud on earth is agriculture," wrote a Mississippi farmer, and then he said the most blasphemous thing ever spoken by one of Jefferson's "chosen people of God"—"No wonder Cain killed his brother. He was a tiller of the ground." [41]

Expressed in mass action, this spirit could break out in fits of insane violence like that at Delhi, Louisiana, where a mob of small farmers "rode into town and demolished the stores of I. Hirsch, S. Blum & Co., Casper Weil, and Mr. Rosenfield." They hoped thus "to cancel their indebtedness," they said.[42] If ever this frustration could be canalized into some plan of action that promised a way out of the morass, it would prove a force to reckon with.

The New-South romanticism had been largely eastern in origin, for it was from the seaboard states of Virginia, Georgia, and the Carolinas that the impulse toward industrialism, recantation, and speculation had been spread over the states to the westward. The agrarian resurgence eventually called forth in response, however, was definitely western in origin. It was from the southwestern and Gulf states of Texas, Louisiana, and Arkansas—especially from Texas—that agrarian radicalism, conducted by the Farmers' Alliance, was to electrify the eastern South.

The Southern Farmers' Alliance was organized by a group of small, frontier farmers of Lampasas County, Texas, who combined to protect themselves against foreign-owned land syndicates and cattle kings about 1875. The organization spread to a few ad-

39 Charleston *News and Courier,* April 30, 1886.

40 Notes for a speech, in Watson Papers.

41 Quoted in Ferguson, "Granger Movement in Mississippi," 5.

42 Jackson *Clarion-Ledger,* October 31, 1889. The incident, however, is not indicative of widespread antisemitism, for there seems to have been very little. Jewish supply merchants were quite common in the region in the period.

joining counties, but in the Greenback campaign of 1878 it split up and disbanded because of political dissension—a chronic disease of the Alliance that was apparently congenital. In 1879, however, a new Alliance was founded on the basis of a copy of the old constitution. At the first meeting "by a decisive vote, all party political features were struck out from the original Lampasas declaration of principles." The following year the "Farmers' State Alliance" was incorporated as "a secret benevolent association." It was later said by its official journal, the *Southern Mercury,* to have consisted in 1880 of "a few of the poorer class of farmers" in six or seven counties of western Texas.[43]

In the mid-eighties a new spirit took possession of the order that was manifested not only in expansion, but in an outburst of long-repressed radicalism. Locally, the county trade committees of the Alliance began to bring pressure to bear on furnishing merchants to exact better terms for the organized patronage of the farmers. Then, in August, 1886, a convention representing 2,700 suballiances from 84 counties met in Cleburne. In a stormy four-day session the convention adopted a new constitution and a series of "demands" calling for legislation against the great foreign and Northern land syndicates and for other laws forbidding speculation in crop futures, taxing and controlling railroads, establishing interstate-commerce regulation, and expanding the currency.[44]

The heritage of political timidity from Reconstruction days, the old taboo against political action on the part of farmers' organization that had kept the Grange in line and broken up the original Alliance in the seventies, had at last been defied. The city press, hitherto tolerant or mildly patronizing, now flamed up with violent denunciation. A Dallas paper called the Alliance "essentially re-

[43] *Southern Mercury* (Dallas), XII (January 5, 1893), 8; William L. Garvin and S. O. Daws, *History of the National Farmers' Alliance and Co-operative Union of America* (Jacksboro, Tex., 1887), 14–16; William L. Garvin, *History of the Grand State Farmers' Alliance of Texas* (Jacksboro, Tex., 1885); J. E. Bryan, *The Farmers' Alliance: Its Origin, Progress and Purposes* (Fayetteville, Ark., 1891), 4–6; W. Scott Morgan, *History of the Wheel and Alliance and the Impending Revolution* (Fort Scott, Kan., 1889), 281.

[44] C. W. Macune, "The Farmers' Alliance" (essay written in 1920, deposited in University of Texas Library, Austin), 4, 10–12; Bryan, *Farmers' Alliance,* 9; Ralph Smith, "The Farmers' Alliance in Texas, 1875–1900," in *Southwestern Historical Quarterly,* XLVIII (1944–1945), 346–69.

pugnant to the spirit, the traditions and the fundamental ideas of Democracy," since it was "dominated by the spirit of class legislation, class aggrandizement, class exclusiveness and class proscription." It was "scarcely less than treason to be indifferent to such a danger," declared the editor.[45] Within the order a large conservative element was similarly alarmed at the demands, on the ground that they represented "a political move." The suspicious minority met after the convention and organized an opposition Alliance that split the order. The malady that had killed the original order was again at work, and the Farmers' Alliance would probably have gone to pieces had it not been for the skillful work of a man then on the verge of a remarkable career—Dr. C. W. Macune.[46]

A tall, handsome figure, Macune was described as "well proportioned, stalwart, with black hair and eyes and moustache setting off a set of strong regular features." Born in Wisconsin in 1851, he was the son of a Canadian blacksmith and Methodist preacher of restless habits, who died on the trail to California when his son was a baby. The son was also versatile and restless, but ambitious, for although he had to go to work at ten, he found time to read law and practice medicine. He lived successively in California, Kansas, and finally Texas, where he settled about 1870.[47]

At the time of the political dissension that threatened to wreck the Texas Alliance, Macune was chairman of the executive committee of the order. By some means the resignation of the president was secured, and Macune became acting president. He called a meeting of the Alliance at Waco in January, 1887, and laid careful plans for a coup that would not only avert the threatened disaster to the Texas Alliance but unite its factions for campaigns and endeavors undreamed of in their official philosophy. At Waco there assembled some five hundred delegates, many of them with instructions that would have made reconciliation impossible. According to Macune, they were "primed and ready and determined to carry out their instructions; a stormy time seemed imminent." Not until

[45] Dallas *Morning News*, August 14, 1886.

[46] Robert Lee Hunt, *A History of Farmer Movements in the Southwest* (n.p., n.d.), 31–33; Macune, "Farmers' Alliance," 12–16.

[47] Annie L. Diggs, "The Farmers' Alliance and Some of Its Leaders," in *Arena* (Boston), V (1891–1892), 598–99; Hicks, *Populist Revolt*, 106–107; Montgomery *Advertiser*, May 6, 1892.

the second day of the turbulent convention, and then only when Macune "rebelled and absolutely refused to recognize any man until the object of the meeting was stated," did the bedlam subside. He then proceeded to dazzle the wrangling delegates with two visions—one, of economic salvation from the lien system by means of "one great giant enterprise" of co-operative buying and selling, and the other, of the expansion of the Alliance into a national organization. Electrified by Macune's speech the factions forgot their feuds, voted to consolidate with the Louisiana Farmers' Union, adopted a new constitution and a new name ("National Farmers' Alliance and Co-operative Union of America"), voted for the co-operative plan, and elected Macune president.[48]

The Alliance immediately sent forth organizers in teams—five men to Alabama, five to Mississippi, seven to Tennessee, three to Arkansas, two to Florida, and so on, to include all the cotton states, as well as Kentucky and Missouri. These Texas missionaries were whirlwinds of zeal. "Only the age that produced the Evangelical Alliance could have given to the religious world a Talmadge, a Moody, or a Sam Jones," said one of them.[49] From distant North Carolina an organizer reported to Texas headquarters that he had held twenty-seven meetings with farmers in Wake County and left twenty-seven suballiances; in twenty-one days he organized eleven more in Harnett, and in fourteen days he launched ten in Moore County. "The farmers seem like unto fruit—you can gather them by a gentle shake of the bush," he reported.[50] The Texans were amazed at their success. Hundreds of thousands flocked to the Alliance.

Not only had the "fruit" been ripened by intensified economic distress, but the way had been prepared for the national organizers by several local orders of independent origin. The Louisiana Farmers' Union that consolidated with the Alliance was only one of many. There were smaller ones like the North Carolina clubs and the Florida unions that threw in their lot with the Alliance.[51] None of these approached in strength and numbers the Agricul-

[48] Macune, "Farmers' Alliance," 16–18; Bryan, *Farmers' Alliance,* 11–16.

[49] Garvin and Daws, *National Farmers' Alliance,* 45.

[50] *Ibid.,* 49–50; Bryan, *Farmers' Alliance,* 11–16.

[51] James O. Knauss, "The Farmers' Alliance in Florida," in *South Atlantic Quarterly,* XXV (1926), 300–15.

tural Wheel, organized in Prairie County, Arkansas, in 1882. Union with the Brothers of Freedom, also of Arkansas, increased the membership to 40,000. The Wheel began a program of expansion to other states two years ahead of the Alliance, extending into Tennessee, Kentucky, Texas, Alabama, Mississippi, Missouri, Oklahoma, and Wisconsin. At its second national convention in November, 1887, the Wheel claimed a membership of half a million. Consolidation of the Wheel and the Alliance was officially agreed upon in December, 1888, and completed the following year.[52]

The power and prestige of the Alliance mounted and membership soared phenomenally. Probably the national officials had no very accurate check upon total membership, but the more conservative estimates placed the total well above a million and a quarter, and some claimed three million at the peak of the movement.

In addition there were reported to be 1,250,000 members of the Colored Farmers' National Alliance and Co-operative Union. Although the Southern Alliance drew the color line, its leaders emphasized the common cause of the races as farmers in all the fundamental aims of the order. The Colored Alliance also originated in Texas. The first group was organized at Houston in December, 1886, and during the years of rapid growth of the white Alliance the Colored Alliance spread with it into all the Southern states. According to President Leonidas L. Polk of the white Alliance, the Negro order was "an entirely distinct organization," although "most of its organizers are white." The Reverend R. M. Humphrey, a white Southerner, was "Superintendent" of the Colored Alliance and took the leading part in organizing it. The ritual and secret work of the order probably appealed to the Negro as much as it did to the white joiner. Although it is usually assumed that the Colored Alliance was a mere tool of the white order, there is considerable evidence of independence among the Negroes.[53]

The word "farmer" is laden with ambiguities that have made it a convenient disguise for a variety of interests. Who were the farm-

[52] Bryan, *Farmers' Alliance*, 21–27; Morgan, *Wheel and Alliance*, 62–64; *National Economist* (Washington), I (1889), 222–23; II (1889), 24–25.

[53] Leonidas L. Polk, quoted in Richmond *Dispatch*, August 19, 1891; *National Economist*, I (1889), 6–7.

ers of the Farmers' Alliance? The constitution adopted in 1888 included as eligible for membership only "a farmer, farm-laborer, country mechanic, country school teacher, country physician, country minister of the Gospel, and editor of strictly agricultural journals." [54] It was at least a pretty strictly "country" affair. Other provisions of the constitution and later "Working Bulletins" specifically excluded as "obnoxious to the Constitution" bankers or bank employees, railroad employers, lawyers, brokers, real-estate dealers, cotton buyers and salesmen, warehouse owners, and operators, and especially "any person who keeps a store, who buys or sells for gain," except those "under supervision of the order." Officials appear to have taken the rules seriously. A Virginia Alliance president went so far as to exclude anyone who was "engaged in farming and in addition thereto follows one of the above named occupations." [55]

But were the farmers predominantly landowners or tenants? This is a more difficult question. Information of this character has been found for only one state Alliance, that of South Carolina. Official figures reported that 54.88 per cent of the members were "engaged in farming and own their land," and that 30.71 per cent "engaged in farming but own no land." Other members were distributed among country doctors, ministers, teachers, and mechanics, the last composing 2.85 per cent of the members.[56] These proportions would seem to represent a fair cross section of the rural white population of the state. If landowners predominated, so did they still in the eighties among white farmers in most states —if by a narrow margin. The larger landowners, who were likely to be supply merchants as well as planters, were often excluded by the Alliance rules of membership. Whether the South Carolina picture was typical is not known, but one gets the impression that nonlandowners bulked larger in the Southwestern Alliances.

The Allianceman, like the Populist, was always more interest-conscious than class-conscious, and there was much to be said for the contention that in a struggle between an industrial capitalism

[54] *National Economist,* I (1889), 3.

[55] Mann Page to Charles H. Pierson, January 16, 1891, in Charles H. Pierson Papers (University of Virginia Library, Charlottesville).

[56] *National Economist,* I (1889), 156–57.

and a colonial agrarianism, farmers big and little were in the same boat. In the words of a South Carolina journalist, "The landowner was so poor and distressed that he forgot that he was a capitalist . . . so weary of hand and sick of spirit that he imagined himself in precisely the same plight as the hired man . . . and so the political blending of white landlord and white laboring man was complete." [57] "We are the mudsills!" declared an Alliance organizer to Georgia farmers, echoing a phrase Ben Tillman had used in South Carolina. "The idea seems to have obtained in the minds of thousands of farmers that every man's hand is against them," other organizers found, "and, hence, there is a kind of war spirit pervading their entire being." [58]

The national headquarters of the Alliance at Washington was a great powerhouse of doctrine, sending pulsations through the most obscure backwoods suballiance. The *National Economist,* a weekly journal begun in March, 1889, as the official organ of the national order, was ably edited by Dr. Macune and had a tremendous influence. Macune also headed the large Alliance publishing house that daily sent out "quantities of documents, pamphlets, reports and educational reform literature." Hundreds of state and local Alliance papers, penetrating the remotest corners, found hundreds of thousands of readers. In 1890 about one thousand of these papers were organized into the National Reform Press Association, the members of which could be suspended from the Alliance by the national president for deviation from the St. Louis platform in any detail.[59] In their references to the opposition press, which poured derision and misrepresentation upon the order, the Alliance leaders minced no words. The policies of such papers, the farmers were told, were "dictated by your monetary enemy, whose interests are just the opposite of yours." The most celebrated exponents of the New South were not spared. In 1890 a formal notice over the signature of President Polk was sent to all Alliances declaring a

[57] William W. Ball, "The Industrial Revolution in South Carolina," in *Sewanee Review,* XIX (1911), 131.

[58] Garvin and Daws, *National Farmers' Alliance,* xi–xii.

[59] Frank M. Drew, "The Present Farmers' Movement," in *Political Science Quarterly,* VI (1891), 310; Diggs, "Farmers' Alliance and Some of Its Leaders," *loc. cit.,* 598–99.

boycott upon papers that "shall seek to impair our strength or unity," and upon advertisers in such papers.[60]

In 1891 the Alliance was reported to have in the field 35,000 official lecturers, classified as national, state, district, county, and sub-alliance lecturers. The first three classes were salaried, and all were on the mailing list of the Lecture Bureau in Washington, which sent them every quarter outlines of "three different and distinct lectures (with full reference for all authorities cited)." There was also a Propaganda Committee to formulate policy. One gathers from yellowed pamphlets that the agrarian ideologists undertook to re-educate their countrymen from the ground up. Dismissing "history as taught in our schools" as "practically valueless," they undertook to write it over—formidable columns of it, from the Greeks down. With no more compunction they turned all hands to the revision of economics, political theory, law, and government.[61]

How well this matter was assimilated up the forks of the creek where the local "lodges" met twice a month is a subject for conjecture. Probably stronger than the appeal of statistics was the fascination of secret work and ritual that was a part of every meeting, not to mention the unusual opportunities for conviviality in districts socially undernourished. Women were eligible for membership, and it was through the Grange and the Farmers' Alliance that Southern women got their first real opportunity for direct participation in public life and politics. County, district, and state "conventions" were much-anticipated occasions. The Texas Alliance held one of its state conventions after crops were laid by, in the open country, camp-meeting fashion, "so that members from all over the state could come in their wagons with tents and enjoy a week's reunion." Delegates were urged to "bring along all the family, so that they may imbibe our principles." [62] If they imbibed anything else—all the merrier! But it is perfectly evident that the farmers drank deeply of old and tested vintages along with new ideas and strange, forbidden mixtures quite alien to the latitude of Possum Trot.

60 *National Economist,* IV (1890), 85.

61 *Ibid.,* V (1891), 34; VI (1891), 116.

62 *Southern Mercury,* XII (May 11, 1893), 8.

One of the most popular Alliance notions was that the co-operatives promised deliverance from the serfdom of the lien system. The idea took hold in many ways and was more widely adopted than it had been under the Grange. Its most simple application was a contract between a local Alliance and a merchant giving him a monopoly of their trade in exchange for better prices and terms. Hundreds of local orders experimented with co-operative stores. There were also co-operative gins, co-operative tanneries, co-operative mills. Texas was reported in 1887 to have twelve flour mills established and five under construction. The Alliance warehouse in the eighties became almost as familiar a feature of the county seat as the courthouse, in parts of the South. Virginia and some other states tried out the Rochedale plan of co-operatives, though its cash basis limited its appeal. For the few who had cash there were the Alliance business agencies, which bought direct from manufacturer and wholesaler. In the periodic reports of the Committee on Manufactures and Agricultural Implements, attesting the comparative worth of sundry wagons, binders, plows, and sewing machines, were the rudiments of a consumer's research service.[63]

None of these schemes could compare in magnificence with the Farmers' Alliance Exchange, sometimes called the "Macune business system." There was more than a touch of kinship between Dr. Macune and his Eastern contemporaries R. H. Edmonds and D. A. Tompkins, presiding visionaries of the Brave New South. The Doctor also had his visions. All farmers were to combine in a "strong, solid, secret, and binding organization," so that "the whole world of cotton raisers might be united for self-protection." Macune would fight monopoly with monopoly. The farmer might then exact a fair price for his product and at the same time drive a better bargain for his purchases. A four-story, "acre-and-a-half hall" was erected at Dallas to house the Exchange headquarters. The city contributed $100,000 in property and money. Each county organization had an exchange business manager and usually an Alliance cotton yard. Collecting cotton samples from all over the

[63] Garvin and Daws, *National Farmers' Alliance*, 58–61; Richmond *Virginia Sun*, February 27, 1892; *National Economist*, IV (1891), 248; Hicks, *Populist Revolt*, 132–34.

state at the Dallas Exchange, the system "brought standard classification and quotations from the markets of the world into competition with local buyers." Much cotton was handled by the Exchange the first year, and 1,500 bales were sold in one shipment to Europe. On an insubstantial footing of credit, the Exchange then began buying and distributing merchandise, doing, it was claimed, a million-dollar business the first year. Macune reported the Exchange had saved farmers 40 per cent on plows, 30 per cent on sewing machines, 30 per cent on wagons, and 50 to 75 per cent on buggies, besides having forced a "reduction in prices of all other commodities in every county, city, town and hamlet of the entire state."[64]

Like other ideas that issued from the Texas hatchery, the Macune Exchange plan took states to the east by storm. State exchanges with experimental variations of the plan were rapidly set up in nearly all the Southern states. In less than a month after it was organized the Mississippi Exchange reported that it was conducting an average business of $700 a day. The Georgia Exchange, commended as the best of the lot, was said to have saved its members $200,000 in fertilizers alone, and other states reported substantial savings. The Florida Exchange successfully marketed citrus. State agents of the associated Alliance agencies in 1890 claimed to have done a business amounting to about $10,000,000 that year. The Colored Farmers' Alliance set up exchanges in Houston, New Orleans, Mobile, Charleston, and Norfolk. Alliancemen were jubilant over their initial successes: there was "almost a universal conviction that financial salvation was come." Enthusiastic plans were announced for Alliance cotton and woolen mills, and an Alliance university. Virginians talked of starting their own foundry to break the plow trust.[65]

The Alliance enjoyed one triumph over the trusts. In the sum-

[64] Macune, "Farmers' Alliance," 18–31; Garvin and Daws, *National Farmers' Alliance*, 66–68; Morgan, *Wheel and Alliance*, 312–13; Clarence N. Ousley, "A Lesson in Co-operation," in *Popular Science Monthly* (New York), XXXVI (1890), 821–28; Ralph A. Smith, "'Macuneism,' or the Farmers of Texas in Business," in *Journal of Southern History*, XIII (1947), 220–44.

[65] *National Economist*, I (1889), 4–5, 13; Dallas *Morning News*, July 3, 1887; A. R. Venable to Pierson, June 17, 1891, in Pierson Papers; Raleigh *Progressive Farmer*, November 3, 1887.

mer of 1888 manufacturers of jute bagging for cotton bales combined to raise the price of jute from seven to eleven cents a yard, thereby laying a tribute of some $2,000,000 on the cotton farmer. Alliance leaders all over the South sprang into action. A convention, called by the national president to meet in Birmingham, unanimously adopted a resolution to substitute cotton bagging for jute. On the strength of this decision and a firmly organized boycott, dozens of mills turned to the manufacture of the cotton substitute. Some of them were organized by the Alliance itself. The fight was carried to all corners of the Cotton Belt, and the trust collapsed.[66]

Henry Grady's paper pictured the "deluded brothers" as headed for socialism and said that "their declaration of principles, if carried out, would revolutionize our entire system of government, shutting out all competition, placing the commerce, the producer and manufacturer in the hands of one man, closing up all stores save their own." [67] Rougher tactics were employed sometimes. In Dothan, Alabama, the keeper of an Alliance store and his clerk were killed.[68] In Mississippi Captain Frank Burkitt, Alliance leader and editor of the official journal of the state order, was seriously wounded by a gunshot and a little later his press was burned to the ground.[69]

As heavy as were the blows from a hostile system surrounding them, the co-operatives suffered more from weaknesses within. The large state exchanges simply undertook too great a volume of business for their capital. Their reliance upon joint notes as collateral got them in trouble with creditors, and frantic efforts to collect assessments upon members proved unavailing. Amateurish management and optimistic plunging were common faults. The Florida Exchange lasted five years, the Georgia Exchange six, but the parent organization in Texas failed in less than two years. Local stores, gins, and warehouses lingered through the nineties, but only in small numbers.[70]

66 Birmingham *Daily Age-Herald*, May 16, 1889; *Manufacturers' Record*, XIV (October 6, 1888), 11; *National Economist*, I (1889), 161.

67 Atlanta *Constitution*, November 22, 1887.

68 Jackson *Clarion-Ledger*, October 24, 1889.

69 *Ibid.*, September 17, October 22, 1891.

70 Macune, "Farmers' Alliance," 18–35; Hunt, *Farmer Movements in the Southwest*, 36–40. The Pierson Papers gave much insight into the decline of co-operatives.

The huge task the Alliance undertook was beyond the capacity of private resources. The core of the problem was still credit, and only the Federal government was to prove powerful enough to cope with it. Realizing this after two years of struggle with their exchanges, the Alliancemen advanced an ingenious plan for Federal relief, known as the "subtreasury plan." This was presented before the national meeting of the Alliance in December, 1889, by the ubiquitous Dr. Macune, who deserves chief credit for its origin. In brief, the plan called for the establishment of a warehouse or elevator and a subtreasury office in every county that offered for sale during the year a half-million dollars worth of farm products. In these warehouses the farmer might store his "nonperishable" crops, including cotton, wheat, tobacco, corn, and sugar, and receive certificates of deposit. The certificates entitled him to a loan for one year in legal-tender notes equal to 80 per cent of the market value of the crop on deposit. The terms of this "commodity credit" were one per cent a year plus a small charge for handling and storing the products. It was argued that this short-term credit would enable the farmer to break the chains of the lien system. The farmer would be relieved of the necessity of selling when the market was glutted and prices at their lowest. The plan was also intended to place a "supplemental volume" of money in circulation to "prevent sudden and violent contractions" that forced down prices during the movement of crops.[71] A similar plan to aid the Russian peasants, put into effect in August, 1888, by a ukase of the Czar, is thought to have influenced the framers of the Southern subtreasury plan.[72]

Presented as "the one most essential thing" upon which the Alliance should now concentrate, the plan was adopted and supported with zeal. It was soon to receive nationwide criticism and to flutter the dovecots of Washington. As happened with other Alliance measures, the features of the subtreasury system most denounced as revolutionary and unconstitutional were later written into Federal legislation—in the Warehouse Act of 1912, and the Commod-

[71] *National Economist,* II (1889), 225–26; VI (1891), 17; S. M. Scott, *The Sub-Treasury Plan, and the Land and Loan System* (Topeka, 1891), 5, 35, 61–62; Macune, "Farmers' Alliance," 43–46.

[72] James C. Malin, "The Farmers' Alliance Subtreasury Plan and European Precedents," in *Mississippi Valley Historical Review,* XXXI (1944–1945), 255–60.

ity Credit Corporation Act of 1933, for example. The subtreasury was to figure as a rallying cry and test of loyalty in Alliance and Populist campaigns to come.

Since 1887 Southern Alliance leaders had turned over the idea of uniting with an order of independent origin that was expanding contemporaneously in the Midwest and Northwest; this was the National Farmers' Alliance, commonly called the Northern Alliance. After three years of whirlwind growth and consolidation the Southern order had far outstripped the Northern in power and numbers, exceeding it perhaps three to one by the end of 1889. Macune had explored the possibilities of union, but from the first, difficulties appeared. The Midwestern farmers enjoyed greater prosperity than those of the South and the newer West. Midwestern agriculture had "attained to a business, capitalistic basis" undeveloped as yet in the other two regions. An additional issue dividing South and Midwest arose over the efforts of the latter to place taxes and restrictive laws upon synthetic food products such as oleomargarine that competed with dairy products. Southern farmers, both as producers of cottonseed and as consumers of cheap foods, felt their interest injured. While Southern Alliancemen hurled sharp resolutions against such measures as the Conger Lard Bill, Northern Alliances supported them with equal force. As "settlement" colonies of the Northeast, the Midwestern states naturally shared more of that region's ideas on finance and politics than did the "exploitation" colonies. They "wanted reform but not revolution," whereas the Southerners tossed that bombshell word about most casually. Contrary to popular impression, the more radical wing of the agrarian revolt of the nineties was Southern rather than Western.[78]

In December, 1889, both Southern and Northern Alliances held their annual meetings in St. Louis simultaneously to attempt a consolidation. The ambitious Southern leaders, by now envisioning a confederation of all farmer organizations and a working agreement with labor, were in a generous mood. Considering their superior numbers and power they could afford generosity. They promptly accepted the Northern order's first condition by adopting the name National Farmers' Alliance and Industrial Union,

[78] Herman C. Nixon, "The Cleavage within the Farmers' Alliance Movement," *ibid.*, XV (1928–1929), 22–33.

and agreed to admit Negroes into the Supreme Council, the national legislative body. The real difficulty centered upon the Northerners' objections to "secrecy" in the Southern order. This objection was less frivolous than it sounded. The secrecy peculiar to the Southern Alliance included a vague body of "unwritten law" that vested great authority in a National Supreme Council. It enabled the Southern Alliance to move with a swiftness and unity unknown to the loosely organized Northern order. Some Northern leaders feared domination by the South. It appears that the old bloody-shirt feeling was more prevalent among the Northern delegates than among the Southern. At any rate, the majority of the Northern delegates left St. Louis without committing themselves. The strong Alliances of the newer West, Kansas, South Dakota, and North Dakota, however, seceded from the Northern Alliance and consolidated with the Southerners. Weakened by these defections the Northern order lost ground rapidly the following year, while Southern organizers poured out through the Northwest.[74] The Southern leaders enjoyed another triumph at St. Louis by gaining the official endorsement of their "demands" by the Knights of Labor, whose leaders pledged close co-operation with the farmers in pressing the demands upon Congress.

It was with considerable justification, therefore, that the Southerners "now assumed the right to direct the whole farmers' movement" [75]—not to mention as much of the labor movement as they could. "Sectionalism in this country will continue," warned retiring President Macune, but it would "assume a different form from that which has so long afflicted the people, and have another purpose." As the new president, Leonidas L. Polk of North Carolina, described the purpose and character of the new sectionalism, "the people of the awakened South and the people of the great agricultural West—aroused and inspired by a common danger—have locked their hands and shields in a common cause." [76]

From the beginning, official pronouncements on the political role of the Alliance had been somewhat confused, not to say jesuit-

[74] Drew, "Present Farmers' Movement," *loc. cit.*, 283–86; Hicks, *Populist Revolt*, 113–27.

[75] Hicks, *Populist Revolt*, 126.

[76] *National Economist*, III (1890), 257; IV (1890), 200.

ical. Conscious of political dissension as the nemesis of the order in the past and fearing it in the future, Alliancemen probably rationalized even to themselves the strong political bent of their organization. The proscriptive one-party system in the South made repeated denial of any action independent of the Democratic-Conservative party almost essential to existence. At any rate Alliance spokesmen, especially in the earlier years, were given to continual reiteration of the "nonpolitical" and "strictly business" character of their constitution. Yet it is difficult to see how the "demands" and "platforms" that issued from their annual conventions, almost all of which were quite out of harmony with the conservative party led by the Redeemers, could be realized by any other than political means. As the membership of the Alliance rolled up into the millions, the thinking of many must have been reflected in a speech made before a farmers' convention of Louisiana. "We are so numerous," said the speaker, "that if we organize in political associations all the powers and functions of the State would pass under our control,"—and then hastened to renounce the thought.[77]

Gradually Alliance leadership lifted the taboo on political aims. Not long before his retirement as president, Macune, customarily circumspect about politics, wrote that "Whatever else this movement may be, a third-party movement it is not"; yet he added that it proposed "to exert a more decisive influence in the primaries of *both parties*." [78] With the succession of Polk to the presidency after the St. Louis meeting, leadership fell to a man who had long been an advocate of political action, though not as yet of independence. "We are not to be intimidated or frightened by the cry that 'the farmers are going into politics,'" his influential paper said.[79]

Early in 1890, without any official announcement, the Alliance began a movement to capture the Southern states by taking control of the state Democratic nominating conventions. All candidates were informed that "The Alliance Yardstick" was being applied, and that even the most solidly entrenched brigadier among the Redeemers had to "stand up and be measured." Usually the measurement took the form of a written pledge in which the candi-

[77] *Proceedings of the Third Annual Session of the* [Louisiana] *State Agricultural Society . . . 1889* (Baton Rouge, 1889), 7.

[78] *National Economist,* I (1889), 145.

[79] Raleigh *Progressive Farmer,* February 16, 1888.

date promised to support all the demands of the St. Louis platform in addition to the subtreasury plan and what local measures the Alliance agreed upon. The Texas nominating convention in 1890 was described by the conservative Dallas *News* as "a stiff sort of semi-revolutionary Democracy . . . with communistic proclivities." [80] In other states it was observed that "the brigadiers, colonels, and 'majahs' are no longer the ruling factors," and everywhere younger men and new faces were noted.

There was reason for the excitement in Alliance circles when the victories of 1890 were totaled. They represented an agrarian triumph. In Tennessee the Alliance named the governor, 14 of the 33 state senators and 40 of the 90 members of the lower house, making the Assembly "distinctly agrarian in character." [81] The North Carolina Alliance claimed 8 Congressmen, and among state officers, "All the Democrats and half the Republicans [were] pledged." The order claimed between 75 and 80 of the 133 Alabama assemblymen and one United States Senator, although Reuben F. Kolb, the state leader, was defeated for the nomination for governor. Alliancemen gained 52 of the 100 seats in the Florida Legislature and elected their candidate for the Senate. Louisiana, Virginia, and Kentucky held no state elections in 1890, but the Virginia Alliance believed it had 5 Congressmen satisfactorily pledged. Kentucky farmers counted 4 Alliance Congressmen and Mississippi 2.[82] Besides turning out 6 incumbent Congressmen, the powerful Georgia Alliance "chose the governor, wrote the platform, named three-fourths of the senators and four-fifths of the representatives." [83] Delegates to conventions called to write new constitutions for Mississippi and Kentucky were elected in 1890, and in each convention Alliance delegates gained the upper hand. A large faction of the Arkansas Alliance anticipated the third-party revolt by departing from the rule of working in the old party and supporting the Union Labor party, which ran a strong race but lost.[84]

80 Quoted in Sam H. Acheson, *Joe Bailey, The Last Democrat* (New York, 1932), 40–41.

81 Robison, *Bob Taylor,* 148.

82 Drew, "Present Farmers' Movement," *loc. cit.,* 307.

83 Arnett, *Populist Movement in Georgia,* 116.

84 Thomas (ed.), *Arkansas and Its People,* I, 222–28.

In 1890 the Farmers' Alliance also made temporary juncture with the rising stars of Benjamin R. Tillman of South Carolina and James S. Hogg of Texas. Both men eagerly sought Alliance endorsement, but they were primarily concerned with the construction of powerful personal machines for their own ends, and they were soon to part ways with the doctrinaire Alliance. Governors-elect Ben Tillman and Jim Hogg were nevertheless conspicuous features of the agrarian uprising of 1890, and their success marked the overthrow in their states of the Redeemers and their pliant understanding with the corporations. The one-eyed, grim-faced farmer from Edgefield and his entire ticket were elected in South Carolina, and by a party revolution the Hampton-Butler-Redemption men were supplanted by Tillmanites. Hogg's sweeping victory, with the support of the Knights of Labor, Grangers, and Alliance, marked the ascendancy of the Reagan-Terrell agrarian faction of the old party in Texas.[85]

"Being Democrats and in the majority," wrote one optimistic Allianceman after the victories of 1890, "we took possession of the Democratic party." It apparently occurred to few Alliancemen that the reverse might be the case: the Democratic-Conservative party might have taken possession of the Alliance. Until it was clear which had happened it would seem to many, as it did to the *National Economist*, that the Alliance together with its Western associates had "by one effort revolutionized the politics of the nation." [86]

[85] Simkins, *Pitchfork Ben Tillman*, 138–68; George M. Bailey, "The Life of James Stephen Hogg" (Manuscript in The University of Texas Library, n.d.), 172–200.

[86] *National Economist*, IV (1890), 133.

CHAPTER VIII

MUDSILLS AND BOTTOM RAILS

IF RECONSTRUCTION ever set the bottom rail on top, it was not for long and never securely. Redemption seemed to leave little doubt that the bottom rail was again on the bottom—whatever its temporary dislocation. It remained for the New South to find what Reconstruction had failed to find: the measure of the emancipated slave's freedom and a definition of free labor, both black and white; for the white worker's place in the New Order would be vitally conditioned by the place assigned the free black worker.

Much discussion about the Negro's civil rights, his political significance, his social status, and his aspirations can be shortened and simplified by a clear understanding of the economic status assigned him in the New Order. Emancipation and Reconstruction had done little to change that picture. The lives of the overwhelming majority of Negroes were still circumscribed by the farm and plantation. The same was true of the white people, but the Negroes, with few exceptions, were farmers without land. Questionnaires from the census of 1880 revealed that in thirty-three counties of Georgia where Negro population was thick, "not more than one in one hundred" Negro farmers owned land; the same proportion was reported from seventeen black Mississippi counties; twelve others reported not one in twenty, and many not one in fifty. From Tennessee as a whole the report was that only "a very small part of the Negroes own land or even the houses in which they live"; also from Louisiana and Alabama came report of "very few" owners.[1]

[1] *Tenth Census, 1880*, V, *Cotton Production*, "Mississippi," 154–55; "Tennessee," 104–105, "Louisiana," 83–84; VI, *Cotton Production*, "Georgia," 172–73.

More specific information is provided for one state by the report of the Comptroller General of Georgia for the year ending October 1, 1880. Of a total of some $88,000,000 in land value, the Negroes, who made up nearly half the state's population, owned around $1,-500,000. Of a total of some $23,000,000 value put upon cattle and farm animals, the Negroes owned about $2,000,000, and of some $3,200,000 in agricultural tools, the Negroes reported a little more than $163,000.[2] It is pretty clear that as a rule the Negro farmer not only worked the white man's land but worked it with a white man's plow drawn by a white man's mule. In the next two decades the race's landholdings improved slightly, but in 1900 black Georgians had taxable titles to only one twenty-fifth of the land; only 14 per cent of the Negro farmers owned their farms, and in 1910 only 13 per cent.[3] In the South as a whole, by 1900, 75.3 per cent of the Negro farmers were croppers or tenants.[4]

The landless Negro farmers, like the landless whites, worked either for wages or for shares, under any of several arrangements. When the Alabama planter furnished tools, animals, and feed, as well as the land, his share was one half of all crops; when he furnished only the land he took one fourth of the cotton and one third of the corn. There were numerous variations, including the "two-day system" on Edisto Island, where the tenant worked two days of the week for the landlord in the feudal manner.[5] The impression of uniformity in the labor system that replaced slavery would seem to have been exaggerated. As late as 1881 it was reported that in Alabama "you can hardly find any two farmers in a community who are carrying on their business alike," and frequently one planter might use several methods at once: "To one he rents, to another he gives a contract for working on shares, to another he pays wages in money, and with another he swaps work, and so *ad infinitum.*" Whatever system was used "there follows the same failure, or partial failure." [6]

The share system called forth especially severe criticism from

2 Quoted in Rainey, "Negro and the Independent Movement," Chap. I.

3 Brooks, *Agrarian Revolution in Georgia*, 44, 122.

4 United States Census Bureau, *Negro Population in the United States, 1790–1915* (Washington, 1918), 571–72.

5 *Tenth Census, 1880*, V, *Cotton Production*, 60–66; VI, *Cotton Production*, 154–55.

6 Montgomery *Advertiser*, August 12, 1881.

all sides as being "ruinous to the soil" and "a disgrace to farming." A large proportion of landlords preferred and used the wage system. From Tennessee in 1880 it was reported that "advocates for shares and wages are about equally divided in number." Census reports of wages paid for labor in cotton production in 1880 make no distinction between white and black workers, and there probably was little difference. Prevalent monthly wages for a man's work "from sun to sun" were $8.00 to $14.00 in Alabama; $8.00 to $15.00 in Arkansas; $6.00 to $10.00 in Florida; $5.00 to $10.00 in Georgia ($4.00 to $6.00 per month for women); $6.00 to $15.00 in Louisiana; $8.00 to $12.00 in Mississippi, South Carolina, and Tennessee; $8.00 to $15.00 in Texas. Daily wages were usually 50 cents with board, or 75 cents without. A year's wages for a man in the central cotton belt of Georgia were $60.00 to $100.00; in Tennessee they were $100.00 to $125.00. Both yearly and monthly wages included rations.[7] In 1888 it was estimated by an authority that "the regular allowance of an ordinary hand is 12 pounds of bacon and 5 pecks of meal by the month," which "would cost him twenty-three dollars in the course of twelve months." [8]

It should be noted that the year 1880, for which the wage rates are quoted, was a relatively "good" year for cotton prices. When the price fell to half that in the nineties the wages could not have been nearly so high. If a yield of only three to six bales per hand could be expected, as estimated in Arkansas in 1880, the product of a year's labor would likely bring little more than $100.00 on the market in the middle nineties. Working on shares, the cropper at that rate received about $50.00 for his year's work. Neither he nor his landlord was likely to see or handle any cash, since both were in all probability deeply enmeshed in the toils of the crop lien. They received instead meager supplies at the prices demanded of credit customers.

The tides of Negro migration that had set in during Reconstruction, as the first and most characteristic expression of freedom, continued to move in the same general directions for some years

[7] *Tenth Census, 1880,* V, *Cotton Production,* "Arkansas," 104–105; "Louisiana," 83–84; "Mississippi," 154–55; "Tennessee," 104–105; "Texas," 160–61; VI, *Cotton Production,* "Alabama," 154–55; "Florida," 70–71; "Georgia," 172–73; "South Carolina," 60–66.

[8] Philip A. Bruce, *The Plantation Negro as a Freeman* (New York, 1889), 200–201.

after Redemption. These movements were of three kinds: from the country to the towns; from the poorer lands to the delta, bottom, and richer lands; and from the older states to the newer states of the Southwest. Intermittent complaint and a few laws against "enticing" labor persisted through the eighties. With one striking exception, however, the Negro migrations were largely from one part of the South to another. The great exodus northward did not begin until a half century after freedom.[9]

A census survey of the relation of land and labor in the cotton state of Alabama in 1880 revealed that the Negroes were most thickly concentrated upon the most fertile soil in the state, and the whites, upon the poorest soil; that the most fertile land, where the sharecropping system was most prevalent, yielded the least product, and was rapidly being exhausted; that poorer lands under cultivation by owners produced greater yield per capita and per acre; and that the white farmer was rapidly gaining on the black in the proportion of cotton produced.[10]

In spite of these facts, there was an almost universal preference among Black-Belt landlords for Negro tenants and workers. "White labor is totally unsuited to our methods, our manners, and our accommodations," declared an Alabama planter in 1888. "No other laborer [than the Negro] of whom I have any knowledge, would be as cheerful, or so contented on four pounds of meat and a peck of meal a week, in a little log cabin 14 × 16 feet, with cracks in it large enough to afford free passage to a large sized cat." [11] "Give me the nigger every time," echoed a Mississippi planter. "The nigger will never 'strike' as long as you give him plenty to eat and half clothe him: He will live on less and do more hard work, when properly managed, than any other class, or race of people. As Arp truthfully says 'we can boss him' and that is what we southern folks like." [12]

The writer who estimated the cash value of freedom for the

[9] The exception was the "Exodus" of 1879. This has been treated by the preceding volume in the present series, Coulter, *South During Reconstruction*, 100–101. On Negro migration, see Wharton, *Negro in Mississippi*, 106–24.

[10] *Tenth Census, 1880*, VI, *Cotton Production*, "Alabama," 64.

[11] A. W. S. Anderson, in *Proceedings of the Third Semi-Annual Session of the Alabama State Agricultural Society* (Montgomery, 1888), 93–95.

[12] Quoted in Wharton, *Negro in Mississippi*, 121.

Negro thirty years after emancipation at a little less than one dollar a year to the individual [13] overstated his point, though not so grossly as it might seem. At least such expensive luxuries as civil liberties and political franchises were beyond his reach. He knew very well that immediate, daily necessities came first—land, mules, plows, food, and clothes, all of which had to be got from a white man who oftener than not had too little himself.

In the working out of a new code of civil rights and social status for the freedman—in the definition of the Negro's "place"—Reconstruction had been only an interruption, the importance of which varied from state to state, but which was nowhere decisive. The transition from slavery to caste as a system of controlling race relations went forward gradually and tediously. Slavery had been vastly more than a labor system, and the gap that its removal left in manners, mores, and ritual of behavior could not be filled overnight. The so-called "Black Codes" were soon overthrown, as were the laws imported by the Carpetbaggers. Redemption and Hayes's policy of *laissez faire* left the code to be worked out by Southern white men. It has already been pointed out that there was no unity of opinion among them concerning the Negro's political rights. There also existed a roughly comparable division with reference to his civil rights.

Hampton, Lamar, Nicholls, and Redeemers of that type gave their solemn pledges in the Compromise of 1877 to protect the Negro in all his rights. They were probably guilty of less hypocrisy than has been charged. The class they represented had little to fear from the Negro and at the same time considerable to gain for the conservative cause by establishing themselves in a paternalistic relationship as his protector and champion against the upland and lower-class whites. This would better enable them to control his vote (against the same white element), not to mention his labor. In 1877 J. L. M. Curry listened to a debate of the Virginia Assembly in Jefferson's neoclassic capitol. "A negro member," he recorded with evident satisfaction in his diary, "said that he and his race relied for the protection of their rights & liberties, not on the 'poor white trash' but on the 'well-raised' gentlemen." [14] Black-Belt

[13] Cooper, *Piedmont Region*, 77.

[14] Diary of J. L. M. Curry, January 13, 1877, in Curry Papers.

white men were casual about their daily intimacy and easy personal relations with Negroes, an attitude that made upland Southerners uncomfortable and shocked Northerners, even Radical Carpetbaggers. So long as this old leadership retained strong influence, the racial code was considerably less severe than it later became.

In the early years of freedom saloons in Mississippi usually served both whites and blacks at the same bar; many public eating places, "using separate tables, served both races in the same room"; public parks and buildings were still open to both to a great extent; and segregation in common carriers was not at all strict.[15] The most common type of discrimination on railways was the exclusion of Negroes from the first-class, or "ladies' " car. The races were accustomed to sharing the second-class coach. In 1877, however, a South Carolinian wrote that Negroes were "permitted to, and frequently do ride in first-class railway and street railway cars" in his state. This had caused trouble at first but was "now so common as hardly to provoke remark." [16] In 1885 George W. Cable, who was sensitive regarding discrimination, reported that in South Carolina Negroes "ride in the first class cars as a right" and "their presence excites no comment," while "In Virginia they may ride exactly as white people do and in the same cars." [17] Even the antebellum practice of using a common cemetery continued for many years. White papers occasionally "mistered" Negro politicians, if they were "good" politicians, and a Richmond paper affirmed in 1886 that "nobody here objects to sitting in political conventions with negroes. Nobody here objects to serving on juries with negroes." [18] Even the Tillman legislation of 1891 defeated a Jim Crow bill for railway cars.

From the beginning, however, concessions to the harsher code and developing phobias of the hillbillies of the white counties had

[15] Wharton, *Negro in Mississippi*, 232. The evolution of "caste as a method of social control" is admirably worked out by this author.

[16] Belton O'Neall Townsend, "South Carolina Society," in *Atlantic Monthly*, XXXIX (1877), 676. Commenting in 1879 on the "perfect equality" of races in Southern tramcars, a member of Parliament wrote: "I was, I confess, surprised to see how completely this is the case; even an English Radical is a little taken aback at first." Sir George Campbell, *White and Black . . .* (New York, 1879), 195.

[17] Cable, *Silent South*, 85–86. Cable was quoting the Charleston *News and Courier* with regard to South Carolina. The observation on Virginia custom is his own.

[18] Richmond *Dispatch*, October 13, 1886.

to be made. There were South Carolinians in numbers who did not share the Charleston *News and Courier*'s feeling that it was "a great deal pleasanter to travel with respectable and well-behaved colored people than with unmannerly and ruffianly white men."

It is one of the paradoxes of Southern history that political democracy for the white man and racial discrimination for the black were often products of the same dynamics. As the Negroes invaded the new mining and industrial towns of the uplands in greater numbers, and the hill-country whites were driven into more frequent and closer association with them, and as the two races were brought into rivalry for subsistence wages in the cotton fields, mines, and wharves, the lower-class white man's demand for Jim Crow laws became more insistent. It took a lot of ritual and Jim Crow to bolster the creed of white supremacy in the bosom of a white man working for a black man's wages. The Negro pretty well understood these forces, and his grasp of them was one reason for his growing alliance with the most conservative and politically reactionary class of whites against the insurgent white democracy. A North Carolina Negro wrote: "The best people of the South do not demand this separate car business . . . and, when they do, it is only to cater to those of their race who, in order to get a big man's smile, will elevate them [*sic*] to place and power." He believed that "this whole thing is but a pandering to the lower instincts of the worst class of whites in the South." [19]

The barriers of racial discrimination mounted in direct ratio with the tide of political democracy among whites. In fact, an increase of Jim Crow laws upon the statute books of a state is almost an accurate index of the decline of the reactionary regimes of the Redeemers and triumph of white democratic movements. Take, for example, the law requiring separate accommodations for the races in trains, said to be "the most typical Southern law." No state [20] enacted such a law for more than twenty years after 1865.

19 Editorial, *Southland* (Salisbury, N.C.), I (1890), 166–67.

20 The Tennessee legislature passed an act in 1875 abrogating the common law and releasing common carriers and other public servants from serving anyone they chose not to serve. A Federal circuit court declared this unconstitutional in 1880. An act of 1881 required separate first-class accommodations for Negroes, but left the two races unsegregated in second-class coaches. Stanley J. Folmsbee, "The Origin of the First 'Jim Crow' Law," in *Journal of Southern History*, XV (1949), 235–47.

Yet in the five years beginning in 1887 one after another adopted some variation of the law: Florida in 1887, Mississippi in 1888, Texas in 1889, Louisiana in 1890, Alabama, Arkansas, Kentucky, and Georgia in 1891. These were the years when the Farmers' Alliance was first making itself felt in the legislatures of these states. Mississippi, in 1888, was the first state to adopt a law providing for the separation of the races in railway stations, and Georgia, in 1891, the first to adopt the law for streetcars.[21] These laws, though significant in themselves, were often only enactments of codes already in practice. Whether by state law or local law, or by the more pervasive coercion of sovereign white opinion, "the Negro's place" was gradually defined—in the courts, schools, and libraries, in parks, theaters, hotels, and residential districts, in hospitals, insane asylums—everywhere, including on sidewalks and in cemeteries. When complete, the new codes of White Supremacy were vastly more complex than the ante-bellum slave codes or the Black Codes of 1865–1866, and, if anything, they were stronger and more rigidly enforced.

Among the institutions of the Old Order that strained to meet the needs of the New, none proved more hopelessly inadequate than the old penitentiaries. The state was suddenly called upon to take over the plantation's penal functions at a time when crime was enormously increasing. The strain was too great. One after another of the states adopted the expedient of leasing the convicts to private corporations or individuals. In Louisiana the convict-lease system had an ante-bellum origin; in the other Southern states it was introduced by the provisional or military governments and retained by the Carpetbaggers and Redeemers.

For a number of reasons the lease system took firm roots in the New Order and grew to greater proportions. For one thing, it fitted perfectly the program of retrenchment, for under it the penitentiary not only ceased to be a heavy burden on the taxpayer but became a source of revenue to the state—sometimes a very lucrative source. The system also fitted conveniently the needs occasioned by the new criminal codes of the Redemption regimes,

21 Franklin Johnson, *Development of State Legislation Concerning the Free Negro* (New York, 1919), 15, 54, 62–207; Gilbert T. Stephenson, *Race Distinctions in American Law* (New York, 1910), 216–17.

which piled up heavy penalties for petty offenses against property, while at the same time they weakened the protection afforded the Negro in the courts. The so-called "pig law" of Mississippi defined the theft of any property over ten dollars in value, or any cattle or swine of whatever value, as grand larceny, with a sentence up to five years. After its adoption the number of state convicts increased from 272 in 1874 to 1,072 by the end of 1877. The number in Georgia increased from 432 in 1872 to 1,441 in 1877. Additional convictions meant additional revenue instead of additional taxes. The system quickly became a large-scale and sinister business. Leases of ten, twenty, and thirty years were granted by legislatures to powerful politicians, Northern syndicates, mining corporations, and individual planters. Laws limiting hours of labor and types of work for convicts were nonexistent in some states and negligible in others, and in two states protective laws were later removed or modified. Responsibility of lessees for the health and lives of convicts was extremely loose. Some states had no inspectors and in others inspection was highly perfunctory if not corrupt. Where the law permitted, the large lessees subleased convicts in small or large gangs for short periods, thus rendering responsibility to the state even more fictitious and protection of the state's prisoners all but impossible. County prisons in many cases adopted the system and in Alabama had twice as many convicts leased as the state. The South's "penitentiaries" were great rolling cages that followed construction camps and railroad building, hastily built stockades deep in forest or swamp or mining fields, or windowless log forts in turpentine flats.[22]

The degradation and brutality produced by this system would be incredible but for the amount of evidence from official sources. A report of the inspectors of the Alabama penitentiary revealed that the prisons were packed with several times the number of convicts they could reasonably hold. "They are as filthy, as a rule, as dirt could make them, and both prisons and prisoners were infested with vermin. The bedding was totally unfit for use. . . . [It was

22 *Report of the United States Commissioner of Labor, 1886, Convict Labor* (Washington, 1887), especially pp. 72–79. For a dispassionate account by a warden, see J. C. Powell, *The American Siberia; or, Fourteen Years' Experience in a Southern Convict Camp* (London, 1891), *passim;* Wharton, *Negro in Mississippi*, 237–40.

found] that convicts were excessively and sometimes cruelly punished; that they were poorly clothed and fed; that the sick were neglected, insomuch as no hospitals had been provided, that they were confined with the well convicts." [23] A grand-jury investigation of the penitentiary hospital in Mississippi reported that inmates were "all bearing on their persons marks of the most inhuman and brutal treatments. Most of them have their backs cut in great wales, scars and blisters, some with the skin peeling off in pieces as the result of severe beatings. . . . They were lying there dying, some of them on bare boards, so poor and emaciated that their bones almost came through their skin, many complaining for want of food. . . . We actually saw live vermin crawling over their faces, and the little bedding and clothing they have is in tatters and stiff with filth." [24] In mining camps of Arkansas and Alabama convicts were worked through the winter without shoes, standing in water much of the time. In both states the task system was used, whereby a squad of three was compelled to mine a certain amount of coal per day on penalty of a severe flogging for the whole squad. Convicts in the turpentine camps of Florida, with "stride-chains" and "waist-chains" riveted on their bodies, were compelled to work at a trot. "They kept this gait up all day long, from tree to tree," reported the warden.[25] The average annual death rate among Negro convicts in Mississippi from 1880 to 1885 was almost 11 per cent, for white convicts about half that, and in 1887 the general average was 16 per cent. The death rate among the prisoners of Arkansas was reported in 1881 to be 25 per cent annually. An indication of what was called "moral conditions" is provided in a report of the Committee on the Penitentiary of the Georgia Legislature: "We find in some of the camps men and women chained together and occupying the same sleeping bunks. The result is that there are now in the Penitentiary twenty-five bastard children, ranging from three months to five years of age, and many of the women are now far advanced in pregnancy." [26] For the Southern convict-lease system a modern scholar can "find parallel only in the persecutions

[23] *Biennial Report of the Inspectors of the Alabama Penitentiary From September 30, 1880 to September 30, 1882* (Montgomery, 1882), *passim.*

[24] Jackson *Clarion,* July 13, 1887.

[25] Little Rock *Daily Gazette,* March 24, 27, 1888; Powell, *American Siberia,* 22.

[26] Georgia *House Journal,* 1879, Pt. I, 386–91.

of the Middle Ages or in the prison camps of Nazi Germany." [27]

The lease system was under bitter attack, especially from the various independent parties, and repeated attempts were made to abolish or reform it. Julia Tutwiler of Alabama was a moving spirit in the reform movement. Almost everywhere, however, the reformers were opposed by vested interests within the Redemption party—sometimes by the foremost leaders of that party. Senator Brown of Georgia was guaranteed by his twenty-year lease "three hundred able-bodied, long-term men" to work in his Dade Coal Mines, for which he paid the state about eight cents per hand per day.[28] Senator Gordon was also a member of a firm leasing convicts. Colonel Colyar, leader of one wing of the Redemption party in Tennessee, leased that state's prisoners at $101,000 a year for the Tennessee Coal and Iron Company. Control over these Southern state "slaves" was the foundation of several large fortunes, and in one case, of a great political dynasty. Robert McKee, who was in a position to know all the workings of the system, wrote that the state warden of Alabama, John H. Bankhead, "grew rich in a few years on $2000 a year," and manipulated the legislature at will. "The 'penitentiary ring' is a power in the party," he wrote privately, "and it is a corrupt power. One of the State officers is a lessee of convicts, and has a brother who is a deputy warden." [29] Former Secretary of State Rufus K. Boyd believed that the convict-lease ring was "as unscrupulous as any radical in the days of their power. . . . Are we all thieves? What is it leading to? Who can submit to these things patiently?" [30] Yet the party continued to submit.

The convict-lease system did greater violence to the moral authority of the Redeemers than did anything else. For it was upon the tradition of paternalism that the Redeemer regimes claimed authority to settle the race problem and "deal with the Negro."

The abandonment of the Negro by his Northern champions

27 Fletcher M. Green, "Some Aspects of the Southern Convict Lease System in the Southern States," in Fletcher M. Green (ed.), *Essays in Southern History Presented to Joseph Gregoire de Roulhac Hamilton* . . . (Chapel Hill, 1949), 122.

28 Georgia *House Journal*, 1879, Pt. I, 386–91.

29 Robert McKee to Boyd, February 3, 1882, in McKee Papers.

30 Boyd to McKee, February 26, 1883; also Morgan to McKee, March 15, 1882; McKee to Thomas R. Roulhac, February 25, 1883, *ibid.*

after the Compromise of 1877 was as quixotic as their previous crusade in his behalf had been romantic and unrealistic. The *Nation* thought the government should "have nothing more to do with him," and Godkin could not see how the Negro could ever "be worked into a system of government for which you and I would have much respect." [31] The New York *Tribune,* with a logic all its own, stated that the Negroes, after having been given "ample opportunity to develop their own latent capacities," had only succeeded in proving that "as a race they are idle, ignorant, and vicious." [32]

The Supreme Court's decision in October, 1883, declaring the Civil Rights Act unconstitutional was only the juristic fulfillment of the Compromise of 1877, and was, in fact, handed down by Justice Joseph P. Bradley, Grant's appointee, who had been a member of the Electoral Commission of 1877. "The calm with which the country receives the news," observed the editor of the New York *Evening Post,* "shows how completely the extravagant expectations . . . of the war have died out." [33] A Republican who held repudiated bonds of South Carolina wrote from New York that the Civil Rights decision came "as a just retribution to the colored people for their infamous conduct" in assisting in the repudiation of the bonds; "if they expect the people of the North to fight their battles for them they can wait until doomsday," he added.[34]

It has already been pointed out that the wing of the Republican party that raised the loudest outcry against Hayes's policy of deserting the Negro promptly abandoned him itself as soon as it came to power under Garfield and Arthur and threw support to white Republicans in alliance with any white independent organization available. Repeated warnings from the South that the Negro voters were "getting demoralized," that they would "make terms with their adversaries," and that the Republican party was "losing its hold on the younger generation" were ignored.[35]

[31] *Nation,* XXIV (1877), 202; Edwin L. Godkin, quoted by Buck, *Road to Reunion,* 295.

[32] New York *Tribune,* April 7, 1877.

[33] New York *Evening Post,* October 16, 1883. [34] Letter, *ibid.,* October 20, 1883.

[35] A. J. Willard, Columbia, S.C., to J. Hendrix McLane, [?] 12, 1882; James E. Richardson to Chandler, September 14, 1884, in Chandler Papers; David M. Key to Hayes, December 31, 1882, in Hayes Papers.

Political leaders of his own race furnished guidance of doubtful value to the Negro in his political quandary. For one thing the average cotton-field Negro voter had little more in common with the outstanding Negro politicians of the South than he had with the corporation lawyers who ran the Republican party in the North. Former Senator Blanche K. Bruce of Mississippi owned "a handsome plantation of 1,000 acres," which he operated as absentee landlord, much as had his predecessor, Senator Jefferson Davis.[36] Former Congressman James T. Rapier of Alabama was "the possessor of extensive landed interests" in that state in which he employed more than a hundred people. Former Congressmen Josiah T. Walls of Florida and John R. Lynch of Mississippi were reported to be "proprietors of vast acres under cultivation and employers of large numbers of men," [37] and Norris Wright Cuney, Negro boss in Galveston, Texas, was the employer of some five hundred stevedores.[38] Former Senator Bruce was quoted in 1883 as saying that his party represented "the brains, the wealth, the intelligence" of the land, and that "the moneyed interests of this country would be seriously affected" by a Republican defeat.[39]

The more successful of the Negro politicians were maintained in some Federal office "of high sounding titles and little importance" in Washington. At home they often came to an understanding with Democratic leaders of the Black Belt called "fusion," which served the interests of both by diminishing the power of the white counties in the white man's party and the authority of white leaders in the black man's party.[40] The confusion in which this policy resulted for the average Negro voter may be imagined from the nature of the instruction Lynch gave Mississippi Republicans at a meeting in 1883. It made no difference whether the county machines decided "to fuse with the Independents instead of the Democrats, or with the Democrats instead of the Independents, or to make straight [Republican] party nomination instead of fusing with either"; it was the duty of all good party men, whatever the decision, to follow the machine, "although they may honestly be-

36 Washington *Bee* (Negro paper), July 21, 1883.

37 Huntsville *Gazette* (Negro paper), February 11, 1882.

38 Maud Cuney-Hare, *Norris Wright Cuney* (New York, 1913), 42.

39 New York *Globe* (Negro paper), February 24, 1883.

40 See above, pp. 103–104.

lieve the decision to be unwise." [41] Such instructions would not have sounded unfamiliar to followers of the white man's party.

Soon after the war Negroes began to break up into differentiated social and economic classes that eventually reproduced on a rough scale the stratified white society. Enough of a Negro middle class had emerged in the eighties to reflect faithfully the New-South romanticism of the white middle class, with its gospel of progress and wealth. A Negro paper named the *New South* made its appearance in Charleston. It warned the race against "following the *ignis fatuus* of politics," and urged the gospel of "real progress"—money-making.[42] The class of 1886 at Tuskegee adopted the motto "There is Room at the Top," [43] and freshman W. E. B. Du Bois found his classmates at Fisk in 1885 of the same blithe turn of mind.[44] No American success story could match the Master of Tuskegee's *Up From Slavery!*

Another considerable Negro element saw nothing better than to take refuge under the paternalism of the old masters, who offered some protection against the extreme race doctrines of the upland whites and sometimes more tangible rewards than the Republican bosses. Cleveland's administration and its Southern lieutenants encouraged this tendency among Negroes. The *Nation,* a Cleveland supporter, rejoiced that "Thousands of them" had discovered "that their true interests are bound up with the interests of their old masters." [45]

Although the majority of the Negro masses remained Republican or potentially Republican voters, suspicion and criticism of the party of liberation were on the increase during the eighties. The Compromise of 1877 was described as "disillusioning"; the Civil Rights decision as "infamous," a "baptism in ice water"; Chandler's politics as "fatuous" and "degrading." There was also a growing tendency to look upon Republican tariff, railroad, and financial legislation more critically. "The colored people are consumers," said the chairman of a Colored People's Convention in Richmond.

[41] Quoted in New York *Globe,* October 20, 1883.

[42] Quoted in *Nation,* XLVIII (1889), 461.

[43] *Southern Letter* (Tuskegee), V (July, 1888), 3.

[44] W. E. Burghardt Du Bois, *Dusk of Dawn: An Essay toward an Autobiography of a Race Concept* (New York, 1940), 25–27.

[45] *Nation,* XLI (1885), 369.

"The Republicans have deserted them and undertaken to protect the capitalist and manufacturer of the North." [46] "Neither of these parties," wrote a Negro editor, "cares a tinker snap for the poor man. They are run in the interest of capital, monopoly and repression." [47] The defeat of the Blair bill was a bitter disappointment. Professor J. C. Price, editor of a Negro journal in Salisbury, North Carolina, pointed out that "the Republican party was committed to the enactment of national legislation for the education of the masses," yet the Blair bill had been "voted down and owed its death in the Senate to Republican opposition." Under the circumstances the Negro was not impressed by the Lodge bill to reenact Reconstruction election laws, and was more disillusioned when it was defeated. "He is beginning to distinguish between real friendship and demagoguery." [48]

In the meanwhile, the movement to make the party "respectable" was gaining ground among "Lily-white" Republicans in the South. A party leader addressing the Lincoln Club of Arkansas on the problem of attracting "persons who have heretofore acted with the Democratic party," announced that he was seeking "a way by which they could act with the Republican party without being dominated over by the negro." [49] The Republican White League of Texas believed that "the union is only safe in the hands of the Anglo-Saxon race, and that a Republican party in Texas to merit the respect of mankind must be in the hands of that race." [50] A New England traveler was grieved to report to the "kinsmen and friends of John Brown, Wendell Phillips, and William Lloyd Garrison" the words of a Southern white Republican who said, "I will not vote to make a negro my ruler. . . . I was a white man before I was a Republican." [51] Even the Northern churches in the South, stoutest proponents of the missionary phase of Northern policy, had drawn the color line by the end of the eighties.[52]

46 Richmond *Dispatch*, April 16, 1890.

47 New York *Globe*, April 5, 1884. See also, *ibid.*, October 13, 20, 27, 1883; May 3, 1884.

48 *Southland*, I (1890), 162–63.

49 Little Rock *Daily Gazette*, July 22, 1888.

50 Dallas *Morning News*, June 9, 1892.

51 Charles H. Levermore, "Impressions of a Yankee Visitor in the South," in *New England Magazine*, N.S., III (1890–1891), 315.

52 Farish, *Circuit Rider Dismounts*, 214–15.

Not long after the inauguration of President Benjamin Harrison in 1889, the Negro press began to accuse him of throwing his support to the Lily-white faction of his party in the South and of not giving the Negroes their fair reward in patronage. The protest soon became bitterly critical. In January, 1890, delegates from twenty-one states met at Chicago and organized the National Afro-American League. Professor Price was elected president and T. Thomas Fortune, who was easily the foremost Negro editor of his day, was chosen secretary. In a militant speech Fortune said of the old parties that "none of them cares a fig for the Afro-American" and that "another party may rise to finish the uncompleted work" of liberation.[53] Inspired by the Chicago meeting, which established numerous branch leagues, other Negro conventions were held. In Raleigh a "Negroes' 'Declaration of Independence' " was proclaimed, declaring that "The white Republicans have been traitors to us," and the Negroes, "the backbone of the Republican party, got nothing" in the way of patronage.[54] Joseph T. Wilson, chairman of a Negro convention in Richmond, protested that his race had been "treated as orphan children, apprenticed to the rice-, cotton-, and tobacco-growers at the South." As for the Negro's political plight, "The Republican party does not know what to do with us and the Democratic party wants to get rid of us, and we are at sea without sail or anchor drifting with the tide." [55] Five such conventions were held in 1890, and all of them were said to have "declared their disaffection with existing political parties." [56] The black man was beginning to feel toward his party much the same as the Southern white man was feeling toward his—that his vote was taken for granted and his needs were ignored.

By 1890 a million Negroes were reported to have joined the Colored Farmers' Alliance. At their annual convention, held at the same time and place as the convention of the white Alliance, the black farmers took a more radical position than their white brethren, substantially affirming the single-tax philosophy that "land is not property; can never be made property. . . . The land belongs to the sovereign people." They also leaned even more toward political independence. Their leader reminded them: "You are a race of farmers, seven-eighths of the colored people being

[53] New York *Age*, January 25, 1890.

[54] Richmond *Dispatch*, April 16, 1890.

[55] *Ibid.*

[56] *National Economist*, IV (1890), 234–35.

engaged in agriculture," and there was "little hope of the reformation of either of the existing political parties." [57]

As the Populist rift in the ranks of white solidarity approached, the Negro race was more prepared for insurgency than at any time since enfranchisement. Leaders shrewdly calculated their opportunities. For some it was the chance to "teach the White Republicans a lesson"; for others, to strike a blow against "our old, ancient and constant enemy—the Democracy"; for still others, an experiment in joint action with white Southerners on a platform of agrarian radicalism. The general temper was perhaps best expressed in the slogan offered by one Negro: "Let the vote be divided; it will be appreciated by the party who succeeds to power." [58]

The appeal that the proslavery argument had for the poorer class of whites had been grounded on the fear of being leveled, economically as well as socially, with a mass of liberated Negroes. Social leveling after emancipation was scotched by sundry expedients, but the menace of economic leveling still remained. The rituals and laws that exempted the white worker from the penalties of caste did not exempt him from competition with black labor, nor did they carry assurance that the penalties of black labor might not be extended to white.

The propagandists of the New-South order, in advertising the famed cheap labor of their region, were not meticulous in distinguishing between the color of their wares. If they stressed the "large body of strong, hearty, active, docile and easily contented negro laborers" who conformed to "the apostolic maxim of being 'contented with their wages,' and [having] no disposition to 'strike,' " they claimed the same virtues for the "hardy native Anglo-Saxon stock." The pledge of the *Manufacturers' Record,* for example, that "long hours of labor and moderate wages will continue to be the rule for many years to come," amounted almost to a clause of security in the promissory note by which the New South got capital to set up business. Additional security was not lacking. "The white laboring classes here," wrote an Alabama booster, "are separated

[57] *Ibid.*

[58] See opinions of several Negro leaders under the title "Will a Division Solve the Problem," in *Southland,* I (1890), 222–44; also Huntsville *Gazette,* March 29, 1890; November 21, 1891.

from the Negroes, working all day side by side with them, by an innate consciousness of race superiority. This sentiment dignifies the character of white labor. It excites a sentiment of sympathy and equality on their part with the classes above them, and in this way becomes a wholesome social leaven." [59]

It was an entirely safe assumption that for a long time to come race consciousness would divide, more than class consciousness would unite, Southern labor. Fifty strikes against the employment of Negro labor in the period from 1882 to 1900 testify to white labor's determination to draw a color line of its own. It is clear that in its effort to relegate to the Negro the less desirable, unskilled jobs, and to exclude him entirely from some industries, white labor did not always have the co-operation of white employers.[60]

In the cotton mills, at least, racial solidarity between employer and employee held fairly firm. By a combination of pressures and prejudices, a tacit understanding was reached that the cotton-mill villages were reserved for whites only. Probably no class of Southerners responded to the vision of the New South more hopefully than those who almost overnight left the old farm for the new factory. The cotton-mill millennium had been proclaimed as the salvation of "the necessitous masses of the poor whites." One enthusiastic promoter promised that "for the operative it would be Elysium itself." Historians have placed the "philanthropic incentive," undoubtedly present in some cases, high in the list of motives behind the whole mill campaign.

The transition from cotton field to cotton mill was not nearly so drastic as that which accompanied the change from primitive agriculture to modern factory in England and New England. For one thing, the mill families usually moved directly from farm to factory, and usually came from the vicinity of the mill. For another, the ex-farmer mill hand found himself in a mill community made up almost entirely of ex-farmers, where a foreigner, a Northerner, or even a city-bred Southerner was a curiosity. As late as 1907 a study revealed that 75.8 per cent of the women and children in

[59] John W. Dubose, *The Mineral Wealth of Alabama and Birmingham Illustrated* (Birmingham, 1886), 109.

[60] Charles H. Wesley, *Negro Labor in the United States, 1850–1925; A Study in American Economic History* (New York, 1927), 235–38.

Southern cotton mills had spent their childhood on the farm, and the 20.2 per cent who came from villages usually came from mill villages.[61]

The company-owned shanties into which they moved differed little from the planter- or merchant-owned shanties they had evacuated, except that the arrangement of the houses was a reversion to the "quarters" of the ante-bellum plantation instead of the dispersed cropper system. As pictured by an investigator in Georgia in 1890, "rows of loosely built, weather-stained frame houses, all of the same ugly pattern and buttressed by clumsy chimneys," lined a dusty road. "No porch, no doorstep even, admits to these barrack-like quarters." Outside, in the bald, hard-packed earth was planted, like some forlorn standard, the inevitable martin pole with its pendant gourds. Inside were heaped the miserable belongings that had furnished the cropper's cabin: "a shackling bed, tricked out in gaudy patchwork, a few defunct 'split-bottom' chairs, a rickety table, and a jumble of battered crockery," and on the walls the same string of red peppers, gourd dipper, and bellows. In certain mill villages of Georgia in 1890 not a watch or clock was to be found. "Life is regulated by the sun and the factory bell"—just as it had once been by the sun and farm bell. The seasons in the vocabulary of the cracker proletariat were still "hog-killin'," "cotton-choppin'," and " 'tween crops." The church was still the focus of social life, and the mill family was almost as migratory as the cropper family. The whole of this rustic industrialism moved to a rural rhythm.[62]

Mill-village paternalism was cut from the same pattern of poverty and makeshift necessity that had served for plantation and crop-lien paternalism. In place of the country supply store that advanced goods against a crop lien there was the company store that advanced them against wages, and since the weaver was as rarely able to add and multiply as was the plowman, accounts were highly informal. Mill-village workers were sometimes little further advanced toward a money economy than were cotton croppers, and

[61] Davidson, *Child Labor Legislation in the Southern Textile States*, 7–8; Thompson, *From the Cotton Field to the Cotton Mill*, 109–10; Mitchell, *Rise of the Cotton Mills*, 173–86.

[62] Clare de Graffenried, "The Georgia Cracker in the Cotton Mill," in *Century Magazine*, N.S., XIX (1891), 487–88.

payday might bring word from the company store that the family had not "paid out" that week. Pay was often scrip, good only at the company store, or redeemable in cash at intervals. Company-owned houses were usually provided at low rent and sometimes rent free. "Lint-head" fealty often carried with it certain feudal privileges like those of gathering wood from company lands and pasturing cows on company fields. The unincorporated company town, in which everything was owned by the mill corporation, was the most completely paternalistic. Here company schools and company churches were frequently subsidized by the corporation, which of course controlled employment of preacher and teacher.[63] In the smaller mills the relationship between owner and employees was highly personal and intimate, with a large degree of dependency on the part of the workers. "Not only are relations more friendly and intimate than at the North," found a Northern writer, "but there is conspicuous freedom from the spirit of drive and despotism. Even New England superintendents and overseers in their Southern mills soon glide into prevailing *laissez-faire* or else leave in despair." [64]

After all allowance has been made for the manna of paternalism, the "family wage," and the greater purchasing power of money in the South, the wages of Southern textile workers remained miserably low. The very fact that the wages of the head of a family combined with those of the other adult members were inadequate to support dependents makes the "family wage" a curious apology for the system. Wages of adult male workers of North Carolina in the nineties were 40 to 50 cents a day. Men constituted a minority of the workers, about 35 per cent in the four leading textile states in 1890; women, 40 per cent; and children between the ages of ten and fifteen years, 25 per cent. The wages of children, who entered into degrading competition with their parents, varied considerably, but there is record of mills in North Carolina that paid 10 and 12 cents a day for child labor.[65] The work week averaged about seventy hours for men, women, and children. Wages were slow to improve, and did not keep pace with mounting capitalization and profits.

[63] Mitchell, *Rise of the Cotton Mills*, 225–26.

[64] De Graffenried, "Georgia Cracker in the Cotton Mill," *loc. cit.*, 487.

[65] Davidson, *Child Labor Legislation in the Southern Textile States*, 8, 16.

Adult male spinners in representative mills of North Carolina who had received $2.53 a week in 1885 were getting $2.52 in 1895, and adult female spinners in Alabama got $2.76 a week in the former and $2.38 in the latter year.[66] Hourly wages for adult male spinners in the South Atlantic states were not quite 3 cents in 1890, only 2.3 cents in 1895, and a little over 3 cents in 1900; for female spinners in the same section the rate declined from about 4.5 cents an hour in 1890 to 4 cents in 1900.[67] Yet with these wages and conditions, there seems to have been no trouble in filling the company houses to overflowing. Few workers ever returned to farming permanently, and strikes were almost unheard of.

The glimpses one gets of life among this sunbonneted, wool-hatted proletariat raise doubts about the sense of *noblesse oblige* and the "philanthropic incentives" with which their employers have been credited. If paternalism sheltered them from the most ruthless winds of industrial conflict, it was a paternalism that could send its ten-year-old children off to the mills at dawn and see them come home with a lantern at night. It could watch its daughters come to marriageable age with "a dull heavy eye, yellow, blotched complexion, dead-looking hair," its "unmarried women of thirty . . . wrinkled, bent, and haggard," while the lot of them approached old age as illiterate as Negro field hands.[68] If white solidarity between employees and employer was to save the white worker from the living standard of the Negro, the results in the cotton mills were not very reassuring.

The extent to which labor in other industries shared in the prosperity of the New South is indicated by the level of wages maintained. In few industries or crafts did wages rise appreciably, and in many they were actually reduced. In the tobacco industry of the South Atlantic states, for example, cigar makers got 26 cents an hour in 1890 and 25 cents in 1900, while stemmers' wages remained at about 10 cents; in representative leather industries of the same states tanners remained on 11-cent wages, while in the South Cen-

66 *Eleventh Annual Report of the Commissioner of Labor, 1895–96* (Washington, 1897), 184, 235.

67 *Nineteenth Annual Report of the Commissioner of Labor, 1904* (Washington, 1905), 385.

68 De Graffenried, "Georgia Cracker in the Cotton Mill," *loc. cit.*, 489–93, 495; Davidson, *Child Labor Legislation in the Southern Textile States*, 12–13.

tral states their wages fell from 12.75 cents in 1890 to 11.5 cents in 1900; compositors' wages in the printing industry advanced from about 24 cents to nearly 26 cents in the South Atlantic states over the decade, from 28 cents to 29 cents in the South Central states; machinists did little better than hold their own in this period; bricklayers' wages declined from 45 cents to 43 cents in the South Central states and rose from 35 cents to about 37 cents in the South Atlantic states; carpenters in the former section got nearly 26 cents in 1890 and over 27 cents in 1900, while in the latter section their wages were raised from about 24 cents to about 26 cents; and wages of unskilled labor in the building trades varied from 8 cents to 12 cents an hour in the nineties.[69]

To a large extent the expanding industrialization of the New South was based upon the labor of women and children who were driven into the mills and shops to supplement the low wages earned by their men. In several states they were being drawn into industry much more rapidly than men. In representative establishments studied in Alabama the number of men increased 31 per cent between 1885 and 1895, that of women increased 75 per cent; girls under eighteen, 158 per cent; and boys under eighteen, 81 per cent. The increases over the same period in Kentucky were 3 per cent for men, 70 per cent for women, 65 per cent for girls, and 76 per cent for boys.[70] Of the 400,586 male children between the ages of ten and fourteen gainfully employed in the United States in 1890, the two census divisions of the Southern states accounted for 256,502, and of the 202,427 girls of that age at work they listed 130,546. The great majority in each case were employed in agriculture, fisheries, and mining.[71] Thousands of women who went to work in the cities lived on subsistence wages. In Charleston shops, where the average weekly earnings for women were $4.22, were "well-born, well-educated girl[s] side by side in the least attractive pursuits with the 'cracker.' " In Richmond, where women's wages averaged $3.93 a week, there was an "almost universal pallor and sallowness of countenance" among working women. In Atlanta "great illiteracy

[69] *Nineteenth Annual Report of the Commissioner of Labor, 1904,* pp. 374, 403, 417, 430–31, 461, 465.

[70] *United States Bureau of Labor Bulletin No. 10* (Washington, 1897), 242.

[71] *Eleventh Census, 1890, Compendium,* Pt. III, 460–62.

exists among the working girls. Their moral condition also leaves much to be desired. The cost of living is comparatively high." [72]

In spite of the contributions of women and children, the working family in the South seemed less able to own a house than that of any other section. Of the eighteen cities in the whole country with a percentage of home tenancy above 80, eleven were in the South. Birmingham, with 89.84 per cent of tenancy had the highest rate in the United States; the percentage in Norfolk was 85.62, and in Macon, 84.66. In the South Atlantic states as a whole, over 75 per cent of home dwellers were tenants.[73] Interlarded with the long, shady boulevards of the "best sections" of Nashville, Norfolk, Macon, Memphis, and Montgomery were alleys lined with one- and two-room shanties of colored domestics. In the "worst sections" of every city sprawled the jungle of a darktown with its own business streets and uproarious, crime-infested "amusement" streets. Beyond, in suburban squalor and isolation, were the gaunt barracks of white industrial workers, huddled around the factories.

Conditions of public health and sanitation under which the urban working classes lived cannot be grasped from general descriptions, since health improvements and safeguards were highly discriminatory within the cities. Richmond justly boasted in 1887 of her relatively high expenditures for municipal improvements, of being "the best-paved city of her population in the Union," and of the splendor of Broad, Main, and Cary streets, "yearly improved by elegant houses built for merchants and manufacturers." Yet in 1888 the United States Commissioner of Labor blamed "bad drainage of the city, bad drinking water, and unsanitary homes" for the appalling conditions of health among the working girls of Richmond.[74] New Orleans, with a long start over her sisters, easily achieved pre-eminence among unsanitary cities by the filth and squalor of her slums. The president of the State Board of Health of Louisiana reported in 1881 that "The gutters of the 472 miles of dirt streets are in foul condition, being at various points choked up with garbage, filth and mud, and consequently may be regarded

[72] *Fourth Annual Report of the Commissioner of Labor, 1888* (Washington, 1889), 13, 16, 24, 68.

[73] *Eleventh Census, 1890, Farms and Homes*, 29.

[74] *Fourth Annual Report of the Commissioner of Labor, 1888*, p. 24.

simply as receptacles for putrid matters and stagnant waters. The street crossings are in like manner more or less obstructed with filth and black, stinking mud." [75]

"We have awakened, or are fast awakening, from our dream," commented a Southern editor. "We have pauperism, crime, ignorance, discontent in as large a measure as a people need. Every question that has knocked at European doors for solution will in turn knock at ours." [76] When work relief was offered at twenty cents a week by private charity in Alexandria, Virginia, "poor women were more than glad to get the work, and came from far and near, and many had to be sent away disappointed every week." [77] In New Orleans "a multitude of people, white and black alike," lived on a dole of thirteen cents a day in the nineties.[78]

Labor in the Southern textile mills, largely unorganized, has claimed a disproportionate share of the attention of scholars. The result has been a neglect of the history of labor in other industries and in the crafts, as well as an encouragement of the impression that no labor movement existed in the region at this period.

A study of the labor movement in the largest Southern city concludes that "the South, to judge by New Orleans, had craft labor movements smaller but similar to those in Northern cities," and that they were growing in power and influence in the eighties and nineties.[79] It was a period of testing unknown strength and challenging tentatively the Old-South labor philosophy of the New-South doctrinaires and their pledge to Northern investors that long hours, low wages, and docile labor were assured.

However appealing white Southern labor found the doctrine of white supremacy, it realized pretty early that "In nearly all the trades, the rates of compensation for the whites is [*sic*] governed more or less by the rates at which the blacks can be hired," and that the final appeal in a strike was "the Southern employer's ability to hold the great mass of negro mechanics *in terrorem* over the heads

[75] *Annual Report of the Board of Health of the State of Louisiana . . . for the Year 1881* (New Orleans, 1881), 5–6. See also, Shugg, *Origins of Class Struggle in Louisiana*, 282–89.

[76] New Orleans *Times*, September 13, 1881.

[77] New York *Tribune*, February 10, 1881.

[78] Shugg, *Origins of Class Struggle in Louisiana*, 297.

[79] Roger W. Shugg, "The New Orleans General Strike of 1892," in *Louisiana Historical Quarterly*, XXI (1938), 559.

of the white." [80] Agreement upon the nature of their central problem did not bring agreement upon the proper means of dealing with it. Two possible but contradictory policies could be used: eliminate the Negro as a competitor by excluding him from the skilled trades either as an apprentice or a worker, or take him in as an organized worker committed to the defense of a common standard of wages. Southern labor wavered between these antithetical policies from the seventies into the nineties, sometimes adopting one, sometimes the other.

The rising aristocracy of labor, the railway brotherhoods, drew a strict color line. On the other hand, the Brotherhood of Carpenters and Joiners claimed fourteen Negro locals in the South in 1886. The coopers', the cigar makers', the bricklayers', the steel workers', and the carpenters' unions had by the eighties adopted the practice of "issuing . . . separate charters to Negro craftsmen wherever existing locals debarred them." The federations of dock workers in the cotton ports of New Orleans, Savannah, and Galveston overrode race barriers and admitted, equally, white and black longshoremen, draymen, yardmen, cotton classers, and screwmen. Especially successful were the efforts to organize the Negroes in New Orleans. The Central Trades and Labor Assembly of that city was said "to have done more to break the color line in New Orleans than any other thing . . . since emancipation of the slaves." [81]

Much of this temporary "era of good feeling" between black and white workingmen has been credited to the guidance of the Knights of Labor. The Knights' doctrine of interracial solidarity and democratic idealism makes the history of the order of particular significance for the central problem of Southern labor. The history of the Knights also confutes the legend of the Southern worker's indifference to unionism. As soon as the national organization of the Knights was established in 1878 it dispatched 15 organizers to the South. A quickening of Southern interest was evident in 1884, and by 1886 there were in ten states 21,208 members attached to the Southern District assembly and perhaps 10,000 more

[80] Bruce, *Rise of the New South*, 164–65.

[81] Sterling D. Spero and Abram L. Harris, *The Black Worker. The Negro and the Labor Movement* (New York, 1931), 22, 43–44; Wesley, *Negro Labor in the United States*, 236–37, 255.

members of locals attached to national trade assemblies or directly to the General Assembly of the Knights. An incomplete list places 487 locals in the South in 1888, but there were many more. Concentrated around such cities as Birmingham, Knoxville, Louisville, New Orleans, and Richmond, locals were also scattered over rural areas and embraced cotton hands and sugar workers, black as well as white. The national convention of the Knights in 1886, the year of their greatest strength, met in Richmond and was attended by delegates of both races from many parts of the South. The convention heard reports that "colored people of the South are flocking to us" and that "rapid strides" have been made in the South.[82]

The Knights were involved in numerous strikes in the South during the latter years of the eighties. These conflicts broke out in the coal mines of Alabama and Tennessee, in the cotton mills of Augusta, Georgia, and Cottondale, Alabama, among the sugar workers of Louisiana and the lumber workers in Alabama. The Knights' greatest strike victory, that against the Missouri Pacific system and Jay Gould in 1885, was won in considerable part in the shops of Texas and Arkansas. The Southwestern strike of 1886, which marked the climax and greatest failure of the order, broke out in Texas, and some of its most violent phases occurred there. The Knights experimented with co-operative enterprises of various kinds, though on no such scale as did the Farmers' Alliance. The order figured conspicuously in the politics of several cities. In 1886 the Workingman's Reform party, backed by the Knights, elected two blacksmiths, a cobbler, and a tanner to the city council of Richmond, and took control of nearly all departments of the government. In 1887 the Knights claimed that they had elected a Congressman and eleven of the fifteen city council members in Lynchburg, a majority of the city and county officers in Macon, and several officers in Mobile. The following year they asserted that they had elected the mayors of Jacksonville, Vicksburg, and Anniston. The mayor of Anniston was a carpenter, and the council included two molders, a brickmaker, a butcher, a watchmaker, and

[82] Frederic Myers, "The Knights of Labor in the South," in *Southern Economic Journal* (Chapel Hill), VI (1939–1940), 479–85. One official asserted that the order had 100,000 members in five Southern states, but this was an exaggerated claim.

a shoemaker. Their reforms were mild enough, but their experimental defiance of the color line was bitterly attacked in the Southern press. Under these burdens and the additional ones of lost strikes, the Knights passed into a decline in the South as in the nation. Co-operation with the Farmers' Alliance gave the order a decided agrarian color by the end of the eighties.[83]

A second peak of activity in the Southern labor movement came in 1892. It therefore coincided with the outburst of the Populist revolt and, like it, was symptomatic of popular discontent with the New Order of the Redeemers. It may be illustrated by two unrelated outbreaks of contrasting character—the general strike in New Orleans and the violent insurrection of Tennessee coal miners against the employment of convict labor.

The general strike in New Orleans, which followed the Homestead strike in Pennsylvania and preceded the Pullman strike in Chicago, has been described as "the first general strike in American history to enlist both skilled and unskilled labor, black and white, and to paralyze the life of a great city." It came as "the climax of the strongest labor movement in the South." [84] New Orleans was about as well unionized as any city in the country when the American Federation of Labor began a successful drive early in 1892 that added thirty new chartered associations, thus bringing the total up to ninety-five. A new unity was achieved in the Workingmen's Amalgamated Council, a centralized but democratically elected body made up of two delegates from each of the forty-nine unions affiliated with the A. F. of L. The New Orleans Board of Trade, an organization of the merchants of the city, was as determined to maintain traditional prerogatives of hiring and firing as the labor council was to establish the right of collective bargaining.

Inspired by a victory of the city streetcar drivers that put an end to a sixteen-hour day and gained a closed-shop agreement, the so-called "Triple-Alliance," consisting of the unions of the teamsters, scalesmen, and packers (which included Negro members), struck

[83] *Ibid.*, 485–87; Frank W. Taussig, "The South-Western Strike of 1886," in *Quarterly Journal of Economics* (Boston, Cambridge), I (1886–1887), 184–222; Dallas *Daily News*, March 2–April 23, 1886; Richmond *Dispatch*, May 18, July 2, September 30, October 3, 1886; Jackson *Clarion*, November 9, 1887; *National Economist*, II (1889), 221; *Tradesman*, XIV (May 15, 1886), 23.

[84] Shugg, "New Orleans General Strike of 1892," *loc. cit.*, 547.

for a ten-hour day, overtime pay, and the preferential closed shop. The Workingmen's Amalgamated Council appointed a committee of five workers, including a Negro, to conduct the strike. The Board of Trade refused to recognize the unions or to deal with them in any way. The workers' committee first threatened, and finally, on November 8, called a general strike in support of the unions of unskilled workers. Forty-two union locals, with over 20,000 members, who with their families made up nearly half of the population of the city, stopped work. Each union on strike demanded recognition and a closed shop. Business came to a virtual standstill; bank clearings were cut in half. The employers openly declared that it was "a war to the knife" and that they would resort to extreme measures, including violence. Yet in spite of the hysteria kept up by the newspapers, the importation of strikebreakers, and the threat of military intervention, the strikers refrained from violence and there was no bloodshed. On the third day of the strike the governor of the state came to the aid of the capitalists with a proclamation that, in effect, set up martial law and implied that the militia would be called unless the strike was ended. The labor committee, never very aggressive, accepted a compromise which, though gaining the original demands of the Triple Alliance concerning hours and wages, forfeited the fight for collective bargaining and the closed shop. The Board of Trade, confident that labor, like the Negro, had been put in its "place," boasted that New Orleans was an open-shop city, and that the old philosophy of labor had been vindicated.[85]

The second labor struggle was fought upon a more primitive level, for the most elemental rights, and fought with savage violence. Competition with convict labor leased by corporations had been a long-standing and often-voiced grievance of labor all over the South. As a conservative paper stated the case in Alabama, "Employers of convicts pay so little for their labor that it makes it next to impossible for those who give work to free labor to compete with them in any line of business. As a result, the price paid for labor is based upon the price paid convicts." [86]

In 1883 the Tennessee Coal, Iron, and Railroad Company leased

[85] *Ibid.*, 547–59; New Orleans *Times-Democrat*, October 25, November 4–11, 1892.
[86] Fort Payne (Ala.) *Herald*, quoted in Birmingham *Age-Herald*, August 8, 1889.

the Tennessee penitentiary, containing some 1,300 convicts. Thomas Collier Platt, the New York Republican leader, was president of the company and Colonel Colyar, the Tennessee Democratic leader, was general counsel. "For some years after we began the convict labor system," said Colyar, "we found that we were right in calculating that free laborers would be loath to enter upon strikes when they saw that the company was amply provided with convict labor." [87]

Tennessee labor protested, and the legislature occasionally investigated, once reporting that the branch prisons were "hell holes of rage, cruelty, despair and vice." But nothing was done. In 1891, the miners of Briceville, Anderson County, were presented by the Tennessee Coal Mine Company with an "iron-clad" contract relinquishing employees' right to a check weigher, agreeing to "scrip" pay, and pledging no strikes. When they turned down the contract the company ordered convicts to tear down their houses and build stockades for the convicts who were to replace free labor. The evicted miners then marched in force on the stockades and, without bloodshed, compelled guards, officers, and convicts to board a train for Knoxville. Governor John P. Buchanan, with three companies of militia, promptly returned the convicts to the stockades. A few days later more than a thousand armed miners packed the guards and convicts off to Knoxville a second time, and those of another company along with them, again without bloodshed. Only after the Governor had promised to call a special session of the legislature were the miners pacified. Labor demonstrations in Chattanooga, Memphis, Nashville, and other towns demanded an end to convict labor and sent aid to the miners. Kentucky and Alabama labor, afflicted with the same evil, also became aroused. The Tennessee state convention of the Farmers' Alliance, which the Governor attended, demanded the repeal of the convict-lease law. In spite of the official position of the Alliance, the fact that there were fifty-four Alliance members of the legislature, and that Governor Buchanan owed his election to the order, the special session of the legislature took no satisfactory action. After a futile appeal to the courts, the miners took the law into their own hands. On the night of October 31, 1891, they forcibly freed the convicts of the

[87] Nashville *Daily American,* August 23, 1892.

Tennessee Coal Mine Company, allowed them all to escape, and burned down the stockades. They repeated the same tactics later at two other mining companies, releasing in all some five hundred convicts. The mine operators of the area then employed free labor, gave up the "iron-clad" contract, and granted a check weigher.[88]

The insurrections of the following year made those of 1891 seem tame by comparison. The Tennessee struggles involved more men and deeper issues than the contemporary Homestead strike, but they got little attention then or later. These insurrections broke out in Middle Tennessee at the mines of the Tennessee Coal and Iron Company, which had put its free labor on half time and employed 360 convicts full time. Miners overcame the Tracy City guards, burned the stockades, and shipped the convicts to Nashville. Inspired by this example, miners of one of the Tennessee Coal, Iron, and Railroad Company mines in Anderson County, at which convict labor had been reinstated, burned the stockades, renewed their war, and laid siege to Fort Anderson, which was occupied by militia and civil guards paid jointly by the company and the state to guard the convicts. Although the miners killed a few of the troops sent to relieve the besieged fort, the convicts were again reinstated. The final insurrection spelled the doom of the convict lease, however, for the following year the system was abolished by the legislature.[89]

By their actions the Tennessee miners, the New Orleans trade unions, and workers in the mines and foundries of Alabama, Georgia, and Virginia gave notice in 1892 that Southern labor was not going to accept the Old-South labor philosophy of the New-South leaders—not without a fight, anyway. The militancy of Southern labor also gave notice to the insurgent Southern farmer that he might seek recruits for the Populist revolt in the mines and factories as well as in the fields.

88 A. C. Hutson, Jr., "The Coal Miners' Insurrection of 1891 in Anderson County, Tennessee," in East Tennessee Historical Society's *Publications* (Knoxville), No. 7 (1935), 105–15; Nashville *Daily American,* July 17–21, August 13, 1891.

89 A. C. Hutson, Jr., "The Overthrow of the Convict Lease System in Tennessee," in East Tennessee Historical Society's *Publications,* No. 8 (1936), 82–103; Nashville *Daily American,* August 15–23, 1892; Memphis *Appeal-Avalanche,* January 3, 7, March 1, 1892.

CHAPTER IX

SOUTHERN POPULISM

THE agrarian resurgence of 1890 revived the old debate over the sectional diplomacy of the South. Conservative Southerners were as devoted to the Northeastern affiliation and as opposed to a Western alliance as they had been in 1878. "To talk of the South making a political alliance" with the West, declared the Charleston *News and Courier,* "is to talk utter nonsense." The Augusta *Chronicle* agreed that "The South has everything to lose and nothing to gain by a league with the West." [1]

Southern Alliancemen, on the other hand, were positive in their Western leanings. Their only serious doubt was whether they could co-operate effectively with their Western brethren so long as the two sections were divided by party lines. Unable to gain the concessions from the old parties that the Southerners had gained from the Democrats, Western Alliancemen had formed a third party in 1890. In Kansas and the Dakotas, the three Western states that had joined the Southern Alliance in 1889, the Populists won striking victories, electing two Senators and several Congressmen. On the face of it, however, the Southern strategy of electing Alliance candidates within the old party appeared much more impressive. Southern Alliancemen claimed a majority in eight state legislatures, six Alliance-elected governors, and more than fifty Congressmen who were pledged to support the Alliance platform. The apparent success of the strategy was the strongest argument conservative leaders of the Alliance had against the radicals who wanted to leave the old party.

At the annual Alliance convention, meeting in Ocala, Florida,

[1] Charleston *News and Courier,* September 23, 1890; Augusta *Weekly Chronicle,* October 22, 1890.

in December, 1890, the debate raged. "The third party project is the uppermost topic of discussion," reported a local paper. Western delegates made it their mission to convert their Southern brothers to Populism. Terence V. Powderly and other Knights of Labor lent a hand. The Colored Alliance, also meeting in Ocala, was reported ready for revolt, and so were several Southern white leaders. After prolonged debate the conservative views of Macune and Leonidas F. Livingston prevailed, and a resolution postponing consideration of a third party until February, 1892, was adopted. President Polk's interpretation of the action, however, gave no comfort to conservatives. "If the Democrats of the Fifty-second Congress do not manifest a willingness to grant our demands," he said, "a third party is inevitable and the Southern Democratic Alliance men will be in. They are determined to gain the ends they are striving for and they will smash any party that opposes them." [2]

The convention revised Alliance demands to emphasize the subtreasury plan and other Southern ideas, and in revised form they became the "Ocala Platform" by which Populists were later to swear. Dissatisfied with the Macune compromise, radical Alliancemen proceeded with plans for the third party, but the great majority of members undoubtedly put aside any thought of revolt until the strategy of working within the old party was given a fair trial. All would depend upon the results achieved.

If the strategy of working within the old party offered fair prospects anywhere it would seem to have been in Georgia, where the Alliance had elected the governor, three fourths of the senators, and four fifths of the representatives. The first achievement of the "Farmers' Legislature," however, was far from reassuring, for it elected Gordon to the Senate seat that Brown had just vacated, thus replacing one member of the old bourgeois Triumvirate with another. Several high Alliance officials even supported Patrick Calhoun of the Richmond Terminal for the place. On the other hand, the farmers extended the powers of the railroad commission, placed restrictions upon banking corporations and railroads, strengthened

[2] Quoted in New York *Herald*, December 9, 1890. See also, Jacksonville *Florida Times-Union*, December 6, 1890; Atlanta *Constitution*, December 2–7, 1890; Raleigh *Progressive Farmer*, December 9, 1890.

state inspection of fertilizers, and established a Negro college. Disappointed Alliancemen pronounced these achievements insufficient and declared that unfair taxation, the lien system, and railroad overcapitalization and discrimination had been left untouched. The leading Alliance paper of Georgia accused the "silk-hat bosses" of deserting the "wool-hat" rank and file.[3]

Tennessee had elected State Alliance President John P. Buchanan governor in 1890 and placed a strong Alliance delegation in the legislature. The discontent of radical agrarians and miners with this administration has been explained by the fact that, on the whole, "Governor Buchanan's administration was as conservative as former Democratic administrations in Tennessee."[4] The Virginia Alliance had been promised a railroad commission by the Democratic state chairman in exchange for a pledge to maintain party unity. The Democratic assembly, however, defeated both the Alliance railroad commission bill and a bill aimed at the American Tobacco Company trust.[5] Kentucky agrarians were similarly disappointed over their experiment with maintaining "party unity." Governor John Young Brown, famous for his part in the Compromise of 1877, "went the whole way with the Alliance" while soliciting votes in 1891, but in his first message to the Alliance legislature he cautioned it "against legislation which will discriminate against the legitimate interests of corporations and property." In spite of a mandate for railroad regulation recently handed down by a constitutional convention, the Kentucky lawmakers left the railroads a free hand and delivered few of their promised reforms.[6]

For all the terror he inspired among South Carolina aristocrats and Redeemers and the number of them he turned out of office, Governor Tillman recommended only moderate changes once in power. In the main, these were of two general categories: measures to enhance the power of the upland counties and to push the Negro

[3] Arnett, *Populist Movement in Georgia*, 118–22; C. Vann Woodward, *Tom Watson: Agrarian Rebel* (New York, 1938), 162–63.

[4] J. A. Sharp, "The Farmers' Alliance and the People's Party in Tennessee," in East Tennessee Historical Society's *Publications*, No. 10 (1939), 91.

[5] Moger, *Rebuilding of the Old Dominion*, 69–73; Sheldon, *Populism in the Old Dominion*, 70–71.

[6] Clark, *History of Kentucky*, 598–99; *National Economist*, VI (1891), 209–10.

farther down the social and political ladder, and measures to encourage agricultural and industrial colleges at the expense of the liberal-arts institution. He did raise taxes on corporate wealth slightly, but the bill to reorganize the railway commission, in which the Alliance was especially interested, failed.[7] He won the praise of conservatives by declaring, "It is sickening to hear the South talk about forming a political alliance with the West." [8] Alliancemen said that "by speech, interview, and letter" Tillman was "scattering seeds of discord and discontent, for the sole purpose of injuring the Alliance," and that he had "consorted with the most violent and vicious enemies of the Alliance." At its annual meeting of 1891 the South Carolina Alliance formally repudiated Tillman by a unanimous vote, in spite of the protests of the Governor, who was present.[9]

Governor Hogg and the Texas Alliance enjoyed a honeymoon of several months during which the legislature approved a railroad commission, an alien land law aimed at foreign syndicates, and laws regulating public and railway securities, increasing educational funds, and abolishing the convict lease.[10] A rift between Hogg and the Alliance appeared when the Governor insisted upon an appointive, instead of an elective, railroad commission and then refused to appoint any Alliancemen to the commission. Another cause of Alliance complaint was the Governor's proposal to invest the permanent public-school fund of Texas in the bonds of railroads yet to be built. Alliancemen divided into pro- and anti-Hogg factions, and the Governor appears to have encouraged the division. His friends issued an "Austin Manifesto" in March, 1891, charging that the opposition leaders were scheming to turn the Alliance into a third party. They also attempted to organize an antisubtreasury Alliance and split the state organization. In October State Democratic Chairman N. W. Finley published a letter denouncing the "subtreasury Alliance political party" as a "treacherous enemy" which would be "kept out of democratic councils and democratic primaries." Alliancemen who adhered to the subtreasury plan were

[7] Simkins, *Pitchfork Ben Tillman*, 170–90.

[8] Quoted in Charleston *News and Courier*, September 23, 1890.

[9] *National Economist*, V (1891), 322; *Southern Mercury*, XI (May 19, 1892), 1; Atlanta *Southern Alliance Farmer*, quoted in Augusta *Chronicle*, July 2, 1891.

[10] Bailey, "Life of James Stephen Hogg," 295–96, 320–26.

thereby expelled from the old party. Governor Hogg congratulated Finley on the "justice and soundness" of his ruling.[11]

The Alliance attempts to gain its ends within the old party were also reported to be going on the rocks in Alabama, Florida, and Mississippi. The North Carolina legislature "made practically no efforts to bring relief to the farmers or to carry out the progressive points of the platform on which the majority had been elected." [12] Instead, it amended the state charter of the Alliance to render it politically impotent.

Southern critics of the Alliance, as if by concerted agreement, chose the subtreasury plan as their main point of attack. Democratic politicians who had been elected on the Alliance platform in 1890 found the subtreasury intolerable a year or two later. Governors Tillman and Hogg pronounced the plan "paternalism" and "class legislation." Alliance-elected Senators Gordon of Georgia and Zebulon B. Vance of North Carolina viewed the subtreasury with alarm, and so did Senators George of Mississippi, Morgan of Alabama, and Reagan and Richard Coke of Texas.[13] Disaffected Alliance members were encouraged to organize an antisubtreasury Alliance. With the avowed object of "overthrowing the old organization," a few hundred delegates from Mississippi, Arkansas, Texas, Kansas, and Minnesota met at St. Louis in September, 1891, but their organization was stillborn.[14]

In spite of the state-rights and constitutional thunder of the politicians, the uneasiness of many Southern members, and the indifference of Western members, the Farmers' Alliance accepted the challenge of the conservatives and proclaimed the subtreasury a test of loyal Alliancemen. This stand was of doubtful political expediency, yet during the summer of 1891 one state Alliance after another held its annual meeting and solidly endorsed the Ocala

[11] James S. Hogg to N. W. Finley, October 31, 1891, in James Stephen Hogg Papers (University of Texas Library, Austin); *Southern Mercury,* XI (April 21, 1892), 5; *ibid.* (May 19, 1892), 9; Dallas *Morning News,* January 22, February 2, May 30, 31, October 25, 1891; Martin, *People's Party in Texas,* 26–27, 36–38.

[12] Philip Weaver, "The Gubernatorial Election of 1896 in North Carolina" (M.A. thesis, University of North Carolina, 1937), 17–18. This legislature was elected in 1892, but is included as one of the Alliance-Democratic experiments.

[13] Scott, *Sub-Treasury Plan and The Land and Loan System,* 63; *National Economist,* IV (1890), 37; Jackson *Clarion-Ledger,* May 7, July 9, 15, November 19, 1891.

[14] Dallas *Morning News,* September 15, 16, 1891; *National Economist,* VI (1891), 2.

Platform and the subtreasury. Announcing the results of thirteen such state conventions, the *National Economist* reported very few votes cast against the subtreasury.[15] These declarations were in effect a challenge to the old party to come over to Alliance demands or face a revolt.

The stiffening tone of Alliance statements and determined conduct of its leaders were causing alarm among old-party leaders. Justice Lamar expressed in 1891 his "deep, intense, and almost tremulous solicitude, mixed with painful regrets" over "the wonderful change which has been going on in the character, spirit and purpose of the farmers of Mississippi, indeed of the whole South." It seems the farmers had adopted "the selfish, ignoble idea of government—namely a means of their own self-enrichment and aggrandizement." [16]

A wonderful change had also taken place in Democratic attitudes toward the Alliance. In 1890 the movement had been widely regarded as a boon to national Democratic party interests at the expense of Western Republicans. A conservative Alabama paper had said the Alliance "will undoubtedly result in great good to the Democratic party," and a Mississippi editor agreed that "the Republican party will feel the shock" while the Democrats would profit.[17] Now that the farmers were proving less tractable than expected, Alliance principles became the target for abuse once reserved for abolitionists and Carpetbaggers. The Nashville *Daily American*, which had supported Alliance candidates in 1890, considered the Ocala Platform a "hideous abortion of demagogy and fanaticism" in 1891, and declared "open war" on the Alliance as "an enemy of the Democratic party." [18] The Augusta *Chronicle* was "delighted to see the Alliance in the West send some farmers to Congress" in 1890, but pronounced its principles "paternalism run mad" in 1891.[19] Senator Vance, recently re-elected with Alliance support, declared the subtreasury and other demands "demagoguism and communism which mark a people as unfit for self-government." [20]

[15] *National Economist*, V (1891), 376.

[16] Quoted in Mayes, *Lucius Q. C. Lamar*, 552–53.

[17] Birmingham *Age-Herald*, July 30, 1890; Jackson *Clarion-Ledger*, July 31, 1890.

[18] Nashville *Daily American*, November 11, 1891.

[19] Augusta *Chronicle*, August 3, 1890; July 17, 1891.

[20] Quoted in Clement Dowd, *Life of Zebulon B. Vance* (Charlotte, 1897), 301.

It had been much easier to make promises to radical agrarians in 1890 than it was in 1892, a presidential election year. The time was approaching to nominate Grover Cleveland and rally the South to "sound money" and Northeastern conservatism. This was more difficult than it had once been. Senator Morgan believed that the nomination of Cleveland might lose certain states. A group of Democratic leaders in Alabama, Georgia, Mississippi, and Virginia sought to placate rebellious farmers with a free-silver platform and the nomination of David B. Hill of New York instead of Cleveland. The scheme was defeated in its early stages.[21] Yet every state Democratic convention of 1892, from Virginia to Texas, endorsed free silver in one form or other, and not one was a "Cleveland" platform. The South Carolina Democrats went so far as to adopt the Ocala Platform word for word and to resolve that the nomination of Cleveland would be "a repudiation of the demands of the Farmers' Alliance, which embody the true principles of Democracy, and a surrender . . . to the financial kings of the country." They carefully added that they would "actively support" any candidate nominated, no matter what his platform.[22]

The numerous Alliance-pledged and Alliance-supported Congressmen the South sent to Washington proved no more susceptible to Alliance control than had state officials elected in the same way. The Supreme Council of the Alliance had requested each Congressman elected with Alliance aid to refuse to enter any party caucus called to nominate a speaker unless "the principles of the Ocala platform are made a test of admission to said caucus." The entire Southern delegation, with the exception of Tom Watson, trooped into the Democratic caucus and was pledged to support for the speakership Charles F. Crisp, a Georgia conservative and an outspoken opponent of Alliance principles. The first Southern leader to shake off the old-party control, Watson was chosen Populist nominee for speaker by his Western colleagues. At home he founded the *People's Party Paper* and proclaimed that "Georgia is ready for the third party." [23]

21 Allan Nevins, *Grover Cleveland: A Study in Courage* (New York, 1932), 467–68, 483.

22 *Appletons' Annual Cyclopaedia . . . 1892*, p. 705.

23 Atlanta *People's Party Paper*, November 26, 1891; Woodward, *Tom Watson*, 186–93.

The success of the third party would be largely determined by the position taken by the Southern Alliance, and this question had become "the all-important subject of discussion from one end of the Order to the other," according to the *National Economist.* To follow the development of President Polk's ideas is to trace the steps that led to rebellion. The presidency of the Southern Alliance was a powerful office, and Polk of North Carolina had held it since 1889. His prestige and influence had spread all over the country. Early in 1891 he was warning the Democrats that the Alliance would not be content with free silver and minor demands of the Order, but would insist upon wholehearted support of the sub-treasury, government ownership of railroads, and the abolition of national banks. In February he pointed out that Cleveland was "a true and consistent friend of the money power" and unacceptable to the Alliance. In June he protested that the Order was not a third party, but that if revolt did come it would be because of "the domineering, intolerant and unreasonable action" of the Democrats. Should intelligent Alliancemen, he asked, oppose a party that adopted its demands and support a party that scorned them? Polk's unanimous re-election as president at the annual meeting of the Alliance in Indianapolis, November, 1891, was widely hailed as a victory by Populist leaders. He was already spoken of as the "most probable" presidential candidate of the new party in 1892.[24] The Confederation of Industrial Organizations, meeting at St. Louis on February 22, 1892, was attended by delegates of many national farmer and labor organizations, but by far the largest delegations were those of the white and colored Alliances of the South. In spite of opposition, third-party sympathizers seated Polk as chairman of the congress and carried the day in a mass meeting after formal adjournment with a resolution calling for a national Populist ticket in 1892.[25] The nearest the National Alliance ever came to official endorsement of revolt was an instruction handed

[24] Raleigh *Progressive Farmer* (Polk's paper), February 24, May 5, June 3, 1891; Richmond *Dispatch,* August 19, 1891; Indianapolis *Journal,* November 16, 1891; Washington *Post,* November 20, 1891; Nashville *Daily American,* November 22, 1891; Atlanta *People's Party Paper,* November 26, 1891; Stuart Noblin, *Leonidas La Fayette Polk; Agrarian Crusader* (Chapel Hill, 1949), 254–71.

[25] St. Louis *Republican,* February 24, 25, 1892; *Southern Mercury,* XI (January 14, 1892), 2.

down by high officials in May that "devotion to our principles" should take precedence over "party affiliations." [26]

The Populists were not able to swing all Alliancemen to the third party, but the movement affected Alliance membership variously. In Virginia there was a "sudden falling off in membership," [27] and the reports of the secretary of the North Carolina Alliance indicate a decline of 10 to 20 per cent in the last quarter of 1891.[28] On the other hand, the official organ of the Georgia Alliance announced in March, 1892, that "membership rolls are larger than they ever have been" and that "the Georgia Alliance is almost unanimously committed to the third party." [29] The National Order was reported to have enjoyed a 33.5 per cent "increase in paying members" in 1891.[30] There is no means of verifying these claims.

The nomination of Cleveland by the Democrats in June, 1892, did as much as anything to encourage revolt in the South. The only concession the Cleveland forces made to Southern Democrats, who pleaded for free silver to carry the South, was a plank denouncing the force bill placed foremost in the platform. This appeal to Southern state rights and race sentiment did little to make the nominee more acceptable to Alliancemen, for Cleveland had been made a symbol of all the reformers opposed in the old party. "Clevelandism," said the *National Economist,* "seeks to get beyond the Republicans in the direction of compliance with the grasping demands of the moneyed and monopolistic interests of this [Northeastern] section." A Virginia Alliance leader declared that the nomination had "snapped the last cord which binds free men to the Democratic party." [31]

The cause of Populism in the South suffered a heavy blow when

26 *Southern Mercury,* XI (May 12, 1892), 5, 9; Richmond *Virginia Sun,* May 11, 1892. According to the Montgomery *Daily Advertiser,* May 4, 5, 1892, the Alliance conference at Birmingham, where these instructions were adopted, voted 21 to 16 against an outright endorsement of the third party.

27 Sheldon, *Populism in the Old Dominion,* 49.

28 "Quarterly Report to the Lecturer of the First District for the Term Ending December 31, 1891," in Marion Butler Papers (University of North Carolina Library, Chapel Hill).

29 Atlanta *Southern Alliance Farmer,* March 21, 1892.

30 *National Economist,* VI (1891), 177.

31 *Ibid.,* VII (1892), 130; Robert Beverley, Jr., quoted in Richmond *Virginia Sun,* July 6, 1892.

Colonel Polk suddenly died on the eve of the third-party convention at Omaha that was expected to nominate him as the first Populist candidate for President. The nomination fell instead to General James B. Weaver of Iowa, the old Greenback campaigner. To balance the Union officer, General James G. Field of Virginia was given second place on the ticket.[32]

The issue of revolt or conformity in the South, however, was not settled in noisy conventions and secret councils. A generation of white-solidarity indoctrination had heightened the emotional content of that issue until it was the most explosive question Southerners had faced since 1861. Changing one's party in the South of the nineties involved more than changing one's mind. It might involve a falling-off of clients, the loss of a job, of credit at the store, or of one's welcome at church. It could split families, and it might even call in question one's loyalty to his race and his people. An Alabamian who had "voted for Democratic candidates for forty years" wrote after breaking with the old party that he had "never performed a more painful duty." [33] A Virginian declared after taking the same step that "It is like cutting off the right hand or putting out the right eye." [34] Old Hickory Alliance, No. 611, of Caroline County, Virginia, was doubtless soothing such troubled spirits when after earnest debate it resolved quaintly "That we pledge our support to the People's Party in a nonpartisan spirit, not for the sake of party, but for the sole purpose of securing the enactment of our demands into law." [35]

The painful transition from the old party to Populism was bridged in some states by a transitional party retaining the old name. Thus, for a few months after they were read out of the Democratic party, Texas Alliancemen found refuge in a party called the "Jeffersonian Democrats," which soon consolidated with the Populists. Another variation was the party organized by Reuben F. Kolb of Alabama, also called "Jeffersonian Democrats," which

[32] "General" James G. Field's actual rank, he said, was that of major. Richmond *Virginia Sun*, July 20, 1892.

[33] McKee to William H. Skaggs, December 29, 1893, "A rough draft of a letter sent," in McKee Papers.

[34] Robert H. Tyler, quoted in Richmond *Virginia Sun*, July 27, 1892.

[35] Minute Book of the Old Hickory Alliance, No. 611, 1889–1894, entry dated July 9, 1892, in Pierson Papers.

never formally merged with the smaller Populist party of the state but always voted with it. In effect they were both Populist. In all Southern states the new party organized and nominated a ticket before the election of 1892.

The conventional caricature of the Populist leader as a fanatical hayseed with insurrectionary whiskers bears small resemblance to the real leaders of the party in the South. The movement drew its leaders from much the same class that earlier agrarian uprisings had drawn upon in that region. The chief difference was that this class enjoyed much less prosperity and prestige in the 1890's than it had in the 1790's or the 1830's. The leaders varied in origin from state to state as they had a century earlier. The leaders of Virginia Populism bore the names Page, Beverley, Cocke, Ruffin, Harrison—than which there were none more honored. Mann Page, unmistakably a gentleman of "family," was president of the Virginia Alliance three years and later president of the National Alliance. Edmund Randolph Cocke, Populist candidate for governor in 1893, had entertained General Lee and his family at his ancestral home, "Oakland," for several weeks after Appomattox. Charles H. Pierson, English by birth, Cambridge graduate, Oxford theological student, and an ordained Anglican priest, was the capable editor of the leading Populist paper of the state, the *Virginia Sun*.[86] A resident of John Taylor's Caroline County, Pierson was conscious that he was sustained by a century-old tradition of agrarian protest. So, for that matter, was General Field, a resident of Jefferson's county of Albemarle. These men brought the traditional sobriety of the Upper South to a movement for which the Lower South could be depended upon to breed its historical quota of ardor.

"Cyclone" Davis and "Stump" Ashby of Texas could supply whatever the patrician Populists of Virginia lacked in the way of color. The towering, rangy figure of Cyclone Davis, six feet three, became known to audiences from Oregon to North Carolina. Schoolteacher, politician, editor, and lawyer by turns, Davis was a born dissenter. With several volumes of Jefferson's works in his arms, he would mount the platform and hold a crowd in his power for hours. Stump Ashby had a background of cowpunching, schoolteaching, preaching, and farming, and the oratorical magic of an

86 Sheldon, *Populism in the Old Dominion*, 33–35, 45, 95–96.

evangelical revivalist. His excessive fondness for liquor alienated many, but on the hustings he was acknowledged to have no peer.[37] The foremost leader of Texas Populists was Judge Thomas L. Nugent, a man of a very different nature. He was described by an opposition newspaper as "a quiet, self-contained, intellectual and scholarly man, and an accomplished lawyer," whose leadership of his party would lend "dignity and moral elevation to the campaign." [38]

More typical of Southern Populism than either Virginians or Texans were the leaders of the movement in Alabama, Georgia, and North Carolina—Reuben F. Kolb, Thomas E. Watson, and Leonidas L. Polk, respectively. Neither patricians nor plebeians, they were all men of substantial landed property, successful farmers and planters, and withal literate, informed, and capable citizens. Each edited a newspaper, and each held important offices as Democrats before becoming Populists: Kolb and Polk as commissioners of agriculture, Watson as Congressman. Of the three, Kolb was the only one who did not rise to prominence in the national movement.

Rank-and-file members of the party sprang from lower economic and social classes. A careful study of the politico-economic geography of Texas has sustained the conclusion that the "prosperous farmers fundamentally were Democrats," and that "it was the poor, small farmer then who constituted, together with thousands of his fellows, the rank and file of the People's party." [39] Maps comparing the Populist vote with the size of landholdings in Georgia indicate that in that state the Populist vote "varied in the rural districts, to a considerable extent, in inverse proportion to the prevalence of the Negroes and the large plantations," although an important exception to this rule was Tom Watson's district, which lay in the Black Belt.[40] In Louisiana the Populists' "great stronghold was in the hill parishes of northwestern Louisiana, peopled

[37] Martin, *People's Party in Texas,* 120–25; James H. Davis, *Memoir, by Cyclone Davis* (Sherman, Tex., 1935), 14–15. "Stump's" name was Harrison Sterling Price Ashby, believe it or not.

[38] Dallas *Morning News,* June 25, 1892; Martin, *People's Party in Texas,* 114–18; Catherine Nugent (ed.), *Life Work of Thomas L. Nugent* (Stephenville, Tex., c. 1896), *passim.*

[39] Martin, *People's Party in Texas,* 61–62, map opposite p. 60, and table on p. 63.

[40] Arnett, *Populist Movement in Georgia,* maps opposite p. 184.

mainly by small white farmers," and the movement "never gained much of a foothold in the cotton parishes of the delta, or in the sugar parishes, and it was never strong in the cities." [41] In Alabama the movement was regarded by one of its leaders as "an effort of the masses of the whites to free themselves from the rule of the black-belt Democratic party of the old slave-owning type," and a student of the same movement considers it a "white county" party.[42] On the other hand, the only section of Virginia upon which Populism laid strong hold was the "Southside," which was in the Black Belt. The Southside, however, was also the center of agricultural depression and unrest.[43] The large-scale farmer and even the farmer with good lands and large yield was not necessarily the prosperous farmer in the middle nineties. Adversity tended to close gaps that once had divided farmers politically.

Southern Populism was one manifestation of American radicalism that even bitter opponents could not stigmatize as "foreign." The leading conservative paper of Texas described the Populists of that state as solid, native white stock "sober and earnest from first to last" and estimated that 90 per cent of them were "ex-democrats whose standing in the party was formerly as undisputed" as any. "Their earnestness," continued the same paper, "bordering on religious fanaticism, has a touch of the kind of metal that made Cromwell's round heads so terrible a force. . . . It would be supreme folly to despise and belittle a movement that is leavened with such moral stuff as this." [44]

No Southern movement ever gave rise to a more colorful press than did Populism. At one time it was a press of considerable strength, though few samples of its publications have found their way to college libraries or reputable archives. An incomplete list gives the names of 195 papers published in Southern states in 1895 that openly declared themselves Populist.[45] This does not accurately

[41] Melvin J. White, "Populism in Louisiana During the Nineties," in *Mississippi Valley Historical Review*, V (1918–1919), 14–15.

[42] Joseph C. Manning, *The Fadeout of Populism* (New York, 1928), 60; Clark, *Populism in Alabama*, 173.

[43] Sheldon, *Populism in the Old Dominion*, 74, 80, and map on p. 105.

[44] Dallas *Morning News*, June 25, 1892.

[45] *American Newspaper Annual*, 1895 (Philadelphia, 1895). There are several indications that the number of papers supporting the party was larger than this. Thus,

reflect the strength of Populist journalism, since many Alliance papers gave full support to the movement, as did many that declared themselves "Independent."

Thirty-five miles from the nearest railroad and twenty-eight from a steamboat landing, in the upland cotton fields of Winn Parish, Louisiana, was published the *Comrade,* edited by Hardy L. Brian, leader of the Populists of his state. In an equally remote corner of Georgia, at Ellijay, was published the *Toiler's Friend,* and in Tennessee appeared the *Weekly Toiler.* Georgia's campaigns were enlivened for a time by the *Revolution* and the *Wool Hat.* The larger and more firmly established journals, such as Watson's *People's Party Paper,* and the Texas papers, *Southern Mercury* and *Weekly Advance,* wielded great influence, but more typical were the small, local weeklies. The majority of them were established to promote the Populist cause, and with great singlemindedness they pursued that purpose. They were uniformly, consistently, and vehemently partisan. Local and national news was crowded to the rear by long editorials expounding government ownership, referendum and recall, and atrocities of the trusts; crude cartoons satirizing the capitalists and the old parties; and columns defending Populist principles. Central agencies, such as the National Reform Press Association, supplied much of editorial material for the local papers and at the same time provided a powerful means of co-ordinating and directing party propaganda. Boycotted by advertisers, dogged by creditors, and handicapped by inexperience, the Southern Populist editors nevertheless played an important part in advancing their party's cause.

Southern Populists and reformers also contributed to the national literature of exposure and polemic that in the middle nineties was directed at monopoly capitalism. More completely forgotten than their Northern counterparts, the Southern books were of much the same character and for their region more effective. In 1894, the worst year of the depression, the same year that Henry

in Alabama as many papers listed themselves "Independent" or "Independent Democrat" as "Populist," and it should be recalled that the great majority of Reuben F. Kolb's supporters in that state never called themselves Populists. The leading Populist organ of North Carolina is described as "Independent." Martin, *People's Party in Texas,* 200 n., places the number of Populist papers in Texas at 100, as a "conservative" estimate.

D. Lloyd's *Wealth Against Commonwealth* and William H. Harvey's *Coin's Financial School* appeared, Charles H. Otken of Mississippi published *The Ills of the South;* Milford W. Howard, Populist Congressman from Alabama, published his *If Christ Came to Congress,* followed in 1895 by *The American Plutocracy;* and in 1894 also appeared Cyclone Davis' *A Political Revelation,* a work buttressing Populist principles with doctrines from the American Revolution.

It would have been difficult to find a climate more hostile to the cultivation of radical movements than the South in the 1890's. For a generation the South had practiced a political romanticism that dissociated politics from realities and masqueraded shabby expedients and doubtful concessions in the garments of the past. A cult of racism disguised or submerged cleavages of opinion or conflicts of interest in the name of white solidarity, and the one-party system reduced political intolerance to a machine of repression.

Southern Populists challenged the New-South romanticism head on. The farmers mingled politics frankly with questions of land, markets, wages, money, taxes, railroads. They spoke openly of conflicts, of both section and class, and ridiculed the clichés of Reconciliation and White Solidarity. The bolder among them challenged the cult of racism with the doctrine of common action among farmers and workers of both races. The very existence of the third party was, of course, a challenge to the one-party system as well as to white solidarity.

Populists would never have overcome their handicaps had they not been able to appeal to a great body of native Southern tradition and doctrine. A mine of such tradition they uncovered in eighteenth-century revolutionary writings and in the ideas upon which Southerners had drawn when they provided the national leadership for the struggle against Hamiltonian Federalism and later against Whiggery.

"We will now look through the volumes of Jefferson's works and see what Mr. Jefferson said on this matter," Cyclone Davis would announce—whereupon he would quote Jefferson to John Taylor on the iniquities of banks, or again confound with the words of Madison the "prating G O P Republicans" or the "so-called States' Rights Democrats," or perhaps expound Jackson on corporate control of Congress. "The crowd that take their politics from Alexander Hamilton is the crowd we have got to beat," he declared and to make the application clear added, "Cleveland is our Hamilton." For that matter, both "the Democrats and Republicans of today are with Hamilton." Listing a long series of Hamiltonian ideas, he followed each with the assertion: "Jefferson opposed; so do the Populists." [46]

Important in the Populist credo, however, was the declaration found in their national platform of 1892: "We believe that the powers of government—in other words, of the people—should be expanded," and this was to be accomplished "as rapidly and as far as the good sense of an intelligent people and the teachings of experience shall justify." The Populists did not intend the expansion to play the Hamiltonian godfather to corporate interests. Rather the expansion was to be at the expense of those interests, especially in the three fields in which the majority of their demands lay—those of money, land, and transportation.

On the question of money the Populists believed that the government had abdicated its sovereign power in favor of private corporations which were manipulating coinage, credit, and public finance to their own gain. They called for abolition of the national banking system, the enlargement of currency in circulation, and a system of commodity credit such as that of the subtreasury plan. Secondly, they believed the government had failed as custodian of public land, "including all the natural sources of wealth," and had permitted rapacious interests to steal the people's heritage. They demanded that large quantities of land and resources be reclaimed from the corporations. Thirdly, they declared for government ownership and operation of railroads and telegraph and telephone systems of the country. So far, they declared, the expansion of government powers should go in 1892, and many were prepared for it to go further in the near future.

The shibboleths and economic doctrines on which the New-South system rested came in for frequent attack by Southern Populists. The social Darwinism preached by Tompkins and Dawson

[46] James H. Davis, *A Political Revelation* (Dallas, 1894), 120, 147, 157, 178–79, 259–60, 267–68.

and spread through the region by the *Manufacturers' Record* was anathema to the stanch Populist. Herbert Spencer's philosophy of *laissez faire* was pronounced "radically wrong" by one writer; [47] and another pointed to tenancy, unemployment, and monopoly as "the logical result of the teaching of Adam Smith, Leon Say, and their school." He called for a "co-operative, instead of a corporative" economy.[48] The Gospel of Progress was nonsense, according to a Texas editor, who viewed as a "century of retrogression" the period in which "corporate greed and monopoly have concentrated the wealth into the hands of a few hundred men, who are as essentially the masters of the people as were the feudal barons of the middle ages the masters of the peasants." [49] As for the industrial expositions, so dear to the New-South developers and expanders, the Populist viewed them with skepticism. "The capitalists and manufacturers of the East and of Europe know more about our resources than we ourselves do!" exclaimed one, who counted an exposition not worth "two whoops in hades." [50]

To a Virginia Populist the developers and expanders appeared to be working to "hand us over bound hand and foot to foreign dividend-hunters." He continued: "But it is said: 'It will never do to drive capital away from the state. You must attract it by offering it inducements'—said inducements being liberty to fleece the people. . . . Our reply to all this loathsome mammon-worship is that you are bartering away Virginia's birthright for a miserable mess of pottage." He was annoyed by the shibboleth that was made of the word "conservatism" in his state, nor was he "to be deterred from the advocacy of government ownership by the cry of 'Socialism.' " [51]

The Southern Populist was enamored of a vocabulary that somewhat misled his critics, shocked many Southerners he sought to win, and frightened his more conservative Western allies. When the *Southern Mercury* proclaimed "a bitter and irrepressible conflict between the capitalist and the laborer," and appealed to "every

[47] *National Economist,* I (1889), 408–409.

[48] *Southern Mercury,* XII (May 4, 1893), 9.

[49] Dallas *Texas Advance,* September 30, 1893.

[50] *Southern Mercury,* XI (April 28, 1892), 3.

[51] Richmond *Virginia Sun,* February 13, 1892; May 17, 1893.

wage earner to combine and march shoulder to shoulder to the ballot box and by their suffrage overthrow the capitalistic class," [52] it was using language that was hardly Fabian. So was General Field when he declared it to be "the eve of the greatest revolution the country has ever known," and Populism to be "the party of the revolution of '92—the logical sequence of that of '76"; and Tom Watson when he called his party's campaign book *Not A Revolt; It is A Revolution;* or the Arkansas author of a history of the Alliance when he referred in his title to "the Impending Revolution."

This language seems misleading today, but it did not seem so to the Alabama historian William Garrott Brown, a close observer of the political upheaval of 1888–1892 in the South. "I call that particular change a revolution," he wrote, "and would use a stronger term if there were one; for no other political movement—not that of 1776, nor that of 1860–1861—ever altered Southern life so profoundly." [53]

The political strategy of Southern Populists was based on combinations and alliances along regional, class, and racial lines—first, an alliance between South and West; second, a combination of farmers and city and factory laborers; and third, a political union with Negro farmers and laborers within the South. Every phase of this strategy was a challenge to the New-South system, which had sought to divide all the elements Populists were trying to unite.

In calling for a Western alliance, the Populists were aware that they had to break the New South's connection with the Northeast that had endured since the Compromise of 1877. Instead of appealing to the vague nationalism of "Reconciliation" and "Reunion," slogans of the New South, they frankly avowed that they were "striving to unite the South and Northwest in a political alliance." They denounced Southerners who were "trying to coerce the people into perpetual submission to the dictation of the Northeast, and to their debasing exactions." By dominating both old parties the rulers of the Northeast had contrived that "every law they have demanded has been enacted, during the past thirty years; and every law they have demanded put cash in their pockets and has

[52] *Southern Mercury*, XI (May 5, 1892), 9.

[53] William G. Brown, "The South and the Saloon," in *Century Magazine*, LXXVI (1908), 463.

taken cash out of the pockets of other sections of the country."[54] The Populist remedy was a combination of exploited colonies against the exploiting empire.

The Southern Populists Ben Terrell, Cyclone Davis, and Tom Watson toured the Western states, and the Westerners James B. Weaver, Jerry Simpson, and Mary E. Lease campaigned in the Southern states. National conventions listened to orators from both sections declare eternal brotherhood. Welcoming General Weaver to Virginia, Julian M. Ruffin, speaking as "the grandson of the man who fired the first gun in the late war," declared that even if the Union general "were the man who fired the shot that made him fatherless, he would vote for him."[55] Nevertheless, it cannot be denied that General Weaver's candidacy was a considerable handicap to the Populist cause in the South, or that Polk, a former Confederate Army officer, had he lived and received the nomination instead, might have meant much to the cause in the South.

The Populist plan of drawing labor into the farmer's party was a continuation of the policy of the Southern Farmers' Alliance, which had effected a union with the Knights of Labor in 1889. Southern Populists took keen interest in the wave of labor unrest and strikes that swept the country, their own section included. Congressman Watson led in calling in 1892 for an investigation of the Homestead strike and the part played by the Pinkerton Agency in breaking it. Tennessee Populists supported the uprising of miners that overthrew the convict-lease system in their state, and the party agitated for the abolition of the system in all Southern states. Other labor measures sponsored by the party included child-labor laws, mechanics' and laborers' lien laws, railway-labor laws, and the establishment of state labor bureaus. Southern Populist papers were often outspoken champions of the rights of organized labor and sharp critics of antilabor measures. Mass meetings of labor were held repeatedly to endorse Populist candidates. In Texas W. R. Lamb and other officials of the state Federation of Labor took the lead in organizing the new party and were strong forces in the movement from the beginning. Lamb served as chairman of

[54] *Southern Mercury*, XI (April 28, 1892), 8–9; *ibid.* (June 2, 1892), 8.
[55] Richmond *Virginia Sun*, July 27, 1892.

the party's state executive committee. It was "a fact of indisputable validity," reports a political scientist, that in Texas "most of the wage earners supported the cause of Populism and voted for the candidates nominated by the People's Party." [56]

More important to the success of Southern Populism than the combination with the West or with labor was the alliance with the Negro. Yet it was the most difficult of the three. That alliance had wrecked the Readjusters and had proved a fatal weakness of the Republicans. In the end, it had been the Redeemers, the party of white supremacy, that had been most successful in controlling the Negro vote. A special difficulty of the Populist-Negro combination lay in the historical position of the upland whites toward the blacks, an antagonism with roots in slavery days. The regions where Populism made its strongest appeal were the very regions that found it most difficult to overcome racial feeling.

One additional difficulty threatened not only the interracial alignment in the South, but the realignment of South and West. In June, 1890, Congressman Henry Cabot Lodge introduced a bill for Federal control of elections, popularly known as the "force bill." In some respects it provided a tighter control of elections than the Act of 1870, for the Federal supervisor was given power to control registration of voters, to pass on qualifications of challenged voters, and to decide between Federal canvassers and state canvassers of an election.[57]

The Lodge bill caused more alarm and excitement in the South than any Federal measure since 1877.[58] "Not for twenty years has the public mind been so much disturbed," declared the Richmond *Dispatch* in a five-column, front-page editorial on the subject. "The South stood one reconstruction," said a Mississippi paper. "It remains to be seen whether it will meekly submit to another." The Atlanta *Constitution* called for a revival of "that glorious era"

[56] Woodward, *Tom Watson*, 205–207; Sharp, "Farmers' Alliance and People's Party in Tennessee," *loc. cit.*, 97–98; Sheldon, *Populism in the Old Dominion*, 62; Dallas *Morning News*, July 2, 5, 1892; Martin, *People's Party in Texas*, 67–68, 217.

[57] *Nation*, LI (1890), 44. For Henry Cabot Lodge on the bill, see *Congressional Record*, 51 Cong., 1 Sess., 6538–45.

[58] For example, Charleston *News and Courier*, September 24, 1890; Dallas *Morning News*, June 16, 1890; Jacksonville *Times-Union*, July 25, 1890; Atlanta *Constitution*, quoted in Richmond *State*, July 19, 1890; Jackson *Clarion-Ledger*, December 5, 1890.

when "the indomitable spirit of the freemen of Georgia was equal to the emergency. . . . What we did twenty years ago we can do again." [59] Governor John B. Gordon advocated a boycott on Northern business in reprisal.

The practical uses of the alarm over the force bill were not lost on the old party. "Its effect will be to draw the color line more intensely and to weld the South more solidly together," observed a Richmond Democrat.[60] "But for the Force Bill," admitted a Democratic paper, "the South might possibly have listened to the appeals of some of the new parties." But so long "as that bill threatens her with all the horrors of reconstruction days," white solidarity was assured.[61] The Lodge bill was defeated in the Senate in January, 1891, but Southerners were not permitted to forget the threat throughout the third-party revolt. The Northeast could hardly have presented the conservative South with better insurance against a working-class combination across race barriers. Lodge was following the Massachusetts precedent of Garrison and Sumner in dividing South and West over race policy, and thereby hindering an alliance of those sections against his own.

Populist journals scoffed at the "humbug" of "Negro domination" raised by Democrats who were using the Negro vote to defeat the third party, but the Populists were perfectly aware of the danger of the issue. They knew that no candidate and no party giving the least encouragement to the force bill could hope for success in the South. At the Ocala convention the white Alliance "with wildest enthusiasm" adopted a protest against the force bill, while the Colored Alliance, meeting separately in Ocala, simultaneously endorsed the bill. Western delegates returned home deeply discouraged. The president of the Kansas Alliance said that "The agitation in the South over the Lodge bill precludes the possibility of an independent movement at this time." [62]

In the face of this ugly situation Populist leaders proceeded in determined fashion to seek an understanding with the Negro. Not all factors were against them. A wave of unrest not unlike that

59 Quoted in Richmond *State,* July 19, 1890. See also, Richmond *Dispatch,* July 24, 1890; Jackson *Clarion-Ledger,* December 5, 1889.

60 Captain Sol Cuthens, in Richmond *Dispatch,* July 24, 1890.

61 *Ibid.,* October 8, 1892.

62 Quoted in Sheldon, *Populism in the Old Dominion,* 73 n.

agitating Southern whites was mounting among Southern blacks; and the Negro was voicing disillusionment with Republican platforms and with the Lily-white policies of that party in the South. There was already a start toward Negro Populism in the Colored Alliance, which claimed more than a million members. "From the very first," said the leader of the organization, speaking optimistically in 1890, "the Colored Alliance has been strongly in favor of the third party movement. They have practically cut away from the Republicans." [63]

The Republican and Democratic parties dealt with the Negro voter through " 'fluence men" and "owl meetings" in which money and liquor figured prominently and violence was not rare. It remained to be seen whether the new party would follow the old pattern. The issue was fought out in the open at the first Populist convention in Texas in the presence of Negro delegates. A white delegate moved a resolution that, in effect, denied the Negro responsible representation in party committees. A Negro delegate from Fort Worth objected, pointing out bluntly that "The negro vote will be the balancing vote in Texas." He continued: "If you are going to win, you will have to take the negro with you. . . . You must appoint us by convention and make us feel that we are men." The white president of the convention agreed. "I am in favor of giving the colored man full representation," he said. "He is a citizen just as much as we are, and the party that acts on that fact will gain the colored vote of the South." These views were applauded and upheld, and two Negroes were elected members of the State Executive Committee of the party.[64]

Populists of other Southern states followed the example of Texas, electing Negroes to their councils and giving them a voice in the party organization. Negroes were also elected as delegates to the national conventions of the party. At the St. Louis convention in February, 1892, William H. Warwick, a colored delegate from Virginia, was placed in nomination for assistant secretary of the body. A white delegate from Georgia moved that the nomination

[63] R. M. Humphry, quoted in New York *Herald,* December 4, 1890. Of course, the Negroes had not "practically cut away."

[64] Dallas *Morning News,* August 18, 1891.

be made unanimous, adding: "I wish to say that we can stand that down in Georgia." The question was put, and there was "a great 'aye' " from the delegates, including over two hundred Southern whites,—one "no" from an Alabama delegate.[65]

In their platforms Southern Populists denounced lynch law and the convict lease and called for defense of the Negro's political rights. Populist officers saw to it that Negroes received such recognition as summons for jury service, which they had long been denied. White and black party workers organized Negro Populist clubs and indoctrinated them in party principles. Picnics, barbecues, and camp meetings were arranged for black Populists, and both races were welcome at party rallies and speeches, blacks to one side, whites to the other. One of the most effective Negro Populists was J. B. Rayner of Calvert, Texas, a man of commanding ability and energy, who renounced Republicanism and with a corps of Negro assistants set out to convert his people to Populism. Even between campaigns Rayner worked "incessantly." [66]

The Populists framed their appeal to the Negro upon the dubious, if popular, theory that "self-interest always controls." "Let it once appear plainly," counseled Tom Watson, "that it is to the interest of a colored man to vote with the white man, and he will do it." He contended that "the accident of color can make no difference in the interest of farmers, croppers, and laborers"; and he told the two races: "You are kept apart that you may be separately fleeced of your earnings." [67] As a white Texan expressed it, "They are in the ditch just like we are." [68] Charles B. Spahr, a Northern scholar, thought that in Georgia and to some extent in Alabama "The colour line seemed to have broken down [by 1894] and the time seemed near at hand when all the political rights of the negro, and all the rights that could be secured to him through political action, would be granted him." [69] An English Fabian journal reported that the Populists gave "negroes of the South a political fel-

[65] *National Economist,* VI (1892), 394–95.

[66] Martin, *People's Party in Texas,* 94–96, 126–27.

[67] Thomas E. Watson, "The Negro Question in the South," in *Arena,* VI (1892), 541–48.

[68] Dallas *Morning News,* August 18, 1892.

[69] Charles B. Spahr, *America's Working People* (New York, 1900), 103.

lowship which they have never obtained, not even from their saviors, the Republicans."[70]

When all that is said, it should at once be added that those gains were limited and that their significance is easily exaggerated. A dilemma with roots as deeply struck in the history of a people as were those of the South's ancient problem could not be expected to yield to political formulas, and certainly not to the Populist formula of "self-interest." "This is a white man's country and will always be controlled by the whites," wrote a Virginia Populist, introducing an essay on the rights of the Negro.[71] Whatever rights the Populists were prepared to give the Negro, the Virginian's premise was pretty universally assumed, tacitly if not openly.[72] Populist organizations of Mississippi and South Carolina made few advances to the Negro save of the type made by the old party. Dusty squadrons of blacks were often marched to the polls after receiving pay in liquor and money, and the guards were not invariably Democrats. The greater temptation for Southern Populists was to secure the Negro vote through deals with Republican bosses by an arrangement known as "fusion." This kind of agreement came at an even greater cost to principle, but later, as despair of coping with Democratic use of the Negro grew, Populists experimented more and more with this method.

For parts of the South the campaign of 1892 was the first since the final contests of Reconstruction in which two parties of anything approaching equal strength had contested an election, and the first since 1860 in which opposing parties had consisted largely of native whites. Tabooed opinions, buried grievances, repressed ambitions, and issues that had been long passed over or tacitly hushed suddenly demanded immediate attention. Readjustment proved a painful and tumultuous business. "A stranger reading

[70] Anonymous, "The Presidential Campaign in America," in *Progressive Review* (London), I (1896), 117–32.

[71] Richmond *Virginia Sun*, December 20, 1894.

[72] "Whatever differences may exist among North Carolinians over a question of national policy, there should be none in the State where Anglo-Saxon rule and good government is the paramount issue," wrote Marion Butler in July, 1892. At that time he was a Democrat, later a Populist, and still later a Republican, and throughout the whole period he edited a paper called the *Caucasian*. Quoted in William A. Mabry, *The Negro in North Carolina Politics Since Reconstruction*, in Trinity College Historical Society *Historical Papers*, Ser. XXIII (Durham, 1940), 32–33.

the Alabama press of the Populist era," writes one historian, "would scarcely be able to dissociate it from the party calumny and vituperation of the late Reconstruction days." [73] The comparison was also drawn by Populists themselves.[74] Reversion to the violent and revolutionary tactics of Reconstruction days was advocated, and to some extent practiced, by both sides.

Cases of political pressure exerted by means of boycott, social ostracism, foreclosure of mortgages, discharge from jobs, withholding of credit and supplies, and discharge of tenants and croppers were reported from various parts of the South.[75] Democratic businessmen and manufacturers appealed to their Northern creditors for funds to fight the Populists, while politicians appealed successfully to Cleveland and the national Democratic organization for money.[76]

The appeal to violence was especially prevalent in the Lower South. Frank Burkitt, leader of Populism in Mississippi, was knocked from a speaker's platform unconscious. He continued his canvass later, guarded by armed friends. Joseph C. Manning, Populist writer and orator of Alabama, was attacked and driven from Florence by a mob, and Kolb was similarly treated in Henry County. Two third-party editors were driven from their towns in Texas, and a third was killed in a duel with a Democratic editor; a political feud in San Augustine County of the same state cost the lives of half a dozen men including the Populist sheriff; Negro Populist speakers were repeatedly molested, and white speakers more than once. In Georgia Watson's life was threatened, and an attempt was made to lynch his foremost Negro speaker; in all, some fifteen Negroes and several white men were killed during the Georgia election. General Weaver, Populist candidate for President, was howled down at Albany, threatened with personal in-

[73] Clark, *Populism in Alabama,* 177.

[74] William H. Skaggs, *The Southern Oligarchy . . .* (New York, 1924), 128. In describing the methods employed by Democrats of Alabama against the Populists, Skaggs wrote: "In the long list of corrupt practices and crimes which have been charged against the carpetbaggers, there is nothing more sordid, more blatantly felonious."

[75] Joseph C. Manning, *Politics of Alabama* ([Birmingham], 1893), 19; Martin, *People's Party in Texas,* 186.

[76] J. Fred Rippy (ed.), *F. M. Simmons, Statesman of the New South: Memoirs and Addresses* (Durham, 1936), 18–19.

dignity at Waycross, and rotten-egged at Macon. He abandoned his campaign of the state when he learned that worse might happen in Atlanta. Populists retaliated by organizing night-riding societies such as "Gideon's Band."

"I am ashamed of the state of opinion in Alabama," wrote Senator Morgan privately. "Access to the truth is denied, free speech is 'boycotted,' envy is made malicious, friends and faithful servants are condemned without a hearing, and filthy demagogues are installed in leadership." He despaired of the state party machine, which "operated in secrecy" and "organized social and class jealousies and distrust into a reckless hatred of all who are not inside the closed circle." [77]

The campaign in the Upper South did not take so violent a turn. In Tennessee Robert L. Taylor, who in 1886 had ushered in a mild and comic type of agrarianism, returned to the stump with his fiddle and bow to lure the "Populites" into line. He would turn a debate into a "revival," sing "Turn, Sinner, Turn," and plead with backsliders to repent and come up to shake his hand: "Come on back, boys. Come on back." The state press took up the refrain: "Come on back! Your hearthstones, your fireside idols, your pride in the past, your hopes for the future all make to you honest appeal." [78]

The Tennessee Populists nominated Governor Buchanan (who had been elected governor in 1890 as an Alliance Democrat) and made a strong appeal to labor, but finished third in the election. Republican and Populist votes together considerably outnumbered those of the Democrats, however, and the old party's victory left it seriously weakened.[79] Confused leadership befuddled Kentucky Alliancemen so badly that their vote came to be divided among Populist, Democratic, Republican, and Independent or "Alliance" candidates in the state election of 1891, though the new party polled a surprisingly large vote, electing one state senator and twelve representatives.[80] North Carolina Populists, who later gained control of their state, were badly handicapped for leadership in 1892 by the

[77] Morgan to McKee, February 4, 1892, in McKee Papers.

[78] Nashville *Daily American,* August 31, September 25, 1892.

[79] Sharp, "Farmers' Alliance and People's Party in Tennessee," *loc. cit.,* 106–10; Robison, *Bob Taylor,* 174.

[80] Prichard, "Popular Political Movements in Kentucky," 140–44.

death of Polk, bungled their nomination for governor, and finished with only eleven seats in the legislature.[81]

The *Virginia Sun* charged that there "never were such bacchanalia of corruption and terrorism" as were practiced against Populists in 1892. Old methods once employed against the Readjusters were revived. The Populists maintained that there was "no doubt at all" that their candidates polled a majority of votes cast in four congressional districts, and that "the Democrats have deliberately thrown out the returns of their own judges in precinct after precinct until the majorities are fixed to suit themselves." [82] These claims are corroborated with regard to the Fourth District by a study that concludes, "it was clear that the Populist had received a majority of the votes," and was deprived of the election by fraud.[83]

In Florida and Mississippi the new party showed surprisingly small strength. Louisiana Populists in combination with Anti-Lottery allies of the Democratic party won an easy victory over the regular Democrats in the state election of 1892. In the national election, in which they reached an understanding with the Republicans, however, the Populists fell down to the level of the votes ordinarily received by the Republican party.[84]

Tillman in South Carolina and Hogg in Texas continued to steer successfully between Populism and conservatism, and each was able to strengthen the powerful political machine he was building. The South Carolina conservatives did not bolt the old party and appeal to the Negro vote as they had done in 1890, but made their peace with Tillman, who supported Cleveland in spite of the state party's endorsement of the Ocala Platform. On the other hand, the right wing of Texas Democracy, unable to endure Hogg's agrarian measures, bolted the party, nominated Judge George Clark for governor, and with the support of the Republicans seriously menaced Hogg's re-election. The Populists nominated Judge Nugent, but torn by reluctance to further a victory of Clark, the Populists did not poll the vote they might have in a simpler contest. Even so, they polled more than 100,000 votes, and probably as many white

81 Mabry, *Negro in North Carolina Politics*, 33–34.

82 Richmond *Virginia Sun*, November 16, 1892.

83 Sheldon, *Populism in the Old Dominion*, 90–92.

84 White, "Populism in Louisiana," *loc. cit.*, 7–8, 11; New Orleans *Times-Democrat*, October 16, 1892.

votes as either of the two opposing candidates. The latter were more successful in controlling the black vote, however, and while the Populists fell to third place, Hogg was re-elected.[85]

The Negro vote and its fraudulent manipulation were likewise decisive in Georgia and Alabama. The election in Georgia has been properly characterized as a "solemn farce," for the old-party managers showed no more reluctance than they had during Reconstruction and the Independent movement in employing bribery, wholesale ballot-box stuffing, and intimidation. The total vote counted in Augusta was about double the number of legally accredited voters. The Populist candidate for governor was defeated, and Watson lost his contest.[86]

In the Alabama state election Governor Jones was declared elected over Kolb by a majority of some 11,000 out of almost 250,000 votes cast. Yet Kolb carried eight more counties than Jones, and it was conceded that Kolb had received a majority of the white votes. The explanation lay in the vote of the Black Belt, where twelve black counties returned Democratic majorities of more than 26,000. "It is needless to attempt to disguise the facts of the Alabama election," said an unusually candid Democratic paper. "The truth is that Kolb carried the state, but was swindled out of his victory by the Jones faction, which had control of the election machinery and used it with unblushing trickery and corruption." [87] Alabama state law provided no means for contesting an election, and the legislature refused to set up such machinery. There followed wild talk of revolutionary measures. "Undoubtedly the defeat of the popular will by the ballot-box stuffers would justify revolution after the manner of our fathers," wrote Robert McKee to William H. Skaggs. "There was the same condition of affairs in the state during the reconstruction period—the same crimes against the ballot-box." [88]

Southern Populism, despite its defeats, had showed surprising strength for a party only a few months old. Leaders professed to be undismayed and determined to continue the fight: "I am deter-

[85] Bailey, "Life of James Stephen Hogg," 463–64, 480.

[86] Arnett, *Populist Movement in Georgia,* 153–55; Woodward, *Tom Watson,* 241–42.

[87] Nashville *Banner,* quoted in Nashville *Daily American,* August 12, 1892.

[88] McKee to Skaggs, February 18, 1894; also Skaggs to McKee, February 22, 1892, McKee Papers.

mined never to give it up as long as I live," declared Watson.[89] The leading Texas spokesman of his party declared, "The results, be what they may, show conclusively that the Populist principles are deeply imbedded in the hearts of the masses."[90]

Unquestionably there remained much fighting spirit in the hearts of the Southern Populists after the defeat of 1892. Their maximum strength and their most important victories were yet to come. It was pretty clear by 1892, however, that the controlling forces in America would be no more reconciled to a Populist South than they had been to a planter-Confederate South or a Carpetbagger-freedman South.

[89] Atlanta *Constitution*, December 11, 1892.

[90] *Southern Mercury*, XI (November 10, 1892), 8.

CHAPTER X

REVOLT AGAINST THE EAST

THE story of the great depression of the nineties has been told too exclusively in terms of the stricken cities of the East and the impoverished plains of the West. There was also a depression in the South, and the indications are that it lasted longer and was more heavily felt, in some respects, than in other parts of the country. The percentage of business failures in the South was considerably higher than the national average throughout the depression years and approximately twice as high as it was in the West, apart from the Pacific Coast states and the territories.[1] Liabilities of failing firms in New England were never so large in those years as in Southern failures. The plight of Kansas was probably as bad as has been pictured, but the percentage of failures in Mississippi one year doubled, and another tripled, that in Kansas. The story that Hamlin Garland told of the Middle Border in his *Main-Traveled Roads* is no more burdened with tragedy than is Charles H. Otken's *The Ills of the South.*

The Panic of 1893 did not mark the beginning of the depression in the South, for there the proportion of failures was exactly the same in 1891 that it was two years later. The panic, however, did bring home to the cities and industrial towns of the South as never before the distress that had gripped the surrounding countryside for years. In the spring of that year savings banks refused money to depositors unless they gave sixty days notice, while other banks

1 The following data are available in *Statistical Abstract of the United States, 1893,* pp. 25–27; *ibid., 1895,* pp. 334–36 (West Virginia is included in the Southern states):

Percentage of failures in:	*1891*	*1892*	*1893*	*1894*	*1895*
National average	1.07	.88	1.28	1.25	1.09
Southern average	1.71	1.48	1.71	1.67	1.59
Western average	.77	.64	.95	.78	.80

suspended the honoring of checks entirely.[2] Marginal industries, some of which were no older than the boom of 1890, began to topple and close their doors. Although the cotton mills fared better than many of the new industries, textile factories in Atlanta, Augusta, Columbus, and Macon, and others in South Carolina and Mississippi shut down a large part of their machinery or closed entirely. Country-bred labor began to suffer its first serious encounter with industrial unemployment and depression. The failure of the Richmond Terminal left the South Atlantic seaboard states without a single large solvent railway system. In Richmond, New Orleans, and Atlanta unemployment became an increasingly serious problem. "Enterprise lags, failures continue," said a Lynchburg paper at the end of 1893. "Workshops are still idle, wages go downward, the unemployed multiply, gold tends outward. Meanwhile the winter closes in upon us, and the poor cry for bread." [3] Hoke Smith's paper reported that in the textile-mill workers' district of Atlanta "famine and pestilence are to-day making worse ravages than among the serfs of Russia." [4]

The attention attracted by labor conflict in the North and West during 1894 tended to obscure closely parallel events of the same violent year in the South. The worst year of the depression opened with unprecedented unemployment and rumors of jobless men roaming in armies through the countryside. Jacob Coxey's "army," which set forth from Ohio for Washington on March 15, was the most publicized. On April 21 a strike of soft-coal miners was called which eventually involved some 160,000 men the nation over. This was followed by violent labor conflict in the textile mills of New England. Overshadowing all these events, however, were the Pullman strike in Chicago, the boycott and strike called by Eugene Debs's American Railway Union for June 26, and Cleveland's intervention with Federal troops at Chicago.

"In this critical time," declared the *Manufacturers' Record* during the Chicago strike, "the South has fortunately demonstrated its freedom from labor riots and from anarchistic teachings." The

[2] Richmond *Dispatch*, January 1, 1894; Arnett, *Populist Movement in Georgia*, 166.

[3] Lynchburg *News*, December 20, 1893, quoted in Moger, *Rebuilding of the Old Dominion*, 102.

[4] Atlanta *Journal*, quoted in Atlanta *People's Party Paper*, April 14, 1892.

editor pictured "the West repelling capital and denouncing the government; the South protecting capital and heartily supporting the government"; then he drew the favorite moral: the South was the ideal place for Northern capital and industry.[5] Senator Gordon echoed these views with a touch all his own: "How comforting, sustaining, and inspiring is the reflection that while these industrial and social storms have been raging around us, we of the South have been resting in peace, in safety, and comparative comfort." [6]

Unfortunately the record contains ample evidence that in 1894 the South was torn by all the varieties of industrial conflict that racked the North—riots, strikes, use of state troops, bloodshed, destruction of property, and, in addition, race conflict. Hundreds of Southern Populists were preaching doctrine that, in the view of Gordon and the *Manufacturers' Record,* was more "anarchistic" than any ever uttered by Governor John P. Altgeld of Illinois.

When the national soft-coal strike was called in April, miners in Northern Alabama walked out and Governor Thomas G. Jones ordered a regiment of state troops to the scene. Pinkerton detectives hired by the Governor reported that "very bitter feeling" against the presence of troops existed among the miners, but the sheriff of Jefferson County assured the Governor that "concentration of troops to this point has had the desired effect, and I think it will soon end the strike." [7] It did. Jones's order dismissing the troops, dated June 29, had hardly been executed, however, when railroad workers in Birmingham and its vicinity walked out on a strike inspired by the Chicago Pullman strike. Governor Jones, formerly an attorney for the Louisville and Nashville, one of the railroads involved in the strike, ordered troops to Birmingham to protect the companies in hiring men to replace the strikers.[8] This affair had not ended when miners struck at the Pratt mines and elsewhere and attempted by force to prevent the use of Negro strikebreakers by the

[5] *Manufacturers' Record,* XXV (July 13, 1894), 385.

[6] Atlanta *Constitution,* August 26, 1894.

[7] Lieut. James B. Erwin to Gov. Thomas G. Jones, June 17, 1894; William A. Pinkerton to J. K. Jackson, secretary to Gov. Jones, June 22, 1894, in Official Records of Governors, File Box No. 32 (Alabama State Archives). See also, Pinkerton to Jones, November 15, 1893; December 18, 1894; George M. Morrow to Jones, May 29, 1894, *ibid.,* File Boxes Nos. 27, 28.

[8] Birmingham *Age-Herald,* July 6, 11, 1894; *Appletons' Annual Cyclopaedia . . . 1894,* p. 4; McKee to Senator Morgan, July 8, 1894, McKee Papers.

Tennessee Coal, Iron, and Railroad Company. Jones ordered troops to the Pratt mines on July 16.

By this time Alabama was aflame with another contest between Conservatives and Populists. The strike was not without its political aspects. An officer of the governor's staff on duty with the troops wrote Jones that Populist miners from Blocton were leading the strike, and that Kolb's race for governor would be affected by the outcome. "The striking miners are the strongest backing he [Kolb] has," reported the lieutenant.[9] The officer co-operated closely with the president of the Tennessee Coal, Iron, and Railroad Company, Nathaniel Baxter, and with De Bardeleben of Birmingham. He was informed by these gentlemen that if the miners did not accept company terms, "it was the intention of the company to open up Blocton, bring down a force of Italians from the North and West, call on the State for protection, and start to work, cost what it might." Additional Pinkerton detectives were employed who were, according to the officer in command, to be "arrested and put into jail in order to get evidence against the prisoners." [10] Drained of funds by the strike and betrayed by secret agents employed at public expense, the miners went down to defeat and returned to work at the company's terms.

In October, 1894, violent labor demonstrations and riots broke out on the wharves of New Orleans when English shippers attempted to substitute Negro for white screwmen, workers who loaded cotton bales on ocean-going ships. Such racial harmony of labor as had marked the strike of 1892 in the same city broke under the depression, and race warfare raged along the levees and was renewed with greater violence the following March. Several men were killed, property valued at $750,000, including 25,000 bales of cotton, was destroyed by fire, and several levees were damaged. Governor Murphy J. Foster called out the militia on March 14, and under its protection the Negroes went to work for the Englishmen of the West Indian Steamship Company.[11]

"Virginia wants a good class of immigrants," declared Governor

[9] Lieut. Erwin to Gov. Jones, August 10, 1894, in Official Records of Governors, File Box No. 32 (Alabama State Archives).

[10] *Ibid.;* Birmingham *Age-Herald,* July 17–August 15, 1894.

[11] *Appletons' Annual Cyclopaedia . . . 1894,* p. 443; *ibid., 1895,* pp. 427–28; New Orleans *Daily Picayune,* March 13, 1895.

Charles T. O'Ferrall in the summer of 1894, "but none of the mongrel proletariat element, which I believe are the real cause of the trouble in the West." [12] When labor trouble came closer to home, however, and a strike began at the Pocahontas coal mine the following May, the Governor's taste in immigrants seems to have changed. O'Ferrall dispatched troops to Pocahontas to protect the 400 Italians whom the mineowners imported by special train from the North to replace the native Virginia miners and break their strike.[13] The Governor was greatly agitated over labor demonstrations in the North, and used the state militia to drive Coxey's Commonwealers of Christ back across the Potomac after their departure from Washington. Invoking "the wisdom of Jefferson," the Governor of Virginia declared, "this blessed old State is famous for stamping out fanaticism, heresies, and fallacies, and for it her name rings throughout the land." His rule in such emergencies was, he said, "Toleration to the winds!" He preferred "war to anarchy," and bade patriots "ask no ornament for your sword but the notches on the blade." [14]

These sentiments were echoed by other Southern leaders during the Pullman strike. At a critical stage of the Chicago crisis, a Populist introduced in the United States Senate a resolution looking to government control of railroads, rates, and wages. "Immediately the South leaped into the saddle with General Gordon in the lead," it was reported. Senator Daniel of Virginia introduced a resolution heartily endorsing Cleveland's intervention in Illinois with Federal troops, which the Senate promptly passed. General Gordon sounded the note of "reconciliation," a favorite theme of his. When the dread day of barricades arrives, declared the General, "the men who wore the gray from 1861 to 1865 and confronted the Stars and Stripes in battle under great convictions will be found side by side with the men who wore the other uniform." [15]

Southern sentiment was by no means united on these matters. While Governor Jones of Alabama (involved with troops and strikes himself at the time) said that there was "no question of state's rights" involved in Cleveland's intervention in Illinois,[16]

[12] Richmond *Dispatch*, July 10, 1894. [13] *Ibid.*, May 16–19, 1895.

[14] *Ibid.*, August 11, 1895. See also, *ibid.*, January 2, 1894.

[15] Little Rock *Arkansas Gazette*, July 14, 1894.

[16] Birmingham *Age-Herald*, July 11, 1894.

Governor Hogg of Texas declared it to be "a fatal blow at State's rights," and announced that he would not tolerate Federal troops crossing the borders of Texas for strikebreaking purposes. "I would be there to stop them," he announced. He openly sided with Governor Altgeld and predicted in a much-quoted utterance that Chicago would be "bespattered with blood, brains, hair, hide, livers and lights" if Cleveland did not change his policy.[17] When the "Desert Contingent" of Coxey's Army began to board Texas freight trains, the Southern Pacific Company appealed to Governor Hogg, only to be told that it was no crime to "bum" a ride. The company then hauled several hundred free passengers into the deserted plains, switched them to a siding, and left them. Hogg ordered the railroad company to rescue the men. When the company refused, the Governor vowed "by gatlins" he would not suffer "such wholesale murder." The company promptly sent a train for the stranded men and sped them on their way.[18]

First and last, however, it was the farmers and the agricultural masses associated with them who suffered most bitterly in this depression. Conditions and prices that were bad enough in the eighties to provoke the angry protest of the Farmers' Alliance movement grew considerably worse in the nineties. "The outlook here is gloomier than since 1873 on account of crop failures and crop prices," wrote an Alabamian in the fall of 1892.[19] Prices fell to less than half those of a decade earlier. The cotton farmers produced a crop in 1894 that exceeded by two million bales any crop previously grown; yet they received $50,000,000 less for it than for the crop of 1882.[20] For people who depended upon cotton as their only source of cash income these prices meant destitution. The tobacco farmer's story was similar. The value placed upon the Virginia tobacco crop of 1894 was less than half the value of any crop since 1880 except 1888, and less than a third of the crop of 1881. The Kentucky crop of 1894 was valued at less than it had been since the seventies, and the 1895 crop went even lower.[21]

17 Quoted in Sam Acheson, *35,000 Days in Texas; A History of the Dallas News and Its Forbears* (New York, 1938), 174.

18 *Ibid.*, 172–73.

19 W. Brewer, Hayneville, Ala., to McKee, October 19, 1892, in McKee Papers.

20 *Statistical Abstract of the United States, 1896*, pp. 296–98.

21 *Ibid., 1895*, pp. 304–305.

Of the 119 counties of Kentucky, 87 could not raise enough money in 1891 to pay the expenses of local government; schools as well as banks closed.

The lien system tightened its grip; mortgages increased and so did tenancy. The farmer fell more deeply into debt; and, as his debt increased, the money in which it was measured appreciated in terms of bales, and bushels, and pounds of his product. The Southern farmer listened with mounting anger to lectures upon his "financial integrity" from his Eastern creditors, who were enriched at his expense. "We have reached the stage where slow, reasoned arguments cannot any longer affect us," wrote a Kentuckian; "neither the ties of partisanship or political loyalty. It is a question of bread and meat, and we are ready to fight." [22]

If Nature piled calamity upon the financial woes of the Western farmer, she was no kinder to the farmer of the South. Flood, drought, and plague competed with debt, mortgage, and bankruptcy as causes of suffering. Crevasses in the levees of the lower Mississippi in 1891, 1892, and 1893 resulted in floods that made thousands homeless and reduced many to the point of starvation. The floods drowned stock, destroyed property valued at several millions, and rendered much of the overflowed land unproductive for years. Drought followed flood. Lack of water cut Louisiana rice production from 182,000,000 pounds in 1893 to 76,000,000 in 1895. Drought in 1896 caused an almost total loss of crops in the hill country of Louisiana, Mississippi, Arkansas, and Texas. The great freeze of 1894–1895 resulted in widespread suffering, and in Florida it brought disaster to the orange growers. Tropical storms lashed the sea islands and the Georgia coast in 1893, and the same year brought a recurrence of the yellow-fever epidemic on the Gulf Coast. In 1892 a new and terrifying enemy began an invasion from Mexico that in future years was to overrun the cotton kingdom—the boll weevil.

The South had every reason to hope for sympathy and aid from the new Democratic Congress and administration that took office in 1893—the first since 1860 in which all branches were in the control of the old party. Not only was there a substantial Democratic

[22] Letter dated February 18, 1895, in the Paris *Bourbon News,* quoted in Prichard, "Popular Political Movements in Kentucky," 161–62.

majority in both houses, but the Speaker of the House and the majority leader in the Senate were both Southerners. Seniority of Southern Congressmen told heavily in congressional committees. Of the 56 standing and select committees of the House, Southern Democrats were chairmen of 27, and of the 46 standing committees of the Senate, Southerners held the chairmanship of 23.[23] In addition, three Southerners sat in Cleveland's cabinet, and others occupied important positions in the administration.

The President's cabinet appointees from the South, however, were men out of touch, or out of sympathy, with the dominant thought and mood of their region. They came of the same school to which the Southern cabinet members of his first administration belonged and represented the temper of the eighties and the Eastern alliance rather than the mood of the nineties and the Western affiliation. They usually saw eye to eye with cabinet members from the Northeast—Daniel S. Lamont, William C. Whitney, and Richard Olney. John G. Carlisle, Secretary of the Treasury, once a silverite, had gone over to the opposition and was regarded as a renegade by many Southerners—"the Judas from Kentucky," Tillman called him. Hilary A. Herbert, Secretary of the Navy, was the editor of the leading apology for the ultraconservative Redeemer regime, *Why the Solid South,* dedicated "to the business men of the North." Hoke Smith, then leader of the conservative wing of his party in Georgia, was appointed Secretary of the Interior "largely and perhaps chiefly" upon the recommendation of Lamar, who held the same office in Cleveland's first administration.[24] The first Southerner appointed to the Supreme Court after Lamar's death was Senator Edward D. White, president of one of the largest sugar refineries and a wealthy planter with conservative views from the Louisiana Delta. The President also found office for several of the older politicians who were overthrown by the agrarian revolt of 1890.

It was not that Cleveland was left in ignorance of conditions and opinion in the South. Even Lamar warned him that "our people are wretchedly poor," and described to him "the poverty and dis-

[23] *Official Congressional Directory* (1st ed.), 53 Cong., 2 Sess., in *Senate Miscellaneous Documents,* 53 Cong., 2 Sess., No. 12, pp. 125–30, 139–46.

[24] Josephus Daniels, *Editor in Politics* (Chapel Hill, 1941), 183.

tress which brood over plantation and field and household. . . . They hear with almost despair that their most trusted Democratic leaders oppose the measures that are offered for their relief. The free coinage of silver and tariff reform have been regarded by them as the only measures of relief which the Democratic party has to propose." While Lamar considered the President's monetary policy "firm" and "wise," he said it "saddened their hearts and frustrated their expectations." [25] Congressman-elect John Sharp Williams wrote the President that no one in the North had "any idea how close many of the congressional districts in the South were" to going Populist in 1892. "Farmers in this section, like drowning men, were willing to catch at straws," he said, and warned of "hundreds of thousands of honest, zealous Democrats, who are tired to death of the 'business interest' of the few being made a pretext to defeat the real interest of the many." [26] Congressman Joseph Wheeler of Alabama pleaded with the President for "moderate concessions" that could be used to combat Populism in the South. Without them he predicted defeat for his party in Alabama.[27]

Instead of making moderate concessions, President Cleveland promptly set about imposing, with the aid of the patronage club and all the powerful resources at his command, a financial program of contraction that the mass of Southern people regarded as legislation to enrich the creditor section at their expense and depress them to the level of a colonial dependency. One unpopular measure followed another: the repeal of the Silver Purchase Act, the first gold bond issue, Cleveland's veto of the seigniorage bill, and the series of gold bond issues that followed. On top of these came the fiasco of the tariff reformers' efforts in the Wilson bill, and later the Supreme Court's decision declaring the income tax unconstitutional. Party leaders of high rank in the South protested bitterly against Cleveland's course from the beginning. Senator Vance declared that the President "could not have carried a single electoral vote south of the Potomac" had his program been known to the electorate in 1892. "For the first time in thirty-three years

[25] Mayes, *Lucius Q. C. Lamar*, 554.

[26] John S. Williams to Grover Cleveland, December 20, 1892, in Grover Cleveland Papers (Division of Manuscripts, Library of Congress).

[27] Dyer, *"Fightin' Joe" Wheeler*, 319.

the Democratic party was intrusted with the power of enacting laws," said the Senator in the last speech of his life. "Now, in fulfillment of these promises, the first thing which is done is to yield to the clamor of the capitalists hostile to silver." [28]

It was even more embarrassing to explain to rebellious constituents and heckling Populists how it was that Cleveland's unpopular measures could be reported out of congressional committees presided over by Southern Democrats and passed by the aid of Southern votes. It was Speaker Charles F. Crisp of Georgia who shut off debate and whipped the House into submission to Cleveland's veto of the seigniorage bill. Many a state delegation solidly pledged to reform split up under pressure and went over in part to the administration.

In one of the most plaintive of the appeals made to Cleveland by distraught Southern Democrats, Governor William J. Northen of Georgia wrote the President in September, 1893, saying, "The conditions of this State are fearful and threatening" and are engendering "a lack of confidence in the party in power." His greatest fear was of the growing power of Populism. "Every election held in this State for the past three (3) months has gone against the Democrats and in favor of the Populists," he wrote. "Ex-Congressman Watson, the leader of the Populists, has taken advantage of the conditions, and is speaking over the State to assemblies never less than 2,000, and sometimes as many as 5,000 people." [29]

Southern Populists, instead of slackening their efforts after the election of 1892, intensified the crusade during the following off-election year. Third-party speakers worked the districts and precincts systematically, keeping up an unremitting fire of ridicule, exposure, and attack against the records of old-party officials, taking full advantage of popular resentment of Cleveland's policies, and doing all they could to widen the split in the Democratic party. New Populist clubs were organized, new party papers founded, and new converts made by the thousands. Local and state as well as congressional elections were contested bitterly, often successfully. Tom Watson spoke during the summer of 1893 in thirty-five Georgia counties to crowds that he estimated to total 150,000 peo-

[28] Dowd, *Life of Zebulon B. Vance*, 267; Richmond *Dispatch*, September 2, 1893.

[29] William J. Northen to Cleveland, September 15, 1891, in Cleveland Papers.

ple. Virginia Populists contested the state election of 1893 under heavy handicaps and added nearly 70,000 votes to the ballot they polled the preceding year.

Texas Populists held huge camp meetings in the open country, attended by several thousand people. Crowds of fifteen thousand were not unheard of. The scene was said to have "resembled that of a great military camp." Local orators Cyclone Davis and Stump Ashby were sometimes supported by General Weaver, Jacob Coxey, Mary E. Lease, and other out-of-state speakers. "For a whole week they literally lived and breathed Reform: by day and by night they sang of Populism, they prayed for Populism, they read Populist literature and discussed Populist principles with their brethren in the faith, and they heard Populist orators loose their destructive thunderbolts in the name of the People's Party." [30]

A Philadelphia reporter discovered "a sequel to the Coxey movement" in a demonstration by the Populists of Arkansas on their way to a convention in Little Rock. "These men all started on their political journey on the same day, July 14," he reported. "By frequent meetings and speeches along the highways and byways an unusual degree of Populistic fervor has been worked up which threatens to give serious trouble to the Arkansas Democrats." Two thousand of these marchers filled the city's wagon yards to overflowing on July 19. They displayed the motto "Keep off the grass," declared their sympathy for Coxey as well as for the Chicago Pullman strikers, and breathed destruction for the Democratic machine, which they denounced as "cowardly, tyrannical and a menace to the rights of the people." [31]

The Populists of Alabama mixed a good deal of horseplay and rustic comedy in their campaign methods. Kolb's opponent in the race of 1894 was William C. Oates, from the Black Belt, described as "a conservative among conservatives, and a party regular par excellence." [32] Strings of corncobs, emblem of the Kolbites, were festooned on wagons, buggies, and platforms. Supporters of his opponent were recognized by garlands of oat straw worn as hat-

[30] Martin, *People's Party in Texas*, 171–72; also *Southern Mercury*, XII (May 11, 1893), 8.

[31] Philadelphia *Ledger*, quoted in Little Rock *Arkansas Gazette*, July 23, 1894. See also, Little Rock *Arkansas Gazette*, July 19, 21, 1894.

[32] Albert B. Moore, *History of Alabama* (University, Ala., 1934), 633.

bands and belts. The campaign took on an uglier aspect when Governor Jones began to use troops against Populist strikers, and Kolbites swore they would "try Winchester rifles and a few hangings." [33] Threats and counterthreats were heard in other states, and it began to look as if the election of 1894 would be more violent than the preceding one.

One refinement of old-party methods took the form of changes in election laws—usually described as reforms. The Sayre election law of Alabama, for example, prohibited assistance in marking ballots, thus providing means of disfranchising thousands of illiterate voters, white as well as black.[34] The Walton law, passed by the Democrats of the Virginia Legislature in 1893, likewise discriminated against the unlettered voter.[35] A new registration law adopted in Georgia the following year placed in the hands of a Democratic registration committee the power to draw up lists of qualified voters. The potentialities of this law were demonstrated in Richmond County, in Watson's district, where more than one third of the Negroes registered (almost as many as whites) were listed as "just attained the age of 21." The leading Democratic paper of Augusta cynically remarked that in an approaching election "the usual methods of securing negro votes" would be employed.[36] The party machine in Arkansas depended upon a new poll tax and exclusion of Populists from county election commissions; the North Carolina system of centralized control was still in effect.

Despairing of victory in a contest of the usual kind and fearing a repetition of the methods used against them in 1892, Populists of several states began to turn to the plan of fusion with local Republican organizations, with which there had been some experimenting in the previous election. Populists were divided over the question of fusion, with both sides represented in each state. The most prominent leader of the antifusionists, or "Middle-of-the-Roaders" (the more radical wing), was Tom Watson, who denounced fusion as a betrayal of party principle, a course that would bring down upon the Populists all the odium attached to the Republican party in the South. Leader of the fusionists was Marion Butler, successor

[33] Quoted *ibid.*, 628.

[34] Clark, *Populism in Alabama*, 146; Montgomery *Advertiser*, August 10, 1894.

[35] Sheldon, *Populism in the Old Dominion*, 106–108.

[36] Woodward, *Tom Watson*, 276.

to Colonel Polk as leader of the party in North Carolina and a politician of a more "practical" type than either Polk or Watson. The fusionists argued that the Democrats were maintaining themselves in power by means of Negro votes obtained by coercion or fraud. According to the *Louisiana Populist,* "in all the hill parishes where the white people are in the majority, the Populists polled big majorities, but in the river parishes where the Negroes were in the majority the Democrats succeeded in maintaining white supremacy (?) with the Negro votes." [87] The same complaint was made in other states. The proper reply to Democratic tactics, urged the fusionists, was an understanding with the state Republican organizations. It was the counsel of expediency and desperation to which the Independents and Readjusters of the seventies and eighties had listened, and it held out the same hope of victory as well as the same risk of confusion of purpose and ultimate downfall.

"Fusion" was a poor name for the policy, for in no case did either party to an agreement give up its identity or merge with the other. The binding force was plainly expediency, and the only principle Republicans and Populists proclaimed in common was the demand for "a free ballot and an honest election." Agreements of one kind or another were made between the two parties in North Carolina, Alabama, Georgia, Louisiana, and Arkansas in 1894, and later in Virginia and Texas. In North Carolina the agreement was formal and public: one ticket, part Populist and part Republican, was to have the support of both parties. In other states the arrangement might be the withdrawal of candidates in certain areas by one party or the other, or in the case of a national election an exchange of support of a state ticket for support of a national ticket.

The growing cleavage within the Republican party between the Lily-whites and the Black and Tans tended to govern the disposition of the minority party votes, for in states where fusion agreements were made Republicans of the white counties generally supported the Populists, and Negro Republicans of the Black Belt, under the usual inducements and compulsions, voted Democratic. Negro Republican leaders in Alabama and Texas campaigned for the party of white supremacy and helped keep the Black Belt

[87] Quoted in Lucia E. Daniel, "The Louisiana People's Party," in *Louisiana Historical Quarterly,* XXVI (1943), 1097.

Democratic, while white Republicans of those states generally supported Populist candidates.[88] Fusion did not prove popular with the Negroes of North Carolina in 1894, and their vote was "not a prime factor in determining the outcome of the election," which was a victory for the fusionists.[89] The Democrats therefore continued to be more successful in controlling the black vote than the Populists, although the latter suffered heavy loss in prestige under attack by the party of white supremacy for alleged racial disloyalty.

Elections of 1894 in the Lower South, especially in Alabama, Georgia, and Louisiana, proved more violent than any since Reconstruction. Kolb of Alabama was again the victim of fraudulent control of election returns in the Black Belt as well as some manipulation in the white counties. Methods used to defeat Watson resulted in such transparent robbery that prominent Democrats joined in the protest against them, and the Democratic candidate thus elected resigned his seat to submit to another election. In Louisiana there was tampering with poll books, debarring of Populist commissioners, intimidation of voters, and the customary manipulation of the Negro vote.

In spite of the methods used against them, Southern Populists with the aid of fusionists made great gains in 1894, outstripping their brethren in the West, where the party went into a decline. Their outstanding victory of the year came in North Carolina where, for the first time in twenty years, the Democrats were driven from control of both houses of the legislature. Populists won control of the Senate and, together with Republicans, a majority in the House. The newly chosen legislature elected the Populist leader Marion Butler to a full term in the United States Senate, and a Republican to the unexpired term of Senator Vance. Of the newly elected representatives to Congress, 3 were Populists, 3 Democrats, 2 Republicans, and one an Independent supported by the fusionists. Although Kolb was declared the loser in the race for governor in Alabama, one Populist was elected to Congress, and 3 other fusionists, one of them a Populist, won seats after contesting the election before the national House of Representatives. The Populists did not gain control of the legislature of Alabama

[88] Martin, *People's Party in Texas*, 243–44; Moore, *History of Alabama*, 635.

[89] Mabry, *Negro in North Carolina Politics*, 34–35.

but swept Democrats out of office in many of the white counties. On the face of the Georgia election returns, which the Populists as well as some Democrats denounced as fraudulent, the Populists polled 44.5 per cent of the vote in the state election, reduced the Democratic majority from 80,000 (which it had been in 1892) to 20,000, carried 46 of the 137 counties, and elected 5 state senators and 47 representatives. In no Western state save Nebraska did Populism muster so much strength in 1894 as it did in these three states in the heart of the "conservative" South.[40]

While the old party had repressed the radical uprising once more, it was doubtful that it could afford to risk a repetition of its methods. Thousands of Populists were convinced that they had been defrauded and cheated. In Alabama, where the Democrats had refused to provide any legal means of contesting an election, the chairman of the Populist campaign committee, William H. Skaggs, issued a revolutionary manifesto: "The condition in this State has reached a climax. There is no doubt that the State ticket headed by Captain R. F. Kolb has been elected. The alternative is presented of submission to wrong, insult and robbery, or to assert the sovereign power, before which thrones totter, Sceptres fall, and the outrages of tyrants cease. . . . A proud and chivalrous people, worthy of freedom, cannot shirk the responsibilities the situation enforces."[41] Kolb declared that he had been "twice elected" governor: "and this time, by the grace of God and the help of the good people of Alabama, I will be Governor." Governor Jones proclaimed it his intention (also "by the grace of God") to prevent this and surrounded the capitol with troops. In the presence of hundreds of his followers Kolb took the oath of office and delivered his "inaugural" in the street before the guarded capitol shortly after the Democratic governor had been inaugurated. Kolb counseled against violence, however, and the forlorn rebellion developed no further than Kolb's advice to his followers to pay no taxes to the "usurpers."[42]

Whatever ideological differences divided President Cleveland from Democratic politicians of the South, the practical question

[40] Western and Southern votes are compared in Hicks, *Populist Revolt,* 337.

[41] Montgomery *Advertiser,* August 10, 1894.

[42] *Ibid.,* November 20, December 2, 5, 1894.

of patronage was the issue over which the greater number of them broke with the administration. Even "Pitchfork" Ben Tillman, who became the most virulent Cleveland-baiter of them all, had in 1893 written the President a mollified letter begging to be consulted on patronage. Cleveland contemptuously made the letter public without answering it and turned the patronage over to Tillman's enemies. This was the "true explanation" of the South Carolinian's extreme bitterness.[43] Openly threatening opponents of his financial policies with the patronage weapon, the President wrote Governor J. M. Stone of Mississippi that "such office holders must not be surprised if they are summarily dealt with." [44] On the other hand, Cleveland was inclined to give ear to the latter-day Carpetbagger Henry M. Flagler, who in behalf of himself and Henry B. Plant begged him to "help us redeem the State" of Florida from "a miserable set of demagogues," by means of patronage; [45] or to the deposed Senator Wade Hampton, who urged the appointment of a judge on the grounds that it "would be a rebuke to the Tillman Legislature." [46]

One by one, and then by droves, Southern Democrats broke with Cleveland. Congressman Joseph W. Bailey's reason was that he "could not name even the post-master of the lowliest village in North Texas." [47] William E. Curtis, Assistant Secretary of the Treasury, observed in 1894 that the President's "former Southern supporters in the Senate . . . cannot abuse him too much." [48] Senator John T. Morgan was heard to remark, "I hate the ground that man walks on," and on the Senate floor he called Cleveland's supporters "cuckoos." [49] Only such utterances from the conservative Morgan could prepare the public for the outbursts of a Tillman. "When Judas betrayed Christ his heart was not blacker than this scoundrel, Cleveland, in deceiving the Democracy," he told his cheering constituents. "He is an old bag of beef and I am going

[43] Simkins, *Pitchfork Ben Tillman*, 312–13.

[44] Cleveland to Stone, April 26, 1895, in New Orleans *Times-Democrat,* May 4, 1895; Stone to Cleveland, April 21, 1895, in Cleveland Papers.

[45] Henry M. Flagler to Daniel S. Lamont, November 9, 1893, in Cleveland Papers.

[46] Wade Hampton to Cleveland, December 4, 1893, *ibid.*

[47] Acheson, *Joe Bailey*, 58–59.

[48] James A. Barnes, *John G. Carlisle, Financial Statesman* (New York, 1931), 341.

[49] Quoted in Nevins, *Grover Cleveland*, 543, 568.

to Washington with a pitchfork and prod him in his old fat ribs." [50] The "rural element" of South Carolina, wrote one of Hampton's correspondents, "hate Cleveland with a regular proletarian hatred." [51] Perhaps Southerners had hated other Presidents as much, but none so articulately.

Hating Cleveland impotently constituted no defense against Populist encroachments and merely widened the split in the old party. Antiadministration Democrats would have to either leave their party or take control of it. At first there was considerable talk in the Southern press of forming a new silver party. Tillman, who had declared the idea of an alliance with the West "sickening" in 1890, publicly endorsed the plan of deserting the Democrats and forming a silver party in league with the West.

These ideas were prominent at the convention of free-silver supporters in Memphis, June 12, 1895. The "strictly nonpartisan" character of the meeting was emphasized by the Democrats promoting it, and an effort was made to attract Populists and Western silver-Republicans. More than 2,200 delegates "from all the Southern and Western states" attended. A few suspicious Southern Populists put in their appearance, and seven of them were appointed to the committee on resolutions, but it was estimated that more than 90 per cent of the delegates were Democrats. The great majority, including seven Senators and several governors, were from the South, and they dominated proceedings. Conspicuous among the Westerners present were former Congressman William J. Bryan of Nebraska, Senator William M. Stewart of Nevada, and Senator David Turpie of Indiana. The convention listened to Tillman predict failure for the free-silver movement within the Democratic party and advocate the formation of a new party. South Carolinians, he said, "had their trunks packed for two years, and were now ready to move from the old house." Somewhat to the prejudice of the "nonpartisan" atmosphere, Senator Isham Harris of Tennessee urged Democratic unity. The convention adjourned without conclusive action after adopting resolutions that rivaled Populist pronouncements for color and vehemence, but declared for nothing more radical than the silver panacea. Silver, the minimum agrarian

[50] Quoted in Simkins, *Pitchfork Ben Tillman*, 315.

[51] Andrew T. Harlee to Hampton, April 22, 1893, in Cleveland Papers.

demand, was the only bait that anti-Cleveland Democrats were prepared to use in their trap for Populists.[52]

After the official adjournment of the Memphis convention prominent delegates put aside their nonpartisan guise and immediately resolved themselves into a strictly partisan caucus of silver Democrats. They definitely tabled the idea of a new silver party in favor of a scheme for "revolutionizing" [53] the old party and capturing control from within. Here was formed the senatorial clique that was eventually to take control of the Chicago Convention of 1896.

To complete details of organization the silver Democrats held a conference at Washington in August. Their avowed purpose was to capture control of the next national convention. Reporters found the delegates "pretty unanimous for a Western man for President and a Southern man for Vice President." Southerners were again the dominant element. The conference issued an "Address to the People," drafted by a committee of six Southerners and two Midwesterners, of which Senator Daniel of Virginia was chairman. The committee on resolutions was composed of fifteen members from the South and border states and five from the West and Middle West. The choice of a national committee was left to a group presided over by Senator Harris and composed of four Southerners and two Midwesterners. The conference earnestly recommended that in each county and precinct bimetallic Democratic clubs be organized.[54]

The silver crusade now went into high gear. Bimetallic Leagues had already been organized in nearly all the Southern states. By July 4, 1895, nearly every parish in Louisiana and fourteen wards in New Orleans had organized. Arkansas Democrats were thoroughly organized in Bimetallic Leagues in August. William Jennings Bryan hurried from one Southern state to another attending silver meetings, leaving behind him a trail of admirers. Early in August official Democratic conventions of Mississippi, Texas, and Missouri endorsed the free-silver platform.

With the strategy focused upon luring Populists back into the

52 Memphis *Commercial Appeal*, June 13–15, 1895.

53 The expression "revolutionize" was used by the secretary of the National Democratic Committee in this connection, in Montgomery *Advertiser*, July 5, 1896. See also, Senator Daniel's interview, in Washington *Post*, August 15, 1895.

54 Washington *Post*, August 14, 15, 1895.

old party, the most popular speakers were pressed into service. Former Governor Hogg was drafted to make "at least ten speeches" in Texas within thirty days "to counteract the influence of Populists" who were "holding camp meetings all over the State." The silver appeal, it was hoped, would make "many Populists 'return unto the house of their fathers.' "[55] Evan Howell, who had fought the third party tooth and nail, was "willing to join hands with any populist in Georgia" in 1895, and he thought Tom Watson "sincere."[56] The conservative Mississippi Senators, Walthall and George, saw the light and became silver men.

It was sometimes doubtful which was the lurer and which the lured. Certain Populist leaders sought to turn the tables on the old party and use the silver panacea as bait for wavering Democrats. The "nonpartisan" silver convention in North Carolina, for example, was dominated by Populists. On the question of *rapprochement* with the Democrats the Populists were divided, as they had been over fusion with the Republicans. Having succeeded with his Republican fusion, Populist Senator Butler of North Carolina turned his talents toward a combination with the Democrats. Butler had been applauded in Memphis for saying "he loved the [silver] cause better than his party" and "would be willing to sacrifice for the time all other policies of the Populist platform."[57] Tom Watson led in opposing this as he had in opposing fusion with Republicans. "The scheme is a trap, a pitfall, a snare, a menace, a fraud," he warned. It would end in "forever checking our advance toward government ownership of railroads" along with other radical demands.[58]

What the silver Democrats lacked in the way of a radical program they made up in violence of language. In his maiden speech to an astonished Senate, Tillman spoke darkly of a new Mason and Dixon's line that would unite "the toiling and now downtrodden masses" of city and farm; "agrarianism and communism will join hands," and if the armed proletariat marched on Washington, the

[55] J. W. Blake to Hogg, August 10, 1895, in Hogg Papers.

[56] Atlanta *Constitution*, July 19, 1895.

[57] Richmond *Dispatch*, September 18, 26, 1895. See also, Butler's own paper, Raleigh *Daily Caucasian*, March 13, 1895.

[58] Woodward, *Tom Watson*, 282–83.

farmers would "lift no hand to stay the march, but join it." [59] He offered nothing but free silver, however, and the Populists were not fooled. They knew his record. Nor were Kentucky Populists deceived when the Democrats offered a true-blue silverite and Confederate as candidate for governor in 1895. Third-party leaders pointed out the candidate's connection with the Louisville and Nashville machine and stuck to their own nominee. As a result the Republicans carried the election, their first victory in the state. The silver strategy had backfired on the Democrats, and it might do so again.

Still another contender for Southern support was President Cleveland, who waged a campaign to recover the South in 1895. In February he was "entirely certain," he said, that Southerners could "be dislodged from their association with the West," and he believed that "a campaign of education . . . would produce quick and abundant results." [60] A few Southern Congressmen enlisted in his cause and toured the South thoroughly, but one of them "found conditions not altogether favorable to the advancement of the plan of education." [61] Secretaries Carlisle and Hoke Smith went South to make speeches. A "sound money" convention held in Memphis shortly before the silver convention of June brought out a crowd of businessmen but no countrymen or prominent politicians. Finally Cleveland carried the war to the South himself, appearing in Atlanta along with six members of his cabinet in October to speak at the Cotton States Exposition. Resolutions poured in from bankers' associations, chambers of commerce, and manufacturers. But by the end of the year it was apparent that Cleveland's cause in the South was hopeless.

In the spring and summer of 1896 one after another of the state Democratic conventions in the South pronounced enthusiastically for silver. Only Florida and Louisiana failed to take a positive stand against the President's monetary policy. All others instructed their delegates to vote for a silver nominee at the Chicago convention. The temper of these gatherings is suggested by the test for delegates from North Carolina proposed by one countryman: "Stand

[59] Quoted in Simkins, *Pitchfork Ben Tillman,* 323.

[60] Quoted in Nevins, *Grover Cleveland,* 679–80.

[61] Josiah Patterson to Cleveland, April 5, May 5, 1895, in Cleveland Papers.

'em up in a row, spit on 'em, and don't let any man go first until he is so hot he sizzles." [62] Cleveland's name was hissed at his party's conventions in Virginia, North Carolina, and Kentucky. The South Carolina convention, with only four dissenting votes, endorsed Tillman as its presidential candidate, denounced the President as "un-Democratic and tyrannical," and condemned his entire administration.

The silver faction from the South and West was well organized in advance of the Chicago national convention, but united on no candidate. Bryan wrote former Governor Hogg, "we do not want any candidate who is satisfactory to the eastern democrats," and urged Hogg to become a candidate himself, with the support of Texas, Arkansas, Louisiana, and Mississippi.[63] Hogg's preference in candidates was Governor Altgeld of Illinois.[64] Richard P. Bland had his supporters, and several Southerners were mentioned for the vice-presidency. It was reported in Chicago that the South was "making more of a fight this year to be represented on the ticket than at any previous convention since the war." [65] Tillman announced that the South was ready to support "any man you please who is a true representative of that [silver] platform—we have no choice."

At Chicago the silverites overthrew tradition at once by rejecting Senator Hill of New York, the choice of the National Committee for temporary chairman, and electing Senator Daniel of Virginia. Senator James K. Jones of Arkansas was made chairman of the committee on resolutions, and it was he who selected Bryan to take charge of debate on the platform for the silver cause. Tillman, who at that time was the more widely known of the two men, was given the larger share of time as Bryan's colleague in the debate. It was the supreme moment in the career of each man and the best opportunity any silver candidate had at Chicago. While it is doubtful that Tillman entertained serious hope of being nominated, he had taken the trouble to speak in thirteen states on his way to Chicago and undoubtedly intended to make his influence felt in a large way.

[62] Daniels, *Editor in Politics*, 162.

[63] William J. Bryan to Hogg, February 24, 1896, in Hogg Papers.

[64] Hogg to John P. Altgeld, June 1, 1896 (copy), *ibid.*

[65] Chicago *Tribune*, July 7–9, 1896.

To the conservative East the South Carolinian seemed a fitting mouthpiece for the shocking and unaccountable temper of the former Confederacy. Rustic in manner and uncouth in speech, Tillman scorned the most elemental tact and blurted out impolitic and unlovely truths that party politics had tabooed for a generation. He snarled at "lying newspapers" in his opening sentence and referred to himself as the "pitchfork man." Hissing greeted his next sentence and recurred throughout his fifty-minute speech. He came from "the land of secession," he said, and if the white man could be liberated by a second secession he was "willing to see the Democratic party disrupted again." The fact was that "the Southern and Western people have been hewers of wood and drawers of water, and that their substance is going to the East." Catcalls and hisses drowned the statistics he shouted to prove his point. To endorse Cleveland would be to make "asses and liars" of themselves. "We of the South have burned our bridges as far as the Northeastern Democracy is concerned," he declared. "We have turned our faces to the West." To those who denied that the issue was sectional he shouted, "I say it is a sectional issue." [66]

Senator Jones hastily rose to deny that there was anything remotely sectional about the issue, and to insist that he loved all sections with utmost impartiality. The delegates sustained his denial by nominating for the vice-presidency Arthur Sewall, a banker from Maine. They defeated Tillman's resolution condemning Cleveland's administration as "tyrannical," and they rejected his agrarian-sectional definition of their cause for the Main-Street compromise of William Jennings Bryan, whose cross-of-gold speech stretched his "broader class of business men" to embrace farmer, lawyer, wage earner, crossroads merchant. They were businessmen all.

Repelled by Tillman, the Democrats nevertheless heeded one piece of his advice. In his Chicago speech he warned party leaders that they must get the Populists to endorse the Democratic platform and candidate—"or you are beaten." Three days before the Populist national convention opened at St. Louis, Senator Jones of Arkansas, newly chosen Democratic national chairman, was on

[66] Quoted in Simkins, *Pitchfork Ben Tillman*, 335–37; and in Chicago *Tribune*, July 10, 1896.

hand promoting a Populist-Democratic fusion. Enthusiastic supporters of his efforts were General Weaver of Iowa and Populist Senator William V. Allen of Nebraska. These, and with them the majority of Western delegates, came to St. Louis committed to the nomination of Bryan and Sewall. Less radical than the Southern Populists, they accepted the silver panacea as a substitute for Populist doctrines and had grown accustomed to the idea of fusion with Democrats in the West. Some of the Western-state fusion agreements of 1896, contended one Westerner, "could only prove effective through a national fusion of Populists and Democrats." [67]

So deep were the resentments aroused by four years of war against the old party in the South that fusion with Democrats had become more abhorrent to many Southern Populists than fusion with Republicans. The majority of the big Southern delegations at St. Louis was militantly opposed to fusion and, above all, determined to rebel rather than accept the banker Sewall. To forestall a bolt of the Southerners the fusionists proposed the unusual procedure of nominating the candidate for Vice-President first. They also circulated the rumor that Democratic Chairman Jones had promised to obtain the withdrawal of Sewall in favor of the Populist nominee, provided Bryan received the Populist endorsement for President. The name of Tom Watson, favorite of the Southern radicals and leading opponent of fusion, was then presented as Bryan's running mate. Chairman Allen repeatedly denied knowledge of a message from Bryan, then in his possession, rejecting such an arrangement. Absent from the convention and misinformed as to its proceedings, Watson weakly consented to the use of his name. His nomination placated the radicals temporarily and assured the nomination of Bryan, but many of them went home saying they had been "sold out."

Disaffection on the left was matched by rebellion on the right of the Bryan Democracy. Leading Democratic city newspapers in Richmond, Charleston, Nashville, Chattanooga, Louisville, Montgomery, Mobile, New Orleans, Galveston, and Dallas refused to support Bryan. The Montgomery *Advertiser*, for example, regarded the Chicago convention as "subversive of everything in the

[67] N. A. Dunning, "An Appeal to Populists," a handbill dated October 20, 1896, in Butler Papers.

history and tradition of the Party," and the platform as "not only Populistic" but "full of socialism." [68] Of the 151 Southern manufacturers who responded to a poll by the *Manufacturers' Record,* 124 were for McKinley and 12 were noncommittal. Daniel A. Tompkins knew of one millowner who swung all his operatives to McKinley, and Professor Edwin Mims knew of several Southern college faculties who voted solidly for him.[69] Southern headquarters of the National, or "Gold," Democrats were managed by W. N. Haldeman of the Louisville *Courier-Journal,* partner of Henry Watterson. Carlisle and Watterson, logical leaders of the Gold party were passed over, and Simon B. Buckner of Kentucky was chosen running mate of John M. Palmer of Illinois. Haldeman and the Gold Democrats made no secret of their plan to draw enough support from the Democrats to elect McKinley and "settle the fate of Bryan and Sewall." [70] Mark Hanna contributed liberally to the new party, spending $160,000 in Virginia alone.[71]

In the meantime, the Populist-Democratic fusion made in St. Louis showed signs of collapse. Democratic Chairman Jones bluntly refused to consider withdrawing Sewall in favor of Watson and told the Populists to "go with the Negroes, where they belong." His policy seemed to confirm Watson's speculation regarding the Southern Democrats: it was "not so much free silver they want as it is the death of the People's party."

Under suspicion by many Populists for the fusion with Republicans that had won him his office, Senator Butler of North Carolina incurred further distrust by his management of fusion with the Democrats as national chairman of the Populists. For two months he refused to give Bryan and Watson official notification of their nomination, and he failed to press the demand that Sewall be withdrawn. Apathy and demoralization spread through Popu-

[68] Montgomery *Advertiser,* July 14, 1896. For a list of bolting Southern newspapers, see *ibid.,* July 15, 1896.

[69] A list of 704 Virginians, chiefly Democrats, who signed a pledge not to support Bryan was printed in Richmond *Dispatch,* August 14, 15, 1896. The list included Governor C. T. O'Ferrall.

[70] Haldeman, Louisville, to Watterson, Geneva, Switzerland, August 22, 1896, in Henry Watterson Papers (Division of Manuscripts, Library of Congress); James A. Barnes, "The Gold-Standard Democrats and the Party Conflict," in *Mississippi Valley Historical Review,* XVII (1930–1931), 441.

[71] Royall, *Reminiscences,* 202–203.

list ranks the South over. "The uncertainty on Watson and Sewall is tearing our party to pieces," wrote the leader of the Tennessee Populists to Butler.[72] A Populist Congressman of Alabama confessed, "We are all at sea." [73] Referring to the treatment of his party, the Populist chairman in Kentucky predicted, "This gives McKinley Kentucky." [74] Bryan lost the state by 142 votes.

Fusion was failing to fuse. Robert McKee reported early in the year that in his state the Democrats and the Populists were "flying at each other's throats with a ferocity neither time nor circumstance can mitigate. Either would prefer the triumph of the common enemy to that of the other." [75] During the state campaign and election in Louisiana armed bands of Democratic "regulators" roved the northern parishes beating, killing, and intimidating. The militia was called out three times to suppress riots and twice to protect ballot counting. The *Times-Democrat* admitted that "in many precincts" the ballots reported were "two, three, and four times as great as the number of males of voting age." This Democratic paper further admitted that the party of white supremacy was able to carry only five of the twenty-five parishes having a white majority, and that in parishes with a three-to-one majority of whites the Democratic vote was almost the reverse. White supremacy had once more been "saved by negro votes." [76] Although the Populists had fought this bitter contest in alliance with the Republicans, they were called upon to fuse with the Democrats in the national election. Hardy Brian, Populist leader, had threatened revolution against the Democrats for stealing the state election in April, and in September he agreed to split the electoral vote for Vice-President with them.[77] The demoralization produced by this policy is indicated by William A. Guthrie, Populist candidate for governor of North Carolina. "I confess," he wrote Senator Butler during the campaign, "that I myself am 'befogged' at present, hardly know where to go, what to say when I speak, or 'where I am at.' " [78] And

[72] John H. McDowell to Butler, August 6, 1896, in Butler Papers.

[73] M. W. Howard to Butler, August 21, 1896, *ibid.*

[74] J. A. Parker to Butler, August 21, 1896, *ibid.*

[75] McKee to James B. Simpson, January 30, 1898, in McKee Papers.

[76] New Orleans *Times-Democrat,* April 25, 26, May 1, 17, 1896.

[77] Hardy Brian to Butler, October 3, 1896, in Butler Papers.

[78] William A. Guthrie to Butler, September 26, 1896, *ibid.*

no wonder! His party was co-operating with the Republicans on the state ticket and with the Democrats on the national ticket at one and the same time. Populist officials from Louisiana, Kentucky, and Georgia warned Butler that thousands of party members would simply "remain away from the polls." [79]

Less than a month before the November election, Governor Charles A. Culberson, Democratic candidate for re-election in Texas, wrote Colonel Edward M. House, his campaign manager, saying *"the situation is critical."* He expected the Populists to support the Republican ticket. "The fight will be very close even if I do not lose," he said. But there was a tested remedy. "Our fight," wrote the Governor, "shall be to get the negro and railroad vote. What have you done as to the last?" [80] The assistance of Negro bosses was sought for the defense of white supremacy in other states also.

The silver Democrats were able to carry every Southern state save Kentucky for Bryan, though the customary margin of the old party vote was seriously reduced in several quarters. In the twelve states the Democratic national ticket received 1,557,120 out of a total of 2,702,088 votes. The large Populist vote of 1894 melted away in 1896. If the primary purpose of the old party was a national victory for silver, the campaign was a failure. If on the other hand the purpose was the destruction of the Populist party, it was a success. "Our party, as a party, does not exist any more," admitted Watson. "Fusion has well nigh killed it. The sentiment is still there, but confidence is gone." [81] The pattern of confusion that had betrayed the Independents and Readjusters in the seventies and eighties had been repeated in the nineties. With the agrarian radicals in alliance with the party of big business and party of white supremacy in combination with Negroes against lower-class whites, it was little wonder that the masses lost confidence and became apathetic. Their frustrated impulses toward revolt were to seek newer and stranger outlets in the future.

The old party had succeeded in throwing off Eastern domination temporarily, but with a few exceptions there was no remark-

79 For example, J. A. Tetts, state secretary of the Populist party, to Butler, October 3, 1896, *ibid.*

80 Charles A. Culberson to Edward M. House, October 12, 1896, in E. M. House Papers (microfilm in University of Texas Library).

81 Atlanta *People's Party Paper,* November 13, 1896.

able regeneration in the leadership. The silver leaders—or, at least, the *new* silver leaders—constructed their machines on the model inherited from the Redeemers. With the opposition demoralized, they were more strongly entrenched than before.

For the broader aspects of the revolt, Henry Adams penned a brusque epitaph. "A capitalistic system had been adopted, and if it were to run at all, it must be run by capital and by capitalistic methods; for nothing could surpass the nonsensity of trying to run so complex and so concentrated a machine by Southern and Western farmers in grotesque alliance with city day-laborers, as had been tried in 1800 and 1828, and had failed even under simple conditions." [82] Even so, the tradition of 1800, 1828, and 1896 remained deeply grooved in the Southern mind. To many it seemed the only logical political expression of the discontents of an unhappy minority region.

[82] Henry Adams, *The Education of Henry Adams, An Autobiography* (Boston, 1918), 344.

CHAPTER XI

THE COLONIAL ECONOMY

THE vision that inspired the Southern businessman was that of a South modeled upon the industrial Northeast. The Richmond banker and railroad president John Skelton Williams, for example, said in 1898 that he was "hoping to see in the South in the not distant future many railroads and business institutions as great as the Pennsylvania Railroad, the Mutual Life Insurance Company, the Carnegie Steel Company or the Standard Oil Company." [1] It was assumed, of course, that as such corporations developed, Southern counterparts of the Morgans, Carnegies, and Rockefellers would rise with them.

Pending the realization of these hopes, it behooved good Southerners to do all in their power to attract the attention and the investments of Northeastern capitalists southward. Deploring "the populistic tendencies of some Southern people" which gave offense to such interests, Williams held up for admiration several of the dominant Northeastern corporations of the day. Southerners, he declared, "ought to be proud of the strength and magnitude of these and similar concerns as the Englishman is of the Bank of England." Richard H. Edmonds of the *Manufacturers' Record* joined with Colonel D. B. Dyer, Augusta industrialist, in organizing the Southern Development Association, the purpose of which, according to Dyer, was "to promote the colonization and improvement of the South." [2] The two ideas were identical in the minds of these gentlemen. The headquarters of the association was in New York.

As the old century drew to a close and the new century progressed

1 Quoted in *Manufacturers' Record*, XXXIV (September 9, 1898), 101.

2 Richmond *Dispatch*, June 22–23, 1894.

through the first decade, the penetration of the South by Northeastern capital continued at an accelerated pace. The Morgans, Mellons, and Rockefellers sent their agents to take charge of the region's railroads, mines, furnaces, and financial corporations, and eventually of many of its distributive institutions. Southern counterparts of the Northeastern masters, however, failed to appear. The number of Southern businessmen increased steadily, and some of them waxed in fortune. But the new men, as well as many of the old, acted as agents, retainers, and executives—rarely as principals. The economy over which they presided was increasingly coming to be one of branch plants, branch banks, captive mines, and chain stores.

Northeastern control over the vast, sprawling railway system of the South was virtually completed within the decade following the Panic of 1893 by a series of large-scale reorganizations. J. Pierpont Morgan, mightiest of the Northern empire builders, opened the era of reorganization and consolidation by creating the Southern Railway out of the ruins of the Richmond and West Point Terminal Company in 1894.

Plundered, mismanaged, and insolvent, the Terminal system was left in great confusion in 1893. Upon undertaking the reorganization, Morgan imposed terms which "virtually meant that the security holders accepted in advance any proposals which he might make." [3] The New York banker took over 4,500 miles of railroad and 150 miles of water line formerly operated by more than thirty separate corporations. The new company owned all but 491 miles of the road, and Morgan retained control. Within a few months the Southern Railway swiftly expanded its holdings to a total of 7,500 miles of rail. In the course of the reorganization "$120,000,000 of common stock was issued to persons who paid not a single dollar in actual value for it"—a transaction that has been called "the classic example" of stock jobbing and watering.[4]

The New York *Sun* said of the reorganization "that the event is the most notable that has taken place in the history of American railroads, and that its bearing upon every Southern business is of

[3] Campbell, *Reorganization of the American Railroad System,* 150.

[4] Maxwell Ferguson, *State Regulation of Railroads in the South,* in Columbia University *Studies in History, Economics and Public Law,* LXVII, No. 2 (New York, 1916), 52.

vital importance." [5] The significance for Southern mining, manufacturing, and commerce is indicated by the facts that Morgan now dominated transportation in the two great coal fields of the region; that he tapped the iron industry from Knoxville to Birmingham, with thirty furnaces on the western division of the system; and that his lines laced the Piedmont cotton-mill country, penetrated the tobacco country of Kentucky and North Carolina, spread branches through the heart of the lumber country, and even dipped into the truck and fruit traffic of Florida. The Southern has been called "the basis of Morgan's empire," but that empire was to include several additional large provinces in the South before it was completed.

Within ten years after the formation of the Southern Railway two great systems of comparable size, the Atlantic Coast Line and the Seaboard Air Line, were consolidated in the same region. In May, 1902, the Atlantic Coast Line, which operated 1,676 miles, the result of the consolidation of several roads by a Connecticut holding company, took over completely the huge Plant System, stretching from Charleston to Tampa. The Plant System itself, the empire of the Connecticut Yankee Henry B. Plant, was the result of a process of consolidation of numerous small roads between 1879 and 1899, when Plant died.[6]

The year it acquired the Plant System the Atlantic Coast Line purchased controlling stock in the Louisville and Nashville Railroad, one of the oldest and strongest systems in the South. In the spring of 1902 John W. Gates of Wall Street, by means of a quiet speculative spree, secured a corner on Louisville and Nashville stock, control of which was immediately taken over by J. P. Morgan and Company. The Company explained that it "consented solely to relieve the general financial condition" and added a rather overemphatic denial: "The Southern Railway has no interest, direct or indirect, present or prospective, in the stock." [7] Morgan then obligingly strengthened his most important competitor, the Atlantic Coast Line, by financing its purchase of the Louisville and Nashville stock. With more than 10,000 miles of rail under its control,

[5] Quoted in *Railway World* (Philadelphia), XXXIX (1894), 756–57.

[6] Howard D. Dozier, *A History of the Atlantic Coast Line Railroad* (Boston, 1920), 140–47; G. Hutchinson Smyth, *The Life of Henry Bradley Plant* (New York, 1898), *passim*.

[7] Quoted in Dozier, *Atlantic Coast Line Railroad*, 149.

the Atlantic Coast Line now connected cities lying between Norfolk and Tampa on the east and New Orleans and Louisville on the west, linking the two areas at Chattahoochee, Montgomery, and Atlanta.

The youngest of the large systems was the Seaboard Air Line, formed in July, 1900, to consolidate eighteen corporations originally owned and operated by three companies. Under the Seaboard these separate roads were united into a continuous system by the construction of some 200 miles of new line. When completed the new road paralleled the Atlantic Coast Line throughout its extent with a 2,600-mile system from Washington south along the coastal plain.[8]

Smaller roads were raided, bankrupted, driven to the wall, or suffered to survive, at the pleasure of the giant systems. The giants divided the Southern colony at their leisure, according to mutual interest. During the heyday of conquest, Milton Hannibal Smith, president of the Louisville and Nashville, wrote Samuel Spencer, president of the Southern, to settle "the future of certain railroads that are, or may be tributary or competitive with roads controlled by the L & N RR and the Southern Ry." Smith playfully opened his remarks with this colloquy between conquistadors:

Pizarro: How shall we divide the new world?

Cortez: I will take North America and you can have all of South America, except ——, and neither of us will do anything to the Isthmus without notice to and cooperation of the other.

Pizarro: While Patagonia is not a very large or important part of the world, yet, perhaps, it is as much as I can tote.

Spencer replied in kind:

Pizarro: Since our last conversation, the division of the New World between us has made some progress.

Cortez: Yes; you seem to have acquired Patagonia, and I have secured a considerable part of North America which touched my former territory, but it seems to me you have acquired a con-

[8] Edward S. Meade, "The Seaboard Air Line," in *Railway World*, XLIX (1905), 895–97.

> siderable neck of the Isthmus which is the connecting link between us.[9]

Presidents Smith and Spencer could have posed more appropriately as corregidors than as conquistadors, for they acted as agents and not as principals. "In the South at the turn of the century," concludes a scholarly account, "there were three large systems, the Southern, the Atlantic Coast Line and the Seaboard Air Line—and Morgan dominated all three to the exclusion of competition." [10] Smith and Spencer were not dividing the New World, but settling administrative boundaries between two provinces of a single empire.

If their title of conquistador stood in question, their methods and ideas were none the less suggestive of that genus. Smith operated the Louisville and Nashville for thirty-eight years on the theory that, in his words, "society, as created, was for the purpose of one man's getting what the other fellow has, if he can, and keep out of the penitentiary." His chief complaint lay against government interference with the game. He was once called upon by Joseph W. Folk, attorney for the Interstate Commerce Commission, to explain certain large expenditures for political purposes:

Smith: We try to get on good terms and cooperate with the State authorities . . . . it is an exceedingly difficult matter to protect the property of a large corporation in 13 different States from confiscation by the people.

Folk: What people?

Smith: The people of the country. . . . People having a democratic government, with a majority rule, create commissions and other forms of government with power to confiscate. . . . All legislative bodies are a menace. . . .

Folk: So, as I understand you, Mr. Smith, you consider government by the people as dangerous, and you conceive it to be your patriotic duty to counteract it?

[9] Milton H. Smith to Samuel Spencer, February 22, 1896; Spencer to Smith, February 29, 1896, in United States Interstate Commerce Commission, *Hearings Relative to the Financial Relations, Rates, and Practices of the Louisville & Nashville Railroad Co., The Nashville, Chattanooga & St. Louis Railway, and Other Carriers*, printed in *Senate Documents*, 64 Cong., 1 Sess., No. 461, pp. 369–73.

[10] Campbell, *Reorganization of the American Railroad System*, 332.

Smith: No. What are we going to substitute? We do not want chaos. We do not want anarchy. . . .

Folk: The anarchist, Mr. Smith, says all legislative bodies are a menace; in action they are a calamity.

Smith: That is my opinion.

Folk: You say all legislative bodies are a menace, and in action they are a calamity. Will you explain the difference between your theory and the theory of the anarchist?

Smith: I don't know about the anarchist. I can not explain the difference.[11]

President Smith had outlined his views to the Commission twenty years earlier and he saw no reason to change them:

Commissioner: You say that the Government ought to leave you and the shipper who resides at those places free to contract. Now, that shipper is obliged to pay whatever you charge?

Smith: No.

Commissioner: What could he do?

Smith: He could walk.[12]

Morgan called his main road the Southern and named as its president a Southerner. Graduate of the University of Georgia and the University of Virginia and a Confederate veteran, President Spencer took personal charge of a large publicity organization that card-indexed newspaper editors according to their usefulness. Money, social pressure, sentiment, and tradition were brought to bear to protect Morgan's interests from legislative action. "Born and reared in the South, and identified by my life's work with Southern interests, I feel that I have a right to speak to you as one of your own people," Spencer told an Alabama audience in 1906. The burden of his message was that "the interests of the railroad and its patrons are identical." [13]

11 United States Interstate Commerce Commission, *Hearings,* in *Senate Documents,* 64 Cong., 1 Sess., No. 461, pp. 404–409.

12 Quoted by Smith, *ibid.,* 353.

13 Samuel Spencer, *Address of Samuel Spencer, President of the Southern Railway Company, before the Alabama Agricultural Association, at Montgomery, Alabama, October 25, 1906* (n.p., n.d.), 2–4, 23. See also, "The Newspapers on 'Tainted News,'" in *Collier's, The National Weekly* (New York), XXXIX (May 4, 1907), 15.

Of the two Yankee empire builders who divided Florida—Plant and Flagler—the mightier proved to be Flagler. Taking the east coast as his half, he started operations in the late eighties after he had accumulated a fortune as a Rockefeller associate in Standard Oil. Flagler opened his first luxury hotel at St. Augustine in 1888. Pushing southward through 300 miles of untamed scrub and hammock with his railroad and hotel chain, the pioneer Flagler flung back the last American frontier—to establish pleasure palaces and playgrounds for the idle rich. The first locomotive pulled into West Palm Beach in 1894, and his Royal Poinciana opened its doors the same year. By 1896 the palace cars from Bar Harbor and Newport could roll unimpeded through the poverty-littered Carolinas and all the way to Miami and its Royal Palm Hotel. Flagler had invested $30,000,000 in Florida to reach Miami. In his next leap he took to sea with his railroad, and with a labor force of 4,000 men and an expenditure of $20,000,000, he spanned the Florida Keys and entered Key West in 1912. Like his contemporary empire-builder James J. Hill, who operated at the opposite corner of the continent, Flagler founded cities and colonies, fostered agriculture, and encouraged immigration. At his death in 1913 his empire included 765 miles of track, hotels to accommodate 40,000 guests, and numerous land companies, newspapers, and utilities.[14]

Since the time it was a colony of England, the South had wrestled with the problem of securing immigrants to fill up its sparsely settled territories, develop its resources, and supplement its labor supply. In the late nineteenth and early twentieth centuries it was the railroad companies that dealt most effectively with the problem that had once been the concern of lords proprietors, London joint-stock companies, and slave traders of the seventeenth and eighteenth centuries. It is true that state bureaus, land companies, and numerous immigration societies of businessmen took part in the movement. Each state had an immigration bureau of some sort by 1900, and most of them had agents in New York and the West, and some in Europe, to spread propaganda. Their effectiveness was limited, however, by small appropriations. Legions of immigration societies sprang up, more than a hundred in Louisiana alone.

[14] S. Walter Martin, *Florida's Flagler* (Athens, 1949), 117–21, 145, 158–67, 202–24, 235, 241–44.

Regional associations with imposing names and important dignitaries as officers held conventions and published annual proceedings. The secretary of the Southern Inter-State Immigration Association revealed the true state of things, however, when he wrote the governor of Alabama that the support of his organization derived "almost wholly from the Railroad Companies of the South" and that he hoped for "little or no financial aid" from state legislatures.[15] While the conventions orated and resolved, the railroads acted.

With millions of acres in their possession and an urgent need for traffic, the railroads had both the incentive and the means of action. The Missouri Pacific and Iron Mountain system, which owned over 1,000,000 acres in Arkansas, employed 300 immigration agents in the West. The Southern Pacific employed twice that number and sold 3,000,000 acres between Corpus Christi and New Orleans in the decade following 1894. The Nashville, Chattanooga, and St. Louis had some 1,000 agents working the Middle West. The Mobile and Ohio labored to dispose of more than 600,000 acres, and the Illinois Central almost that amount, in Mississippi, Alabama, Kentucky, and Louisiana. In 1903 Morgan's Southern Railway settled 2,000 families on 2,270,018 acres. The Louisville and Nashville, working with land companies, sold 105,154 acres of farm lands and 255,540 acres of timber and mineral lands along its lines in 1903. Each of the large roads had its own immigrant newspaper or journal and distributed quantities of state and local propaganda literature. Twice a month all the main railroads with lines into the South ran special "homeseekers' trains" at half rates. Small colonies of Midwesterners, Italians, Danes, Swedes, Hungarians, and Germans sprinkled the South along the railroads. Dunkers and other religious or socialistic colonies settled in Georgia and Alabama.[16]

Considering the amount of effort put into the immigration

[15] J. G. Patrick, Secretary of the Southern Inter-State Immigration Association, to Governor Jones, May 18, 1894, in Official Records of Governors, File Box No. 31 (Alabama State Archives).

[16] Walter L. Fleming, "Immigration to the Southern States," in *Political Science Quarterly,* XX (1905), 278–94; Bert James Loewenberg, "Efforts of the South to Encourage Immigration, 1865–1900," in *South Atlantic Quarterly,* XXXIII (1934), 377–84. The L and N figures are taken from an unpublished seminar paper on colonization activities of the railroad by Jean Keith of the Johns Hopkins University.

movement, the results were insignificant. While the greater part of the railroad campaign was in the West, where some success was attained, much of the propaganda attempted to divert southward part of the great tide of European immigration. The flood tide of European immigration, in 1899–1910, swept past the South leaving it almost untouched and further isolating it in its peculiarities from the rest of the country. New Hampshire received more European immigrants in that decade than the total received by North Carolina, South Carolina, Tennessee, Mississippi, Georgia, and Kentucky; Connecticut got many more than the whole South combined and New Jersey twice as many.[17] In the interchange of native population by internal migration, moreover, all the Southern states, save Oklahoma, Florida, and Virginia, lost more than they gained. The railroads were a path of emigration as well as immigration.[18]

The Southern iron and steel industry between 1893 and 1913 repeated in a general way the pattern followed by railroad history. The Panic wrecked many marginal companies built up in the boom period. Then came a wave of reorganization and consolidation which made a few large companies out of many small ones, and finally the hand of the New York banker grasped control.

While production in other Southern states was declining or making slow progress, that in the Birmingham area of Alabama expanded rapidly. The Tennessee Coal, Iron, and Railroad Company, easily the dominant operator in the Alabama fields, was in 1887 "the largest single holder of ore lands and furnace plants in the United States." Consolidations and mergers later brought into the Tennessee Company twelve rival companies, including the huge De Bardeleben interests, in 1892. By that time the company owned seventeen large furnaces, thirteen in Alabama and four in Tennessee, all fed from its own mines, and an imperial domain of 400,000 acres of coal and iron lands. The company weathered the Panic of 1893, broke the strike of 1894 with the aid of Governor Jones's militia, and reduced operating costs by cutting wages. To

[17] United States Immigration Commission, *Abstracts of Reports*, in *Senate Documents*, 61 Cong., 3 Sess., No. 747, I, 105. According to immigrants' report of their final destination.

[18] C. Warren Thornthwaite, *Internal Migration in the United States* (Philadelphia, 1934), Plate II, opposite p. 8; Plate III, opposite p. 12.

dispose of surplus pig iron, a foreign market was built up in England, Europe, and Japan that made Birmingham the largest shipping point for pig iron in the country by 1898, and the third largest in the world—in spite of the 200 miles that separated the city from tidewater.[19]

Faced with acute depression in pig iron and growing competition for the domestic market from the great corporations of the Pittsburgh area, officials of the Tennessee Company decided in 1897 that their only salvation lay in the production of steel. President Nathaniel Baxter began at once the construction of a modern open-hearth steel plant with a capacity of 1,500 tons a day at Ensley, Alabama.[20] Market conditions were propitious. Because of defects of Bessemer-steel rails, railway companies the country over were turning to open-hearth steel, and within a few years the plant at Ensley was turning out the greater part of open-hearth rails produced in the United States. In the spring of 1907 the Harriman lines placed an order for 150,000 tons of open-hearth rails with the Tennessee Company for all its roads, "an order that riveted the attention of the entire steel world on the new Ensley plant." [21] Here was a direct challenge to Pittsburgh steel masters and their New York bankers.

In the library of J. Pierpont Morgan, on the evening of November 5, 1907, the United States Steel Corporation concluded the purchase of all but a fraction of the stock of the Tennessee Coal and Iron Company from the Wall Street syndicate currently in possession. For the princely Southern domain the corporation paid $35,317,632, nearly all of it in U.S. Steel bonds. The purchase was represented by the Morgan firm as a public service, "solely to prevent the further spread of the panic," said George W. Perkins [22] —and all monopolistic motives were disclaimed. President Theodore Roosevelt not only sanctioned the absorption but justified it in the language of the corporation officials. On the day before the purchase Judge Elbert H. Gary and Henry C. Frick assured him, said the President, "that under ordinary circumstances they would

19 Clark, *History of Manufactures in the United States*, II, 242–43; III, 111.

20 Armes, *Story of Coal and Iron in Alabama*, 465.

21 *Ibid.*, 515.

22 *Absorption of the Tennessee Coal & Iron Co.*, in *Senate Documents*, 62 Cong., 1 Sess., No. 44, p. 66.

not consider purchasing the stock, because but little benefit will come to the Steel Corporation from the purchase," and that they were merely trying "to prevent a panic and general industrial smash-up." [23]

Others have taken a sharply contrasting view. John Moody, an authority on trusts, wrote that the purchase "added an almost unheard-of value to the equity back of the Steel Corporation stocks," and considered that "A very conservative estimate of the values of the ore and coal deposits" would be "hardly less, in all probability, than $1,000,000,000." "If they checked the panic by this transaction," continued Moody, "they did it by taking a few dollars out of one pocket and putting millions into another." [24] A Senate-committee investigation found that the purchase constituted a violation of the Sherman Antitrust Act, and that "the President was not authorized to permit the absorption." The committee report continued: "To sum the matter up briefly, we think the property is very valuable, worth probably several hundred million dollars, and that among the larger benefits which the steel corporation derives from the merger are the control of the open-hearth output of steel rails, the ultimate control of the iron-ore supply of the country, the practical monopoly of the iron and steel trade of the South, and the elimination of a strong and growing competitor." [25]

In Birmingham the coming of U.S. Steel was hailed as the fulfillment of the millennial promises of a generation. The Birmingham *Age-Herald* declared that it would "make the Birmingham District hum as it never hummed before," and the Birmingham *News* prophesied that it would "make the Birmingham District the largest steel manufacturing center in the universe." [26] The often-quoted predictions of Hewitt and Carnegie about the matchless future of the city were once more reprinted. Birmingham had long lived in an atmosphere of expectancy. It continued to do so.

One of the first acts of the new owners was to install as president of the Tennessee Company a genial young Southerner named George Gordon Crawford, who like Samuel Spencer of the South-

[23] Theodore Roosevelt to Attorney General Charles J. Bonaparte, November 4, 1907, quoted *ibid.*, 4.

[24] John Moody, quoted *ibid.*, 13.

[25] Committee report, *ibid.*, 16.

[26] Quoted in Armes, *Story of Coal and Iron in Alabama*, 520–21.

ern Railway, came from Georgia. Crawford assisted in crushing a coal miners' strike in 1908.

The iron-age millennium had yet to arrive at the end of the period under survey, and the splendid promises remained to be fulfilled. In fact, between 1903 and 1913 the production of pig iron in the South "remained almost stationary, while that of the United States as a whole increased more than 70 per cent." While in 1893 the South's proportion of the national production had been 22 per cent, it had fallen to 11 per cent by 1913. Steel fared somewhat better, but under the Pennsylvania rules of "Pittsburgh Plus" and "Birmingham Differential," the captive industry came far from living up to possibilities obviously unexploited.[27]

In the strictly extractive industries the South functioned in the role traditionally assigned it, and in producing fuels, ores, and raw materials the economy met with fewer artificial restrictions and curbs. Production of minerals soared as new resources were discovered. Control and development of the new resources, however, usually fell into the hands of Eastern bankers and industrialists.

The modern era of oil production in America opened on January 10, 1901, when the Lucas "discovery well" at Spindletop, near Beaumont, Texas, came in with an unprecedented gusher. In many ways Spindletop deserved the popular title of "the world's greatest oil well." Each of the nine days before it was capped, the wild well gushed between 70,000 and 110,000 barrels.[28] When it is recalled that the discovery well of 1859 in the Pennsylvania fields came in at ten barrels a day, and that the average daily production of the Eastern wells was less than two barrels each in 1901, something of the hysteria of the Texas oil boom can be grasped. Special trains ran from Philadelphia, New York, and other Eastern cities. By the end of the year 500 wells had been drilled pepperbox fashion within five acres, divided into "tracts as small as one square yard," and a forest of wooden derricks covered the low mound. The second year of production the Spindletop Pool produced 17,500,000 barrels.[29]

27 Clark, *History of Manufactures in the United States,* III, 26.

28 *Manufacturers' Record,* XXXIX (January 24, 1901), 5.

29 Gerald Forbes, *Flush Production, The Epic of Oil in the Gulf-Southwest* (Norman, 1942), 7–19; Carl Coke Rister, *Oil! Titan of the Southwest* (Norman, 1949), 50–65.

Spindletop was only the beginning of the great Southwest oil boom. New Texas pools were opened at Powell (1901), Sour Lake (1902), Petrolia (1904), Beaver Switch (1909), and Burkburnett (1912). Oklahoma, with a series of spectacular discoveries at Red Fork (1901), Glenn (1905), Cushing (1912), and Healdton (1913) soon surpassed Texas. By 1907, the year she became a state, Oklahoma led the nation, and by 1913 she produced one fourth of the country's oil. Louisiana pools discovered in the same period were Jennings (1901), Anse-la-Butte (1902), Caddo (1906), Vinton (1910), Pine Prairie (1912), and De Soto (1913).[30]

Hustling from one of these boom pools to the next was a traveling carnival of wildcatters, well drillers, mule skinners, and sharpers who enriched the vernacular, folklore, local color, and even a few of the pockets of the Southwest for an era. "Never before was a region assaulted by so numerous, desperate, determined, and plunging an army of wildcatters," writes one who followed the army.[31] Ephemeral shantytowns sometimes vanished along with the army: one clapboard hotel turned up in five different Texas towns under as many different names. Tulsa and Port Arthur were among the more permanent creations of the oil boom.

Early in the century three nominally competing pipeline and refining companies, presided over by Standard Oil, established themselves in the Southwest. The Mellons of Pittsburgh entered in 1901 with their Gulf Company; the Texas Company was organized by John W. Gates soon afterward; Standard Oil operated through various subsidiaries already established. With complete monopoly over transportation, these pipeline companies found it a simple matter to drive down or fix the price at will, and squeeze out the independents by counterdrilling or refusing transportation. The first 5,000,000 barrels drawn from Spindletop yielded producers between three and seventeen cents a barrel. One lot of 100,000 barrels at the Sour Lake Pool in Texas sold for one cent a barrel, and sometimes thousands of barrels simply flowed "down the creek." When the great Healdton Pool was discovered, a Standard Oil company agreed to run in a pipeline provided production

[30] Forbes, *Flush Production*, 23, 42, 46; Rister, *Oil!*, 66–142.

[31] Samuel W. Tait, Jr., *The Wildcatters, An Informal History of Oil-Hunting in America* (Princeton, 1946), 127.

was raised to 10,000 barrels. Then within a few weeks it was announced that the company would transport only 4,000 of the 10,000 barrels then being produced and pay only fifty cents a barrel.[32] The profits of the pipelines are indicated by the dividends of the Mellon Company, which paid 35 per cent in 1911, 22 per cent in 1912, and 27 per cent in 1913.[33]

The *Manufacturers' Record* was given to boasting of the "Southern monopoly" of the nation's deposits of certain vital minerals, such as manganese, bauxite, phosphate rock, fuller's earth, and sulphur. These rich mineral deposits, however, were "Southern" monopolies only in the sense that the sulphur of Sicily, owned by a British syndicate, was once a "Sicilian" monopoly. Protected by patent laws, franchises, options, or outright possession of mineral lands, the Mellons, Rockefellers, Du Ponts, and other capitalists monopolized "Southern monopolies."

Locked under hundreds of feet of sea mud and quicksand along the Gulf Coast of Louisiana and Texas lay some 95 per cent of the nation's deposits of sulphur. These riches were unlocked in 1903 by the combination of a process of pipeline extraction developed in Standard Oil laboratories and the opening of the nearby Spindletop oil pool, which provided cheap fuel for the process. Within a few years the Union Sulphur Company was producing 80 per cent of the world's output of this important mineral by an unprecedentedly cheap process.

Cheap sulphur could have been a tremendous boon to farmers of the Southeast, who spent some 10 per cent of their gross income for fertilizers, a larger amount than farmers of any other part of the country. If sulphuric acid is "the golden key which unlocked the door of modern industry," the Louisiana deposits should have meant much to the South's industrial hopes. But the sulphur was not cheap. It was cheaply produced—at costs varying from $3.75 to $4.50 per ton—but it was sold by the monopoly at a fixed price of $18.00. It took a big pipeline to siphon off the profits of the South's sulphur. In 1913 the Union Sulphur Company produced 491,000 tons and sold it at a profit of $13.85 per ton, a total profit of $6,800,-

[32] *Transportation of Oil by Pipe Lines: Hearings before the Committee on Interstate and Foreign Commerce,* House of Representatives, 63 Cong., 2 Sess., on H.R. 16581, May 15 and 16, 1914 (Washington, 1914), 41–42, 51–55.

[33] *Ibid.,* 33; Harvey O'Connor, *Mellon's Millions* (New York, 1933), 107.

350. Earnings of the company that year were $3,400 per share. According to one study, annual profits of the company varied between 150 and 400 per cent of its total investment.[34] A good part of these profits came out of the huge fertilizer bill of the Southern farmer. By means of a patent monopoly the Union Company held complete mastery of America's sulphur until 1913. Thereafter Mellon and Morgan managed to move in to new Texas sulphur fields. After a brief flurry of competition, the price was amicably fixed at a high level again.

The entire domestic supply of bauxite, the ore from which aluminum is made, was mined in four Southern states—Arkansas, Georgia, Alabama, and Tennessee. Easily the largest and most important producer was Arkansas, where deposits were discovered around the beginning of the century. The new Southern mineral province of bauxite became a tributary, and ultimately the property, of Pittsburgh and the Mellon aluminum monopoly. Numerous independent producers held out for a time, but one by one they were bought up, squeezed out, or brought under control by the Aluminum Company of America. By 1909 the Mellon monopoly of known bauxite deposits suitable for profitable exploitation was almost complete. In 1912 an independent firm, the Southern Aluminum Company, backed by French capitalists, set up an expensive plant in North Carolina, but gave up after two years and sold out to the Mellon Company.[35]

To the blight of the depression of the nineties the new cotton mills of the Piedmont, unlike other industries of the South, seemed relatively immune. Their immunity was probably due to the stability of their foreign market for coarse cloth. The factories of North Carolina and South Carolina continued to run at full capacity, for the most part, many of them both day and night. They competed successfully in the markets of Philadelphia, New York, and Boston, shipped large quantities of coarse cotton cloth to the Orient, and reported profits of 25 and 30 per cent. Bankrupt croppers and tenants, despairing of making a living from 5-cent cotton, left the land for the mill. Even some landowners joined the exodus.

34 Robert H. Montgomery, *The Brimstone Game; Monopoly in Action* (New York, 1940), 48–50.

35 O'Connor, *Mellon's Millions*, 88–92; *The Mineral Industry . . . during 1913* (New York), XXII (1914), 13–25, 47–52.

The phenomenal pace of new mill construction slackened temporarily in 1893 but gathered new momentum in the mid-nineties. "Cotton-mill building made greater progress in the South during 1895 than ever before," reported the *Manufacturers' Record,* estimating an increase of approximately a million spindles, "or probably twice as great as ever before recorded in one year." The increase in spindles in the South between 1890 and 1897 was 151 per cent, and only 20 per cent in New England.[36]

The plight of the New England textile industry was a subject of intense interest in the South. Early in January, 1895, representatives of three of Lowell's largest corporations appeared before the Massachusetts legislature seeking amended charters permitting them to do business below the Potomac.[37] During the next few years, millions of dollars of New England capital went into Southern plants and investments, mainly in South Carolina, Georgia, and Alabama. A committee of Fall River manufacturers, replying to their workers' protests, attributed a sharp wage cut to the competition of Southern mills. The Boston *Transcript* carried gloomy articles on the "crisis" and the "impending ruin," and in the spring of 1896 a score of New England mill presidents and managers conceded numerous advantages of the South.[38]

Among the advantages debated or conceded were the South's newer machinery, cheaper labor, lower taxes, proximity to raw materials, cheap water power, milder climate—the list grew with the controversy and was enlarged upon by Southern boomers and capital seekers. In a spirit of candor, however, the *Manufacturers' Record* advised New England to seek the real explanation in the answer to the question "why England is shipping textile machinery to India and other parts of the East." [39] Edwin L. Godkin, who viewed economics from the standpoint of empire, made the same comparison: "The condition of the Massachusetts mills," he observed, "finds its parallel in England. The greatest market for British cotton is India, but cotton spinning in India has been advancing slowly during the same time and by the same means that

[36] *Manufacturers' Record,* XXVIII (January 3, 1896), 337; Thompson, *From the Cotton Field to the Cotton Mill,* 70–71; Cooper, *Piedmont Region,* 59–60.

[37] Richmond *Dispatch,* January 18, 1895.

[38] Boston *Transcript,* December 16, 1897; Boston *Journal,* April 12, 1896.

[39] *Manufacturers' Record,* XXXII (December 24, 1897), 335.

the industry has been growing in the Carolinas. Nearness to the raw material, which the India spinner enjoys, is the smallest part of his advantage. Here too, the wage question is the great factor. Wages of the Indian operative are only ten to twenty cents per day, and the hours of labor are such as the employer chooses to make." [40]

Dismissing the South's other advantages as of minor importance, a committee of the influential Arkwright Club of New England came to the following conclusion: "We have, therefore, practically to consider only the problem that is presented by the fact that labor is cheaper in the South; that the hours of labor are longer, and that there is neither any of the restrictive legislation urged among us by the labor unions, and very generally placed upon our statute-books, nor any prospect even of an early agitation in behalf of such restrictions. . . . So far as we could learn there is no disposition to organize labor unions." [41] The report estimated that the cost of labor was 40 per cent lower in the South than in New England, and that the working day in North Carolina was 24 per cent longer than in Massachusetts.

Trained economists, while assigning some credit to other factors, especially to the new and improved machinery of the Southern mills, have fixed upon labor costs and working hours as the chief initial advantage of the South, although they differ among themselves as to the extent of that advantage. One investigator goes so far as to say that "the corner-stone of the structure has been the supply of cheap and tractable labor." [42] Until 1906 the lowest legal minimum in any Southern state was sixty-six hours a week, a seventy-five–hour week was not uncommon, and the average week in North Carolina in 1906 was sixty-nine. After 1900 the Southern operator's advantage in cheap labor tended to diminish as wages rose and labor became scarcer.[43] The movement of New England capital southward slowed down somewhat thereafter.

[40] New York *Evening Post,* December 15, 1897.

[41] *Manufacturers' Record,* XXXII (December 24, 1897), 335.

[42] Melvin T. Copeland, *The Cotton Manufacturing Industry of the United States,* in *Harvard Economic Studies,* VIII (Cambridge, 1912), 39. Cf. Mitchell, *Rise of Cotton Mills,* 180–81, 224–25; Clark, *History of Manufactures in the United States,* III, 173.

[43] Thompson, *From the Cotton Field to the Cotton Mill,* 133; Kohn, *Cotton Mills of South Carolina,* 63–64.

The race between the two sections nevertheless continued. Upon the economic plane rivalry became as keen as it had once been upon a political level. Since Massachusetts and South Carolina led the opposing sides, the dispute was enlivened by moral recriminations which—as in the ante-bellum struggle—centered about the labor systems of the two rivals. The South continued to roll up statistical gains. In 1904 she took the lead over New England in cotton consumed by her mills, and by 1914 was consuming more than all the rest of the country. By 1904 the challenger was surpassing the champion in the production of cotton yarn and five years later was outproducing the rest of the country.[44] In the number of active spindles the Southern states rose from 27.6 per cent of all in the country in 1899 to 35.5 per cent in 1914, while New England declined from 60.1 per cent to 54.4 per cent of the total in the same decade.[45]

In spite of these relative gains in production, the textile industry of the South did not escape the general pattern of colonialism to which other industries of the region were prone to conform. The chief products of the Southern cotton mills were yarn and coarse or unfinished cloth, much of which was shipped north for final processing before going to the consumer. This fact plus the investment of Northern capital and the dependence upon Northern commission houses for selling and even for financing brought the cotton mills into line with the colonial trend.

The only Southern colossus of finance comparable with Rockefeller was the master of the tobacco monopoly. Buck Duke transferred his headquarters and his ablest lieutenants from North Carolina to New York in the eighties, however, and operated thereafter under the corporation laws of New Jersey. In New Jersey he built his mansion and planted his bronze statue of William McKinley, three times life-size. Duke's story is one of high finance on a national and international rather than on a regional scale. His agents pushed as aggressively into Egypt, India, China, and the remote reaches of the Orient as did those of Standard Oil. Duke's methods, in fact, paralleled those of Rockefeller. By the use of rebates, discrimination, a country-wide secret service, and price manipulation, Duke crushed one competitor after another. In

[44] *United States Census of Manufactures*, 1914, II, 31, 35.

[45] *Ibid.*, 37.

1907 the American Tobacco Company was estimated to control, in parent and subsidiary companies, a capitalization of $500,000,000. "The circle of the Trust organization," wrote an investigator in that year, "is now practically complete from the ownership or control of tobacco lands to the manufacture of products and the marketing of goods. In no other industry has there been developed so complete and so splendid an organization as the Tobacco Trust." [46]

The tobacco industry in the South was early subject to the domination of the trust. As the number of establishments diminished, the size and output of the remaining ones increased rapidly. The number of tobacco factories in North Carolina declined from 253 in 1894 to 33 in 1914, though not all the failures should be attributed to the tobacco trust. The nominal breaking up of the trust in 1911 did not appreciably change the situation. The South's share of the industry tended to grow as the factories gravitated toward the source of raw material and cheaper labor. Factories were dismantled in the North, where wages were higher, and transferred to the South. The majority of the factory workers were women and children, who worked long hours at low wages. Measured by the value of product, the South's output increased from about 22 per cent of the national production in 1899 to 30 per cent in 1909 and nearly 40 per cent ten years later.[47]

Other industries, too numerous to examine in detail, increased production in their Southern factories or were established in the South for the first time in those years, and usually for the same reasons. They were of one general type—the "low wage, low-value-creating industries." The South seems to have had a fatal attraction for them. They were the industries that gave the first rough processing to the South's chief crops and resources, the physical bulk of which often made it economical to do the manufacturing near the source of the raw material. Manufacturers of these products sought large supplies of cheap, unskilled labor. Cotton yarn and coarse cloth, cane sugar, turpentine and rosin, polished rice, cottonseed oil, fertilizers, wood-distillation products, liquors, lum-

[46] Jacobstein, *Tobacco Industry in the United States*, 116, 117–23, 136.

[47] *Thirteenth Census, 1910*, X, *Manufacturers, General Report and Analysis*, 639–41; Tilley, *Bright-Tobacco Industry*, 596; Jacobstein, *Tobacco Industry in the United States*, 125.

ber and timber, and tobacco products bulked large in the vaunted industrialization of the New South. In general, they were the type of industry which added the lowest value of product per wage earner. Only rarely did the South develop an industry, such as furniture manufacturing in North Carolina, which finished goods for the ultimate consumer.[48] Even the *Manufacturers' Record,* in spite of a tendency to greet each new smokestack with hosannahs, admitted that "much of the manufacturing of the South is still largely a case of production of materials that are used elsewhere as materials in manufactures bringing largest returns in proportion to the capital invested." [49]

Rupert Vance has noted the "evil companionship" into which the perfectly legitimate and laudable cause of Southern industrialization has fallen.[50] The regrettable association had its origins in the propaganda of the New-South school. Seeking to overcome the artificial barriers and natural handicaps to healthy industrial development, this school evolved a program widely adopted in the region. "To recapitulate," ran a typical statement, "we must induce capital for manufactures to come here by offering cheaper money, cheaper taxation, cheaper labor, cheaper coal, and cheaper power, and much more public spirit." [51] The program included tax exemptions, municipal subsidies, tacit commitments against wage-and-hour laws and social legislation, and a "co-operative" spirit regarding the handling of labor troubles. The social costs were charged up to "progress."

The New South did not pause in its crusade to ponder a friendly letter from Lowell, Massachusetts, published in the *Manufacturers' Record:* "Our capitalists are going into your country because they see a chance to make money there, but you must not think that they will give your people the benefit of the money they make. That will come North and enrich their heirs, or set up public libraries in our country towns. . . . Your people should not be dazzled by the glamour nor caught with the jingle of Northern gold, but they

[48] Harriet L. Herring, *Southern Industry and Regional Development* (Chapel Hill, 1940), 31–35.

[49] *Manufacturers' Record,* LXV (May 7, 1914), 56.

[50] Rupert B. Vance, *All These People; The Nation's Human Resources in the South* (Chapel Hill, 1945), 277.

[51] Samuel H. Pullman to editor, Richmond *Dispatch,* January 1, 1897.

should exact terms from these men that will be of benefit to the communities in which they may select to establish themselves." [52]

By far the greater part of the products from the South's mines, farms, and forests continued to leave the region in the form of raw or crudely processed materials to be fabricated at factories in the North or abroad. The abundant natural resources that the New-South school predicted would develop Ruhr Valleys, Pittsburghs, and Detroits from the Potomac to the Gulf produced no such results. Like republics below the Rio Grande the South was limited largely to the role of a producer of raw materials, a tributary of industrial powers, an economy dominated by absentee owners.

In 1910 the great majority of the gainfully employed workers in the Southern states was engaged in extractive industries—agriculture, forestry, animal husbandry, fishing, mining. These workers, 62 per cent of the total of the gainfully employed, were producers of raw materials. It is true that this represents a decline in the proportion of such workers in the South. But in New England only about one sixth of the South's percentage, or 10.7 per cent, and in the Middle Atlantic states about one fourth, or 14.2 per cent, were classified as workers in extractive industries by the census. The percentage of Southern workers employed in manufacturing, transportation, trade, public service, professional service, and clerical occupations was lower than in any other region of the country. The percentage in manufacturing was very markedly lower.[53] The abundance of natural resources and industrial opportunities was widely advertised and the desperate need of an industrialized and diversified economy was acknowledged, but in spite of thirty years of intensive propaganda and effort the South remained largely a raw-material economy, with the attendant penalties of low wages, lack of opportunity, and poverty.

In the midst of the depression of the nineties, when Carolina textiles and Alabama iron were showing gains, the Philadelphia *Times* remarked that "it begins to look as if the Eastern States would need less protection against European competition and more against the enterprise of Southern progress." [54] But as a mat-

[52] *Manufacturers' Record,* XXVII (June 7, 1895), 285.

[53] *Thirteenth Census, 1910,* IV, *Population, Occupational Statistics,* 44–45.

[54] Quoted in *Manufacturers' Record,* XXV (March 2, 1894), 65.

ter of fact, there were barriers along the banks of the Potomac, the Ohio, and the Mississippi as well as along the Atlantic coast. The protective walls to the eastward, being subjects of public policy and debate, were simply more conspicuous than those to the southward and westward.

One set of barriers was the freight-rate differential. The Interstate Commerce Commission recognized the connection between industrial development and freight-rate differentials as early as 1889. In an opinion concerning a case from the South, the Commission held freight-rate inequalities "in a very great degree responsible for the lack of local development in that region, except at favored localities." [55]

Justifying their policy on the grounds of low population density, seasonal fluctuations, low-grade cargo, and the predominance of one-way and local traffic, the Southern carriers had from the beginning charged higher rates per mile than Northern carriers. The distinctive Southern freight rates and classifications were institutionalized on a regional basis in the seventies and eighties by railway associations and pools that established "boundaries more tangible than the Confederacy ever achieved," with a capital in Atlanta and a rate sovereignty extending from the Chesapeake to the Gulf.[56] After 1887 the Interstate Commerce Commission gave legal sanction to the railway-association rates and classifications and recognized a "Southern Territory" with boundaries running along the Ohio and Potomac and dipping into Virginia on the north and following the Mississippi on the west. Similarly, an "Official Territory" north of the Ohio and east of the Mississippi, and a "Southwestern Territory" including Arkansas, Louisiana, Texas, and a slice of New Mexico, as well as two other western rate territories were evolved and recognized.

The disparity of rates between territories, the resulting economic discrimination, and the advantages of shippers in Official Territory were acknowledged by the beginning of the twentieth century, but

[55] "In re Tariffs and Classifications of the Atlanta and West Point Railroad Company and Other Companies," in *Interstate Commerce Commission Reports* (New York, 1890), III, 46–47.

[56] David M. Potter, "The Historical Development of Eastern-Southern Freight Rate Relationships," in *Law and Contemporary Problems* (Durham), XIV (1947), 429.

no scientific comparison of rates was made in that period.[57] The spread between regional levels has been reduced since 1913, but a careful study made twenty-five years later revealed that, on the average, shippers of classified goods still had to pay rates which were 39 per cent higher in the Southern Territory and 75 per cent higher in the Southwestern Territory than shippers in the favored Official Territory paid for the same services.[58] These differentials were to an extent evaded for a time by arrangements with small independent lines in Official Territory that enabled some Southern producers to compete in the Northern market. Railroads in Official Territory, however, began quite early to use rate differentials to bar competition from Southern producers and monopolize the big markets for their own shippers. "It was done at the request of the Pennsylvania iron men," replied the general freight agent of the Pennsylvania Railroad when asked why rates on Southern iron were advanced in 1890.[59]

Certain trade advantages accrued from these rate differentials. Since a little over half of the population and considerably more than half of the wealth and buying power of the country was located in Official Territory, that region became a powerful magnet for goods. It was a market in which all manufacturers of a national scale had to compete. Manufacturers within the favored region moved their products much greater distances for an equal amount of money than could those in outlying territories. Nor did the bar-

57 United States Interstate Commerce Commission, *Railways in the United States in 1902 . . .* (Washington, 1903), Pt. II, *A Forty-Year Review of Changes in Freight Tariffs, passim;* William H. Joubert, *Southern Freight Rates in Transition* (Gainesville, Fla., 1949), especially Chaps. I–IV, illuminates the history of rate-making in this period.

58 J. Haden Alldredge, *The Interterritorial Freight Rate Problem of the United States*, in *House Documents*, 75 Cong., 1 Sess., No. 264, p. 13. Disadvantage of Western Trunk-Line Territory is placed at 47 per cent, that of Mountain-Pacific at 71 per cent. Cf. lower estimates of a study five years later: *Report on Interterritorial Freight Rates*, in *House Documents*, 78 Cong., 1 Sess., No. 303, pp. 55–57. "The territorial differences in the levels of first-class rates . . . are large, but they have apparently been even greater in the past. The trend during the past 25 or 30 years has been toward reducing the spreads in class-rate levels." *Ibid.*, 21.

59 *Tradesman*, XXII (August 15, 1890), 40. The Interstate Commerce Commission has recognized that Northern carriers have for the most part controlled interterritorial rates from the South to the North. Joubert, *Southern Freight Rates*, 337.

riers operate reciprocally, for Official Territory shippers could penetrate into the Southern market at a somewhat lower rate, mile for mile, than their competitors in the South had to pay for shipping similar articles wholly within their own territory. "Thus, one has here something remarkably similar to the working of a protective tariff, to the extent that certain favored interests effectively strive to protect themselves at home while retaining privileges elsewhere." [60]

Special or "commodity" rates for raw materials and primary manufactures were generally lower than rates for finished goods. The special rates were arranged to facilitate the flow of raw materials, agricultural staples, fuel, and lumber into distant manufacturing plants. The commodity rates were sometimes said to "offset" the higher rates for manufactured goods, but they were a dubious blessing to the South. The chief beneficiary was the Northeastern manufacturer—not the actual or potential manufacturer of the outlying territory, who lost whatever advantage lay in nearness to raw materials. Low rates for raw materials at once encouraged and perpetuated the South's old pattern of raw-material economy and its dependence upon outside sources for manufactured goods. Economists have pointed out a general tendency, subject to exceptions, for the burden of freight rates to grow "progressively heavier in proportion to the degree of processing carried through" in the unprivileged territory. Thus, while raw cotton and cottonseed oil moved eastward at low rates, the rates mounted steeply in proportion to fineness of textiles or food products manufactured from those same raw materials.[61] In view of the success with which the Northeast used its advantages to retain the profitable functions of manufacturing, it has been suggested that it assumed a position "like the mother country in an empire." [62] "For nearly three generations," writes J. Haden Alldredge, ". . . the country has been accepting influences and conditions which have made a workshop region of one section of the country, with the other sections, as

60 Alldredge, *Interterritorial Freight Rate Problem of the United States*, 48.

61 Henry B. Kine, *Freight Rates, The Interregional Tariff Issue*, in Vanderbilt University *Papers of the Institute of Research and Training in the Social Sciences*, No. 3 (Nashville, 1942), 8–11.

62 *Regionalized Freight Rates: Barrier to National Productiveness*, in *House Documents*, 78 Cong., 1 Sess., No. 137, p. 17.

marked off by the present territorial rate boundaries, being largely in a position of contributors of raw materials and semifinished products to the industrialized region." [63] Those who attempt to account for the South's retarded economic development largely in terms of freight rates encounter difficulties, however, in the case of Virginia. Although nearly all of that state lies in Official Territory, the lower-class rates do not seem to have given Virginia any advantage over her sister states to the south.[64]

There were other "differentials" that barred the way to industrialization. The United States Steel Corporation took control of Birmingham steel production and imposed on the output of Alabama mills the system of "Pittsburgh Plus," that is, the price of steel at Pittsburgh plus the freight charge from Pittsburgh to the place of delivery. In 1909 the Corporation exchanged this system for that of the "Birmingham Differential," which meant that the consumer of Alabama steel had to pay the price at Pittsburgh plus a differential of $3.00 a ton, plus freight from Birmingham. Straight Pittsburgh Plus was retained by the Corporation in pricing its Birmingham wire, making the differential $18.30 per ton on this product. The general sales agent of the American Steel and Wire Company advised the Corporation in 1908 that to sell wire produced in Alabama on the Birmingham-Differential basis might result in giving Southern manufacturers some advantage over certain Northern competitors, "which, of course, would not be advisable," he said.[65]

The effort to justify the steel differential on the ground that the cost of production was higher in the South was under even more handicap than the justification of the freight-rate differential by similar claims. An investigation by the Federal Trade Commission demonstrated that the cost of producing steel at Birmingham was lower than at any other point in the country, 26 per cent lower than at Pittsburgh, in fact. Yet consumers of Birmingham steel paid

[63] Alldredge, *Interterritorial Freight Rate Problem of the United States,* 51.

[64] A treatment of barriers to Southern development that disparages the significance of freight rates is Calvin B. Hoover and B. U. Ratchford, *Economic Resources and Policies of the South* (New York, 1951), 65–88.

[65] *Federal Trade Commission vs. United States Steel Corporation et al.,* Docket No. 760 (Washington, 1924), "Brief and Argument by Attorneys for Federal Trade Commission," 273–74.

$3.00, and after 1920 $5.00, more per ton than Pittsburgh steel cost. The buyer of steel bars at Pittsburgh paid only $2.10 above the cost of production, while the buyer at Birmingham paid $8.00 more than the cost of production for bars and $18.30 more for Birmingham wire products.[66] It was the contention of the Commission that the Birmingham Differential was conceived for the "purpose of protecting the Pittsburgh mills, and in turn the Pittsburgh steel users, so that they can still buy steel from Pittsburgh." [67]

The steel price differential enabled the Northern fabricator to penetrate deeply into Southern territory and narrowly constricted the zone in which the Southern operator could compete. Thus a Birmingham rivet company found that the differential amounted to 9 per cent of the price of its product and that it was excluded from competition in Kentucky, Virginia, Missouri, and Arkansas because of this. A bridge company in Chattanooga discovered that the Birmingham Differential placed it under a disadvantage of 7 per cent in competition with Pittsburgh for construction in Winston-Salem and prohibited it from competing with the same city for business in Memphis. A Nashville company purchasing steel from Birmingham was excluded from construction in Kentucky, and the Pittsburgh-Plus handicap restricted an Alabama mattress company to the northern part of Alabama and a part of Mississippi. A boatbuilder of New Orleans was driven to buying steel from Pittsburgh and to curtailing the scale of his construction.[68] These and many similar examples were offered in support of the Federal Trade Commission's view that the steel differential was choking established industries and preventing or discouraging the establishment of new ones: "It is retarding not only the growth of the consumers in the South but also the producers." [69]

In urging the end of Pittsburgh Plus, one of the attorneys of the Commission said: "Let us now give the people of the South some of the advantages of their location where iron ore, coal, and limestone deposits all meet at the door of the steel mill. . . . Let us

[66] *Ibid.*, 375–76, and Commission's Exhibit No. 6853, Appendix, 1.

[67] *Ibid.*, 378.

[68] *Ibid.*, "Statement of Case," I, 130–32, 173–78, 217–21, 281–85.

[69] *Ibid.*, "Brief of Commission," 377.

enable the steel users of the South to put up at least reasonably decent shops; let us take New Orleans out of the slough of industrial despair, where the once big shops are now but repair shops because of the insatiable desire to protect Pittsburgh." [70]

It would be an oversimplification of the South's problem to attribute its industrial deficiencies entirely to artificial barriers. There were "natural" economic difficulties as well—the scarcity of liquid capital, technical ability, and skilled labor, for example, not to mention the handicap of a late start. In addition there were the chains of habit and custom and the deep groove of agrarian tradition that confined thought in ancient patterns. For the most part, however, these were transitory barriers, characteristic of any economy in the early phases of industrialization. The cotton-mill crusade demonstrated that none of them was insuperable and that the time had already passed when the lack of industrialization could be explained by them. Of the old "natural" handicaps that remained, there were none but were intensified by the new artificial restraints and barriers.

The British Board of Trade, which once supervised the economic destinies of the South, would probably have found much to admire in the neomercantilism under which the region entered the twentieth century. As a means of discouraging the rise of competing manufacturers, building up a monopoly of the carrying trade, promoting an ample supply of cheap raw materials, and eliminating foreign competition in colonial markets, the combination of regionalized freight rates, basing-point system, Pittsburgh Plus, Birmingham Differential, patent control, and Federal tariff schedules was rather more effective than the combination of Navigation Acts, Wool Act, Iron Act, and Hat Act. Patent laws were less easily evaded than parliamentary acts prohibiting the importation of skilled craftsmen and trade secrets into the colonies, and the protective tariff assured the manufacturers and merchants of Official Territory the monopoly of a market sealed off almost airtight from the cheaper products of foreign manufacturers. The metropolitan North retained for its tradesmen and fabricators the more profitable functions of transporting, processing, and distributing of goods. The large extent to which ownership of the South's trans-

[70] *Ibid.*, 378.

portation, communication, financial, and manufacturing corporations was centralized in the cities of the Northeast, as well as the considerable degree to which ownership of the region's natural resources and its certificates of public indebtedness was concentrated there, no doubt contributed much to the stability of the system. The control exercised by the British merchant over the tobacco colonies was extensive, but it never equaled that of the Northeastern banker.

Undoubtedly some of the wealth created by the new factories, furnaces, mines, and wells did remain in the South. The railroads reorganized by the bankers did solve some basic regional problems of transportation—as well as maintain discriminatory rates. Manufacturing establishments did maintain big payrolls and increase job opportunities—as well as exploit cheap labor. Northern investment and development of Southern industries did give states more taxable resources—even if legislatures were inclined to grant generous tax exemptions. Without doubt the concentration of industry in the Piedmont helped retail trade and brought a new degree of prosperity and growth to many towns of the area. Toward the end of the period under survey, even with the low wage scale that prevailed, many workers began to enjoy a little better living standard. In other words, under the new economic order the South was making some strides toward solving the fundamental economic problems of increasing the production of wealth and, in some degree, equalizing distribution. That was certainly part of the picture.

On the other hand, the penalties attached to the colonial and more primitive economy are apparent from almost any regional comparison of the distribution of wealth, income, wages, and goods. The estimated per capita wealth of the United States in 1900, for example, was $1,165 and that of the South, $509, or less than half. In 1912 the disparity was $1,950 to $993 in the South. Per capita wealth in the Middle Atlantic states in the latter year was $2,374.[71] These figures do not accurately reflect true distribution of wealth, since they include valuations of all railroads, mines, mortgages, and other properties in the South owned by outside interests. The earliest per capita income estimates available, those

[71] *Statistical Abstract of the United States, 1933*, p. 259.

for 1919, indicate that per capita income in the Southern states was about 40 per cent lower than the national level, a difference that may be presumed to have existed earlier. The eleven states with lowest per capita income were all Southern, from Alabama at $321, on the bottom, to Louisiana at $412. The highest state average in the country, $929, was New York's. The national average was $614, that of the thirteen Southern states, $405. No Southern state came near the national average, and the seven bottom states, with 15 per cent of the nation's population received scarcely 2 per cent of the national income.[72] The first income-tax returns under the new Federal law of 1912 were filed in 1913. Of the 357,598 persons reporting a net income in excess of $2,500 for the ten months ending December 31, 1913, only 41,016 were from the South. With 28 per cent of the population, the region had only 11 per cent of the taxable incomes. The higher the incomes reported, the smaller the South's share: 46 of the 1,598 incomes above $100,000, and only 17 of the 813 above $150,000.[73] Another indication of the distribution of wealth was the South's proportion of the nation's bank deposits, which in 1914 was $1,491,106,598 out of $16,707,486,486.[74] More important for the mass of people was the South's celebrated wage differential, which in manufacturing industries was 12 per cent in 1909: $452 per wage earner in the South as against the national average of $518. The differential in the extractive industries, where more than 60 per cent of Southern wage earners were employed, was greater.[75]

There were undoubtedly inequalities of wealth and opportunity between classes and races within the South that were rightly attributed to faults in Southern policy, leadership, and society, but in considering them critics sometimes overlooked the plight of the region as a whole.

Cut off from the better-paying jobs and the higher opportunities, the great majority of Southerners were confined to the worn grooves of a tributary economy. Some emigrated to other sections, but the

72 Maurice Leven and Willford I. King, *Income in the Various States, Its Sources and Distribution, 1919, 1920, and 1921* (New York, 1925), 264–67.

73 *Statistical Abstract of the United States, 1914*, pp. 603–604.

74 *Manufacturers' Record*, LXV (May 14, 1914), 41.

75 *Thirteenth Census, 1910*, VIII, *Manufactures, General Report and Analysis*, 57, 542.

mass of them stuck to farming, mining, forestry, or some low-wage industry, whether they liked it or not. The inevitable result was further intensification of the old problems of worn-out soil, cut-over timber lands, and worked-out mines.

CHAPTER XII

THE MISSISSIPPI PLAN AS THE AMERICAN WAY

As LATE as 1879 three foremost spokesmen of the South, Lamar of Mississippi, Hampton of South Carolina, and Stephens of Georgia, agreed in a public statement that the disfranchisement of the Negro was not only impossible but undesired. Lamar declared that it was "a political impossibility under any circumstances short of revolution," and that even if it were possible the South would not permit it. Hampton, who claimed the distinction of being "the first man at the South" to advocate suffrage for the emancipated slave, remarked that the Negro "naturally allies himself with the more conservative of the whites."[1] These gentlemen obviously hoped for a good deal from this new ally of conservatism.

The century had scarcely ended, however, before the prophesies of these statesmen were overturned throughout the South. Lamar's own state, famous for her "Mississippi Plan" of 1875, again led the way in race policy with a "Second Mississippi Plan," but this time by means "short of revolution." Disfranchisement was accomplished by a constitutional convention in 1890. Mississippi was the only state that took this step before the outbreak of the Populist revolt. South Carolina was next with a convention in 1895, Louisiana in 1898, North Carolina by means of an amendment in 1900, Alabama in 1901, Virginia in 1901–1902, Georgia by amendment in 1908, and Oklahoma in 1910. Over the same years Tennessee, Florida, Arkansas, and Texas accomplished disfranchisement by means of the poll tax and other devices.

1 A symposium, "Ought the Negro to be Disfranchised," in *North American Review*, CXXVIII (1879), 231–32, 241–42. "He will never be disfranchised," wrote Bishop Haygood in *Our Brother in Black*, 81.

The Second Mississippi Plan stirred immediate interest throughout the South, and had the times been favorable the other states would probably have followed the example much more quickly than they did. Conservatives of neighboring states, grappling with powerful Populist opposition, eyed the results of the Mississippi Plan enviously. An Alabama journal remarked in 1892 that "we would do well to imitate the wise politicians of Mississippi." [2] Ben Tillman boasted, after putting through a successful imitation, that South Carolina and Mississippi were the only Southern states to avoid a strong challenge from the third party. There were several abortive attempts at constitutional revision in the early nineties, but no further extension of the Mississippi Plan until after the collapse of Populism.[3]

For a number of reasons disfranchisement was delayed elsewhere. In the first place, faced with a mounting tide of agrarian radicalism, "with the wildest Populist ideas so prevalent," conservatives hesitated to call conventions that might seize the opportunity to write into organic law clauses that "smacked of socialism and communism" and "Kansas ideas." [4] In the second place, once Southern whites were split into two parties both the Populists and the Democrats sought to win the Negroes to their cause. The Populists were engaged in a crusade to unite both races upon a platform of democratic reform in behalf of the common man. The conservatives at the same time found in the Negro vote the most effective means of defeating the Populists. And finally, the Lodge force bill of 1890 indicated that a Northern conscience had been reawakened on the subject of Negro suffrage, and that it might resist or overthrow disfranchisement measures of doubtful constitutionality.

In 1898 these doubts and fears and constitutional qualms were largely laid to rest. In that year, for one thing, the United States Supreme Court, in the case of *Williams* v. *Mississippi*, passed fa-

[2] Mobile *Register*, quoted in Jackson *Clarion-Ledger*, June 23, 1892.

[3] As noted above, page 275, Virginia, Alabama, and Georgia passed new election codes after 1892 which put new restrictions on the voters.

[4] Southern press, quoted in McDanel, *Virginia Constitutional Convention of 1901–1902*, pp. 9–10; in William A. Mabry, "Louisiana Politics and the 'Grandfather Clause,'" in *North Carolina Historical Review* (Raleigh), XIII (1936), 292; and in Malcolm C. McMillan, "A History of the Alabama Constitution of 1901" (M.A. thesis, University of Alabama, 1940), 58.

vorably upon the new plan and adopted the views of the Mississippi court.[5] By that time, also, conservatives had little to fear from agrarian radicals and the influence they might exert on new constitutions. Reaction was in the air. Some Populists favored disfranchisement in the belief that once the Negro was removed from politics, white men could divide, one-party domination would cease, and the way would lie open for white radicalism. Other Populists blamed the Negro's defection to conservativism for their defeat. The exciting vision of 1892, picturing black and white farmer and laborer marching together toward a new era, had by 1898 become dimmed by old prejudices and suspicions. It had been a precarious and handicapped experiment from the start.

On the whole, the Wade Hampton type of alliance came easier for the Negro. Writing of the situation in Georgia, the Negro educator John Hope made the claim that "Populism was defeated by the colored voters espousing the Democratic side," and that "this fact is acknowledged and to an extent appreciated by the party now in power—to the extent at least of staving off any further disfranchisement measures thus far." [6] The gratitude of the Georgia Democrats, as it turned out, meant a respite of only three more years. A Northern investigator came to the conclusion that Kolb and the Populists were defeated by Negro votes in Alabama also, where he "found, on the testimony of negroes as well as whites, that the mass of negroes had actually voted the Democratic ticket." [7]

Booker T. Washington announced to the Southern white man in 1895 a doctrine of profound significance for the future of racial relations. The implications of the so-called "Atlanta Compromise" will be explored later, but it should be noted at this point that in so far as Washington's pronouncement constituted a renunciation of active political aspirations for the Negro it had an important bearing upon the movement for disfranchisement.[8]

[5] 170 U.S. 213 (1898).

[6] John Hope, "Negro Suffrage in the States whose Constitutions Have Not Been Specifically Revised," in *American Negro Academy Occasional Papers*, No. 11 (Washington, 1905), 53.

[7] Spahr, *America's Working People*, 104.

[8] Another Negro the same year published a book in which he concluded that "Our failure [as voters] . . . was humiliating and complete all along the line" and that

Southern white Republicans were divided on the question of disfranchisement. The Lily-white faction, which gained ground during the nineties, more or less openly welcomed the movement in the belief that the removal of the Negro would make the party respectable in the South and permit white men to divide. With the white Republicans indifferent, the Populists divided, and the Negro himself apathetic, resistance to disfranchisement from within the South reached a low point by 1898.

In the meantime, the North had taken up the White Man's Burden, and by 1898 was looking to Southern racial policy for national guidance in the new problems of imperialism resulting from the Spanish war. Commenting on the Supreme Court's opinion upholding disfranchisement in Mississippi, the *Nation* pronounced it "an interesting coincidence that this important decision is rendered at a time when we are considering the idea of taking in a varied assortment of inferior races in different parts of the world"—races "which, of course, could not be allowed to vote." [9] Senator Morgan of Alabama was chairman of the committee of the Hawaiian Commission that framed the voting restrictions for one "assortment of inferior races." To reject the property and literacy tests recommended for Hawaiians, reported the Senator, would be to "turn the legislature over to the masses" and "deprive the more conservative elements and property owners of effective representation." [10] Senator Morgan's advice was also sought by the white-supremacy advocates of his own state who were currently debating additional franchise restrictions for Alabama. A speech in defense of American imperialism by George F. Hoar "most amply vindicated the South," said Senator John L. McLaurin of South Carolina. He thanked the Massachusetts statesman "for his complete announcement of the divine right of the Caucasian to govern the inferior races." The Boston *Evening Transcript* reluctantly admitted that the Southern way was "now the policy of the Adminis-

"white leadership is preferable." Jerome R. Riley, *The Philosophy of Negro Suffrage* (Hartford, 1895), 19, 34.

[9] *Nation*, LXVI (1898), 398–99.

[10] *Report of the Hawaiian Commission*, in *Senate Documents*, 55 Cong., 3 Sess., No. 16, pp. 149–50.

tration of the very party which carried the country into and through a civil war to free the slave." [11]

Events in the Philippines soon indicated that the Mississippi Plan had become the American Way. "If the stronger and cleverer race," said an editorial in the Boston *Atlantic Monthly,* "is free to impose its will upon 'new-caught, sullen peoples' on the other side of the globe, why not in South Carolina and Mississippi? The advocates of the 'shotgun policy' are quite as sincere, and we are inclined to think quite as unselfish, as the advocates of 'benevolent assimilation.' The two phrases are, in fact, two names for the same thing." [12] Professors John W. Burgess and William A. Dunning of Columbia University brought academic authority to the support of Southern policy. Burgess thought "that the Republican party, in its work of imposing the sovereignty of the United States upon eight millions of Asiatics, has changed its view in regard to the political relations of races and has at last virtually accepted the ideas of the South upon that subject." He assured the South that the leaders of the party of emancipation would never "again give themselves over to the vain imagination of the political equality of man." [13] Dunning deprecated "the trite generalities of the Rights of Man," and declared "The enfranchisement of the freedmen [to be] as reckless a species of statecraft, as that which marked 'the blind hysterics of the Celt' in 1789–95." [14]

The implications of the new American imperialism for Southern race policy were not lost upon the leaders of the disfranchisement movement. Sympathetic views from the North were quoted in the constitutional conventions and the press, and campaign orators drew the lessons of imperialism for the people. "Mr. President, this is not a sectional issue, the race problem is no longer confined to the States of the South," said a delegate to the Alabama disfranchisement convention. It was the same problem from Cuba and Ala-

11 Boston *Evening Transcript,* January 14, 1899.

12 Anonymous, "Reconstruction and Disfranchisement," in *Atlantic Monthly,* LXXXVIII (1901), 435.

13 John W. Burgess, *Reconstruction and the Constitution, 1866–1876* (New York, 1902), 298.

14 William A. Dunning, *Essays on the Civil War and Reconstruction and Related Topics* (New York, 1898), 250–51.

bama to Hawaii and the Philippines, and "we have the sympathy instead of the hostility of the North." [15] With the sections in rapport, the work of writing the white man's law for Asiatic and Afro-American went forward simultaneously.

Repugnance for corrupt elections was put forward everywhere as the primary reason for disfranchisement. Popular disgust with fraudulent elections was sincere and widespread. It probably reached its peak during the repression of the third party, although it was given as an important motive of the disfranchisement convention of Mississippi in 1890. The president of the convention said that fraud had become "chronic," that it was "used even as between the whites themselves," and that "Fourteen years of fraud excited nausea." [16]

Of the 183 cases of contested elections in the United States House of Representatives between 1875 and 1901, 107 came from twelve Southern states, the great majority of them involving charges of fraud.[17] And these were states from a presumably "solid" section.

"I told them to go to it, boys, count them out," admitted former Governor Oates to the constitutional convention of Alabama, recounting the methods of the conservatives in that state. "But we have gone on from bad to worse until it has become a great evil," he added. "White men have gotten to cheating each other until we don't have any honest elections." [18] It was this point of whites cheating whites that became sorest during the Populist struggle. "It is true that we win these elections," explained the leading conservative paper of Louisiana, "but at a heavy cost, and by the use of methods repugnant to our idea of political honesty and

[15] Emmett O'Neal, in *Official Proceedings of the Constitutional Convention of the State of Alabama, May 21st, 1901 to September 3d, 1901* . . . (Wetumpka, Ala., 1941), III, 2783. See also, Alfred P. Thom, quoting Dunning and *Atlantic Monthly,* in *Report of the Proceedings and Debates of the Constitutional Convention, State of Virginia . . . June 12, 1901, to June 26, 1902* (Richmond, 1906), II, 2966–67; George H. Rountree, quoted in Raleigh *News and Observer,* February 18, 1899.

[16] S. S. Calhoon, "Causes and Events that Led to the Calling of the Constitutional Convention of 1890," in *Mississippi Historical Society Publications* (Oxford), VI (1902), 109.

[17] Chester H. Rowell, *Digest of Contested Election Cases* . . . (Washington, 1901).

[18] *Proceedings of the Constitutional Convention of . . . Alabama,* 1901, III, 2788–89.

which must, in time, demoralize the people of Louisiana." [19] A "prominent Democrat" of Virginia shared this fear. "Cheating at elections is demoralizing our whole people," he said. "We are deteriorating as a people, and the principal cause of our deterioration is this idiotic nonsense about 'preserving white civilization' by cheating." [20] Others feared that corruption in political life would contaminate business and social relations.

The remedy, declared the reformers, was the disfranchisement of the Negro. A white Republican of Virginia found the argument paradoxical. "The remedy suggested here is to punish the man who has been injured," he said. The Negroes were to be disfranchised "to prevent the Democratic election officials from stealing their votes." [21] To a Democrat of Alabama, it was not a matter of ethics but of economy. "Now we are not begging for 'ballot reform' or anything of that sort," he said, "but we want to be relieved of purchasing the Negroes to carry elections. I want cheaper votes." [22]

Behind the "White Supremacy" slogans and the front of racial solidarity there raged a struggle between Southern white men that is usually overlooked. It is essential to examine this before the disfranchisement movement can be understood. The parties to the struggle were variously described as the Black Belt and the Hill Country, or the Lowlands and the Uplands, but lines of cleavage usually separated the counties predominantly black from those mainly white in population. It was not a new struggle. When the Negro was a slave, the white counties sought to tax him as property and prevent his owners from counting him as a basis for Black-Belt representation in state legislatures and party conventions. Opposing these measures, the slaveowners often fought to retain property qualifications for officeholding and prevent upland counties from increasing their quota of representatives.

By 1860, but for a few exceptions, property qualifications had

[19] New Orleans *Times-Democrat,* January 11, 1898. The same paper of May 8, 1892, referred to Louisiana as "the head center of ballot box stuffing."

[20] Quoted in Richmond *Virginia Sun,* June 14, 1893.

[21] Delegate Albert P. Gillespie, in *Proceedings and Debates of the Constitutional Convention . . . of Virginia,* 1901–1902, II, 3014.

[22] Delegate William A. Handley, in *Proceedings of the Constitutional Convention of . . . Alabama,* 1901, III, 2276–77.

been removed, universal white manhood suffrage prevailed, and representation was generally apportioned according to white population. Thus the slaveowner was partly deprived of the advantage of counting the slaves. Reconstruction and the Carpetbag constitutions upset the ante-bellum arrangement and restored the Black Belt to power. The white minority in the black counties, heirs to the Carpetbag system, often defended the Radical constitutions. Vetoing a bill calling for a new constitution, Governor Robert Lowry of Mississippi said, of the Carpetbag document: "True it is that it was prepared and submitted to us in large part by aliens, but 'good can come out of Nazareth,' as was long ago proved." [23] Attacking that veto, a hillbilly paper declared that "the carpetbaggers so framed our present constitution . . . as to give a preponderance of representation to the negro counties" and that the Black-Belt whites "hypocritically raised the howl of white supremacy while debauching the ballot-boxes and through this infamous means made themselves potent factors in our State and county governments." [24]

Each side to the dispute was beset by fears and suspicions of its opponent and maneuvered for advantage. "I ask you gentlemen of the black belt," exclaimed a white-county Virginia delegate, "How do you happen to be here if the Negroes control down there?" [25] "What are we here for?" asked an Alabama delegate. "Not to preserve white supremacy. White supremacy is secure in Alabama." [26] The real question was *which whites* should be supreme. The vote for the conventions of Virginia and Alabama were decidedly sectional, with the white counties and the remnants of the Populist party largely in opposition and the black counties in sup-

[23] Jackson *Clarion-Ledger,* January 26, 1898.

[24] Okolona (Miss.) *Chickasaw Messenger,* quoted *ibid.,* March 14, 1889. Using total population as a basis for representation, the white man of the Black Belt often exceeded two and three times the power of his brother in the white counties. Thus eleven Black-Belt counties with a white population of 56,659 were entitled to 144 votes in the Democratic party conventions of Alabama, while eleven white counties with a white population of 61,376 were entitled to only 44 votes. Moore, *History of Alabama,* 582 n.

[25] D. C. O'Flaherty, in *Proceedings and Debates of the Constitutional Convention . . . of Virginia,* 1901–1902, I, 140.

[26] Robert J. Love, in *Proceedings of the Constitutional Convention of . . . Alabama,* 1901, III, 2826.

port—a circumstance that led skeptics to comment upon the eagerness of the Negroes for their own disfranchisement.[27]

In the case of the first two disfranchising conventions the Black Belt was the more reluctant section, and leaders of the white farmers took the initiative. It was not Negro domination but white domination from the Black Belt that the white counties of Mississippi sought to overthrow in 1890. The two jealous factions worked together only by means of elaborate compromise. "You gentlemen of the black counties must sacrifice power, and you of the white must give up principle," declared Judge Wiley P. Harris. The "power" was the advantage enjoyed by the Black-Belt whites as a result of the voteless Negroes, and the "principle" was that of universal white manhood suffrage. The black-county delegation yielded to the creation of thirteen new seats of the state legislature, all of which were expected to be assigned to white counties, while the latter accepted the poll tax and the literacy test as limits upon suffrage.[28] A similar compromise was effected in the Alabama convention which gave the white counties of that state five additional representatives and two additional senators. The western counties of Virginia were "very much more interested in economic questions" than in "questions of suffrage," in "railroad domination" than in "Negro domination," said their delegates,[29] and as the price of their support of disfranchisement demanded and got a corporations commission.

As important as were these compromises, the storm center of the great debate was always disfranchisement. Some delegates were troubled with the uneasy awareness that they had assembled to reverse the tendency of half a century of democratic history and deprive from half to two thirds of their fellow citizens of the ballot. The sharp conflict between deep-rooted convictions and the work at hand gave rise to much searching of soul and explaining of votes.

[27] *Ibid.*, 260; McMillan, "History of the Alabama Constitution," 93–94.

[28] J. S. McNeilly, "History of the Measures Submitted to the Committee on Elective Franchise, Apportionment, and Elections in the Constitutional Convention of 1890," in *Mississippi Historical Society Publications*, VI (1902), 134–35; Vicksburg *Commercial Herald*, quoted in New Orleans *Times-Democrat*, December 18, 1895.

[29] See especially, Allen C. Braxton of Staunton, in *Proceedings and Debates of the Constitutional Convention . . . of Virginia*, 1901–1902, II, 2451; other delegates, *ibid.*, 2996, 3007.

Views were often stated with revealing frankness. Delegate J. Thomas Heflin, whose conscience was emphatically not troubled by the work at hand, nevertheless opposed the publication of full records of debates. "We will say things down here in our Southern way, and in the great old commonwealth of Alabama," he suggested, "that we do not want read and criticised day after day as we deliberate in this body." [30] The records of these debates, more than any comparable documents, disclose the tortured conscience of the South.

In the campaigning stage of the movement, disfranchisement leaders in all states—for example, Charles B. Aycock of North Carolina, Ben Tillman of South Carolina, and Hoke Smith of Georgia—gave repeated assurances that no white man would be disfranchised. Once deliberations began, however, it became apparent that powerful elements of the movement saw in it an opportunity to establish in power "the intelligence and wealth of the South," which would, of course, "govern in the interest of all classes." [31] Oates, who had fought the Populists, informed his Alabama colleagues that he favored eliminating "all those who are unfit and unqualified, and if the rule strikes a white man as well as a negro, let him go. There are some white men who have no more right and no more business to vote than a negro and not as much as some of them." [32] A delegate from a Tidewater county told the Virginia convention that it was "not the negro vote which works the harm," but "the depraved and incompetent men of our own race." [33]

The conservative press urged the conventions to forget their pledges and eliminate the undesirable white voters. According to Edgar Gardner Murphy, the Alabama convention, "largely at the suggestion of the Press Association of Alabama, practically ignored any literal interpretation of the unfortunate pledge, and the completed instrument did, in effect, result in the disfranchisement of a large number of white voters." [34] "The *Times-Democrat* has all along strenuously contended that what is sauce for the goose must

[30] *Proceedings of the Constitutional Convention of . . . Alabama*, 1901, I, 71.

[31] J. A. P. Campbell to editor, Jackson *Clarion-Ledger*, April 3, 1890.

[32] *Proceedings of the Constitutional Convention of . . . Alabama*, 1901, III, 2789.

[33] *Proceedings and Debates of the Constitutional Convention . . . of Virginia*, 1901–1902, II, 2864.

[34] Edgar Gardner Murphy, *Problems of the Present South* (New York, 1904), 193 n.

be made sauce for the gander," wrote the editor of the New Orleans paper, who believed that all tests "must be applied with equal rigor in the case of poor or illiterate whites and in the case of poor or illiterate Negroes." [35] Likewise the *Picayune* of the same city was "just as desirous to shut out every unworthy white man" as it was to exclude "every unworthy negro." [36] The Charlotte *Observer* described the movement as "the struggle of the white people of North Carolina to rid themselves of the dangers of the rule of negroes and the lower class of whites." [37] John B. Knox, president of the Alabama constitutional convention, denied that the Negro was the exclusive concern in his state. "The true philosophy of the movement," he later wrote, "was to establish restricted suffrage, and to place the power of government in the hands of the intelligent and virtuous." [38] The background of Populist agitation against which certain of these conventions were held suggests comparison with the Shaysite upheaval that served as a background of the Federal convention at Philadelphia in 1787.

The two commonest barriers erected against voters of the lower class by the disfranchisers were the literacy and property qualifications. Literacy was made one means of qualifying for the franchise in eight states, and in four of these property was an alternative.[39] The standards of both literacy and property would appear at first to be low—the ability to read and write, and the possession of taxable property worth from $300 to $500. But it should be borne in mind that illiteracy and poverty were far more generally characteristic of the lower class in the South then than now. In some states the per capita wealth did not equal the property qualification, and the general practice of undervaluation for tax assessment meant that property worth several times the minimum requirement would not be assessed high enough to qualify a voter.[40] Of the 231 counties in the United States in which 20 per cent or more

[35] New Orleans *Times-Democrat,* January 18, 1898.

[36] New Orleans *Daily Picayune,* March 23, 1898.

[37] Quoted in Asheville *Gazette,* July 3, 1900.

[38] John B. Knox, "Reduction of Representation in the South," in *Outlook,* LXXIX (1905), 171.

[39] Possession of taxable property was an alternative qualification in South Carolina, Louisiana, Alabama, and Georgia.

[40] David D. Wallace, *The South Carolina Constitution of 1895* (Columbia, 1927), 34.

of the whites of voting age were illiterate, 204 were in the South.

Advocates of property and literacy tests for the franchise first attempted to appeal to the patriotism of the poorer whites on somewhat the same basis that the slaveowners had appealed to them for support of the Confederacy. "Thousands of gallant sons of the South," a delegate told the Mississippi convention, "had no property in slaves or otherwise, and yet they offered their lives to protect their neighbor's property, and the same noble spirit is now ready for any concession or sacrifice that will secure and perpetuate white supremacy in Mississippi. (Great and long continued applause.)" [41]

The yeomanry, some of them graduates of the Populist school, seemed less eager for self-sacrifice in the nineties than they had been in the sixties. Their spokesmen would have no part in this type of patriotism. Delegate Monroe McClurg declared that Mississippi had "tried property qualifications in three different forms," but that "in the Constitution of 1832 the State returned to the American principle of [white] manhood suffrage" and did not intend to retreat.[42] Frank Burkitt of Chickasaw County, with other Alliancemen, fought and defeated the property qualification. Thomas L. Long of an Alabama white county where many crops were made "by white women and oxen" declared that in his part of the country "not one in ten" would ever own enough to qualify under the $300 property test.[43] In the western and mountain districts of Virginia and North Carolina suspicion and resentment flamed up fiercely against property and literacy tests.

It was apparent from the outset that loopholes through the literacy and property barriers would have to be provided for the underprivileged whites. The first and most-common loophole was the "understanding clause," invented by the Mississippi convention. It permitted illiterates to register and vote who could "understand" any section of the state constitution read to him, "or give a reasonable interpretation thereof." The obvious subterfuge of the understanding clause was offensive to men of conscience. It was

41 Jackson *Clarion-Ledger*, September 18, 1890. See similar appeal of E. H. Bristow, in letter to editor, *ibid.*, August 14, 1890.

42 Quoted in Jackson *Clarion-Ledger*, September 18, 1890.

43 *Proceedings of the Constitutional Convention of . . . Alabama*, 1901, III, 3137.

denounced unsparingly on the floor of the Mississippi convention. The Southern press called it a "disgraceful absurdity," a "manifest sham," a "shameless fraud," a "cowardly and evasive makeshift." [44] In the South Carolina convention, which was the next to adopt the clause, Ben Tillman dealt with the problem with characteristic candor: "Some have said there is fraud in this understanding clause. Some poisons in small doses are very salutary and valuable medicines. . . . The [registration] officer is responsible to his conscience and his God; he is responsible to nobody else. There is no particle of fraud or illegality in it. It is just simply showing partiality, perhaps, (laughter) or discriminating. Ah, you grin." [45] Carter Glass was even more outspoken in the Virginia convention. "Discrimination!" he exclaimed. "Why that is precisely what we propose; that exactly is what this convention was elected for." [46]

The moral dilemma of the disfranchisers induced some painful rationalization. In effect, these gentlemen undertook to reform fraudulent elections by means that winked at fraud. Alfred P. Thom of Norfolk first opposed the understanding clause, "the great storm center" of debate, then accepted it as "not the horrible thing it is painted to be," and finally concluded that it was a positive good. In a fraudulent election, he argued, a man "does not know whether he has been defrauded or not"; whereas with the understanding clause, "he cannot be defrauded without notice and knowledge." Between the two, Thom persuaded himself, there was "a vast difference, a vast distinction." [47] To the majority of the Louisiana convention, however, this distinction was not at all clear. As one member remarked, to adopt the understanding clause would be "to send word to the registrars to do what you will not do yourself. We are told," he continued, "that it is more honorable to permit highway robbery than to rob a hen roost. I see no honor in either." [48]

[44] Raymond *Gazette*, Memphis *Appeal*, Vicksburg *Post*, and Lexington *Advertiser*, quoted in Jackson *Clarion-Ledger*, October 9, 1890.

[45] *Journal of the Constitutional Convention of the State of South Carolina . . . 1895* (Columbia, 1895), 469.

[46] *Proceedings and Debates of the Constitutional Convention . . . of Virginia*, 1901–1902, II, 3076.

[47] *Ibid.*, 2968–72.

[48] F. P. Stubbs, quoted in New Orleans *Times-Democrat*, March 20, 1898.

President Knox of the Alabama convention held that the clause "perpetuates the very form of abuse we are seeking to escape," [49] yet he was compelled to see his state adopt the scheme.

Persuaded that the understanding clause was "based on fraud," the Louisiana convention invented the "grandfather clause." This exempted from the literacy and property tests those entitled to vote on January 1, 1867, together with their sons and grandsons. Opponents of the measure fought it as "vicious," "glaringly unconstitutional," "undemocratic," and "unamerican," and both Senators from Louisiana pronounced the clause unconstitutional.[50] A New Orleans editor could not conceive of "a more undemocratic scheme than to create a hereditary class of voters." [51] The plan was nevertheless adopted and became a model for other Southern states.

By the time North Carolina came to debate the grandfather clause, the following year, white-supremacy theorists had rationalized the new doctrine and incorporated it into the racial dogma. George H. Rountree, chairman of the committee on constitutional amendments, disclosed that "fitness for self-government was largely a matter of heredity. It must be obtained by inheritance and not by schools and learning." Whereupon a Negro member called him to terms on his history: "This talk of inheriting the power of self-government," he said, "is nothing but a revival of the doctrine of the divine right of kings. . . . The doctrine of this country is that all men are created free and equal. This doctrine must and will prevail." [52]

State conventions borrowed freely from each other, and as inventions multiplied there was a tendency for franchise provisions and especially "loophole" clauses to become more numerous and complex. Thus, Josephus Daniels went to Louisiana to study the workings of the recently adopted plan of that state. He reported that "the educational requirements softened by the Mississippi 'understanding clause,' and the Louisiana 'grandfather clause,' and

[49] *Proceedings of the Constitutional Convention of . . . Alabama,* 1901, I, 11.

[50] "Explanation of Votes," in *Official Journal of the Proceedings of the Constitutional Convention of the State of Louisiana . . . 1898 . . .* (New Orleans, 1898), 142–47.

[51] New Orleans *Times-Democrat,* March 26, 1898.

[52] Raleigh *News and Observer,* February 18, 1899.

the poll tax receipt, will do the work." [53] Virginia, Alabama, and Georgia also borrowed the principle of the grandfather clause but applied it to war veterans, and, in the case of Alabama and Georgia, to their lineal descendants. The president of the Alabama convention claimed that the work of that body represented an improvement on previous efforts, since it included not only the property and educational qualifications and the understanding and grandfather clauses but the "good character clause," an additional loophole for whites later imitated by Georgia.

The special clauses to which so much attention was devoted were, for the most part, of limited duration. In the case of South Carolina, for example, the understanding clause opened the way for permanent registration of the underprivileged for only two years. "What about the illiterates after two years?" asked one delegate. "If they do not care to read and write they should not be bothered with," was the answer.[54]

However varied the franchise qualifications and loopholes of the several constitutions, they all contained the poll tax, and it was in all cases a part of the permanent, not the temporary, plan. Nor were there for the indigent any such loopholes as accompanied literacy and property tests.[55] The poll tax was not confined to those states that revised their constitutions around the turn of the century, but was adopted by Tennessee, Florida, Arkansas, and Texas as well and imbedded in their existing constitutions.[56]

To explain the poll tax as a disfranchiser it would be necessary to explore all the procedures artfully attached to its payment. It is possible here only to suggest their nature. All states required payment well in advance of elections, one as much as eighteen months beforehand. The tax receipt usually had to be preserved and

[53] Editorial, *ibid.*, January 13, 1899.

[54] Quoted in Charleston *News and Courier*, October 31, 1895.

[55] Some states exempted men over sixty years of age, others, the disabled and in certain cases war veterans.

[56] Tennessee's constitution of 1870 authorized a poll tax, but not until 1890 did the legislature adopt one; a tax authorized by the Florida constitution of 1885 was put into effect in 1889. Arkansas in 1892 and Texas in 1902 adopted poll tax amendments. Virginia adopted a poll tax amendment in 1876, but the Readjusters secured its repeal in 1882. Georgia had long required voters to have paid all their taxes for the year preceding the election.

sometimes presented twice, once to the registrar and once to the election official. Annual state rates ranged from $1.00 to $2.00, with an additional county levy permitted in some states. More significant was the cumulative feature of the tax. The tax was cumulative for the entire period of liability in two states, for three years in one, and two in another. Great effectiveness was expected of this feature in the case of the "vicious voter" of both races. "We want that poll tax to pile up so high that he will never be able to vote again," said an Alabama disfranchiser. Compulsory collection would "destroy the objects and purposes" of the tax.[57] The penalty for nonpayment was, of course, disfranchisement. Since the payment of the poll tax was optional, complicated, and burdensome, and since additional tests and hurdles might still deprive prospective voters of their ballots even if they paid the tax, it is little wonder that thousands lost the suffrage. Thorough investigation has indicated, however, that both the advocates and the opponents of the poll tax have exaggerated its effectiveness as a disfranchiser.[58]

In the Mississippi convention the Delta counties had insisted upon the poll tax, said one of their spokesmen, "as their *sine qua non,* knowing that as a means of negro disfranchisement, it is worth all the rest." [59] But there were more important possibilities in the poll tax. "It reduces the electorate and places the political control of the State in the hands not of a minority of the voters alone, but of *the minority of the whites,*" said a poll-tax proponent of Louisiana. "Take the case of Mississippi, for instance. . . . The poll tax gets rid of most of the negro votes there, *but it gets rid of a great many whites at the same time—in fact a majority of them.* . . . The total vote in the last State election [1896] when the Populists made a hot fight, was only 64,339, including the Negroes. Less than half of the whites voted—the law 'discouraged' probably 6,000 negroes who would have been qualified, but who might have voted but for the poll tax; but it discouraged 60,000 or more white

[57] *Proceedings of the Constitutional Convention of . . . Alabama,* 1901, III, 3381.

[58] The most sensible and penetrating analysis of the poll tax is V. O. Key, Jr., *Southern Politics in State and Nation* (New York, 1949), 578–618.

[59] Vicksburg *Commercial Herald,* quoted in New Orleans *Times-Democrat,* December 18, 1895.

men from voting." [60] A Louisianian who opposed the tax as "undemocratic" and "un-American" observed that "the men who want the white men eliminated are advocating the imposition of a poll tax." [61] An association between the poll tax and white disfranchisement was also pointed out in the Virginia and the Alabama constitutional conventions.[62]

The Negro, supposedly the primary concern of the white-supremacy conventions, was often forgotten in the struggle of white man for supremacy over white man. In the first place, the Negro was all but completely excluded from the conventions called to consider his disfranchisement. One colored member was elected to the Mississippi convention, a wealthy planter and businessman, who differed in no important way on fundamental issues from the dominant white element. No other disfranchising convention contained any Negro members save that of South Carolina, which had six. They defended their race eloquently from Tillman's onslaughts, but acknowledged their helplessness. "You have the power here to do as you please," said one. "There are only six of us." [63] Replying to the charge that ignorance disqualified his race as voters, a Negro member of the North Carolina legislature asked his white colleagues during the debate over the disfranchising amendment, "Why is the Negro ignorant? Is it not your fault? Wasn't there a law on the books in 1831 making it a crime for a Negro to learn to read and write?" [64] There was no answer from the white side.

Booker T. Washington, spokesman of conservative middle-class Negroes, opposed, not qualified suffrage as such, but only discrimination between races by such devices as the understanding and grandfather clauses. "The Negro does not object to an educational or property test," he told the Louisiana convention in 1898; only let the tests fall equally upon black and white. Such a law, of

[60] Editorial, *ibid.*, March 8, 1898. Italics added.

[61] R. C. Wickliffe of West Feliciana Parish, quoted *ibid.*, March 17, 1898.

[62] *Proceedings and Debates of the Constitutional Convention . . . of Virginia, 1901–1902*, II, 2979; Knox, "Reduction of Representation in the South," *loc. cit.*, 171.

[63] Charleston *News and Courier*, October 26–27, 1895.

[64] Representative of Vance County, quoted in Raleigh *News and Observer*, February 18, 1899.

course, would permit the educated and propertied Negro class to vote, while the mass of propertyless and illiterate blacks would be disfranchised along with the whites of the same class. In this position he followed exactly the same line as that taken by such conservative whites as J. L. M. Curry, who addressed a similar appeal to the same convention.[65] Whether because of the position he took or because of a general apathy among his race, Washington met with a discouraging response from his people when he made the same appeal to the legislature of Georgia the following year.[66] To a friend he wrote privately: "I am almost disgusted with the colored people of Georgia. I have been corresponding with leading people in the state but cannot stir up a single colored man to take the lead in trying to head off this movement. I cannot see that they are doing a thing through the press. . . . It is a question how far I can go and how far I ought to go in fighting these measures in other states when the colored people themselves sit down and will do nothing to help themselves. They will not even answer my letters." [67]

Deprived of a representative in the conventions, Negroes elsewhere resorted to petitions. Washington joined with several middle-class Negroes, bankers, doctors, and politicians, in a conciliatory and somewhat humble petition to the Alabama convention, begging fair treatment.[68] A Negro convention in Birmingham resorted to the threat of mass migration to states "where the rights of manhood will be respected." They also appealed over the heads of the white leaders to the lower-class whites, warning them that they were "being used as instruments to effect their own political destruction." [69] These petitions and appeals received scant attention.

The racial attitudes of the whites, however, did not present the solid uniformity that the white-supremacy campaigns advertised. The disparity between white attitudes is illustrated in the Alabama

[65] Booker T. Washington and Curry, quoted in T. Thomas Fortune, "Immorality of Southern Suffrage Legislation," in *Independent* (New York), L (1898), 1576–77.

[66] Washington's appeal to the legislature of Georgia, in Atlanta *Constitution*, November 10, 1899.

[67] Washington to Fortune, November 7, 1899, in Booker T. Washington Papers (Division of Manuscripts, Library of Congress).

[68] *Proceedings of the Constitutional Convention of . . . Alabama*, 1901, I, 189–92. See also, petition of W. H. T. Holtzclaw, *ibid.*, II, 2069–71.

[69] Resolutions of the convention, in Birmingham *Age-Herald*, September 26, 1901.

debates. D. C. Case, a Populist member, was howled down when he somewhat quaintly proposed as the first article of the disfranchising constitution the words: "That all men are created free and independent; that they are endowed by their Creator with certain inalienable rights." [70] A white Republican also interposed somewhat ineffectually in the Negro's behalf. But the most commanding and effective voice raised in defense of the submerged race was that of the patrician. He represented the extreme right in social and economic doctrine but, at the time, carried on the Wade Hampton tradition of paternalism. Two former governors of the state, Jones and Oates, spoke in that tradition in the Alabama debates.

Asked why he took so much interest in a worthless soldier, Robert E. Lee, according to Jones, replied, "Because he is under me." The Governor continued: "The Negro race is under us. He is in our power. We are his custodians. . . . we should extend to him, as far as possible, all the civil rights that will fit him to be a decent and self respecting, law-abiding and intelligent citizen. . . . If we do not lift them up, they will drag us down." [71] He insisted upon a respectful hearing of Booker Washington's petition. Oates could shake an empty sleeve and say with impunity (and the support of history) against the grandfather clause that "there were a good many who wore the grey who did not wear it very honorably . . . for a large number of them deserted." [72] The indiscriminate enfranchisement of poor whites, believed Oates, was as vicious as the blanket disfranchisement of all Negroes, "the better element" of whom he would encourage to vote. *"It is not a racial question,"* declared the Governor, thereby denying the very premise of the whole movement. As for the low white man, "I would not trust him as quickly as I would a negro of intelligence and good character." [73]

The opposite school represented the true temper of the white-supremacy movements and the constitutional revision they produced. Gesnard Williams of Marengo County believed that no Negro was the equal of "the least, poorest, lowest-down white man I ever knew." Tom Heflin of Chambers County, on the threshold of a successful political career, spoke the idiom of the new era. "I believe as truly as I believe that I am standing here that God Al-

[70] *Proceedings of the Constitutional Convention of . . . Alabama,* 1901, I, 168.
[71] *Ibid.,* IV, 4303. [72] *Ibid.,* III, 2797. [73] *Ibid.,* II, 2793–94. Italics added.

mighty intended the negro to be the servant of the white man," he said. In view of the coming race conflict, said Heflin, "I do not believe it is incumbent upon us to lift him [the Negro] up and educate him and put him on an equal footing that he may be armed and equipped when the combat comes." [74] The immediate future of Southern policy belonged neither to the fallen Populists nor to the old Jones-Oates type of patrician—but to the Heflins.

When they had completed their labors the framers of the disfranchising constitutions looked upon their work with something less than complete satisfaction. Divisions had been close and debate bitter. Some members had refused to sign the completed documents, and many openly voiced dissatisfaction. There were misgivings about the constitutionality of some clauses and an uneasy awareness that the moral dilemma of the franchise had not been solved. There were half measures and compromises that pleased no one entirely, and clauses that were at cross-purposes with the solemn promises of the Democratic party.

"We have not drafted the exact constitution that we would like to have drafted," admitted E. B. Kruttschnitt, president of the Louisiana convention, in a farewell address to the members. But he was content with the franchise section. "What care I whether it be more or less ridiculous or not? Doesn't it meet the case? Doesn't it let the white man vote, and doesn't it stop the negro from voting, and isn't that what we came here for? (Applause)." [75] The press was less complacent. Kruttschnitt complained that the papers had "criticised, in the most hostile manner, almost every act of this Convention." A New Orleans paper reported that "indignation over the suffrage ordinance is limited to no section of the State," and quoted press comment to indicate that "North Louisiana joins hands with Central and South Louisiana in protest." [76]

The Mississippi convention had suffered similar treatment. Not only had it been authorized by undemocratic methods, but it had disfranchised many thousands of whites along with the blacks. Furthermore, instead of redressing the gross inequality of representation that penalized the white counties and was their main reason

[74] *Ibid.*, III, 2837, 2841; IV, 4302–4303.

[75] *Journal of the . . . Constitutional Convention of . . . Louisiana,* 1898, p. 380.

[76] New Orleans *Times-Democrat,* March 8, 1898. See also, *ibid.*, March 29, 1898.

for agreeing to the convention and submitting to the poll tax and disfranchisement plan, the Mississippi convention actually perpetuated and solidified the power of the Black-Belt oligarchy. Its work was therefore doubly undemocratic: it disfranchised the race that composed a majority of the population, and it delivered a large majority of whites into the control of a minority of their own race in the black counties.[77] The Mississippi press bitterly attacked the franchise provision as a fraud and a disgrace. Thirty-four papers, including all the leading journals save the Vicksburg *Herald,* "which had the convention's patronage," were listed in absolute opposition.[78] Faced with this hostility, the convention decided that it was "unnecessary and inexpedient" to submit the new constitution to the electorate for ratification and instead simply proclaimed it to be the law of the land.[79]

Mississippi set a precedent that was followed by all the Southern conventions save one, that of Alabama. In avoiding ratification by popular vote, these conventions made "a wide departure," according to an authority, from what had been "prevailing practice" since 1829, except for a period during and immediately after the Civil War.[80]

The Virginia convention was doubly obligated to submit its work to the electorate. After two unsuccessful attempts to gain consent of the people for a convention, the Democrats wrote into their platform of 1900 a pledge proposed by Carter Glass that the new constitution "shall be submitted to a vote of the people for ratification or rejection." [81] According to a party leader, "it was put there for the purpose of securing the votes of the people of Virginia in favor of holding a constitutional convention." [82] To make sure that suspicion was allayed, the General Assembly in its act providing

77 Albert D. Kirwan, "Apportionment in the Mississippi Constitution of 1890," in *Journal of Southern History,* XIV (1948), 234–46.

78 Wharton, *Negro in Mississippi,* 213–14.

79 *Journal of the Proceedings of the Constitutional Convention of the State of Mississippi . . . 1890* (Jackson, 1890), 549–50, 567–68.

80 Walter F. Dodd, *The Revision and Amendment of State Constitutions,* in Johns Hopkins University *Studies in Historical and Political Science,* Extra Volumes, N.S., No. 1 (Baltimore, 1910), 64–67.

81 Richmond *Dispatch,* May 3, 1900.

82 Alfred P. Thom, in *Proceedings and Debates of the Constitutional Convention . . . of Virginia,* 1901–1902, II, 3254–55.

for the election of delegates to the convention stipulated that the constitution be submitted. Once the convention was in session, however, there was talk of the "inexpediency" of submission. Glass himself declared that "no body of Virginia gentlemen could frame a constitution so obnoxious . . . that I would be willing to submit its fate to 146,000 ignorant Negro voters (great applause)." [83]

This was the usual argument against ratification. Yet in Alabama, the only state in which the constitution was submitted to the voters, the white counties turned it down flatly and the black counties carried it by majorities often exceeding the white voting population. The Alabama vote, indicating heavy white opposition, was cast while the question of ratification was being debated by the Virginia convention—which was well aware of strong white opposition at home. By a small majority the Virginia convention decided against popular ratification. It was the general opinion that the new constitution would have been rejected had it been submitted and that the convention's "action was a negation of democracy." [84] "It is best to do it this way," wrote an editor who supported the decision. "The whole movement is revolutionary, and the simplest and quickest way of disposing of the subject is the best." [85]

The precise effect of the new constitutions is difficult, and in some states virtually impossible, to determine for lack of adequate registration figures.[86] Louisiana registration before and after the new constitution was as follows: [87]

	White	*Negro*	*Total*
Registered on January 1, 1897	164,088	130,344	294,432
Registered, March 17, 1900 (new constitution)	125,437	5,320	130,757

83 *Ibid.*, 3257.

84 McDanel, *Virginia Constitutional Convention of 1901–1902*, p. 129.

85 Richmond *Times*, May 30, 1902.

86 For some interesting samples of registration figures, see Lewinson, *Race, Class, & Party*, Appendix II, 214–21.

87 *Biennial Report of the Secretary of State of the State of Louisiana . . . 1896 to 1898* (Baton Rouge, 1898), 26–27; *ibid., 1898 to 1900*, pp. 25–27; *Report of the Secretary of State to the Governor of Louisiana* (Baton Rouge, 1904), 52–53. The presidential election year 1904 was chosen because there was a tendency for registration to fall off in other years.

	White	*Negro*	*Total*
Reduction in registration	38,651	125,024	163,675
Registration of 1904 (first Presidential election year after poll tax was required)	91,716	1,342	93,058

The voters qualified to register in 1900 as follows: [88]

	White	*Negro*	*Total*
Under the "educational" qualifications	86,157	4,327	90,484
Under the "property" qualifications	10,793	916	11,709
Under the "grandfather clause"			29,189

The case of Texas, however, strongly suggests the use of caution in interpreting the decline in Southern voting, and particularly in attributing the decimation of the electorate entirely to formal devices of disfranchisement. For in Texas, which used only the poll tax as a means of disfranchisement—and that not until 1904, the percentage of the potential electorate actually voting in 1900 fell to less than half of what it had been in the hot election of 1896. Voting continued to decline gradually after the poll tax became effective, but the great decimation occurred before that. This instance has suggested to V. O. Key, Jr., the possibility that formal measures of disfranchisement in the Southern states merely "recorded a fait accompli brought about, or destined to be brought about, by more fundamental processes." [89] Among these processes he mentions the suppression of the Populist revolt, appropriation of some Populist slogans by the Democrats, reaction against Negro voting during the agrarian uprising, and consolidation of the one-party system. In all probability this pattern of events accounts for many of the phenomena often attributed to the poll tax and other formal restrictions. The force of the "fait accompli" suggestion,

88 The figures indicate that a few voters qualified in more than one way; hence the discrepancy between total registered and totals qualified under the three headings. Registration under the grandfather clause was not broken down according to race in 1900, but an official list of persons qualified under the clause in 1902 gives 37,877 white and 111 colored people. It is presumed that a few Negroes qualified similarly in 1900. *Report of the Secretary of State . . . Louisiana. May 12th, 1902* (Baton Rouge, 1902), 558.

89 Key, *Southern Politics in State and Nation,* 533–35.

however, is diminished by the experience of Mississippi, where disfranchisement was accomplished before the Populist revolt broke out and the accompanying pattern developed.

Mississippi's understanding clause, in contrast to Louisiana's grandfather clause, proved to be a veritable poor man's "eye of the needle" instead of the wide gate to the franchise it was represented to be. Only 1,037 whites and 1,085 blacks were registered by means of the famous clause in Mississippi by 1892.[90] "Ignorant whites are in most instances reluctant," it was explained, "to expose their illiteracy or to subject themselves to an examination in respect to their knowledge of the constitution." [91] Under the provisions of the new constitution of Mississippi 68,127 of the 110,100 male whites over 21 were registered along with 8,615 of the 147,205 male Negroes over 21. Roughly one Negro in seventeen and two whites in three were therefore qualified to vote provided they paid their poll tax—and kept the receipt! By this means a potential electorate of 257,305 was reduced to a potential electorate of 76,742, and a Negro majority of 37,105 was converted into a white majority of 58,512.[92] The actual number of votes in the heated election of 1892, contested by four parties, was only 52,809.

Registration figures do not tell the whole story, for reduction in the number of voters was even more marked than the reduction in those qualified to vote. Between the presidential elections of 1900 and 1904 the franchise restrictions of the Virginia constitution went into full effect. The total vote of Virginia in 1900 was 264,240, while in 1904 it was 130,544—a decline from 147 voters per 1,000 population to 67 per 1,000. Nor can it be assumed that this decrease is to be explained by the elimination of the Negro voter, for while only about 35 per cent of the males of voting age were colored, the poll was reduced by 51 per cent. Not until 1928 did Virginia cast as large a vote in a Presidential election as she did in 1888. This was a temporary rise. When Franklin D. Roosevelt defeated Wendell Willkie in 1940, Virginia cast 61,000 fewer votes than when Harrison defeated Cleveland, and in 1944, fewer by 37,166 than she cast 56 years earlier. Many factors in addition to

90 *Appletons' Annual Cyclopaedia . . . 1892*, p. 472.

91 Jackson *Clarion*, August 25, 1892.

92 *Nation*, LIV (1892), 139.

the formal devices of disfranchisement contributed to this decima tion. In the meanwhile, however, the electorate had been doubled by the enfranchisement of women, and the population had increased by approximately 1,000,000. In 1940 fewer than 10 in every 1,000 of population were voting, as against 147 in 1900.[93] A Richmond editor wrote in 1924 that never since the constitution of 1902 had more than 20 per cent of the *whites* of voting age named a winning candidate in that city. "Twenty per cent of the electorate rules—20 per cent at the maximum," he concluded. "And it is called democracy!" [94]

Virginia elections usually brought out a higher percentage of voters than did those of some of her sister states to the south—even those that relied upon nothing more than the poll tax as a disfranchiser. While in Virginia the average vote cast for Congressmen declined about 56 per cent between 1892 and 1902, in Alabama the decline was 60 per cent; in Mississippi, 69 per cent; in Louisiana, 80 per cent; and in North Carolina, 34 per cent. Of the states relying upon the poll tax or the white primary the decline was 69 per cent in Florida, 75 per cent in Arkansas, 50 per cent in Tennessee, and 80 per cent in Georgia.[95]

During the same years there was a general falling-off in the number of voters in the country as a whole. It has been estimated that 76.4 per cent of the potential electorate took part in the Presidential election of 1892 and only 65.8 per cent in that of 1904.[96] But this represents a decline of only 10.6 per cent. On the other hand, it is often said that the general election figures in the South are misleading, because after the primary system was adopted the real issues were settled and the significant voting done before the general election was held. It is true that there was usually more interest taken and more voting done in the primaries than in general elections. Thus, there were 72,070 votes cast in the Louisiana Democratic primary in 1904 and only 54,222 in the general election; the governor's race of 1906 in Alabama brought out

93 *World Almanac*, 1888–1946; McDanel, *Virginia Constitutional Convention of 1901–1902*, pp. 50–58.

94 Richmond *Times*, November 8, 1924.

95 Francis G. Caffey, "Suffrage Limitations at the South," in *Political Science Quarterly*, XX (1905), 60.

96 Charles H. Titus, *Voting Behavior in the United States* (Berkeley, 1935).

94,661 votes in the primary and only 71,616 in the general election; and in the Texas race the same year the primary vote was 294,106 and the general election 185,840.[97] Both primaries and general elections brought out only a fraction of the potential electorate, and it occasionally happened that the primary went uncontested. As one writer described the psychology of nonvoters in Virginia, "If they were Republicans their votes would be thrown away and if they were Democrats their votes would not be needed." [98] The disfranchisers had prepared the atmosphere in which apathy and indifference grew and spread.

In states that carried constitutional revision beyond franchise changes, the pervading distrust of the electorate and of popular government was manifest in other departments. There was, for example, a tendency to favor the executive over the legislative branch, to prefer appointive to elective offices, and to remove the judiciary further from popular influence. Mississippi, one of the first states in the Union to have an elective judiciary, defeated the principle in her new constitution. The same fight was also lost in the convention of Virginia. In both Virginia and Alabama the struggle for an elective railroad commission was lost, although the new appointive Corporation Commission of Virginia was a commendable achievement. Mississippi put an end to the election of the governor by direct popular vote, substituting an electoral college scheme.

The patronage and appointive power of the executive was enormously increased in some cases. The governor of Louisiana was given a long list of officers to appoint. Under the rule of the disfranchisers, North Carolinians were again virtually deprived of local self-government, which had been restored temporarily by the Fusionists, and were returned to the Redeemer system. "The counties of western North Carolina," as Governor Charles B. Aycock put it, "gave up their much-loved right of local government in order to relieve their brethren of the east from the intolerable

[97] *Report of the Secretary of State . . . of Louisiana* (Baton Rouge, 1905), "Statistical Tables of Registrations and Elections," x–xi, xiv–xv; Thomas M. Owen (ed.), *Alabama Official and Statistical Register, 1907* (Montgomery, 1907), 250, 272; *Texas Almanac and State Industrial Guide, 1947–1948* (Dallas, 1948), 423–24.

[98] McDanel, *Virginia Constitutional Convention of 1901–1902*, p. 50.

burden of negro government." [99] At least, that was the theory.

In Virginia, where the first representative assembly in the New World had met in 1619, the convention of 1901 questioned the very principle of representative government. The General Assembly was described as "a wild rabble" which was an enemy of "business interests" and did more harm than good. As for the people's interest in the matter, said one member, "if you did not have a Legislature for ten years they would not know anything about it, nor care anything about it." [100] The suggestion of reducing the number of members of the Assembly was discussed, and by a very narrow margin the motion to make both the elections and the sessions of the Assembly quadrennial was defeated. The quadrennial election and brief session of the legislature once every four years had just been adopted by the convention of Alabama, which thus became the only state in the Union with such a system. Ten years earlier Mississippi had adopted the quadrennial election but retained biennial sessions. The whole argument for the quadrennial legislature, contended a member of the Alabama body, was based "on a want of confidence in the capacity of the people to govern themselves," or upon "the assumption that the people are not to be trusted." [101] Whether the member was correct or not, those attitudes and assumptions were fairly common in the disfranchising conventions.

The hopes and prejudices and fears of millions of people were involved in disfranchisement, and the motives behind the movement were undoubtedly many and complex. In general, however, the leaders held up above all others three justifications for disfranchisement: (1) The removal of the Negro vote, they argued, would put an end to the corrupt elections that had long disgraced Southern politics; (2) the removal of the Negro as arbiter between white factions would enable the white men to divide freely again on basic issues and enjoy a vigorous political life; (3) disfranchisement would force the Negro to abandon false hopes, find his

[99] Quoted in R. D. W. Connor and Clarence Poe, *The Life and Speeches of Charles Brantley Aycock* (New York, 1912), 65.

[100] Quoted in McDanel, *Virginia Constitutional Convention of 1901–1902*, pp. 89, 93.

[101] Emmett O'Neal, in *Proceedings of the Constitutional Convention of . . . Alabama*, 1901, IV, 4708, 4711.

"place," and as a consequence race relations would improve. The extent to which the last of these three hopes was realized will be examined in the following chapter. As for the first two, one was to a qualified degree realized and the other was not.

While their remedy somewhat suggests throwing out the baby with the bath, the disfranchisers could claim with a degree of truth that after their work was done Southern elections were more decorous. Disgraceful scenes of ballot-box stealing, bribery, and intimidation were much rarer after disfranchisement. One effective means of stopping the stealing of ballots, of course, is to stop the people from casting them. Elections are also likely to be more decorous when the electorate of the opposition parties has been disfranchised or decimated and the election becomes a formality in a one-party system. Opponents of the new system held that it perpetuated old evils in a legalized form. "Elections under it would turn," said one critic, "not primarily upon the will of the people but upon the partisan or factional allegiance of the registrars." [102] The debates of the conventions indicate what the registration officials were expected to do, whether they did it or not. "At best it is an enamelled lie," wrote John Spencer Bassett of the North Carolina law. To him it was "one more step in the educating of our people that it is right to lie, to steal, & to defy all honesty in order to keep a certain party in power." [103] The majority of Southerners, however, were taught to regard disfranchisement as reform.

As for the promise that disfranchisement would enable white men to divide freely on fundamental issues, it simply failed to materialize. The spirit of intolerance and proscription aroused by the white-supremacy campaigns did not stop at the bounds of race. North Carolina Red Shirts pulled white Populists from platforms, beat them up, and ran them out of town. Furnifold M. Simmons, Democratic state chairman and later United States Senator, boasted that he sent "some of our boys" to terrorize the Populist Senator Marion Butler, that they "scared him almost to death," and that the Republican governor of the state "was so badly frightened that he

[102] Newman H. Freeman, *ibid.*, III, 2809–10.

[103] John S. Bassett to Herbert B. Adams, February 18, 1899, in W. Stull Holt (ed.), *Historical Scholarship in the United States, 1876–1901: As Revealed in the Correspondence of Herbert B. Adams*, in Johns Hopkins University *Studies in Historical and Political Science*, LVI, No. 4 (Baltimore, 1938), 265.

slipped away from Raleigh immediately after the election."[104] Dissident whites were watched shrewdly for their reaction to white-supremacy propaganda. Josephus Daniels observed with obvious satisfaction the presence of "quite a number of white Populists and white Republicans" in a Red-Shirt parade of 1,000 in 1898.[105] When three Populist members of the legislature cast their votes for the disfranchisement amendment the following year, Daniels reported that "the applause was long and deafening, shouts and yells being added to the hand clapping."[106] The next year he remarked that while "in 1892–94 and '96 the Populist convention was like a mighty torrent pouring down the mountain side; in 1900 it is like an old mill-pond after the water has been turned off."[107]

White supremacy enjoyed a success second only to that of the silver panacea as a discourager of political independence and a uniter of the Solid South.

104 Rippy (ed.), *F. M. Simmons*, 24–26.

105 Quoted in Richmond *Times*, November 5, 1898.

106 Raleigh *News and Observer*, February 18, 1899.

107 *Ibid.*, April 19, 1900.

CHAPTER XIII

THE ATLANTA COMPROMISE

IN PLACE of the improvement in race relations promised by the disfranchisers as a result of their work there occurred a serious deterioration in almost all departments. In part this was a direct result of the methods used by the disfranchisers themselves. It became standard practice to support disfranchising campaigns with white-supremacy propaganda in which race hatred, suspicion, and jealousy were whipped up to a dangerous pitch. Politicians and newspapers co-operated in circulating Negro atrocity propaganda in the form of feature stories, cartoons, photographs, and posters.

Aycock's campaign managers staged "White Supremacy Jubilees," in which hundreds of armed men paraded in red shirts. Ben Tillman came up from South Carolina to lend a hand, and sympathizers in Richmond told of 50,000 rounds of ammunition and a carload of firearms shipped to North Carolina a few days before the election of 1898. The Negroes remained quiet. Shortly after the whites of Wilmington won the election over a thoroughly cowed black majority, a mob of 400 men led by a former Congressman demolished a Negro newspaper office, set it on fire, shot up the Negro district, killed 11 Negroes, wounded a large number, and chased hundreds into the woods. The leader of the mob was then elected mayor of the city. He proclaimed that "all further violence" should cease.[1]

The sequel of the white-supremacy election in Georgia was similar, except that the Atlanta mobs looted, plundered, lynched, and murdered for four days. Race riots were not transient products of

1 Wilmington *Morning Star*, November 10, 11, 1898.

propaganda that passed with the campaigns. Three years after Tillman's disfranchising constitution went into effect some twelve Negroes were killed and several wounded during an election near his home. In 1900, two years after Louisiana adopted the grandfather clause, several mobs of white men roamed the city of New Orleans for three days, assaulting Negroes, looting, burning, and shooting. "The bloody horseplay of the mobs is full of instruction for the whole South," observed a New Orleans paper. "It is evident that the grand idea of white supremacy has become the stalking-horse of anarchy in this part of the Union." [2]

But mob rule and race riots were not confined to one part of the Union. Within a month of the riot in New Orleans race riots occurred in New York City and Akron, Ohio. "Rioting in the North," according to a Negro historian, "was as vicious and almost as prevalent as in the South." [3] With the cry, "Lincoln freed you, we'll show you where you belong," mobs took possession of Lincoln's home town of Springfield, Illinois, for two days in 1908 and waged brutal war on Negro life and property. Governor James K. Vardaman of Mississippi believed the experience would "cause people of the North to look with more toleration upon the methods employed by the Southern people." [4]

Lynch law still took a savage toll of Negro life, though the number of lynchings in the country declined markedly from the peak reached in the nineties, a tendency happily not in conformity with the deterioration in race relations already noted. From 1889 to 1899 the average number of lynchings per year was 187.5, while in the following decade the number was 92.5, or less than half. Two other significant changes, however, occurred over the same period. The proportion of the lynchings taking place in the South increased from about 82 per cent of the total in the earlier decade to about 92 per cent in the period 1900–1909. At the same time, the proportion of lynching victims who were white decreased from 32.2 per cent in the earlier decade to 11.4 per cent in the latter. In other words, while lynching was decreasing in the South, it was decreasing more

[2] New Orleans *Times-Democrat,* July 27, 1900.

[3] John Hope Franklin, *From Slavery to Freedom* (New York, 1947), 435.

[4] Quoted in William E. Walling, "The Race War in the North," in *Independent,* LXV (1908), 534.

slowly than elsewhere. It was becoming an increasingly Southern and racial phenomenon.[5]

In the first decade of the new century the extremists of Southern racism probably reached a wider audience, both within their own region and in the nation, than ever before. Thomas Dixon's popular "series of historical novels . . . on the race conflict," as the author described the trilogy, appeared between 1902 and 1907.[6] One of them, *The Clansman,* a bitter indictment of the Negro, was dramatized on the stage and later on the screen for an even wider audience. Within the same five-year period were published such works as *"The Negro a Beast": or, "In the Image of God," The Caucasian and the Negro in the United States, The Color Line: A Brief in Behalf of the Unborn,* and *The Negro, A Menace to American Civilization,* books characterizing the race as degraded, bestial, and incapable of improvement.[7] Between 1901 and 1909 Ben Tillman made "countless speeches" to Chautauqua audiences in all parts of the country, popularizing his racial views. The Negroes were "akin to the monkey," an "ignorant and debased and debauched race," declared the Senator, and "To hell with the Constitution" if it interfered with lynching rapists.[8] Ten years removed from the equalitarianism of his Populist days, Tom Watson was preaching *"the superiority of the Aryan"* and the "HIDEOUS, OMINOUS, NATIONAL MENACE" of Negro domination.[9]

Southerners of the older generation were sometimes shocked at the fierce, ungovernable passions abroad in the South. Old Governor Oates thought "the change in public opinion in regard to the status of the Negro" was "most startling" in Alabama. "Why,

[5] Arthur F. Raper, *The Tragedy of Lynching* (Chapel Hill, 1933), 25, 480–83. The "South" in this instance includes Missouri.

[6] Thomas Dixon, Jr., *The Leopard's Spots: A Romance of the White Man's Burden —1865–1900* (New York, 1902); *The Clansman: An Historical Romance of the Ku Klux Klan* (New York, 1905); *The Traitor: A Story of the Fall of the Invisible Empire* (New York, 1907).

[7] Charles Carroll, *"The Negro a Beast": or, "In the Image of God"* (St. Louis, 1900); William P. Calhoun, *The Caucasian and the Negro in the United States* (Columbia, 1902); William B. Smith, *The Color Line: A Brief in Behalf of the Unborn* (New York, 1905); Robert W. Shufeldt, *The Negro, A Menace to American Civilization* (Boston, 1907).

[8] Quoted in Simkins, *Pitchfork Ben Tillman,* 394–96.

[9] *Watson's Jeffersonian Magazine* (Atlanta), III (1909), 97.

sir," he exclaimed to the men of Heflin's generation, "the sentiment is altogether different now, when the Negro is doing no harm, why the people want to kill him and wipe him from the face of the earth." [10] Edgar Gardner Murphy, one of the young humanitarians, deplored the same fateful trend. Extremists, he said, had proceeded "from an undiscriminating attack upon the Negro's ballot to a like attack upon his schools, his labor, his life—from the contention that no Negro shall vote to the contention that no Negro shall learn, that no Negro shall labor, and (by implication) that no Negro shall live." They ended by preaching an "all-absorbing autocracy of race," an "absolute identification of the stronger race with the very being of the state." [11]

It was little wonder that in the speeches at a Southern conference on race problems held in Montgomery in 1900, "The overruling note sounded through all their words is pessimistic." According to a report of the conference, "Economically, morally, religiously, even physically, this sad key was struck time and again." [12] The pessimism of the Montgomery conference persisted in the South for more than a decade. It pertained not only to the relations between races, but to the condition and progress of the Negro himself. William Garrott Brown reported evidence of the sentiment everywhere in his tour of the South in the spring of 1904. "The great majority of those with whom I have talked," he wrote, "declare that the Negro is not adapting himself to the new era, that he is not 'making good.' " Three Southern governors agreed that the Negro was deteriorating as a laborer.[13] Two Northern investigators, Ray Stannard Baker and Albert Bushnell Hart, encountered sentiment of the same kind in the South.[14] Three British travelers with experience in race problems of South Africa and the West

10 *Proceedings of the Constitutional Convention of . . . Alabama*, 1901, IV, 4441.

11 Edgar Gardner Murphy, *The Basis of Ascendency* (New York, 1909), 25, 29–30.

12 *Publications of the Southern History Association* (Washington), V (1901), 171; *Race Problems of the South: Report of the First Annual Conference . . . of the Southern Society for the Promotion of the Study of Race Conditions and Problems in the South at Montgomery, Alabama* (Richmond, 1900), 52–56, 144–45, 148–49, 187–93.

13 William G. Brown, under the name "Stanton," in Boston *Evening Transcript*, March 19, 21, 1904.

14 Ray Stannard Baker, *Following the Color Line; An Account of Negro Citizenship in the American Democracy* (New York, 1908), *passim;* Hart, *Southern South, passim.*

Indies took an extremely discouraging view of relations in the South and saw in complete segregation or colonization of the Negro the only alternative to disaster.[15] In the North it was "generally acknowledged" in 1903 "that the new negro at the South is less industrious, less thrifty, less trustworthy, and less self-controlled than was his father or his grandfather." [16]

Upon one opinion both whites and blacks, Northerners and Southerners appeared to be in agreement—that the transition from the slavery system to the caste system had been accomplished at the cost of grave deterioration in race relations. The intimacy of contact under slavery, especially that between the better type of both races, was succeeded by a harsh and rigid separation. Under slavery, as W. E. B. Du Bois, for example, pointed out, the two races sometimes "lived in the same home, shared in the family life, often attended the same church, and talked and conversed with each other," while under the caste system there was "little or no intellectual commerce" between races.[17] "Ours is a world of inexorable divisions," wrote Murphy. Segregation had "made of our eating and drinking, our buying and selling, our labor and housing, our rents, our railroads, our orphanages and prisons, our recreations, our very institutions of religion, a problem of race as well as a problem of maintenance." [18]

As the old type of Negro bred in slavery died off and the new type bred to caste increased, it seemed from within the white world that the Negro was losing his manners and his morals. Crowding into the slums of the cities in great numbers, the Negro population of Southern urban communities increased 32 per cent between 1890 and 1900 and 35.8 per cent in the following decade. As the urban Negro population increased, the proportion of crime committed by the race mounted—from 256 imprisoned per 100,000 Negro population in 1904 to 1,079 in 1910.[19] Homicide rates in Atlanta,

[15] Archer, *Through Afro-America;* William Pringle Livingstone, *The Race Conflict; A Study of Conditions in America* (London, [1911]); Maurice S. Evans, *Black and White in the Southern States; A Study of the Race Problem in the United States from a South African Point of View* (London, 1915).

[16] "The Negro Problem and the New Negro Crime," in *Harper's Weekly,* XLVII (1903), 1050.

[17] W. E. Burghardt Du Bois, *The Souls of Black Folk* (Chicago, 1903), 183–85.

[18] Murphy, *Basis of Ascendency,* 122, 138.

[19] Monroe N. Work, *Negro Year Book, 1914–1915* (Tuskegee, 1914), 314, 350.

Birmingham, Memphis, and New Orleans reached appalling heights, and in the country at large the rate for colored persons became almost seven times the rate for whites.[20]

The walls of segregation and caste were raised higher and higher by law and custom. Between 1900 and 1911 ten Southern states elaborated their laws requiring separation of races in transportation facilities, all of them including laws for street railways, and some for ferries and steamboats.[21] Atlanta carried the tendency to the point of having separate elevators, though not by compulsion of law, by 1908.[22] Between 1911 and 1914 the cities of Norfolk, Richmond, Ashland, Roanoke, Winston-Salem, Greensboro, Greenville, Augusta, and Atlanta passed ordinances segregating residential areas, and in 1913 an agitation was started by Clarence Poe of the *Progressive Farmer* for the segregation of farm lands in North Carolina.[23]

On both sides of the wall of caste grew suspicion, uneasiness, and mistrust. Governor N. B. Broward told the Florida legislature in 1907 that "relations between the races are becoming more strained and acute." Writing in 1903, John Spencer Bassett concluded that "there is today more hatred of whites for blacks and blacks for whites than ever before." [24] Speaking for the Negro, Charles W. Chesnutt said the same year that "the rights of the Negroes are at a lower ebb than at any time during the thirty-five years of their freedom, and the race prejudice more intense and uncompromising." [25]

Over the years there evolved along with the caste system a generally accepted credo of race among white Southerners. In 1913 Thomas Pearce Bailey, a Southern educator, set down this "racial creed of the Southern people" with such candor and accuracy that it may serve as the best available summary: "1. 'Blood will tell.' 2. The white race must dominate. 3. The Teutonic peoples stand for race purity. 4. The Negro is inferior and will remain so. 5. 'This

20 Harrington C. Brearley, *Homicide in the United States* (Chapel Hill, 1932), 97.

21 Johnson, *State Legislation Concerning the Free Negro*, 54, 62–207.

22 Baker, *Following the Color Line*, 28–29.

23 Work, *Negro Year Book, 1914–1915*, pp. 31–34.

24 John S. Bassett, "Stirring Up the Fires of Race Antipathy," in *South Atlantic Quarterly*, II (1903), 304.

25 Charles W. Chesnutt, "The Disfranchisement of the Negro," in Booker T. Washington *et al.*, *The Negro Problem* (New York, 1903), 104.

is a white man's country.' 6. No social equality. 7. No political equality. 8. In matters of civil rights and legal adjustments give the white man, as opposed to the colored man, the benefit of the doubt; and under no circumstances interfere with the prestige of the white race. 9. In educational policy let the Negro have the crumbs that fall from the white man's table. 10. Let there be such industrial education of the Negro as will best fit him to serve the white man. 11. Only Southerners understand the Negro question. 12. Let the South settle the Negro question. 13. The status of peasantry is all the Negro may hope for, if the races are to live together in peace. 14. Let the lowest white man count for more than the highest Negro. 15. The above statements indicate the leadings of Providence." [26]

Not all Southern whites subscribed to the credo. Men of Murphy's school struggled in perplexity with the race question, always conscious that their motives and honesty might be impugned at home and abroad. Occasionally an outsider perceived and sympathized. "Deeply religious and intensely democratic as are the mass of whites," wrote Du Bois, "they feel acutely the false position in which the Negro problems place them." [27] And Henry James breathed "a soft inward dirge over the eternal 'false position' of the afflicted South." [28]

It was an ex-slave who eventually framed the *modus vivendi* of race relations in the New South. Booker T. Washington was more than the leader of his race. He was also a leader of white opinion with a national following, and he propounded not merely an educational theory but a social philosophy. The historical stage was set for the entrance of this remarkable man. It was a time when the hope born of Reconstruction had all but died for the Negro, when disfranchisement blocked his political advance and the caste system closed the door to integration in the white world, when the North had abandoned him to the South and the South was yielding to the clamor of her extremists. The defiant spirit of the old Negro

[26] Thomas P. Bailey, "Race Orthodoxy in the South," in *Neale's Monthly Magazine* (1913), reprinted in his *Race Orthodoxy in the South* (New York, 1914), 93. For a good survey, see Guion G. Johnson, "The Ideology of White Supremacy, 1876–1910," in Green (ed.), *Essays in Southern History*, 124–56.

[27] Du Bois, *Souls of Black Folk*, 186.

[28] James, *American Scene*, 362.

leaders of emancipation and Reconstruction appeared increasingly quixotic under these circumstances.

The year 1895 marked both the death of Frederick Douglass and the acclaim of Booker Washington as the new leader of the race. The new doctrine came to be known as the "Atlanta Compromise," so called because in a famous speech before an audience of both races at the opening of the Atlanta Cotton States and International Exposition Washington gained instantaneous and nationwide recognition.[29] "Nothing has happened since Henry Grady's immortal speech before the New England society in New York that indicates so profoundly the spirit of the New South," reported James Creelman in the New York *World*.[30] The comparison was not without historical validity. Washington's life mission was to find a pragmatic compromise that would resolve the antagonisms, suspicions, and aspirations of "all three classes directly concerned—The Southern white man, the Northern white man, and the Negro." It proved, he admitted, "a difficult and at times a puzzling task." [31] But he moved with consummate diplomacy, trading renunciation for concession and playing sentiment against interest.

To the white South (always "of the better class") he made a disarming concession. "I was born in the South," he said, "and I understand thoroughly the prejudices, the customs, the traditions of the South," and, he added, "I love the South." He had learned that "these prejudices are something that it does not pay to disturb," [32] and "that the agitation of questions of social equality is the extremist folly." [33] In the second place, he had early renounced Northern intervention and subscribed to Southern white views on that sore point. "My faith is that reforms in the South are to come from within," he said.[34] He gave assurances that the Negro was more interested in industrial education and economic oppor-

29 The invitation to make the address was secured only with great difficulty and pressure. See Garland Penn to Washington, August 19, 23, September 9, 1895, in Washington Papers.

30 Quoted in Booker T. Washington, *Up from Slavery* (New York, 1901), 238.

31 Booker T. Washington, *My Larger Education; Being Chapters From My Experience* (Garden City, 1911), 50, 24–25.

32 *Ibid.*, 178–79.

33 Washington, *Up from Slavery*, 223.

34 E. Davidson Washington (ed.), *Selected Speeches of Booker T. Washington* (Garden City, 1932), 6. From a speech delivered in 1884.

tunity than in political rights and privileges, and he agreed that property and educational qualifications were desirable for the franchise. This did not mean that he gave up ultimate realization of any kind of rights, but he said nothing of ultimate aims. He appealed to sentiment, reminding the South of the "fidelity and love" of the Negro during the Civil War, and, identifying his race with the industrial hopes of the region, asked consideration for those who "without strikes and labour wars" had built up the South's industries.[35]

To the Northern whites Washington, like the older type of Negro leader, came in search of friends for his race. He fully appreciated "those Christ-like philanthropists" who opened their pockets to his people.[36] But instead of appealing to the agitators and doctrinaires he sought out the very type of men whom Southern whites were trying to interest in the development of Southern industry. He thus identified himself with the Eastern affiliations of the conservative South. These Northern capitalists were actual or potential investors in the region and sometimes large-scale employers of black labor. Washington found his way with amazing ease among such men. He was more than once a guest aboard the yacht of H. H. Rogers of Standard Oil, a man he admired for his "practical grasp of public and social questions." William H. Baldwin, Jr., vice-president of the Southern Railway, employer of thousands of Negroes, spent hours with Washington over the latter's speeches, "going into minute details of verbal expression." He was an intimate of Collis P. Huntington, builder of Newport News and railway owner, and a guest of Andrew Carnegie at Skibo Castle.[37] Again and again he pointed out the practical significance of his message for labor problems. Speaking to a convention of industrialists in Alabama, he said: "It is here alone, by reason of the presence of the Negro, that capital is freed from the tyranny and despotism that prevents you from employing whom you please." [38] Elsewhere he expressed unfriendliness for labor unions, revolu-

[35] Washington, *Up from Slavery,* 221. From the Atlanta speech of 1895.

[36] Washington (ed.), *Selected Speeches of Booker T. Washington,* 14.

[37] Washington, *My Larger Education,* 73, 78, 257; John G. Brooks, *An American Citizen: The Life of William Henry Baldwin, Jr.* (Boston, 1910), 177.

[38] Washington (ed.), *Selected Speeches of Booker T. Washington,* 81–82, and also see pp. 46–47.

tionary tactics, and socialism, and professed devotion to the laissez-faire theory of government.[39]

To his own race he preached a gospel of conservatism, patience, and material progress. "I fear that the Negro race lays too much stress on its grievances and not enough on its opportunities," he told a Fisk University audience.[40] The prejudices and injustices of the caste system and the barbarities of the mob (subjects he rarely mentioned) should be met with "few words and conservative action"; it was wise "to suffer in silence" and exercise "patience, forbearance, and self-control in the midst of trying conditions." He was "not asking that the Negro act the coward," he added; "we are not cowards." The friendship of the conservative, upper-class Southern whites and wealthy Northern capitalists, however, offered more hope than agitation and protest. Security and recognition would follow material gain, and his people should begin not at the top, but at the bottom, in both education and industry, and work up in the American way. "This country demands that every race shall measure itself by the American standard," he said. All Negroes admitted that "the black man has far better opportunity to rise in his business in the South than in the North." [41]

The power this man came to wield over the destinies of his race and over the New South stood in striking contrast to his incorrigible humility. The man who abjured "social equality" in the South moved in circles of the elite in the North and aristocracy abroad that were opened to extremely few Southern whites.[42] The man who disparaged the importance of political power for his race came to exercise political power such as few if any Southern white men of his time enjoyed. A sampling of his vast correspondence indicates the extent of this power. As chief patronage referee in the South for Federal appointments during the administrations of Roosevelt and Taft, he was consulted on virtually all Negro appointments and on the merits of many Southern whites.[43] He cor-

39 Booker T. Washington, *The Man Farthest Down* (New York, 1912), 102–103; Booker T. Washington, "The Negro and the Labor Unions," in *Atlantic Monthly*, CXI (1913), 756.

40 Washington (ed.), *Selected Speeches of Booker T. Washington*, 40–41.

41 *Ibid.*, 40–41, 52–53.

42 Washington, *My Larger Education*, 177.

43 See letters of Theodore Roosevelt to Washington, 1901–1909 (e.g., December 25,

rected the messages of Presidents and blighted careers by his silence. His influence was sought in all parts of the United States, and his power over the Negro press was known and feared.[44] More directly he influenced the distribution of the vast patronage of Northern philanthropy.

During the two decades from 1895 to Washington's death in 1915, Negro thought and policy in matters of race relations, labor, education, and business enterprise conformed in large measure to the Tuskegee philosophy. This was not due so much to the genius and personal influence of Booker Washington as to the remarkable congeniality between his doctrines and the dominant forces of his age and society, forces that found an eloquent voice in the brown orator, but that would have made themselves felt in any case. Negro labor history illustrates the tendency.

The caste system, the color line, and the new spirit of racial aggression were strongly felt in labor relations and in trade unions. Caste sanctioned a division of labor into white men's jobs and black men's jobs. Sometimes aided by employers' policy of hiring, sometimes encouraged by politicians, white labor kept up an unremitting pressure to drive Negroes out of the better paid, more attractive work, and further down in the job hierarchy. While at the end of the Civil War Negro artisans are said to have outnumbered white by five to one, they made up only a small proportion of the labor force in most crafts by 1890. From that time to 1910 the Negroes held their own fairly well in some of the crafts. Between 1890 and 1910 the total of Negro male workers in all nonagricultural pursuits increased by two thirds, but this was to be explained by the great expansion of "Negro-job" industries—saw mills, coal mining, and railroad construction and maintenance.[45] The increasing mechanization of tobacco manufacturing converted many "Negro jobs" into "white work," and broke what had once been al-

1906); William Loeb (secretary to Roosevelt) to Washington, 1909–1911; and entire correspondence of Charles W. Anderson to Washington, in Washington Papers.

44 For example, Washington to T. Thomas Fortune, April 9, 1906; Washington to Anderson, June 9, 1911, *ibid.*

45 Spero and Harris, *Black Worker*, Table IX, 160; Gunnar Myrdal, *An American Dilemma; The Negro Problem and Modern Democracy* (New York, 1944), I, Table I, 285; Baker, *Following the Color Line*, 249–50.

most a Negro monopoly. The mounting employment of white women, and the more rigid segregation of races this always implied, also eliminated Negro workers in other industries. Early in the twentieth century there was much comment upon the disappearance of the Negro from trades he had traditionally monopolized, or very largely so. "It is possible now," wrote one Southerner in 1904, "to live in New Orleans as free from any dependence on the services of Negroes as one could be in New York or Boston." While in 1870 the city directory had listed 3,460 Negroes as carpenters, cigar makers, painters, clerks, shoemakers, coopers, tailors, bakers, blacksmiths, and foundry hands, not 10 per cent of that number were employed in the same trades in 1904. Yet the Negro population had gained more than 50 per cent.[46]

The national trade unions did not create racial discrimination, but finding it widespread they acquiesced pretty generally in it and therefore share responsibility for perpetuating it on an organized basis. In spite of many fine pronouncements that recall the idealistic policy of the Knights of Labor, the American Federation of Labor proved to be no serious hindrance to the practice of racial exclusion and separation among its affiliated unions. In 1900 President Samuel Gompers suggested that since it seemed impracticable to insist on the acceptance of Negro members, separate unions be organized for them. Ten years later Gompers was quoted as favoring the exclusion of Negroes from unions because they could not "understand the philosophy of human rights." [47] Only some twelve national unions, the majority of them railway brotherhoods, openly excluded the Negro. But while the other unions carried no such provision in their charters, they bowed to local preference and sanctioned tacit agreements to exclude, or discriminate against, the Negro. In 1910 only six national unions were estimated

[46] William Garrott Brown, "The White Peril" (1904), in *The New Politics and Other Papers* (Boston, 1914), 116–17. Washington discounted the tendency and wrote Brown that "the Negro has shifted occupations rather than lost them." Washington to Brown, June 20, 1904, in William Garrott Brown Papers (Duke University Library, Durham).

[47] Samuel Gompers, quoted in New York *World*, November 19, 1910. See Gompers' report, in *Report of the Proceedings of the Twentieth Annual Convention of the American Federation of Labor . . . 1900* (Louisville, 1900), 22–23.

to have more than a thousand Negro members, and of those having any at all a large number reported less than a hundred.[48]

In a few unions colored labor managed to retain a stronger position in the South than in the North. This was particularly true of coal mining and the older building trades, such as bricklaying and plastering, in which the Negro had a large number of craftsmen when the unions moved into the South. In such cases the unions were compelled to treat them with some respect. Barred from the railway unions from the start, the Negro was compelled to work unorganized in the midst of a highly organized industry. He was made ineligible for promotion on the usual basis of seniority, paid less than the white man for the same work, and was often used by Southern railway management to keep wages down and to weaken and undermine the unions that barred him from membership. A strike tied up the Georgia Central Railroad in 1909 over the issue of hiring Negro firemen, and another on the Cincinnati, New Orleans, and Texas Pacific in 1911 over the same issue resulted in the killing of ten firemen.[49] One revival of interracial solidarity occurred in the independent Brotherhood of Timber Workers. Started in 1910 among the lumber camps of Louisiana, Texas, and Arkansas, the union attained a membership of 35,000, half of it Negro. Joining the Industrial Workers of the World in 1912, the Brotherhood attempted to force some minor concessions from Louisiana operators, only to be met with a lockout in forty-six mills. After a three-year struggle against the operators and against latent race feeling, the I.W.W. union disintegrated.[50]

Negroes held a strong position in Alabama coal mines from the beginning and had been organized in some degree since the Knights of Labor. The United Mine Workers sent organizers into the Southern fields in the nineties with the difficult assignment of uniting Negro, native white, and foreign miners. The long campaign was an intermittent warfare against determined operators, fought under handicaps of racial antagonism. Remarkable gains were made in

48 French E. Wolfe, *Admission to American Trade Unions,* in Johns Hopkins University *Studies in Historical and Political Science,* XXX, No. 3 (Baltimore, 1912), 122–33.

49 Spero and Harris, *Black Worker,* 286–91.

50 *Ibid.,* 331–33; *Bill Haywood's Book; The Autobiography of William D. Haywood* (New York, 1929), 241.

Tennessee and Alabama between 1899 and 1902. In the latter year the union claimed about 65 per cent of the Alabama miners as members, a majority of them Negroes. Many operators in that state signed contracts with the union in 1900. Four years later a writer who had predicted earlier that "the Negro would never be anything but a scab" was amazed to find Birmingham unions "strong and defiant and they control blacks as well as whites." [51]

The miner's union fought a battle for existence in 1908, when the Alabama operators, strengthened by the recent arrival of United States Steel in the territory, refused to renew expired contracts and announced wage cuts. The National Executive Board of the United Mine Workers called a strike for July 6 and threw its enormous resources and prestige into the struggle. In ten days 18,000 men were out and every mine in the state, save those worked by convicts, was closed down. Operators imported strikebreakers by the train loads. Three trains were ambushed by strikers who fought pitched battles with guards. Strikers were reported patrolling highways, dynamiting houses, and intimidating nonunion workers. Hundreds of union men were jailed, threatened, and mistreated, and for nearly eight weeks shootings, beatings, or riots were reported almost daily. Strikers evicted from company houses were sheltered in a tent encampment erected by the union near Birmingham. Since it housed both Negro and white families, the camp became the target for an outburst of race propaganda. Here the industrialist, reform Governor Braxton B. Comer (a former lessee of convict labor) struck the fatal blow to the miners' hopes when he forbade public meetings, ordered the state militia to cut down the tents, and threatened to lock up pickets. Faced with the Governor's ultimatum, the union capitulated and called off the strike. The humiliating defeat cost the United Mine Workers $407,500, spent in relief to Birmingham strikers. Vice-President John P. White, in charge of the strike, confessed his discouragement to the national convention of his union. "We who live in well organized districts," he said, "and who are surrounded by better influences and have more industrial liberty cannot conceive of the condi-

[51] William Garrott Brown, under the name "Stanton," in Boston *Evening Transcript,* April 13, 1904; Spero and Harris, *Black Worker,* 352–57; Frank J. Warne, *The Coal Mine Workers* (London, 1905), 220–21.

tions there." He blamed the skillful use of race prejudice for the defeat. Union membership in Alabama fell from 18,000 to 700 the year following the strike, and no attempt at reorganization was made for a decade. Thousands of white miners fled the district and were replaced by nonunion Negroes.[52]

Booker Washington was certainly not responsible for the Negro's diminishing position in the crafts, his exclusion from unions, and his employment as a strikebreaker. Finding Negro labor in this plight, he plotted what seemed to him the most practical course. "The Negro is not given to 'strikes,' " he said. "His policy is to leave each individual free to work when, where, and for whom he pleases." [53] He pronounced trade unionism "that form of slavery which prevents a man from selling his labor to whom he pleases on account of his color." [54] The Negro worker should rely not upon collective bargaining but upon the paternalism of well-disposed employers. "You should remember," he reminded Southern industrialists, "that you are in debt to the black man for furnishing you with labor that is almost a stranger to strikes." [55]

After the strike of 1908 was crushed, the big Alabama operators, Tennessee Coal and Iron (United States Steel) and the De Bardeleben Coal Company, introduced an elaborate welfare and educational program for their labor. In order to convert illiterate common Negro workers into efficient skilled workers and assure a stable bulwark against unionism, the operators built schools, hospitals, welfare and recreational centers, and improved housing on a grand scale. This welfare capitalism, according to a journal of the Hampton Institute, was working toward "the same ends as those which Hampton and Tuskegee and the whole system of education they represent are striving for. Moreover, in many cases, these parallel efforts and aims are drawn closer together by the fact that Hampton and Tuskegee graduates are having a large part in such work." Alumni of these institutions did in large measure direct the program of welfare work and company unionism, and one of

[52] *Proceedings of the Twentieth Annual Convention of the United Mine Workers of America, 1909* (Indianapolis, 1909), I, 65–67; II, 863–64, 873; Birmingham *Age-Herald*, July 6, August 31, 1908.

[53] Booker T. Washington, *The Negro in Business* (Boston, 1907), 354.

[54] From a speech to the Southern Industrial Convention in 1899, in Washington (ed.), *Selected Speeches of Booker T. Washington*, 81.

[55] *Ibid.*, 82.

the companies established annual scholarships to Tuskegee for children of its employees.[56]

Washington's "industrial" education philosophy was an integral part of his labor philosophy. By teaching the crafts he hoped to encourage the Negro to recoup to some extent his position of post-emancipation days. "A large element of people at the South favored manual training for the Negro," he said, "because they were wise enough to see that the South was largely free from the restrictive influences of the Northern trade unions, and that such organizations would secure little hold in the South so long as the Negro kept abreast in intelligence and skill with the same class of people elsewhere." [57] Such a concept, he believed, would appeal to men of wealth and position who "see the close connection between labor, industry, education and political institutions." [58] Brickmaking, blacksmithing, wheelwrighting, harness making, basketry, tinsmithing—the type of crafts taught at Tuskegee—had more relevance to the South of Booker Washington's boyhood than to the South of United States Steel, but his teachings of orderliness, cleanliness, discipline, and a "cooperative spirit" had relevance for the new era as well.

The enormous vogue that industrial education enjoyed among Negro educators in the South and the extent to which the older institutions, some of them without enthusiasm, fell in with the movement are to be explained to some degree by the influence that Washington exercised over the distribution of Northern philanthropic funds. There is considerable evidence to support the view of an unfriendly critic that Washington's influence became so powerful that "almost no Negro institution could collect funds without the recommendation or acquiescence of Mr. Washington." [59]

One of the most important developments in Negro history, not to say the history of the South, was the rise of a whole separate system of society and economy on the other side of the color line. Excluded from equal participation in the white world, the Negro

[56] Spero and Harris, *Black Worker,* 246–47, 363–66; Bond, *Negro Education in Alabama,* 230–33.

[57] Washington, *Negro in Business,* 333.

[58] Washington, *My Larger Education,* 59–60.

[59] Du Bois, *Dusk of Dawn,* 73; Bond, *Negro Education in Alabama,* 217–19.

constructed a copy of it—of its churches, schools, banks, theaters, professions, services, and other institutions. Beginning as a largely undifferentiated class of former slaves, the race was soon sorted out into all the social and economic classes of the white capitalistic society upon which it was modeled. And as in the white society of the time, the businessman occupied a foremost rank of prestige. The Negro middle and upper class was caught in the curious dilemma of suffering from segregation and at the same time having a vested interest in it, since it provided what opportunity and protection from white competition the Negro did enjoy in the uphill struggle for the patronage and business of his own race.[60] The Negro middle class, like the working class, therefore stood in need of a philosophy that could somehow reconcile the disadvantages and the advantages of segregation.

In 1900 Booker Washington took the leadership of the rising Negro business community of the country by organizing the Negro Business League and serving as president for several years. By 1907 there were 320 local Business Leagues with a wide influence in the Negro world. In speeches and books Washington held up the self-made black capitalist as a hero of his race. The businessman's gospel of free enterprise, competition, and *laissez faire* never had a more loyal exponent than the master of Tuskegee. Washington went back to a bygone day for his economic philosophy. It consisted of the mousetrap-maker-and-beaten-path maxims of thrift, virtue, enterprise, and free competition. It was the faith by which the white middle-class preceptors of his youth had explained success, combined with a belief that, as he expressed it, "there is little race prejudice in the American dollar." Washington's individualistic doctrine never took into account the realities of mass production, industrial integration, financial combination, and monopoly. Since the Negro capitalist was nearly always a small capitalist, he was among the first to suffer and the last to rally under the new pressures. He was largely confined to petty trade and a declining proportion of that.[61]

[60] Guy B. Johnson, "Negro Racial Movements and Leadership in the United States," in *American Journal of Sociology*, XLIII (1937–1938), 57–71; Myrdal, *American Dilemma*, I, 305.

[61] Washington, *Negro in Business*, 268–75, and *passim;* Booker T. Washington, "Negro Disfranchisement and the Negro in Business," in *Outlook*, XCIII (1909),

The shortcomings of the Atlanta Compromise, whether in education, labor, or business, were the shortcomings of a philosophy that dealt with the present in terms of the past. Not that a certain realism was lacking in the Washington approach. It is indeed hard to see how he could have preached or his people practiced a radically different philosophy in his time and place. The fact remains that Washington's training school, and the many schools he inspired, taught crafts and attitudes more congenial to the premachine age than to the twentieth century; that his labor doctrine was a compound of individualism, paternalism, and antiunionism in an age of collective labor action; and that his business philosophy was an anachronism. It is hardly necessary to add that white leaders of the South adhered pretty generally to the same doctrines and that the larger part of them subscribed to Washington's race policy.

While Washington's leadership of ten million American Negroes was generally conceded, it did not go undisputed. Leadership of the opposition fell to W. E. Burghardt Du Bois, born in Massachusetts of a line of free ancestry and educated at Fisk, Harvard, and Berlin. Narrowly missing a teaching appointment at Tuskegee, for which he applied, Du Bois went instead to Atlanta University in 1896 and started a school for the scientific study of the Negro in the South. Here he published, in a series of reports, the first adequate social studies of the Negro in his changed condition. Science soon proved an inadequate vehicle for the message of a poet and prophet. He began to write with brooding passion and a brilliant pen of the peonage of his people, of the wretchedness in which they lived, of the white man's law and the black man's wrongs, of the harsh code of caste and the brutality of the mob. He challenged the "Tuskegee Machine" and attacked what he believed to be Washington's equivocations on political rights, his submissive concessions to Southern caste discriminations, his silence in face of injustice, and his narrowly materialistic conception of Negro education.[62] In 1905 Du Bois issued a call from Atlanta to those of like mind, demanding "aggressive action." The ensuing conference organized the

311; Washington (ed.), *Selected Speeches of Booker T. Washington*, 40–41, 52–53; Spero and Harris, *Black Worker*, 50–52; Myrdal, *American Dilemma*, I, 306–307.

[62] Du Bois, "Of Mr. Booker T. Washington and Others," in *Souls of Black Folk*, 41–59, and *passim*.

"Niagara Movement" and demanded for the Negro "every single right that belongs to a freeborn American, political, civil and social." [63] The picture of the Niagara adherents marching barefooted the following year to the scene of John Brown's raid offered a bold contrast to the spirit of the Atlanta Compromise. Antagonism between the two movements and their leaders became quite bitter and personal.[64] In 1910 Du Bois left Atlanta and moved to New York to become the only Negro official in the newly organized National Association for the Advancement of Colored People, which absorbed the Niagara people and incorporated their militant spirit. The leadership of Du Bois and the ascendancy of the new movement over the old was not acknowledged until after the First World War. Booker Washington remained impregnable in his authority until his death in 1915.

The year 1913 was known among Negroes as a "Year of Jubilee" —the fiftieth anniversary of emancipation. All over the South there were held celebrations and expositions to commemorate the progress of the race over a half century. The achievements of 128,557 colored farm owners in the South,[65] the ownership by Negroes of 38,000 business enterprises and 550,000 homes, and the accumulation of $700,000,000 of wealth by Negroes in the country as a whole were held up as evidence of the progress of the race.[66] The reduction of illiteracy among Negroes from more than 90 per cent in 1865 to some 30 per cent in 1913 did represent something approximating a race-wide accomplishment. Essentially, however, the material progress of which the Jubilee boasted represented the rise of a colored middle class of businessmen, farmers, and professional people—the accumulations of a "brown middle class" that had arisen out of a "black proletariat."

[63] Du Bois, *Dusk of Dawn*, 88–93.

[64] For a man of mild address, the language Washington used to describe his opponents was pretty strong. See Washington to Anderson, September 29, 1905; Washington to J. C. Asbury, October 2, 1905, in Washington Papers. For his published opinion, see *My Larger Education*, 110–27.

[65] United States Census Bureau, *Negro Population . . . 1790–1915*, p. 585.

[66] Work, *Negro Year Book, 1914–1915*, p. 4, estimates as of 1913.

CHAPTER XIV

PROGRESSIVISM—FOR WHITES ONLY

THE crusade for Cuba broke the South's preoccupation with reform and scotched the radicalism of the nineties. Southerners responded with customary impetuosity to the upsurge of martial spirit and put aside sectional grievances. Silverites were among the most prominent jingoes. "We are crusaders again, as we were in 1861 and in 1846," wrote an Alabama Congressman who opposed the war.[1] Senator Tillman celebrated the newly imposed unity of war and nationalism in a jingle he recited to his colleagues:

Populists, Democrats, Republicans are we,
But we are all Americans to make Cuba free.[2]

"The Spanish War finished us," declared Tom Watson. "The blare of the bugle drowned the voice of the Reformer." [3] After a blast at imperialism and war, he retired from public life for six years. No other Populist was available to assume leadership of the moribund party. Polk of North Carolina and Nugent of Texas were dead. Reuben Kolb was making his peace with the old party in Alabama, and Cyclone Davis was spellbinding Western states with war speeches. Senator Marion Butler of North Carolina was vying with conservative patriots in support of the war. Even Milton Park, editor of the *Southern Mercury,* and most undaunted Populist of them all, confessed his discouragement in 1898. The election of that year, he wrote, proved that "the Democratic party can declare for anything it likes and win. It shows, too, that the people of Texas are suffering from a state of mental lethargy." He fretted

1 Willis Brewer to McKee, April 23, 1898, in McKee Papers.

2 *Congressional Record,* 55 Cong., 2 Sess., 3888.

3 *Watson's Jeffersonian Magazine,* V (1910), 817.

peevishly about "the kind of cattle reformers have to deal with in Texas," and raged at the prevailing reactionism of Southerners: "Had they lived in the old colonial days," he continued, "they never would have rebelled against King George or kicked against the stamp tax. . . . To them Patrick Henry would have been a crank and Sam Adams an incendiary. They would have all been Tories in 1776. They are all Tories now." [4] Park veered off toward the Socialist party the following year, taking with him an element of the Populists.

While Park exaggerated the depth of the reactionary trend in the South, the tendency toward it was undoubtedly strong. Texas reverted to the control of a succession of conservative governors. Former Governor Hogg, firebrand of 1890, was touring Northeastern states in 1898 seeking to convince capitalists that Texas was the safest possible place for investment and corporate enterprise.[5] A few years later he was amassing a fortune as an oil-company promoter. The contemporary rulers of Georgia, from 1898 to 1906, were probably as conservative as any of their predecessors in the eighties.[6] The victory of the silver faction of the old party in the South had worked no profound regeneration in its nature. The new men were frequently of a familiar type. Joseph F. Johnston, elected governor of Alabama in 1896, described himself as "a silver man from tail to snout," yet he was a Birmingham banker and a former president of the Sloss Iron and Steel Company, owned by a New York syndicate.[7] Under his administration the Alabama compromise of Birmingham industrialists and Black-Belt conservatives thrived unimpaired. South Carolina retained Tillman in the Senate but sent John L. McLaurin to join him in 1897. Unlike the senior Senator, McLaurin defended the gold standard, the ship subsidy, and the annexation of the Philippines, and contended that "business men must fill the offices and administer affairs of government in the South as in the East, the North, and the West." [8]

[4] *Southern Mercury*, XVI (November 17, 1898), 9.

[5] Hogg to House, May 16, 1898, House Films, Roll 111.

[6] John C. Reed, "The Recent Primary Election in Georgia," in *South Atlantic Quarterly*, VI (1907), 27–36.

[7] Armes, *Story of Coal and Iron in Alabama*, 248–50.

[8] Quoted in Wallace, *History of South Carolina*, III, 387.

If the South fell into the mood of McKinleyism for a season, it also developed its own variety of progressivism in the era that followed hard upon McKinley. The latter phenomenon has been pretty universally ignored—or misconstrued. "I don't know of any progressive sentiment or any progressive legislation in the South," said Senator Robert M. La Follette in 1912, and William Allen White echoed the denial in 1914.[9] If the progressives themselves did not recognize and acknowledge their Southern kin, it is little wonder that writers since that day have uncritically accepted the stereotype of a Reactionary South.

The Southern counterpart of a Northern progressivism developed nearly all traits familiar to the genus, but it was in no sense derivative. It was a pretty strictly indigenous growth, touched lightly here and there by cross-fertilization from the West. It sprouted in the soil that had nourished Populism, but it lacked the agrarian cast and the radical edge that had frightened the middle class away from the earlier movement. Southern progressivism was essentially urban and middle class in nature, and the typical leader was a city professional man or businessman, rather than a farmer. Under the growing pressure of monopoly, the small businessmen and urban middle class overcame their fear of reform and joined hands with the discontented farmers. They envisaged as a common enemy the plutocracy of the Northeast, together with its agents, banks, insurance companies, public utilities, oil companies, pipelines, and railroads. Southern progressivism often took a sectional character, identifying the popular enemy with "foreign" interests. These interests were defended by Southern apologists who were strongly entrenched within the old party and frequently controlled it through bosses and state machines. William E. Dodd, then a college professor in Virginia, described the situation in his state to Walter Clark, a critic of machine rule in North Carolina. "This state," wrote Dodd, "is no more self-governing to-day than the Catholic Church. Thomas F. Ryan is our master and he lives

9 Robert M. La Follette, quoted in Arthur S. Link, "The Progressive Movement in the South, 1870–1914," in *North Carolina Historical Review,* XXIII (1946), 173; William Allen White to Judge J. A. Burnette, Topeka, March 7, 1914, in Walter Johnson (ed.), *Selected Letters of William Allen White, 1899–1943* (New York, 1947), 154.

in New York. Thomas S. Martin is his henchman and we have powerful newspapers to defend both with none to oppose either." [10] The struggle for progressive democracy was directed against such bosses as Martin and was carried on within the old party between conservative and reform factions.

Several circumstances favored the reform factions in the first decade of the new century. The Populist party, bearing the odium attached to any threat to white solidarity, had in large measure constituted an obstruction to the spread of reform ideas in the South. The collapse of the third party not only removed a stigma from reformism, but it brought back into the old party its disaffected left wing. Returning, the Populists brought along with them their ideological baggage, for which room had to be found.

Whether as a cause or a result, the direct-primary system of nominating party candidates appeared with progressive movements all over the South. The direct primary was not invented in Wisconsin in 1903, as is sometimes said, for by that time a majority of the Southern states were already practicing the system, and by 1913 all the remaining ones had adopted it except North Carolina, which fell into line in 1915.[11] A part of the paraphernalia of progressivism in all sections, the primary was one of the first demands of the reformers. "In the South this demand was even stronger than at the North," [12] because in the one-party system nomination meant election. The adoption of the primary was in part the fulfillment of the implied pledge of the disfranchisers that once the Negro was removed from political life the white men would be given more voice in the selection of their rulers. In part also it was a gesture of

[10] William E. Dodd, Ashland, Va., to Walter Clark, September 7, 1906, in Hugh T. Lefler (ed.), "Selected William E. Dodd–Walter Clark Letters," in *North Carolina Historical Review*, XXV (1948), 91–92.

[11] Local and county primaries appeared even earlier, but reference here is to Democratic state-wide primaries, whether mandatory or not. The system was adopted in South Carolina in 1896, Arkansas in 1897, Georgia in 1898, Florida and Tennessee in 1901, Alabama and Mississippi in 1902, Kentucky and Texas in 1905, Louisiana in 1906, Oklahoma in 1907, Virginia in 1913, and North Carolina in 1915. Link, "Progressive Movement in the South," *loc. cit.*, 188–90.

[12] Charles B. Spahr, "Method of Nomination to Public Office: An Historical Sketch," in *Proceedings of the Chicago Conference for Good City Government and the Tenth Annual Meeting of the National Municipal League* (Philadelphia, 1904), 324.

welcome to the returning Populist prodigals. The great hope of the progressives was that since the old convention system of nomination had facilitated boss and machine control, the substitution of the primary would restore popular control. In at least five states, Alabama, Arkansas, Florida, Mississippi, and Texas, the change to the primary was an immediate, or nearly immediate, antecedent of the victory of a reform administration. It is probable that in those cases the primary paved the way for reform.

The joker in the Southern primaries was the fact that they were *white* primaries. Southern progressivism generally was progressivism for white men only, and after the poll tax took its toll not all the white men were included.[18] The paradoxical combination of white supremacy and progressivism was not new to the region, but it never ceased to be a cause of puzzlement and confusion above the Potomac—and not a little, below. The paradox nevertheless had its counterpart in the North, where it was not uncommon for one man to champion both progressivism and imperialism. In such instances it was a matter of white supremacy over browns instead of blacks. Hiram Johnson was apparently no more troubled by his advocacy of proscription of Japanese in California than Hoke Smith by his treatment of Negroes in Georgia. The Southern leader who professed reactionary racial views and advanced political and economic reforms in the same breath was known as a "demagogue," unless he happened to be a political ally, in which case he was a "progressive."

Had La Follette and White undertaken the most casual survey of legislation and platforms in the South they would have discovered there all the progressive doctrines and experiments familiar to Wisconsin and Kansas and their latitudes. Southern reformers sought to "bust the trusts" and regulate them at the same time. They strengthened their railroad and public-utility commissions, hauled railroads and other malefactors into court, reduced rates, fought discrimination, and passed unfair-practice laws, safety and inspection laws for mines and factories, pure-food and drug bills, penitentiary reforms, and much humanitarian legislation. Progressives here and there experimented with all the political inventions associated with the movement. Besides the direct primary, these

18 The poll tax payment was not a prerequisite for voting in Tennessee primaries.

included the initiative, referendum, and recall; preferential primaries; and corrupt-practices and antilobby acts.

In command of the movement was a group of "reform governors" who were almost as picturesque a lot of leaders as those who arose in the nineties. Like their contemporaries and counterparts, the Western reform governors La Follette of Wisconsin and Albert B. Cummins of Iowa, the Southern governors had no co-ordinated, interstate organization, although their programs were similar. The men themselves ranged in type from a spellbinder to a dignified factory owner.

Napoleon Bonaparte Broward came of a line of planters, soldiers, and theologians impoverished by the war. He was left an orphan at the age of twelve in the palmetto scrub of eastern Florida. The boy worked through the hard-bitten, hungry years of Reconstruction on the St. Johns River as raftsman, cook, deck hand, and fireman. In his teens he shipped north to Boston on a freighter. For two years he followed the sea as a fisherman off the Newfoundland Banks or aboard oyster boats and lumber vessels. Returning to the Florida river life, he became a bar pilot and later the skipper of a steamboat. Broward entered politics in 1888 at the age of thirty-three as sheriff of Duval County, in which Jacksonville lies. In 1896 he returned to the sea and became an evader instead of an enforcer of the law. As designer, part-owner, and sometimes captain of the steamer *Three Friends,* the erstwhile sheriff turned filibusterer and ran the blockade with arms and ammunition for the Cuban revolutionists. His adventures brought him fame and popularity. But it was Broward's championship of the "crackers" against the predatory railroads, his efforts to save the remaining public lands from the "land pirates," and his Paul Bunyan–like ambition to drain the Everglades which made him a folk hero, elected the former deck hand governor in 1904, and founded Broward progressivism in Florida.[14]

Born in 1856, William Goebel of Kentucky was the son of a German immigrant cabinetmaker and his German wife who moved to Covington from Carbondale, Pennsylvania, in 1863. Goebel escaped a jeweler's apprenticeship, studied law, and rose rapidly

[14] Samuel Proctor, "Napoleon B. Broward, The Years to the Governorship," in *Florida Historical Quarterly,* XXVI (1947), 117–34.

and brilliantly in the profession. His political career opened in the state senate, where he served twelve years and rose to leadership of the reform faction of the Democratic party. Outwardly a cold and taciturn man with no oratorical gifts and few intimates, Goebel succeeded by his consummate political ability and the popular appeal of his struggle to tax and regulate the corporations and railroads.

Charles B. Aycock and James K. Vardaman, though men of very different types, both rose to power on the white-supremacy issue and waves of racial bitterness. The youngest of ten children of a small farmer and local politician, Aycock was born in Wayne County, North Carolina, in 1859. His mother was unable to write her own name. Aycock managed to attend the state university and qualify for the bar. In 1893 he became United States attorney for the eastern district of his state. His great political passion, aside from white supremacy,[15] was education, and apparently he meant education for both races. Beyond that he rarely ventured. The party boss and Aycock's campaign manager, Furnifold M. Simmons, frankly admitted that Aycock had reached an understanding with "the large corporations." [16] In comparison with the simple, unassuming figure of Aycock, Vardaman presented a spectacular contrast, with his long, flowing hair and long, flowing coattails. The Mississippian campaigned for the hillbilly vote mounted upon a lumber wagon drawn by oxen and won the devotion of this element both by his reactionary race doctrine and his progressive program of economic and social reform. Even his opponents found it "impossible to determine where his idealism ended and his demagoguery began." [17] He was defeated twice in his attempts to secure the Democratic nomination for governor but was successful in 1903 after the adoption of the direct primary.

In August, 1906, within the same week, Braxton Bragg Comer of Alabama and Hoke Smith of Georgia were elected governors in those states by strong reform movements. Smith, the Atlanta editor and publisher, and Comer, the Birmingham manufacturer,

[15] According to his biographers, "Aycock believed in the right of the white man to rule as profoundly as he believed in God. He knew that the instinct of race is divinely implanted." Connor and Poe, *Life and Speeches of Charles Brantley Aycock*, 160.

[16] Rippy (ed.), *F. M. Simmons*, 29.

[17] Percy, *Lanterns on the Levee*, 144.

were both prosperous members of the urban middle class. Like the earlier reform governor Altgeld and the Cleveland mayor Tom Johnson, Comer was a man of considerable wealth, reported to have been worth a half million or more at the time of his election.[18] Yet under Comer's leadership the Democratic party of Alabama for the first time since Reconstruction dropped the word "Conservative" from its official title. Comer was jolted out of the complacency of his class by the impact of freight rates and railroad discriminations upon his interests as a planter, banker, and cotton manufacturer. Hoke Smith was probably carried farther along the road to reform than was his natural inclination by his coalition with Tom Watson, who swung the old Populists to his support. These oddly matched teammates—a former member of Grover Cleveland's cabinet and the leader of the Populist party—pulled together awkwardly until Watson kicked over the traces, but while they pulled they carried Georgia farther toward progressivism than Watson and all the hosts of Populism had in the nineties.

Southern progressivism had a fringe that was less lunatic than comic, less radical than burlesque. It is best typified by Jeff Davis of Arkansas. In the dialectics of this "Karl Marx for Hill Billies," [19] the class struggle was waged between the "red necks" and their mortal enemies, the "high-collared roosters" of the city. In that struggle, so he assured the dispossessed, the "one-gallus" proletariat had nothing to lose but their plowlines—whereas the trusts had plenty. Jeff Davis tilted with the corporation monster at every crossroad in Arkansas and made trustbusting the favorite sport of the rustic barbecue. If his battles were largely bloodless and the results intangible, the same was often true of more celebrated combats in far-off Washington, and Jeff's were more exciting. There was a compensatory satisfaction in watching the enemy being bullied and slain in pantomime, especially when one had fought in vain for years without so much as coming to grips with the foe.

Jeff Davis loved his trade and practiced it with gusto and without shame. He abjured all elegancies save his habitual Prince Albert

[18] Herbert Quick, "Comer of Alabama," in *The Reader* (Indianapolis), X (1907), 497.

[19] Rupert B. Vance, "A Karl Marx for Hill Billies, Portrait of a Southern Leader," in *Social Forces* (Chapel Hill), IX (1930–1931), 180–90.

suit of Confederate gray, and he could demolish an opponent by calling him a gentleman. "If you red-necks or hillbillies ever come to Little Rock," he would say, "be sure and come to see me. . . . If I am not there tell my wife who you are, that you are my friend and belong to the sunburned sons of toil. Tell her to give you some hog jowl and turnip greens. She may be busy making soap, but that will be all right." [20] And they loved him with a devotion unshaken by his defiance of both Baptists and prohibitionists and elected him governor and then to the Senate, where he died unbeaten and unbeatable.

The first Southern reform movement to make a determined fight for power ended in an assassination and came near plunging a state into civil war. This was the fight led by William Goebel of Kentucky in 1899–1900. A man of remorseless determination, Goebel fought ruthlessly against equally ruthless foes and inspired hatred as well as devotion. In the Democratic convention of 1899, he outmaneuvered the L and N machine, which led the fight against him, and won the nomination for governor in a struggle that split the party. Goebel then faced the opposition not only of a strong Republican party, which nominated William S. Taylor, but also of the bolting Democrats who nominated former Governor John Young Brown, a friend of the railroads.[21]

Goebel campaigned on his reform record in the state senate, where he had labored to tax hidden capital, to increase the taxation of railroads and public utilities, and to secure labor and franchise laws. He also demanded a new state antitrust law and increased power for the state railroad commission. Above all, however, he carried home his fight against the Louisville and Nashville Railroad, its president Milton H. Smith, its lobbyist Basil W. Duke, and the chairman of its board of directors, August Belmont. In scarcely a speech did Goebel fail to mention the railroad or one of its officials.[22] It was time, he declared, that "the Louisville and Nash-

20 Charles Jacobson, *The Life Story of Jeff Davis, The Stormy Petrel of Arkansas Politics* (Little Rock, 1925), 234, and *passim.*

21 Urey Woodson, *The First New Dealer, William Goebel* . . . (Louisville, 1939), 236–37; Thomas D. Clark, "The People, William Goebel, and the Kentucky Railroads," in *Journal of Southern History,* V (1939), 34–48.

22 Louisville *Commercial,* October 17–November 12, 1899; also the Louisville *Evening Post* and the Cincinnati *Enquirer* of the same dates.

ville became the servant instead of the master of Kentucky." He charged that Brown had entered the race only "after Basil Duke had called at the office of August Belmont in New York City, and found out what the attitude of the L & N Railroad would be in this fight." [23]

There is no question that the railroad was deeply interested in the election. Belmont published correspondence revealing that Goebel's campaign had been the subject of resolutions by the board of directors.[24] The fight centered in Louisville, where the power of the Louisville and Nashville was concentrated and where tension was so great that the Republican governor called out the militia to police the polls. William Jennings Bryan toured the state speaking in Goebel's behalf. In spite of Bryan's aid the Republican candidate Taylor won by a plurality of 2,383 votes and was inaugurated on December 12.

Goebel was not to be stopped by the inauguration of an opponent. Contending that the election had been corrupted by the railroads, he organized his forces in the legislature to contest the election. When it became apparent that the Democratic majority in that body intended to unseat the Republican administration, tension in the capital became dangerous. Threats and insults had been loosely exchanged during the campaign. In answer to Goebel's charge that he was a "corruptionist" for the Louisville and Nashville, Basil Duke replied that he would "not submit to an attack from a liar, slanderer and an assassin because he happens to be a self-selected candidate for governor." [25] This was the customary challenge to a duel. It was a day of hair-trigger politics. Goebel himself had killed a political opponent three years before in an exchange of shots. Toward the middle of January a train loaded with more than a thousand armed men from the mountains pulled into the capital, transported by the Louisville and Nashville. On the thirtieth, as Goebel was approaching the state capitol, several shots rang out from one of the offices occupied by a Republican

[23] Cincinnati *Enquirer*, October 19, 1899.

[24] R. E. Hughes, F. W. Schaefer, and E. L. Williams, *That Kentucky Campaign; or the Law, the Ballot and the People in the Goebel-Taylor Contest* (Cincinnati, 1900), 283.

[25] *Ibid.*, 110.

official and Goebel dropped in his tracks, fatally wounded. His assassin was never identified.[26]

Ignoring the Governor's order, the Goebelite members of the legislature met and proclaimed the wounded man governor. Goebel died four days after taking the oath and was succeeded by his lieutenant governor, J. C. W. Beckham. Kentucky now had two governments, one of which proclaimed a state of insurrection. The deadlock was eventually broken by the courts, which decided in favor of the Democrats. Governor Taylor became an exile from the state. The reformers pushed through their bill extending the powers of the railroad commission, but the death of their leader and the very violence of their struggle for power seemed to leave them enervated. They failed to rally to the support of the commission during its prolonged litigation with the Louisville and Nashville, which virtually tied its hands for nearly fifteen years.[27]

While no other reform movement encountered resistance that went to the extreme of assassination, they all met stiff opposition. This was always supported and often led by the railroads. It was natural that railroad regulation should have headed the list of reforms. The lobbyists and lawyers of the large systems were in many cases closely allied with the political machines which the reformers were seeking to overthrow. Moreover, the farmers and the urban middle class nursed long-accumulated grievances against the railroads. In the lexicon of the reformers, the locomotive came to replace the steam roller as a symbol of oppression.

The development of railroad regulation in the various states was closely parallel. In the seventies and eighties the nine Southern states east of the Mississippi River created railroad commissions. They ranged in type from the weak Virginia commission of 1877, which had only advisory capacity and narrowly restricted jurisdiction, to the powerful Georgia commission of 1879, which had authority to fix and enforce uniform rates, prevent discrimination, and establish freight classifications. These early commissions, although they performed useful functions in their day, came under

[26] Caleb Powers, Republican secretary of state, was tried and convicted four times for the crime, but was eventually pardoned. Caleb Powers, *My Own Story* (Indianapolis, 1905), *passim*.

[27] Ferguson, *Regulation of Railroads in the South*, 115–27.

attack toward the end of the century. The reformers were dissatisfied, not only with the law, but with the performance of the commissions. From Georgia came the cry that the comparatively strong commission of that state was "nothing more than a pretense, a sham, an imposition on the tax payers and an insidious prop to the present system of corporative robbery." [28]

Within the decade beginning in 1897 nearly all the Southern states revised their commissions, increased the authority they exercised, and usually made the members elective instead of appointive.[29] Florida and Tennessee, both of which had repealed their earlier commissions, revived them in 1897 in a strengthened form and made membership elective. Louisiana in 1898 and Arkansas in 1899 created their first commissions, and Kentucky revised her old one in the following year. North Carolina pioneered with "the first corporation commission created in the United States" [30] in 1899, extending jurisdiction not only to all carriers of freight and passengers but to other public utilities, private and public banks, and loan and trust companies. Virginia followed her example in 1901, Georgia and Alabama in part in 1907, and Oklahoma in her new constitution of the same year. A comparison of state commissions in 1902 revealed that those with strongest authority were in the South and Middle West.[31]

The fierce antimonopoly and antirailroad spirit probably reached its climax in the South, as it did in other parts of the country, in 1906 and 1907. In the latter year, wrote a North Carolina college professor, the various state legislatures of the South were furiously at work "reducing freight and passenger rates, prohibiting discriminations and rebates, establishing penalties for delay in the transportation of goods, enforcing liability for damages to passengers, prohibiting free passes, reducing the hours of labor of railroad employees, requiring the introduction of safety appliances, pro-

[28] Quoted in Frank Parsons, *The Railways, the Trusts, and the People* (Philadelphia, 1905), 243.

[29] All state commissions between 1890 and 1902 are described and compared in elaborate tables in the *Sixteenth Annual Report of the Interstate Commerce Commission*, Appendix G, Pt. IV, in *House Documents*, 58 Cong., 2 Sess., No. 253, Pt. V, 45–113. Earlier and later developments are also discussed in Ferguson, *Regulation of Railroads in the South*.

[30] Ferguson, *Regulation of Railroads in the South*, 170–71.

[31] *Report* in *House Documents*, 58 Cong., 2 Sess., No. 253, Pt. V, 15.

hibiting combinations and traffic agreements." [32] The commissions or legislatures of Alabama, Arkansas, Georgia, Mississippi, North Carolina, South Carolina, Tennessee, Texas, and Virginia were considering drastic reductions in passenger fares, while before the Texas legislature alone were pending eighty-three antirailroad measures.[33]

In considerable degree the railroads had themselves to blame for the bitterness of the crusades against them in the South. Practices of discrimination, rebates, stockjobbing and stock watering, favoritism, and overcharging continued in spite of regulations against them. Certain of the larger roads, in particular, evaded or ignored the orders of the state commissions, or tied them up in litigation. Scarcely an order of importance made by the Louisiana commission was left uncontested. Resentment was aroused by the way in which railroads punished certain states—for example, Georgia and Texas—by retaliating against their commissions through control over interstate rates.[34] The fighting blood of the reformers was especially stirred by the ease with which the railroads, after they had lost a long struggle over some piece of legislation, would secure an injunction from a Federal judge. This happened repeatedly.

North Carolina reformers in the legislative session of 1907 had as their *cause célèbre* a uniform reduction of passenger rates to two and one-fourth cents a mile. Josephus Daniels, who had recently adopted red-ink headlines, led a sensational campaign in the press. In spite of a multitude of lobbyists, a subsidized opposition press, and the threats and promises of the railroads, the reformers won their new law by a narrow margin. Daniels proclaimed it "the most brilliant victory in the history of legislation in North Carolina." [35] Some of the carriers complied promptly with the law, but a group headed by the Southern Railway quickly obtained an injunction. The reformers were outraged. Daniels called on state officials to

[32] William H. Glasson, "The Crusade Against the Railroads," in *South Atlantic Quarterly*, VI (1907), 174.

[33] *Ibid.*, 165–69.

[34] Parsons, *Railways, the Trusts, and the People*, 246; Daniel A. Tompkins, "The Real Grievances Against the Railroads," in *South Atlantic Quarterly*, VI (1907), 317–22.

[35] Daniels, *Editor in Politics*, 502.

indict the railroads and ignore the Federal judge, and the speaker of the house of the state legislature declared that state officials would have to "choose between obeying Federal decisions and their oaths to enforce the state laws." [86] Governor Robert B. Glenn, though a former employee of the Southern Railway, was prepared to enforce the law if it took "every dollar in the treasury and put arms in the hands of every available man in the state." Shades of Calhoun and nullification were invoked when a North Carolina superior-court judge then defied the Federal-court injunction, indicted and imprisoned a railroad agent for violating the state law, and fined the Southern Railway $30,000. The president of the Southern and other railroad officials were also arrested. According to a contemporary review of the proceedings, "never before has so sharp a conflict between the State and the United States Courts been presented." [87] Fortunately, Roosevelt was denied the opportunity of playing Jackson to Daniels' Calhoun, for the Southern capitulated to state authority, and differences were adjusted by compromise.

The Southern, the Seaboard, and the Atlantic Coast Line came to adopt a more conciliatory policy toward state commissions and legislatures—an example that came to be generally followed by railroads. But not by the Louisville and Nashville, not while President Milton Hannibal Smith had breath in his body and "legislative agents" on his payroll. A stocky figure with a pointed beard and an unconcealed contempt for "demagogues" and "blatherskites," Smith charged head on through the age of reform bearing the banner of *laissez faire*. At one and the same time his railroad was defying regulations and orders of the four sovereign states of Kentucky, Florida, Tennessee, and Alabama.[88] In Governor Comer of Alabama, a man of his own class who had gone over to the reformers, Smith met something like his match, and in that state the battle was fought to a finish.

Comer's position was that high freight rates were thwarting the development of manufactures in cotton, lumber, iron, and steel, and keeping the state on a raw-material economy.[89] The new re-

[86] *Ibid.*, 505.

[87] Robert W. Winston, "The Passenger Rate War in North Carolina," in *South Atlantic Quarterly*, VI (1907), 346.

[88] Ferguson, *Regulation of Railroads in the South*, 120–24, 136–38, 145–46, 161–62.

[89] Governor's message, Alabama *Senate Journal*, Extra Sess., 1907, p. 23.

form legislature of 1907, elected on Comer's platform, rapidly enacted his program, greatly expanding the authority of the railroad commission, reducing rates, and prohibiting passes to public officials, lobbying, and various unfair practices. Passenger rates were reduced and maximum freight rates were fixed on 110 commodities.

Milton Smith descended upon Montgomery with an army of retainers and lobbyists and took the field in person, touring the state denouncing the Governor as a "highwayman" and his legislation as "populistic." He later admitted that he directed the expenditure of $34,800 in one campaign against Comer, that he subsidized a newspaper to the extent of $15,000, and that these were not his only political expenditures in Alabama.[40] The very thought of Comer enraged the railroad president: "An impossible man," he declared. "A disordered mind. He will not be placated." [41] The Governor replied in an address to the legislature that Smith "admitted that his road has dominated the policies and politics of Alabama for years," and charged that his corporation had "done more to debauch the State of Alabama than any other interest in the State." [42]

The railroads applied to the Federal district court in Montgomery for an injunction against enforcement of certain of the new acts. This court was presided over by Judge Thomas G. Jones, inveterate foe of the Populists in the nineties, moderate champion of the Negro in the convention of 1901, and now Federal judge by grace of the support of Booker Washington.[43] The reformers had not forgotten Jones's long service as attorney for the Louisville and Nashville, and perhaps with that in mind enacted their "Outlaw Bill," a measure revoking the license of any foreign corporation that instituted in the Federal court a suit that had started in a state court. Jones not only declared this act unconstitutional but on the same ground enjoined the enforcement of all but one of the acts complained of, and for good measure declared the rate-making power of the railroad commission unconstitutional. Off the bench,

40 *Railway Age,* LXIV (1918), 446; also Milton H. Smith to Braxton B. Comer, November 7, 1907, in Birmingham *Age-Herald,* November 9, 1907.

41 *Senate Documents,* 64 Cong., 1 Sess., No. 461, p. 362.

42 Alabama *Senate Journal,* Extra Sess., 1907, p. 23.

43 Birmingham *Age-Herald,* October 8, 1901.

he said that Comer was inciting the people to riot and sedition and that in all probability he was slightly mad.[44]

After a conference with Governor Smith of Georgia and Governor Glenn of North Carolina, both of whom had succeeded in bringing the railroads to terms, Comer appeared before a special session of the legislature with what he believed a means of evading Judge Jones. The assembly enacted an "injunction-proof" bill, so called because in order to be effective against it an injunction would have to extend to every citizen of the state—a manifest absurdity, so it was thought. But that was precisely the kind of injunction Judge Jones granted, upon the application of the Louisville and Nashville, thereby nullifying the work of the special session completely.[45] The battle continued, and after governor and judge were both retired from office, Milton Smith was still defying the law of Alabama. He did not give up the struggle until 1913. The capitulation of this fortress of *laissez faire* might almost mark the end of an era.

The railroads were only one of several strongholds of economic privilege attacked by the Southern reformers. The high rates and overcharge of the great insurance companies, nearly all of which were located in the Northeast, were a subject of resentment and agitation. Insurance was identified as one of the pipelines which siphoned off to another region capital and savings needed at home. Of the many insurance reforms of the period, those originating in Florida and Texas were the most interesting. Governor Broward estimated that the excess of premiums paid out over the amount received in return "would equal a ten mill tax on the present assessed valuation of Florida," and that losses paid in twelve years had only been about 30 per cent of the gross receipts of companies doing business in the state. He therefore proposed that the state go into the life-insurance business itself and issue state policies.[46] Broward's plan was not carried through, but a more indirect attack on the problem succeeded in Texas in the form of the Robertson Law of 1907. This law required every life-insurance company doing busi-

[44] On the whole controversy, see Allen J. Going, "The Governorship of B. B. Comer" (M.A. thesis, University of Alabama, 1940), 34–40.

[45] Birmingham *Age-Herald,* November 28–29, 1907.

[46] Florida *House Journal,* 1905, pp. 41–43.

ness in Texas, no matter what its home state, to invest in Texas securities and real estate at least 75 per cent of the legal reserve required by the laws of the state of its domicile and to keep these investments.[47]

The big oil companies and their subsidiaries bore the brunt of much antimonopolistic sentiment in the Southwest. From the time Governor Hogg sought the arrest of Rockefeller and Flagler as fugitives from Texas justice in 1895, the state was intermittently embroiled in antitrust proceedings against a succession of oil companies. The most famous of these cases was that against the Waters-Pierce Company, which was compelled to forfeit its charter in 1900. Within the same year the company was supposedly purged of its Standard Oil connections, reorganized, and, with the assistance of Senator Joseph W. Bailey, whose political fortunes were thereby involved with the company, again licensed to do business in the state. Five years later it developed that the Standard Oil Company had retained control over Waters-Pierce all along. The state again brought suit against the company and in 1909 collected $1,808,483 in penalties and dissolved the company.[48] In the meantime, Standard Oil was doing business in Texas through several other affiliates, and in 1907 the state filed suit against eleven such concerns, demanding a total of $75,900,000 in fines. Four of the companies were enjoined from doing business in the state as a result of the suit, and $201,650 in fines was collected.[49]

If the antitrust laws on the statute books of the states were any indication, the monster of monopoly would have been slain forever in the South.[50] The statutes of North Carolina, for example, forbade virtually all of the practices by which the tobacco trust built up and maintained its monopoly. Yet the American Tobacco

47 *Revised Civil Statutes of the State of Texas, . . . 1911* (Austin, 1912), Arts. 4775–86, pp. 976–81.

48 Waters-Pierce Oil Company, Appellant, *v.* State of Texas, Appellee, In the Court of Civil Appeals, Third Supreme Judicial District of Texas, *Transcript of the Record* (Austin, 1909), *passim;* also Galveston *Daily News,* April 25, 1909.

49 Ralph W. Steen, *Twentieth Century Texas, An Economic and Social History* (Austin, 1942), 107.

50 Compare, for example, William F. Kirby (comp.), *A Digest of the Statutes of Arkansas . . . 1903* (Austin, Tex., 1904), Secs. 1976–82, pp. 555–83; *North Carolina Statutes, Revisal of 1908* (Charleston, S.C., 1908), Art. 3028, pp. 1628–29; *Revised Civil Statutes of the State of Texas, . . . 1911,* Arts. 7796–7818, pp. 1691–98.

Company continued to thrive without embarrassment in that state. It remained for Jeff Davis of Arkansas to press the antitrust crusade to its logical and preposterous conclusion. As attorney general he filed 126 suits against fire-insurance companies, and while he was in the mood he brought action against express companies, tobacco companies, oil companies, and cotton-oil companies. The metropolitan press of the East was indignant. Representatives of the leading insurance companies of the United States and Great Britain resolved to boycott Arkansas and immediately began canceling policies and withdrawing from the state. Representatives of the budding business community of the state met in convention and desperately implored relief.[51] But Jeff was adamant.[52] When the courts ruled against his construction of the law, he took the issue to the people and was elected governor. He made the trust "the paramount issue" in three campaigns, but nothing very practical came of his efforts.[53]

The only effective fight made on the trust was extralegal, not to say illegal, and it was inspired by zeal for no theory but by desperate economic pressure. It started in the Kentucky and Tennessee "Black Patch" among the dark-leaf tobacco farmers as a protest against the market monopoly of the American Tobacco Company, which had driven the price of tobacco down below the cost of production and threatened the farmers with ruin. Organized at Guthrie, Kentucky, in September, 1904, the Planters' Protective Association took in all classes of farmers from planters to share-

[51] Little Rock *Arkansas Gazette,* April 11–13, 1899; Jacobson, *Life Story of Jeff Davis,* 43–49.

[52] The "poet laureate" of the legislature replied to petitioners in verse, in Little Rock *Arkansas Gazette,* April 13, 1899:

> The business men, on Wednesday next,
>   Will meet at Glenwood Park,
> To see what lies within their power
>   To make us toe the mark.
>
> But I can inform them now
>   That we came here by nature,
> And they can't control a single man
>   Of the Arkansas Legislature.

[53] Governor's message, in Arkansas *Senate Journal,* 1905, p. 15; Jacobson, *Life Story of Jeff Davis,* 49, 71–72.

croppers. At its peak it was estimated to have 30,000 members in western Kentucky and Tennessee and 8,000 in Virginia. A similar association was organized in Henderson, Owensboro, and Bowling Green, Kentucky, which reached a total of about 20,000 members, and another of Burley-tobacco growers in Central Kentucky attained a membership of approximately 35,000.[54] Finding no satisfactory relief in the peaceful methods originally adopted, and obtaining no help from the heirs to Goebel's reform movement, the farmers in 1906–1908 took the law in their own hands. Masked bands of night riders dynamited factories, burned down scores of warehouses, and destroyed hundreds of thousands of dollars worth of property belonging to the tobacco trust and its friends. In order to compel co-operation, the night riders scraped plant beds, laid waste to crops and farms, brutally whipped, beat, and sometimes murdered men and women, intimidated courts, and terrorized whole towns and counties. Frankly revolutionary in method, the night riders justified their lawlessness by invoking the spirit of the Boston Tea Party. Before violence was curbed by military force in 1908, the movement spilled over into the cotton states of Arkansas, Mississippi, Alabama, and Louisiana and threatened to awaken such a spirit of lawlessness as had not existed since the time of the Ku Klux. The farmers secured higher prices, but their victory was bought at an appalling cost in property, suffering, life, and moral deterioration.[55]

In 1907, while the reform wave in the South was at its crest, the new state of Oklahoma entered the union. The latent radicalism in Oklahoma, long repressed under territorial government, was released with the sudden force of one of her gushers, a brash and precipitant flood that shocked Eastern conservatives and startled some who considered themselves reformers. To the editor of the *Outlook* the new state's constitution appeared to be "undoubtedly the most radical organic law ever adopted in the Union." President Roosevelt was quoted as saying his opinion of it was "not fit for publication," and Secretary Taft censured the constitution

[54] James O. Nall, *The Tobacco Night Riders of Kentucky and Tennessee, 1905–1909* (Louisville, 1939), 121, 131, 135.

[55] John G. Miller, *The Black Patch War* (Chapel Hill, 1936), 18–23, 42, 47, 86; Nall, *Tobacco Night Riders*, 104–19.

strongly. On the other hand, William Jennings Bryan, one of the advisers of the framers, called it "the best State Constitution ever written." [56] One of the influences strongly at work upon the constitutional convention consisted of organized farmers and workers. They drew up a list of twenty-four "demands" that were to be their criteria in voting for delegates to the convention, and pledged themselves to "support a brother farmer or laborer in preference to any other profession." [57] Thirty members of the Farmers' Union and several labor spokesmen were elected delegates, and virtually all of the twenty-four "demands" were written into the constitution. In a scholarly study of the document Charles A. Beard called it "a mosaic in which the glittering new designs of 'advanced democracy' appear side by side with patterns of ancient English make." Among the former were the Oregon system of initiative and referendum, the compulsory direct primary, a powerful corporation commission, home rule for municipalities, and a formidable array of provisions for the protection of labor, public health, and public welfare. Professor Beard discovered among the Oklahomans a deficiency in that "wholesome anxiety to protect and safeguard private property" which James Bryce viewed as typical of our state constitutions. But "in almost every article of the Oklahoma constitution" he found a "spirit of fierce opposition to monopolies" and a "jealousy of large business enterprises." [58] In fact, it required all of 7,000 words for the framers to list their restrictions and limitations upon corporations, railroads, and public utilities, and for good measure they added protection of "the right of the state to engage in any occupation or business for public purposes," agriculture excepted. Without any doubt the Southern reformers could count Oklahoma in their column.

In municipal reform progressives held up two innovations as the cures for the "shame of the cities." These were the commission plan and the city-manager plan of municipal government. Both of them originated in the South. The first city in the country to adopt the

[56] "Oklahoma's Radical Constitution," in *Outlook*, LXXXVII (1907), 229–30; Guthrie *Oklahoma State Capital*, September 5, 1907.

[57] Albert H. Ellis, *A History of the Constitutional Convention of the State of Oklahoma* (Muskogee, Okla., 1923), 45–58.

[58] Charles A. Beard, "The Constitution of Oklahoma," in *Political Science Quarterly*, XXIV (1909), 95–104.

commission plan was Galveston, Texas. The devastating hurricane and tidal wave of September, 1900, not only swept away a large part of the city but the antiquated city-council form of government as well. In the crisis of reconstruction and relief that followed, the city commission proved its efficiency by rebuilding the city, restoring its credit, and constructing a mighty sea wall. Houston followed the example of her neighbor in 1903, and by 1907 Dallas, Denison, Fort Worth, El Paso, Greenville, and Sherman had adopted the commission plan. The movement spread eastward and was taken up by Memphis, New Orleans, Jackson, Birmingham, and Charlotte. By 1913 most of the larger cities in the South and many of the smaller ones were using the new type of government. Des Moines, Iowa, adopted it in 1907 and from there it spread over the North and West under the name of the "Des Moines Idea." [59] Likewise, the city-manager plan was first tried by Staunton, Virginia, in 1908, then by Sumter, South Carolina, in 1911, but it spread over the rest of the country under the name of the "Dayton Idea" after that city adopted it in 1914.[60]

Partly by chance the prohibition crusade made juncture with the progressive movement in the South, and the two forces marched together for a time. Occasionally they quarreled, but common enemies more often drew them together, and they fought many of their battles in close alliance.

Until 1907 no state-wide prohibition law existed in the South; only three survived in the country, and none had been passed since 1889. Then in August, 1907, Georgia passed a drastic statewide law that touched off the third national prohibition wave, the first since the eighties. In rapid succession within the next nine months Oklahoma, Alabama, Mississippi, and North Carolina followed Georgia's example, and Tennessee joined them in January, 1909. Four of the six states acted through their legislatures, two by popular vote. Florida and Texas came within a handful of popular votes of adopting prohibition, and the remaining states crowded the saloons into the cities and diminishing pockets of territory.[61]

59 John J. Hamilton, *The Dethronement of the City Boss* (New York, 1910), 17–25.

60 Leonard D. White, *The City Manager* (Chicago, 1927), 125–28.

61 For a time it appeared that the Southern plan would be the state or local dispensary system, first introduced into the country by Georgia in 1891, and adopted more widely by South Carolina and on a limited basis by three other states. The plan

The suddenness with which the prohibitionists appeared to seize whole states was deceptive. For years they had besieged the demon rum in county campaigns by the local-option method. In Georgia 125 of the 145 counties were already dry before state-wide prohibition was adopted, and in Alabama, 90 per cent of the state. In Mississippi 69 of the 76 counties, and in North Carolina 62 of the 97 counties had banished the saloon before the states took action.

Even in Kentucky the cause of good bourbon whisky had been lost in 94 of the 119 counties by 1908. One computation at the beginning of 1907, before the prohibition "wave" was heard of, found 825 of the 994 counties in the ex-Confederate states under prohibition laws.[62]

The remarkable success of the movement in the South was often attributed to the presence of the Negro, but a close study of the region concludes that "the negro has been an inconsiderable factor" and that "the saloon has been abolished and retained in the communities of the South without apparent reference to the presence of the negro." [63] There was, however, a pronounced correlation between the success of prohibition and a high percentage of native-born, rural, Protestant elements in the population. In Georgia, Alabama, Mississippi, North Carolina, and Tennessee, which were among the strongest and earliest prohibition states, the native-born constituted 99 per cent or more of the population, the rural element ranged from 88 to 79 per cent, and Protestants comprised from 99 to 92 per cent of the church population.[64] More specifically, it was the nine tenths of the Protestants included in the Baptist and Methodist folds who filled the dry ranks, for their ministers carried the crusade into their pulpits and preached not temperance but teetotalism. Hand in hand with the Anti-Saloon League and the temperance organizations, the parsons gradually perfected their methods in local campaigns. They tapped the sources of reformism

---

was discredited by administrative scandals in South Carolina, and it never satisfied the genuine prohibitionists.

62 John E. White, "Prohibition: The New Task and Opportunity of the South," in *South Atlantic Quarterly*, VII (1908), 133; Frank Foxcroft, "Prohibition in the South," in *Atlantic Monthly*, CI (1908), 627–31; D. Leigh Colvin, *Prohibition in the United States* (New York, 1926), 333–34, 344.

63 Blakey, *Sale of Liquor in the South*, 32.

64 Peter H. Odegard, *Pressure Politics* (New York, 1928), 32.

that sustained the contemporary education and child-labor crusades, but they also used revival tactics and stormed polls with mobs of singing and praying women and children. Their success earned for the South the name of being "the mainspring" and "the propagandic base of the national agitation." The region was "well-nigh puritanized" by the White Ribboners.[65]

Even though prohibition was primarily a countryman's cause, it won converts among the urban progressive leaders. Reform governors Glenn of North Carolina, Comer of Alabama, and Smith of Georgia took up the cause, and their reform legislatures enacted state prohibition. The farmer-labor coalition that wrote the most advanced shibboleths of progressivism into the Oklahoma constitution also wrote in prohibition. It was a simple matter to lump the rum demon with the railroad monster as enemies of the people. An identification of prohibition with progressivism was furthered by a tendency of the bosses and machines to join with the liquor interests and fight prohibition. This was not invariably true, for in Virginia, Boss Thomas S. Martin and his machine worked harmoniously with the Anti-Saloon League and its Methodist leader, James Cannon, against the progressives. Where the prohibitionists did infiltrate the progressive ranks they tended to subordinate all other reforms to a single-minded and sometimes reckless drive toward their goal. Governor Comer, after his limited railroad reforms were achieved, proclaimed the saloon to be the only remaining enemy worthy of his steel. Child-labor reformers could get no support for their bill from the millowning governor nor divert any attention of the electorate from the emotional prohibition crusade. Comer and prohibition both went down to defeat in the election of 1910, and the progressives were driven from office in Alabama by conservatives.[66] The prohibition issue completely disrupted the Democratic party in Tennessee and returned the Republicans to power. Malcolm R. Patterson, conservative, antiprohibitionist machine candidate, defeated Edward R. Carmack, prohibitionist candidate for governor, in a violently fought Democratic primary

[65] William Garrott Brown, "The South and the Saloon," in *Century Magazine*, LXXVI (1908), 463, 465; White, "Prohibition: The New Task," *loc. cit.*, 133.

[66] James B. Sellers, *The Prohibition Movement in Alabama, 1702–1943* (Chapel Hill, 1943), 129–48; Davidson, *Child Labor Legislation in the Southern Textile States*, 224–26.

in 1908. In November of that year two close friends of Governor Patterson shot and killed Carmack in the streets of Nashville, and the Governor pardoned one of them. In the name of their martyred leader, the prohibition Democrats passed their bill over the Governor's veto. When the machine threatened to renominate Patterson on an antiprohibition platform in 1910, the prohibitionists bolted their party, organized the Independent Democrats, and endorsed Ben W. Hooper, the dry candidate of the Republican party. Hooper became the first Republican governor of Tennessee in thirty years.[67]

The ephemeral victories of the White Ribboners over the saloons, like those of the shippers over railroads, independent oilmen over pipelines, policyholders over insurance companies, and righteous amateurs over political bosses, constituted satisfactions of a tangible sort to a considerable class of Southerners. But there were other Southerners, many of them, who were relatively unmoved by these triumphs of the righteous and whose political urges were not fulfilled by progressivism. They had nothing to ship by classified freight rates, no oil wells to protect against pipelines, and no insurance policies to bother about. Perhaps they were also deficient in righteousness, for come Saturday night they wouldn't mind if they had a drink. But they did harbor deep and abiding grievances and powerful, if inarticulate, political urges. Those of them who had sought satisfaction in the independent rebellions and the Populist revolt came away frustrated and cheated. It is doubtful that many of them were later able to identify themselves completely with citified reformers like Comer the manufacturer, and Smith the publisher, nor with Glenn, Campbell, Goebel, and Broward. Jeff Davis they could claim as their very own, and Vardaman and Tillman could speak their idiom. But Tillman, harsh and ascetic as ever, drew away from them, and both he and Vardaman ascended unto Washington and left their flocks untended. In their absence, a new type of shepherd took charge of the fold.

By some obscure rule of succession, Bleases tended to follow Tillmans and Bilbos to succeed Vardamans. The new type of leader

67 George A. Gates, "Democratic Insurgency in Tennessee," in *Independent*, LXIX (1910), 866–68; Hamer (ed.), *Tennessee; A History*, II, 704–706.

could hardly be said to have had a program or a party. Instead, he had prejudices and a following. Abuse by the city press was grist to his mill, and the more he was badgered and set upon by respectable politicians, reforming parsons, and Northern liberals, the more readily and joyfully did a slandered, misunderstood, and frustrated following uphold his cause and identify themselves with the persecuted leader. The leader often flouted sober conventions, sometimes consorted with lewd company, and in numerous ways proclaimed himself one of the boys. Cole Blease, Jeff Davis, and Tom Watson were periodically embroiled with parsons, missionaries, and prohibitionists. But they oftener tilted with foes more vulnerable and farther afield.

In one instance the transition from the old to the new type of leadership was accomplished by a single individual, though at tragic cost to his integrity and mental health. Tom Watson, who in his Populist days had stepped forth alone like a young David to battle the Goliath of his people's foe, spent his latter days rallying villainous mobs to bait and hound minorities. Turning against the progressive Hoke Smith, whom he had helped to elect, he defeated him in 1908 by combining with the reactionary Joseph M. Brown. Meanwhile, he diverted his following with a seven-year crusade against the Pope, forays upon the Socialists, and tirades against his onetime allies of the Negro race that were matchless in their malevolence. For two years he poured forth a flood of obscene and incendiary slander against the Jewish defenders of Leo Frank, who was eventually lynched and brutally mutilated by a mob that drove the Governor from the state. By such devices he recouped his lost political power and for sixteen years virtually bossed the Democratic party of Georgia while acknowledging no loyalty to it.

As an understudy of Tillman, Cole L. Blease imitated the master but improved his technique and expanded his appeal. For Blease embraced within his fold the people the master had described as "the damned factory class," and with them the large depressed rural element that had been entranced by the violence of Tillman's language but disappointed by the mildness of his performance. Agricultural colleges were very nice, but these people, when they were so much as literate, rarely aspired to more than grade school. Not that Blease gave them anything more tangible than Tillman, but he was more lavish with the intangibles—which were better than nothing. In vain his opponents pointed out that Blease had knifed labor bills, opposed child-labor laws, and repeatedly betrayed the classes he professed to love.[68] Those classes cherished him for voicing their bitter hatreds and frustrations and for his unabashed defiance of the self-righteous and respectable. They loved him when he humiliated the old state by praising lynchers before the Governors' Conference of 1912 and threatening to "wipe the inferior race from the face of the earth." [69] After two Blease administrations, Tillman had more than he could stand. "It makes me sad and angry," he said in a premature "farewell address" in 1914, "to be told that Tillmanism is the direct cause of Bleaseism," though he admitted that "there is just enough likeness to deceive the ignorant." To defeat Blease and save his own failing political fortunes, Tillman joined hands with his old conservative enemies, the very people he had taught the Bleaseites (and onetime Tillmanites) to hate. Blease's rise was temporarily scotched, but the future of Calhoun's onetime Greek Democracy lay in Cole Blease's hand as surely as it had once lain in Tillman's.[70]

The relationship between Vardaman and his heir apparent Theodore G. Bilbo was much the same as that between Tillman and Blease. Perhaps the difference between master and understudy was not so great, and Vardaman could never be persuaded to renounce his successor. But even Vardaman's enemies, whom Bilbo inherited along with his following, admitted that the Great White Chief had mixed a modicum of idealism with his demagoguery. On the other hand, the majority of them would never admit that his heir ever rose above the level of an obscene clown. An extensive reading in the literature of billingsgate by which such offenders have been characterized leads to the conclusion that the invective employed to describe Bilbo set a new mark. In 1910 the Mississippi senate resolved by a vote of twenty-five to one that he was "unfit to sit with honest upright men in a respectable legisla-

[68] Columbia *State*, September 3, 5, 8, 15, 1910. For an autobiographical sketch, see Cole Blease's message, in *Reports and Resolutions of the General Assembly of the State of South Carolina, Regular Session Commencing January 12, 1915* (Columbia, 1915), III, 198–205.

[69] Richmond *Times-Dispatch*, December 6, 1912.

[70] Simkins, *Pitchfork Ben Tillman*, 485–503.

tive body" and called upon him to resign. But he thrived on abuse and was even then on the threshold of a long career.[71]

Progressivism had its day in the South as elsewhere, but it no more fulfilled the political aspirations and deeper needs of the mass of people than did the first New Deal administration. Otherwise, there is no explaining the rise of the Bleases in the earlier instance —nor of Huey Long in the latter.

71 Albert D. Kirwan, "A History of Mississippi Politics, 1876–1925" (Ph.D. dissertation, Duke University, 1947), 380, 398–99, 404, 339–42, 460.

CHAPTER XV

PHILANTHROPY AND THE FORGOTTEN MAN

"HUMAN society needs constructive management," observed Walter Hines Page and made a memorandum lest it slip his mind. This led the busy editor to another observation: "One of the best examples of organization in our time was done by John D. Rockefeller when he organized the Standard Oil Company. . . . Talks on the reconstruction of society with him might yield ideas. Worth trying, if I get time." [1]

The baffling social problems of the South, which had frustrated Radical Reconstruction missionaries in the seventies, Redeemers of the New-South school in the eighties, and Populists in the nineties, became in the first decade of the new century the main laboratory for sociological experiments of organized Northern philanthropy and its Southern agents. Philanthropic funds and investment capital, sometimes from the same sources, penetrated the South simultaneously. In the spring of 1901 Robert C. Ogden took southward his first special train loaded with philanthropists—an annual event of the ensuing decade. A New York paper printed the story under the headline "MEN OF MILLIONS TO REDEEM THE SOUTH." [2] And the old region prepared for redemption in a new form and a new set of redeemers.

The new redemption had its Southern wing of redeemers. They were not men of millions, and for the most part they kept their skirts clear of politics. They were middle-class, professional people—schoolmen, churchmen, editors—inspired with humanitarian zeal and a passion for uplift. Among the leaders were churchmen

1 Hendrick, *Earlier Life and Letters of Walter H. Page,* 380.

2 New York *World,* April 28, 1901, quoted in Allan Nevins, *John D. Rockefeller; The Heroic Age of American Enterprise* (New York, 1940), II, 483.

like the young Arkansan Edgar Gardner Murphy, the North Carolinian Alexander J. McKelway, and the old crusader J. L. M. Curry, of Alabama and Virginia. There were college presidents like Charles W. Dabney of Tennessee, Edwin A. Alderman of North Carolina and Virginia, Charles D. McIver of North Carolina, and David F. Houston of Texas. They included expatriate Southerners like Page and George Foster Peabody, transplanted Yankees like Seaman A. Knapp, and Negroes of Booker T. Washington's turn of mind. Estimable gentlemen with high collars and fine principles, they were very much in earnest, but the changes they envisioned included no basic alteration of social, racial, and economic arrangements. Over such matters there was no contretemps between them and the men of millions with whom they collaborated.

The philosophy of redemption by philanthropy was formulated as well as anywhere in Walter Hines Page's "The Forgotten Man" and other addresses. "Since both the politician and the preacher have failed to lift this life after a century of unobstructed opportunities," said Page in 1897, "it is time for a wiser statesmanship and a more certain means of grace." [3] Education, uplift, philanthropy, and up-to-dateness were Page's "more certain means of grace." He would furnish the "wiser statesmanship" in his spare time. To him old Southern communities seemed filled with "contemporary ancestors," whom he and his up-to-date friends were bound to modernize. Once the job was done, the old towns would seem "very like hundreds of towns in the Middle West," he promised. "What an interesting field for sociological experiment!" he exclaimed. He would grasp the sorry scheme of things entire! He would "rebuild old commonwealths!"

"Well," wrote Page to Wallace Buttrick, the plump and benign secretary of Rockefeller philanthropies, "Well, the world lies before us. It'll not be the same world when we get done with it that it was before: bet your last penny on that will you!" [4]

There was, in truth, enough to keep trainloads of philanthropists and battalions of uplifters busy in the South. Antiquated social institutions protruded like primeval rock from smooth pavement to obstruct the traffic of progress. The date on the cornerstone of the

[3] Walter Hines Page, *The Rebuilding of Old Commonwealths* (New York, 1902), 26.
[4] Page to Wallace Buttrick, February 10, 1907, in Page Papers.

Virginia penitentiary was 1797. "Mr. Jefferson gave considerable study to the details," observed a Richmond editor, who regretted that the feet of inmates tended to stick out the windows. Conditions in the new factories and industrial slums recalled those of England in Dickens' boyhood. Southern labor toiled for the most part in the preunion stage of its development, and Southern farmers still followed the furrows and practices of remote ancestors. The prevalent reactionism in race policy returned that question approximately to the era of the Black Codes. All the talk of public education had yet to produce anything approaching adequate schools. One could assume that every other Negro and one of five white men he met could not read and write. It was natural that the first and most abiding concern of the philanthropists should be the schools.

The labors of such crusaders for public education as Curry, McIver, and Alderman, and the campaigns of the Farmers' Alliance had produced small results by 1900. Nor had the Peabody and Slater funds, small in comparison with philanthropic foundations of the twentieth century, succeeded materially in priming the pump of state and local taxes. The public schools of the South at the opening of the new century were for the most part miserably supported, poorly attended, wretchedly taught, and wholly inadequate for the education of the people. Far behind the rest of the country in nearly all respects, Southern education suffered from a greater lag than any other public institution in the region.

In 1900–1901 Alabama school funds averaged only $3.10 for each child attending school. This was less than one tenth the amount spent upon the average school child the same year in the North Atlantic states. In North Carolina the expenditure per child was $4.56; in South Carolina, $4.62; and in no Southern state was the amount spent half as much as the national average of $21.14 per student. The reformer's protest against "five cents worth of education per child" was supported by official statistics that showed a range from four cents a day per child in Alabama to ten cents, in Texas. The amount of school funds raised per capita of the whole population in the South was little more than a third of the national average and one fourth of the average in the North Atlantic States.[5]

[5] *Report of the Commissioner of Education for the Year 1900–1901* (Washington, 1902), I, lxxxix–xciii; *ibid., 1914* (Washington, 1915), II, 18.

On the top of the sectional differential was a large racial differential, for while the amount provided for the average white child in the former slave states was $4.92, the average Negro child had only $2.21 spent on his education.[6]

The sectional differential between abilities to pay, however, was even more marked than the difference between the amounts raised for education. The special difficulties which beset the South placed her educational problem in a unique category. In the first place the greater proportion of children to adults in the South made her burden heavier. In New York there were 125 adult males to every 100 children of school age; in Massachusetts, 135; and in Connecticut, 134; but there were only 66 in North Carolina and Mississippi and 61 in South Carolina. The average adult in the Southern states had about twice as many children to educate as the adults of the Northern states. Moreover, there was much less money with which to do it. The amount of taxable wealth per child of school age in Massachusetts was $6,407 as compared with $1,301 per child in North Carolina. This meant a tax more than five times as great in the Southern as in the Northern state in order to provide equal school funds. Even that would not produce equality of schooling, since the South had the extra expense of two separate school systems for the two races, with two corps of teachers and two sets of physical equipment. In addition to these burdens, there was the great Southern problem of sparsity of settlement, for approximately 80 per cent of the population was rural.[7]

Inadequate as the schools were, less than half of the children of school age were regularly attending them. By 1900 all states outside the South, except two, had adopted some kind of compulsory school-attendance law, while Kentucky was the only one of the Southern states with such a law.[8] The percentage of white children of school age in daily attendance in Southern states ranged from 37 in Virginia to 56 in Texas, with only three states having more than 50 per cent. Attendance among Negro children ranged from 23 per cent in Texas to 46 per cent in Tennessee, and in no state

[6] *Report of the Commissioner of Education . . . 1900–1901*, I, cii.

[7] *Report of the Commissioner of Education for the Year 1903* (Washington, 1905), I, lxxviii; Charles L. Coon, *Facts About Southern Educational Progress . . .* (Durham, 1905), 67–70; G. S. Dickerman, *The South Compared with the North in Educational Requirements* (New Haven, 1901), 15–16.

[8] *Report of the Commissioner of Education for . . . 1913* (Washington, 1914), II, 21.

were so many as half of them regularly in school. The length of the school term in the South in 1900–1901 was not 100 days a year, and in the rural districts it was much less than that.[9] Charles W. Dabney in 1901 summarized conditions forcefully. "In the Southern states," he said, "in schoolhouses costing an average of $276 each, under teachers receiving the average salary of $25 a month, we are giving the children in actual attendance 5 cents' worth of education a day for eighty-seven days only in the year." His conclusion was that such means would "never educate the people." [10]

Judging by almost any measurable result of the educational system in 1900, Dabney was right. There were 1,198,774 illiterate native-white and 2,637,774 colored people ten years of age and over in the Southern states in 1900. The proportion of native-white illiterates in the South was approximately 12 per cent, as compared with 1.6 per cent in the North Atlantic states and 4.6 per cent in the United States. North Carolina led with 19.5 per cent, Louisiana followed with 17.3, then Alabama with 14.8, and Tennessee with 14.2. Negro illiteracy stood at approximately 50 per cent, having decreased from about 75 per cent since 1880.[11] Between the elementary schools and the colleges and universities was a gap virtually unbridged by the public schools. Outside of a few cities, the high schools were, according to Dabney, "nothing more than an addition of a few miscellaneous courses to the common school." The students who qualified for college work were prepared largely in the numerous private schools and academies—the existence of which was, incidentally, a factor in delaying the establishment of public schools.[12]

The great educational awakening in the South did not come until the dawn of the twentieth century. If any one state was more prominent than another in fostering the origins it was probably North Carolina, the home state of some of the foremost leaders in

[9] Coon, *Facts About Southern Educational Progress,* 17; *Report of the Commissioner of Education . . . 1900–1901,* I, lxxxii. The school attendance figures are for the year 1902–1903.

[10] *Proceedings of the* [Sixth] *Conference for Education in the South . . . 1903* (New York, 1903), 42.

[11] *Twelfth Census, 1900, Population,* II, ciii–cv.

[12] Dabney, *Universal Education in the South,* II, 408–12.

the South—Page, Alderman, McIver, and Aycock. Starting from further behind than almost any other state, North Carolina began her movement earlier, and by the time the regional crusade was under way her leaders were in a commanding position. From other states came Charles W. Dabney, president of the University of Tennessee, and Edgar Gardner Murphy, who took up the cause in Alabama. The aged pioneer J. L. M. Curry, who had campaigned for education since 1865, lived until 1903, long enough to see the new movement launched and give it his blessing.

The zeal that animated the education crusade was that mixture of paternalism and *noblesse oblige* which is the nearest Southern equivalent of Northern humanitarianism. The spirit was the most authentic heritage the dominant middle class got from the old ruling class. It was alike implicit in the doctrine of Curry and in Page's address of 1897, "The Forgotten Man," which Dabney called "the gospel of the campaign that followed." [13] For Murphy the gospel was "that real spirit of *noblesse oblige* which has so largely dominated the development of Southern life." [14] Page spoke of redeeming the "illiterate, neglected, forgotten" white man, but he and his associates included the Negro among the disinherited.

The successful launching of the campaign was the result of the combined efforts of Southerners of this class and organized Northern philanthropy. The man chiefly responsible for bringing the two groups together was Robert Curtis Ogden, wealthy merchant capitalist and churchman of New York City, who preached a gospel of "business idealism" to his own class in the North. A lifelong friend of General Samuel C. Armstrong and for forty-five years a trustee of the Hampton Institute, Ogden was familiar with the Armstrong-Washington philosophy and acquainted with the more conservative white leaders of education.[15]

[13] *Ibid.*, 238.

[14] Edgar Gardner Murphy, *Problems of the Present South* (New York, 1904), 7.

[15] Robert C. Ogden, "Business Idealism," in *Business World* (New York), XXV (1905), 277–81. John S. Bassett wrote of Ogden: "Intellectually he measures up to the Sunday School type. . . . He is a philosopher of sunny faces and well-filled bellies. Everyone must like him, but he is no Moses for a great people." Bassett to William E. Dodd, May 7, 1907, in William E. Dodd Papers (Division of Manuscripts, Library of Congress).

The meeting place of Northern and Southern leaders was the Conference for Southern Education. This informal organization grew out of the annual gatherings, mainly of Christian ministers, at Capon Springs, West Virginia, which began in the summer of 1898. The annual sessions attracted little attention until the fourth conference, held at Winston-Salem in April, 1901. Delegates came from all over the South, and President Ogden brought in his private train a number of prominent Northerners, including John D. Rockefeller, Jr., and William H. Baldwin, Jr. The session was greeted by Governor Aycock, fresh from his victorious education (and white-supremacy) campaign. Dabney woke the delegates up with an uncompromisingly frank exposure of the deficiencies of the Southern schools, and they promptly began to organize a Southwide campaign. The Conference resolved to promote "a campaign of education for free schools for all the people," black as well as white.[16]

Ogden appointed the Southern Education Board as the executive committee of the Conference in 1901. It consisted largely of Southerners, though Ogden remained president until his death in 1913, the year before the Board was dissolved. At the outset the Board decided that none of its funds should go as assistance to schools and institutions, but that all should be applied "exclusively for the purpose of stimulating public sentiment in favor of more liberal provision for universal education in the public schools." It was strictly a propaganda and publicity organization. Among the objectives agreed upon were voluntary local taxation for better schools, compulsory education, longer school terms, consolidation of weak schools, and industrial and agricultural education.[17]

George Foster Peabody guaranteed funds of about $40,000 a year for the first two years, but from its inception the Board anticipated the donation of big money. It was known that John D. Rockefeller, Jr., after attending the Winston-Salem meeting in 1901, had

[16] *Proceedings of the Fourth Conference for Education in the South* (n.p., 1901), 12, and *passim.* The best brief account of the early years of the Conference is by Wyckliffe Rose, "The Educational Movement in the South," in *Report of the Commissioner of Education for . . . 1903,* I, 359–90.

[17] "A Brief Statement Concerning the Origin and Organization of the Southern Education Board," in Dabney, *Universal Education in the South,* II, Appendix V, 538–41.

interested his father in the new movement. The "General Education Board" was organized shortly after the Southern Education Board to hold and disburse funds for the benefit of education. In the hands of this Board, Rockefeller placed $53,000,000 in a series of large gifts made between 1902 and 1909. While other philanthropic work was contemplated, the donor indicated his "special interest" in the needs of Southern education.[18] The General Education Board was closely associated with the Southern Education Board, serving in effect as an interlocking directorate or holding company for vast philanthropic interests.[19]

With a fervor reminiscent of the cotton-mill crusade of the eighties, Southerners embraced the educational panacea and began the campaign in 1902 that eventually swept the region. The propagandists took pains to eradicate the suspicion that this was all a Yankee notion by proclaiming it to be the fulfillment of Jefferson's command to "Preach a crusade against ignorance." Dabney and his able assistant, Philander P. Claxton, started the propaganda mills of their Bureau of Investigation and Information at Knoxville on February 1, 1902. By the following year they were regularly mailing handouts to 1,700 newspapers in the South, besides turning from their presses thousands of bulletins, circulars, reports, and documents for use in the various state campaigns.[20] With a subsidy from the General Education Board, Dabney opened a

18 *The General Education Board; An Account of its Activities, 1902–1914* (New York, 1915), 12–17. See Appendix II, 216–23, for the correspondence between John D. Rockefeller, Jr., or his agent, and the General Education Board concerning the gifts from 1902 to 1909.

19 Thus, William H. Baldwin, Jr., was a member of the Southern Education Board and president of the General Education Board. George F. Peabody was treasurer of both, Curry was a member of both as well as the agent of the Peabody and Slater funds, while Ogden was president of the Southern board and the Southern Conference, a member of the General Board, and a member of the Hampton and Tuskegee boards of trustees, as were several other members of the General Education Board. The interlocking nature of the several boards of directors, of which these are only a few examples, indicates that the disposal of large funds was in the hands of relatively few people. Two additional funds were established in this period to promote Negro education in the South: the Jeanes Fund established by Anna T. Jeanes, who gave, among other donations, $200,000 to the General Education Board in 1905 and an endowment fund of $1,000,000 to a separate board in 1907. Caroline Phelps Stokes left part of an estate of $1,000,000 for Negro education in 1909.

20 Report of Charles W. Dabney, in *Proceedings of the* [Sixth] *Conference for Education in the South . . . 1903,* p. 45.

summer school for teachers in 1902 at the University of Tennessee, which was attended in the next five years by more than 11,000 students. "Its object," he wrote Page, was "to fill them with our gospel and make them missionaries for the cause." [21] Other subsidies were provided for the payment of rural school and school improvement work supervisors in eleven Southern states. Professors of education were subsidized in ten states.

The effective force of the educational crusade was exerted not by the boards and central agencies but from within the several states in campaigns planned and led by their own people. The state campaigns were conducted independently and were of varied origin and duration. The campaign in North Carolina began before 1902 and the campaigns of Tennessee and Virginia in 1903, Georgia in 1904, Alabama, South Carolina, and Mississippi in 1905, Louisiana in 1906, Kentucky and Arkansas in 1908, and Florida in 1909. In some states these were but the first of several annual or biennial campaigns that continued until, or after, 1913. The Southern Education Board contributed literature, advice, the assistance of its agents, and a small subsidy, ranging from about $20,700 in Virginia to $2,600 in Florida, to help support each state campaign.[22]

The campaign in North Carolina would probably have occurred without outside stimulation. Advising Page what to say in his Forgotten-Man speech, McIver said the state was "just going into a great educational campaign" at that time. Aycock was determined to redeem his pledges of 1898, and took personal command of the crusade. In the summer of 1902 an organized corps of speakers held more than 350 rallies in 78 of the 97 counties of the state. "Men of every profession and business volunteered their services, and in open-air meetings, in courthouses, in churches, in schoolhouses, wherever the people could assemble, they gathered." [23] Claxton advised the campaigners of Tennessee that "people have not yet

[21] Dabney to Page, February 8, 1902, in Page Papers; Andrew D. Holt, *The Struggle for a State System of Public Schools in Tennessee, 1903–1936,* in Teachers College, Columbia University *Contributions to Education,* No. 753 (New York, 1938), 180–82.

[22] *Southern Education Board: Activities and Results, 1904 to 1910* (Washington, 1911), 26. Expenditures on the campaigns were reported to be "from $30,000 to $40,000 a year" between 1902 and 1910.

[23] Charles D. McIver to Page, April 15, 1897, in Page Papers; Connor and Poe, *Life and Speeches of Charles Brantley Aycock,* 122; Edgar W. Knight, *Public School Education in North Carolina* (Boston, 1922), 335–36.

outgrown, certainly in Tennessee and the Southern states, appeals through the mouth and through the ear, the appeal of the great mass meeting." In that state the crusade was preached "from the pulpit, the bar, the stump; at picnics, barbecues, circuit and county courts, school commencements, country fairs, race tracks and even at a wedding ceremony." [24] Mass-meeting, revival tactics were found effective in the "whirlwind campaign" in Kentucky and the "May campaign" in Virginia. To an all-day meeting twenty-five miles from a railroad in a mountain county of Alabama "families of from three to twelve persons came in plain farm wagons with straw-covered beds, chairs from the fireside as seats, drawn by a yoke of oxen." The picture was repeated from Virginia to Texas—throngs of blue-denimed men and bonneted women sweating quietly through the periods of country orators or responding in true revival pattern.[25]

At the opening of the crusade a Virginia campaigner reported that it was "by no means uncommon to find men of intelligence and influence who are out and out opposed to free public education for all the people." [26] Following Aycock's example, campaigners met the opposition to Negro education with vigorous argument. In several other states strong movements to apportion educational funds between the races according to the proportion of taxes each paid—thus emasculating Negro schools—were defeated. The popular appeal of the mass campaigns brought the politicians into line, and the number of men who called themselves "educational governors" multiplied rapidly. Among them were James B. Frazier of Tennessee and Andrew J. Montague of Virginia, in addition to the reformers Aycock, Broward, Comer, and Hoke Smith. Some of them actually contributed effectively to the movement.

Southern educators and Northern philanthropic agents could (and often did) boast of impressive achievements for their campaigns. The total annual expenditures for public schools in the Southern states mounted from $21,372,543 in 1900 to $71,420,338

[24] Holt, *Struggle for a State System of Public Schools in Tennessee*, 209–10.

[25] Cornelius J. Heatwole, *A History of Education in Virginia* (New York, 1916), 315–16; Stephen B. Weeks, *History of Public School Education in Alabama*, United States Bureau of Education *Bulletin*, 1915, No. 12 (Washington, 1915).

[26] Robert Frazer, in *Proceedings of the Fifth Conference for Education in the South* (Knoxville, 1902), 35.

in 1913, while the amount per capita of the total population more than doubled. In the same period North Carolina's expenditures more than quadrupled, rising from $950,317 to $4,067,793, and Georgia's from $1,980,016 to $5,403,927.[27] Virginia was devoting approximately a half and Alabama more than a half of their net state revenues to education in 1914. The estimated value of public-school property in the South better than tripled in this period. North Carolina built an average of more than one new schoolhouse a day during the years 1902–1910. Teachers' salaries, school attendance, and the length of school terms all made corresponding advances as a result of the campaigns. Illiteracy among white children of school age was reduced to less than half of what it had been at the opening of the century. Illiteracy was also sharply reduced among Negroes, but they did not share equitably in the improved facilities. The school laws of Virginia, Kentucky, Tennessee, North Carolina, and other states were extensively revised, compulsory-attendance laws were adopted, and many antiquated provisions thrown out.[28] For all the improvements achieved by zeal and self-sacrifice and philanthropy, the public-education system of the South still remained far below the national average at the end of this period. The peculiar Southern combination of poverty, excessive numbers of children over adults, and duplication for two races proved in the end more of a problem than Southern resources, philanthropy, and good intentions could solve.

Had Page's imaginary Forgotten Man materialized in flesh and blood he would probably have been a wan figure clad in blue denim, clearly recognizable as a farmer—most likely, a tenant farmer. He was an entirely appropriate symbol. For there were two sides to the new picture of agricultural prosperity of the first decade of the twentieth century that replaced the old picture of the depressed nineties.

One side was the picture of soaring land values, rising crop prices, declining bankruptcies, and an easing of the tight-credit plight of the debtor. Between 1900 and 1910 the value of all farm property

[27] *Report of the Commissioner of Education . 1914*, II, 18–19.

[28] *Ibid.*, 8–21; *General Education Board . . . 1902–1914*, pp. 181–82; *Southern Education Board . . . 1904 to 1910, passim;* Dabney, *Universal Education in the South*, II, 510–11; Wharton, *Negro in Mississippi*, 249.

in the three Southern census divisions increased 110 per cent, the value of land, 131 per cent. While farm property of the South Atlantic states had climbed in value a meager 9 per cent in the nineties, the increase of the following decade was 103 per cent. The operating scale of some landlords in 1910 was indicated by a study of 226 plantations in the Black Belt, each with 50 or more tenants. Their average size was 4,216 acres and their average value, $114,000.[29] Mississippi, Alabama, and Georgia each contained more than 5,000,000 acres of land organized in plantations of five or more tenants. The percentage of farmer bankruptcies out of the total bankruptcies declined all over the South, especially in the central states, where the percentage in 1913 was less than a fifth of what it had been in 1899.[30] "The landlord, whether he have one hundred acres or two thousand, is contented and prosperous," reported a South Carolinian in 1911.[31]

But there was a contrasting side to the picture, for landowners were a minority of the farmers, and the prosperity was unequally distributed. The soaring land values that brought prosperity to the landowner at the same time made it more difficult than ever for the tenant to become a farm owner. The percentage of Southern farms operated by tenants increased in the prosperity decade as it had in every decade since the Civil War. The number of Southern states having a majority of their farms operated by tenants increased from four in 1900 to eight in 1910. The Cotton Belt contained half the tenant farmers in the country, and in no other large region were tenant farmers in a majority. Much of this increase was due to the transfer of hired labor to the status of sharecropper, actually a type of supervised labor for the plantation.[32]

A marginal farmer on the lowest rung of the economic ladder, the tenant farmer could well pose as the Forgotten Man. He shared little of the new prosperity and continued a relic of the depressed

29 *Thirteenth Census, 1910*, V, *Agriculture*, 42–44, 84, 884.

30 David L. Wickens, *Farmer Bankruptcies, 1898–1935*, United States Department of Agriculture, *Circular* No. 414 (Washington, 1936), 11.

31 William W. Ball, "The Industrial Revolution in South Carolina," in *Sewanee Review*, XIX (1911), 133–34, 137.

32 Lewis C. Gray *et al.*, "Farm Ownership and Tenancy," United States Department of Agriculture, *Agricultural Yearbook, 1923* (Washington, 1924), 513, 531–32; *Thirteenth Census, 1910*, V, *Agriculture*, 112–13; McKitrick, *Public Land System of Texas*, 144–46.

nineties in the new century. "He struggles on from year to year, being able to exist solely because of his deplorably low standard of life, using the least efficient stock and implements and the most antiquated methods of cultivation." [33] The wretched inefficiency of the system is revealed by figures showing that in 1906, when the annual productive power of each worker on the farms of Iowa equaled $1,088.11, the average amount per worker was $147.46 in South Carolina, $159.75 in North Carolina, and $150.98 in Alabama.[34] Unlike many of the landowners, who managed to escape the chains of the lien system by means of loans from the bank, the tenant merely traded masters, for the landowner now discounted his tenant's account with the merchant and shifted the 20 or 25 per cent difference to his own pocket.[35] It appeared to one writer in 1913 that the tenant system was "the most vital of the rural problems" of the South, "the foundation of all others." "The result of this tenant system is poor agriculture, exhausted soils, small crops, poor roads, decaying bridges, unpainted homes, and unkept yards." [36]

The philanthropists arrived at their interest in the plight of the Southern farmer indirectly. In the course of their campaign for public schools they came gradually to realize that the main obstacle in the South was not apathy but poverty. "The great bulk of the people of the Southern states was simply not earning enough to provide proper homes and to support good schools," concluded the General Education Board. "Whatever the other deficiencies, the prime need was money." [37] Neither philanthropy nor government could come near supplying that deficiency, so great was its extent. If it were to be supplied at all it would have to be done by the people themselves. This obviously meant greatly increasing the earnings of the average farmer. According to the hopeful analysis of the philanthropists and their agents this worthy objective was to be achieved by persuading the farmer to adopt new

[33] Brooks, *Agrarian Revolution in Georgia,* 61–62.

[34] Seaman A. Knapp, "An Agricultural Revolution," in *World's Work,* XII (1906), 7733.

[35] Enoch M. Banks, "Tendencies Among Georgia Farmers," in *South Atlantic Quarterly,* III (1904), 113–14.

[36] John L. Coulter, "The Rural Life Problem of the South," *ibid.,* XII (1913), 63.

[37] *General Education Board . . . 1902–1914,* p. 21.

and efficient methods of cultivation and thus increase his productivity.

For a generation the land-grant agricultural colleges had been at work in the South. Agricultural-experiment stations were set up in all the Southern states and scores of farmers' institutes and agricultural journals strove to spread enlightenment. Yet, according to an authority on agricultural education, less than 5 per cent of the farmers of some states of the South had been appreciably affected by these teachings, while "the great masses" of Southern farmers were "as wedded to their old systems as before these educational movements were inaugurated." [38]

After considering the plan of addressing itself to future farmers and teaching agriculture in the common schools, the General Education Board rejected the approach as impracticable. Instead the Board "deliberately decided to undertake the agricultural education not of the future farmer, but of the present farmer." [39] Secretary Buttrick searched almost a year for some means of accomplishing this huge task before he discovered Seaman A. Knapp.

A grizzled Victorian of seventy with white muttonchop whiskers, piercing eyes, and indomitable energy, Dr. Knapp already had behind him several distinguished careers. After many years as editor, teacher, and college president in Iowa, he had moved to Louisiana in 1885 to take charge of colonizing with Midwestern farmers holdings half the size of Connecticut that belonged to an English syndicate. On the side he developed the rice industry of the Southwest, preached agricultural innovations through the West and South, and carried out missions in the Orient and the West Indies for the Department of Agriculture. It was while employed part time by the department as special agent in the South that Knapp in 1903 developed his famous "demonstration" technique of agricultural education at Terrell, Texas. Abandoning the government model farm and other methods of demonstration, Knapp went directly to the dirt farmer with a simple and ingenious proposition. The farmer was selected by a local committee that guaranteed him against loss if he would undertake to conduct on his own

[38] Seaman A. Knapp, quoted in Oscar B. Martin, *The Demonstration Work* (Boston, 1926), 22.

[39] *General Education Board . . . 1902–1914*, p. 22.

land a demonstration of new methods. He agreed to plant selected seed furnished by the government and follow certain instructions. The farmer himself was to pocket all profits, and the community had an interest in watching results. The plan thus enlisted the farmer's self-interest and pride as well as that of his community. No land was leased nor money exchanged, and the government was sent to the sidelines. Knapp's theory was that "What a man sees or hears he may doubt, but what he does he cannot doubt." The results were an immediate and startling success, both in production and in pedagogy. The Terrell farm became the model for hundreds of thousands of similar demonstration farms established over the following decade.[40]

Neither Dr. Knapp nor the combined hosts of philanthropy and government could have diffused the demonstration technique with such lightning speed through the South had it not been for the inestimable assistance of the Mexican cotton-boll weevil. The weevil panic seized Texas in the summer of 1903, a decade after the insect crossed the Rio Grande. A disastrous season, the worst in a quarter century, cut per-acre yield in half and frightened hundreds of families into flight. "I saw hundreds of farms lying out," wrote Knapp; "I saw wretched people facing starvation; I saw whole towns deserted." Merchants refused credit, stores closed their doors, and labor migrated in droves as demoralization spread. The boll weevil was recognized as a menace threatening ruin to the entire cotton economy, for the pest was spreading eastward.[41]

Scientists had already developed a "cultural remedy" that would enable farmers to grow cotton in weevil-infested areas. Dr. Knapp's demonstration technique had been developed without reference to the weevil problem, but Washington officials saw that with slight modifications it could be used in this crisis and placed Knapp in command of an emergency demonstration program in January, 1904. Knapp inspired a small corps of agents with his zeal and mobilized support from railroads, businessmen, everybody. By the end of the year more than 7,000 farmers had conducted demon-

[40] Bailey, *Seaman A. Knapp*, 149–68; Martin, *Demonstration Work*, 19, 23.

[41] Martin, *Demonstration Work*, 169–77; Seaman A. Knapp, *Demonstration Work in Cooperation With Southern Farmers*, United States Department of Agriculture, *Farmers' Bulletin* No. 319 (Washington, 1908), 5–6.

strations of their own and influenced other thousands to adopt improved methods. Not only had Knapp proved that cotton could be grown in spite of the weevil but that production in infested lands could outstrip and even double production on land free of the weevil but cultivated by old-fashioned methods. It became apparent, moreover, that there was no quick method of exterminating the boll weevil, that it was a more-or-less permanent evil that would spread throughout the cotton kingdom, and that the only effective way of dealing with the problem was the way Knapp had developed in Texas. This meant educating the man behind the plow handles in the essentials of sound agriculture—diversification, rotation, seed selection, more intensive cultivation, deeper plowing, better stock, and better implements.[42]

Secretary Buttrick was still seeking a way to educate the Southern farmer into prosperity when David F. Houston remarked to him in 1905, "There are two universities here in Texas; one is in Austin, the other is Dr. Knapp." [43] After hearing Knapp expound his demonstration method, Buttrick was convinced that right here had "the General Education Board found the answer." The weevil could be regarded as "a sort of blessing in disguise," an ally of science, education, and philanthropy, by means of which an agricultural revolution could be extended, as no amount of propaganda could extend it, throughout the South. Knapp was enthusiastic, but the Federal government adhered to the theory that its funds were available only on the grounds that the weevil was an interstate menace, and could not be expended for educational uses beyond the infected area. Philanthropy stepped into the constitutional breach in April, 1906, with an agreement between the Secretary of the General Education Board and the Secretary of Agriculture by which the Board was to supply funds for demonstration work in the noninfected states, and leave control of both areas in the hands of the government.[44]

In 1907, while the government confined its work to Texas, Arkansas, and Louisiana, the Board conquered new territory in Mississippi, Alabama, and Virginia; in 1908 the government added Oklahoma, and the Board, Georgia and the Carolinas. As the weevil and the government advanced eastward, philanthropy retreated to

[42] Bailey, *Seaman A. Knapp*, 177–86. [43] *Ibid.*, 214.

[44] *General Education Board . . . 1902–1914*, pp. 23–27.

break new ground, until by 1913 demonstration work was in progress in all the Southern states. Though the number of agents grew from 24 in 1906 to over 1,000 in 1913, the method remained that devised by Knapp, who supervised it closely until his death in 1911. Farm by farm throughout the back country the demonstration work progressed, until by the end of 1912 it was established in 636 out of 1,163 counties in the Southern states. In Alabama every county was included and in South Carolina 95 per cent of the counties. Knapp's missionaries reached over 14,000 farms in 1908, 63,622 in 1910, and 106,621 in 1912, and each demonstration was visited by 30 to 100 farmers annually. State and local aid was enlisted to such an extent that between 1903 and 1914 it outstripped philanthropy, contributing in those years $1,069,405 to the General Education Board's $925,750, and the Federal government's $1,922,300.[45]

Exorbitant claims were made for the demonstration work. Even after such claims are discounted, however, the recorded achievements are astonishing. Generally speaking, demonstration methods doubled average production wherever applied. Thus the average acre in Mississippi yielded 17 bushels of corn or 228 pounds of lint cotton, while the demonstration acre yielded 35 bushels of corn or 445 pounds of cotton. Nor were results entirely measurable in bushels and pounds. Houses, barns, and equipment brightened and improved with crops, and progress was made toward diversification. The boys-club and girls-club movement was launched by Knapp to mobilize youth. Stagnant communities all over the South were vitalized as they made the transition from the agricultural age of Chaucer to that of the twentieth century. Thousands of debt-ridden farmers, hard bitten with pessimism or despair, took on new life and hope.[46] In the end, however, the clinching argument of the demonstration method was more pounds and bushels. More and more cotton. Always more cotton.

Prophets of agricultural reform have long been at odds concerning the true way of salvation for the South. While one has preached abundance, another has called for scarcity. While Knapp was per-

[45] *Ibid.*, 35–49.

[46] See, for example, farmers' letters in Knapp, *Demonstration Work in Cooperation with Southern Farmers*, 18–22; *General Education Board . . . 1902–1914*, pp. 50–70.

forming miracles in an attempt to double crop production, other organizations were straining every nerve to curb production. Of the several cotton-crop control schemes of this period those of the Southern Cotton Association and the Farmers' Union were the most important. A bumper crop and rapidly declining prices in 1904 were the immediate occasions of a convention at New Orleans in January, 1905, to which "all persons of all professions interested in cotton" were invited. The president of the newly formed Southern Cotton Association declared that "we must, and will, reduce the present cotton acreage from 25 to 40 per cent on every cotton farm in the South for 1905." Elaborate plans were announced, and several state associations were formed. Production did fall about 14 per cent the following season, but it is impossible to say how much of this was due to the Association's efforts. Unable to work through local units, to command unified support, or to reconcile contradictory interests among its membership, the Association expired in 1908.[47]

A hardier and more durable growth, the Farmers' Union, like all major agrarian movements of the period, sprang up in Texas. It was founded in 1902 by Newt Gresham, once active in the old Farmers' Alliance. The new order revived many Alliance doctrines and methods, and some of the old militancy, but whether because it had more cautious leaders or appealed to a different class of farmers, it lacked the edge of radicalism typical of the Alliance. Like the old movement, the Farmers' Union excluded from membership merchants, bankers, lawyers, and speculators, but it strove to "make farmers into businessmen." By 1905 state organizations were completed in Arkansas, Oklahoma, Alabama, Georgia, Mississippi, and Louisiana, and a national Farmers' Union was established. Under the leadership of Charles S. Barrett of Georgia, elected president in 1906, the Union in the next three years spread with "wonderful swiftness and impelling force" through all the cotton states, into the Middle West and out to the West Coast. The national secretary reported 935,837 active members in 1907, and

[47] *Report of the Commissioner of Corporations on Cotton Exchanges* (Washington, 1908–1909), III, Pt. V, "Influence of Producers' Organizations on Prices of Cotton," 325–27, 330, 334; Theodore Saloutos, "The Southern Cotton Association, 1905–1908," in *Journal of Southern History*, XIII (1947), 492–510.

in 1909 Barrett claimed a "floating membership" of 3,000,000. Accurate records were lacking, however, and treasury receipts indicate nowhere near this number of dues-paying members.[48]

Inspired to a certain extent by the example of farmers' movements in Ireland and Denmark [49] and the experience of the old Alliance, the Farmers' Union launched a wide variety of co-operative enterprises. Among them were co-operative warehouses, gins, stores, fertilizer factories, flour mills, oil mills, and banks. The Texas Union had 136 gins in operation, and Alabama boasted 29, as well as 41 stores and 5 fertilizer factories. The largest co-operative effort went into warehouses, a system of which was established in each cotton state. President Barrett reported more than 2,000 of them in operation in 1907, though many were small; combined, they could take care of only a fraction of the cotton crop.[50] Politically, the Farmers' Union was very conscious of its power, but less open in the use of it than the Alliance had been. "We are strong enough," declared one Union spokesman, however, "to force into the platform of any political party, anything we demand, and strong enough to force them to carry out our demands." [51] In several states the Farmers' Union played a vital role in the educational crusade.

According to the United States Commissioner of Corporations, the Farmers' Union represented "the most comprehensive movement ever undertaken by farmers to control the production and marketing of their crops." [52] In their efforts to reduce production

48 Treasurer's reports, in *Minutes of the National Farmers' Educational and Co-operative Union of America*, 1906–1912 (Texarkana, 1906–1912); Charles S. Barrett, *The Mission, History and Times of the Farmers' Union* (Nashville, 1909), 22–24, 107, 158–62, 196; Commodore B. Fisher, *The Farmers' Union*, in University of Kentucky *Studies in Economics and Sociology*, No. 2 (Lexington, 1920), 5–6, 12, 16–17; *Report of the Commissioner of Corporations on Cotton Exchanges*, III, Pt. V, 321–24.

49 Clarence Poe, *How Farmers Cooperate and Double Profits* (New York, 1915), 57; Fisher, *Farmers' Union*, 40–43.

50 A. C. Davis, *The Farmers' National Education, Cooperative, and Industrial Union, What it is and What it is Doing* (Texarkana, 1912), 31–36; *Minutes of the National Farmers' Educational and Cooperative Union of America*, 1907, p. 5; A. C. Davis, *Co-operative Enterprises of the Farmers' Union* (n.p., n.d.), *passim*; *Report of the Commissioner of Corporations on Cotton Exchanges*, III, Pt. V, 354.

51 J. Y. Callahan, *The Burning Issue* (Enid, Okla., 1908), 57; Barrett, *Mission, History and Times of the Farmers' Union*, 45, 88, 257; Davis, *Farmers' Union*, 16.

52 *Report of the Commissioner of Corporations on Cotton Exchanges*, III, Pt. V, 321.

and fix prices Union officials resorted to the calling of international conferences of manufacturers of cotton, holding cotton from the market, plowing under crops, cutting acreage, destroying surplus, and threatening banks with mass withdrawal of deposits as a defense against foreclosure. "We are following the example of organized wealth" was the defense of officials who sought "to fight fire with fire." Once in the spring of 1907 and once the following spring Barrett issued a "manifesto" to members asking that they plow up 10 per cent of their cotton crops. Though production continued to mount, prices held fairly high. Government investigators were skeptical of the amount of credit claimed by the Farmers' Union for such improvement as occurred.[53]

The old Populist formula of agrarian solidarity to which the Farmers' Union appealed was put under increasing strain by the burden of rising tenancy. While the Union occasionally passed a resolution of sympathy with the tenant, the order was predominantly of landowner leanings, and there were plenty of signs that conflict between landless and landed were not resolved in the new fraternity. Flashes of strife appeared from time to time in Texas, where the percentage of tenant farmers had increased from 37.6 in 1880 to 52.6 in 1910. Barnburning and other violence, accompanied by protest meetings in fifty counties, were reported in the late nineties.[54] Rumblings of tenant distress continued in the following decade. In 1911 a convention of tenant farmers at Waco organized the Renters' Union of America. They passed drastic resolutions of single-tax flavor "favoring a tax 'to the limit on all land held for speculation or exploitation,' " declared "that 'use and occupancy' was the only just basis for title to land," protested against rising rents, and called for an end to cash payments of rent. The movement subsided after another convention.[55]

Philanthropists, government experts, agrarian agitators, and politicians all had their turns at doctoring the sick man of Southern agriculture. Whether because of, or in spite of, the doctors' pre-

[53] Barrett, *Mission, History and Times of the Farmers' Union*, 128–29; Callahan, *Burning Issue*, 15; *Minutes of the National Farmers' Educational and Cooperative Union of America*, 1908, p. 25; Thomas J. Brooks, *Origin, History, and Principles of the Farmers' Educational and Cooperative Union* (Greenfield, Tenn., 1908?), 2–10.

[54] *Southern Farmer* (New Orleans), IV (December 25, 1897), 1.

[55] Benjamin H. Hibbard, "Tenancy in the Southern States," in *Quarterly Journal of Economics*, XXVII (1913), 494–95; Steen, *Twentieth Century Texas*, 48–50.

scriptions, the patient rallied for a time. But his subsequent case history is proof that none of the doctors effected a cure—not one that lasted, at any rate.

The educational crusaders struck the first blow against the old fortress of laissez-faire doctrine while the advocates of child-labor legislation were preparing the second. Both movements went forward simultaneously, sometimes with common objectives and foes, and at times with the same captains. In the child-labor crusade, however, it was not the Northern philanthropic foundations but the labor unions and Southern humanitarians who took the initiative and furnished the sinews of war.

Child labor in the South of the new century was not an occasional abuse or a passing phenomenon. It was an entrenched interest, a growing evil that had become a normal feature of the textile industry and the foundation of fortunes. In 1900 three out of ten workers in the mills of the South were children under sixteen years of age, and 57.5 per cent of those children were between ten and thirteen. Those under ten, of whom there were many, were not enumerated.[56] A former president of the American Cotton Manufacturers' Association declared that the adoption of an age limit of fourteen would close every mill in North Carolina, because 75 per cent of the spinners in that state were fourteen or younger; the preceding president of the Association estimated that only 30 per cent of the cotton-mill operatives of the South were adults over twenty-one years of age.[57] The number of children under sixteen in the mills increased 600 per cent between 1880 and 1900, and in the next five years, during which the number of spindles in the South increased by half a million, 3,133 children were added.[58]

In 1894 the only child-labor law on the books of the leading

[56] United States Census *Bulletin* No. 69, *Child Labor in the United States* (Washington, 1907), 42–44. These figures include Delaware and Maryland. North Carolina, South Carolina, and Georgia mills employed 49.6 per cent of the child cotton-mill operatives in the United States.

[57] R. M. Miller, Jr., and G. B. Hiss, both of the Charlotte, quoted by Alexander J. McKelway, "Child Labor in Southern Cotton Mills," National Child Labor Committee, *Publications,* Larger Ser., No. 20 (New York, 1906), 8.

[58] United States Bureau of Labor, *Report on Condition of Woman and Child Wage-Earners in the United States,* I, 28, 33, in *Senate Documents,* 61 Cong., 2 Sess., No. 645. Referred to hereinafter as *Woman and Child Wage-Earners.*

Southern textile states, an Alabama law of 1887 limiting the working day to eight hours, was repealed upon the demand of a Massachusetts company that began the construction of a large mill in the state in 1895.[59] "Eastern capital may now be invited South without having the disadvantage of the restriction in the hours of labor of women and children," an advocate of repeal was reported to have said.[60] Eastern capital was, of course, not the only interest concerned. Children along with adults were worked eleven and twelve hours a day and even longer, often reporting to work before dawn and leaving after sunset. Murphy of Alabama had "seen children of eight and nine years of age leaving the factory as late as 9:30 o'clock at night, and finding their way with their own little lanterns." [61] Night shifts were more common in the South than in the North. Of thirty-one North Carolina mills operating at night in 1908, twenty-seven had children under sixteen on the night shift. "Mothers complain that the children who work at night are nervous," it was found. Illiteracy among mill-village children was from three to four times that among white children at large, yet over three fifths of the mill-village children between six and fifteen years of age who were investigated were at work, and only about one fifth were attending school.[62]

By 1900, Samuel Gompers and the American Federation of Labor had campaigns for child-labor legislation under way in Alabama, Georgia, and the Carolinas, in which states more than 90 per cent of the child labor in Southern textiles was employed. Gompers employed Irene Ashby, a young Englishwoman of education and social standing, who made the first extensive investigation of conditions in the South and sought to win support for labor among upper-class Southerners. Murphy, then a young minister of thirty-one in Montgomery, turned aside from work in race relations to give wholehearted and effective support to the cause of child labor. Other Protestant ministers, women's clubs, and humanitarian groups joined with labor to crusade for the child in Alabama and in North and South Carolina. In Georgia, where Northern textile investments were especially strong, labor cam-

59 Davidson, *Child Labor Legislation in the Southern Textile States,* 20–21.

60 *American Federationist,* IV (1897–1898), 278. The writer was quoting from memory.

61 Murphy, *Problems of the Present South,* 119.

62 *Woman and Child Wage-Earners,* I, 237, 249–51, 284, 289.

paigned without important upper-class support and met with a series of failures. In the three other leading textile states, however, with the decisive support of Governor Aycock and a timely decision by Chief Justice Walter Clark of North Carolina, the agitators gained the adoption of child-labor laws in 1903. Weak compromises, far below the hopes of reformers, the laws of 1903 set an age limit of twelve but contained loosely defined exceptions in two states and provisions for enforcement in none. At best they were only a start.[63]

In the cotton manufacturer the reformer met an antagonist of formidable prestige and influence. For twenty years the manufacturer had been popularly acclaimed as the restorer of prosperity to the South, who ran a philanthropic enterprise for the salvation of the "poor white." As McKelway satirized the theme, the mill was "an orphan asylum, a children's training school, a playground, a hospital, a college and a trip to Europe, all in one." Finding himself suddenly condemned as an exploiter of children, the manufacturer reacted violently. The *Manufacturers' Record* attacked the gentle Murphy as "bryanesque," "inflammatory," "radical," and "unreasonable," and John C. Cary, president of a South Carolina mill, wrote that the reformers were tools of the New England textile industry plotting to "cripple" Southern mills and destroy their advantage of cheap labor.[64] Daniel A. Tompkins called the movement New England's second crusade, compared it with abolitionism, and declared work good for children "even at ages below fourteen." [65] Asa G. Candler, Atlanta capitalist, told a convention of reformers that "The most beautiful sight that we see is the child at labor; as early as he may get at labor the more beautiful, the more useful does his life get to be." [66] The path of the Southern reformer was rugged.

[63] These campaigns receive definite treatment in Davidson, *Child Labor Legislation in the Southern Textile States*, Chaps. II, IV, V, and VI.

[64] *Manufacturers' Record*, XLII (August 28, 1902), 93–95; John C. Cary's article, *ibid.* (September 18, 1902), 150–51; Edward Ingle's summary of the whole case, *ibid.* (October 9, 1902), 201–20.

[65] Quoted in Winston, *Builder of the New South . . . Daniel Augustus Tompkins*, 264–67.

[66] *Proceedings of the Fourth Annual Meeting*, National Child Labor Committee, *Publications*, Larger Ser., No. 69 (New York, 1908), 159.

Under the leadership of Murphy the National Child Labor Committee was organized in 1904, and state movements were coordinated under central direction. Murphy later retired from leadership to move on to the educational crusade, and Alexander J. McKelway, a young minister and editor from North Carolina, became secretary for the Southern states. Labor-union agitators stepped to the rear ranks, and the names of prominent middle-class Southerners appeared on the Committee's letterhead.[67] Reform propaganda became more skilled and turned the tables on conservatives by its own appeal to Southern tradition and prejudice. While little white Anglo-Saxons were toiling in the mills, said reformers, little Afro-Americans were attending school or growing tall in the sun. And was it not Jefferson Davis who had said, "Do not grind the seed corn"? As for the sectional argument, were not New England owners of Southern mills exploiting Southern children and acting as "conspicuous opponents" of child-labor laws?[68] As students of English factory laws, the Southern reformers knew that although the first law of 1802 placed English law ahead of the Southern-state laws of 1903, the struggle in England continued a century later. They were undismayed by the first years of repeated failure, and by 1909 could with some justice claim that progress "in the last six years has been more rapid than any similar advance either in America or Europe, for a similar large population."[69] By 1912 all Southern states had adopted an age-and-hour limit and some sort of prohibition against night work for children, though in the leading textile states the age limit was still only twelve and the hours sixty a week. Southern laws lagged behind the national standard generally, and enforcement provisions were totally inadequate.[70] An investigation by the Federal Bureau of Labor revealed that the age-limit laws were "openly and freely violated in

[67] Davidson, *Child Labor Legislation in the Southern Textile States,* 122–26.

[68] Alexander J. McKelway, "Legislative Hints for Social Reformers," manuscript in the Alexander J. McKelway Papers (Division of Manuscripts, Library of Congress), sketches the author's methods and experiences in legislative campaigns all over the South.

[69] McKelway, in *Proceedings of the Fifth Annual Conference,* National Child Labor Committee, *Publications,* No. 94 (New York, 1909), 66.

[70] Child-labor laws of all states as of 1912 are conveniently summarized in National Child Labor Committee, *Child Labor Bulletin,* I, No. 2 (New York, 1912), 1–77.

every State visited," that out of 143 mills in five Southern states, 107 employed children under 12 years of age illegally.[71] The struggle for child-labor protection continued through the New Freedom and into the New-Deal era, but the reformers of the first decade proved worthy pioneers.

Beyond the enactment of child-labor laws the Southern reformers made no inroads against the barriers of mill-village paternalism. Part of the millowner's resentment toward the humanitarians was his indignation against the presumptions of a rival, for he continued to regard himself as the only philanthropist worthy of the name. It was the philanthropy of the fief, a village privately owned and policed. Eighty-seven per cent of cotton textile workers in the South were living in company-owned houses in 1908. Mill management had been long accustomed to subsidizing or supporting one or more churches and preachers, and about the time of the public-school crusade, the mills expanded their investments in education. At the same time a few began to employ welfare workers in recreation and community work.[72] If paternalism proved benevolent in some instances, the average mill family nevertheless remained upon an appallingly low living standard. Taking as a "minimum standard" an income "so low as to furnish a standard of living that would exclude everything except the bare necessaries of life," and as a "fair standard" one step above this level, the United States Bureau of Labor made a detailed study of Southern mill families in 1907–1908. It found that about one fifth had incomes at or below the "minimum standard," just over half were above the "minimum" but below the "fair standard," and almost 30 per cent had more than the "fair standard." In less than half of the families of another sampling of North Carolina and Georgia mill families did the food standard come up to that set by the Atlanta prison dietary.[73] A high incidence of pellagra and other dietary diseases in the mill villages was an ugly evidence of wage rates. The sectional wage differential continued throughout the period: in 1912 and 1913

[71] *Woman and Child Wage-Earners*, I, 171–72.

[72] *Ibid.*, 519; Harriet L. Herring, *Welfare Work in Mill Villages* (Chapel Hill, 1929), 26–31, and *passim*.

[73] Herbert J. Lahne, *The Cotton Mill Worker* (New York, 1944), 130–32.

hourly earnings in New England were 37 per cent above those in the South.[74]

In spite of their celebrated "docility" and an almost-hopeless bargaining position, the "lint-heads" showed signs of contesting with the paternalists control over their own welfare. For a dozen years after the collapse of the Knights of Labor, unionism was a dead cause among Southern textile workers. Trade unionism was at a low ebb generally in the South. In January, 1898, Eugene V. Debs could find but a single trades assembly in Georgia. "The few who are still organized dare not say their soul is their own," he reported. "At Rome competent printers are working for one dollar per day. Railroad employees are afraid of their own shadows. Their slavery is pitiable in the extreme. Children in the cotton mills of Georgia get for their wages 57 cents a week." [75] Later that year Prince W. Greene, a handsome young Southerner, hurriedly organized a local union and took his men out in a large strike against wage cuts at the Columbus, Georgia, mills. Applying for affiliation with the American Federation of Labor, Greene was directed to join the National Union of Textile Workers. To their surprise the Southerners found themselves in control of this weak union and elected Greene president.[76]

Concerned over recent wage reductions in New England mills and the menace of low wages in the South, Samuel Gompers was on the point of launching a general campaign below the Potomac. He promptly appointed Greene to head the campaign, and under his command a team of organizers worked the South from Richmond to Mobile in the spring of 1899. They reported encouraging results in organizing locals of plumbers, typographers, marble cutters, gas fitters, and other trades, but their main efforts were among the mill villages of the Piedmont. In some areas they reported mill employees " 'so ignorant, that the greatest difficulty is experienced

[74] For a detailed study of wage differential, see Abraham Berglund, George T. Starnes, and Frank T. De Vyver, *Labor in the Industrial South* (University, Va., 1930), 69–104; A. F. Hinrichs, "Historical Review of Wage Rates and Wage Differentials in the Cotton Textile Industry," in *Monthly Labor Review* (Washington), XL (1935), 1170–80.

[75] Chicago *Social Democrat,* January 20, 1898. Courtesy of Dr. Howard Quint.

[76] George S. Mitchell, *Textile Unionism in the South* (Chapel Hill, 1931), 26.

in organizing them,' " but awakened sufficient interest to start more than thirty new locals and revive old ones.[77]

The fledgling textile unions began under the handicap of lost strikes. The determined management of eleven cotton mills in Augusta crushed a strike in eight of the mills by concerted lockout in the winter of 1898–1899. The following year the Carolinas were shaken from end to end of the Piedmont by strikes and lockouts involving thirty mills in North Carolina alone. The trouble started near Greensboro, where Caesar Cone of the Proximity Mill closed his factory and company store with the announcement that he had recently come South to avoid labor unions and would tear down his mill rather than submit to them. After a short lockout he resumed work with nonunion labor under a yellow-dog contract. The sharpest struggle occurred in Alamance County, textile center of the state. There seventeen mills combined in joint resistance to a strike by discharging all union members and evicting them from company houses. "Nearly every mill in the state has pronounced against union labor," wrote an investigator in 1901. In the spring of that year, another strike was lost at Danville, Virginia, in spite of Gompers' personal assistance.[78]

Retreating from crushing defeats in the upper Piedmont, unionism made its last stand in Augusta in 1902 with a strike at the John P. King mill, the biggest in the city. Organized management, with the support of the Southern Manufacturers' Association, replied with a complete lockout of some 8,000 employees from all mills in the vicinity. Evicted from their homes, strikers built a tent colony on the banks of the Savannah and took up hunting and fishing to provide victuals. Northern unions poured about $10,000 into the Augusta strike, but after a struggle of fifteen weeks the fight was lost. It was the old story of an empty war chest and the overwhelming power of management. From Danville to Augusta organizers reported "a woeful lack of interest" among Southern mill villages after the defeat of 1902. Once again the *Manufacturers' Record* could boast that "in its immunity from labor troubles the

[77] *American Federationist,* IV (1897–1898), 275–76; VI (1899), 57–59, 77; VII (1900), 17; *Southern and Western Textile Excelsior* (Charlotte, N.C.), VII (1899), 9.

[78] Jerome Dowd, "Strikes and Lockouts in North Carolina," in *Gunton's Magazine* (New York), XX (1901), 139; Thompson, *From the Cotton Field to the Cotton Mill,* 191–93; *American Federationist,* VIII (1901), 167–69.

South is conspicuously in contrast with other sections of the country." Textile unions virtually disappeared from the region until a revival in 1913.[79]

Following the example set by the philanthropists, child-labor reformers, and educators, the social-welfare people also undertook to launch their movement on a South-wide scale. The initiative was taken by Kate Barnard, who according to McKelway was "to Oklahoma what Jane Addams is to Chicago, its First Citizen." A pretty and apparently irresistible champion of the underdog, Miss Barnard at the age of twenty-seven was made state commissioner of charities and corrections of Oklahoma by the Farmers' Union and labor-union men, who controlled the reform government of the new state, and cheered her every utterance. She explained her indifference to woman suffrage to McKelway by saying that "the boys have always done what she asked them to do." [80]

In 1911 Miss Barnard persuaded Governor Hooper of Tennessee to call a Southern conference on social problems. Seven hundred people from all states of the region met at Nashville in May, 1912, and organized the Southern Sociological Congress. The "object" of the Congress was "To enlist the entire South in a crusade of social health and righteousness." Its "Social Program" included the abolition of child-labor and the convict-lease system, better provision for the welfare of children and defectives, higher standards of public health and education, and the improvement of race relations. The call for "closest cooperation with the church" indicated the leaning of a large number of the members.[81] Like Dr. J. T. Mastin, father of the welfare awakening in Virginia, and A. J. McKelway, acting president of the Congress for a time, many Southern welfare leaders were former preachers or prominent laymen. The Sociological Congress established an office to serve as a clearing-

[79] *Proceedings of the Second Annual Convention of the United Textile Workers of America*, 1902 (n.p., n.d.), 9–10, 18, 20–21; *Proceedings of the Third Convention of the United Textile Workers of America*, 1903 (n.p., n.d.), 47–48; Lahne, *Cotton Mill Worker*, 189–90; *Manufacturers' Record*, XLV (March 31, 1904), 224.

[80] A. J. McKelway, "Kate," in *American Magazine* (New York), LXVI (1908), 587–93.

[81] James E. McCulloch (ed.), *The Call of the New South* (Nashville, 1912), 7–17; James E. McCulloch (ed.), *The South Mobilizing for Social Service* (Nashville, 1913), 13–15; Lydia Shivers, "The Social Welfare Movement in the South" (Ph.D. dissertation, University of North Carolina, 1935), 50–51.

house for information on social-welfare work and provided the occasion for an annual convention. The founding of the Congress by no means marked the opening of social-welfare work in the South, for in every field in which the Congress took an interest the work was already under way.

One of the mightiest strongholds of privilege and social evil besieged by the welfare reformers was the convict-lease system, still in existence in one form or another in all the Southern states in 1900. Official investigations in Georgia revealed sickening "evidences of cruelty" and "inhuman neglect," and concluded that the system was "barbaric," "worse than slavery," and "a disgrace to civilized people." [82] Sporadic and sometimes vigorous opposition to the lease system from the time of its origins had achieved little, but between 1900 and 1913 the reformers overthrew the convict lease in six states and weakened it in others. The Louisiana Prison Reform Association, organized in 1897, gained the ear of the state constitutional convention of 1898, which prepared the way for the final eradication of the lease in Louisiana in 1901.[83] Mississippi finally succeeded in prying her last convicts from the plantation of an influential politician in 1906. The constitution written by Oklahoma progressives in 1907 forbade the selling of convict labor in any way. In the same year Georgia reformers under Hoke Smith's administration, aided by ministers, labor unions, newspapers, and the Prison Reform Association, aroused great popular indignation at mass meetings against the brutality of the lease system and abolished it completely.[84] Texas followed the example of Georgia in 1910 by an act that reformed her whole prison system and ended the lease as well. Thwarted by the state legislature, Governor George W. Donaghey of Arkansas attracted national attention in 1912 by pardoning 360 convicts at one time "for the purpose," he said, "of forever breaking up the convict lease system in this state." [85] Within the next six years this bar-

[82] "Report of the Convict Investigating Committee," in Georgia *Acts and Resolutions*, 1908, pp. 1059–1104.

[83] Elizabeth Wisner, *Public Welfare Administration in Louisiana* (Chicago, 1930), 162–63.

[84] A. Elizabeth Taylor, "The Abolition of the Convict Lease System in Georgia," in *Georgia Historical Quarterly* (Athens), XXVI (1942), 273–87.

[85] George W. Donaghey, "Why I Could Not Pardon the Contract System," in *Annals of the American Academy of Political and Social Science*, XLVI (1913), 28.

barous relic disappeared from all but one of the remaining Southern states.[86]

The low standard of public health in the South, like the low standard of public education, was a challenge to both welfare worker and philanthropist. The shortage of physicians, low income, a high incidence of typhoid and malaria, a large Negro population with aggravated problems of venereal disease and tuberculosis, and a virtual monopoly within the nation of hookworm and pellagra all combined to make the South's public-health problem unique in the country. From 1872, when Virginia established the first state health board in the South, until 1905, when the last yellow-fever epidemic occurred, public-health work in the region was largely concerned with yellow jack and other epidemics. Preventive medicine was handicapped by niggardly appropriations, public indifference, and political interference. There were no county health departments, and only two state boards, those of Florida and Mississippi, were spending as much as one cent per capita in 1898.[87]

A series of medical discoveries near the end of the nineteenth century altered the whole conception of communicable diseases and prepared the way for a new era of public health, beginning in the South about 1906. Ronald Ross, an Englishman, identified the carrier of malaria in 1898; Walter Reed, a native of Virginia, made the same discovery for yellow jack in 1899; and Charles Wardell Stiles, a New Yorker, established the existence of widespread hookworm infection in the Southern states in 1902. The awakening of a new era in public health was reflected in the decade beginning in 1906 in the establishment of state boards in all Southern states still lacking them, the reorganization and strengthening of the older boards in the Southeast, substantial increases in appropriations for

[86] By 1919 Alabama alone retained the system. Hastings H. Hart, "Prison Conditions in the South," in *Proceedings of the Annual Congress of the American Prison Association . . . 1919* (Indianapolis, 1919?), 201. The common substitute was the large state prison farm or the county chain gang. As for the latter, the superintendent of the North Carolina state prison in 1908 believed the chain gang "in every respect as defective and as full of possibilities for wrongdoing, cruelty and inhumanity as was the old convict-lease." Quoted in Jesse F. Steiner and Roy M. Brown, *The North Carolina Chain Gang* (Chapel Hill, 1927), 41.

[87] Francis R. Allen, "Public Health Work in the Southeast" (manuscript in possession of its author), 27–29, 72, 113.

state-wide work, and a start in the founding of county health departments. Antituberculosis work began about 1906 with the founding of bureaus of control and sanitariums. The first diagnosis of pellagra in the country is said to have been made in Alabama in 1906. Florida set up the first bacteriological laboratory in the region in 1903, an example soon followed by the other Southeastern states. Distribution of serums, vaccines, and antitoxins was undertaken by several states in this period.[88]

While the public-health awakening in the South clearly antedated the hookworm campaign, it is evident that a tremendous stimulus derived from the highly publicized work of the Rockefeller Sanitary Commission. An aggressive state campaign against hookworm infection was already under way in Florida before the entrance of the Commission, which imitated the methods of that state. The investigations of Dr. Stiles revealed that this parasite, like so many phenomena, microscopic and otherwise, was in this country confined almost entirely to the boundaries of the Southern states and was widespread in all of them.[89]

Walter Hines Page, gadfly of philanthropy, was infected with Dr. Stiles's new panacea for the South's ills while the two men were serving on Roosevelt's Commission on Country Life in 1908. Convinced that he had at last found the cure for the South's ills (as well as the key to its history), Page stung Wallace Buttrick into action, and the idea took hold of the Rockefeller advisers.[90] They organized the Rockefeller Sanitary Commission for the Eradication of Hookworm Disease in October, 1909, and with a fund of a million dollars, supplemented by state appropriations, launched a new crusade to save the South. By that time the strategy, tactics, and high command of the Southern philanthropic campaign had settled into a pattern which was closely followed. Aside from Dr. Stiles and two other physicians, the Sanitary Commission consisted mainly of members of one or another of the education boards. It included Page, Alderman, Claxton, James Y. Joyner, and Wyckliff Rose, adminis-

[88] Charles V. Chapin, *A Report on State Public Health Work Based on A Survey of State Boards of Health* (Chicago, 1916?), 8–57; Allen, "Public Health Work in the Southeast," Chaps. VIII–XI.

[89] Chapin, *Report on State Public Health Work,* 105–107.

[90] Hendrick, *Earlier Life and Letters of Walter H. Page,* 369–73.

trative secretary. The field work, organized by states as was the education work, moved forward, as Page said, with "the efficiency of an admirable business organization and the fervor of a religious propaganda." [91] The work included the placating of a sensitive South, suspicious of this new salvation from Rockefeller. In spite of derision and ridicule, the people, reassured by their newspapers and schools, flocked by the hundreds to the itinerant dispensaries. "It looks like the days of Galilee," reported Rose. Numerous photographs of the diseased are convincing documentation of the need for the work and the impressiveness of its accomplishment. In its final report in 1914, the Commission recorded the results of work in 578 counties in eleven Southern states, where 1,087,666 persons were examined and 440,376 treated. Of more than half a million children examined, 39 per cent were found to be infected.[92] Undoubtedly stimulated by the hookworm commission, public-health measures in other directions were greatly intensified in the years 1910–1914. Within those years, expenditures by the health departments in eleven Southern states were increased 81 per cent.[93]

Each succeeding conquest of uplift—whether over yellow jack, illiteracy, boll weevil, convict lease, hookworm, or barefootedness—was published forth as the eradication of the last historical handicap of a feckless region. "Now, for the first time," Page would announce, in this instance with respect to the hookworm, "the main cause of their long backwardness is explained and it is a removable cause." Innumerable photographs of washed, wormed, and weevilless Southerners were printed by Page and the foundations as evidence of the salvation they had wrought. Not everyone regarded this salvation as final. Gazing out of his Pullman at the small stations, "where the social scene might be sufficiently penetrated, no doubt, from the car window," Henry James viewed "the subject populations on the road to Charleston" with a mixture of detach-

[91] Walter H. Page, "The Hookworm and Civilization," in *Worlds' Work,* XXIV (1912), 507. Hookworm study became a part of the public-school curriculum in eight Southern states.

[92] *Fifth Annual Report of the Rockefeller Sanitary Commission for Eradication of Hookworm* (Washington, 1915), 11–15, 26, 90–117. See also, the four previous annual reports.

[93] Chapin, *Report on State Public Health Work,* 8, 33, 50.

ment and dismay. Perhaps it was "the misery of subject populations" everywhere, but undoubtedly the social scene was "shabby and sordid." [94] Other observers fell back upon the "poor-white" theory in a pinch.

[94] James, *American Scene*, 382–83.

CHAPTER XVI

BONDS OF MIND AND SPIRIT

BY THE turn of the century it was time for the generation that had grown up in the post-Reconstruction period to take command of the cultural life of the South. As a rule, people of this generation were unprepared for the task. They were the children of the cultural famine that blighted the land of their youth, and they came to manhood bearing the marks of intellectual malnutrition. The bread of learning and leisure and art and travel had been dealt out to them scantily, if at all. From the example set them by their fathers they could but conclude that achievement was something measured pretty strictly in material terms and that one looked northward for the standard of comparison. Sterility and imitation were marks of the culture they produced.

The Southern literary awakening that had lighted the national skies in the eighties subsided to a dull afterglow before the end of the century. None of the major luminaries and few of the lesser lights of the post-Reconstruction period were entirely extinct. Many of them were in evidence down to the World War period, industriously and sometimes profitably exploiting reputations gained in their youth. An exile in Massachusetts since 1886, George W. Cable lectured and wrote feverishly, turning out books for four decades, but adding nothing to his reputation thereby. Charles Egbert Craddock (Mary Noailles Murfree) continued to mine the old veins of local color in her Tennessee mountains and repeat old formulas of character and situation. Additional Negro books came from the pen of Joel Chandler Harris. Thomas Nelson Page settled prosperously in Washington, undisputed champion among the glorifiers of the Old South and the plantation legend. Critics are generally agreed that few if any of them equaled in later years the quality of their earliest work.

Even Southern critics, ordinarily generous to a fault with writers of their own region, were speculating upon "the reason why one hears so many people say of late that the Southern novels are becoming tiresome." One believed it was because the writers did "not represent truly the condition of Southern society since the war," and in their effort "to exalt the old planter" had given "a false color to existing Southern life." [1] Another lamented that the promise of the regional literary revival had not been fulfilled because "of the want of any adequate representation of typical Southern life of *to-day*." [2] William P. Trent deplored the monotonous emphasis of the local colorists upon the Negro, the mountaineer, and other primitive types, who had "been simply worked to death," while the great themes of social upheaval in the South had "been, comparatively speaking, untouched." "Of careful analysis of social conditions, of profound study and comprehension of the principles of human action, and of serene, self-contained art there are still few traces in the Southern literature of the present generation," he wrote.[3]

The fact was that Southern letters simply shared in the doldrums into which national literature had fallen. Between the short-lived revival of the eighties and the literary flowering of the South that was to begin in the twenties stretched a period of comparative barrenness. Originating no themes or schools themselves, Southern writers divided their allegiance among various national movements and literary fads. The school of social protest and muckraking claimed no important adherents below the Potomac in spite of vigorous Southern participation in the political activities of which muckraking was a reflecton. Nor did any Southern Hamlin Garland appear to record in fiction the agrarian upheaval of the nineties. The early naturalism of Theodore Dreiser and Jack London found no contemporary counterpart in the South.

1 John Raper Ormond, "Some Recent Products of the New School of Southern Fiction," in *South Atlantic Quarterly*, III (1904), 287.

2 John B. Henneman, "The National Element in Southern Literature," in *Sewanee Review*, XI (1903), 359, 365.

3 William P. Trent, "Tendencies of Higher Life in the South," in *Atlantic Monthly*, LXXIX (1897), 768.

In the vogue of the historical novel, which reached its peak in the four years following the Spanish-American War and continued to dominate the scene for a decade, Southern romancers found full scope and a ready market for their outpourings. Out of some 400 historical novels published between 1895 and 1912, 72, all dealing with American themes, have been chosen "on the basis of popularity at the time of publication and of inclusion in histories of American literature" for a detailed study.[4] Of the selected novels 34 were written by 12 Southern authors,[5] and 38 by 15 Northern authors. The disproportionate number of historical novelists from the South gave the whole literary movement a particularly sectional emphasis. In spite of their sectional point of view, the Southern authors appear to have been quite as popular with the national public as the Northern, for they accounted for 19 of the 35 titles among the annual lists of "ten best sellers" of this period. Four of the 7 historical novels that sold more than 500,000 copies were by Southern writers.[6] The air was heavy with romance in 1900, and the national heart throbbed with the emotions of idealized heroes and reveled in settings of mahogany, old silver, and gold lace.

The Southern romancers came almost entirely from the Upper South and the border states. Thomas Nelson Page, Mary Johnston, and Ellen Glasgow were Virginians; Thomas Dixon and John Fox, Jr., moved from neighboring states to Virginia; and George W. Cable and Maurice Thompson were of Virginian ancestry. The Deep South was represented by Cable alone, and he left Louisiana quite early. In fact, all 12 of the novelists save Glasgow left their native states to live elsewhere, 8 of them in the North and West. Glasgow again excepted, none of the 12 represented anything essentially new in the New South. All of them came of old families, 11 of which had been prosperous in ante-bellum days.

[4] Sheldon Van Auken, "The Southern Historical Novel in the Early Twentieth Century," in *Journal of Southern History*, XIV (1948), 161. The figures that follow are taken from this study, which includes the border states.

[5] F. Hopkinson Smith, George W. Cable, Maurice Thompson, James Lane Allen, Mary Noailles Murfree (Charles Egbert Craddock), Thomas Nelson Page, John Fox, Jr., Thomas Dixon, Jr., Mary Johnston, Winston Churchill, Ellen Glasgow, and Upton Sinclair.

[6] John Fox, Jr., *The Little Shepherd of Kingdom Come* (New York, 1903); Winston Churchill, *The Crisis* (New York, 1901), and *Richard Carvel* (New York, 1899); and Mary Johnston, *To Have and to Hold* (Boston, 1900).

Eight of the families had belonged to the wealthy class of slave-holding planters and had lost their wealth primarily as a result of the war. Twenty of the 34 successful historical novels these authors produced in the period 1895–1912 dealt with the Civil War or Reconstruction.[7] If the Southern aristocracy lacked literary defenders in the days of its dominance, it had no dearth of them in the days of adversity, when the old culture was in ashes. For almost with one voice the romancers spoke in vindication of the society, ideals, and values of the ancient regime.

The most persistent and prolific of the historical novelists was Mary Johnston, a frail Virginia woman who made her literary debut in 1898 with *Prisoners of Hope*. She followed it with her record-breaking best seller, *To Have and to Hold*. Both books dealt with seventeenth-century Virginia—with pirates, cavaliers, Roundheads, Indians, a shipload of prospective brides. Miss Johnston turned from one colorful episode to another in the history of her native state, to early eighteenth-century Williamsburg in *Audrey* (1902), to Jeffersonian Virginia in *Lewis Rand* (1908). The niece of General Joseph E. Johnston and the daughter of a Confederate army major, she found sympathetic materials in the Civil War, which she exploited in *The Long Roll* (1911) and *Cease Firing* (1912).

While the historical vogue lasted it infected almost the entire Southern literary group, the old local colorists along with certain newcomers who were tampering with realism. James Lane Allen illustrated the trend in *The Choir Invisible* (1897), Page in *Red Rock* (1898), Cable in *The Cavalier* (1901), Ellen Glasgow in *The Battle-Ground* (1902), and Craddock in *A Spectre of Power* (1903), to mention only selected examples. The Reconstruction period, a preoccupation of many Southern academic historians of that day, was also a subject of special fascination for the novelists. Contemporary race agitation and disfranchisement naturally heightened interest in the more dramatic elements of the story. The romancers, for the most part, wrote in passionate vindication of the conservative South and produced melodrama crowded with sensational crime and peopled with malevolent villains, wicked turncoats, and sterling heroes. Harris' *Gabriel Tolliver* (1902), Cable's *John*

[7] Van Auken, "Southern Historical Novel," *loc. cit.*, 173–75.

March, Southerner (1894), and Walter Hines Page's *The Southerner, A Novel* (1909) took some exception to the prevailing stereotypes, but the others tended to deepen and confirm them.

Through the long Victorian twilight that lingered over the South there moved with composure a Tennysonian gentleman from Kentucky: James Lane Allen, the last champion of the Genteel Tradition. In his writing career, from the eighties to the twenties, he compassed a whole cycle of American literature and epitomized several of its stages. He scored his first success as a romanticist of the local color school with *Flute and Violin and Other Kentucky Tales* (1891), followed by *The Blue Grass Region of Kentucky* (1892), essays chronicling a departed glory. In the years of the Pullman strike and the Populist struggles he was publishing *A Kentucky Cardinal* (1894) and its sequel, *Aftermath* (1895), an idyl of provincial life. *The Choir Invisible* (1897), a novel depicting as its hero a Galahad in buckskins from the eighteenth-century frontier not only did much to start the vogue of historical romance but gained the author an immense following at home and abroad. The book produced for Allen an income equal to that of President McKinley and made each of his new volumes for thirteen years a literary event. No provincial in outlook, he introduced to American readers the techniques and themes of English and French naturalism in elegant and fastidious prose tinted with idealism. His *Summer in Arcady: A Tale of Nature* (1896), reflecting Hardy's influence, dealt boldly with sex for its time. *The Reign of Law: A Tale of the Kentucky Hemp Fields* (1900) grappled frankly with the conflict of science and religion and the crumbling of orthodoxy and brought down upon him abuse from the pulpit and press. *The Mettle of the Pasture* (1903), which treated realistically the "double standard," did not mend matters with offended critics. Next he turned to symbolism and more science in *The Bride of the Mistletoe* (1909) and its sequel, *The Doctor's Christmas Eve* (1910), both of which evoked criticism of a violence incomprehensible in the present day. For these subtle, symbolic tales of modern marriage, spun out of anthropological lore from *The Golden Bough,* the puritanical, aristocratic Allen was accused of "voluptuousness" and "eroticism." [8]

[8] Knight, *James Lane Allen and the Genteel Tradition,* 118, 153, 177–79, and *passim.*

After his flirtation with naturalism, Allen drew tighter about him his cloak of tradition and the aloofness of the gentleman aristocrat. For the pushing, vulgar South that surged about him he had nothing but disdain. "With the strainings and sweatings, the hardships and wrongs of his fellows he would have nought to do," says his biographer. His young friend Ellen Glasgow, whom he tried to understand, called him "the most gallant figure" she had ever known.

Certain enthusiasts hailed the rising star of O. Henry as the answer to the critic's prayer for a Southern writer with a genius for the common touch. To be sure, the North Carolinian was not inhibited by any of the formidable traditions of the gentleman novelist of Kentucky. Ex-beachcomber, ex-jailbird, consorter-with-highwaymen, and man about town, William Sydney Porter greeted the common man with a slap on the back. To the Tarheel writer the Big City meant *The Four Million* rather than "The Four Hundred" of Ward McAllister, the preposterous Georgian. He wrote in the slang of the day, drew tears of sympathy for the underdog, and counted William James among his admirers. O. Henry's literary show enjoyed an uninterrupted run of a decade, ended only by his death in 1910. His two hundred and more tales were packed with tricks and travesties, bubbling with fun, and abounding in gusto. His highest moments were probably reached in the stories of his native South, but no one could fairly expect O. Henry to assume the role of prophet to the new age. The discipline of high art and the dignity of tragedy were not for him.

The forerunner of the new age did arise, but in a most improbable place. The standard of revolt was lifted in a Richmond rose garden of the nineties, and the bearer was neither beachcomber nor jailbird, but the sheltered daughter of an aristocratic, Victorian home. The rebellion of Ellen Glasgow can, as yet, only be recorded, not explained, for of all the strange mutations in this age of the South's transition hers was the most unaccountable. It began in 1897 with the publication of *The Descendant,* her rather immature first novel. The twenty-two-year-old author chose as her central figure a bastard son of the disinherited white trash, who was a "sullen Socialist" to boot. The title page bore a quotation from Haeckel. She was conscious, she later wrote, of "beginning a solitary revolt against the formal, the false, the affected, the sentimental, and the pretentious, in Southern writing." [9] Only later was revolt "subdued to the civilized uses of irony." All around her South she saw lying "untouched" materials such as had never challenged the technique of realism. "The world was full of fermenting processes, of mutability and of development, of decay and of disintegration," she wrote. "The old agrarian civilization was passing; the new industrial system was but beginning to spring up from chaos." [10] Scornfully rejecting "the colored spectacles of evasive idealism," she declared that "What the South needs is blood and irony."

Ellen Glasgow conceived the ambition, after her first publication, of writing "a well-rounded social record of Virginia" in the form of realistic fiction. This series, which she called "Novels of the Commonwealth," treated the period from 1850 to 1912, and the task occupied her from 1899 until it was completed in 1916.[11] She turned first, in *The Voice of the People* (1900), to the drama of agrarian upheaval about her, chronicling the rise of the son of a shiftless illiterate farmer and underlining the clash between the spirit of caste and democracy. Only one of her books, *The Battle-Ground,* dealt with the period before 1870. Though it came as close to the spirit of romance as anything she wrote, it treated civilian life in the Richmond of the war years in realistic fashion. She returned to the problem of caste in *The Deliverance* (1904), the story of a tenant tobacco farmer of aristocratic background who is torn between a fierce passion for revenge against his landlord, formerly the overseer of his plantation, and love of the ex-overseer's granddaughter. *The Romance of a Plain Man* (1909), also concerned with intermarriage of poor white and aristocrat, recounts the rise of a city worker, paralleling the story of the rural lower class in *The Voice of the People.* Both the remaining novels in the series, *Virginia* (1913) and *Life and Gabriella* (1916), have as their central

9 Ellen Glasgow, *A Certain Measure* (New York, 1938), 8.

10 Ellen Glasgow, *The Voice of the People* (Virginia ed., New York, 1938), xvi.

11 Miss Glasgow listed the "Novels of the Commonwealth" according to the period covered as follows: I, *The Battle-Ground* (1850–1865); II, *The Deliverance* (1878–1890); III, *The Voice of the People* (1870–1898); IV, *The Romance of a Plain Man* (1875–1910); V, *Virginia* (1884–1912); VI, *Life and Gabriella* (1894–1912). She later added three "Novels of the Country" and four "Novels of the City." Glasgow, *Certain Measure,* 3–4, 59.

figures Southern women and express the feminist revolt against chivalry. The only conspicuous element in Southern society which is not made the special subject of one of Ellen Glasgow's novels is the Negro, and he enters freely into all her Virginia books, though usually as a servant. No caste nor class, nor race nor creed in the Southern world created by Ellen Glasgow is granted a monopoly of either the virtues or the vices. There are brutal, greedy poor whites as well as heroic ones, and there are charming and wise aristocrats as well as degenerate and cruel ones. There were times in this early phase of her work when her skepticism did not seem quite broad enough to include the Brave New South, and when she appeared on the point of embracing the gospel according to Walter Page. Her later work proved that she outgrew this tendency, however, and that she could be as skeptical of the New Order as of the Old.

"Realism crossed the Potomac twenty-five years ago, going north!" observed Stuart P. Sherman in 1926, referring to Glasgow's early work.[12] When eventually the bold moderns of the South arrested the reading and theatrical world with the tragic intensity of the inner life and social drama of the South, they could find scarcely a theme that Ellen Glasgow had wholly neglected. She had bridged the gap between the old and the new literary revival, between romanticism and realism.

Scholarship and the higher learning were slower than letters to recover lost ground and establish sure footing in the New Order. For one thing, the scholar was more dependent than the man of letters on libraries and laboratories, endowments and salaries—expensive luxuries only remotely accessible. He required a community of mind that understood his purposes, defended him from church and state, and won him tolerance and support from the public. The scholar needed powerful universities, and none existed in the South.

"I am so tired of trying to make bricks without straw," exclaimed Edwin A. Alderman. "I am so weary of trying to carry out ideas without means." Alderman had been president of the University of North Carolina, then of Tulane, and was considering a move to Virginia. "Virginia is poor," he continued. "The University of

[12] Stuart P. Sherman, *Critical Woodcuts* (New York, 1926), 76.

Virginia is poor." [13] Yet the institutions he served were affluent in comparison with others of the region. The discouragements of less-favored presidents are recorded in their annual reports. For the year 1900–1901 the University of Alabama reported an income of $10,000 from the state, while the universities of Kentucky, Mississippi, and Tennessee reported no state appropriation at all.[14] President Thomas D. Boyd labored from 1898 to 1904 to remove the constitutional provision that limited the annual appropriation for Louisiana State University to $15,000. Until 1898 the limit had been $10,000.[15] Alderman's theory was that penury had become a habit, "a stunting inheritance from the days of want and poverty." [16]

Endowments were pitifully inadequate or totally lacking. None of the eighteen American institutions that had endowments of $1,500,000 or more at the beginning of the century were in the South; and of the thirty with as much as $1,000,000 the South had only two, Vanderbilt and Tulane. Of the $157,000,000 of productive funds held by the universities and colleges of the country, Southern institutions held about $13,500,000, or less than half of the funds held by the colleges of New York State alone. Seven of Alabama's nine colleges and eleven of the sixteen in Texas had no endowment whatever. The twenty-four colleges of Tennessee enjoyed an endowment income of $138,653 as compared with $1,228,-132 for the twenty-three New York institutions. Income from any source was extremely low. The total available annual income for the sixty-six colleges and universities of Virginia, North Carolina, South Carolina, Georgia, Alabama, Mississippi, and Arkansas was $65,843 less than that of Harvard in 1901.[17]

The Southern professoriate was not impressed by references to Mark Hopkins and his log or Moses Waddel and his log school. The average professor's salary in forty-four of the better white

13 Alderman to Page, April 4, 1904, in Page Papers.

14 *Report of the Commissioner of Education . . . 1900–1901*, II, 1688–1707.

15 Marcus M. Wilkerson, *Thomas Duckett Boyd; The Story of a Southern Educator* (Baton Rouge, 1935), 155, 181, 185.

16 Alderman to Page, January 18, 1905, in Page Papers.

17 *Report of the Commissioner of Education . . . 1900–1901*, II, 1622, 1631–32, 1696–98. These figures do not include technological and professional colleges nor women's colleges, in which the disadvantage of the South is even greater. Figures for Delaware, Maryland, West Virginia, and the District of Columbia have been deducted from the Census "South."

colleges in ten Southern states was estimated by a study in 1901 to be about $840.[18] The value of buildings and grounds of Southern colleges represented only $19,000,000 of a national total of $146,000,000; the South's share of scientific apparatus valued at $17,500,000 was $1,500,000, while her share of the 8,500,000 books in college libraries was less than 1,250,000.[19] The Carnegie Foundation found in the Lower South only one institution, Tulane, which measured up to its requirements for institutions of college rank—at least six professors giving full time to college work, admission requirements of four years of high school, and a course of four years of liberal arts and sciences.[20] After a survey of the plight of higher learning in the South in 1910, one Southern college president found "No university well enough equipped to do genuine research work, and twice as many professional and polytechnic schools as are needed, and none of them able to give our people the advantages that northern and western institutions offer." [21]

Poverty was only one difficulty, for compounding its ills was the necessity of spreading such meager funds as were available among a multitude of superfluous institutions that hung on in a dying condition from the Old Order or sprouted up thickly in the New. This evil was not confined to the South, but its effects there were pronounced. One study estimated that twenty colleges of fair standards could fill the needs of the region, but there were more than twenty of various kinds in several states. Scores of miserably equipped colleges competed among themselves and with high schools for the only revenue available—tuition fees. Great numbers of them depended largely upon their preparatory departments for income and were colleges in name only. Six of Tennessee's twelve "universities" and ten of her twelve "colleges" reported that a majority of their students were below the college level. At the U. S. Grant University in Athens, 258 of the 284 students were

[18] E. H. Babbitt, "The Problems of the Small College in the Southern States," in *Proceedings of the Seventh Annual Meeting of the Association of Colleges and Preparatory Schools of the Southern States* (Chicago, 1901), 58. The author estimated the average Harvard professor's salary at only $1,200.

[19] *Report of the Commissioner of Education . . . 1900–1901*, II, 1631.

[20] Hart, *Southern South*, 300.

[21] Robert E. Blackwell of Randolph-Macon College, quoted in *Report of the Commissioner of Education for . . . 1911* (Washington, 1912), I, 255–56.

so classified.[22] As a consequence of confusing high-school and college work, standards of admission and graduation were widely debased. In 1913 the bachelor's degrees of thirty-eight Southern women's colleges were adjudged approximately "equivalent to one year of college work," while the degree of fifty-eight others did "not apparently represent any standard work at all." [23]

"When we think of the heavy handicaps of the South," said President Robert E. Blackwell of Randolph-Macon College in 1910, "it is simply disheartening to contemplate our situation." [24] Nevertheless, there were Southern educational leaders who were keenly aware of debased standards and determined to raise them. This work was aided by four organizations, two of which were Southern and two, Northern. In 1895 Chancellor James H. Kirkland of Vanderbilt took the lead in organizing the Southern Association of Colleges and Secondary Schools. Its purpose was "to elevate the standard of scholarship and to effect uniformity of entrance requirements," as well as to enforce a sharp distinction between colleges and secondary schools. By 1913 twenty-eight colleges and universities had been accepted as members by the association, but of these only seven could be said strictly to require of all students four years work for the bachelor's degree.[25] The Southern Methodist church in 1898 created an Educational Commission, whose duty it was to fix minimum requirements of admission and graduation for all its numerous affiliated colleges and secondary schools.[26] The Carnegie Foundation for the Advancement of Teaching exerted some influence by rating colleges according to their admission requirements and by withholding benefits from colleges failing to conform to its standards. A more direct result was obtained through the endowment gifts of the General Education Board. As a part of its national program of college aid, the Board contributed to thirty-two Southern institutions by June, 1914, about $3,000,000,

22 *Ibid., 1900–1901*, II, 1668–69.

23 Elizabeth A. Colton, "The Approximate Value of Recent Degrees of Southern Colleges," in *Proceedings of the Nineteenth Annual Meeting of the Association of Colleges and Secondary Schools of the Southern States* (Nashville, 1913), 73–82.

24 Quoted in *Report of the Commissioner of Education for . . . 1911*, I, 255.

25 Guy E. Snavely, *A Short History of the Southern Association of Colleges and Secondary Schools* (Durham?, 1945?), 3, 10.

26 Farish, *Circuit Rider Dismounts*, 280.

which was supplemented by private donors to make a total of some $12,000,000.[27] This with other gifts had by 1913 more than doubled the endowments of 1901, but the South's proportion of the sum of national college endowments was no greater in 1913 than in 1901.[28]

In spite of handicaps and hardships, men of learning were somehow assembled in Southern faculties. Before the end of the century William P. Trent reported, somewhat prematurely, perhaps, that in the better colleges "The day of the broken-down clergyman-professor is over, and the trained specialist has taken his place," and by 1904 William Garrott Brown discovered that "a growing percentage of the instructors" in Southern colleges were "young men who have travelled and studied in other parts of the country and abroad." [29] German seminars, and particularly the University of Leipzig, trained a considerable number of them. At one time in the nineties there were five members of the Vanderbilt faculty who had studied in Leipzig.

Undisputed primacy, however, belonged to the Johns Hopkins University as dispenser of the higher learning to Southern scholars in the last quarter of the nineteenth century. Attracted in part by the large proportion of Southerners on the faculty of the new university and in part by the scholarships that the founder established for candidates from Maryland, Virginia, and North Carolina, Southern students crowded the Hopkins seminars. Returning with their degrees to fill posts in the South, they founded Hopkins "colonies" from Virginia to Texas. With the pardonable exaggeration of a loyal alumnus, the editor of the *Sewanee Review* wrote in 1901 that "so far as the Southern States are concerned, one might almost say that their educational history for the past quarter of a century has been largely that of the Johns Hopkins University. It is rare, indeed, to find at the South any college of note whose faculty has not been drawn largely from Baltimore." [30] A more matter-of-fact tabulation in 1896 listed sixteen colleges below Mason and Dixon's line that had employed three or more Hopkins-trained men on

[27] *General Education Board . . . 1902–1914*, pp. 147–59.

[28] *Report of the Commissioner of Education for . . . 1913*, II, 192.

[29] Trent, "Tendencies of Higher Life in the South," *loc. cit.*, 722–73; Brown, in Boston *Evening Transcript*, March 12, 1904.

[30] Burr J. Ramage, in *Sewanee Review*, IX (1901), 379.

their faculties and suggested that the list would have been doubled by the inclusion of colleges employing one or two.[31]

The new learning was spread beyond the limits of the classroom by the editorial activities of William Peterfield Trent, John Spencer Bassett, and Walter Hines Page, three of the most zealous Hopkins apostles. In 1892, Trent and a group of associates at the University of the South launched the *Sewanee Review,* a quarterly literary journal of comparatively high critical standards. At Trinity College ten years later Bassett took the lead in establishing the *South Atlantic Quarterly,* which under his editorship sought to break down sectional and traditional barriers to thought. As editor successively of the *Forum,* the *Atlantic Monthly,* and the *World's Work,* Page kept an ear cocked southward to discover talent adaptable to his predilections and point of view.[32] Chapel Hill stirred from "the unchanging charm of that academic circle of eighteenth-century life," of which Page complained, to launch *Studies in Philology* in 1906 under the editorship of C. Alphonso Smith. The critical study of Southern letters, begun by the thirty-year-old Trent in his revisionist biography, *William Gilmore Simms* (1892), was carried on more sympathetically by William Malone Baskervill of Vanderbilt in his two-volume *Southern Writers: Biographical and Critical Studies* (1897–1903).

Historical scholarship in the South experienced an awakening toward the end of the century comparable to the literary revival of the eighties. Like the men of letters, the Southern historians turned to their own region for subject matter. Academicians for the most part, they participated in a national movement to establish the ascendancy of the college professor over the field of history. They tended to regard history as a branch of industry rather than of art, laying great stress on the "exploitation of raw materials," the importance of "production," and the "scientific" method. Professor Herbert Baxter Adams, maestro of the school, was eulogized by his student Woodrow Wilson as "a great Captain of Industry, a cap-

31 *Twenty-First Annual Report of the President of The Johns Hopkins University . . . 1896* (Baltimore, 1896), quoted in Wendell H. Stephenson, "Herbert B. Adams and Southern Historical Scholarship at the Johns Hopkins University," in *Maryland Historical Magazine* (Baltimore), XLII (1947), 3, n. 6.

32 The Page Papers in the Houghton Library, Harvard University, are filled with letters from Southern writers.

tain in the field of systematic and organized scholarship." [33] The production record of his Johns Hopkins seminar from 1877 to 1901 was reported in the manner of the Baltimore *Manufacturers' Record* boasting of the output of Southern mills: "fifty-three Southern members of the Department of History have written 748 monographs, books or articles, of which 316 have been specifically on the South, while non-Southern men have written 51 articles in addition upon the South." [34]

The debt of Southern historians to Professor Adams was undoubtedly large. After the death of Adams in 1901, the center of Southern historical scholarship shifted from the Hopkins to Columbia University under the direction of William Archibald Dunning. Young Southerners were attracted to Dunning by the genial professor's interest in Reconstruction and by his sympathetic conservatism. Among those who sat at his feet were Walter L. Fleming, James W. Garner, William K. Boyd, Ulrich B. Phillips, Benjamin B. Kendrick, Charles W. Ramsdell, J. G. de Roulhac Hamilton, and C. Mildred Thompson. The most popular subject of investigation was Reconstruction. Garner's *Reconstruction in Mississippi* (1901) set a relatively high standard, for the times, in detachment and fairness toward conflicting races, classes, and parties. Those who followed with studies of other states did not invariably meet with the same success in these respects. The work of the Columbians was, nevertheless, some improvement over the pioneering efforts of the Hopkins group.[35]

William E. Dodd of North Carolina and Ulrich B. Phillips of Georgia were both historians of the new type: Dodd was trained at Leipzig, Phillips at Columbia; but they represented divergent traditions, each deeply rooted in the Southern past. Dodd, a passionate champion of the democratic tradition, sought to give the people back their heritage of egalitarianism in interpretative stud-

[33] Quoted in Richard T. Ely, "A Sketch of the Life and Services of Herbert Baxter Adams," in *Herbert B. Adams: Tributes of Friends, with a Bibliography of the Department of History, Politics and Economics of the Johns Hopkins University, 1876–1901* (Baltimore, 1902), 46.

[34] William K. Boyd, "Southern History in American Universities," in *South Atlantic Quarterly,* I (1902), 241; Stephenson, "Herbert B. Adams and Southern Historical Scholarship at the Johns Hopkins University," *loc. cit.,* 1–20.

[35] Wendell H. Stephenson, "A Half Century of Southern Historical Scholarship," in *Journal of Southern History,* XI (1945), 17–23.

ies of democratic leaders from Jefferson to Wilson. The tradition of the conservative South came more naturally to the pen of Phillips, who sifted the ruins of the plantation-slavery economy for artifacts of ante-bellum civilization. William Garrott Brown and Philip Alexander Bruce managed to escape the academic life and some of its limitations. Between 1895 and 1910 Bruce published three creditable volumes on the early economic, social, and institutional history of his native Virginia. Brown of Alabama won immediate acclaim from the academicians for his studies on the Lower South in spite of his rebellion against the professors' dry-as-dust models and his insistence that there was need for grace and humor in so human an affair as history writing. More in conformity with the times were the thirteen volumes of *The South in the Building of the Nation* (1909–1913), a venture in organized, co-operative history headed by Julian A. C. Chandler. Containing work of solid merit, the volumes were highly uneven in quality.

When the newly trained scholars returned to the South to air their views in sleepy college towns, there were alarms and explosions that raised the issue of academic freedom. Battles in the seventies and eighties had occurred over the new sciences, particularly Darwinism, and the offenders against academic freedom had been denominational colleges. The Methodists had been involved in Vanderbilt's dismissal of Alexander Winchell from the chair of geology in 1878; the Baptists, in the removal of Crawford H. Toy from their seminary at Louisville in 1879; and the Presbyterians, in the action against James Woodrow at their seminary in Columbia, South Carolina, in 1883.[36] The twentieth century posed dangers from powerful new industrial interests that dominated college boards and contributed to endowments as well as the risk of interference from popular political idols.

Professor William E. Dodd of Randolph-Macon College was less concerned over the restraints that religious and race orthodoxy put upon freedom than he was over the menace of beneficiaries of economic privilege who had "found places on college boards of control, and now threaten both legislator and teacher who speak

[36] Howard K. Beale, *History of Freedom of Teaching in American Schools* (New York, 1941), 204; Virginius Dabney, *Liberalism in the South* (Chapel Hill, 1932), 190–96. Within a few years James Woodrow was elected president of the state university of South Carolina.

the truth about their doings." He declared that "many subjects which come every day into the mind of the historian may not with safety even so much as be discussed." Dodd warned particularly of the danger to freedom that he saw in the millions poured into colleges and educational funds by the Ogden movement, the General Education Board, and its subsidiary, the Southern Education Board. "Not one of the colleges that has profited by this new movement, not one whose officials affiliated with Mr. Ogden and his board, has done anything to encourage freedom of speech on economic subjects," he wrote. While the General Education Board proclaimed the ideal of freedom, he added, "none of their supporters in the South have found it possible to condemn publicly the methods of Mr. Rockefeller, their great benefactor." [37] Certain Negro educators who opposed Booker Washington's scheme of industrial training and demanded higher education for their race charged that the Rockefeller and other foundations exerted pressure by withholding funds from liberal arts colleges, though the justice of their charge has been disputed.[38]

Others were alarmed at the influence that native Southern men of wealth gained over the faculty and administration of colleges they endowed. In the middle nineties Trinity College, an impoverished Methodist institution of North Carolina, gained a new president and soon afterward the renewed favor of a generous benefactor. The president was John C. Kilgo, evangelistic preacher and Tillmanite from South Carolina. The benefactor was Washington Duke, tobacco-trust magnate and Republican. Kilgo was soon exciting wonder by sensationally attacking Bryan and the silverites, advocating the gold standard, denouncing Thomas Jefferson as a "monster" and "infidel," and defending trusts and monopolies as a blessing. The president and members of his faculty eulogized their benefactor publicly and profusely. Among the qualities attributed to Washington Duke by Professor William P. Few, who was to become Kilgo's successor in 1910, were "an unequalled sense of proportion," an "instinctive recognition of the eternal fitness

[37] William E. Dodd, "Freedom of Speech in the South" (letter to the editor), in *Nation*, LXXXIV (1907), 383–84. The following year Dodd accepted a professorship at the Rockefeller-endowed University of Chicago. Randolph-Macon College later accepted an endowment from the General Education Board.

[38] Beale, *History of Freedom of Teaching*, 189–95.

of things," an "intuitive knowledge of what is right and proper," together with "the most useful gift vouchsafed to men on earth—the gift of unerring wisdom"—a gift he shared with Abraham Lincoln.[39] When Judge Walter Clark, a member of the Trinity Board of Trustees, criticized Kilgo for "an affluence of sycophancy" and "deification of wealth," the president demanded and, with the support of the Board, secured Clark's resignation.[40]

An occasional utterance on the race issue by an emboldened professor sometimes aroused a clamor so furious that college administrations weakly yielded. On one issue of this sort Trinity College appeared to somewhat better advantage. In 1903 when Professor Bassett pronounced Booker Washington "the greatest man, save General Lee, born in the South in a hundred years," faculty and administration joined in successful resistance to the demand for the professor's head.[41] Emory College, another Methodist institution, had set an unfortunate example the year before when it "accepted the resignation" of Professor Andrew Sledd, who had published an innocuous dissent from the prevailing doctrine of race proscription.[42]

Among those who took a hopeful view, Professor Mims of Vanderbilt wrote in 1907 that "In spite of ecclesiastical influences on the one hand and political influences on the other, the best colleges are moving toward tolerance in all things." [43] And the same year Professor W. Le Conte Stevens of Washington and Lee, who had moved to the North in 1877 "because of the shackles to which he was subjected in his Southern home," found after returning to teach in the South that "a professor is now tolerated where a

39 William P. Few, "Washington Duke," in *South Atlantic Quarterly*, IV (1905), 207–208.

40 On the Kilgo-Clark controversy, Aubrey L. Brooks, *Walter Clark, Fighting Judge* (Chapel Hill, 1944), 102–28, and Paul Neff Garber, *John Carlisle Kilgo: President of Trinity College, 1894–1910* (Durham, 1937), 212–29, take opposing views, each favoring his own subject. For correspondence on the subject, see Aubrey L. Brooks and Hugh T. Lefler (eds.), *The Papers of Walter Clark, 1856–1901*, I (Chapel Hill, 1948), 361–418.

41 Bassett, "Stirring Up the Fires of Race Antipathy," *loc. cit.*, 299.

42 Andrew Sledd, "The Negro: Another View," in *Atlantic Monthly*, XC (1902), 65–73; Henry M. Bullock, *A History of Emory University* (Nashville, 1936), 240. Professor Sledd was reinstated several years later.

43 Edwin Mims, "The South's Intellectual Expression," in *World's Work*, XIV (1907), 8984.

generation ago his head would have fallen." [44] These gentlemen, however, did not have to reckon with the new type of politician, as did their colleagues in state institutions. Only a year after their complacent views were recorded, Governor Charles N. Haskell suddenly fired the president and more than one fifth of the faculty of the University of Oklahoma without offering any reason connected with scholarship or ability. The president, a man with a Harvard doctorate, was replaced by a man with no college degree.[45] In 1911 Professor Enoch M. Banks of the University of Florida boldly contended that "the South was relatively in the wrong" in the secession crisis, and in the same article congratulated his native region upon "The new spirit of liberality toward opposing views," which was "perhaps the greatest incipent triumph of the twentieth century South." Professor Banks was peremptorily fired for his pains.[46]

Offenses against academic freedom were no more numerous in the South than in other regions during this period, however, a fact that is the more remarkable when the long ante-bellum and post-bellum embargo against new ideas is taken into account.[47]

The church was a serious competitor of the state and the philanthropic capitalist for influence over higher education in the South. In 1906 the Methodist Episcopal Church South counted twenty colleges under its wing, while the Southern Baptists had forty colleges under some degree of control, and the largest Presbyterian sect in the South reported eighteen colleges a decade later.[48] Jealous of secular encroachments, the denominational colleges, with church support, sometimes struck at state universities and occasionally grappled with millionaires for control of colleges.

Denominational war against state institutions was waged sporadi-

[44] W. Le Conte Stevens, "Intellectual Freedom in the South" (letter to the editor), in *Nation,* LXXXIV (1907), 430.

[45] "Do the People Rule in Oklahoma," in *Outlook,* XC (1908), 242–44.

[46] Enoch M. Banks, "A Semi-Centennial View of Secession," in *Independent,* LXX (1911), 299, 303; also editorial note, *ibid.,* LXXI (1911), 79.

[47] Dabney, *Liberalism in the South,* 343; Beale, *History of Freedom of Teaching, passim.*

[48] Bureau of the Census, *Religious Bodies: 1906* (Washington, 1910), Pt. II, 68, 470; Bureau of the Census, *Religious Bodies, 1916* (Washington, 1919), Pt. II, 590. The Presbyterians in the report of 1906 did not distinguish the secondary from the higher schools.

cally in several states, but in none more bitterly than in North Carolina in the nineties. There the Baptist, Methodist, and Presbyterian colleges, with considerable support from their churches and the aggressive leadership of such men as Josiah W. Bailey of the Baptist *Biblical Recorder* and President Kilgo of Trinity College, attacked the state university at Chapel Hill as a seat of ungodliness and an unfair competitor of church colleges. They demanded that the state institutions be reduced to the "voluntary principle" for support, and that all taxes for education should go to the public schools.[49] During the white-supremacy and public-school campaign to restore the Democrats to power in 1898, the denominational colleges and the large corporations exacted a secret promise from Furnifold M. Simmons, state Democratic chairman, that the legislature would not increase the appropriation of the state university nor the taxes of the corporations.[50] The denominational war subsided with the return of prosperity.

The cultivation of millionaire patrons for the denominational colleges posed something of a dilemma: while desperately eager for endowments, the colleges were at the same time jealous of secular control. Doctrinal harmony between patron and college sometimes facilitated compromise, as at Trinity, which later changed its name to Duke. In the struggle for control of Vanderbilt, the central university of Southern Methodism, the issue was openly joined, however, and the embattled bishops were arrayed against the plutocracy. The fight, which raged for a decade, opened in 1904 when Bishop Warren A. Candler challenged faculty appointments of Chancellor Kirkland on the grounds of church membership. Bishop Elijah Embree Hoss stirred the hosts of Methodism with ceaseless agitation and in 1910 gained the endorsement of the General Conference for the claims that the Church and not the Commodore had founded Vanderbilt, that the General Conference had the

[49] Luther L. Gobbel, *Church-State Relationships in Education in North Carolina since 1776* (Durham, 1938), 132–71; Garber, *John Carlisle Kilgo*, 43–83; Daniels, *Editor in Politics*, 102–11, 230–34, 318–24.

[50] Rippy (ed.), *F. M. Simmons*, 29.

[51] Elijah E. Hoss, "The Matter of Church Schools," in *Methodist Quarterly Review* (Nashville), LIX (1910), 230–45; James H. Kirkland, "Recent History of Vanderbilt University," *ibid.*, 343–58; Edwin Mims, *History of Vanderbilt University* (Nashville, 1946), 291–318.

right to elect its trustees, and that the College of Bishops had the power of veto over actions of the trustees. When the University refused to acknowledge their authority, the bishops brought suit to establish their claims. In 1913, while the case was still before the court, it was announced that Andrew Carnegie had given a million dollars to the Vanderbilt Medical School on condition that its board and administration should not be selected for denominational reasons. Three years earlier Bishop Hoss had denounced Rockefeller and Carnegie, especially the latter, as "the most terrible menace to religious education that our country has ever seen." Candler likewise spurned "the agnostic steel-monger," and the College of Bishops vetoed the acceptance of his gift. The court decided the case against the bishops, however; the gift was accepted, and the University cast off ecclesiastical control. The defeated bishops then retired to make strongholds of Emory University in Georgia and Southern Methodist University in Texas. Endowed with a million dollars in 1914 by Bishop Candler's brother Asa, Coca-Cola magnate and fundamentalist, Emory was able for a time to resolve conflict between clergy and plutocracy in the bosom of the family.[51]

Neither learning nor literature of the secular sort could compare with religion in power and influence over the mind and spirit of the South. The exuberant religiosity of the Southern people, the conservative orthodoxy of the dominant sects, and the overwhelming Protestantism of all but a few parts of the region were forces that persisted powerfully in the twentieth century. They were a large element in the homogeneity of the people and the readiness with which they responded to common impulses. They explained much of the survival of a distinctive regional culture, and they went far toward justifying the remark that the South was solid religiously as well as politically.[52]

Instead of withering away before the advance of industry, science, and urbanization, the Southern legions of Christian soldiers multiplied in numbers and, to judge from appearances, waxed in zeal.

[52] Edwin McNeill Poteat, Jr., "Religion in the South," in William T. Couch (ed.), *Culture in the South* (Chapel Hill, 1934), 248–69, has an illuminating discussion of the subject.

Church membership in the South increased from 6,139,023 in 1890 to 9,260,899 in 1906. In those sixteen years church membership increased 51 per cent while population grew 39 per cent. The building of new churches paralleled the construction of the new factories and rivaled their rate of growth. In the decade after 1906 the South was the only region, apart from the Far West and the mountain states, which showed marked increase in the number of churches.[53]

With the exception of one state, these gains in church membership represented very largely the growth of Protestant sects—the most rapid growth they enjoyed in any part of the country. The exception was Louisiana, the only Southern state in which Protestants were in a minority, and where by 1906 the Catholics made up 61 per cent of the church membership. In the Southern states east of the Mississippi River, Kentucky excepted, 96.6 per cent of the church members were Protestant. They ranged from 99.4 per cent in North Carolina to 90.3 in Florida. The great area of these eight states contained the most solidly Protestant population of its size in the Western Hemisphere. In the states of the trans-Mississippi South, Protestants made up only 67.8 per cent of the church members, and in Kentucky 80 per cent. Approximately nine out of ten Protestants in the eastern South were either Methodists or Baptists. The Baptists were the largest and most rapidly growing group. Together, the Methodists and Baptists accounted for more than 87 per cent of the Protestant membership in the states east of the Mississippi, and 80 per cent in Kentucky and the trans-Mississippi South.[54]

The significance of numbers in measuring the strength of Southern churches is strongly modified by circumstances peculiar to the region. A study made in 1915 shows that of some 44,400 Baptist and Methodist churches in the South, 36,500, or 82 per cent, were in the open country or small towns. Four fifths of these rural churches were served by absentee pastors, and nine tenths of them held

[53] Bureau of the Census, *Religious Bodies: 1906,* Pt. I, 520–21; Bureau of the Census, *Religious Bodies, 1926* (Washington, 1930), Pt. I, 57.

[54] Bureau of the Census, *Religious Bodies, 1926,* Pt. I, 46–47. The percentage of Protestants was 41.7 in the North Atlantic Division, 62.1 in the North Central division, and 36.6 in the Western Division.

services only once a month.[55] The pioneer tradition of the circuit rider, who served two to six churches at a time, persisted strongly. The tenure of the average rural preacher, about two years within a parish, was as impermanent as that of his tenant-farmer parishioner. Nearly half of the preachers supplemented their income by another occupation, though in no other region did more than 15 per cent do so.[56] The average salary reported for Baptist ministers outside the principal cities was $334 for whites and $227 for Negroes in 1906.[57] Not more than one fifth of the rural white preachers of that denomination had any special vocational training.[58]

Upon good authority one learns that there were three tendencies "clearly discernible" in American Christianity of this period: "a trend toward church unity, a further liberalizing of theology and an increasing emphasis upon socialized religion." [59] Yet one searches vainly for important manifestation of any one of these three tendencies in the annals of Southern Christendom. Instead, there is evidence that the current in the South ran counter to all three tendencies.

Northern and Southern branches of the dominant Protestant churches made little progress in this period toward healing the schisms that had divided them originally over the slavery issue in the mid-nineteenth century. Objections to reunion came from both sides. Competition and overlapping of the white branches of Northern and Southern Baptists and Methodists were continuous sources of bitterness. In 1906 the Southern Baptists had planted 1,899 churches in states outside the South, and the Southern Methodists had 1,645 such churches.[60] The Northern branches likewise waged imperialistic expansion in the South. In 1912 40 per cent of the Southern Methodist church organizations in the North and West were in direct competition with churches of the Northern

[55] Victor I. Masters, *Country Church in the South* (2d ed., Atlanta, 1917), 111–13. See also *ibid.*, Appendix C, 204.

[56] Edmund deS. Brunner, *Church Life in the Rural South* (New York, 1923), 51, 58–60, 65.

[57] Bureau of the Census, *Religious Bodies: 1906,* Pt. I, 94–95.

[58] Masters, *Country Church in the South,* 89.

[59] Harold U. Faulkner, *The Quest for Social Justice, 1898–1914* (New York, 1931), 207.

[60] Bureau of the Census, *Religious Bodies: 1906,* Pt. II, 69, 471. The Census divisions of the South are used here.

Methodists while 34 per cent of the Northern Methodist churches in the far South were in places served by Southern Methodism. The two denominations had $12,000,000 invested in property in the same communities and paid $750,000 to preachers of competing churches.[61] The Baptists took no significant step toward reunion in this period. A loose federation was agreed upon by the Methodists in 1898, but in 1916 Bishop Collins Denny pronounced friction worse than it had been when federation was proposed. Northern and Southern Methodists of Japan succeeded in abolishing Mason and Dixon's line in 1907, but union in the home country was not to be achieved for more than thirty years.[62]

Unity within the South between denominations and splinters of denominations made even less progress than union of sectional schismatics. In the North and West a decline in sectarianism enabled many churches in depleted country districts to combine in federated, affiliated, or interdenominational churches. A study in the twenties revealed 977 such churches in the North and West, but mentioned the South only to say the region was omitted "because it had very few united churches." [63] Denominational orthodoxy was as strict and obstinate in the South as theological orthodoxy, and a fierce competitive spirit kept alive hundreds of depleted rural churches to waste duplicated effort. Imperceptible differences over doctrine and policy split up larger denominations into rival splinters. A half-dozen kinds of Baptists and at least that many kinds of Presbyterians called to mind Milton's "subdichotomies of petty schisms." If there was a "solid religious South," it was not a denominational solidarity.[64]

Theological orthodoxy came nearer being the essence of Southern religious solidarity, for in spite of ecclesiastical differences the basic theology of the region was remarkably uniform. "Scratch any sectarian skin and the same orthodox blood flows," wrote a Southern clergyman.[65] Modernism and liberalized theology were rejected,

[61] Paul N. Garber, *The Methodists Are One People* (Nashville, 1939), 91.

[62] *Ibid.*, 84–87, 95.

[63] Elizabeth R. Hooker, *United Churches* (New York, 1926), x, 289; Bureau of the Census, *Religious Bodies, 1926*, Pt. II, 642–43.

[64] Brunner, *Church Life in the Rural South*, 51; Poteat, "Religion in the South," *loc. cit.*, 254–55.

[65] Poteat, "Religion in the South," *loc. cit.*, 261.

or ignored, in favor of "the old-time religion." Unorthodox sects such as Unitarianism and Christian Science made no more progress in the South of this period than did the movement for united and federated churches. Evangelistic revivalism, reported by an authority to be "largely abandoned" in the nation,[66] continued to flourish in the town as well as the country. Two North Carolina counties held 211 revival meetings in the course of a year, and even city denominations sometimes retained and used their camp-meeting grounds. When Bishop Candler thundered against "the dainty forms of ritualism" and "the timid utterances of rationalism," only a tiny number of the faithful trembled. Pulpit demagogues matched those of the new political variety in the methods they used and the crowds they drew, and a half-dozen successful revivalists competed for the mantle of Sam Jones, when he died in 1906.

The social-gospel movement that swept Protestant denominations in the North was not unknown to Southern clergymen, and even had a few spokesmen among them. This was evident in 1912 at the Southern Sociological Conference, largely a ministerial affair, which adopted a "Social Program," and at the Conference of 1913, which listened to Walter Rauschenbusch, Samuel Z. Batten, and other leaders of the movement.[67] The dominant conservatism of the Southern church, however, was expressed by the editor of the Nashville *Christian Advocate,* when he wrote in the midst of the suffering of a depression that "No amount of interest in matters that are occur[r]ing in this world can be an effective substitute for an intelligent concern in matters that lie within the sphere of the world to come." [68] He was echoed a decade later by Candler, who called for "great revivals" as "the cure for congested wealth and consuming poverty. This will extinguish the fires of socialism." [69]

The socially undistinguished, the poor, and the illiterate, neglected by the more respectable sects, found refuge in premillennial

[66] Henry K. Carroll, *Religious Forces of the United States* (rev. ed., New York, 1912), lxxxiv.

[67] McCulloch (ed.), *Call of the New South* and *South Mobilizing for Social Service,* and Charles R. Zahner, *Social Christianity, The Gospel for an Age of Social Strain* (Nashville, 1912), were published by the Methodist publisher and inspired by the social gospel.

[68] Quoted in Farish, *Circuit Rider Dismounts,* 104.

[69] Warren A. Candler, *Great Revivals and the Great Republic* (Nashville, 1904), 258.

cults. Despairing of blessings in this world, they generally looked forward to a cosmic cataclysm that would cast down the mighty and exalt the humble. Lumped together as "Holy Rollers" by "respectable" parishioners, they were given to uproarious practices that had characterized some of the older sects in their more primitive days. In the words of an official description of the Pentecostal Holiness Church, organized originally in the mill town of Anderson, South Carolina, in 1898, "Joyous demonstrations frequently characterize the services, and this is to some extent disagreeable to persons accustomed to a quiet form of worship." [70] Such sects sprouted thickly among the depressed masses of the South in the nineties. In 1895, C. H. Mason, a Negro, founded the Church of God in Christ and established the first congregation in an old ginhouse on the banks of a creek near Lexington, Mississippi. Thirty years later Mason was "general overseer and chief apostle" of over seven hundred churches.[71] In 1896 William S. Crowdy, an Oklahoma Negro cook, established the Church of God and Saints of Christ, which grew to ninety-four churches in twenty years. The Holiness Church was founded in Tennessee in 1902; the Free Christian Zion Church of Christ, at Redemption, Arkansas, in 1905; and the Churches of the Living God, in Texas in 1908.[72]

Apart from religion, literature, and scholarship, the South of this period found extraordinarily meager means of expression. Painters there were, as well as sculptors, musicians, and architects. Aside from expressions of a strictly folk level of art, however, this generation of Southerners was almost totally devoid of any aesthetic achievement that can be recorded as a permanent contribution to the culture of which they were a part. The region was as dependent aesthetically as it was economically. It imported its art—what little it got—as it did other consumers' goods, from the North or from abroad. Standard art museums, like standard Carnegie libraries, appeared on town squares—mausoleums to house the remains of

[70] Bureau of the Census, *Religious Bodies, 1916,* Pt. II, 543. The Southern origin of these sects was called to the writer's attention by Simkins, *South Old and New,* 324–25.

[71] Bureau of the Census, *Religious Bodies, 1926,* Pt. II, 380–81.

[72] Bureau of the Census, *Religious Bodies, 1916,* Pt. II, 204–205, 210, 217, 290. For the best description of the primitive parson, see Robert Penn Warren, *At Heaven's Gate* (New York, 1943).

picked-over collections from the estates of the wealthy. They rarely contained a single worthy example of the masters or anything vital from the studios of living artists. Scarcely any generation of Southerners, save that which wrestled with the frontier, was so completely isolated from the main streams of Western culture. Gentlemen from the court at Versailles, philosophers from revolutionary Paris, novelists from Victorian London had all at one time or another been able to find congenial company, creditable wines, and intellectual stimulation in Southern manor houses and plantations, even in the howling woods. But wilderness towns of the eighteenth-century South were often in closer touch with the wellsprings of Western civilization than were the industrial cities of the late nineteenth and early twentieth centuries.

Some slight advantages derived from isolation. The South was too poor, for example, to do much building in the period when architectural taste reached its lowest ebb. Prosperity did bring on a building boom in the first decade of the twentieth century. Surveying the new crop of structures in 1911, an architectural critic discovered little but stereotypes and imitations. He reported that "the staple Southern skyscraper" was "on the same footing with the staple skyscraper of the North." Having even less commercial justification, it appeared to be "erected as a matter of local or individual pride." He found "less than he expected" of "local color" and adaptation to regional needs. "Even the special physical requirement of the Southern climate, the greater need for shade, does not pervade the domestic architecture. As a rule, the good houses in the South might as well be in New England." [73] The visiting architect failed to comment on Florida, where Flagler was hanging stuccoed Spanish scenery on his luxury hotels, or on numerous examples of collegiate architecture decked out in frills from Renaissance Venice, medieval Oxford, and maybe Persia.

To find anything vital and original in Southern arts a tourist would have had to pass up the prosperous suburbs and either head for the backwoods or plunge back into the slums. In either place he would have found people who could not buy their art as con-

[73] Russell F. Whitehead, "The Old and the New South; A Consideration of Architecture in the Southern States," in *Architectural Record* (New York), XXX (1911), 34, 44, 56.

sumers' goods, and people who had plenty of sorrows of their own to sing about. They made their own art, started new religions, and sang their own songs. Enthusiasts had already begun to discover the folk songs of the Southern highlands. Singers from Fisk University and Hampton Institute were making the beauty of Negro spirituals known throughout the country and abroad. A public was slower to form for an art which originated in the few spots of the South where the nineties were gay. In the lower slums of New Orleans there began to appear Negro "spasm" bands or "jass" bands that put on sidewalk performances in front of saloons, theaters, dives, and whorehouses. The musicians, who could neither read nor write music, used homemade instruments and were given to wild improvisations, "cutting," "bucking," and "breaks." Louis Armstrong, the famous trumpeter, and Clarence Williams, the "swing" pianist, developed in this school. In 1910 W. C. Handy published his "Memphis Blues," and in 1911 one of the spasm bands of New Orleans played an engagement in New York under the name "Jazz Band." Four years later the "Dixie Land Jazz Band" toured the country.[74] In a very few years "American" music meant jazz in Paris, Cairo, Shanghai.

[74] Federal Writers Project, *New Orleans City Guide* (Boston, 1938), 136–38.

CHAPTER XVII

THE RETURN OF THE SOUTH

AT THE end of the first decade of the twentieth century the South looked back upon fifty years of isolation and impotence in national politics. Southerners could boast of the recovery of agricultural, commercial, or industrial power, but not the recovery of political power and prestige. Politically the South remained humbled, and its half-century of abasement was nowhere more evident than in its paltry share of place and power.

Between 1861 and 1912 no Southerner, except Andrew Johnson, served as President or Vice-President, nor did one achieve so much as the nomination of a major party for either office. Of the 133 cabinet members appointed during that period, only 14 were from the South, and of the 31 justices of the Supreme Court, only 7. The South furnished 2 of the 12 speakers of the House of Representatives during those years, and fewer than one tenth of the diplomatic representatives to the major powers. Whether because of the caliber of men chosen or the weakness of their party, the record of Southern delegations in Congress was lacking in distinction. "If for fifty years," wrote William Garrott Brown in 1910, "there has been a single great general law or policy initiated by Southerners or by a Southerner, or which goes or should go by any Southerner's name, the fact has escaped me." [1]

In contrast with the power and glory of the ante-bellum South, the impotence and frustration of the post-bellum period is all the more striking. For almost fifty of the seventy-two years between the inauguration of Washington and that of Lincoln, Southern men

[1] William Garrott Brown, "The South in National Politics," in *South Atlantic Quarterly*, IX (1910), 106.

had held the presidency, and for sixty of those years a Southern chief justice presided over the Supreme Court. During the period, the South furnished 20 of the 35 justices of the Supreme Court, 56 of the 119 men of cabinet rank, 13 of the 23 speakers of the House of Representatives, and more than half of the diplomatic representatives to major powers.[2]

Never in the history of the country, and rarely in the history of any country, had there been a comparable shift in the geography of political power. The phenomenon fascinated Southern strategists, and they speculated endlessly as to its causes. Although the explanation was undoubtedly complex, and included, besides a lost war, some account of shifts in economic power and the balance of population, Southern thinkers were inclined to oversimplify the problem and to seek in the realm of political action an explanation and a solution.

Debate over sectional diplomacy continued intermittently from the time the South turned its back on the Eastern alliance and embraced the West in 1896. The party revolution of that year, while resulting in the defeat of Bryan, had left his friends, the champions of a Western alliance, in command of the Southern wing of the party. Southern conservatives, friends of Cleveland and the East, remained discredited, for their desertion was remembered against them. The Bryanites found little difficulty in persuading their section to renew the alliance of 1896 in the next presidential election. The depression had left deep wounds upon the mind of the Southern people, and for years thereafter they nursed old scars and prescribed old remedies. The Democratic conventions of all the Southern states in 1900 either instructed their delegates to vote for Bryan at the national convention or heartily endorsed his candidacy. Imperialism, militarism, and expansion were favorite subjects for denunciation.[3]

The weakness of the strategy of a Western alliance was made apparent by the election of 1900. In all the West, so recently aflame with agrarian discontent, only Colorado, Idaho, Montana, and Nevada—four mountain states representing thirteen electoral votes

[2] Maryland is included in the ante-bellum South.

[3] Summaries of the conventions will be found under the names of the states, in *Appletons' Annual Cyclopaedia . . . 1900, passim.*

—joined the South in supporting Bryan. The South was left in greater isolation than it had been since 1872.

As in 1878, when the "Left-Forkers," advocates of a Western alliance, were silenced by the collapse of their experiment, the Bryanites of 1900 were overwhelmed by an outburst of abuse calling for a repudiation of the West, of radicalism, and of liberal tendencies generally. "What can the South expect," demanded the Louisville *Evening Post,* "from such a party and such leaders?" Two former members of Cleveland's cabinet, John G. Carlisle and Hoke Smith, called for a reorganization of the party to place conservatives in strict control. The Macon *Telegraph* pronounced the strategy of 1896 a "stupendous blunder" and that of 1900 "almost deliberate suicide," and the Richmond *Times* urged the party to "purge itself of Populism and Bryanism." [4] Conservatives and reactionaries who had not enjoyed a hearing in the South for eight years now burst into print to demand a revival of the New York–Atlanta axis. "Back to the Eastern alliance" was their cry.[5]

Thomas Fortune Ryan, Wall Street operator and onetime Virginian, was ready to point the way and assume the command lost by the Tillmans and Hoggs. He reminded Southerners that the only victories their party had won since the Civil War were won with New York nominees, conservative platforms, and the diplomacy of the Lamars, Hamptons, and Wattersons. Ryan recalled the glorious days of 1894, when the party was "the conservator of property rights and government by law," when its "fundamental policy" was "industrial freedom" and a repudiation of "The ball and chain of government interference with manufactures." The South, he adjured, should "with unflinching faith" set its face "Against these new follies of budding state-socialism." [6]

Unable to stem the tide of reactionism, Southern leaders reversed course with what grace they could and sailed with the cur-

[4] These and numerous other reactions to the results of the election are quoted in the New Orleans *Picayune,* November 8, 1900, and in *Public Opinion* (New York), XXIX (1900), 644–46.

[5] See, for example, S. S. P. Patteson, "The Political Isolation of the South," in *Sewanee Review,* IX (1901), 94–96; John L. McLaurin, "Breaking Up the Solid South," in *World's Work,* II (1901), 985–86; Perry Belmont, "The Plight of the Democratic Party," in *North American Review,* CLXXII (1901), 268–78.

[6] Thomas F. Ryan, "The Political Opportunity of the South," in *North American Review,* CLXXVI (1903), 161–72.

rent. Among those who sacrificed principle to expedience were fiery Bryanites as well as future Wilsonites. John W. Daniel of Virginia, Colonel Edward M. House of Texas, W. W. Kitchen of North Carolina, John Sharp Williams, House minority leader, along with James K. Vardaman, Albert S. Burleson, and even Ben Tillman co-operated with August Belmont and David B. Hill of New York to subvert liberal Democratic preachments of the past decade and promote the nomination of the ultraconservative New York banker, Judge Alton B. Parker.[7] "Certainly the bonds between the South and the extreme West have been dissolved," observed a Southern editor even before the Democratic national convention; "it is plain that we have elected to resume our friendship with the Democrats of the East." [8] To the conservatives of the South the counterrevolution within the Democratic party was welcome enough, but the palpable stultification of Southern sentiment in 1904 was unhappily illustrated by the picture of Ben Tillman pleading Parker's cause before the national convention after the nominee's "gold telegram" had offended all silverites.[9]

To Tom Watson it seemed "a colossal piece of effrontery" for the Democrats to admit that "for eight years they have been wrong and the Republicans have been right, and at the same time demand that the crowd which has been wrong shall be substituted for the party that has been right." Returning to politics after eight years of retirement, Watson accepted the Populist nomination for President and barnstormed the country from California to Boston, ridiculing the transmogrified Democracy and appealing to discontented Bryanites. He polled an insignificant vote. His own section submitted tamely to the old party.[10]

The strategists of reaction were even more thoroughly discredited by the results of their experiment in 1904 than the radicals had been in 1896 and 1900. In place of the thin Western support which they forfeited, they gained by their truckling to the conservative East a grand total of seven of Maryland's eight electoral votes—and

[7] House to Albert S. Burleson, June 4, 1904; Williams to Burleson, May 13, 1904, in Albert S. Burleson Papers (Division of Manuscripts, Library of Congress); Bryan to Hogg, July 10, 1902, in Hogg Papers; House to August Belmont, n.d. (copy), House Films, Roll 111.

[8] Jacksonville *Florida Times-Union,* June 15, 1904.

[9] Simkins, *Pitchfork Ben Tillman,* 390–92.

[10] Woodward, *Tom Watson,* 357–63.

nothing more. The South's isolation now seemed complete. As Senator Augustus O. Bacon of Georgia viewed the situation, "the South was as effectually cut off from all influence in the management of the United States Government as it would be if it was a British Crown colony." [11] There seemed to be nothing better to do in 1908 than to execute another about-face and return to Bryan for a third forlorn crusade. This merely resulted in the loss of one of Maryland's votes and the recovery of three Western states.

It was clear that the very solidarity of the South was one important source of its political impotence. Not only did it stake all its political fortunes upon the chances of a single party but those of a consistently losing party at that. Neither of the major parties was obliged to consult seriously the needs and wishes of the South: one found it unnecessary; the other, virtually useless. The indifference of its own party was the more maddening, for nothing was expected of the other. The only President the Democrats succeeded in electing in more than a half century appeared to turn a deaf ear to all but the conservative minority of the South. In the four presidential elections from 1896 to 1908, all of them Republican victories, the Democratic candidates polled a total of 633 electoral votes, 521 of which came from the Southern states.[12] In each of these contests, the party relied confidently upon the 130 or more votes of the South and succeeded in polling an average of only 28 votes outside the region. Yet for all its dogged constancy, the South's voice was far from decisive in party councils. Every four years found the South anxiously asking, complained Clark Howell, " 'What does New York want?' 'How does Tammany like this?'—or, 'Can we carry this, that, or the other doubtful Eastern state, by doing this, that, or the other thing'—and never stopping to make any reasonable and just demand as a matter of principle." [13]

Renouncing sectional alliances and balance of power politics as futile, one school of political thinkers placed the blame for the South's political plight entirely upon its one-party system. The South's rigid solidarity, they contended, stultified thought, pro-

11 Quoted in *Public Opinion*, XXXVII (1904), 644.

12 Edgar E. Robinson, *The Presidential Vote, 1896–1932* (Stanford University, 1947), Table X, 402–403.

13 Clark Howell to Page, August 29, 1908, in Page Papers.

moted intolerance, fostered indifference and nonvoting, and deprived the people of a wholesome political experience. It drove men of strong and independent minds out of politics and left the people prey to demagogues. It even robbed them of influence in the party to which they were blindly committed. The South had forfeited its freedom of choice, and loss of freedom generally means loss of power. The remedy, so they held, lay in the restitution of the two-party system and political independence.

By "independence" these gentlemen did not mean Populism and Socialism, nor by the "two-party system" did they mean restoration of Negro suffrage. They were inclined to be orthodox in their view of white supremacy and more orthodox in their economic views than their fellow Southerners. They were unhappy over the dominance of the Bryan element in the South, and their "independence" usually consisted of voting the national Republican ticket whenever the Democrats nominated Bryan. The most articulate people of this school were intellectuals who, for the most part, had moved North or had attached themselves to wealthy patrons or endowed institutions in the South. They included such men as Walter Hines Page, William Garrott Brown, James W. Garner, William P. Few, and Edwin Mims.[14]

Two other Southern elements pined for a rebirth of Republicanism in the South. One was the capitalist. The Southern Industrial League met in Atlanta in July, 1900, and expressed a strong preference for protective tariff, ship subsidies, the gold standard, and retention of the Philippines.[15] The other element was the Lily-white Republican organizations. These varied in character and respectability and were strongest in the Upper-South states of North Carolina, Tennessee, Kentucky, and Virginia, though they were present in all the states. Especially after disfranchisement took effect did

[14] See, for example, Page's introduction of the President at his speech to the North Carolina Society of New York, in William H. Taft, *The South and the National Government* (New York, 1908), 5–7; Brown, "South in National Politics," *loc. cit.*, 103–15; James W. Garner, "New Politics for the South," in *Annals of the American Academy of Political and Social Science*, XXV (1910), 172–83; Edwin Mims, "The Independent Voter in the South," in *South Atlantic Quarterly*, V (1906), 1–7; Edwin Mims, "President Theodore Roosevelt," *ibid.*, IV (1905), 48–62; William P. Few, "President Eliot and the South," *ibid.*, VIII (1908), 184–91.

[15] *Manufacturers' Record*, XXVIII (July 26, 1900), 1.

the Lily-whites gain the upper hand over the Black-and-Tan Republicans. "The fact is," wrote Ray Stannard Baker in 1908, "the Republican party, as now constituted in the South, is even a more restricted white oligarchy than the Democratic party. In nearly all parts of the South, indeed, it is a closed corporation which controls or seeks to control all the federal offices." [16]

These elements were not very harmonious, but they had enough in common to enable them to agree upon a sort of standing petition to Republican presidents, renewed from one administration to the next. This petition urged the appointment of white men to Federal offices in the South, the complete abandonment of the threat of Federal intervention in behalf of the Negro, and reassurances of any and all kinds that would overcome the Southern trauma of Negro domination. On a high plane this petition was framed in the searching articles of William Garrott Brown, and especially in his letters to President Taft. "What is needed," he wrote, "is fuller and fuller proof of an entirely sympathetic attitude on the part of the Republican party and its national leaders." [17] Brown, more than certain of the Lily-white politicians, was concerned that the party be made "respectable" in the South, but like them he was virtually demanding that the Republican Presidents adopt white supremacy. In the sixteen years of Republican rule that followed 1897, and especially in the latter half of the period, the Southern petitioners made rather remarkable progress toward the realization of their aims.

The significant changes in the Southern policy of the Republican party were made by Roosevelt and Taft. McKinley made two rather successful tours of the South, but the appeal he made to the people was largely sentimental in nature. He left the political policy developed by his predecessors largely unaltered and outstripped them in the appointment of Negroes to office.[18]

16 Baker, *Following the Color Line*, 261. See also, Lewinson, *Race, Class, & Party*, *passim*.

17 Brown to Charles D. Norton, Taft's secretary, October 13, 1910 (copy), in Brown Papers. Brown, however, wished to see "a few good Negroes put, with the consent of their communities, into inconspicuous places." See also, Taft to Brown, November 3, 1910; Brown to Taft, May 30, 1911 (copy), *ibid.*

18 Henry L. West, "The President's Recent Tour," in *Forum*, XXXI (1901), 661–69; Charles S. Olcott, *The Life of William McKinley* (Boston, 1916), II, 301–302. McKinley scotched a proposal to reduce the representation of the Southern "rotten

The way of Roosevelt with the South was as tortuous as the proverbial way of a man with a maid. Simultaneously, or by turns, he wooed the mutually hostile Black-and-Tans, Lily-whites, and White-Supremacy Democrats. Quixotic reformism mingled strangely with an old brand of practical politics from the start. One of his first acts as President was a move to elevate the quality of Federal appointments in the South. Publicly acknowledging Booker T. Washington as his adviser, he appointed to the Federal bench in Alabama former Governor Thomas G. Jones, conservative Gold Democrat. There followed a series of such appointments, "all of them democrats and all of them men of the highest standing," boasted the President.[19] It was the only way, he said, "to make a Republican party in the South which shall be even respectable." [20] It was, therefore, an appeal to conservative whites of both parties.

Yet Roosevelt's Southern policy in its early stages seems to have been more fundamentally dictated by his fear that Senator Mark Hanna would contest his nomination in 1904. Knowing the powerful hold that Hanna had upon the Negro delegations, which could prevent his nomination, Roosevelt sought to gain control of the Republican "rotten boroughs" of the South in order to ensure his nomination—just as his predecessors, who were less dedicated to reform, had done. James S. Clarkson of Iowa, a man he had once denounced as a spoilsman, was appointed surveyor of customs in New York and assigned the duty of securing Negro fealty.[21]

In the autumn of 1902 the Lily-white Republicans of the South moved against the Negro with an aggressiveness similar to that with which the White-Supremacy Democrats had driven him from political life. In North Carolina and Alabama, shortly after the disfranchisement campaigns, the Lily-white machines drew the color line and excluded Negro members from Republican conventions.[22]

---

boroughs" in Republican national conventions. Dorothy G. Fowler, *The Cabinet Politician; The Postmasters General, 1829–1909* (New York, 1943), 264–65.

19 Roosevelt to Howell, February 24, 1903, in Atlanta *Constitution,* March 2, 1903.

20 Roosevelt to Postmaster General Henry C. Payne, July 8, 1902, quoted in Fowler, *Cabinet Politician,* 266.

21 Henry F. Pringle, *Theodore Roosevelt, A Biography* (New York, 1931), 343–44; Henry F. Pringle, "Theodore Roosevelt and the South," in *Virginia Quarterly Review,* IX (1933), 14–25.

22 New York *Times,* October 25, 1902; Washington *Star,* November 18, 1902; Moore, *History of Alabama,* 656–57.

Fearing a general revolt of the Negroes against the President, who was reported to have favored the blow against them in North Carolina, Booker Washington hurried to New York to see Clarkson. After a conference with Roosevelt, Clarkson assured Washington of the President's "displeasure and disapproval over the attempt to form a white man's party" of "Jim Crow" Republicans in the Southern states.[23] The President did much more. He called in groups of Negro leaders and reassured them; he released to the press Washington's letter recommending Judge Jones and revealing the Negro's influence over patronage; he punished the Lily-whites by removing one of their officeholders in Alabama and replacing him with a Gold Democrat. More striking yet was his appointment of William D. Crum, a Negro, to a conspicuous Federal office at Charleston and his stubborn fight against the Senate's refusal to confirm the appointment. Then early in January, 1903, he closed the post office at Indianola, Mississippi, because of white demonstrations against the Negro postmistress.

The disaffected Negroes were delighted at the President's change of course. Meeting in Washington in January, the National Afro-American Council resolved to "commend Theodore Roosevelt to the affection and confidence of our people regardless of party affiliation." On the other hand, certain Lily-white Republican leaders angrily repudiated the President and endorsed Hanna as their candidate for 1904.[24]

In the meantime, the wooing of Southern white Democrats had gone from bad to worse. The reaction to Booker Washington's dinner at the White House in the first month of Roosevelt's presidency was startling in its violence, even in a day of high-pitched racial propaganda.[25] No amount of Federal offices for respectable Gold Democrats—including one for a grandson of Stonewall Jackson and another for a son of Jeb Stuart—seemed to allay the rancor it aroused. John Temple Graves declared that Roosevelt had "destroyed the sectional peace and fraternal harmony which McKinley

[23] James S. Clarkson to Washington, October 11, 1902, in Washington Papers.

[24] New York *Herald*, January 26, 1903; Washington *Post*, January 12, 26, 31, 1903. See also, Roosevelt to Washington, May 9, 1904, in Washington Papers.

[25] Examples quoted in New York *Times*, October 19, 1901. It *was* a dinner, not a luncheon, as Southern folklore modified the story after Roosevelt regained his popularity.

builded,"[26] and a New Orleans editor called him "the worst enemy to his race of any white man who has ever occupied so high a place in this republic."[27] Watterson's paper pronounced him "infinitely a worse enemy of the white men and women of the south than any of the radical leaders of the past."[28]

Disturbed at the bitterness, Roosevelt wrote long letters of remonstrance. He maintained that he had appointed fewer Negroes and more white Democrats and showed more solicitude for Southern feelings than any previous Republican President, yet he had been rewarded with more hatred than any of them. He seems to have been genuinely bewildered at what he called "the incomprehensible outcry."[29] One thing Roosevelt failed to take into account was the change in the South itself: his first administration happened to coincide with the climax of Southern racism and propaganda that accompanied and followed disfranchisement. In the second place, although his challenges to Southern mores were fewer, they were more spectacular and considerably more widely publicized than those of any recent President.

If in his policies Roosevelt was repugnant to the South, in person he was to prove irresistible. With the "rotten boroughs" under control, the Hanna threat dispelled, and the election of 1904 handsomely won, he returned to the task of winning the South. In April, 1905, he stormed across Texas, making some thirty speeches, and left the politicians amazed at what he had done. "I have never witnessed anything like the change which has occurred toward him," one of them wrote Albert S. Burleson. The tour was a continuous ovation and a personal triumph.[30] In the fall he returned

[26] Quoted in Jacksonville *Florida Times-Union,* March 8, 1903.

[27] New Orleans *Daily Picayune,* March 8, 1903.

[28] Louisville *Courier-Journal,* quoted in *Public Opinion,* XXXVII (1904), 645. The Roosevelt Scrapbooks (Widener Library, Harvard University), especially "Events of Interest," Vol. V, contain ample illustration of Southern sentiment.

[29] Roosevelt to Howell, February 24, 1903, in Atlanta *Constitution,* March 2, 1903. Roosevelt's fullest and most interesting letter on the Negro and the South was written to Owen Wister, April 27, 1906, and published in Wister, *Roosevelt, the Story of a Friendship, 1880–1919* (New York, 1930), 248–57. See also, Roosevelt to Wister, May 3, June 21, 1906, *ibid.,* 258–62.

[30] W. G. S. Sterett to Burleson, April 20, 1905, in Burleson Papers; C. Arthur Williams, "The President in Texas," in *Collier's,* XXXV (April 24, 1905), 16; Acheson, *35,000 Days in Texas,* 218–19.

to complete the conquest in speeches from Richmond to New Orleans. The President's railroad, trust, and Panama Canal policies were mentioned to explain his wildly enthusiastic reception, but they were as nothing compared with his brash emotional appeal. Roosevelt paid homage to Lee and the Confederacy and praised the Southern people for loyalty to their traditions. He advised the Negroes at Tuskegee to stay out of the professions and trust Southern whites as their best friends. He sent roses to Stonewall Jackson's widow and had himself photographed with three picturesque Negro servants of the Bulloch family before the columns of the ancestral mansion in Georgia. "One would suppose that the President himself fired the last two shots from the *Alabama* instead of his uncle," wrote one reporter who heard talk of a Democratic nomination for Roosevelt.[31]

Little more was heard against Roosevelt's racial views. "If there has been any conversion on that subject, it is rather the President than the South that has seen a new light," observed William Garrott Brown. He congratulated Roosevelt on his "new attitude on the Southern question." [32] Thomas Nelson Page thought the President was "more a Democrat than a Republican," [33] and Edwin Mims believed he was "as much opposed to negro domination as any Southerner." [34]

On the other hand, the Negro reaction to the Southern tour was one of disillusionment. Out of fifty Negro leaders who were asked for their opinion of the President's course by the *Voice of the Negro,* only ten approved. A majority of the Negro newspapers that commented were critical. Du Bois condemned his silence on disfranchisement, and an unidentified leader thought him guilty of "national treachery to the Negro." Only Booker Washington and a few others wholly approved.[35] The following year, when Roosevelt ordered three companies of Negro troops dishonorably

[31] "Visit of the President to the South," in *Confederate Veteran* (Nashville), XIII (1905), 488–90; "Roosevelt's Tour Through the South," in *Voice of the Negro* (Atlanta, Chicago), II (1905), 823–24; Pringle, *Theodore Roosevelt,* 371.

[32] William Garrott Brown, "President Roosevelt and the South," in *Independent,* LIX (1905), 1086–89.

[33] Thomas N. Page, "President Roosevelt from the Standpoint of a Southern Democrat," in *Metropolitan Magazine* (New York), XXI (1905), 680.

[34] Mims, "President Theodore Roosevelt," *loc. cit.,* 62.

[35] "A Canvass for Opinion," in *Voice of the Negro,* II (1905), 827.

discharged as a result of the riot in Brownsville, Texas, for which the Negroes disclaimed responsibility, even Washington wavered. "Within a few days—I might almost say hours—as a consequence of this order, the songs of praise of ten million people were turned into a chorus of criticism and censure," he wrote.[36]

The revised Southern policy was wholeheartedly embraced by Taft. As Secretary of War he uncomplainingly shouldered the indignant criticism of Roosevelt's Brownsville order.[37] In a speech at Greensboro, North Carolina, in 1906, he "delighted the Democrats and infuriated the Republicans," according to Josephus Daniels, by declaring that his party in that state would be stronger "if all the Federal offices were filled by Democrats." [38] While he denounced the influence of Southern rotten boroughs upon the Republican party as roundly as Roosevelt, Taft depended upon patronage to secure Southern delegates pledged to support his nomination.[39] In his presidential campaign, however, Taft broke with party precedent. Declaring that he would not be President of half the country, he invaded the South. "I am proud," he told Atlantans, "to have been the first Republican candidate for the Presidency who, in the course of his campaign, visited states south of Mason and Dixon's line." [40] Roosevelt contributed his bit by appointing Luke E. Wright, an ex-Confederate soldier and Democrat from Tennessee, his Secretary of War. "With the President and three members of the cabinet either Southern bred, Southern born or Southern biased; with the first Secretary of War since Jefferson Davis an ex-Confederate soldier [*sic*]; with the present Republican candidate so Southern in sentiment that many Negroes are forsaking his standard," the South could at last divide its vote, declared one patriot.[41]

Whether because of the unpopularity of Roosevelt's racial policy in his first term or the attraction Parker held for Southern conserva-

36 Washington, *My Larger Education*, 181.

37 Henry F. Pringle, *The Life and Times of William Howard Taft* (New York, 1939), I, 323–28.

38 Daniels, *Editor in Politics*, 488.

39 Fowler, *Cabinet Politician*, 291–96; Pringle, *William Howard Taft*, I, 347.

40 William Howard Taft, *Political Issues and Outlooks* (New York, 1909), 231.

41 Thornwell Jacobs, in *Taylor-Trotwood Magazine* (Nashville), VIII (1908), 7. See also, Silas McBee, "The South and Mr. Taft," in *Sewanee Review*, XVI (1908), 486–94.

tives, the Republican vote in the South declined markedly in 1904. On the other hand, whether due to the overtures of Taft or conservative reaction against Bryan's third campaign, the Republicans gained significantly in 1908. The Republican vote increased in all Southern states, varying from a few hundred in some to more than 12,000 in Tennessee, more than 17,000 in Georgia, 18,000 in Texas, nearly 30,000 in Kentucky, and more than 32,000 in North Carolina. The change of a few thousand votes in Tennessee and North Carolina would have delivered them to Taft. Since few Negroes were voting any longer, these gains very largely represented an increase of white votes. One estimate held that more than 100,000 of the 114,000 Republican votes in North Carolina were white votes.[42]

Declaring that he had "only just begun," Taft returned to the South shortly after his election to make several speeches, one of which he hopefully entitled "The Winning of the South." In this and other pronouncements he reiterated the shibboleths of White Supremacy: "the best friend that the Southern Negro can have is the Southern white man," the history of Reconstruction was "painful," the fear of Federal enforcement of social equality was "imaginary," and—most emphatically—there was nothing inconsistent between the Fifteenth Amendment and Southern safeguards against "domination . . . by an ignorant electorate"—that is, disfranchisement.[43] Taft secured the resignation of Dr. Crum, replaced him with a white man, and declared that thenceforth he would find the more prominent offices for the Negro in the North.[44]

Excited by such pronouncements and by the vote in 1908, William Garrott Brown went so far as to say that it was "only a question of time" until one or more Southern states went Republican, and Walter Hines Page hailed "the impending and inevitable breaking of the Solid South." [45] Until well into 1910 there was no

[42] Robinson, *Presidential Vote,* Table II, 47–54; William Garrott Brown, "President Taft's Opportunity," in *New Politics and Other Papers* (Boston, 1914), 177–80.

[43] Taft, "The Winning of the South," in *Political Issues and Outlooks,* 237; also his address to the North Carolina Society of New York, in *South and the National Government,* especially pp. 10–12; and quotations in Henry L. West, "President Taft and the South," in *Forum,* XLI (1909), 289–96.

[44] Pringle, *William Howard Taft,* I, 390.

[45] Brown, "President Taft's Opportunity," *loc. cit.,* 182–83; Page in his introduction of Taft in the latter's address to the North Carolina Society of New York, in Taft, *South and the National Government,* 6.

lack of prophets who were ready to stake their reputations upon predictions of the eventual, imminent, or immediate dissolution of the Solid South.[46] By the end of that year, however, Taft had revealed a position on the tariff that was highly unpopular in the South; the Democrats had won a sweeping victory in congressional elections, and the progressive crusade was fighting for control of both the old parties.

There was plenty of tinder lying loose in the South to catch the sparks of a national progressive crusade. The South was, after all, the most thoroughly Bryanized region in the country. Nor were all the sparks struck off by the Crolys, Weyls, and Brandeises up North. The patrician radical Walter Clark had used the North Carolina supreme court bench for twenty years as a platform for ringing pronouncements that placed him in the vanguard of progressive thought of his time and to the left of Herbert Croly and Louis D. Brandeis. Member of an aristocratic planter family and a Confederate veteran, Clark enjoyed the unique distinction in the nineties of having his candidacy officially endorsed by Populists and Republicans as well as Democrats. He battled relentlessly against the monopolies and railroads and worked tirelessly to protect the health and life of factory workers. No measure, he thought, should be rejected merely because it was socialistic. "Every civilized government is to a large extent, and almost in proportion to its degree of civilization, socialistic," declared Judge Clark.[47] At the other end of the South, Colonel Edward M. House of Texas moved more silently toward his ends. He embodied his dreams and ideals in an anonymous novel, *Philip Dru: Administrator,* published in 1912, but begun before he met Woodrow Wilson. A utopian yarn describing the realization of a progressive's paradise, the novel has as its hero a young Southerner who rallies a rebel army and overthrows an Eastern oligarchy of "masterful and arrogant wealth." After the revolution the hero rewrites the constitution, enacts every heard-of reform, and sails off to organize a "League of Nations."

[46] For example, Enoch M. Banks, "The Passing of the Solid South," in *South Atlantic Quarterly,* VIII (1909), 101; E. N. Vallandigham, "The Solid South in Dissolution," in *Putnam's Magazine* (New York), VII (1909–1910), 803–808.

[47] Brooks and Lefler (eds.), *Papers of Walter Clark,* I, 449; and II, 535–53, for a foretaste of the New Deal in 1903. See also, Brooks, *Walter Clark: Fighting Judge, passim.*

Besides these Southern progressives, there was in every Southern state from Virginia to Texas a progressive wing of the old party with leaders seasoned by years of fighting the bosses and machines. In some states the progressive wing was in the ascendancy in 1910, in others it was struggling toward power. In a majority of cases, these elements in the South were eventually recruited by the Wilson movement. But not at first.

The first Southern "president-makers" whom Wilson attracted were precisely the same sort he originally attracted in the North—the most conservative elements in the Democratic party. When Colonel George Harvey experimentally raised the Wilson banner in New York in 1906, Henry Watterson of the Louisville *Courier-Journal*, James C. Hemphill of the Charleston *News and Courier*, and John G. Carlisle, Cleveland's Secretary of the Treasury, responded enthusiastically. These gentlemen, together with August Belmont, Thomas Fortune Ryan, and Harvey, saw Wilson as A Parker, perhaps, for 1908." [48] The logic of casting Wilson in this role is apparent when it is recalled that three weeks after the election of 1904 he had publicly called on the South to renounce the Bryanites, whom he wished "utterly and once for all thrust out of Democratic counsels." [49] Southern conservatives, who framed their campaign to prevent Bryan's nomination in 1908 under the slogan "A Southerner for President," looked hopefully to Wilson. One such group, meeting in Nashville in 1907, cheered "every reference to Bryan's unfitness," issued an address to the Democrats of the country declaring that "the South has always been regarded as the bulwark of conservatism," and invited Wilson to address them.[50]

Failing to have their way in 1908, the original Wilson men, encouraged by their candidate's election as governor of New Jersey, continued their efforts. As late as December, 1910, Harvey and Watterson, the ranking generals of the campaign, conferred with Thomas Fortune Ryan at the latter's Virginia estate to persuade the millionaire to back their plans for 1912. "Marse Henry," who was one of the chief architects of Tilden's nomination in 1876,

48 Baker, *Woodrow Wilson, Life and Letters*, III, 4, 21–22.

49 *Ibid.*, 9–10; New York *World*, December 1, 1904.

50 Wilson, however, was "forced to decline." Nashville *American*, November 13, 1907; "A National Democrat," "Has the Conservative South a Presidential Candidate?" in *North American Review*, CLXXXV (1907), 475–84.

seemed on the point of rounding out a brilliant career of thirty-six years of conservative sectional diplomacy by consolidating another East-South alliance. Then, within a brief period, the whole conservative Wilson organization evaporated. Governor Wilson had revealed himself as a smasher of political machines and bosses and an uncompromising reformer. The bosses of other states, who had previously shown great sympathy, quickly lost interest. Even Harvey, Watterson, Hemphill, and Ryan were soon involved in schemes to discredit their former candidate and ruin his chances. The Wilson presidential movement, so recently manned by eager advisers, was by January, 1911, left without pilot or crew.[51]

Early the following spring an entirely new organization was formed by new men. The key figures were William F. McCombs, Walter F. McCorkle, and Walter Hines Page. William G. McAdoo joined them in the summer. Southerners all, they were yet Southerners of a type different from that represented by Watterson and Hemphill. Uprooted, transplanted, and urbanized provincials, they lived as exiles in New York. Insofar as they represented the progressive South, it was the new urban-progressive group which they led instead of the agrarian wing. McCombs of Arkansas had become devoted to Wilson as his student at Princeton. Able, erratic, and inordinately ambitious, he quickly assumed command of the organization.[52] McCorkle, a Virginian and president of the Southern Society of New York, was less active in the work. McAdoo of Georgia and Tennessee, the third member of this Scotch-Irish conspiracy, was famous in New York as the builder of the Hudson Tunnels. He soon became second only to McCombs in the organization.[53] Page, the expatriate Tarheel, was privy to the plot from the start and active to the end.[54] The role of Colonel House of Texas, as Professor Link has shown, was peripheral and unimportant to this phase of Wilson's fortunes.[55]

As vital as was the work of the Southerners-in-exile, the work of

51 Arthur S. Link, *Wilson: The Road to the White House* (Princeton, 1947), 310–11.

52 Maurice F. Lyons, *William F. McCombs, The President Maker* (Cincinnati, 1922), and William F. McCombs, *Making Woodrow Wilson President* (New York, 1921), give the McCombs side of the story.

53 He tells his own story in *Reminiscences of William G. McAdoo.*

54 Wilson to Page, February 10, 1911, in Page Papers, is the opening document in the story of the organization.

55 Link, *Wilson: The Road to the White House,* 334–35.

Southerners-in-domicile was more decisive in the prenomination phase of the Wilson movement. For however secure the South was to a Democratic nominee, it was a wide-open field of contest for three candidates for the nomination—all claiming varying degrees of Southernness. Wilson made the capture of the state delegations of his native South a primary objective. A onetime resident of four states of the Southeast, he enjoyed numerous advantages. The Southern press had followed his fight in New Jersey closely, devoting much space to it; and with remarkable unanimity both conservative and progressive editors had sided with him against the bosses. There was, in fact, a curious ambivalence in Wilson's appeal to the South. While the progressives hailed him as their hero, the conservatives, their eyes fixed upon his record up to 1911, clung lingeringly to him as the new symbol of an old Tilden-Cleveland-Parker system of alliance. Southern progressives, on the other hand, breaking the old mold of sectional thinking, looked to him to head an alliance of the urban middle class and the workers in the North with which the South could deal. As the preconvention campaign developed, however, Southern conservatives fell away from Wilson, and he became increasingly the issue over which the two wings of Democrats divided and fought. Between them differences were as marked in several states as between Old-Guard and Progressive Republicans in the North.

Wilson's own reading of the situation at the opening of his campaign in the South is remarkable. He wrote in April, 1911: "The South is a very conservative region—just now probably the most (possibly the only) conservative section of the country—and I am *not* conservative. I am a radical." [56] Which leaves it a moot question whether his misunderstanding of himself or of his native region was the greater.

The Governor opened his national campaign for the nomination with an address in Atlanta in March, 1911, to the Southern Commercial Congress, which had also listened to President Taft and former President Roosevelt. The liberal press of the state reported that the Governor was received with more enthusiasm than either the President or the former President. Wilson skirted the

[56] Wilson to Mary A. Hulbert, April 30, 1911, quoted in Baker, *Woodrow Wilson*, III, 198–99.

edges of a dynamic issue when he warned the South to guard against the domination of financial imperialism of Northeastern capital and brought cheers by calling on the region to "take its place in the councils of the Nation." He was closeted long with Senator-elect Hoke Smith, who like Wilson, had been converted from a Cleveland conservative to a progressive. Soon afterward Smith announced publicly in favor of Wilson's nomination. He was the first figure of political importance in the country to do so.[57]

Before the end of 1911 Wilson had campaigned extensively in Georgia, South Carolina, North Carolina, Virginia, Kentucky, and Texas. During the hottest part of the preconvention campaign, from January to April, 1912, he took time to speak in Virginia, Florida, Georgia, and Tennessee. His cure for the ills of the South differed in no important respect from that he offered the rest of the country. It was largely a matter of replacing machine rule by popular rule. He returned very rarely to the issue of the heedless exploitation of Southern resources and people by Northeastern capital. In fact, he had little to say of economic questions, even showing reluctance to allow tariff reform to become one of his issues. Nor did he talk in the forthright manner of the old Populists about the everyday economic concerns of the people. He did castigate the trusts, and once in South Carolina spoke severely about the "money power." A recurrence to the latter theme called forth a letter of remonstrance from William Garrott Brown. "Don't, we beg of you," he wrote Wilson, "—I will be old fashioned and *implore* you—don't throw away what Cleveland kept, what Roosevelt lost—the confidence of men of your class." [58] Whether he heeded such remonstrances as this or the promptings of his own conscience, Wilson ceased firing, save for an intermittent shot, on economic malefactors and concentrated his barrage upon political miscreants—bosses, machines, lobbyists. While this was a needless forbearance so far as it concerned the typical Southern progressive (whose leaders had been as unsparing in their attacks on business and finance as had any in the country), it no doubt spared the feel-

[57] Arthur S. Link, "The Democratic Pre-Convention Campaign of 1912 in Georgia," in *Georgia Historical Quarterly*, XXIX (1945), 145–47; Atlanta *Journal*, March 10, 11, 1911.

[58] Brown to Wilson, October 30, 1911 (copy by Bassett), in Brown Papers.

ings of his more timid admirers. The Governor's crusade against bosses and machines, on the other hand, fitted exactly the platforms and slogans of the progressive wing of the Democratic party in a majority of the Southern states. They proceeded forthwith to combine a movement to capture state delegations for Wilson with a renewed onslaught upon state bosses.[59]

"How like the conditions in Tennessee are the conditions in New Jersey, as related by Dr. Wilson," observed a Tennessee reform editor. Were the Doctor in that state, declared the editor, "he would be fighting the James Smiths." [60] The "Jim Smith" of Tennessee was former Governor Malcolm R. Patterson, against whom the progressive Democrats had been in rebellion since 1908 and whom they had succeeded in overthrowing in 1910, the year Wilson was elected in New Jersey. They had achieved this by an insurgency similar to that which was tearing the Republican party apart in the North at the same time. The insurgent Democrats, or Independents, led by Senator Luke Lea, refused to follow the regular Democrats in supporting Wilson's opponents, and carried their fight for Wilson to Baltimore.

Texas progressives, like their brothers in Tennessee, were embattled against a conservative state machine over the control of the Democratic party, and like them also the Texans came to look upon their struggle against the bosses and their support of Wilson as one and the same fight. Senator Joseph W. Bailey, boss of the conservative machine, furthered this view by opposing the "revolutionary" Wilson as vigorously as the progressives supported him. Bailey's opponents, Thomas B. Love, Thomas W. Gregory, and Albert S. Burleson, with the aid of Senator Charles A. Culberson and the old Hogg and Bryan faction, constructed "the most effective state Wilson organization in the nation," and won a victory that was

[59] The following account of the Wilson movement in the South is based, in addition to the sources cited, largely upon the investigations of Arthur S. Link. Besides his publications cited above, these include "Tennessee Politics and the Presidential Campaign of 1912," in East Tennessee Historical Society's *Publications*, No. 18 (1946), 107–30; "The Wilson Movement in Texas, 1910-1912," in *Southwestern Historical Quarterly*, XLVIII (1944–1945), 169–85; and "The Wilson Movement in North Carolina," in *North Carolina Historical Review*, XXIII (1946), 483–94.

[60] Nashville *Tennessean and Nashville American*, January 8, 1911. See also, *ibid.*, January 10, 13, 1911.

probably decisive in the preconvention campaign.[61] In North Carolina and Virginia the cleavage over Wilson's candidacy between progressive and conservative Democrats, between the antimachine faction and the machine was as clear-cut as in Tennessee and Texas. Josephus Daniels, Walter Clark, and the Kitchin brothers led North Carolina progressives of the Bryan tradition in a spirited Wilson campaign against the opposition of the machine of Furnifold M. Simmons, whom they sought to retire from the Senate.[62] "The machine in Virginia, as elsewhere," wrote Carter Glass, "is utterly opposed to Wilson." [63] Glass, former Governor Andrew J. Montague, and Henry St. George Tucker carried their war against the machine of Senators Thomas S. Martin and Claude A. Swanson into the presidential contest. Martin worked assiduously with Thomas Fortune Ryan and Congressman Hal D. Flood for the defeat of Wilson.[64] South Carolina was unique in having no serious, organized opposition to Wilson, and although Governor Cole Blease opposed him personally, the state was united for Wilson.

Wilson workers generally assumed that Bryan followers in the South could be relied upon to support Wilson,[65] but this was not true in all states. In Kentucky, where issues were greatly confused, they supported Champ Clark, while in Oklahoma Bryanites and progressive Democrats were divided between Wilson and Clark, and in Arkansas, where no organized contest for Wilson was made, they supported Clark.

Oscar W. Underwood of Alabama represented the most formidable opposition confronting Wilson in the South, and it was around him that conservative anti-Wilson elements generally rallied after

[61] Link, "Wilson Movement in Texas," *loc. cit.*, 171. On the decisiveness of the Texas vote there is an interesting editorial in the Galveston *Daily News*, May 3, 1912.

[62] Raleigh *News and Observer*, April 29, May 10, 1911; May 12, 16, 25, 1912; Brooks, *Walter Clark: Fighting Judge*, 182–85; Josephus Daniels, *The Wilson Era: Years of Peace—1910–1917* (Chapel Hill, 1944), 16.

[63] Carter Glass to Professor Richard H. Dabney, January 10, 1912; Glass to Stuart G. Gibboney, January 10, 1912, copies in Carter Glass Papers (University of Virginia Library).

[64] Thomas S. Martin to R. W. Perkins, March 19, 1912, in Burleson Papers; Norfolk *Ledger-Dispatch*, May 24, 1912; Richmond *Times-Dispatch*, July 4, 1912.

[65] In an interesting analysis of Wilson's strength in various Southern states in February, 1912, Alexander J. McKelway makes this assumption. McKelway to Wilson, February 8, 1912, copy in McKelway Papers.

the cause of Governor Judson Harmon of Ohio became hopeless. The Alabama Congressman burst into national prominence in 1911 upon the calling of the special session of Congress. Underwood was chairman of the powerful Ways and Means Committee and House Leader of the Democratic majority elected in 1910. His skillful management of the free-list bills, which Taft vetoed, was proof of his ability, and the tact and assurance with which he marshaled the new Democratic majority into a unified and effective party, for the first time in a generation, demonstrated genius for leadership. Underwood regarded Bryan as the symbol of frustration and ineffectuality. Bryan challenged the new leader with a savage attack on his tariff decisions, but Underwood's reply from the floor of the House was so effective that Bryan's closest friends were unable to defend him. Here was a Southerner of a new type —without perorations and frills, but not without effectiveness, a type that was to fill the high command of the Wilson administration.[66]

Underwood's contest for the presidential nomination began modestly as a "favorite son" movement in Alabama. Wilson managers conceded that state, but the movement spread afield. In addition to the tariff record of their candidate, the Underwood strategists stressed his Southernness, raised the cry of "The South for a Southerner," and adjured ex-Confederates to "assert their manhood," and "vote for the South." In reply to a challenge of his Confederate antecedents, Underwood's friends publicized the report that his father had been "imprisoned for Southern sympathies." No connection of any of the candidates with secession and rebellion which might attest their qualifications for President was too remote to be neglected. Wilson was held up as "the true Southerner," while Clark was dismissed as "a professional Southerner, a type not uncommon in the North." The controversy (conducted in all seriousness) rapidly became an absurd reversal of the historic rule that a Southern connection was fatal to a Presidential candidacy.[67]

[66] Burton J. Hendrick, "Oscar Underwood, A New Leader from the New South," in *McClure's Magazine* (New York), XXXVIII (1911–1912), 416–20; Claude G. Bowers, "Oscar W. Underwood: A Portrait," in Oscar W. Underwood, *Drifting Sands of Party Politics* (New York, 1931), vii–xiv; *Congressional Record*, 62 Cong., 1 Sess., 3511–13.

[67] For examples, see Atlanta *Constitution*, March 24, May 1, 3, 4, 9, 1912; Atlanta *Journal*, March 31, April 23, 1912; Mobile *Register*, February 4, 7, 1912; Dallas *Morning News*, March 4, 1912.

For less sentimental reasons Underwood's cause was embraced by a number of powerful state machines that were fighting rebellious Wilson factions. The Clark Howell–Joseph M. Brown machine of Georgia, the Martin-Swanson machine in Virginia, the Simmons machine in North Carolina, and the Flagler group with Governor Albert W. Gilchrist of Florida were enlisted in Underwood's campaign. More than three fifths of the funds expended in his behalf were, according to his manager, contributed by Thomas Fortune Ryan.[68] These forces and men enjoyed no wide popular appeal in the South of 1912. They were identified in the public mind with Eastern finance capital, Southern corporate interests and railroads, and reactionary politics. They could never have commanded the popular support marshaled for Underwood had it not been for an incongruous alliance with the very elements in the South which were their bitterest traditional enemies.

Politically confused and demoralized, the defeated legions of Southern Populism had wandered restlessly and homelessly since the nineties. Demagogues had usurped command and diverted them with sham battles against assorted "menaces." Progressivism was essentially urban and its leaders were city men who did not understand nor speak their language. The Wilson movement was in charge of these very same citified progressives, and Wilson's smooth, academic shibboleths of progressivism found less lodgment in the rural than in the urban mind. Rural leaders of the new type —Vardaman of Mississippi, Tom Heflin of Alabama, and the latter-day Watson of Georgia—had no difficulty in leading their followers into an alliance with the machines in support of Underwood. Watson illuminated the campaign by charges that Wilson "kow-towed to the Roman hierarchy," and was "*ravenously fond of the Negro.*' The primary in Georgia illustrated the urban character of Wilson's strength and the rural appeal of Underwood, for while the former carried all but one of the larger cities and most of the towns, the rural counties swept the state into the Underwood camp.[69]

The contest for the Presidential nomination in 1912 was the first

[68] Arthur S. Link, "The Underwood Presidential Movement of 1912," in *Journal of Southern History*, XI (1945), 236, 240.

[69] Woodward, *Tom Watson*, 426–27; Link, "Democratic Pre-Convention Campaign of 1912 in Georgia," *loc. cit.*, 157.

in half a century in which the South played a conspicuous and perhaps even decisive part, and it was the most heated contest of the kind in that period. Insofar as the preconvention struggle was a contest between Wilson and Underwood, the result was very nearly a tie, with Wilson commanding 109 votes and Underwood 111½. Only Texas and South Carolina gave their entire vote to Wilson, while approximately half of Louisiana's vote, three fifths of North Carolina's, half of Oklahoma's, a quarter of Tennessee's, and a third of Virginia's went to him. The four Lower-South states, Alabama, Mississippi, Georgia, and Florida, cast all their votes for Underwood while North Carolina contributed about one third of hers, Tennessee a quarter and Virginia two thirds. Wilson's vote did not accurately reflect progressive strength in the South, for the issue was confused by Clark, who appealed for progressive support and won 70 votes in the Southwestern states.[70]

In the first ballot at the Baltimore convention the Southern vote for Wilson constituted a little more than one third and, with that of Pennsylvania and New Jersey, was the mainstay of the Wilson forces. During the marches and countermarches of forty-six ballotings, the unshakable firmness of the Southern Wilson delegates, the skilled strategy of Albert S. Burleson of Texas, Wilson's floor leader at Baltimore, and the work of his lieutenants Thomas W. Gregory and Luke Lea, as well as the generalship of McCombs, commander of the Army, and McAdoo, were of immense importance in overcoming the almost insuperable odds against Wilson. Of crucial importance was the bargain the Southern Wilson leaders made with the Underwood leaders, which prevented a landslide that would have given the nomination to Clark. Indeed, without the aid of Bankhead, Martin, and some of the Northern bosses against whom he had directed his whole campaign, Wilson would not have been nominated.[71]

The campaign that followed was enlivened by the first serious third-party effort in the South since the nineties. In his eagerness to "carry one of the eleven ex-Confederate States" for the Progressive party, Roosevelt went to even greater lengths than he had

70 *Official Report of the Proceedings of the Democratic National Convention . . . 1912* (Chicago, 1912), 196–97.

71 Link, *Wilson: The Road to the White House*, 431–65.

during his second administration to placate Southern white racism. In effect he adopted the policy of the state Democratic progressive movements—progressivism for whites only. The Bull Moose convention of 1912 categorically refused to seat any Negro delegates from the South, though four states sent Negro delegations to contest the seats of rival white delegations. While turning his back on the Southern Negro, Roosevelt welcomed Northern Negroes as "the peers of white men." A "Lily-white Progressive party" was organized in every Southern state except Oklahoma, and Roosevelt carried his appeal to "the best white men in the South" in speeches at Little Rock, Memphis, New Orleans, Montgomery, Atlanta, Chattanooga, and Raleigh. He was cheered as warmly as he had been during his presidency, but he only succeeded in splitting the Republican vote in the Upper South and in getting about one fifth of the total vote in Georgia, Arkansas, and Alabama.[72]

The Georgia–New Yorkers, Arkansas–New Yorkers, and other hyphenated Southerners who figured in Wilson's preconvention campaign also took charge of his campaign for election. McCombs served as national chairman until he collapsed and was replaced by McAdoo. Josephus Daniels commanded the publicity bureau, Senator Thomas P. Gore of Oklahoma the organization bureau, and Burleson the speakers bureau. Spellbinders from the South, no longer needed where the victory was already won, swarmed northward to lend a hand. While every Southern state save Oklahoma gave Wilson a majority of its popular votes, Arizona was the only state outside the South to do so. So large was Wilson's majority of electoral votes, however, that he could have easily won without a single vote from the South. After hearing for half a century that her political impotence was the result of her solidarity, the South was to triumph finally by the breakup of a solid North.

While Southern progressive Democrats were able to swing their section to Wilson after his nomination, they were less successful in their efforts to overthrow the conservative machines and leaders who had opposed the Wilson movement. The election of 1911 had

[72] George E. Mowry, "The South and the Progressive Lily White Party of 1912," in *Journal of Southern History*, VI (1940), 237–47; Arthur S. Link, "Theodore Roosevelt and the South in 1912," in *North Carolina Historical Review*, XXIII (1946), 313–24.

resulted in "a complete victory for the Machine" in Virginia, according to former Governor Montague, leader of the opposition to Senator Martin. "I am very disconsolate and distressed," he wrote William E. Dodd. "I have done the best I could . . but it all seems to count for nothing." [73] In spite of his well-known opposition to the Wilson movement, Martin remained unshaken in his power by the landslide of 1912. Other conservative anti-Wilson leaders the progressives failed to dislodge in 1912 were Senator Simmons of North Carolina, Governor Oscar B. Colquitt of Texas, Governor Blease of South Carolina, and Senator Bankhead of Alabama. Vardaman of Mississippi claimed a Senate seat in 1912 he had won the previous year in a campaign advocating repeal of the Fourteenth and Fifteenth amendments, and Watson, imp of the perverse, wound up by voting the Bull Moose ticket though still boss of the Democratic party of Georgia. The progressive Democrats were vastly heartened, however, by the prospect of having a powerful friend in the White House.

"All the way from styles in head-gear to opinions on the tariff, the flavor and the color of things in Washington are Southern," remarked an observer not long after Wilson's inauguration. Evidence of the change was everywhere. "It is the spirit and disposition, the purpose and inspiration, the tendency and direction which we note in the guiding forces of affairs. All these point unerringly to the South. In Washington you feel it in the air, you note it in the changed and changing ways of business." [74]

A Southern accent was unmistakable in Wilson's new cabinet. McAdoo and James C. McReynolds were hyphenated Southerners whose accents had been blurred by New York. But Daniels of North Carolina and Burleson and David F. Houston of Texas spoke the unmistakable idiom. In the lesser hierarchy of appointive offices—assistant secretaries, bureau chiefs, and commissioners—the South received "a vastly larger proportion of big and influential posts than it has held since the Civil War." [75] Walter Hines Page went to the Court of St. James and Thomas Nelson Page to Italy, as

[73] Andrew J. Montague to Dodd, September 8, 1911, in Dodd Papers.

[74] Judson C. Welliver, "The Triumph of the South," in *Munsey's Magazine* (New York), XLIX (1913), 738, 740.

[75] *Ibid.*, 733. See also, A. Maurice Low, "The South in the Saddle," in *Harper's Weekly*, LVII (February 8, 1913), 20.

ambassadors. Over the Supreme Court, Chief Justice White of Louisiana continued to preside, and at the elbow of the President there appeared with increasing frequency a gentleman of mild address from Texas, Colonel House.

At the congressional end of Pennsylvania Avenue, the nation's business was transacted in several varieties of the accent predominating at the other end. Martin of Virginia was majority leader in the Senate, Underwood of Alabama in the House. Almost all of the important committees of the Senate and fifteen of the seventeen House committees of the first order were presided over by Southern chairmen. Virginia, Tennessee, and Alabama among them accounted for nine of the seventeen important House chairmanships.

The change in the atmosphere at Washington represented a revolution in the geographical distribution of power. For the contrast between the South's position in 1913 and the humble place it had occupied during the previous half century was almost as marked as the contrast between the South of the ante-bellum period and the South of the era that followed. Nothing like this had occurred upon the accession of Cleveland, though he, unlike Wilson, owed his election largely to Southern votes. The change recalled to some minds the resurgence of the South upon the inauguration of Jefferson and of Jackson. Whether the comparison had any validity beyond the matter of accents remained to be seen.

CRITICAL ESSAY ON AUTHORITIES

A FULL-DRESS bibliography of the period 1877–1913 in Southern history has never been attempted. The closest approach is an unpublished bibliography of the economic history of the South since 1865 compiled by Lester J. Cappon, who very kindly permitted the author to make use of his work. Also of great assistance is Dr. Cappon's *Bibliography of Virginia History Since 1865,* University of Virginia Institute for Research in the Social Sciences, *Monograph No. 5* (University, Va., 1930), a work that has unfortunately not been matched in any other Southern state. The following essay, because of limitations on space, does not even attempt to list all the sources with which the text is documented. It is intended, however, to point out and comment briefly upon materials of major significance.

MANUSCRIPT COLLECTIONS

Since biographies of this period have only recently emerged from the commemorative stage and published correspondence is all but nonexistent, the historian is driven to manuscripts by necessity rather than by zeal. Collections scattered from the Houghton Library at Harvard to the Huntington Library in California have been examined. The collections that proved richest for the present purposes were those of the Division of Manuscripts, Library of Congress; the Hayes Memorial Library, Fremont, Ohio; the state universities of North Carolina, Virginia, Louisiana, and Texas; and Duke University. Material of value was found in the state archives of Alabama, Georgia, North Carolina, Texas, and Mississippi. It was manifestly impossible to use all available manuscripts. Some valuable ones had to be passed up and others only sampled. The following paragraphs refer only to those papers used in preparing this book, and naturally make no pretense of exhaustiveness.

The extent to which manuscript sources are used to document Chapter II of the text makes it unique in that respect. This came about through efforts to unravel the story behind the Compromise of 1877, which remained hidden in manuscript collections. Among the more revealing are the Rutherford B. Hayes Papers in the Hayes Memorial Library. The intelligent administration of this large collection has made it indispensable to students of this period of Southern history. Among other papers in the Hayes Memorial are microfilms of the William Henry Smith Papers, the originals of which are in the William Henry Smith Memorial Library at the Indiana State Historical Society, Indianapolis. Of greatest importance in the decision of 1877 are the Grenville M. Dodge Papers in the Iowa Historical and Memorial Building, Des Moines, particularly General Dodge's letter-books. The Samuel J. Tilden Papers and the John Bigelow Papers are in the New York Public Library. Numerous letters of Henry Van Ness Boynton are in the Benjamin H. Bristow Papers, and important letters of Montgomery Blair are found in the Blair-Gist Papers, both in the Division of Manuscripts, Library of Congress. Other Northern figures of importance in Southern history whose papers are in the Library of Congress are James A. Garfield, John Sherman, William E. Chandler, and Grover Cleveland.

A collection of unexpected richness in political history was the Robert McKee Papers in the Department of Archives and History, Montgomery, Alabama. An obscure figure himself, McKee was an intelligent and candid observer of his times, strategically situated to watch developments from the inside. The official files of several Alabama governors, particularly Governor Thomas G. Jones, were quite illuminating. They are also in the Montgomery archives. The Mississippi State Department of Archives and History in Jackson yielded material from the L. Q. C. Lamar–Edward Mayes Papers and the correspondence of governors. The John B. Gordon Papers and the William J. Northen Scrapbooks (containing numerous manuscripts) are in the Georgia Department of Archives and History in Atlanta.

Among the many manuscripts at the University of North Carolina three large collections of a political character are of especial importance. These are the papers of conservative Senator Matthew W. Ransom, the Populist Senator Marion Butler, both of North Carolina, and the Georgia Populist Thomas E. Watson. The papers of Butler and Watson, the two most prominent Southern leaders of the third party, constitute the most valuable manuscript sources on Southern Populism.

The Carter Glass Papers at the University of Virginia and the Josephus Daniels Papers at the Library of Congress were both damaged by fires that destroyed the mass of material concerning the years prior to 1912. The John Tyler Morgan Papers in the Library of Congress are limited largely to material on foreign affairs. Papers of other Southern political figures consulted in the Division of Manuscripts, Library of Congress, were those of Henry Watterson, John Sharp Williams, and Albert S. Burleson. Some use was made of the James S. Hogg Papers at The University of Texas and of those Edward M. House Papers that have been microfilmed by the Library of the University. The collection of William Garrott Brown Papers at Duke University is rich in intellectual as well as political history of the early twentieth century.

Manuscript sources of social, educational, and economic history are found in the Jabez L. M. Curry Papers, part of which are at the Alabama Department of Archives and History in Montgomery and part at the Library of Congress. University affairs and cultural history are reflected in the William E. Dodd Papers at the Library of Congress, the Edwin A. Alderman Papers at the University of Virginia, and the Daniel C. Gilman Papers and Herbert Baxter Adams Papers at the Johns Hopkins University. An exceptionally rich source of the history of philanthropy, education, letters, and politics is the Walter Hines Page Papers in the Houghton Library, Harvard University. Additional materials on humanitarian movements were found in the Alexander J. McKelway Papers, the Robert C. Ogden Papers, and the Booker T. Washington Papers, all at the Library of Congress. One of the largest manuscript collections in the Library of Congress, the Booker T. Washington Papers, consists of more than 2,500 boxes in various states of disarray and can only be said to have been sampled. The Daniel Augustus Tompkins Papers, divided between the University of North Carolina and the Library of Congress, contain much data on cotton textile history. Information on agricultural organizations, the Farmers' Alliance, and co-operatives was found in the Charles H. Pierson Papers at the University of Virginia. Another valuable source is "The Farmers' Alliance," a manuscript history of the movement written in 1920 by C. W. Macune and now in the library at The University of Texas.

GOVERNMENT PUBLICATIONS

A revolutionary expansion took place in government publications in the early years of the period under survey. For example, the Census of 1880 was published in 21,458 pages, compared with 3,473 pages for the previous census. Other official publications expanded in something like that proportion, and newly created commissions and bureaus of labor, interstate commerce, and corporations started voluminous series of reports. All these series contain data on the South. Helpful guides are Anne M. Boyd, *United States Government Publications, Sources of*

Information for Libraries (2d ed., New York, 1941); and Laurence F. Schmeckebier, *Government Publications and Their Use* (2d rev. ed., Washington, 1939). Of greatest value were the publications of the Bureau of the Census, particularly the *Tenth Census of the United States, 1880*, 22 vols. (Washington, 1883–1888), through the *Fifteenth Census of the United States, 1930*, 32 vols. (Washington, 1931–1934), and the various statistical atlases, especially those of 1900 and 1914. The atlas for 1880 was not printed officially, but much material gathered for it appeared in Fletcher W. Hewes and Henry Gannett, *Scribner's Statistical Atlas of the United States* (New York, 1883). A useful handbook is W. Stull Holt, *The Bureau of the Census; Its History, Activities and Organization* (Washington, 1929).

The annual *Reports* of the Commissioner of Labor and the Bureau of Labor have invaluable data, especially the *Second Annual Report of the Commissioner of Labor, 1886, Convict Labor* (Washington, 1887); and also the *Reports* of *1888, Working Women in Large Cities* (Washington, 1889); *1895–96, Work and Wages of Men, Women, and Children* (Washington, 1897); and *1904, Wages and Hours of Labor* (Washington, 1905). On child labor nothing is so essential as the Bureau of Labor, *Report on Condition of Woman and Child Wage-Earners in the United States*, 19 vols. (Washington, 1910–1913), especially Volume I, *Cotton Textile Industry*, and Volume VI, *The Beginnings of Child Labor Legislation in Certain States; A Comparative Study*. On educational history the *Report of the Commissioner of Education for the Year 1877* (Washington, 1879), and succeeding *Reports* through 1913 are exceptionally rich in Southern data. The Department of Agriculture *Yearbooks*, especially the *Yearbook of the Department of Agriculture, 1899* (Washington, 1900), and *ibid., 1940* (Washington, n.d.), have historical essays of value. Regarding economic conditions around the turn of the century a great source of testimony is the *Report* of the Industrial Commission, 19 vols. (Washington, 1901), particularly Volume II on agriculture and Volume VII on labor and capital. Valuable data on railroad history are packed in the United States Interstate Commerce Commission, *Railways in the United States in 1902. A Twenty-Two Year Review of Railway Operations; A Forty-Year Review of Changes in Freight Tariffs; A Fifteen-Year Review of Federal Railway Legislation; A Twelve-Year Review of State Railway Regulation*, 3 vols. (Washington, 1903). For testimony of Southern railroad executives, see Interstate Commerce Commission, *Hearings Relative to the Financial Relations, Rates, and Practices of the Louisville & Nashville Railroad Co., The Nashville, Chattanooga*

& St. Louis Railway, and Other Carriers, in *Senate Documents,* 64 Cong., 1 Sess., No. 461. On the freight-rate differential J. Haden Alldredge, *The Interterritorial Freight Rate Problem of the United States,* in *House Documents,* 75 Cong., 1 Sess., No. 264; and *Supplemental Phases of the Interterritorial Freight Rate Problem of the United States, ibid.,* 76 Cong., 1 Sess., No. 271, are important guides. Documentation of the entry of United States Steel into the South is provided by *Absorption of the Tennessee Coal & Iron Co.,* in *Senate Documents,* 62 Cong., 1 Sess., No. 44, and of "Pittsburgh Plus" in *Federal Trade Commission vs. United States Steel Corporation, et al.,* Docket 760 (Washington, 1924).

Congressional investigations are often rich in testimony on Southern affairs. Depressions are the subject of *Investigation Relative to the General Depression,* 1878–1879, in *House Miscellaneous Documents,* 45 Cong., 3 Sess., No. 29, and *Report of the Committee on Agriculture and Forestry on Condition of Cotton Growers in the United States,* 2 vols., in *Senate Reports,* 53 Cong., 3 Sess., No. 986. Political history is the subject of the *Report of the United States Senate Committee to Inquire into the Alleged Frauds and Violence in the Elections of 1878,* in *Senate Reports,* 45 Cong., 3 Sess., No. 855. For the *Pan-Electric Investigation,* see *House Reports,* 49 Cong., 1 Sess., X, No. 3142. The *Report of the Country Life Commission* (1909) is printed as *Senate Documents,* 60 Cong., 2 Sess., No. 705.

Official publications of thirteen states, including House and Senate journals, reports of secretaries of state, treasurers, health commissioners, prison commissioners, public-school commissioners, immigration commissioners, and other officials are too numerous for detailed listing. A useful guide to some of this material is Grace E. Macdonald, *Check-List of Legislative Journals of States of the United States of America* (Providence, 1938), and the same author's *Check-List of Statutes of States of the United States of America* (Providence, 1937). Data on voting and on primaries, particularly hard to come by, are found in *Biennial Report of the Secretary of State of the State of Louisiana . . . 1896 to 1898* (Baton Rouge, 1898); *Report of the Secretary of State to the Governor of Louisiana* (Baton Rouge, 1904); Thomas M. Owen (ed.), *Alabama Official and Statistical Register, 1907* (Montgomery, 1907); and a non-official publication, *Texas Almanac and State Industrial Guide, 1947–1948* (Dallas, 1948). Nearly all of the state constitutions of this period are conveniently assembled in Francis N. Thorpe (comp.), *The Federal and State Constitutions, Colonial Charters, and Other Organic Laws,*

7 vols. (Washington, 1909). Constitutional conventions are especially significant in the period, but official records of the debates have been published for only a few states, for which see above, Chapter XII.

AUTOBIOGRAPHIES, MEMOIRS, AND PUBLISHED CORRESPONDENCE

Three volumes of Josephus Daniels' memoirs span the entire period 1877–1913: *Tar Heel Editor* (Chapel Hill, 1939), *Editor in Politics* (Chapel Hill, 1941), and *The Wilson Era: Years of Peace—1910–1917* (Chapel Hill, 1944). Another famous editor, Henry Watterson, *"Marse Henry", An Autobiography*, 2 vols. (New York, 1919), is less rewarding. Defenses of the conservative order in South Carolina are engagingly written by the Charleston editor William W. Ball in *The State that Forgot; South Carolina's Surrender to Democracy* (Indianapolis, 1932). The same tradition is upheld by Virginians in Beverley B. Munford, *Random Recollections* (New York?, 1905); John Goode, *Recollections of a Lifetime . . .* (New York, 1906); and William L. Royall, *Some Reminiscences* (New York, 1909). Social history of the period is enriched by Robert W. Winston, *It's A Far Cry* (New York, 1937); William A. Percy, *Lanterns on the Levee; Recollections of a Planter's Son* (New York, 1941); John A. Rice, *I Came Out of the Eighteenth Century* (New York, 1942); Susan D. Smedes, *Memorials of a Southern Planter* (Baltimore, 1887); John Hallum, *The Diary of an Old Lawyer* (Nashville, 1895); *The Autobiography of Nathaniel Southgate Shaler* (New York, 1909); Grace King, *Memories of a Southern Woman of Letters* (New York, 1932); and Ward McAllister, *Society As I Have Found It* (New York, 1890). Emily L. Bell, *My Pioneer Days in Florida, 1876–1898* (Miami, 1928), tells of settling the east coast. *The Natural Bent: The Memoirs of Dr. Paul B. Barringer* (Chapel Hill, 1949) unfortunately stops in 1881. A few Confederate figures left memoirs that should be consulted: *Reminiscences of General Basil W. Duke, C.S.A.* (New York, 1911); General John B. Gordon, *Reminiscences of the Civil War* (New York, 1903); and John H. Reagan, *Memoirs: With Special Reference to Secession and the Civil War* (New York, 1906).

Other prominent figures who wrote autobiographical works include *Crowded Years, The Reminiscences of William G. McAdoo* (Boston, 1931); Champ Clark, *My Quarter Century of American Politics*, 2 vols. (New York, 1920); William F. McCombs, *Making Woodrow Wilson President* (New York, 1921); J. Fred Rippy (ed.), *F. M. Simmons, Statesman of the New South: Memoirs and Addresses* (Durham, 1936); *The*

Memoirs of Cordell Hull, 2 vols. (New York, 1948); and William H. ("Alfalfa Bill") Murray, *Memoirs of Governor Murray and True History of Oklahoma . . . ,* 3 vols. (Boston, 1945). The voice of political dissent is heard in the Virginia Readjuster John E. Massey, *Autobiography* (New York, 1909); the Georgia Independent Rebecca L. Felton, *Memoirs of Georgia Politics* (Atlanta, 1911); and the Populists Thomas E. Watson, *Life and Speeches of Thomas E. Watson* (Nashville, 1908); Joseph G. Manning, *The Fadeout of Populism* (New York, 1928), and *Politics in Alabama* ([Birmingham], 1893); and James H. Davis, *Memoir, by Cyclone Davis* (Sherman, Tex., 1935). The more important autobiographical works of Negroes are John R. Lynch, *The Facts of Reconstruction* (New York, 1913), which extends past the period indicated; Booker T. Washington, *Up From Slavery* (New York, 1901), and *My Larger Education; Being Chapters From My Experience* (Garden City, 1911); James W. Johnson, *Autobiography of an Ex-Colored Man* (Boston, 1912), and *Along This Way* (New York, 1933); and W. E. Burghardt Du Bois, *Dusk of Dawn, An Essay toward an Autobiography of a Race Concept* (New York, 1940).

No period of Southern history since the American Revolution is so poor in published correspondence as this one. One hopeful sign of improvement in this respect is the recent appearance of Aubrey L. Brooks and Hugh T. Lefler (eds.), *The Papers of Walter Clark,* 2 vols. (Chapel Hill, 1948–1949). Charles Seymour (ed.), *The Intimate Papers of Colonel House,* 4 vols. (Boston, 1926–1928), contains little material on this period. Ray S. Baker's biography of Wilson and Burton J. Hendrick's work on Page, both cited below, contain many letters. Charles R. Anderson (ed.), *The Centennial Edition of Sidney Lanier,* 10 vols. (Baltimore, 1945), supersedes earlier editions. Ulrich B. Phillips (ed.), *The Correspondence of Robert Toombs, Alexander H. Stephens, and Howell Cobb,* in American Historical Association, *Annual Report,* 1911, II (Washington, 1913), includes a few letters of the period concerned. W. Stull Holt (ed.), *Historical Scholarship in the United States, 1876–1901: As Revealed in the Correspondence of Herbert B. Adams,* in Johns Hopkins University *Studies in Historical and Political Science,* LVI, No. 4 (Baltimore, 1938), is rich in intellectual history.

LITERATURE OF CONTROVERSY

The detractors and defenders are subject to serious discount, but the historian cannot neglect them. In the seats of the scornful are Robert C. O. Benjamin, *Southern Outrages; A Statistical Record of Lawless Doings* (Los Angeles?, 1894), voicing the charges of an indignant Negro author; and Albert W. Bishop, *What is the Situation Now? A Review of Political Affairs in the Southern States* (Buffalo, 1894), presenting the jaundiced views of a one-time adjutant general of Arkansas. Attacks upon the Southern politicians and President Hayes's Southern policy are found in Jesse P. Bishop, *The Southern Question. A View of the Policy and Constitutional Powers of the President, as to the Southern States* (Cleveland, 1877); William E. Chandler, *"Can Such Things Be and Overcome Us Like A Summer Cloud, without Our Special Wonder?"* (n.p., n.d.); and *Letters of Mr. William E. Chandler Relative to the So-Called Southern Policy of President Hayes, Together with a Letter to Mr. Chandler of Mr. William Lloyd Garrison* (Concord, N.H., 1878). (Miss) E. B. Emery, *Letters from the South, on the Social, Intellectual, and Moral Conditions of the Colored People* (Boston, 1880), is unhappy about the situation. W. Scott Morgan, *The Red Light; A Story of Southern Politics and Election Methods* (Moravian Falls, N.C., 1904), is the dim view an old Populist took of later developments. James W. Rogers, *The Great Mug-Wump. Canto I. Pan-Electric Sale of Government Property* (Bladensburg, Md., 1886), is an exposure of questionable practices of Southern Democrats prominent in Cleveland's first administration. Henry E. Tremain, *Sectionalism Unmasked* (New York, 1907), is a bitter and sensational exposure of Southern political evils. D. Augustus Straker, *The New South Investigated* (Detroit, 1888), is a more even-tempered critique by a man who had lived in the South from 1875 to 1887.

From the South came a literature of vindication, defense, and recrimination. Perhaps the most elaborate and influential apology for the Redeemers and their regime is Hilary A. Herbert (ed.), *Why the Solid South? or, Reconstruction and Its Results* (Baltimore, 1890), which takes the form of an intemperate attack on Reconstruction, with the obvious inference that Redemption was a reform movement. A reply to South-haters is N. Dumont (ed.), *Convention of Northern Settlers in the South. What Northern Men Say of the South. . . . Proceedings of the Convention of Northern Residents of the South, Held at Charlotte, North Carolina, January 15, 1879 . . .* (Charlotte, N.C., 1879). Tracts of a similar nature are W. Robbins Falkiner, *The South and Its People.* (Richmond, 1890); and Jacobus D. Droke, *From the Old South to the New . . .* (Harriman, Tenn., 1895). Charles H. J. Taylor, *Whites and Blacks; or, The Question Settled* (Atlanta, 1889), is the view of a Negro Democrat and minister to Liberia under Cleveland. J. Milton Waldron and J. D. Harkless, *The Political Situation in a Nut-Shell, Some Un-Colored Truths for Colored Voters* (Washington, 1912), is anti-Republican and encourages political independence among Negroes. Southern writers took the offensive against a hostile national economy in A. W. Terrell, *The Cormorant, the Commune and Labor* (Austin, 1886?); in such Populist tracts as Milford W. Howard, *If Christ Came to Congress* (Washington, 1894), and *The American Plutocracy* (New York, 1895); James H. Davis, *A Political Revelation* (Dallas, 1894); Thomas E. Watson, *Not A Revolt, It Is A Revolution* (Washington, 1892); and a later dissent, Frank J. Bivins, *The Farmer's Political Economy. "The Dead Horse in Our Spring Branch." Farmer Dan Luke's Exposure of Cotton Marketing* (Macon, 1913). Examples of conservative Southern literature on financial questions are Gilbert C. Walker, *Virginia's Debt. Its Origin, History and Present Status* (Richmond?, 1877?); Robert W. Hughes, *A Popular Treatise on The Currency Question Written from a Southern Point of View* (New York, 1879); and John S. Williams, *The Credit of the South: Viewed from a State, Municipal and General Standpoint* (Richmond, 1892). Two antithetical reactions to the New Order by Southern churchmen are Robert L. Dabney, *The New South. A Discourse Delivered at the Annual Commencement of Hampden Sidney College, June 15th, 1882* (Raleigh, 1883), a solemn rejection; and Atticus G. Haygood, *The New South: Gratitude, Amendment, Hope . . .* (Oxford, Ga., 1880), an eager affirmation.

Of the numerous pamphlets on the Texas and Pacific scheme at the library of the Bureau of Railway Economics, Washington, D.C., and the Hayes Memorial Library, the following are most important: *The Press and the People on the Importance of a Southern Line Railway to the Pacific and in Favor of Government Aid to the Texas and Pacific Railway Co.* (Philadelphia, 1875); *Proceedings of the National Railroad Convention at St. Louis, Mo., November 23 and 24, 1875, in Regard to the Construction of the* TEXAS & PACIFIC RAILWAY *as a Southern Trans-Continental Railway Line from the Mississippi Valley to the Pacific Ocean on the Thirty-Second Parallel of Latitude* (St. Louis, 1875); *The Texas and Pacific Railway. Invitation to Thomas A. Scott from Citizens and Business Men of Chicago, to Address Them on the Subject of the Texas & Pacific Railway, and Reply Thereto. April 2nd, 1878* (Philadelphia, 1878). Two other items on the same subject are L. Q. C. Lamar, *The Texas Pacific Railroad. Speech . . . in the Senate of the United States, May 22, 1878* (Washington, 1878); and *The Texas and Pacific Railway Argument of Thomas A. Scott, before the Committee on Railroads of the U. S. Senate, February 7th, 1878* (n.p., n.d.).

TRAVELS AND VISITS

Travelers from abroad did not always venture across the Hudson, fewer still across the Potomac. Of those who came South the greater number concentrated on the race question. The British, because of their experience with numerous races, were perhaps most interesting. Sir William Archer, *Through Afro-America: An English Reading of the Race Problem* (London, 1910), was interested in analogies. In one edition of Sir James Bryce, *The American Commonwealth,* 2 vols. (New York, 1910), there are three chapters on the Negro and the South. Sir George Campbell, *White and Black; the Outcome of a Visit to the United States* (London, 1879); Sir William Laird Clowes, *Black America; a Study of the Ex-Slave and His Late Master* (London, 1891); Maurice S. Evans, *Black and White in the Southern States; A Study of the Race Problem in the United States from a South African Point of View* (London, 1915); and William Pringle Livingstone, *The Race Conflict; A Study of Conditions in America* (London, [1911]), were all more or less concerned with comparisons between the South and various corners of the British Empire. Edward A. Freeman, *Some Impressions of the United States* (New York, 1883), gave little attention to the South; Lady Duffus Hardy, *Down South* (London, 1883), was an exclaimer and appreciator, especially of Florida; and James F. Muirhead, *The Land of Contrasts* (New York, 1898), a professional sight-seer. P. H. B. d'Estournelles de Constant, *America and Her Problems* (New York, 1915), had little space for the South. Ernst von Hesse-Wartegg, *Mississippi-fahrten. Reisebilder aus dem Amerikanischen Süden, 1879–1880* (Leipzig, 1881), was interested mainly in the picturesque; and Max Schüller, *In Den Südstaaten Nordamerikas. Erinnerungen und Eindrücke . . .* (Berlin, 1893), was written to interest immigrants in Dixie.

Visitors from the Northern states sometimes revived Reconstruction themes. Henry Ward Beecher, *A Circuit of the Continent: Account of a Tour Through the West and South . . .* (New York, 1884); George C. Benham, *A Year of Wreck; a True Story, by a Victim* (New York, 1880); Albert T. Morgan, *Yazoo; or, on the Picket Line of Freedom in the South. A Personal Narrative* (Washington, 1884); and Carl Shurz, *The New South* (New York, 1885), are of a type in this respect. The majority, however, exuded the goodwill of "reconciliation." Among these were two books of Henry M. Field, *Blood is Thicker Than Water: A Few Days Among Our Southern Brethren* (New York, 1886), and

Bright Skies and Dark Shadows (New York, 1890); and also William D. Kelley, *The Old South and the New* (New York, 1888); Charles H. Levermore, "Impressions of a Yankee Visitor in the South," in *New England Magazine*, N.S. (Boston, 1889–1917), III (1890–1891), 311–19; A. D. Mayo, "The Third Estate of the South," *ibid.*, 299–311; Alexander K. McClure, *The South: Its Industrial, Financial, and Political Condition* (Philadelphia, 1886); and Charles Dudley Warner, *Studies in the South and West, With Comments on Canada* (New York, 1889). Two journalists gave lively descriptions of surface aspects of the social scene: Julian Ralph, *Dixie; or, Southern Scenes and Sketches* (New York, 1896); and Julian L. Street, *American Adventures; a Second Trip "Abroad at Home"* (New York, 1917). For penetration and authority, two travel books belong in a class by themselves: Mark Twain, *Life on the Mississippi* (Boston, 1883); and Henry James, *The American Scene* (New York, 1907). A new edition of *Life on the Mississippi*, edited by Willis J. Wager (New York, 1944), includes opinions of the South deleted from earlier editions.

PROMOTIONAL LITERATURE

The most prolific writers about the South of this period were the promoters—promoters of immigration, tourist trade, industrialization, investment, railroads, land speculation: all with something to sell. The historian, like the purchaser, should observe the most ancient rule of the market place, *caveat emptor*. The following is a sampling of wares, recommended with reservations. George M. Barbour, *Florida for Tourists, Invalids, and Settlers . . .* (New York, 1882), is one of the better Florida handbooks, of which there are dozens. Walter G. Cooper (ed.), *The Piedmont Region, Embracing Georgia, Alabama, Florida and the Carolinas* (Atlanta, 1895), is an immigration promoter with enough valid information to make it worth while. George B. Cowlam, *The Industrial Future of the South* (n.p., 1891), and *The Undeveloped South. Its Resources, and the Importance of Their Development as a Factor in Determining the Future Prosperity and Growth of Wealth in the United States* (Louisville, 1887), advertises natural resources, as also does E. A. Ford, *A Handbook of the South* (Chicago, 1890). William H. Gannon (comp.), *. . . The Land Owners of the South, and the Industrial Classes of the North . . .* (Boston, 1882), pictures opportunities for Northern capital and labor in South Carolina and Georgia. James A. Green, *The Dream of "Ellen N"; An Illustrated Descriptive and Historical Narrative of Southern Travels* (Louisville, 1886), is a railroad brochure. H. H. Hargrove, *Louisiana and Mississippi's Prosperity to* *be Sought in "Cotton Mills." They Should Seek the Cotton Fields. How Cotton Manufacturing Can Be Made to Pay in Small Country Towns and Enrich the Cotton Grower* (New Orleans, 1899), should be explained by the title, as should Theophile Harang, *The National Syndicates of Capital and Labor. A Scheme for the Rapid Development of . . . Louisiana and the New South* (New Orleans, 1884); William H. Harrison, Jr., *How to Get Rich in the South. Telling What to Do, How to Do It, and the Profits to be Realized* (Chicago, 1888); Thomas P. Janes, *Manual of Georgia: For Use of Immigrants and Capitalists* (Atlanta, 1878); and John E. Land, *Pen Illustrations of New Orleans, 1881–82, Trade, Commerce and Manufacturers* (New Orleans, 1882). Arkansas climbed on the booster's bandwagon with T. B. Mills & Co. [*sic*], *The New Arkansas Travelers* (Little Rock, 1876); and Alabama with John T. Milner, *Alabama: As it Was, As it Is, and As it Will Be* (Montgomery, 1876). Other lures for immigrants are Frank S. Presbrey, *The Southland; An Exposition of the Present Resources and Development of the South* (New York?, 1898); James L. Rock, *Southern and Western Texas Guide for 1878* (St. Louis, 1878); and Eugene C. Robertson, *Road to Wealth Leads Through the South; Solid Facts from Settlers Along the Line* (Cincinnati, 1894). Industrial expositions, the promoter's delight, are reported in Hannibal I. Kimball, *International Cotton Exposition, 1881. Report of the Director General* (New York, 1882); Herbert S. Fairall, *The World's Industrial and Cotton Centennial Exposition, New Orleans, 1884–1885* (Iowa City, 1885); and Walter G. Cooper, *The Cotton States and International Exposition and South Illustrated. Including the Official History of the Exposition* (Atlanta, 1896).

CONTEMPORANEOUS ANALYSES

Between Reconstruction and the First World War the South produced several social critics whose observations on their own times deserve serious attention from the historian. Philip A. Bruce, *The Rise of the New South* (Philadelphia, 1905), was the most ambitious contemporary effort at historical analysis of the New Order. Written by a historian of some distinction, it relied mainly upon statistical data, emphasized economic progress, and neglected political affairs. William Garrott Brown, an intelligent conservative, published many essays on current affairs, some of which were collected posthumously in *The New Politics, and Other Papers* (Boston, 1914). A more radical point of view was expressed in George W. Cable, *The Silent South* (New York, 1885), and *The Negro Question* (New York, 1890). Edgar Gardner Murphy, *Problems of the Present South* (New York, 1904), and *The Basis of Ascendency* (New York, 1909), are among the most interesting ventures in social criticism. Other expressions of the humanitarian and reformist philosophy are Walter Hines Page, *The Rebuilding of Old Commonwealths* (New York, 1902); and Edwin A. Alderman, *The Growing South* (New York, 1908).

Race questions claimed more attention from contemporaneous critics than any other social problems. Atticus G. Haygood, *Our Brother in Black: His Freedom and His Future* (Nashville, 1881), expressed Christian responsibility for the underdog. Philip A. Bruce, *The Plantation Negro as a Freeman* (New York, 1889), was pessimistic, and so was Paul B. Barringer, *The American Negro; His Past and Future* (Raleigh, 1900). Thomas Nelson Page, *The Negro: The Southerner's Problem* (New York, 1904), voiced conventional, conservative attitudes of paternalism. White opinion ranged from William B. Smith, *The Color Line; A Brief in Behalf of the Unborn* (New York, 1905), which considered the Negro subhuman, to Alfred H. Stone, *Studies in the American Race Problem* (New York, 1908), which professed to be scientific and objective. William A. MacCorkle, *Some Southern Questions* (New York, 1908), wrote mainly on problems of Negro franchise and education. Several examples of the more extreme expression of Southern racism are discussed above in the earlier pages of Chapter XIII. Thomas P. Bailey, *Race Orthodoxy in the South, and Other Aspects of the Negro Question* (New York, 1914), summed up popular white dogma without clearly revealing his own opinion.

The Negro side of the discussion is represented by George W. Williams, *History of the Negro Race in America,* 2 vols. (New York, 1882), the work of a neglected historian. T. Thomas Fortune, *Black and White: Land, Labor, and Politics in the South* (New York, 1884), stressed economic and class struggles as the key to the race problem. Booker T. Washington, *The Future of the American Negro* (Boston, 1899), and *The Negro in Business* (Boston and Chicago, 1907), are two of many expressions of the Tuskegee philosophy. W. E. Burghardt Du Bois, *The Souls of Black Folk* (Chicago, 1903), is in part a reply to the Tuskegee challenge. Washington and Du Bois were among several Negro contributors to *The Negro Problem* (Chicago, 1903). Kelly Miller, *Race Adjustment; Essays on the Negro in America* (New York, 1908), contains among other protests an arraignment of Theodore Roosevelt's treatment of the race; and his *Out of the House of Bondage* (New York, 1914), is an account of struggles against race proscription. Irvine G. Penn, *The Afro-American Press and Its Editors* (Springfield,

Mass., 1891), is large and laudatory. The Atlanta University *Publications,* Nos. 1–17 (Atlanta, 1896–1912), edited by W. E. Burghardt Du Bois, constitute a pioneer attempt to establish race studies on a scholarly basis.

Northern contributions on the race question include Ray Stannard Baker, *Following the Color Line; An Account of Negro Citizenship in the American Democracy* (New York, 1908), the report of an intelligent observer; William H. Thomas, *The American Negro* (New York, 1901), a Northern Negro's criticism of his own race; and Albert B. Hart, *The Southern South* (New York, 1910), a Harvard professor's efforts to understand.

Charles H. Otken, *The Ills of the South* (New York, 1894), is an analysis of agrarian troubles. Carl Kelsey, *The Negro Farmer* (Chicago, 1903), is a survey of tenancy. The Farmers' Alliance and its principles are expounded in William L. Garvin and S. O. Daws, *History of the National Farmers' Alliance and Co-operative Union of America* (Jacksboro, Tex., 1887); J. E. Bryan, *The Farmers' Alliance: Its Origin, Progress and Purposes* (Fayetteville, Ark., 1891); and W. Scott Morgan, *History of the Wheel and Alliance and the Impending Revolution* (Fort Scott, Kan., 1889). The Farmers' Union had as one of its contemporary historians Thomas J. Brooks, *Origin, History and Principles of the Farmers' Educational and Co-operative Union of America* (Greenfield, Tenn., 1908?). Statistics of industrial advance are the theme of Richard H. Edmonds, *The South's Redemption, From Poverty to Prosperity* (Baltimore, 1890); the same author's *Facts About the South* (Baltimore, 1902); and M. B. Hillyard, *The New South. A Description of the Southern States, Noting Each State Separately* (Baltimore, 1887). The words of a major prophet may be read in Henry W. Grady, *The New South* (New York, 1890). Though it was published later, William H. Skaggs, *The Southern Oligarchy; An Appeal in Behalf of the Silent Masses of Our Country Against the Despotic Rule of the Few* (New York, 1924), belongs with this generation. It is the malediction of an old Populist. J. C. Powell, *The American Siberia; or, Fourteen Years' Experience in a Southern Convict Camp* (London, 1891), is a remarkable exposure by the captain of a Florida convict camp.

NEWSPAPERS

The trade annual, N. W. Ayer & Son's *Directory of Newspapers and Periodicals . . .* (Philadelphia, 1880–), is useful in determining dates, circulation, and political affiliations of newspapers. Winifred Gregory (ed.), *American Newspapers, 1821–1936: A Union List of Files Avail-*

able in the United States and Canada (New York, 1937), gives changes in titles and location of files as well as dates of publication. Variations in titles below have been noted only when changes after 1877 might lead to confusion. The Library of Congress has the best collection of the larger Southern newspapers, but does not have the obscurer journals. On the latter much light is shed by Thomas D. Clark, *The Southern Country Editor* (Indianapolis, 1948).

In the Upper South the Richmond newspapers that were found most useful were the *Dispatch* (1850–1903), the *Times* (1886–1903, when it was united with the *Dispatch*), the *State* (1876–1897), the Populist-controlled *Virginia Sun* (1891–1897), and the Richmond *Whig* (1824–1888), which became a Readjuster party paper in 1879. The Norfolk *Virginian-Pilot and Norfolk Landmark* (1865–1911) was occasionally consulted. Among North Carolina newspapers used were the Raleigh journals, *Caucasian* (1882–1913), *Progressive Farmer* (1886–, title varies), *Observer* (1876–1880), *News and Observer* (1872–), and *Times* (1879–); the Charlotte *Observer* (1886–), the Durham *Sun* (1889–), and the Wilmington *Morning Star* (1867–). Tennessee newspapers consulted include the Chattanooga *Daily Times* (1869–), Knoxville *Republican Chronicle* (1879–1886), Memphis *Commercial Appeal* (1889–), Nashville *American* (1875–1910), and Nashville *Banner* (1876–). The Louisville *Courier-Journal* (1868–) had an influence that extended beyond Kentucky and gave the paper something of a regional significance. Edited by Henry Watterson, it was probably more widely quoted than any other Southern sheet.

In the Lower South the Charleston *News and Courier* (1803–, with changes in title) is one of the oldest and, for the post-Reconstruction period, most indispensable newspapers. The Columbia *State* (1891–) was also consulted. Among the newspapers of Georgia those of greatest usefulness were the Atlanta *Constitution* (1868–), the Atlanta *Journal* (1883–), the Augusta *Chronicle* (1785–, title varies), and the Macon *Telegraph* (1860–, title varies). Tom Watson's Populist sheet, the *People's Party Paper* (1891–1898), was published in Atlanta and his weekly journal, the *Jeffersonian* (1906–1917) at Thomson. Two Florida journals, the Jacksonville *Florida Times-Union* (1875–, title varies) and the Tallahassee *Floridian* (1828–, title varies; published in Jacksonville after 1898) proved useful. In Alabama, the Birmingham newspapers, the *Age-Herald* (1887–), the *Iron Age* (1874–1887), and the *News* (1888–) were searched with profit, and so also was the Montgomery *Advertiser* (1850?–). Some use was made of the Mobile *Register* (1821–, title varies). Of special value on Mississippi affairs is the Jackson

Weekly Clarion-Ledger (1837–1912), of which a daily edition was published beginning in 1888. Other Mississippi papers quoted are the Natchez *Democrat* (1865–) and the Vicksburg *Herald* (1865–).

In the Southwest there was no more colorful press than that of New Orleans. The *Democrat* (1875–1881) of that city was united with the *Times* (1863–1881) to form the *Times-Democrat* (1881–1914), Major E. A. Burke's paper for a time. Other useful New Orleans papers were the *Item* (1877–), the *Daily Picayune* (1837–1914), and the *Republican* (1867–1878). The *Arkansas Gazette* (1865–) and the *Arkansas Democrat* (1871–), both of Little Rock, were found helpful. Of the Texas press, the Dallas *Morning News* (1885–) and the Galveston *Daily News* (1842–) were consulted most often, with occasional reference to the Houston *Post* (1880–). The Dallas *Texas Advance* (1890?–) was a Populist weekly. The most available and frequently used Oklahoma newspapers were the Guthrie *Oklahoma State Capital* (1889–1911?) and the Oklahoma City *Daily Oklahoman* (1894–).

Research among Negro newspapers has been greatly facilitated recently by the microfilming of scattered files of more than 250 Negro papers of the nineteenth and twentieth centuries, a work sponsored by the General Education Board and the American Council of Learned Societies and filmed by the Photoduplication Service of the Library of Congress. The bulk of this film falls within the period 1877–1913. Much of the research for this volume was completed before this film was available. Negro papers most frequently consulted were the Washington *Bee* (1882–1922), the New York *Age* (1880–, which changed to the *Globe* in 1884 and *Freeman,* 1884–1887, then back to *Age*), Huntsville *Gazette* (1879–1894), and Richmond *Planet* (1883–).

Several Northern papers kept up a running comment on Southern affairs. Prominent among them were the New York *Tribune* (1841–1924), the New York *Herald* (1835 until it united with the *Tribune* in 1924), the Boston *Evening Transcript* (1830–19?), the Chicago *Inter-Ocean* (1872–1914), and the Washington *National Republican* (1860–1888).

PERIODICALS

None of the more ambitious Southern periodicals founded in the postwar years 1865–1869 proved able to survive the seventies. *Scott's Monthly Magazine* (Atlanta, 1865–1869), *The Land We Love* (Charlotte, 1866–1869), the *XIX Century* (Charleston, 1869–1871), the *Southern Review* (Baltimore, 1867–1879), and the *Southern Magazine* (Baltimore, 1868–1875) crumbled one after another. Even the old landmark

De Bow's Review gave up in 1880 after two attempts to come back. Throughout the eighties, a period of intense literary activity in the region, the South was without a single respectable literary periodical. The *Sunny South* (Atlanta, 1875–1907) commanded no important talent until Joel Chandler Harris took it over in 1907 and named it *Uncle Remus's Magazine* (Atlanta, 1907–1913?, title varies). The first journal with reasonably high critical standards to appear in the new era was the *Sewanee Review* (Sewanee, Tenn., 1892–), edited in its early years by William P. Trent. Ten years later the *South Atlantic Quarterly* (Durham, 1902–) was launched under the editorship of John S. Bassett. Both periodicals have proved of great value in the present work.

For a period in the eighties no popular Northern journal of opinion or literature was complete without at least one article about the South or by a Southern author. Throughout the period of thirty-six years, in fact, the South received an unusual share of attention from periodicals of national circulation. There is neither space nor need for a complete list, since it would include all the better-known journals. Three of them become of particular significance while they were under the editorship of Walter Hines Page, because of the lively interest the editor took in Southern authors and affairs. The three periodicals and the dates of Page's editorship are the *Forum* (New York, 1886–1930), 1891 to 1898; the *Atlantic Monthly* (Boston, 1857–), 1898 to 1900; and the *World's Work* (New York, 1900–1932), 1900 to 1913. But *Scribner's* (New York, 1887–1939), *Century* (New York, 1870–1930), *Harper's* (New York, 1850–), and *Lippincott's* (Philadelphia, 1868–1915) were frequently packed with meat for the historian, as were also the weekly journals *Harper's Weekly, A Journal of Civilization* (New York, 1857–1916), the *Nation* (New York, 1865–) and the *Independent* (New York, Boston, 1848–1928). For relations of Northern magazines and their Southern authors, see Paul H. Buck, *The Road to Reunion, 1865–1900* (Boston, 1937), 221–35.

Southern industrialists and businessmen were less backward than Southern literary folk in establishing and maintaining periodicals. Foremost among these is the *Manufacturers' Record* (Baltimore, 1882–). The long shelves of its volumes constitute a basic reference work in Southern industrial history of the period—always to be used with caution. The magazine, its policy, and its original editor, Richard H. Edmonds, are discussed in Chapter VI. Other trade and industrial journals that were found useful are the *Tradesman* (Chattanooga, 1879–1915), the *Virginias, a Mining, Industrial and Scientific Journal . . .* (Staunton, Va., 1880–1885), the *Industrial South* (Richmond,

1881–1887?), and the *Southern and Western Textile Excelsior* (Charlotte, N.C., 1893–1907). Data on railroad history was gained from the *Railway World* (Philadelphia, 1856–1915) and the *Railway Age* (Chicago, 1876–1908).

The *Southern Workman* (Hampton, Va., 1872–1939) was the organ of the Hampton-Tuskegee school of race and labor philosophy. Information on organized labor in the South was obtained from the *American Federationist* (Washington, 1894–), the *Tobacco Worker* (Louisville, 1897–1924), the *Southern Economist and Trade Unionist* (New Orleans, 1897–1900?), and the *United Labor Journal* (New Orleans, 1897–1903?). *Figaro* (New Orleans, 1883–1884?) was hostile to the unions.

The official organ of the Southern Farmers' Alliance was the *National Economist* (Washington, 1889–1894?), and another important periodical of the Alliance was the *Southern Mercury* (Dallas, 1882–1902). The *Farmers' Union News* (Union City, Ga., 1903–1912?) was the national organ of the Farmers' Union. Other agricultural journals consulted were the *American Farmer: A Monthly Magazine of Agriculture and Horticulture* (Baltimore, Washington, 1819–1897), the *Southern Farmer* (New Orleans, 1896–1902), and the *Cotton World* (New Orleans, 1887–1888?).

The following periodicals spoke for a variety of Southern organizations and interests: the *Confederate Veteran* (Nashville, 1893–1932), voice of the United Confederate Veterans; the *Christian Advocate* (Nashville, 1832–1940), chief organ of the Methodist Episcopal Church South, and the *Taylor-Trotwood Magazine* (Nashville, 1905–1910), published as *Bob Taylor's Magazine* in 1905–1906 and in 1912 merged with *Watson's Magazine* (New York, Atlanta, and Thomson, Ga., 1905–1917, with various changes in title). The Negro periodicals *Voice of the Negro* (Atlanta, Chicago, 1904–1907) and the *Crisis* (New York, 1910–) contain much material on the South; and the *Southland* (Salisbury, Winston, N.C., 1890–1891?) has been quoted on Negro opinion.

BIOGRAPHIES

A list of prominent figures of the post-Reconstruction South who have yet to find competent biographers would probably be longer than a list of those who have been so fortunate. Still standing in need of satisfactory biographies are Wade Hampton, John B. Gordon, George W. Cable, Daniel A. Tompkins, and James S. Hogg, to mention only a few. On the other hand, the historian's task is lightened by several biographical studies of recent years.

Among biographies of political figures, those of greatest usefulness were Francis B. Simkins, *Pitchfork Ben Tillman, South Carolinian* (Baton Rouge, 1944); Raymond B. Nixon, *Henry W. Grady: Spokesman of the New South* (New York, 1943); Nelson M. Blake, *William Mahone of Virginia, Soldier and Political Insurgent* (Richmond, 1935); and James A. Barnes, *John G. Carlisle, Financial Statesman* (New York, 1931). Wirt A. Cate, *Lucius Q. C. Lamar* (Chapel Hill, 1935), is a scholarly work; and Edward Mayes, *Lucius Q. C. Lamar: His Life, Times, and Speeches, 1825–1893* (Nashville, 1896), is still of great value for the large number of documents it contains. Similarly, Herbert Fielder, *A Sketch of the Life and Times and Speeches of Joseph E. Brown* (Springfield, Mass., 1883), is not entirely displaced by Louise B. Hill, *Joseph E. Brown and the Confederacy* (Chapel Hill, 1939), which devotes only one chapter to the post-Reconstruction years. On Woodrow Wilson both Arthur S. Link, *Wilson: The Road to the White House* (Princeton, 1947), and the first three volumes of Ray S. Baker, *Woodrow Wilson; Life and Letters,* 8 vols. (Garden City, 1927–1939), were illuminating. Burton J. Hendrick, *The Training of an American; The Earlier Life and Letters of Walter H. Page, 1855–1913* (Boston, 1928), was of more value than the same author's *The Life and Letters of Walter H. Page,* 3 vols. (Garden City, 1922–1925). C. Vann Woodward deals with one of the two Southern Populists so far treated by biographies in *Tom Watson: Agrarian Rebel* (New York, 1938); Stuart Noblin, with the other in *Leonidas La Fayette Polk: Agrarian Crusader* (Chapel Hill, 1949). Other political biographies of varying degrees of usefulness are Sam H. Acheson, *Joe Bailey, The Last Democrat* (New York, 1932); Aubrey L. Brooks, *Walter Clark, Fighting Judge* (Chapel Hill, 1944); R. D. W. Connor and Clarence Poe, *The Life and Speeches of Charles Brantley Aycock* (New York, 1912); Clement Dowd, *Life of Zebulon B. Vance* (Charlotte, 1897); John P. Dyer, *"Fightin' Joe" Wheeler* (University, La., 1941); George C. Osborn, *John Sharp Williams, Planter-Statesman of the Deep South* (Baton Rouge, 1943); Haywood J. Pearce, Jr., *Benjamin H. Hill, Secession and Reconstruction* (Chicago, 1928); Ulrich B. Phillips, *The Life of Robert Toombs* (New York, 1913); Arndt M. Stickles, *Simon Bolivar Buckner, Borderland Knight* (Chapel Hill, 1940); and Manly W. Wellman, *Giant in Gray, A Biography of Wade Hampton of South Carolina* (New York, 1949). Daniel M. Robison, *Bob Taylor and the Agrarian Revolt in Tennessee* (Chapel Hill, 1935), and Alex M. Arnett, *Claude Kitchin and the Wilson War Policies* (Boston, 1937), combine biography and history.

Several unpublished political biographies were read in manuscript, including George M. Bailey, "The Life of James Stephen Hogg" (copy in The University of Texas Library, n.d.); Benjamin H. Good, "John Henninger Reagan" (Ph.D. dissertation, University of Texas, 1932); Diedrich Ramke, "Edward Douglas White, Statesman and Jurist" (Ph.D. dissertation, Louisiana State University, 1940); and Charles G. Summersell, "A Life of Reuben F. Kolb" (M.A. thesis, University of Alabama, 1930). Commemorative works of some help were Archibald S. Coody, *Biographical Sketches of James Kimble Vardaman* (Jackson, 1922); Charles Jacobson, *The Life Story of Jeff Davis, The Stormy Petrel of Arkansas Politics* (Little Rock, 1925); James W. Madden, *Charles Allen Culberson, His Life, Character and Public Service* (Austin, 1929); Farrar Newberry, *A Life of Mr. Garland of Arkansas* (Arkadelphia, Ark., 1908); Catherine Nugent (ed.), *Life Work of Thomas L. Nugent* (Stephenville, Tex., c. 1896); Cadwell W. Raines (ed.), *Speeches and State Papers of James Stephen Hogg* (Austin, 1905); and Urey Woodson, *The First New Dealer, William Goebel; His Origin, Ambitions, Achievements, His Assassination, Loss to the State and Nation; The Story of a Great Crime* (Louisville, 1939).

Men prominent in Southern economic history are treated in Joseph C. Bailey, *Seaman A. Knapp, Schoolmaster of American Agriculture* (New York, 1945); John G. Brooks, *An American Citizen; The Life of William Henry Baldwin, Jr.* (Boston, 1910); J. Evetts Haley, *George W. Littlefield, Texan* (Norman, 1943); John W. Jenkins, *James B. Duke, Master Builder* (New York, 1927); S. Walter Martin, *Florida's Flagler* (Athens, 1949); Allan Nevins, *John D. Rockefeller; The Heroic Age of American Enterprise*, 2 vols. (New York, 1940); G. Hutchinson Smyth, *The Life of Henry Bradley Plant* (New York, 1898); Harold F. Williamson, *Edward Atkinson; The Biography of An American Liberal, 1827–1905* (Boston, 1934); John K. Winkler, *Tobacco Tycoon: The Story of James Buchanan Duke* (New York, 1942); and George T. Winston, *A Builder of the New South; Being the Story of the Life Work of Daniel Augustus Tompkins* (Garden City, 1920).

Southern college presidents of the post-Reconstruction period are the subjects of several biographies, among them Paul N. Garber, *John Carlisle Kilgo, President of Trinity College, 1894–1910* (Durham, 1937); Dumas Malone, *Edwin A. Alderman, A Biography* (New York, 1940); Edwin Mims, *Chancellor Kirkland of Vanderbilt* (Nashville, 1940); Arthur M. Shaw, *William Preston Johnson, a Transitional Figure of the Confederacy* (Baton Rouge, 1943); and Marcus M. Wilkerson, *Thomas Duckett Boyd; The Story of a Southern Educator* (Baton Rouge, 1935). Two figures of first importance in the educational crusade are treated in Edwin A. Alderman and Armistead C. Gordon, *J. L. M. Curry, A Biography* (New York, 1911); and Charles L. Lewis, *Philander Priestly Claxton; Crusader for Public Education* (Knoxville, 1948). Alester G. Holmes and George R. Sherill, *Thomas Green Clemson, His Life and Work* (Richmond, 1937), and Philip W. Wilson, *An Unofficial Statesman—Robert C. Ogden* (Garden City, 1924), deal with philanthropists.

Church leaders are the subjects of Alred M. Pierce, *Giant Against the Sky: The Life of Bishop Warren Akin Candler* (Nashville, 1948); Thomas Cary Johnson, *The Life and Letters of Benjamin Morgan Palmer* (Richmond, 1906), and *The Life and Letters of Robert Lewis Dabney* (Richmond, 1903); William M. Polk, *Leonidas Polk, Bishop and General* (New York, 1915); and Henry A. White, *Southern Presbyterian Leaders* (New York, 1911).

To the shame of Southern historians and Negro scholars, there is no adequate biography of Booker T. Washington. Basil J. Mathews, *Booker T. Washington, Educator and Interracial Interpreter* (Cambridge, 1948), falls somewhat short of expectations. Of other books on Washington, Emmett J. Scott and Lyman B. Stowe, *Booker T. Washington, Builder of a Civilization* (Garden City, 1916), is probably the most useful. Benjamin Quarles, *Frederick Douglass* (Washington, 1948), is the best book on that leader. Other Negroes are pictured in Frederic Ridgely Torrence, *The Story of John Hope* (New York, 1948), and Maud Cuney-Hare, *Norris Wright Cuney, A Tribune of the Black People* (New York, 1913).

Among the studies of Southern authors used are Grant C. Knight, *James Lane Allen and the Genteel Tradition* (Chapel Hill, 1935); Lucy L. C. Biklé, *George W. Cable: His Life and Letters* (New York, 1928); Julia C. Harris, *The Life and Letters of Joel Chandler Harris* (Boston, 1918); Aubrey H. Starke, *Sidney Lanier. A Biographical and Critical Study* (Chapel Hill, 1933); Edd W. Parks, *Charles Egbert Craddock (Mary Noailles Murfree)* (Chapel Hill, 1941); Daniel S. Rankin, *Kate Chopin and Her Creole Stories* (Philadelphia, 1932); and Edward L. Tinker, *Lafcadio Hearn's American Days* (New York, 1924). The best authority on Glasgow is Ellen Glasgow, *A Certain Measure* (New York, 1938).

Biographies of non-Southern figures consulted most often were Allan Nevins, *Grover Cleveland: A Study in Courage* (New York, 1932); Henry F. Pringle, *Theodore Roosevelt, A Biography* (New York, 1931), and *The Life and Times of William Howard Taft,* 2 vols. (New York, 1939); Leon B. Richardson, *William E. Chandler, Republican* (New

York, 1940); Theodore C. Smith, *The Life and Letters of James Abram Garfield,* 2 vols. (New Haven, 1925); Charles C. Tansill, *The Congressional Career of Thomas Francis Bayard, 1869–1885* (Washington, 1946); and Charles R. Williams, *The Life of Rutherford Birchard Hayes, Nineteenth President of the United States,* 2 vols. (Boston, 1914).

GENERAL HISTORIES AND MONOGRAPHS

There are a few chapters on Southern history in the national histories that are of value, particularly in the three volumes devoted to the period 1878–1914 in Arthur M. Schlesinger and Dixon R. Fox (eds.), *A History of American Life,* 13 vols. (New York, 1927–1948). A superior book that provides what might be called the necessary "foreground" of Southern history is V. O. Key, Jr., *Southern Politics in State and Nation* (New York, 1949).

Of the general works on Southern history some are too much a product of the period concerned, or too near to it, to have adequate perspective. This is true of the collaborative work, Julian A. C. Chandler *et al.* (eds.), *The South in the Building of the Nation; A History of the Southern States Designed to Record the South's Part in the Making of the American Nation . . . ,* 13 vols. (Richmond, 1909–1913), though it contains essays of a scholarly nature that have been useful. James W. Garner (ed.), *Studies in Southern History and Politics Inscribed to William Archibald Dunning* (New York, 1914), contains the conclusions of an older generation of Southern historians. Among recent syntheses of comprehensive scope, the most successful is Francis B. Simkins, *The South Old and New; A History, 1820–1947* (New York, 1947); some two thirds of its lucid and informing pages are devoted to the period after the Civil War. Benjamin B. Kendrick and Alex M. Arnett, *The South Looks at Its Past* (Chapel Hill, 1935), is an interpretation by ripe scholars; and Wilbur J. Cash, *The Mind of the South* (New York, 1941), contains the sometimes penetrating estimates of a journalist.

Of the general treatments of the post-Reconstruction period, Bruce, *The Rise of the New South,* has been discussed above under "Contemporaneous Analyses." Coming a few years later, Holland Thompson, *The New South* (New Haven, 1921), attained a somewhat broader perspective; but because the agrarian uprising was assigned to another author in the Yale *Chronicles* series, Thompson was compelled to leave out the heart of his story. An analysis of several broad aspects of the subject is Buck, *The Road to Reunion.*

Among the state histories found useful on the period after 1877 are

Albert B. Moore, *History of Alabama* (University, Ala., 1934); David Y. Thomas (ed.), *Arkansas and Its People, A History, 1541–1930*, 4 vols. (New York, 1930); Kathryn T. Abbey, *Florida, Land of Change* (Chapel Hill, 1941); Thomas D. Clark, *A History of Kentucky* (New York, 1937); Henry E. Chambers, *A History of Louisiana*, 3 vols. (Chicago, 1925); David D. Wallace, *The History of South Carolina*, 4 vols. (New York, 1934); Philip M. Hamer (ed.), *Tennessee; A History, 1673–1932*, 4 vols. (New York, 1933); and Rupert N. Richardson, *Texas, The Lone Star State* (New York, 1943).

Some of the monographs on special subjects are classified under other headings, but there are others covering broader phases. Three highly valuable studies of Virginia history are Charles C. Pearson, *The Readjuster Movement in Virginia* (New Haven, 1917); Allen W. Moger, *The Rebuilding of the Old Dominion* (Ann Arbor, 1940); and George M. McFarland, "The Extension of Democracy in Virginia, 1850–1895" (Ph.D. dissertation, Princeton University, 1934). Francis B. Simkins, *The Tillman Movement in South Carolina* (Durham, 1926), has been superseded by the same author's biography of Tillman, cited above. Robison, *Bob Taylor and the Agrarian Movement in Tennessee*, has been classified under biographies. Roger W. Shugg, *Origins of Class Struggle in Louisiana; A Social History of White Farmers and Laborers During Slavery and After, 1840–1875* (University, La., 1939), makes pertinent comments about the period beyond the limits of the dates in the title. Albert D. Kirwan, "A History of Mississippi Politics, 1876–1925" (Ph.D. dissertation, Duke University, 1947), is one of the best things that has happened to Mississippi history in some time. Edward F. Prichard, Jr., "Popular Political Movements in Kentucky, 1875–1900" (Senior thesis, Princeton University, 1935), was helpful. Three studies of Texas history are recommended: Ralph W. Steen, *Twentieth Century Texas, An Economic and Social History* (Austin, 1942); Reuben McKitrick, *The Public Land System of Texas, 1823–1910*, University of Wisconsin *Bulletin* No. 905 (Madison, 1918); and Ernest W. Winkler, *Platforms of Political Parties in Texas*, University of Texas *Bulletin* No. 53 (Austin, 1916). Other useful studies are Garnie W. McGinty, *Louisiana Redeemed: The Overthrow of Carpet-Bag Rule, 1876–1880* (New Orleans, 1941); Horace Kephart, *Our Southern Highlanders; A Narrative of Adventure in the Southern Appalachians and a Study of the Life Among the Mountaineers* (New York, 1922); George M. Reynolds, *Machine Politics in New Orleans, 1897–1926* (New York, 1936); and John L. O'Connor, *History of the Kentucky Derby, 1875–1921* ([New York], 1921). On state debts and their settlement, see William A.

Scott, *The Repudiation of State Debts; A Study in the Financial History of Mississippi, Florida, Alabama, North Carolina, South Carolina, Georgia, Louisiana, Arkansas, Tennessee, Minnesota, Michigan, and Virginia* (New York, 1893); Reginald C. McGrane, *Foreign Bondholders and American State Debts* (New York, 1935); and Benjamin U. Ratchford, *American State Debts* (Durham, 1941).

Some of the better histories of Southern cities are Gerald M. Capers, Jr., *The Biography of a River Town; Memphis: Its Heroic Age* (Chapel Hill, 1939); William K. Boyd, *The Story of Durham, City of the New South* (Durham, 1925); Angie Debo, *Tulsa: From Creek Town to Oil Capital* (Norman, 1943); and Thomas J. Wertenbaker, *Norfolk, Historic Southern Port* (Durham, 1931). Two brilliant essays in urban history are George R. Leighton, "Birmingham, Alabama: The City of Perpetual Promise," in *Harper's Magazine,* CLXXV (1937), 225–42, and by the same author, "Louisville, Kentucky: An American Museum Piece," *ibid.,* 400–21.

RAILROADS, MANUFACTURERS, AND LABOR

The broader aspects of the industrialization of the South are discussed in Harriet L. Herring, *Southern Industry and Regional Development* (Chapel Hill, 1940), and from another point of view in Broadus Mitchell and George S. Mitchell, *The Industrial Revolution in the South* (Baltimore, 1930). The best general history of manufactures in the period is Victor S. Clark, *The History of Manufactures in the United States,* 3 vols. (New York, 1929). Older general works that are still helpful for some aspects are *The South in the Building of the Nation,* VI, and Bruce, *The Rise of the New South.* Almon E. Parkins, *The South, Its Economic-Geographic Development* (New York, 1938), and Rupert B. Vance, *Human Geography of the South* (Chapel Hill, 1932), are useful works of reference.

Among the most helpful books on railway history are Edward G. Campbell, *The Reorganization of the American Railroad System, 1893–1900. A Study of the Effects of the Panic of 1893, the Ensuing Depression, and the First Years of Recovery on Railroad Organization and Financing* (New York, 1938); and the older works, Stuart Daggett, *Railroad Reorganization* (Boston, 1908); William Z. Ripley (ed.), *Railway Problems* (Boston, 1907); and Lewis H. Haney, *A Congressional History of Railways in the United States 1850–1887,* University of Wisconsin *Bulletin* No. 342 (Madison, 1910). Maxwell Ferguson, *State Regulation of Railroads in the South,* in Columbia University *Studies in History, Economics and Public Law,* LXVII, No. 2 (New York,

1916), provides an extremely useful summary. Individual roads are chronicled in Howard D. Dozier, *A History of the Atlantic Coast Line Railroad* (Boston, 1920); Kincaid A. Herr, *The Louisville & Nashville Railroad, 1850–1942* (Louisville, 1943); John L. Kerr, *The Story of a Southern Carrier . . . The Louisville and Nashville* (New York, 1933); and Peter S. McGuire, "The Seaboard Air Line," in *North Carolina Historical Review* (Raleigh, 1924–), XI (1934), 94–115. Two state studies are Charles S. Potts, *Railroad Transportation in Texas,* University of Texas *Bulletin* No. 119 (Austin, 1909), and Tom Finty, Jr., *Anti-Trust Legislation in Texas* (Dallas, 1916). On the freight-rate question an excellent historical survey is David M. Potter, "The Historical Development of Eastern-Southern Freight Rate Relationships," in *Law and Contemporary Problems* (Durham, 1933–), XIV (1947), 416–48. A more exhaustive work is William H. Joubert, *Southern Freight Rates in Transition* (Gainesville, Fla., 1949).

On cotton-textile history Broadus Mitchell, *The Rise of Cotton Mills in the South,* in Johns Hopkins University *Studies in Historical and Political Science,* XXXIX, No. 2 (Baltimore, 1921), is still the basic monographic study. Older books consulted on the subject are Melvin T. Copeland, *The Cotton Manufacturing Industry of the United States,* in *Harvard Economic Studies,* VIII (Cambridge, 1912); Thomas M. Young, *The American Cotton Industry* (London, 1902); and Holland Thompson, *From the Cotton Field to the Cotton Mill; A Study of the Industrial Transition in North Carolina* (New York, 1906). Works written or inspired by the industrialists are Daniel A. Tompkins, *Cotton Mill, Commercial Features. A Text-Book for the Use of Textile Schools and Investors* (Charlotte, N.C., 1899); August Kohn, *The Cotton Mills of South Carolina* (Charleston, 1907); and Richard E. Walker, *The Problem of the Southern Cotton Mill* (Winston-Salem, 1915). One large aspect of the tobacco industry has been covered with an exemplary thoroughness in Nannie May Tilley, *The Bright-Tobacco Industry, 1860–1929* (Chapel Hill, 1948), a work displacing all others in its field. Useful in other respects are Benjamin W. Arnold, *History of the Tobacco Industry in Virginia from 1860 to 1894,* in Johns Hopkins University *Studies in Historical and Political Science,* XV, Nos. 1–2 (Baltimore, 1897); and Meyer Jacobstein, *The Tobacco Industry in the United States,* in Columbia University *Studies in History, Economics and Public Law,* XXVI, No. 3 (New York, 1907). The uprising against the tobacco monopoly is described in John G. Miller, *The Black Patch War* (Chapel Hill, 1936), and James O. Nall, *The*

Tobacco Night Riders of Kentucky and Tennessee, 1905–1909 (Louisville, 1939).

Mining and heavy industry receive treatment in Ethel M. Armes, *The Story of Coal and Iron in Alabama* (Birmingham, 1910), valuable in spite of its chamber-of-commerce auspices. A more recent work of value is Homer B. Vanderblue and William L. Crum, *The Iron Industry in Prosperity and Depression* (Chicago, 1927). Recent books have clarified many aspects of the Southern oil industry. These are Carl Coke Rister, *Oil! Titan of the Southwest* (Norman, 1949); Gerald Forbes, *Flush Production, The Epic of Oil in the Gulf-Southwest* (Norman, 1942); Samuel W. Tait, Jr., *The Wildcatters; An Informal History of Oil-Hunting in America* (Princeton, 1946); and Boyce House, *Oil Boom* (Caldwell, Idaho, 1941). Robert H. Montgomery, *The Brimstone Game; Monopoly in Action* (New York, 1940), exposes the origin and development of the sulphur monopoly.

Among the labor studies most liberally used are Elizabeth H. Davidson, *Child Labor Legislation in the Southern Textile States* (Chapel Hill, 1939), an excellent job; George S. Mitchell, *Textile Unionism in the South* (Chapel Hill, 1931); Herbert J. Lahne, *The Cotton Mill Worker* (New York, 1944); Sterling D. Spero and Abram L. Harris, *The Black Worker. The Negro and the Labor Movement* (New York, 1931); Charles H. Wesley, *Negro Labor in the United States, 1850–1925; A Study in American Economic History* (New York, 1927); and French E. Wolfe, *Admission to American Trade Unions,* in Johns Hopkins University *Studies in Historical and Political Science,* XXX, No. 3 (Baltimore, 1912). Also consulted was Frederic Meyers, "The Knights of Labor in the South," in *Southern Economic Journal* (Chapel Hill, 1933–), VI (1939–1940), 479–87.

AGRICULTURE AND FARMERS' MOVEMENTS

There is no comprehensive agricultural history of the South in the post–Civil War period comparable with that of Lewis C. Gray's history of the ante-bellum period. Fred A. Shannon, *The Farmer's Last Frontier, Agriculture, 1860–1897* (New York, 1945), is a good recent survey on a national scale with two chapters and many references on the South. Rupert B. Vance, *Human Factors in Cotton Culture* (Chapel Hill, 1929), is a penetrating analysis. An old work still of value is Matthew B. Hammond, *The Cotton Industry; An Essay in American Economic History* (New York, 1897); and another is Charles W. Burkett and Clarence H. Poe, *Cotton, Its Cultivation, Marketing, Manu-*

facture, and the Problems of the Cotton World (New York, 1906). Tilley, *Bright-Tobacco Industry,* is not only the most thorough treatment of the manufacture, but also of the culture, of the leaf. Several articles by qualified writers on various other crops of the region appear in *The South in the Building of the Nation,* VI, and in the *Yearbook of the Department of Agriculture, 1899.*

Two illuminating studies of agriculture in one state are Robert P. Brooks, *The Agrarian Revolution in Georgia, 1865–1912,* University of Wisconsin *Bulletin* No. 639 (Madison, 1914); and Enoch M. Banks, *The Economics of Land Tenure in Georgia* (New York, 1905). Other studies in land tenure are William B. Bizzell, *Farm Tenantry in the United States* (College Station, Tex., 1921); Benjamin H. Hibbard, "Tenancy in the Southern States," in *Quarterly Journal of Economics* (Boston, Cambridge, 1886–), XXVII (1913), 482–96; and H. A. Turner, "A Graphic Summary of Farm Tenure," United States Department of Agriculture, *Miscellaneous Publications* No. 261 (Washington, 1936). An invaluable correction of earlier error regarding the tenure and labor system in the Black Belt is a special study in the *Thirteenth Census, 1910,* V, *Agriculture,* 477–89; see also Roger W. Shugg, "Survival of the Plantation System in Louisiana," in *Journal of Southern History* (Baton Rouge, 1935–), III (1937), 311–25. On the lien system the most interesting reading is two articles by Thomas D. Clark, "The Furnishing and Supply System in Southern Agriculture since 1865," *ibid.*, XII (1946), 24–44, and "Imperfect Competition in the Southern Retail Trade after 1865," in *Journal of Economic History* (New York, 1941–), III (*Supplement,* December, 1943), 38–47.

On government activities in Southern agriculture, see Oscar B. Martin, *The Demonstration Work* (Boston, 1926); and Alfred C. True, *A History of Agricultural Education in the United States, 1785–1925,* United States Department of Agriculture, *Miscellaneous Publications* No. 36 (Washington, 1929).

Many works on farmers' organizations and movements also contain valuable chapters on agricultural history. Solon J. Buck, *The Granger Movement; A Study of Agricultural Organization and its Political, Economic and Social Manifestations, 1870–1880* (Cambridge, 1913), gives less attention to Southern aspects than does John D. Hicks, *The Populist Revolt; A History of the Farmers' Alliance and the People's Party* (Minneapolis, 1931). Investigation of Southern movements have been conducted almost entirely on state lines. James S. Ferguson, "The Grange and Farmer Education in Mississippi," in *Journal of Southern History,* VIII (1943), 497–512; Ralph A. Smith, "The Grange

Movement in Texas, 1873–1900," in *Southwestern Historical Quarterly* (Austin, 1897–), XLII (1938–1939), 297–315; and Roscoe C. Martin, "The Greenback Party in Texas," *ibid.*, XXX (1926–1927), 161–77, are all valuable articles. The Farmers' Alliance is generally treated in studies of the Populist movement. Of the latter the most useful are Roscoe C. Martin, *The People's Party In Texas, A Study In Third Party Politics,* University of Texas *Bulletin* No. 3308 (Austin, 1933); Alex M. Arnett, *The Populist Movement in Georgia,* in Columbia University *Studies in History, Economics and Public Law,* CIV, No. 1 (New York, 1922); William D. Sheldon, *Populism in the Old Dominion* (Princeton, 1935); John B. Clark, *Populism in Alabama* (Auburn, 1927); James A. Sharp, "The Entrance of the Farmers' Alliance into Tennessee Politics," in East Tennessee Historical Society's *Publications* (Knoxville, 1929–), No. 9 (1937), 77–92; and the same author's "The Farmers' Alliance and the People's Party in Tennessee," *ibid.*, No. 10 (1938), 91–113; Kathryn T. Abbey, "Florida Versus the Principles of Populism, 1896–1911," in *Journal of Southern History,* IV (1938), 462–75; Lucia E. Daniel, "The Louisiana People's Party," in *Louisiana Historical Quarterly* (New Orleans, 1917–), XXVI (1943), 1055–1149; and Simeon A. Delap, *The Populist Party in North Carolina,* in Trinity College Historical Society *Papers,* Ser. XIV, No. 2 (Durham, 1922). The Farmers' Union stands in need of scholarly investigation. Commodore B. Fisher, *The Farmers' Union,* in University of Kentucky *Studies in Economics and Sociology,* No. 2 (Lexington, 1920), is not very satisfactory. One must turn also to such works as that of the president of the Union, Charles S. Barrett, *The Mission, History and Times of the Farmers' Union* (Nashville, 1909).

RACE RELATIONS

Recent scholarship has illuminated the history of race relations as well as present conditions by a collaborative work under the direction of Gunnar Myrdal, *An American Dilemma; The Negro Problem and Modern Democracy,* 2 vols. (New York, 1944). A superior synthesis of Negro history is John Hope Franklin, *From Slavery to Freedom* (New York, 1947); and an authoritative work in the sociological interpretation of history is E. Franklin Frazier, *The Negro in the United States* (New York, 1949). W. E. Burghardt Du Bois, *Black Folk, Then and Now; An Essay in the History and Sociology of the Negro Race* (New York, 1939), is especially interesting on certain phases of race history. Among the older histories, Carter G. Woodson, *The Negro in Our History* (8th ed., Washington, 1945) is still useful for reference.

Of outstanding excellence among monographs on special subjects is Vernon L. Wharton, *The Negro in Mississippi, 1865–1890,* in the *James Sprunt Studies in History and Political Science,* XXVIII (Chapel Hill, 1947). On legal aspects of race relations reliable data are supplied in Charles S. Mangum, Jr., *The Legal Status of the Negro* (Chapel Hill, 1940); Franklin Johnson, *The Development of State Legislation Concerning the Free Negro* (New York, 1919); and Gilbert T. Stephenson, *Race Distinctions in American Law* (New York, 1910). Of the several sociological studies of caste and race behavior, Bertram W. Doyle, *The Etiquette of Race Relations in the South* (Chicago, 1937), is most conscious of historical movement and change. Arthur F. Raper, *The Tragedy of Lynching* (Chapel Hill, 1933), is a study of race violence.

The most comprehensive treatment of race factors in Southern politics is Key, *Southern Politics,* already cited, and an older work is Paul Lewinson, *Race, Class, & Party. A History of Negro Suffrage and White Politics in the South* (New York, 1932). Special studies include a competent monograph by William A. Mabry, *The Negro in North Carolina Politics Since Reconstruction,* in Trinity College Historical Society, *Historical Papers,* Ser. XXIII (Durham, 1940); Richard L. Morton, *The Negro in Virginia Politics, 1865–1902* (Charlottesville, 1919); Ralph W. Wardlaw, *Negro Suffrage in Georgia, 1867–1930,* in University of Georgia *Bulletin,* XXXIII (Athens, 1932); and Samuel D. Smith, *The Negro in Congress, 1870–1901* (Chapel Hill, 1940). The most exhaustive study of disfranchisement, William A. Mabry, "The Disfranchisement of the Negro in the South" (Ph.D. dissertation, Duke University, 1933), has been published only in fragments, some of which are "Disfranchisement of the Negro in Mississippi," in *Journal of Southern History,* IV (1938), 318–33; "Ben Tillman Disfranchised the Negro," in *South Atlantic Quarterly* (Durham, 1902–), XXXVII (1938), 170–83; and "Negro Suffrage and Fusion Rule in North Carolina," in *North Carolina Historical Review,* XII (1935), 79–102. The movement is also described in Robert E. Martin, *Negro Disfranchisement in Virginia* (Washington, 1938); and George B. Tindall, "The Campaign for the Disfranchisement of Negroes in South Carolina," in *Journal of Southern History,* XV (1949), 212–34.

On the Atlanta Compromise and Booker T. Washington's philosophy of race relations the best source is still Washington himself, particularly E. Davidson Washington (ed.), *Selected Speeches of Booker T. Washington* (Garden City, 1932). Some discerning essays on the subject are Guy B. Johnson, "Negro Racial Movements and Leadership in the United States," in *American Journal of Sociology* (Chicago,

1895–), XLIII (1937–1938), 57–71, and Charles S. Johnson, "The Social Philosophy of Booker T. Washington," in *Opportunity* (New York, 1923–), VI (1928), 102–105, 115. Mary W. Ovington, *How the National Association for the Advancement of Colored People Began* (New York, 1914), and Du Bois in *Dusk of Dawn* tell of protest movements. Horace M. Bond, *Negro Education in Alabama; A Study in Cotton and Steel* (Washington, 1939), has some penetrating observations on racial leaders and movements. On race relations in labor, Wesley, *Negro Labor in the United States,* and Spero and Harris, *The Black Worker,* have good studies. Abram L. Harris, *The Negro As Capitalist, A Study of Banking and Business Among American Negroes* (Philadelphia, 1936), is highly worth while.

PHILANTHROPY, EDUCATION, AND HUMANITARIANISM

One of the best sources on the philanthropic foundations is their official proceedings. Particularly valuable are the Conference for Education in the South *Proceedings* (New York, 1898–1914). There are several useful summaries. Jabez L. M. Curry, *A Brief Sketch of George Peabody, and a History of the Peabody Education Fund through Thirty Years* (Cambridge, 1898), is one. An invaluable official account is *The General Education Board; An Account of its Activities, 1902–1914* (New York, 1915), which reports all the Board's numerous activities in the South. *Southern Education Board: Activities and Results, 1904 to 1910* (Washington, 1911), is a similar publication. Of some help is Ullin W. Leavell, *Philanthropy in Negro Education,* in George Peabody College for Teachers *Contributions to Education,* No. 100 (Nashville, 1930).

The most comprehensive history of education in the South is written by one of the leading participants in the "crusade" for public schools—Charles W. Dabney, *Universal Education in the South,* 2 vols. (Chapel Hill, 1936). Edgar W. Knight, *Public Education in the South* (Boston, 1922), is a textbook. Two older items are of interest: Charles L. Coon, *Facts About Southern Educational Progress. A Present Day Study in Public School Maintenance for those Who Look Forward* (Durham, 1905); and G. S. Dickerman, *The South Compared with the North in Educational Requirements* (New Haven, 1901). The United States Commissioner of Education *Reports* contain much data on the South, particularly an article of Wyckliffe Rose, "The Educational Movement in the South," in the *Report of the Commissioner of Education for . . . 1903,* 2 vols. (Washington, 1905), I, 359–90. The old series of state histories of education published by the United States Bureau of Education are for the most part outmoded by more recent studies. See particularly Andrew D. Holt, *The Struggle for a State System of Public Schools in Tennessee, 1903–1936*, in Teachers College, Columbia University *Contributions to Education*, No. 753 (New York, 1938); Moses E. Ligon, *A History of Public Education in Kentucky, A Study of the Development and Control of Public Education Based upon the Constitutional Provisions and the Legislative Acts of the General Assembly* (Lexington, 1942); Marcus C. S. Noble, *A History of the Public Schools of North Carolina* (Chapel Hill, 1930); Frederick Eby, *The Development of Education in Texas* (New York, 1925); Stuart G. Noble, *Forty Years of the Public Schools in Mississippi, with Special Reference to the Education of the Negro*, in Teachers College, Columbia University *Contributions to Education*, No. 94 (New York, 1918); Cornelius J. Heatwole, *A History of Education in Virginia* (New York, 1916); Thomas H. Harris, *The Story of Public Education in Louisiana* (New Orleans, 1924); Oscar W. Hyatt, *The Development of Secondary Education in Alabama Prior to 1920* (Nashville, 1933); and Stephen B. Weeks, *History of Public School Education in Arkansas*, United States Bureau of Education, *Bulletin* No. 27 (Washington, 1912). On Negro education the best monograph is Bond, *Negro Education in Alabama*, cited above; and see also the same author's *The Education of the Negro in the American Social Order* (New York, 1934).

The humanitarian impulse may be traced in the proceedings of the Southern Sociological Congress published in James E. McCulloch (ed.), *The Call of the New South* (Nashville, 1912); and by the same editor, *Battling for Social Betterment* (Nashville, 1914). The development of social welfare work is treated in Lydia Shivers, "The Social Welfare Movement in the South" (Ph.D. dissertation, University of North Carolina, 1935); Harriet L. Herring, *Welfare Work in Mill Villages* (Chapel Hill, 1929); and Elizabeth Wisner, *Public Welfare Administration in Louisiana* (Chicago, 1930). On the rise of public-health work, Francis R. Allen has an unpublished study, "Public Health Work in the Southeast," in his possession. Other materials of value are Charles V. Chapin, *A Report on State Public Health Work Based on a Survey of State Boards of Health* (Chicago, 1916?); and John F. Kendrick, *Public Health in the State and Counties of Virginia* (Richmond, 1939).

On the hookworm campaign the best source is the Rockefeller Sanitary Commission for the Eradication of Hookworm, *Annual Reports* (Washington, 1910–1914). The numerous publications of the National Child Labor Committee are very useful, especially *Child Labor Bul-*

letin, I, No. 2 (New York, 1912), 1–77, which summarizes the child-labor laws of all the states as of 1912. Davidson, *Child Labor Legislation in the Southern Textile States,* is invaluable on this subject.

CULTURAL HISTORY

The more elusive qualities of Southern life, its deep loyalties and provinciality, its violence and religiosity, its creeds of family, race, and caste, and its abiding romanticism have all but eluded the professional historian. Howard W. Odum, *An American Epoch* (New York, 1930), captured some of these intangibles with an impressionistic analysis, and Cash, *The Mind of the South,* had a few flashes of intuition. In the main, the scholars have left this broad field to the novelists, to Glasgow, Robert Penn Warren, William Faulkner, and others. Even so striking a reality as the violence of Southern society in this period has attracted no historian, except for its racial aspects. Horace V. Redfield, *Homicide, North and South* (Philadelphia, 1880), is an invidious comparison of dubious statistics.

Religious history has also been neglected, but there is at least one study of genuine merit in the field. This is Hunter D. Farish, *The Circuit Rider Dismounts; A Social History of Southern Methodism, 1865–1900* (Richmond, 1938). There is no study of comparable quality of other churches. The majority of studies in the field are of a sociological cast, for example, Victor I. Masters, *Country Church in the South* (2d ed., Atlanta, 1917); Edmund deS. Brunner, *Church Life in the Rural South* (New York, 1923); and Liston Pope, *Millhands & Preachers, A Study of Gastonia* (New Haven, 1942). National histories of religion for the most part deal with tendencies conspicuously lacking in the South. Studies of some value for Southern problems are Carter G. Woodson, *The History of the Negro Church* (2d ed., Washington, 1945); Elmer T. Clark, *The Small Sects in America* (Nashville, 1937); and Stewart G. Cole, *The History of Fundamentalism* (New York, 1931). George P. Jackson, *White Spirituals in the Southern Uplands* (Chapel Hill, 1933), tells sympathetically of primitive faith. Paul N. Garber, *The Methodists Are One People* (Nashville, 1939), gives a short history of unification. There is a suggestive essay by Edwin McNeill Poteat, Jr., "Religion in the South," in William T. Couch (ed.), *Culture in the South* (Chapel Hill, 1934), 248–69. Winfred E. Garrison, *The March of Faith; The Story of Religion in America since 1865* (New York, 1933), has some space for Southern aspects of the story.

College life and its troubles are chronicled in Edwin Mims, *History of Vanderbilt University* (Nashville, 1946); Philip A. Bruce, *History of the University of Virginia, 1819–1919,* 5 vols. (New York, 1920–1922); Kemp P. Battle, *History of the University of North Carolina,* 2 vols. (Raleigh, 1907–1912); and Henry M. Bullock, *A History of Emory University* (Nashville, 1936). Quarrels between denominational schools and state schools are treated in Luther L. Gobbel, *Church-State Relationships in Education in North Carolina since 1776* (Durham, 1938). Guy E. Snavely, *A Short History of the Southern Association of Colleges and Secondary Schools* (Durham?, 1945?), tells of efforts to raise standards. Other problems of collegiate and intellectual life are examined in Edwin Mims, *The Advancing South; Stories of Progress and Reaction* (Garden City, 1926); and Virginius Dabney, *Liberalism in the South* (Chapel Hill, 1932). Higher education for the Negro is treated in Dwight O. W. Holmes, *The Evolution of the Negro College* (New York, 1934).

Southern letters are the most written-about and the least-illuminated aspect of regional culture. There is great need for a good study of the local color school and the literary revival of the eighties. The bibliography which constitutes the third volume of the new *Literary History of the United States,* 3 vols. (New York, 1948), edited by Robert E. Spiller *et al.*, is a great boon to investigation. Gregory L. Paine, *Southern Prose Writers* (New York, 1947), has a helpful critical bibliography, and so does Edd W. Parks, *Southern Poets* (New York, 1936). Of the many older histories of Southern letters, William M. Baskervill, *Southern Writers: Biographical and Critical Studies,* 2 vols. (Nashville, 1897–1903); Montrose J. Moses, *The Literature of the South* (New York, 1910); and C. Alphonso Smith, *Southern Literary Studies; A Collection of Literary, Biographical, and Other Sketches* (Chapel Hill, 1927), were found of some value. Two monographs, Shields McIlwaine, *The Southern Poor-White from Lubberland to Tobacco Road* (Norman, 1939); and Francis P. Gaines, *The Southern Plantation: A Study in the Development and the Accuracy of a Tradition* (New York, 1924), threw light on the writings of the period. Discerning essays are found in Edd W. Parks, *Segments of Southern Thought* (Athens, 1938); David K. Jackson (ed.), *American Studies in Honor of William Kenneth Boyd* (Durham, 1940); Couch (ed.), *Culture in the South;* and Donald Davidson, *The Attack on Leviathan; Regionalism and Nationalism in the United States* (Chapel Hill, 1938). Sheldon Van Auken, "The Southern Historical Novel in the Early Twentieth Century," in *Journal of Southern History,* XIV (1948), 157–91, is a thorough piece of research.

Other corners of cultural history are lighted by Russel F. Whitehead, "The Old and the New South; A Consideration of Architecture in the

Southern States," in *Architectural Record* (New York, 1891–), XXX (1911), 1–56. Two lively histories of newspapers are Thomas E. Dabney, *One Hundred Great Years; The Story of the Times-Picayune From Its Founding to 1940* (Baton Rouge, 1944); and Sam Acheson, *35,000 Days in Texas; A History of the Dallas News and Its Forbears* (New York, 1938). On the music of the South, see Jackson, *White Spirituals in the Southern Uplands;* Arthur P. Hudson, *Folksongs of Mississippi and Their Background* (Chapel Hill, 1936); Maud Cuney-Hare, *Negro Musicians and Their Music* (New York, 1936); Louis Armstrong, *Swing That Music* (New York, 1936); and William C. Handy, *Father of the Blues; An Autobiography* (New York, 1941).

Any historian of this period must acknowledge, even belatedly, his obligation to the volumes of the Federal Writers' Program of the Works Project Administration, *American Guide Series.*

[illegible]

INDEX

INDEX